Personality Assessment Methods and Practices

Lewis R. Aiken

Personality Assessment Methods and Practices

3rd revised edition

Hogrefe & Huber Publishers
Seattle • Toronto • Bern • Göttingen

Library of Congress Cataloging-in-Publication Data

is available via the Library of Congress Marc Database under the
LC Catalog Card Number 99-71723

Canadian Cataloguing in Publication Data

Aiken, Lewis R., 1931–
   Personality assessment methods and practices
3rd ed.
First ed. published under title: Assessment of personality
Includes bibliographical references and index.
ISBN 0-88937-209-8
1. Personality assessment. I. Title. II. Title: Assessment of
personality.
BF698.4.A54   1999   155.2'8   C99-930602-2

© Copyright 1999 by Hogrefe & Huber Publishers
USA: P.O. Box 2487, Kirkland, WA 98083-2487
                   Phone (425) 820-1500, Fax (425) 823-8324
CANADA: 12 Bruce Park Avenue, Toronto, Ontario M4P 2S3
                   Phone (416) 482-6339
SWITZERLAND: Länggass-Strasse 76, CH-3000 Bern 9
                   Phone (031) 300-4500, Fax (031) 300-4590
GERMANY: Rohnsweg 25, D-37085 Göttingen
                   Phone (0551) 49609-0, Fax (0551) 49609-88

Printed and bound in the USA
ISBN 0-88937-209-8

Contents

PART I: FOUNDATIONS OF PERSONALITY ASSESSMENT

Chapter 1: History and Theories 3

Chapter 2: Psychometrics I:
Measurement, Statistics, and Test Design 39

Chapter 3: Psychometrics II:
Standardization, Reliability, and Validity 65

Chapter 4: Administration, Interpretation, and Reporting . 91

PART II: OBSERVING, INTERVIEWING, AND RATING

Chapter 5: Observations and Interviews 125

Chapter 6: Checklists and Rating Scales 159

PART III: PERSONALITY INVENTORIES

Chapter 7: Rational-Theoretical and Factor-Analyzed Inventories 191

PART IV: PROJECTIVE TECHNIQUES

PART V: PERSONALITY ASSESSMENT TODAY AND TOMORROW

Preface

This book is a survey of concepts, methods, procedures, and materials concerning the assessment of personality. It emphasizes the means and methods of assessment, but theories, research, and issues concerning human personality that have influenced psychological assessment are also considered.

The term *personality assessment* refers to procedures designed to assess a person's characteristic modes of thinking and acting. The assessment of personality is not limited to the classification and measurement of types, traits, and temperaments, but also includes measures of interests, values, attitudes, perceptual and cognitive styles, and other internal dynamics and behaviors characterizing the uniqueness of an individual.

Personality Assessment Methods and Practices (3rd ed.) is divided into five sections. The four chapters in Part I provide an overview of the foundations of personality assessment, including history, theories, and psychometric methods. Construction and administration of assessment instruments, as well as the interpretation and reporting of findings, are also described.

The two chapters in Part II are concerned with basic principles of behavioral observations, interviewing, ratings, and checklists. Personality inventories, including rational-theoretical, factor-analytic, and criterion-keyed inventories, are considered in detail in the first two chapters of Part III. Inventories for measuring interests, values, and attitudes are surveyed in the third chapter—Chapter 9—of this section. The three chapters in Part IV are concerned with projective methods, including association, completion, and drawing techniques, as well as inkblot and apperceptive methods.

The single chapter—Chapter 13—in Part V begins with a consideration of physiological, perceptual, and cognitive measurements of personality. The second part of the chapter deals with applications, and the third part with issues in personality assessment.

Each of the 13 chapters of the book ends with a summary, a set of exercises and activities, and a list of suggested readings for further study of the topic. Numerous illustrations and examples provide students with a background for selecting and using a variety of personality assessment devices and an understanding of their assets and limitations. Students are urged to scrutinize the psychometric qualities (reliability, validity, standardization, etc.) of the various instruments carefully and to become thoroughly familiar with the administration, scoring, and interpretation procedures. The necessity for making multiple observations and measurements, depending on the goals of the psychological assessment, and integrating findings from different sources are stressed as well. Procedures for reporting assessment results to appropriate persons and subsequent follow-up and retesting are also discussed.

Personality Assessment Methods and Practices (3rd ed.) is designed primarily for use in a one-semester course on personality assessment at the upper undergraduate or beginning graduate level. It is also appropriate to combine the text with lectures or readings on personality theories and research or with material on cognitive assessment. It can be used in courses on personality or in a comprehensive course on psychological testing and assessment.

In addition to being a textbook, this volume is a useful source book, providing coverage of a wide range of instruments and procedures, a comprehensive glossary, an appendix of test publishers and addresses, a extensive bibliography, and complete indexes of authors, subjects, and tests. These features add to the book's value as a reference source for professional psychologists and researchers in the behavioral sciences. The book is, however, written primarily as an integrated, survey text.

An *Instructor's Manual for Personality Assessment Methods and Practices* (3rd ed.) containing hundreds of multiple-choice and essay test items, in addition to other instructional resources, is available to course instructors. A diskette of computer programs that may prove interesting and useful in understanding the methods and practices of personality assessment is also available.* These programs are described in the *Instructor's Manual.*

---

* Instructors who adopt the text and are interested in obtaining a copy of the diskette are asked to contact the publisher at Hogrefe & Huber Publishers, P.O. Box 2487, Kirkland, WA 98083-2487, Tel. 425-820-1500, Fax 425-823-8324, e-mail hh@hhpub.com.

■ PART I

FOUNDATIONS OF PERSONALITY ASSESSMENT

CHAPTER 1

History and Theories

No two people are exactly alike; everyone is unique. Even identical twins, who originate from the same fertilized egg and therefore have identical heredities, differ in significant ways. This is true whether they are reared in the same or different environments. On the other hand, everyone is similar in certain respects. Despite differences in heredity, experiences, and culture, people share certain physical and psychological qualities that distinguish them as human beings. Thus, we are both similar and different, equipped with a complex set of dispositions and abilities that identify us as human beings with individual personalities.

The term *personality* is derived from the Greek *persona*, or mask, associated with a role played by an actor. The dictionary defines personality in several ways. One definition emphasizes the public, social stimulus, or behavioral characteristics of a person that are visible to other people and make an impression on them. Another definition stresses a person's private, central, inner core. Included within this private core are the motives, attitudes, interests, beliefs, fantasies, cognitive styles, and other mental processes of an individual. Some definitions of personality emphasize its "person" quality, personal existence, or identity features. An extreme example is the view that personality is a mysterious charisma possessed only by movie stars and other celebrities. Other meanings of personality are associated with specific disciplines or professions. Among these are selfhood, the ideal of perfection, and supreme value (philosophy); the individual members of the Trinity (theology); and a person having legal status (law) (Hunt, 1982).

A more global, or *holistic*, definition of personality views it as an organized composite of qualities or characteristics—the sum total of the physical, mental, emotional, and social qualities of a person. This is the way in which the term is employed in this book, and as such it is essentially synonymous with the psychology of the individual. More specifically, we shall use the term *personality* to refer to a unique composite of inborn and acquired mental abilities, temperaments, attitudes, and other individual differences in thoughts, feelings, and actions. This collection of cognitive and affective characteristics, as it exists in a particular person, is associated with a fairly consistent, predictable pattern of behavior.

Such a broad definition implies that the measurement, or more precisely *assessment*, of personality encompasses a wide range of variables. Among these are not only affective characteristics such as emotion, temperament, character, and stylistic traits, but also cognitive variables such as achievement, intelligence, and specific aptitudes and various psychomotor abilities or physical skills and mannerisms. To assess these variables means to appraise or estimate their level of magnitude by methods such as observations, interviews, rating scales, checklists, inventories, projective techniques, and psychological tests.

This book focuses on the assessment of affective characteristics, encompassing the traditional, albeit somewhat limited, conception of personality variables. Reference is also made to cognitive and psychomotor variables, but they are not discussed at length. For a more complete description of the measurement of cognitive and psychomotor abilities, the reader should consult the *Assessment of Intellectual Functioning* (Aiken, 1996), *Tests and Examinations* (Aiken, 1998), or similar volumes on psychological testing in general and the assessment of human abilities in particular.

■ Historical Foundations

The history of personality assessment goes back to a time when people first noticed individual differences in ways of behaving and thinking. In fact, the analysis and evaluation of individuals is probably as old as humanity itself. Descriptions of character and personality are found in many ancient myths and stories dating back thousands of years before the common era. These legends describe the deeds and personalities of heroes and other famous persons.

Although there are no written records of the earliest behavioral observations, the *Epic of Gilgamesh* (c. 2000 B.C.) and the Bible contain passages indicating an awareness of personality differences. For example, in Judges 7:3–7:7, God says to Gideon:

> You have too many men for me to deliver Midian into their hands. In order that Israel may not boast against me that her own strength has saved her, announce now to the people: "Anyone who trembles with fear may turn back and leave Mount Gilead." So twenty-two thousand men left, while ten thousand remained.

> But the Lord said to Gideon, "There are still too many men. Take them down to the water, and I will sift them for you there. If I say, 'This one shall go with you,' he shall go; but if I say, 'This one shall not go with you,' he shall not go."
> So Gideon took the men down to the water. There the Lord told him, "Separate those who lap the water with their tongues like a dog from those who kneel down to drink." Three hundred men lapped with their hands to their mouths. All the rest got down on their knees to drink.
> The Lord said to Gideon, "With the three hundred men that lapped I will save you and give the Midianites into your hands. Let all the other men go, each to his own place." And the Lord said unto Gideon, "By the three hundred men that lapped will I save you, and deliver the Midianites into thine hand; and let all the other people go every man unto his place."

Presumably God knew that the men who lapped the water with their hands to their mouths were more alert or wary and hence would prove to be more effective than a larger, less vigilant fighting force.

This biblical story is one of the earliest recorded instances of the use of a situational test of personality for the purpose of personnel selection, but it was not the first such procedure to be employed. As early as 2200 B. C., the Chinese had begun using oral examinations to select government workers and to determine periodically if civil servants remained fit to perform their duties. What the examinee said and how he said it were both important in determining whether he passed or failed.

Ancient Greece and Rome

Attempts to analyze and assess human personality can also be seen in the writings of the ancient Greeks and Romans. The Greek physician Hippocrates (460–377 B. C.), who believed that natural rather than supernatural forces are the causes of disease, proposed that there are four "humors" in the human body—blood, black bile, yellow bile, and phlegm. Hippocrates also devised the first formal system for classifying mental disorders, a forerunner of the system proposed by Emil Kraepelin some 2,300 years later. The major categories of Hippocrates' classification system were mania (overexcitability), melancholia (depression), and phrenitis (brain fever).

Around A. D. 200, Galen, a Roman physician who subscribed to Hippocrates' humoral theory, concluded from his observations that four types of temperament correspond to an overabundance of each of the four humors. The four temperament types were sanguine, melancholic, choleric, and phlegmatic. According to Galen, an individual with a *sanguine* temperament has an excess of blood and is forceful, direct, and courageous. An individual with a *melancholic* temperament, who is generally brooding, moody, and withdrawing, was said to have a predominance of black bile. A person with a *choleric* temperament was thought to have

BOX 1-1

Sample Descriptions of the Characters of Theophrastus

The Garrulous Man

The Garrulous man is one that will sit down close beside somebody he does not know, and begin talk with a eulogy of his own life, and then relate a dream he had the night before, and after that tell dish by dish what he had for supper. As he warms up to his work he will remark that we are by no means the men we were, and the price of wheat has gone down, and there's a ship of strangers in town ... Next he will surmise that the crops would be all the better for some more rain, and tell him what he is going to grow on his farm next year, adding that it is difficult to make both ends meet ... and "I vomited yesterday" and "What day is it today?" ... And if you let him go on he will never stop (Edmonds, 1929, pp. 48–49)

The Penurious Man

A Penurious man is one who goes to a debtor to ask for his half-obol interest before the end of the month. At a dinner where expenses are shared, he counts the number of cups each person drinks, and he makes a smaller libation to Artemis than anyone. If someone has made a good bargain on his account and presents him with the bill he says it is too much. When his servant breaks a pot or a plate, he deducts the value from his food. If his wife drops a copper, he moves furnitures, beds, chests, and hunts in the curtains. If he has something to sell he puts such a price on it that the buyer has no profit. He forbids his wife to lend anything—neither salt nor lampwick nor cinnamon nor majoram nor meal nor garlands nor cakes for sacrifices ... To sum up, the coffers of the penurious men are moldly and the keys rust; they wear cloaks which hardly reach the thigh; a very little oilbottle supplies them for anointing; they have hair cut short and do not put on their shoes until midday; and when they take their cloak to the fuller they urge him to use plenty of earth so that it will not be spotted so soon. (Quoted by Allport, 1937, p. 57)

an excess of yellow bile, and was characterized as irritable, bitter, and resentful. Finally, a habitually weak, fragile, and indecisive individual, referred to as a *phlegmatic* personality, was said to have an overabundance of phlegm in the body.

The ancient Greeks were greatly interested in human characteristics and wrote extensively on the subject. Famous philosophers such as Plato (c. 428–347 B. C.) and Aristotle (384–322 B. C.), for example, had much to say on the subject of individual differences. Plato's distinction between rational and irrational human behavior and his analyses of conflict and repression undoubtedly influenced nineteenth-century psychoanalytic theorizing. The doctrine of the soul, which was introduced by the Pythagoreans, was also developed by Plato and Aristotle. To Plato the soul had three functions—nutritive, sensitive, and rational. *Nutritive souls* are characteristic of plants, *sensing souls* of animals, and *rational souls* of humans. Aristotle viewed the soul as a spirit moving in the body, a "perfect unity toward which bodily functions are directed."

Of particular interest to personality assessment are the 30 descriptions or sketches provided by Theophrastus (372–287 B. C.). These sketches, like the Hippocrates-Galen humor theory, were based on overgeneralized observations of human behavior. Examples of the character types described by Theophrastus were the Flatterer, the Garrulous Man (a chatterbox), the Liar, the Penurious Man (a miser), the Surly Man (bad-tempered), and the Tasteless Man (unrefined). Excerpts from two of these sketches, which describe the dominant characteristics and typical style of action of certain types of individual, are given in Box 1–1. Theophrastus presented no scientific evidence for the existence of such character types, although his sketches are entertaining and even thought provoking.

The Middle Ages and Renaissance

A number of other historical events that contributed to the interpretation and assessment of personality are listed in Table 1-1. As this chronology suggests, little genuine progress in the scientific analysis of personality was made until fairly recent times. Descriptive characterizations having a semblance of truth were presented by writers such as Miguel de Cervantes, William Shakespeare, and Charles Dickens. These writings led to such descriptive terms as quixotic and Falstaffian to the English language. The characterizations of famous novelists and playwrights are, however, like those of Theophrastus, usually stereotypes or overgeneralizations. The scientific exploration and measurement of human personality did not begin in earnest until the late nineteenth century.

Until the Renaissance, the study of individuality and personality was held back by the same social and religious forces that hampered progress in art and science. The Middle Ages, which lasted approximately from the fall of the Roman Empire (late fifth century A. D.) until the fourteenth century, was, for most people, a time of unquestioning faith and a struggle to survive and do one's duty. Theologians such as Augustine emphasized introspective reflection, and materialism and science were considered to be enemies of the Church. Due to a combination of social and economic forces, the authority of the Catholic Church began to weak-

TABLE 1–1   **Selected Events in the History of Personality Assessment**

4th cent. B.C.	Theophrastus describes 30 personality or character types
2nd cent. A.D.	Galen relates Hippocrates's theory of body humors to temperament.
1800	F. Gall and J. Spurzheim establish the pseudoscience of phrenology, relating bumps on the skull to personality.
1884	F. Galton describes word association technique, behavior sampling, and other methods for measuring character.
1892	E. Kraepelin uses word association technique in clinical contexts.
1896	E. Kraepelin proposes new classification of mental disorders.
1905	C. Jung uses word-association test for analysis of mental complexes. First practical intelligence test, the Binet-Simon Scale, by A. Binet and T. Simon, published.
1906	Heymans and Wiersma develop list of symptoms indicative of psychopathology.
1910	Kent-Rosanoff word lists published.
1919	R. Woodworth's Personal Data Sheet, the first standardized personality inventory, used in military selection. S. Pressey's X-O Test published.
1921	H. Rorschach's Psychodiagnostic Test first published.
1925	E. Kretschmer describes his observations on the relationships of body build to personality and mental disorders.
1926	F. Goodenough's Draw-a-Man Test published.
1927	First edition of E. K. Strong's Vocational Interest Blank for Men published.
1928	H. Hartshorne and M. May studies of character reported.
1930s	L. Levy and S. Beck popularize Rorschach Inkblot Test in the United States.
1935	Thematic Apperception Test (TAT) developed by H. Murray and his collaborators. Humm-Wadsworth Temperament Scale published.
1938	H. Murray publishes *Explorations in Personality*, describing theoretical foundations of the Thematic Apperception Test. Bender Visual-Motor Gestalt Test for assessing personality and organic brain damage published. First edition of *Mental Measurements Yearbook* published.
1939	Kuder Preference Record and Wechsler-Bellevue Intelligence Scale published.
1940	J. Guilford applies factor analysis to the construction of a personality inventory.
1941–45	Situational tests developed by U. S. Office of Strategic Services.
1942	W. Sheldon and S. Stevens report their research on the relationships between body build and temperament.
1943	Minnesota Multiphasic Personality Inventory, by S. Hathaway and J. McKinley, published.
1949	R. Cattell's 16 Personality Factor Questionnaire published.
1953	Q-sort technique developed by W. Stephenson.
1954	P. Meehl's *Clinical Versus Statistical Prediction* published.
1955	G. Kelly's *Psychology of Personal Constructs* published.
1958	L. Kohlberg publishers the first version of his Moral Judgment Scale.

Table 1-1 continued

1970–90	Increasing use of computers in designing, administering, scoring, and interpreting personality assessment instruments and procedures.
1972	J. Holland's Self-Directed Search, a measure of interests and personality, published. Model Penal Code rule for legal insanity is published and widely adopted in the U. S.
1974	Results of research on Type A coronary-prone personality published and popularized by Friedman and Rosenman.
1975–80	Growth of behavioral assessment methods.
1985	*Standards for Educational and Psychological Testing* published.
1987	Revision of California Psychological Inventory published.
1989	MMPI-II published.
1994	*Diagnostic and Statistical Manual, Fourth Edition (DSM-IV)* published.
1997	Third edition of the Wechsler Adult Intelligence Scale (WAIS-III) published.
1998	*Thirteenth Mental Measurements Yearbook* published.

en during the fifteenth century. As a result, supernatural views and a preoccupation with death, demons, and the hereafter gave way to more temporal, earthly concerns.

The Renaissance, which lasted from the fourteenth to the seventeenth century A. D., together with the subsequent period of Enlightenment during the eighteenth century, witnessed a return to the ancient Hellenistic perspective on the value and worth of the individual. According to this ideal, people are capable of influencing their situation and circumstances. Freed from the constraints of intolerance and censorship, they can use their abilities to understand the world and themselves, and thereby improve the human condition.

Traditional church doctrine held that life is a battleground between the forces of good and evil. People were seen as basically evil, born in sin with only a hope and not a guarantee of salvation. In contrast, many philosophers during the Enlightenment and the succeeding Age of Romanticism maintained that human beings are not bad by nature. The French philosopher Jean-Jacques Rousseau (1712–1778) believed that people are born in a state of goodness and that naturalness is virtuous. He argued that society makes people bad, and that a return to the natural state of the "noble savage" is desirable. This point of view influenced a number of modern humanistic psychologists, who saw the human struggle as an attempt to realize the good or growth potential within oneself. On the other hand, the notion that people are born in neither a state of goodness nor evil, that each person's mind is a "blank tablet" (*tabula rasa*) at birth, was espoused by John Locke, Voltaire, and certain other philosophers. The writings of these men influenced the conceptions of many developmental and experimental psychologists during the twentieth century.

Pseudoscience and Personality Assessment

Most people are curious about what makes them "tick" and how they will turn out. Before the modern era, people often relied on oracles, soothsayers, and other fortune tellers to diagnose their character and foretell their futures. For example, the Oracle at Delphi's advice to "Know thyself" was widely quoted and believed. Unfortunately, much of the "knowledge" of the time, as well as the pseudosciences that perpetuated it, was based on false assumptions and biased observations. Pseudosciences such as astrology, numerology, palmistry, graphology, phrenology, and physiognomy, which have ancient origins, are still espoused by many people. Astrology, numerology, and palmistry are more concerned with forecasting the future or fate of individuals than with analyzing personality and character, but inasmuch as personality affects one's future, these pseudosciences form a part of the history of personality assessment.*

Astrology. Among the oldest of the pseudosciences is *astrology*, which is based on the notion that the relative positions of the moon and planets in relation to the sun affect the fortunes and characteristics of individuals. Each of the twelve

TABLE 1-2 **Personality Characteristics Allegedly Related to the Zodiac**

Constellation	Planet	Birth Date	Personality Characteristics
Capricorn	Saturn	12/21–1/20	Ambition, caution, work
Aquarius	Uranus	1/21–2/19	Humane, unconventional, high and low spirits
Pisces	Neptune	2/21–3/20	Inspiration, easily influenced, dreaming
Aries	Mars	3/21–4/20	Impulsiveness, adventure, disputes
Taurus	Venus	4/21–5/21	Endurance, obstination, labor
Gemini	Mercury	5/22–6/21	Skill, versatility, good relationships
Cancer	Moon	6/22–7/23	Appreciates home life, imagination, indecision
Leo	Sun	7/24–8/23	Generality, pride, desire for power
Virgo	Mercury	8/24–9/23	Analytical, studious, modest
Libra	Venus	9/24–10/23	Justice, artistic sense, sensitivity
Scorpio	Mars	10/24–11/22	Critical sense, secrecy, fights
Sagittarius	Jupiter	11/23–12/20	Idealism, mobility, open-mindedness

* Other pseudosciences concerned with the art of divination, or predicting political and natural events, are hydromancy, geomancy, haruspicy, and necromancy. *Hydromancy* consists of reading the airs, winds, and waters, and *geomancy* of reading geographical features, figures, or lines; *haruspicy* consists of reading the entrails of animals killed in sacrifice; *hepatoscopy*, reading the livers of sacrificial sheep; and *necromancy*, communicating with the dead.

signs of the *zodiac*, or constellations of these heavenly bodies, is supposedly associated with certain aspects of character, temperament, and aptitude (see Table 1–2). Given the exact time and place of a person's birth, an astrologer can prepare an individualized chart, or *horoscope*, of the planetary positions associated with that person. From this information, astrologers claim to be able to predict the person's future and advise him or her on decisions and actions.

Palmistry. Similar in some respects to astrology, and equally old, is *palmistry*. Palmists claim to be able to interpret the character and predict the destiny of a person by analyzing the features of his or her hand. Special attention is given to the seven mounts (Jupiter, Saturn, Apollo or the Sun, Mercury, Mars, the Moon, and Venus) located at the bases of the thumb and fingers and the sides of the hand (see Figure 1–1). The following are examples of characteristics that are purportedly associated with the development of five of these mounts:

Apollo (the sun): Related to intelligence.
Jupiter: Ambition, concern for honor, interest in religion; overdevelopment reveals pride and superstition.
Mars: High development indicates bravery and a martial character; low development suggests cowardice.
Saturn: Related to luck and wisdom.
Venus: Related to amorousness.

In addition to the seven mounts, palmists study the relative length and depth of the head line, the heart line, the life line, and the fortune line of the hand. A short or broken life line points to an early death or serious illness; the head line is associated with intelligence, the heart line with affection, and the fortune line predicts success and failure.

Phrenology. Related to palmistry, but focusing on the head instead of the hand, is *phrenology*. Presumably, relatively few people today believe in phrenology, but it was taken quite seriously by Thomas Jefferson, Edgar Allan Poe, and certain other learned men in the nineteenth century. Pioneered by Franz Gall and his student Johann Spurzheim, phrenology is a pseudoscience in which abstract mental qualities such as acquisitiveness, agreeableness, artistic talent, courage, greed, and pride are associated with the development of over three dozen "organs" of the brain. Phrenologists believe that overdevelopment of one or more of these brain "organs" results in a protuberance (bump) on the skull over the corresponding area (see Figure 1–2). For example, having a head that is thick and full behind the top of the ears was said to denote courage, whereas a head that is thin and depressed in that region was supposedly indicative of cowardice (Fowler, 1890, p. 1).

FIG. 1-1   **Benham's System of Hand-Zone Nomenclature.**

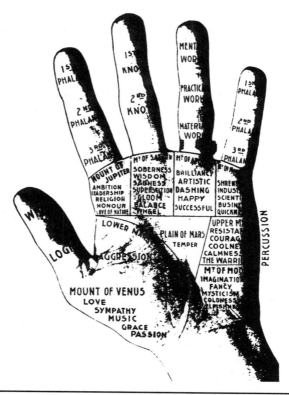

(From *The Book of Palmistry* by Fred Gettings. Triune Books, London, England.)

If the claims of phrenologists are correct, then personality or character should be interpretable by fingering the skull to analyze the configuration of bumps. A number of nineteenth-century physicians believed that it might even be possible to diagnose mental disorders in this manner. By the end of the nineteenth century, however, research in neurophysiology had disproved the notion that specific brain areas are associated with the personality traits or complex functions of the sort described by Gall and Spurzheim.

Physiognomy. Another pseudoscience that proposes to determine temperament and character from external bodily features, especially the face, is *physiognomy*. A kind of guide to physiognomic personality assessment can be found in the interesting chapter by Hett (1936). Dating back at least to Pythagoras in ancient

Phrenologists' Chart of Brain Functions (Corbis).   **FIG. 1–2**

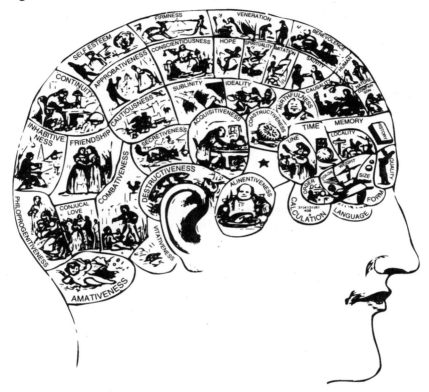

Greece, remnants of physiognomy exist in contemporary personality assessment. Examples are the requirement that a personal photograph be submitted with an employment application and in the Szondi Test. The Szondi Test consists of six sets of photographs with eight pictures per set, of mental patients having different psychiatric diagnoses (catatonia, depression, hysteria, mania, etc.). In taking the test, examinees select the two pictures they like most and the two they like least in each set. The basic assumption underlying the Szondi Test is that the facial features of the mental patients depicted in the 12 selected and 12 rejected photographs have special meaning for the examinee: the needs and personality of the examinee are thought to be similar to those of patients in the photographs that the examinee likes most and dissimilar to those of the patients that the examinee likes least.

Physiognomy should not be confused with the analysis of meanings or messages communicated by facial expressions such as smiling and crying (Ekman &

Friesen, 1984). Physiognomy is concerned with determining personal characteristics from the form or features of the body, especially the face. The analysis of facial expression is a more scientifically accepted and valid effort to determine the meanings and origins of nonverbal behavior.

Many physiognomic descriptions are contained in the English language, for example, a "disarming smile," an "honest expression," a "poker face," or "shifty eyes." Furthermore, certain actors pride themselves on being able to make facial expressions indicative of certain feelings and emotions while playing "character roles."

Graphology. For hundreds of years, and by studying dozens of books written on the subject, people have tried, without notable success, to assess individual personality by analyzing handwriting samples. The pseudoscience of *graphology* as a systematic procedure did not emerge, however, until the nineteenth century in continental Europe. Some *graphologists* attempt to interpret handwriting intuitively on the basis of overall, or global, impressions, whereas others are more analytic in stressing certain signs or clues such as the way the writer dots *i*'s or slants letters. Graphology is not viewed as representing quite the same degree of quackery as astrology or phrenology, and it continues to attract many proponents. For example, thousands of business organizations in the United States, Europe, and Israel use the services of graphologists in employee selection (Fowler, 1991; Sackheim, 1991). Unfortunately, the claims of the proponents of graphology are more often than not just as wrong as those of the phrenologists.

It makes sense that handwriting, which is a type of stylistic behavior, could reflect personality characteristics to some extent. Graphologists are, however, not noted for the validity of their analyses. Even attempts to analyze handwriting by means of computers have failed to demonstrate that handwriting analysis can be a valid method of personality assessment (Rothenberg, 1990). One problem in using handwriting as a diagnostic tool is its inconsistency: a person's handwriting is affected by alcohol, drugs, aging, disease, and many other factors (Kelly, 1994). A perusal of the research literature on graphology leads to the conclusion that graphologists typically do no better than chance in predicting job success (Neter & Ben-Shakhar, 1989).

The Late Nineteenth and Twentieth Centuries

After the French Revolution in the late eighteenth century, a more humane attitude toward the mentally ill developed through the influence of Philippe Pinel, who "struck the chains from the limbs of the insane" and instituted reforms in mental hospitals throughout France. The emphasis of early nineteenth-century psychiatry was on an *organic* basis for mental illness. This was a marked improvement over the older belief that the mentally ill are possessed of demons that must be driven out by beating or burning the body or some other form of *exorcism*. Many late nineteenth- and early twentieth-century psychiatrists focused on *functional* causes of mental illness, such as faulty habits acquired by experience. As a consequence, psychological forms of treatment—hypnosis, reeducation, and psychotherapy—rather than medicine or surgery, were recommended in many cases of mental illness. The French psychiatrists Jean-Martin Charcot and Pierre Janet were pioneers in the development of the concept of functional causes of mental disorders and the use of hypnosis in treatment. In addition to treatments for psychopathological conditions, methods of diagnosing them—including various observational and testing techniques—were devised by French psychiatrists and psychologists.

By the end of the nineteenth century, psychology had been formally christened a science, and the scientific study of human behavior and mental life was well underway. Despite the disinterest of Wilhelm Wundt, experimental psychology's founding father, in the study of motivation, emotion, intelligence, thought, personality, and other individual-difference variables, certain psychologists began conducting research on these topics.

In 1884, Francis Galton, who was actually more interested in intelligence than personality, proposed to measure emotions by recording changes in heartbeat and pulse rate and to assess good temper, optimism, and other so-called character traits. Among the methods described by Galton for measuring these traits was the behavior sampling technique of observing people in contrived social situations.

Galton was also the first scientist to propose using the *word association technique* for personality assessment purposes. In this technique, a series of words is spoken to the examinee, who is directed to respond by saying the first word that comes to mind. The psychiatrist Emil Kraepelin, who became famous for the diagnostic system of classifying mental disorders into organic versus functional and psychoneurotic versus psychotic categories, also developed a word association technique in 1892. Several years later (1905), the psychoanalyst Carl Jung used the word association technique to detect and analyze mental complexes.

The extensive observations and descriptions of mental disorders provided by Emil Kraepelin, Richard von Krafft-Ebing, Eugen Bleuler, and other psychiatrists during the late nineteenth and early twentieth centuries also provided a framework for later development of personality assessment instruments such as the Rorschach Inkblot Test and the Minnesota Multiphasic Personality Inventory (MMPI).

Alfred Binet, a psychologist whose primary claim to fame came from the measurement of intelligence, was also interested in the assessment of personality. Prior to his work in co-authoring the Binet-Simon Intelligence Scale (1905), Binet had devised methods for studying the personality characteristics of eminent persons. One technique that he used involved verbal responses to inkblots and telling stories about pictures (fantasy life); another technique was to collect and analyze writing samples. In one study, Binet asked seven graphologists to analyze handwriting samples obtained from 37 highly successful men and 37 less successful men. In contrast to the results of later scientific studies of graphology, Binet concluded that the diagnostic conclusions drawn by graphologists were fairly accurate (Rothenberg, 1990).

Of particular significance in the history of personality assessment during the early twentieth century was the development and use of the first personality inventory—the Woodworth Personal Data Sheet—for military selection in World War I. This paper-and-pencil, single-score inventory, which was a kind of standardized psychiatric interview, was designed to screen U. S. Army recruits for emotional disorders.

Other noteworthy events in personality assessment were the publication of the Rorschach Psychodiagnostic Test in 1920, the Thematic Apperception Test (TAT) in 1935, and the Minnesota Multiphasic Personality Inventory (MMPI) in 1943. All three of these instruments, which remain popular even to this day, are discussed at length in later chapters. Also related to personality assessment is the extensive work during the late 1920s and succeeding years on the measurement of interests, attitudes, and values. Experimental research on conflict, frustration, and aspiration level conducted by Kurt Lewin and his co-workers also demonstrated how personality could be studied and assessed scientifically.

A great number and variety of single-score and multiscore personality assessment instruments were developed during the 1920s and 1930s. Some of these instruments were designed to diagnose psychopathology, whereas others emphasized the analysis of personal adjustment, values, and other affective characteristics in normal individuals. During the 1940s and 1950s, the growth of clinical, educational, industrial, and other fields of applied psychology, coupled with the development of more sophisticated procedures for constructing, scoring, and interpreting psychometric instruments, led to an even greater number of measures of human abilities and personality. Among the personality variables that were measured and investigated extensively during the 1950s and 1960s were the *authoritarian personality* (Adorno, Frenkel-Brunswik, Levinson, & Sanford, 1950), *field-independence/dependence* (Witkin, Lewis, Hertzman, Machover, Meissner, & Wapner, 1954), *achievement motivation* (McClelland, 1961), *repression-sensitization* (Byrne, 1961), and *locus of control* (Rotter, 1966).

A significant factor in psychological testing and assessment today is the application of high-speed computing machinery in administering, scoring, and interpreting psychological assessment instruments. The use of computers in connection with personality assessment, which began during the 1960s, has broadened and facilitated applications of these instruments in various contexts.

As revealed by literally thousands of articles in popular and professional sources, interest in personality assessment has continued to grow. In addition to periodicals devoted exclusively to personality assessment, dozens of professional journals contain articles dealing with new personality tests and techniques and adaptations of older personality assessment instruments and procedures. The relationships of personality study to psychological assessment is the principal concern of the Society for Personality Assessment, but a number of other professional organizations also concentrate, at least in part, on the measurement of personality. Particularly noteworthy with respect to research on personality is the International Society for the Study of Individual Differences (ISSID), and the associated journal *Personality and Individual Differences.*

Despite, or perhaps because of, the extensive applications of personality assessment instruments, the validity and practical consequences of using these instruments have not gone unchallenged. Criticism can, of course, be healthy if it is not unwarranted or petty. Personality assessment, like any applied scientific enterprise, should be open to examination and evaluation. Consequently, the last section of Chapter 13 of this book is devoted to criticisms and controversies of personality assessment.

■ Theories of Personality

Although it is possible to adopt a fairly atheoretical, empirical approach to assessing personality, even psychologists who profess no great devotion to theories make some assumptions or have some preconceptions with regard to the nature and expected outcomes of their research. At the other extreme from the radical empiricist, who prefers to avoid psychological theories altogether, is the extreme rationalist who attempts to develop an intricate, all-encompassing theoretical model of human motives and actions. Unfortunately, such grandiose theories are frequently based on a minimum of actual observations of the objects of their efforts. Somewhere in the middle of the rational-empirical continuum is the personality psychologist who uses theories in an *eclectic* manner, selecting what he or she perceives as the most useful features of different theories to assist in interpreting the results of observations and other assessments.

At the very least it should be recognized that some frame of reference, some conceptual guidelines, can be helpful in assessing and explaining personality. Almost everyone has a pet theory as to why people behave in certain ways. Like the descriptions of Theophrastus and Shakespeare, these theories of human nature and behavior typically consist of stereotypes or other overgeneralizations. Nevertheless, they provide rough guidelines as to what can be expected of people and how we should act toward them. It is obviously important to have some explanation as to why people do the things they do and expectations of what they may do under certain circumstances. Our comfort and sometimes our very survival depend on our ability to understand and predict the behavior of other human beings and adjust to their idiosyncrasies.

Psychologists realize that everyone is different from everyone else, and that human behavior is very complex and sometimes inconsistent. Consequently, the professional personality theorist is usually cautious in accepting the truth and explanatory power of common-sense theories. The idiosyncrasies and complexities of human behavior and mental life are so impressive to certain psychologists that they have abandoned efforts to discover general principles or laws to explain the seeming vagaries of human nature. They have dismissed the so-called *nomothetic approach*—a search for general laws of behavior and personality—as unrealistic and inadequate to the task of understanding the individual. Rather, they advocate an *idiographic approach* of viewing each person as a lawful, integrated system worthy of analysis in his or her own right (Allport, 1937).

One of the major issues with which personality theorists have wrestled is the explanation of motivation—what drives people to behave in certain ways and to what extent this behavior is based on nature rather than nurture. Certain personality theorists seem to be more concerned with the structure than the dynamics of personality, but almost all realize that accounting for human motivation is an important part of the task of theory construction. Another concern is how social and nonsocial experiences shape personality both during childhood and later, and why certain aberrations or behavioral abnormalities occur. Finally, theorists ask how the different characteristics or facets of personality are organized and integrated to produce unique patterns of perceiving, thinking, and acting. Not all personality theorists have attempted to answer these questions, or even the same questions, in the same ways. There are many differences among theories of personality, differences that often seem to reflect the theorist's own personality as much as the actual nature of human behavior and cognition.

One important difference among personality theorists is the relative emphasis accorded to heredity and environment as molders of behavior. Another difference is the extent to which internal, personal characteristics of the individual rather than external, situational variables are considered to be the major determinants of human action. As these and other points of dispute among personality theorists indicate, there is no comprehensive theory of personality that is supported by all psychologists. On the contrary, theories and research findings in the field of personality and its assessment are constantly developing and changing. Still, it is important for students of personality assessment to have some acquaintance with representative theories of personality and to be aware of the strengths and weaknesses of those theories.

Despite their shortcomings, theories can serve as guides to the measurement and understanding of personality. Certainly one must have some *apperceptive*

Personality Assessment Methods Associated with Specific Theorists   **TABLE 1-3**

Alfred Adler—Analysis of birth order, early recollections dream analysis, social interest (Crandall, 1975)
Gordon Allport—Idiographic content analyses of letters and diaries. Dominance-Submission Test, Study of Values
Albert Bandura—Various measures of self-efficacy
Raymond Cattell—Factor analysis (I-data, Q-data, T-data), psychological tests (16 Personality Factor Questionnaire and other personality inventories)
Erik Erikson—Psychohistorical analysis; Inventory of Psychosocial Balance (Domino & Affonso, 1990); scale to measure development of sense of identity (Ochse & Plug, 1986).
Sigmund Freud—Free association, dream analysis, analysis of transference, analysis of resistance
Carl Jung—Word associations, method of amplification, symptom analysis, dream analysis, painting therapy
George Kelly—Role Construct Repertory Test
Abraham Maslow—Personality Orientation Inventory: A Measure of Self Actualization
David McClelland—Projective measures of need for achievement and need for power
Henry Murray—Thematic Apperception Test, situational (OSS) tests; concept of *needs* also used in Edwards Personal Preference Schedule and Adjective Check List
Carl Rogers—Q-Sort (Stephenson, 1953), Experience Inventory (Coan, 1972). Experiencing Scale (Gendlin & Tomlinson, 1967; Klein et al., 1969).
Julian Rotter—I-E Scale, Interpersonal Trust Scale
William Sheldon—Somatotyping and temperament-typing
Herman Witkin—Body Adjustment Test, Rod and Frame Test, Embedded Figures Test

---

mass, some ideational framework concerning personality and behavior, in order to interpret individual assessment findings. For this purpose, the theories constructed and tested by professional psychologists are probably more useful than the common-sense notions of laypersons.

The five groups of theories discussed here—type, trait-factor, psychoanalytic (or psychodynamic), phenomenological (humanistic), and social learning—have not been equally influential in the development of personality assessment instruments and procedures. However, theorists of all persuasions have devised and/or stimulated the design of various assessment techniques. Sometimes these have been fairly basic procedures, such as painstaking observations of behavior, and at other times quite complex, such as projective techniques. Table 1–3 lists the most prominent personality theorists and some of the assessment methods that are associated with them.

Type Theories

As seen in the discussion of the characters of Theophrastus, one of the oldest explanations of personality is that there are fixed categories or types of people.

The Hippocrates-Galen conception of four body humors and four corresponding temperaments is such a *type theory*. Although this theory is now only of historical interest, there is some overlap between it and more modern conceptions (see Figure 1-4).

The notion that body build is related to personality has captured the imagination of many writers. For example, in Shakespeare's *Julius Caesar* (Act I, Scene II), Caesar observes:

> Let me have men about me that are fat,
> Sleek-headed men, and such as sleep a-nights.
> Yond Cassius has a lean and hungry look;
> He thinks too much, such men are dangerous.
> ... ...
> Would he were fatter! ... He reads much;
> He is a great observer, and he looks
> Quite through the deeds of men: He loves no plays,
> As dost thou Antony; he hears no music;
> Seldom he smiles, and smiles in such a sort
> As if he mock'd himself, and scorn'd his spirit
> That could be mov'd to smile at anything.
> Such as he be never at heart's ease
> While they behold a greater than themselves;
> And therefore are they very dangerous.

Three centuries later, after making extensive measurements of the physiques of mental patients and others, Ernst Kretschmer (1925) concluded that both a thin, lanky, angular body build (asthenic physique) and a muscular body build (athletic physique) are associated with withdrawing tendencies (schizoid temperament). In contrast, a rotund, stocky body build (pyknic physique) was said to be associated with emotional instability (cycloid temperament). Kretschmer maintained that the cycloid and schizoid temperament types are transitional stages, the cycloid leading to manic-depressive psychosis and the schizoid to schizophrenia.

Another body typologist, the criminologist Ceasare Lombroso (1836–1909), believed that the physical characteristics of criminals are different from those of other people. Conceiving of criminals as at a lower stage in biological development, he noted that they had large jaws, receding foreheads, and other primitive physical traits. Lombroso interpreted the presence of such physical features as demonstrating that these individuals were born to become criminals. However, the fact that many criminals do not possess the characteristics listed by Lombroso led to doubts about the credibility of his assertions.

William Sheldon and S.S. Stevens (Sheldon, Stevens, & Tucker, 1940; Sheldon & Stevens, 1942) also proposed a typological theory. The Sheldon *somatotype* system classifies human physiques into three components according to their degree of *endomorphy* (fatness), *mesomorphy* (muscularity), and *ectomorphy* (thin-

Sheldon's Somatotypes.   **FIG. 1–3**

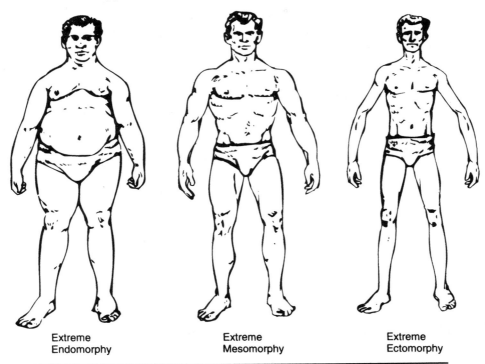

| Extreme | Extreme | Extreme |
| Endomorphy | Mesomorphy | Ectomorphy |

(From *Elements of Psychology* (2nd ed.) by David Krech, Richard Crutchfield, and Norman Livson. Copyright © 1969 by Alfred A. Knopf, Inc. Reprinted by permission of Hilda Krech and Mary Crutchfield.)

ness) on a scale of 1 to 7 (see Figure 1–3). Thus, an extreme endomorph might be a 7–1–1, an extreme mesomorph a 1–7–1, and an extreme ectomorph a 1–1–7. The degree of each component was judged by measurements taken from photographs of the person at various angles.

An excess of any one of the three somatotype components in the Sheldon-Stevens system was found to be related to the temperament types of *viscerotonia*, *somatotonia*, and *cerebrotonia*. An individual's scores on these temperament dimensions were determined from ratings made on the basis of observations and responses to questionnaires. Viscerotonics are jolly, sociable, and loving comfort and eating. Somatotonics are assertive, dominating, noisy, callous, have a youthful orientation, and love physical adventure and exercise. Cerebrotonics are restrained, fast in reacting, introversive, hypersensitive to pain, have difficulty sleeping, and are oriented toward later periods of life. Moderate to high correlations were obtained between ratings on endomorphy and viscerotonia, meso-morphy and somatotonia, and ectomorphy and cerebrotonia.

Body-type theories are interesting, but because of the many exceptions to the hypothesized relationships between body build and personality, their scientific status is not very high. Different interpretations have also been given to the correlations between physique and personality. Contemporary psychologists also object to typologies because they assign people to categories and attach labels to them. Not only does labeling overemphasize internal causation of behavior, but it may also act as a self-fulfilling prophecy in which people tend to become what they are labeled as being. Thus, a person who is designated as an introvert may be left alone by would-be friends, causing him or her to become even more socially isolated. Similarly, a so-called extrovert may become more outgoing or sociable because other people expect such a person to behave in an extroversive manner.

Trait Theories

Among professionals and laypersons alike, a seemingly natural and popular way of describing personality is in terms of traits. A personality *trait* is a predisposition to respond in a particular way to persons, objects, or situations. Traits are narrower or less general than *types*. Whereas traits are possessed in different amounts by different people, types are combinations or clusters of traits.

Gordon Allport. One of the first and most prominent trait theorists was Gordon Allport (1897–1967). Allport visualized human personality as consisting of the dynamic organization of those traits that determine a person's unique adjustment to the environment. Allport and Odbert (1936) began their research on traits by listing 17,953 words in the English language that refer to characteristics of personality. Then they combined and classified the words according to their order of pervasiveness or generality of influence across different situations, and thereby reduced them to a smaller number of trait names. In order of pervasiveness across situations, there are cardinal traits, central traits, and secondary traits. *Cardinal traits*, such as authoritarianism, humanitarianism, Machiavellianism (striving for power), sadism, and narcissism (self-love) are so pervasive in a person's life that they are expressed in almost all behavior. Next in order of pervasiveness are *central traits*—tendencies such as affectionateness, assertiveness, distractibility, honesty, kindness, reliability, and sociability that influence behavior in various situations but not as generally as cardinal traits. In last place according to pervasiveness are *secondary traits,* such as preferences for food or music. A typical individual has few cardinal traits, more central traits, and even more secondary traits.

In terms of the degree to which they are general or shared among different people, Allport also differentiated among common traits, individual traits, and personality dispositions. *Common traits, such as* aggressiveness, are widely shared, *but individual traits* and *personality dispositions* are more specific to particular individuals. Although common traits and individual traits can be measured by standardized assessment instruments, personal dispositions are determined only by careful study of a person.

R.B. Cattell. Another trait theorist, R.B. Cattell (1905–) adopted a holistic position in which personality encompasses both affective and cognitive variables. Cattell classified personality traits in four different ways: common versus unique, surface versus source, constitutional versus environmental-mold, and dynamic versus ability versus temperament. Like Allport, Cattell saw *common traits* as characterizing all people, and *unique traits*, which are the same as Allport's individual traits, as peculiar to the individual. Regarding the surface-source distinction, surface traits are easily observed in a person's behavior, but *source traits* can be discovered only by the statistical processes of factor analysis (see Chapter 2). Furthermore, source traits may be general or specific, depending on the number of situations in which they exert their influence.

Cattell's trait-factor theory also includes *constitutional traits* that depend on heredity, and *environmental mold traits* that are derived from the environment. Finally, *dynamic traits* are those that motivate the individual toward a goal, *ability traits* determine the ability to achieve the goal, and *temperament traits* pertain to the emotional aspects of goal-directed activity. Cattell's trait-factor theory, which is much more elaborate than the brief description provided here, has served as a framework for constructing several personality inventories.

Hans Eysenck (1916–1997). Many other psychologists have theorized and conducted research on personality traits and designed instruments to measure them. Factor-analytic methods have been applied in much of this research, yielding a variety of personality dimensions. The three basic dimensions, or supertraits, in Hans Eysenck's system are introverted versus extraverted, emotionally stable versus emotionally unstable (neurotic), and psychoticism. The first two of these supertraits, which Eysenck believed to be a biologically-based, are depicted in Figure 1–4. The positions of the 32 traits on the circle in this figure indicate the magnitude and direction on the two supertraits. Persons who are on the extraverted side of the horizontal scale are interested primarily in people or things outside themselves. A highly extraverted individual is "sociable, likes parties, has many friends, needs to have people to talk to, and does not like reading or studying by himself" (Eysenck & Eysenck, 1975, p. 5). In contrast, the focus of persons who are closer to the introverted end of the scale is primarily on themselves and their private, inner lives. A typical introvert is characterized as "a quiet, retiring

FIG. 1–4 A Two-Dimensional Classification of Personality.

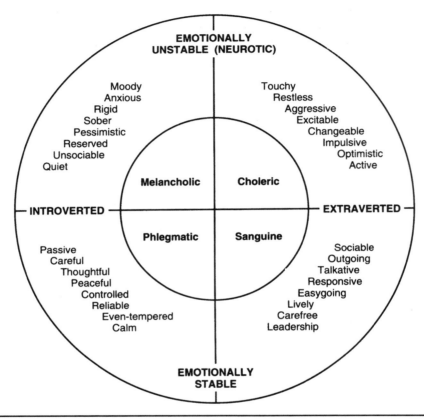

(From *Personality and Individual Differences* by H. J. Eysenck and M. W. Eysenck, Plenum Publishing, 1958. Reprinted by permission of Plenum Publishing.)

sort of person, introspective, fond of books rather than people, reserved and distant except to intimate friends" (p. 5). Also of interest are the locations of Galen's four temperament types on the circle. A melancholic individual is an unstable introvert; a choleric individual, an unstable extravert; a phlegmatic person, a stable introvert; and a sanguine person, a stable extravert.

Psychoanalytic Theories

As pioneered by Sigmund Freud (1856–1939), psychoanalysis is a method of psychotherapy, a method of research on human personality, and a theory of personality. As a theory of personality, psychoanalysis is dynamic, developmental, and intrapsychic. It is dynamic in that it deals with motivation—both conscious and unconscious. It is developmental in that it conceives of personality as changing in response to biological and environmental forces. And it is intrapsychic in that it views the interaction of various motives as producing mental conflicts and psychological disorders.

Sigmund Freud. Freud saw human personality as a kind of battleground where three combatants—id, ego, and superego—struggle for supremacy. The *id*, a reservoir of instinctive drives of sex and aggression housed in the unconscious part of the mind, acts according to the *pleasure principle*. It runs into conflict with the *superego* (conscience), which acts according to the *moral principle*. Although the id is innate, the superego develops as the child internalizes the prohibitions and sanctions that parents place upon his or her behavior. Meanwhile, the *ego*, acting according to the *reality principle*, serves as a mediator between the unrelenting struggle between the id and superego for supremacy. It is as if the id says, "Now!", the superego says "Never!", and the ego says "Later" to the person's basic desires. Although id impulses and the conflict of id with superego and ego usually take place in the unconscious mind, they are expressed in thoughts and behavior in various disguised forms. The expression of unconscious drives and conflicts can occur in dreams (the so-called "royal road to the unconscious), under hypnosis, by having patients say whatever comes into their minds (*free association*), or by using projective techniques and other methods.

Freud also believed that human personality develops through a series of *psychosexual stages*. During each stage, a different area of the body (*erogenous zone*) is the focus of sexual stimulation and gratification, and at that stage conflicts pertaining to the particular body region predominate. The *oral stage* occurs from birth to one and a half years. At this stage pleasure is derived primarily from stimulation of the mouth and lips, as in sucking, biting, and swallowing. During the *anal stage*, from about age one and a half to three years, interest and conflict center on the retention and expulsion of feces. Negativism, manifested by defiance of parental orders, and frequently associated with toilet training, is most pronounced during this stage. Next in order is the *phallic stage*, from ages three to six years, when the body region of greatest interest is the genital area. During the phallic stage—when rubbing, touching, exhibiting oneself, and looking are emphasized, the Oedipus complex develops. The *Oedipus complex*, consisting of a composite of sexual feelings toward the mother and dislike of the father in three- to six-year-old boys, was viewed by Freud as a universal phenomenon. The comparable situation in girls—disliking the mother and loving the father—is referred to as the *Electra complex*.

Freud's theory of personality was based almost entirely on clinical observations of approximately 100 patients, and many parts of the theory have not been confirmed by subsequent research. Certain assumptions, for example, the universality of the Oedipus complex and the notion of a latency period, have been shown to be incorrect. Nevertheless, Freud and his followers rendered an important service in recognizing the existence of infant and child sexuality and its significance for personality development. But recognition of this contribution does not imply acceptance of the idea that all children invariably go through the sequence of psychosexual stages outlined above or that adult personality structure is critically dependent on childhood sexual conflicts.

Classical (Freudian) psychoanalysis has employed such techniques as clinical observations, interviews, and dream analysis in the assessment of personality, but a number of projective techniques have also been applied to get at deeper, less conscious needs, feelings, and conflicts. Word associations, inkblot tests, and even various rating scales and inventories have been designed for the purposes of psychoanalytic research and practice.

Carl Jung. Among the colleagues and disciples of Freud who deviated from his views were Carl Jung, Alfred Adler, Karen Horney, Erik Fromm, and Erik Erikson. In his *analytic psychology*, Jung differentiated between the *personal unconscious*, which was essentially the same as Freud's *unconscious*, and the *collective unconscious*. Jung's collective unconscious is a part of the mind that is shared with all humanity, a storehouse of archaic molds (*archetypes*) and inherited propensities. The collective unconscious contains both frightening memories and ancestral wisdom; it is the source of human creativity. Jung also distinguished between various personality types or dimensions—introversion versus extroversion, sensing versus intuition, thinking versus feeling, and judging versus perception. These dimensions form the theoretical basis of a personality inventory known as the Myers-Briggs Type Indicator (see Chapter 7).

Alfred Adler. Alfred Adler's *individual psychology* minimizes the effects of frustrated or repressed impulses and biological factors on the personality and stresses social factors instead. Adler is best known for his emphasis on feelings of inferiority (the *inferiority complex*) as determiners of personality adjustment, and on the mechanism of compensation as a way of coping with these feelings. According to Adler, feelings of inferiority, which consist of a sense of incompleteness or imperfection in one's life, result from frustration of the drive to mastery (the *will to power*). In psychologically healthy individuals these feelings are replaced with a greater *social interest*, as manifested by being helpful, sympathetic, and tolerant.

Erik Erikson. Compared with Freud, modern psychoanalysts attribute greater importance to social learning and culture than to biological instincts as determiners of personality and behavior. These neoanalysts, or *ego psychologists*, admit their intellectual debt to the founding father, but they have diverged substantially from Freud in stressing the importance of the ego and social factors, and focusing on cross-cultural studies for understanding human personality. One of the most famous of the neoanalysts is Erik Erikson, whose psychohistorical analyses of Martin Luther and Mahatma Gandhi (Erikson, 1958, 1969), in particular, stimulated research on personality assessment through an analysis of the writings of and about famous people. Erikson is even better known for his description of stages and crises in psychological development (Erikson, 1963).

According to Erikson, psychological development consists of eight stages: infancy, early childhood, play age, school age, adolescence, young adulthood, middle age, and old age. At each of these stages the individual is confronted with a particular crisis or conflict that must be resolved if one is to progress to the next level of development. The main crisis or conflict is between trust and mistrust in infancy, between autonomy and doubt in early childhood, between initiative and guilt in the play age (preschool age), between industry and inferiority in the school age, and between identity and role confusion in adolescence. In young adulthood, the conflict is between intimacy and isolation, in middle age it is between generativity and self-absorption, and in old age it is between integrity and despair. A self-report inventory, the Inventory of Psychosocial Balance (IPB) was designed by Domino and Affonso (1990) to assess an individual's standing on all eight psychosocial stages.

Phenomenological Theories

Stemming from a philosophical tradition that emphasizes the analysis of immediate, personal, subjective experience, *phenomenological* (humanistic or "self") *theorists* maintain that trait theorists and others who attempt to interpret personality in terms of a set of components do an injustice to its integrated, dynamic organization. Consequently, phenomenological theorists have been quite critical of psychoanalytic, trait-factor, and behavioral theories of personality. In contrast to traditional psychoanalysis, which emphasizes the fundamental important of sexual and aggressive impulses, the unconscious, and psychosexual stages of development, phenomenologists stress perceptions, meanings, feelings, and the self. Phenomenologists see a person as responding to the world in terms of his or her unique, private perceptions of it. These perceptions are determined by individual experiences and the meanings placed on those experiences in an effort to realize one's potentialities. That part of the environment that is perceived and has meaning for a person is known as the *phenomenal field*, a portion of which (the *self*) is related to the individual in a personal way. Finally, the evaluations, good or bad, that the individual places on the self are referred to as the *self-concept*.

According to Abraham Maslow, Carl Rogers, and other phenomenological theorists and practitioners, the individual strives to attain a state of *self-actualization*, a congruence between the real and ideal selves. The basic direction of a person's existence is toward self-actualization and pleasant relations with other people, but that effort can be disrupted in various ways. Rogers pointed out that most people are not open to or willing to accept the full range of their experiences. In the process of growing up, they learn that they are objects of *conditional positive regard*: parents and other significant people accept the child's behavior only if it conforms to expected standards *(conditions of worth)*. Consequently, the child, who eventually becomes an adult, learns to recognize and accept only a part of his or her experiences. The result is an individual who cannot become totally functioning unless she or he receives *unconditional positive regard* from other people—a state in which the person is accepted regardless of what he or she is or does.

Clinical practitioners of the phenomenological persuasion have tended to reject more objective psychological tests and procedures in favor of case studies and open or unstructured interviews as means of assessing human personality. Carl Rogers was not a great believer in the use of personality assessment instruments, and the influence of phenomenology on the construction of personality assessment instruments has not been nearly as great as that of psychoanalytic and trait-factor theories. However, designers of instruments for assessing feelings and attitudes toward the self usually follow a phenomenological theory of personality. Illustrative of instruments in this category are *Q sorts* (Stephenson, 1953) and inventories such as the Tennessee Self-Concept Scale, the Piers-Harris Children's Self-Concept Scale, and the Coopersmith Self-Esteem Inventories.

Murray's Personology

As described in Murray's book *Explorations in Personality* (1938), *personology* was never a unique, fully developed theory of personality in the same sense as Freud's psychoanalytic theory. Murray's theoretical position was more holistic, incorporating ideas from psychoanalysis, trait theory, and other psychological systems. Murray also believed that the field of personality would best be served by intensive study of the single case, and the 20 "needs" described by him are reminiscent of Allport's "traits." A basic principle of Murray's theorizing is that human beings are driven to reduce tensions generated by forces that are internal *(needs)* and external *(press)* to the person. Thus, behavior is a function of both needs and press, defined as follows:

> A need is a construct . . . which stands for a force (the physico-chemical nature of which is unknown) in the brain region, a force which organizes perception, apperception, intellection, conation, and action in such a way as to transform in a certain direction an existing unsatisfying situation.
>
> The press of an object is what it can *do to the subject or for the subject*—the power that it has to affect the well-being of the subject in one way or another. The cathexis of an object . . . is what it can make the subject do. (Murray, 1938, p. 121).

Murray labeled the actual, objective press from the environment *alpha press*, whereas the perceived press is *beta press*.

The analysis of Thematic Apperception Test stories in terms of needs and press, which is discussed in Chapter 12, was an important application of Murray's concepts in the area of personality assessment. His list of physiogenic and psychogenic needs has also been used in scoring more objective instruments such as the Edwards Personal Preference Schedule and the Adjective Check List.

Two other concepts, or *hypothetical constructs*, in Murray's theory are thema and vector-value. A *thema*, of which behavior is a function, results from a combination of a particular need and a particular press. The concept of *vector-value*, or simply *vector*, was added by Murray to emphasize the fact that needs, rather than existing alone, operate to serve some value or intent. To a large extent, the notion of *vector*, as a force that serves some value, came to replace that of *need* in Murray's thinking. Examples of such vectors, or behavioral tendencies, are avoidance, expression, reception, and rejection.

Social Learning Theories

Many other theoretical conceptions have influenced the development of personality assessment procedures and instruments. Among these are the behavioral concepts discussed in Chapter 5, George Kelly's (1955) theory of personal constructs (see Chapter 6), and the cognitive-behavioral approaches of social learning theorists such as Julian Rotter, Albert Bandura, and Walter Mischel. Only Rotter's and Bandura's ideas will be discussed here; detailed descriptions of other social learning theories are given in Aiken (1993).

Rotter's Social Learning Theory. The first *social learning theory* per se was that of Julian Rotter (1954), who attempted to integrate the traditional behavioristic position on the role of reinforcement in learning with the cognitive conceptions of field theorists such as Kurt Lewin. Rotter was certainly not the first psychologist to note that much human behavior is learned in a social context, but he made a more conscious effort than his predecessors to develop a systematic theory of how this takes place. The theory begins by differentiating between *reinforcement* (motivation) and *expectancy* (cognition); reinforcements result in movement toward or away from a goal, whereas cognitions are internal states such as expectancy and reinforcement value. The term *expectancy* refers to a subjective probability held by a person that a specific behavior performed in a certain situation will lead to reinforcement. Two *generalized expectancies* that have been measured and investigated by Rotter and others are internal-external locus of control and interpersonal trust. *Locus of control* refers to the typical direction from which people perceive themselves as being controlled—internal, or from within oneself, versus external, or by other people. *Interpersonal trust* is concerned with the extent to which a person believes that other people are truthful.

Reinforcement is important for performance, but not all reinforcements are equally valued by the individual. Even when the probabilities of occurrence of different reinforcements are equal, certain objects or actions will have greater *reinforcement value* than others. Both reinforcement value and expectancies are affected by the psychological relevance or meaning of the situation to the individual, which must be understood in order to predict a person's behavior in that situation.

Bandura's Cognitive Social Learning Theory. More important for its development of techniques for modifying maladaptive behavior than for the design of personality assessment instruments is Albert Bandura's (1977) *cognitive social learning theory*. Conceptualizing psychological functioning as the reciprocal interaction of behavior, person variables (cognitions and other internal states), and environmental variables, Bandura emphasizes the fact that the individual is not a passive push-button apparatus which only acts when acted upon. People both influence and are influenced by the social environment, in which learning takes place by observation, imitation, and modeling. Unlike more traditional behaviorists such as Clark Hull and B. F. Skinner, Bandura maintained that much learning takes place without reinforcement—in the absence of rewards and punishments, but that reinforcement determines when the learned behavior will occur. Particularly important to learning is the process of *modeling* the behavior of others. The effectiveness of modeling depends on such factors as the personal characteristics of the model and the learner's motivational level. Aggression, fears, sex-typed behaviors and many other emotional and stylistic reactions are, according to Bandura, learned by observation and modeling.

Bandura underscores the fact that learning and behavior are mediated by perceptions and cognitions. People form internal, symbolic representations of their environments, and these representations mediate changes in behavior. By manipulating these internal symbols, the individual learns to visualize the consequences of certain actions and hence to regulate his or her behavior. Also important in Bandura's theory is the concept of *self-efficacy*, a person's expectation that he or she is capable of learning or performing the particular behaviors that will result in desirable outcomes in a certain situation (Bandura, 1986). Whether or not a person decides to strive toward a particular goal depends greatly on his or her perceived self-efficacy to do what is required to attain the goal. Self-efficacy is affected by the person's history of reinforcement, vicarious experiences, verbal persuasion, and emotional arousal. Also important in Bandura's social learning theory is the concept of *self-system*—an internal frame of reference for perceiving, evaluating, and regulating one's behavior. A part of the self-system is made up of self-efficacy and performance standards acquired during the process of growing up.

Other Approaches to Personality Assessment

A number of assessment instruments have been developed in the context of investigations of personality and behavior disorders.

These efforts, although not totally devoid of theoretical foundations, have not been restricted to a particular theoretical position. There are many examples of this approach: the research of the Harvard personologists, which resulted in the Thematic Apperception Test and other instruments (Murray, 1938); research on the authoritarian personality with the F scale (Adorno et al., 1950); research conducted at the Institute for Personality Assessment and Research in Berkeley, California, which produced the Omnibus Personality Inventory (MacKinnon, 1962); Kohlberg's (1974) research on morality using his Moral Judgment Scale; research on cognitive styles conducted by Witkin and his coworkers (e.g., Witkin & Goodenough, 1981) with their measures of field independence/dependence and by Kagan (1966) with his Matching Familiar Figures Test; and Zuckerman's (1994) research on sensation seeking using his Sensation Seeking Scale. A number of personality assessment instruments were also developed and refined in connection with investigations of genetic factors in personality, continuity of personality across the life span, and the relationships of personality to demographic variables (gender, ethnicity, social class, culture, birth order, etc.).

Finally, rather than being designed in accordance with a specific theory or hypothesis concerning personality, or even in connection with a particular research program, many assessment instruments have been constructed on a purely empirical basis. For example, the items on the Minnesota Multiphasic Personality Inventory (MMPI) were selected on the basis of their ability to distinguish between contrasting groups of normal adults and groups of psychiatric patients. No specific theory of personality was implied or involved in this empirical procedure; MMPI items were simply validated against the specific criterion of psychiatric diagnoses of various samples of mental patients (see Chapter 8).

Another popular assessment instrument that was developed on a purely empirical basis was the Strong Vocational Interest Blank, the grandfather of the current Strong Interest Inventory (see Chapter 9).

■ Summary

The study of personality is concerned with the unique patterns of psychological characteristics that are descriptive of people. A holistic definition of personality deals with both the affective and cognitive, behavioral and mental variables that differentiate between individuals. Various methods—observations, interviews, rating scales, inventories, projective techniques, tests—are used to assess the structure and function of personality, how it develops, and what causes it to function inappropriately.

The assessment of personality is as old as humanity; the earliest methods were observation and situational testing. Descriptions of types of character or temperament are found in the writings of the ancient Greeks, Romans, and people of other cultures and nationalities. Such generalized descriptions also appear in famous works of literature written during medieval, Renaissance, and modern times. One of the most widely cited typologies in ancient times was Hippocrates's humoral theory and the corresponding four temperaments (sanguine, melancholic, choleric, and phlegmatic).

Among the pseudosciences that have been concerned with the analysis of human personality, character, and destiny are astrology, palmistry, phrenology, physiognomy, and graphology. With the possible exception of graphology, none of these pseudosciences is now considered by psychologists to have any factual basis.

The scientific assessment of personality began during the late nineteenth century in the research of Francis Galton, Alfred Binet, and other psychologists and psychiatrists. The first projective technique, the word association test, was introduced by Galton and applied by Emil Kraepelin and Carl Jung for psychodiagnostic purposes. The first personality inventory, a set of questions pertaining to psychopathological symptoms, was devised by Robert Woodworth and his collaborators during World War I. This inventory, the Personal Data Sheet, was designed to identify men who were most likely break down under the stress of military life.

The Rorschach Psychodiagnostic Test, the most widely used of all projective techniques, was devised by Hermann Rorschach during the early 1920s. The second most popular projective technique, the Thematic Apperception Test, was constructed by Henry Murray and his collaborators during the 1930s. The most widely used personality inventory, the Minnesota Multiphasic Personality Inventory (MMPI), was published initially in the early 1940s.

One or more theories of personality stimulated or guided the construction, scoring, and interpretation of many different personality assessment instruments. Psychoanalytic theories and various type and trait-factor theories have exerted the greatest influence on personality assessment, but a number of instruments also owe their development to phenomenological (self) and social learning (behavioral) theories. Different theories place different emphases on the structural and dynamic aspects of personality, and on the relative importance of biological and environmental determinants in its development.

As examples of theories that have stimulated the development of various personality assessment methods, the chapter considers the body-type theory of Sheldon and Stevens, the trait-factor theories of Allport, Cattell, and Eysenck, the psychoanalytic theories of Freud, Jung, and Adler, and the self theory of Rogers.

Three other theoretical, or rational, explanations of personality are described briefly: Murray's need/press conception and the social learning theories of Rotter and Bandura.

In contrast to assessment devices stemming from a specific theory of personality, instruments such as the MMPI and the Strong Vocational Interest Blank were designed on an empirical basis according to their ability to differentiate among specific groups of people. Nevertheless, the construction of these empirically derived instruments was guided by certain assumptions concerning what constructs the instrument should measure and what kinds of items it should contain. Thus, the invention of techniques for assessing personality does not occur in a vacuum but is founded on preconceptions concerning the nature of personality and its development in a particular sociocultural context.

■ Questions and Activities

1. The relationships between body build and personality that were noted by Kretschmer, Sheldon and Stevens, and others do not *prove* that physique causes temperament, or vice versa. Correlation does not imply causation; it only implies prediction. In what way does body build influence personality development? In what way does personality influence physical development? Might not the relationship between personality and physique be dynamic, reciprocal, and interactive? Explain.

2. Rank, from 1 to 12, each of the following sets of three adjectives in terms of how descriptive each set is of you personally. A rank of 1 means that the three adjectives are completely descriptive of you, and a rank of 12 means that the three adjectives are not at all descriptive of you.

_____ 1. pioneering, enthusiastic, and courageous
_____ 2. stable, stubborn, and well-organized
_____ 3. intellectual, adaptable, and clever
_____ 4. sensitive, nurturing, and sympathetic
_____ 5. extraverted, generous, and authoritative
_____ 6. critical, exacting, and intelligent
_____ 7. harmonizing, just, and sociable
_____ 8. secretive, strong, and passionate
_____ 9. honest, impulsive, and optimistic
_____10. ambitious, hard-working, and cautious
_____11. original, open-minded, and independent
_____12. kind, sensitive, and creative

Read the following paragraph for an "interpretation" of your responses:

According to astrology, your personality characteristics are determined by the zodiacal sign of your birthdate. The 12 zodiacal signs and the corresponding dates are as follows:

_____ 1. Aries: March 21–April 19
_____ 2. Taurus: April 20–May 20
_____ 3. Gemini: May 21–June 21
_____ 4. Cancer: June 22–July 22
_____ 5. Leo: July 23–August 22
_____ 6. Virgo: August 23–September 22
_____ 7. Libra: September 23–October 22
_____ 8. Scorpio: October 23–November 21
_____ 9. Sagittarius: November 22–December 21
_____10. Capricorn: December 22–January 19
_____11. Aquarius: January 20–February 18
_____12. Pisces: February 19–March 20

Does the number of the item triad that you gave a rank of 1 correspond to the number of your zodiacal sign? Are the numbers of any of the other item triads that you gave high ranks close to the number of your zodiacal sign? Why or why not? Does astrology really work? Is this a fair test of the validity of analyzing personality in terms of zodiacal signs?
(Adapted from Balch, W.R., 1980). Testing the validity of astrology in class. *Teaching of Psychology*, 7(4), 247–250.)

3. Both classical and modern literature are replete with descriptive examples of the presumed relationships of personality characteristics to facial form and movement. List as many illustrations as you can from the writings of William Shakespeare, Charles Dickens, and other famous writers of such presumed relationships. These writers also created many stereotypic characters, such as Falstaff, Othello, Uriah Heep, Mr. Micawber, and The Artful Dodger, whose names have become synonymous with particular personality characteristics or syndromes. List as many stereotypes of this kind as you can. In what way does popular fiction rely on the successful description of stereotypic characters?

4. Collect anonymous handwriting samples other than signatures from members of a college class and attempt to match the students with their handwriting. What information or techniques did you use in making these matches, and how successful were you? Were you at least able to differentiate between the handwriting of males and females? A colleague of mine and I (Aiken & Zweigenhaft, 1978) found that, in a sample of men and women in Iran, not only were the signatures of women smaller than those of men, but people of higher social status had larger signatures than people of lower social status. Does this make sense? Would you expect similar results in more democratic countries such as the United States? Why or why not?

5. Of what does an effective theory of personality, or any psychological theory for that matter, consist? What does it attempt to do, and what are the criteria of its effectiveness?
6. Make a case for physiognomy and graphology as legitimate areas of research and application in personality assessment.
7. Certain adjectives and nouns are likely to go together in English to describe the behavioral or personality characteristics of certain individuals. Consider the following matching test item:

Directions
On each of the line segments in the *Adjective* column, write the letter corresponding to the associated word in the *Noun* column.

Adjective	*Noun*
___ 1. brown	a. arm
___ 2. disarming	b. eyes
___ 3. fast	c. face
___ 4. glad	d. forehead
___ 5. golden	e. gaze
___ 6. high	f. hand
___ 7. intense	g. lips
___ 8. poker	h. nose
___ 9. sensuous	i. palms
___ 10. shifty	j. shuffle
___ 11. silver	k. smile
___ 12. strong	l. smirk
___ 13. sweaty	m. tongue
	n. voice

After you have made your matches, indicate which adjective-noun combinations are indicators or signs of deception (lying). Can you think of any other adjective-noun combinations that describe other behaviors or personality? Key: 1-h, 2-k, 3-j, 4-f, 5-n, 6-d, 7-e, 8-c, 9-g, 10-b, 11-m, 12-a, 13-i. The following pairs are suggestive of deception: 1-h, 2-k, 3-j, 4-f, 8-c, 10-b, 11-m, 12-a, 13–i. Why do you think there are so many?
8. As long as people have walked the earth, they have depended on other animals for their very existence. Recognition of the importance of animals—for food, clothing, transportation, various household objects, companionship, and even as objects of worship, is seen in the drawings, paintings, and carvings of animal images from prehistoric times to the modern era. Early humans undoubtedly spent a great deal of time watching animals and wondering what they were thinking and what spirits possessed them. Animals were thought to have personalities, and some of these same personality characteristics, perhaps through

reincarnation, were seen in humans. For example, consider the following animals: (1) eagle, (2) fox, (3) lion, (4) mule, (5) owl, (6) peacock, (7) pig, (8) rabbit, (9) sheep, (10) skunk, (11) snake, (12) vulture, (13) wolf. Can you associate one or more of the following personality characteristics with each of these animals: wise, blindly obedient, stubborn, courageous (bold), timid, sly, flirtatious, devouring, gluttonous, sharp-eyed, disreputable (untrustworthy), proud, mean? Can you think of any other personality traits that are associated with these animals or any other animals that are associated with particular personality traits?

9. Interpret the following "Days of Birth" poem, which is of unknown authorship:

> Monday's child is fair of face,
> Tuesday's child is full of grace,
> Wednesday's child is full of woe,
> Thursday's child has far to go,
> Friday's child is loving and giving,
> Saturday's child works for its living,
> And a child that's born on the Sabbath day
> Is fair and wise and good and gay.

How do you think that the poem originated, that is, in what pseudoscience or "theory of personality?"

■ Suggested Readings

Aiken, L.R. (1993). *Personality: Theories, research, and applications* (pp. 1–25). Englewood Cliffs, NJ: Prentice-Hall.

Aiken, L.R. (2000). *Human differences.* Mahwah, NJ: Erlbaum.

Ben-Porath, Y.S., & Butcher, J.N. (1991). The historical development of personality assessment. In C.E. Walker (Ed.), *Clinical psychology: Historical and research foundations* (pp. 121–156). New York: Plenum.

Exner, J.E., Jr. (1995). Why use personality tests: A brief historical view. In J.N. Butcher (Ed.), *Clinical personality assessment: Practical approaches* (pp. 10–18). New York: Oxford University Press.

Frick, W.B. (Ed.). (1995). *Personality: Selected readings in theory.* Itasca, IL: F.E. Peacock.

Harkness, A.R., & Hogan, R. (1995). The theory and measurement of traits: Two views. In J.N. Butcher (Ed.), *Clinical personality assessment: Practical approaches* (pp. 28–41). New York: Oxford University Press.

Hergenhahn, B.R. (1994). *An introduction to theories of personality* (4th ed.). Englewood Cliffs, NJ: Prentice-Hall.

Megargee, E.I., & Spielberger, C.D. (1992). *Personality assessment in America: A retrospective on the occasion of the fiftieth anniversary of the Society for Personality Assessment.* Hillsdale, NJ: Erlbaum.

Pervin, L.A. (1990). A brief history of modern personality theory. In L.A. Pervin (Ed.), *Handbook of personality theory and research* (pp. 21–65). New York: Guilford.

Rorer, L.B. (1990). Personality assessment: A conceptual survey. In L.A. Pervin (Ed.), *Handbook of personality theory and research* (pp. 693–720). New York: Guilford.

Westen, D. (1990). Psychoanalytic approaches to personality. In L.A. Pervin (Ed.), *Handbook of personality theory and research* (pp. 21–65). New York: Guilford.

Wiggins, J.S., & Pincus, A.L. (1992). Personality structure and assessment. *Annual Review of Psychology, 43,* 493–504.

CHAPTER 2

Psychometrics I: Measurement, Statistics, and Test Design

Various procedures and materials are used to collect personality assessment data—observations, checklists, rating scales, personality inventories, projective techniques, and tests. The value of the obtained information depends on the effectiveness with which the associated data-collection instruments and procedures are devised and applied. This chapter and the next one consider some of the more technical features of instrument construction and selection, providing the reader with an introduction to the concepts and methods of psychological measurement.

■ Measurement and Statistics

Measurement, the assignment of numbers to events, is one of the foundations of science. Almost any effort to describe and classify natural phenomena involves measurement of a sort, albeit sometimes at a rather low level. Measurements in psychology and other social sciences are admittedly not as precise as those in natural sciences such as physics, but they can be useful in summarizing data on human behavior and drawing inferences from those data. The quantification of observations provides a more objective basis for making intra- and interindividual comparisons, which is critical to an understanding of individual differences.

Scales of Measurement

The lowest level of measurement, in which numbers are arbitrarily assigned to designate specific objects or events, is on a *nominal scale*. An example of nominal measurement are the numbers on athletic uniforms; these are arbitrary numbers that reveal nothing about the player's skill or position on the team. Illustrative of personal/social variables measured on a nominal scale are biological gender (male vs. female) and ethnicity (black, white, Hispanic, etc.).

At a somewhat higher level is measurement on an *ordinal scale*: ordinal numbers represent the rank orders or orders of merit of some object, person, or situation. Order (place) of finishing in a contest of some kind is an example of ordinal-level measurement. In personality assessment, scales for rating behavior and personal characteristics represent measurement at an ordinal level.

Although many social science variables are measured on ordinal scales, this type of measurement is rather limited. Consider a contest in which John finishes second, Sue fourth, and Joe sixth. It is true that $4 - 2 = 6 - 4$, but it is not correct to conclude that the difference between John and Sue is the same as the difference between Sue and Joe on whatever characteristic is being assessed. The reason is that, on an ordinal scale, equal numerical differences do not necessarily correspond to equal differences in the characteristic being measured.

Justification of a statement such as "the difference between a score of 2 and a score of 4 equals the difference between a score of 4 and a score of 6" requires that the measurements be on an interval or ratio scale. A common example of an *interval scale* is the Celsius scale of temperature. On such a scale, if the temperature is 10° Celsius on Monday, 15° on Wednesday and 20° on Friday, it is correct to say that the difference in temperature (i. e., warmth) on Monday and Wednesday is equal to the difference in temperature on Wednesday and Friday. On the other hand, in order to conclude that it is twice as warm on Friday as on Monday, it is necessary for the measurements to be on a *ratio scale*. On a ratio scale, the number "0" is not an arbitrary zero (as on an interval scale) but rather an absolute zero. Since the "0" on the Celsius scale is an arbitrary zero, another type of instrument—a Kelvin thermometer, on which "0" represents a true zero—the absence of molecular motion—is needed to measure temperature on a ratio scale. Thus, it is correct to say that 20° Kelvin is twice as hot as 10° (both are quite cold!).

Though personality variables are typically measured on an ordinal scale, or somewhere between an ordinal and an interval scale, we frequently employ interval-level statistics in personality measurement. Thus, we may choose to summarize our data with interval-level statistics such as the arithmetic mean, the standard deviation, or standard scores rather than ordinal-level statistics such as the median, the semi-interquartile range, and percentile ranks. No great harm is done by this practice, as long as it is clearly understood that personality measurements are inexact indicators or predictors. As we shall see, however, under certain circumstances it is more appropriate to employ statistics that assume a lower level of measurement than interval or ratio.

Frequency Distributions and Percentiles

A number of questions need to be answered in order to describe psychological measurements obtained from a group of people: How many people made a given score? What is the average score? How spread out or variable are the scores? How is one set of measurements related to another set of measurements? When the number of scores is sizable, answers to these and other statistical questions may be obtained more efficiently by grouping the measurements in the form of a *frequency distribution*. To illustrate the construction of a frequency distribution, consider the 90 numbers in Table 2–1. These are composite scores obtained from ratings assigned by 90 college students to eleven personality characteristics of a political science professor. For each of the following characteristics, the students were instructed at midterm to indicate, on a five point scale (1 = lowest rating on the characteristic through 5 = highest rating on the characteristic), the extent to which the professor was

1. considerate
2. courteous
3. creative
4. friendly
5. interesting
6. knowledgeable
7. motivating
8. organized
9. patient
10. prepared
11. punctual

Thus, the possible sum of ratings assigned to the eleven items ranged from 11 to 55.

It would be possible to group the scores in Table 2–1 into intervals having any desirable numerical width (say 5), yielding the intervals 10 to 14, 15 to 19, 20 to 24, and so on. To do so, however, would distort the data somewhat and is unnecessary when the number of scores in not unduly large. Consequently, as

Raw Scores on Instructor Personality Rating Scale.														**TABLE 2–1**
26	28	40	37	35	33	33	37	29	42	38	35	38	39
39	28	29	28	39	40	36	45	33	37	29	35	36	31
52	34	24	41	41	33	40	33	39	42	37	34	51	48
54	49	38	55	42	47	46	53	31	38	40	27	35	47
39	40	42	42	37	42	43	41	39	44	31	36	34	36
40	39	31	36	28	41	40	32	36	28	39	50	43	34
34	37	35	50	41	42								

TABLE 2–2 Frequency Distribution of Composite Ratings in Table 2–1.

Score Interval Midpoint	Frequency on Interval	Cumulative Percentage (Percentile Rank of Upper Real Limit)
55	1	100.00
54	1	98.89
53	1	97.78
52	1	96.67
51	1	95.56
50	2	94.44
49	1	92.22
48	1	91.11
47	2	90.00
46	1	87.78
45	1	86.67
44	1	85.56
43	2	84.44
42	7	82.22
41	5	74.44
40	7	68.89
39	8	61.11
38	4	52.22
37	6	47.78
36	6	41.11
35	5	34.44
34	5	28.89
33	5	23.33
32	1	17.78
31	4	16.67
30	0	12.22
29	3	12.22
28	5	8.89
27	1	3.33
26	1	2.22
25	0	1.11
24	1	1.11

shown in Table 2–2, we have constructed a frequency distribution having an interval width of 1. The actual (real) limits of an interval range from .5 below the lowest score to .5 above the highest score falling within the interval. Because the width of the interval for the frequency distribution in Table 2–2 is 1, the highest and lowest scores on an interval are identical. Consequently, the real limits range from 23.5 to 24.5 for the first interval, 24.5 to 25.5 for the second interval, and so on. Figure 2–1 is a pictorial representation (a *histogram*) of this frequency distribution.

A Histogram of the Frequency Distribution in Table 2–2.   **FIG. 2-1**

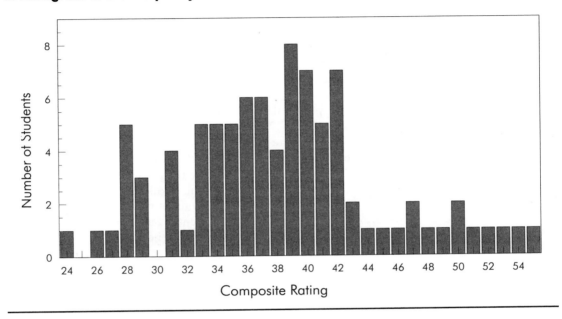

In addition to listing the frequency of each score or score interval, Table 2–2 gives the cumulative percentage or *percentile rank* associated with that score. The percentile rank of a given score is the percentage of people who obtained that score or a lower score. For example, 15 people (1 + 0 + 1 + 1 + 5 + 3 + 0 + 4) gave a total rating of 31 or below to the instructor. So the upper real limit of a score of 31, namely 31.5, corresponds to a percentile rank of 100(15/90) = 16.67. Another way of saying the same thing is that 31.5 is the 16.67th (approximately 17th) *percentile*. Likewise, the percentile rank of the score of 43.5 is 100(76/90) = 84.44 ≈ 84. Alternatively, we can say that 43.5 is the 84.44th percentile.

To determine the percentile rank of the midpoint of a given interval, we (1) divide one-half of the frequency on that interval by the total number of scores in the distribution and multiply it by 100, and then (2) add the resulting product to the percentile rank of the preceding interval. Thus, the percentile rank of a score of 31 is 100(2/90) + 12.22 = 14.44, and the percentile rank of a total rating of 43 is 100(1/90) + 82.22 = 83.33.

Averages

One of the first statistics to be computed from a set of scores is an *average* or *measure of central tendency*. The three averages encountered most often are the mode, the median, and the arithmetic mean. The *mode*, or most frequently occurring score, is the easiest of the three to compute. The mode of the data in Table 2–2 is 39, because more students (8) gave the instructor a total rating of 39 than any other score.

The *median*, or 50th percentile, is the score below which 50 percent of the scores fall. It can be seen that 47.78 percent of the scores in Table 2–2 fall below a score of 37.5 and 52.22 percent fall below a score of 38.5. Therefore, the median can be computed by interpolating within the interval 37.5 to 38.5. This is done by subtracting 47.78 from 50, dividing the remainder by the difference between 52.22 and 47.78, and adding the resulting quotient to 37.5: $37.5 + (50 - 47.78)/(52.22 - 47.78) = 38.00$. Formulas for computing the median from a frequency distribution, in addition to other percentiles and percentile ranks, are given in textbooks on elementary statistics and psychological testing (e. g., Pagano, 1994; Aiken, 1997a).

The mode is the least popular and usually the least representative measure of central tendency. More popular is the median, which is an appropriate measure of central tendency whenever measurements are made on an ordinal scale or the frequency distribution of scores is markedly skewed (asymmetrical). Despite the fact that it can be greatly affected by extremely high or extremely low scores, the most popular of all measures of central tendency is the *arithmetic mean*. The arithmetic mean ($\overline{X}$) is computed as the sum of the scores divided by the number of scores, $\overline{X} = \Sigma X/n$, where the Greek letter capital sigma (Σ) means "the sum of" and n is the total number of scores. Adding all the scores (sum of ratings) in Table 2–1 yields 3,438. So the arithmetic mean is $3428/90 = 38.09$.

Measures of Variability

It is important to know not only the average of a set of scores but also how much the scores vary from each other or from the average. One such measure of variability is the *range*, computed as the highest minus the lowest score. The range of the scores in Table 2–2 is $55 - 24 = 31$. Unfortunately, this simple statistic is greatly affected by extreme scores and consequently tends to be unstable. Another kind of range is the *semi-interquartile range (Q)*, defined as half the difference between the 75th percentile and the 25th percentile. The 75th percentile of the scores in Table 2–2 can be computed by interpolating within the score interval 41.5 to 42.5: $41.5 + (75 - 74.44) / (82.22 - 74.44) = 41.57$. Similarly, the 25th percentile is computed as $33.80 + (25 - 23.33) / (28.89 - 23.33) = 33.80$. Therefore, $Q = (41.57 - 33.80) / 2 = 3.89$.

Q is an appropriate measure of variability when the median is the measure of central tendency. A third measure of variability, the *standard deviation*, is more suitable when the arithmetic mean is the reported measure of central tendency. The standard deviation (s) of a set of scores is computed from

$$\sqrt{\Sigma (X - \overline{X})^2/n},$$

which is the square root of the sum of the squared deviations of the raw scores from the mean divided by the number of scores.

For the data in Table 2–1, $s = \sqrt{3913.29/90} = 6.59$. The square of this number, $s^2 = 43.48$, is the *variance* of the 90 scores.

Standard Scores

Because the measurements obtained from different psychological variables may not be expressed in the same numerical units, it is convenient to have a uniform scale of measurement to which scores on different variables may be converted. Then an individual's performance on one variable can be compared directly with his or her standing on another variable. One popular score transformation that utilizes the mean and standard deviation is the standard z *score*, defined as $z = (X - \overline{X})/s$. Just as the gram and centimeter are standard units of measurement of weight and length in the metric system, the z score is used as a standard unit in psychological statistics. The z score corresponding to a given raw score *(X)* indicates the number of standard deviation units that X is above (+) or below (–) the mean of all scores in the group.

To illustrate the computation of z scores, the z score corresponding to a raw score of 45 from the data in Table 2–2 is $(45 - 38.09) / 6.59 = 1.05$; the z score corresponding to a raw score of 35 is $(35 - 38.09) / 6.59 = -.47$. The arithmetic mean and standard deviation of the z scores for a complete set of data are 0 and 1, respectively.

Correlation and Regression

A correlation coefficient is an index number, ranging from –1.00 to +1.00, that indicates the degree and direction of the relationship between two variables. The closer the correlation is to +1.00 or –1.00, the greater the relationship between the two variables and the more accurately scores on either variable can be predicted from scores on the other variable. When the correlation is positive, low scores on one variable tend to go with low scores on the other variable, and high scores go with high scores. When the correlation is negative, low scores on one variable are associated with high scores on the other variable.

There are many types of correlation coefficients, but we shall restrict our attention to two that are used frequently in the construction of personality assessment instruments and in research involving such instruments—the *product moment coefficient* and the *point-biserial coefficient*. It should be noted that both of these coefficients are based on the assumption of a linear (straight line) relationship between the two variables. If the relationship is nonlinear (or curvilinear) as it may be with variables such as performance efficiency and level of motivation, then the product-moment and point-biserial coefficients give a distorted picture of the true relationship. However, even when they are not precisely linear, the relationships between many psychological variables are sufficiently close to being linear to justify the use of these coefficients.

Product-Moment Coefficient. Consider the 90 pairs of scores in the X and Y columns of Table 2–3, where X is a composite student rating of the personality of an instructor at midterm and Y is an end-of-term student evaluations of the course. The eleven items on the composite personality rating were listed earlier in the chapter. The six items included in the course evaluation score consist of five-point scale ratings of the extent to which the student considered the course:
1. helpful
2. informative
3. interesting
4. motivating
5. stimulating
6. valuable

The formula for determining the product-moment correlation coefficient between the X and Y variables is

$$r = [n\Sigma XY - (\Sigma X)(\Sigma Y)]/\sqrt{[n\Sigma X^2 - (\Sigma X)^2]\,[n\Sigma Y^2 - (\Sigma Y)^2]}.$$

Note that the six values needed in the formula are the number *(n)* of X–Y pairs, the sum of the X scores (ΣX), the sum of the Y scores (ΣY), the sum of squares of the X scores (ΣX^2), the sum of squares of the Y scores (ΣY^2), and the sum of the cross-products of the X and Y scores (ΣXY). Substituting the appropriate values (see last row of Table 2–3) in the above formula yields

$$\frac{90(62,637) - (3,428)(1,610)}{\sqrt{[90(134,482) - (3,428)^2][90(30,952) - (1,610)^2]}} = .4529.$$

The correlation between composite midterm student ratings of instructor personality and end-of-term evaluations of the course is positive but moderate. This suggests that students who assign positive midterm ratings to the instructor's personality also tend to give high course evaluations at term's end.

Composite Ratings of Instructor (X) and Course (Y) by Student.

TABLE 2–3

Student	X	Y	X^2	Y^2	XY
1	26	6	676	36	156
2	28	10	784	100	280
3	40	28	1600	784	1120
4	37	14	1369	196	518
5	35	14	1225	196	490
6	33	12	1089	144	396
7	33	21	1089	441	693
8	37	20	1369	400	740
9	29	18	841	324	522
10	42	21	1764	441	882
11	38	22	1444	484	836
12	35	19	1225	361	665
13	38	18	1444	324	684
14	39	23	1521	529	897
15	39	21	1521	441	819
16	28	19	784	361	532
17	29	12	841	144	348
18	28	9	784	81	252
19	39	15	1521	225	585
20	40	22	1600	484	880
21	36	22	1296	484	792
22	45	25	2025	625	1125
23	33	15	1089	225	495
24	37	15	1369	225	555
25	29	18	841	324	522
26	35	11	1225	121	385
27	36	16	1296	256	576
28	31	16	961	256	496
29	52	30	2704	900	1560
30	34	18	1156	324	612
31	24	11	576	121	264
32	41	21	1681	441	861
33	41	21	1681	441	861
34	33	10	1089	100	330
35	40	16	1600	256	640
36	33	16	1089	256	528
37	39	21	1521	441	819
38	42	19	1764	361	798
39	37	15	1369	225	555
40	34	13	1156	169	442
41	51	23	2601	529	1173
42	48	24	2304	576	1152
43	54	21	2916	441	1134
44	49	20	2401	400	980
45	38	20	1444	400	760

Student	X	Y	X²	Y²	XY
46	55	22	3025	484	1210
47	42	19	1764	361	798
48	47	19	2209	361	893
49	46	22	2116	484	1012
50	53	24	2809	576	1272
51	31	19	961	361	589
52	38	5	1444	25	190
53	40	19	1600	361	760
54	27	12	729	144	324
55	35	15	1225	225	525
56	47	20	2209	400	940
57	39	23	1521	529	897
58	40	17	1600	289	680
59	42	13	1764	169	546
60	42	20	1764	400	840
61	37	18	1369	324	666
62	42	20	1764	400	840
63	43	18	1849	324	774
64	41	19	1681	361	779
65	39	16	1521	256	624
66	44	24	1936	576	1056
67	31	15	961	225	465
68	36	15	1296	225	540
69	34	21	1156	441	714
70	36	18	1296	324	648
71	40	20	1600	400	800
72	39	23	1521	529	897
73	31	23	961	529	713
74	36	10	1296	100	360
75	28	20	784	400	560
76	41	18	4681	324	738
77	40	17	1600	289	680
78	32	19	1024	361	608
79	36	18	1296	324	648
80	28	14	784	196	392
81	39	13	1521	169	507
82	50	7	2500	49	350
83	43	8	1849	64	344
84	34	19	1156	361	646
85	34	14	1156	196	476
86	37	22	1369	484	814
87	35	23	1225	529	805
88	50	21	2500	441	1050
89	41	17	1681	289	697
90	42	30	1764	900	1260
Sums	3428	1610	134482	30952	62637

Simple Linear Regression. Although correlation does not imply causation, it does imply prediction: the larger the value of r, in either a positive or a negative direction, the more accurate the prediction of Y from X (or X from Y). The prediction of Y from X is facilitated by substituting the appropriate values of b, X, and a in the equation $Y_{pred} = bX + a$, where $b = [n\Sigma XY - (\Sigma X)(\Sigma Y)] / [n\Sigma X^2 - (\Sigma X)^2]$, and $a = \overline{Y} - b\overline{X}$. For the data in Table 2–1, $b = [90(62,637) - 3,428(1,610)] / [90(134,482) - (3,428)^2] = .3358$ and $a = 17.89 - .3358(38.0889) = 5.1005$. Entering a value for X, say 50, into the resulting *regression equation* yields Y_{pred} $= .3358(50) + 5.1005 = 21.89$, or approximately 22. This is only a predicted value, not necessarily an obtained Y value; a person who makes an X score of 50 may obtain a quite different Y score than 22. What the predicted Y score of 22 represents is the approximate mean Y score of all individuals whose X score is 50. Therefore, some individuals with X scores of 50 will score below 22 and others will score above 22 on Y.

Coefficient of Determination. Because correlation implies prediction, a useful index of the accuracy of prediction can be derived by squaring the correlation coefficient. The resulting statistic (r^2), which is known as the *coefficient of determination*, is the proportion of variance in the predicted (criterion) variable that can be accounted for (explained) by variability in the predictor variable. For the example, $r^2 = (.4529)^2 = .2051$, showing that approximately 21% of the variance in end-of-course ratings can be accounted for by variability in midterm ratings of the instructor's personality. This leaves $100 - 21 = 79\%$ of the variability in end-of-course ratings unaccounted for—a substantial percentage.

Multiple Regression Equation. As noted above, only 21% of the variance in the criterion variable *(Y)* is accounted for by variation in the predictor variable *(X)*. One possible way of improving the predictability of Y from X is to include more independent variables in the regression equation. Thus, if we include two more independent variables in the equation, the form of the prediction equation, now referred to as a *multiple regression equation*, will be $Y_{pred} = b_1X_1 + b_2X_2 + b_3X_3 + a$. Determination of the numerical values of the b's and a is somewhat complex and almost always done by a computer.

There is no guarantee that including scores on other independent variables in the regression equation will improve the accuracy of prediction, but this is more likely to occur when the independent *(X)* variables have low correlations with each other and high correlations with the dependent *(Y)* variable. It is also important to realize that a multiple regression approach assumes that each independent variable is linearly related to all other variables in the equation and that scores on the dependent variable have a normal (bell-shaped) distribution.

Point-Biserial Coefficient. The point-biserial coefficient is equivalent to the product-moment coefficient when one of the variables is continuous and the other variable is dichotomous. The dichotomous *(X)* variable consists of two discrete groups of people, numerically designated 0 and 1. A formula for computing the point-biserial coefficient is

$$r_{pb} = (\overline{Y}_1 - \overline{Y}) \sqrt{n_1/(n - n_1)}/s,$$

where n = total number of examinees, n_1 = number of examinees in group 1, $\overline{Y}_1$ = the Y mean of group 1, $\overline{Y}$ = the Y mean of both groups combined, and s = the Y standard deviation of both groups combined.

The point-biserial coefficient is useful in a number of contexts, particularly in analyzing the functioning of the individual items that make up a test. To illustrate the application of the point-biserial formula, let gender (female = 0, male = 1) be the dichotomous variable to be correlated with the 90 composite personality ratings in Table 2–4. Then

$$r_{pb} = (36.4722 - 38.0889) \sqrt{36/54}/6.59 = -.2003.$$

The direction and magnitude of this coefficient indicate a very low negative relationship between student gender and ratings of instructor personality; males viewed the instructor slightly less positively than females.

TABLE 2–4 **Composite Ratings of Instructor by Gender of Student.**

Females (n = 54)

26	40	35	33	33	37
38	38	39	28	29	28
39	36	45	29	35	36
31	34	40	33	37	51
54	49	38	55	42	47
46	53	38	35	47	39
42	42	43	39	34	36
40	36	41	40	50	43
34	34	35	50	41	42

Males (n = 36)

28	37	29	42	35	39
40	33	37	52	24	41
41	33	39	42	34	48
31	40	27	40	37	42
41	44	31	36	39	31
28	32	36	28	39	37

Factor Analysis

Table 2–5 is a matrix of correlations among the ratings assigned by the 90 students to the 11 instructor personality items described earlier in the chapter. If the matrix is divided into two triangular portions by drawing a line from the upper left to the lower right corner, it can be seen that it is a symmetric matrix in which the first row contains the same values as the first column, the second row contains the same elements as the second column, and so on. Also notice that all the numbers on the principal diagonal (upper left to lower right) are 1.00, the presumed correlation of each item with itself.

Matrix of Correlations among 11 Instructor Personality Items.   **TABLE 2–5**

Item	1	2	3	4	5	6	7	8	9	10	11
1	1.000	.727	.424	.573	.343	.294	.458	.200	.425	.091	.078
2	.727	1.000	.304	.620	.287	.258	.363	.075	.459	.115	.127
3	.424	.304	1.000	.470	.510	.080	.691	.206	.304	.129	.112
4	.573	.620	.470	1.000	.336	.195	.390	.061	.528	.026	.022
5	.343	.287	.510	.336	1.000	.171	.638	.374	.203	.243	.244
6	.294	.258	.080	.195	.171	1.000	.108	.227	.159	.490	.430
7	.458	.363	.691	.390	.638	.108	1.000	.218	.314	.108	.065
8	.200	.075	.206	.061	.374	.227	.218	1.000	.085	.524	.421
9	.425	.459	.304	.528	.203	.159	.314	.085	1.000	.114	.187
10	.091	.115	.129	.026	.243	.490	.108	.524	.114	1.000	.611
11	.078	.127	.112	.022	.244	.430	.065	.421	.187	.611	1.000

Computation of the correlation coefficients in this matrix is the first step in a *factor analysis*, a statistical procedure for reducing the number of variables (items or tests) to a smaller number of dimensions, or factors, by taking into account the overlap (correlations) among the various measures. In psychological testing, the goal of a factor analysis is to find a few salient factors that account for the major portion of the variance in a group of scores on different tests or other psychometric measures. Thus, the factors extracted by a factor analysis should account for a large percentage of the overlap among the variances of the items or tests represented in the correlation matrix.

In this case, there are 11 items, or variables, so the object of the factor analysis is to find the matrix of *factor loadings*, or correlations between factors and items, that most effectively account for the correlations among the items. There are many factor-analytic procedures, but all involve two stages: (1) factoring the matrix of correlations to produce an initial, unrotated factor matrix; (2) *rotating* the factor matrix to provide the simplest possible configuration of factor loadings. The purpose of the factoring stage of this process is to determine the number of factors required to account for the relationships among the various tests and provide initial estimates of the numerical loadings of each test on each factor. The purpose of factor rotation is to make the factors more interpretable by producing a configuration in which only a few tests have high loadings on any given factor and the majority of tests have low loadings on that factor. One of the most common factoring procedures is the *principal axis* method, and a popular rotation procedures is *varimax rotation*. These are the procedures that will be applied here.

TABLE 2-6 **Unrotated and Rotated Factor Matrices of Instructor Personality Ratings.**

| | Factor Loadings | | | | | | |
| | Unrotated Matrix | | | Rotated Matrix | | | Commu- |
Item	A	B	C	A′	B′	C′	nality
1	.754	−.271	.250	.783	.090	.288	.704
2	.708	−.281	.415	.853	.089	.131	.752
3	.689	−.206	−.440	.303	.015	.786	.710
4	.702	−.392	.240	.790	−.041	.280	.704
5	.674	.063	−.500	.148	.243	.792	.708
6	.442	.477	.402	.353	.669	−.113	.585
7	.714	−.216	−.485	.298	.009	.838	.791
8	.434	.573	−.257	−.082	.649	.392	.582
9	.594	−.201	.330	.691	.102	.120	.502
10	.408	.769	.063	.011	.867	.100	.762
11	.388	.718	.122	.052	.822	.048	.681

Procedure FACTOR of the *Statistical Package for the Social Sciences* (Norusis, 1992) was used to factor the correlation matrix in Table 2–5. The matrix of three factors that were extracted is shown in the columns labeled A, B, and C of Table 2–6. The decimal numbers listed under each factor column are the *loadings*, or correlations, of the 11 items on that factor. For example, item 1 has a loading of .754 on Factor A, −.271 on Factor B, and .250 on Factor C. The sum of the squared loadings for each item is the item's *communality*, or proportion of the item variance that is accounted for by the three common factors. Thus, the communality of item 1 is $(.754)^2 + (−.271)^2 + (.250)^2 = .704$. This means that 70.4% of the variance of the scores on item 1 is accounted for by these three factors.

It is also of interest to determine the proportion of total test (or item in this case) variance that is specific to a given test. To determine the *specificity* of a test or test item, we apply the equation specificity = reliability − communality. Although the topic of reliability is not discussed until the next chapter, let it suffice for now to say that *reliability* is the extent to which test scores are free from errors of measurement. A *reliability coefficient* is an index number ranging from

.00 (complete unreliability) to 1.00 (perfect reliability). Like communality and reliability, specificity ranges from .00 to 1.00; the greater a test's specificity, the more specific whatever that test measures is to the test itself. The greater a test's communality, the more common whatever that test measures is to the other tests in the group of tests being factor analyzed.

The rotated factor matrix is shown in columns A', B', and C' of Table 2–6. The communality of each item is the same as in the unrotated factor matrix, but the rotated factors are much easier to interpret than the unrotated ones. Varimax rotation is an *orthogonal rotation* procedure, in that the factor axes remain at right angles to each other. In contrast, the factor axes in *oblique rotation* make acute or obtuse angles with each other. Orthogonal factors are usually easier to interpret than oblique factors because the factors are uncorrelated, or independent.

In interpreting the rotated factor matrix, we pay particular attention to the items that have loadings of .50 or greater on a given factor. Four items—item 1 (considerate), item 2 (courteous), item 4 (friendly), and item 9 (patient)—have high loadings on factor A'. Consequently an appropriate label for this factor might be "considerateness" or "politeness." Four items also have high loadings on factor B': item 6 (knowledgeable), item 8 (organized), item 10 (prepared), and item 11 (punctual). Hence an appropriate name for Factor B' might be "preparedness." Lastly, three items have high loadings on factor C': item 3 (creative), item 5 (interesting), and item 7 (motivating). An appropriate label for this factor might be "stimulating" or "motivating." These three factors make psychological sense in terms of the kind of personality students prefer in a teacher.

There is much more to factor analysis that has been indicated here; entire books have been written on the subject. As these books reveal, factor analysis is a complex topic that involves higher mathematics such as matrix algebra and the analytic geometry of space. The topic is also a controversial one: not only is there disagreement concerning the best procedures for factoring and rotation, but the interpretation of factors and their psychological foundations have been the source of dispute for many years. At the very least, however, factor analysis provides psychometricians and researchers with a tool for understanding the relationships among psychological variables or events. It has proven to be particularly useful in the design of psychological assessment instruments and in research concerned with the meaning and validity of these instruments.

Other Statistical Methods

The analysis of personality assessment data is not and should not be restricted to descriptive statistics, correlations, and related techniques. Many other univariate and multivariate statistical procedures for analyzing the results of observational, survey, and experimental investigations are available. Constructs measured by personality assessment instruments serve as independent, dependent, and control (covariate) variables in numerous studies, the results of which can be statistically analyzed by analysis of variance, multivariate analysis of variance, and other complex methods. Unfortunately, personality researchers do not always avail themselves of the variety of statistical techniques that are open to them. For example, a survey of 449 articles published in the *Journal of Personality Assessment* from 1990–94 that included some form of data analysis found that approximately 13% used only descriptive statistics. Most of the studies employed only *t* tests, analysis of variance, chi-square, or simple correlation. Factor analysis, multiple linear regression, and multivariate analysis of variance and covariance were employed by a sizable percentage of the studies, but discriminant analysis, logistic regression, and structural equation modeling were used by an even smaller percentage (Schinka, LaLone & Broeckel, 1997). According to the authors, the seeming reluctance of researchers who make use of personality assessment devices to employ advanced statistics procedures limits understanding and generalization of the results of their research. Of course, advanced statistical methods entail more complex assumptions than simpler procedures, and are no solution to the problems of inadequate sampling and control that plague much personality research. One should always beware of the temptation to use a cannon to shoot a fly in order to cover up deficiencies in research design or merely to impress journal reviewers and editors!

■ Constructing and Item-Analyzing Assessment Instruments

The design and construction of personality assessment instruments involves a number of approaches, some based on theoretical or common-sense conceptions of the nature of personality and others on item- and test-criterion relationships. Almost all of these efforts employ some sort of statistical procedures to determine or demonstrate the validity of the instruments.

The construction of projective techniques such as the Rorschach Inkblot Test and the Thematic Apperception Test has typically relied on some theory or theory-based ideas pertaining to personality structure and dynamics, but common sense and a kind of trial-and-error or hit-or-miss empiricism have also played a role in their development. Details on how the best-known projectives were designed are discussed in chapters 10 through 12. Likewise, the design of personality and interest inventories is discussed in chapters 7 through 9. However, because the construction of personality inventories and rating scales has adhered more closely than projectives to statistical and psychometric methods, strategies for constructing these instruments will be considered briefly at this point.

Strategies for Constructing Inventories and Rating Scales

Burisch (1984) described three major strategies for constructing personality inventories and rating scales—deductive, inductive, and external. The *deductive*, or content-based strategy (also referred to as the rational, intuitive, or theoretical approach), entails quite a bit of sophisticated language about personality; a few theoretical conceptions concerning the structure and functioning of personality can also prove helpful. Using this knowledge base as a starting point, the person who is constructing the instrument collects or devises items that he or she hopes will assess the psychological construct(s) under consideration. This was the method used in preparing the 11-item instructor personality scale described earlier in the chapter.

A second strategy, the *inductive* one, involves the use of factor analysis or other correlation-based procedures. Though designers of personality inventories and rating scales typically have some initial ideas about what they desire to measure, the major feature of the inductive approach is to let the data speak for themselves. In other words, a large collection of items is first administered to an appropriate sample of examinees. Then a statistical and/or rational analysis of the responses determines the number of variables being measured by the item aggregate and which items contribute to the assessment of which variables. This approach to inventory construction has also been labeled internal, internal consistency, or itemetric.

A third strategy, known as the *external, empirical*, or *criterion group* approach, has been characterized as the most accurate and most generally valid. Various statistical procedures, including correlational methods, chi square, multiple regression analysis, and factor analysis, have been applied in selecting items by the empirical methods of test construction. In the empirical strategy, as exemplified in the construction of the Minnesota Multiphasic Personality Inventory (MMPI) and the Strong Vocational Interest Blank, items are selected or retained according to their ability to differentiate between two or more criterion groups of persons. In designing the schizophrenia scale on the MMPI, for example, an item was selected for inclusion if the responses given to the item by a group of known schizophrenics were significantly different from those given by a group of normal people. The other clinical scales on the MMPI were constructed in a similar manner. In constructing the Strong Vocational Interest Blank for Men, an item became part of a particular occupational scale (e. g., the "Banker" scale) if the criterion group (bankers) answered the item in a significantly different way from a criterion group of men in general.

It is not always clear which of the three approaches to the development of personality inventories or rating scales is best. Burisch (1984) maintained that scales developed by the deductive approach are more economical to construct and communicate information more directly to the personality assessor. He admitted, however, that deductively developed scales can also be more easily faked and may not be as appropriate as empirically derived scales when it is advantageous for the examinee to fake answers. In any case, a combination of the three strategies has been employed in the construction of many personality inventories and rating scales. Even in the development of the simple 11-item instructor personality inventory discussed previously, two approaches—the deductive and the inductive—were employed.

Item Analysis and Item Response Theory

The process of constructing a personality test or inventory does not end with the initial administration of the instrument to a sample of people. Whatever strategy may have been employed in the construction process—deductive, inductive, external, or more likely some combination of the three, the designer of the instrument will almost always conduct a *post hoc* analysis to determine whether the test items are functioning properly. That is, are the items measuring what the designer wants them to measure? Careful construction of items, a critical inspection of the instrument by psychometricians and subject-matter experts, and preliminary tryouts with small groups of examinees can minimize the number of poorly constructed items. But try as they may, test designers never anticipate all of the problems that occur when a test is actually administered to a large, representative group of people. An empirical item analysis usually reveals that a number of items are functioning in a different way than they are supposed to.

Traditional Item Analysis Procedures. Various statistical indexes may be computed in an item analysis of a test designed to measure a specific psychological characteristic. Among these are measures of item difficulty (What percentage of the examinees gave the keyed answer to the item?) and item discrimination (To what extent does the item discriminate between high and low scorers on the test as a whole or on some external criterion?). If the test or section of the test was meant to measure a single characteristic, then scores on the items comprising the test or section should have high correlations with each other. An alternative procedure is to determine the correlation between scores on each item and scores on the test as a whole. Items having low correlations with other items, or with total test (or section) scores, should then be revised or discarded. Tests on which the items have high correlations with each other or with total test scores are said to have high *internal consistency* or *internal validity*. Tests on which the items are highly correlated with other variables that presumably measure the same characteristic as the test are said to have high *external validity*.

Other statistical methods, such as constructing frequency distributions of the various responses to the item and conducting factor analyses of the item scores, can reveal the weaknesses (and strengths) of the test or other psychometric instrument. But the analysis process is a never-ending one; published and unpublished tests are still being item-analyzed years after they first appeared. There are good reasons for the repetition: the results of an item analysis often vary markedly with the group that is tested, as well as when and under what conditions they are tested. For example, certain items may be answered differently by males than by females, by one ethnic group than another or by one socioeconomic group than another. Scores on particular items may also correlate highly with one criterion measure (e. g., course grades) but not with another criterion (e. g., job performance).

In constructing a standardized test of personality or cognitive ability, it has become common practice to examine each item and its associated statistics for indications of group discrimination or bias. The fact that test items are answered differently by one group than by another does not necessarily mean, however, that the items are biased against one of the groups. An item is biased, in a technical sense, only when it measures something different—a different characteristic or trait—in one group than in another group. If item scores reflect true differences in whatever characteristic or trait the item was designed to measure, then the item is not biased.

Item Characteristic Curves. A somewhat more complex item-analysis method with dichotomously-scored (0 or 1) items begins with the construction of an item characteristic curve for each item. An item characteristic curve provides a detailed picture of the relationship between the proportion of examinees who answered the item in the keyed direction right and their scores on a criterion measure. In constructing an *item-characteristic curve*, the proportion of examinees who responded to the item in a specified way (on an ability test those who got the item right) is plotted against scores on an internal criterion (e. g., total test scores) or performance on some external criterion (e. g., academic or occupational adjustment measures). Once the characteristic curve for a particular item has been constructed, difficulty and discrimination indexes for the item are determined. The *item difficulty index* is the criterion score for which 50 percent of the examinees gave the keyed answer to the item; the *item discrimination index* is the slope of the item characteristic curve at that 50-percent point.

Item Response Curves and Theory. Item characteristic curves are purely empirical, non-theoretical approaches to evaluating the effectiveness of test items. *Item* *response curves*, on the other hand, are based on *item response theory (IRT)*. In constructing an item-response curve, the proportion of examinees who answer the item in a specified way is plotted against estimates of the true standing of those individuals on a latent trait or characteristic of interest. These estimates are derived from a mathematical function known as a logistic equation. The precise mathematical equations involved in IRT vary with the assumptions and estimation procedures prescribed by the approach.

Item-response theory, which has been employed extensively in the development, administration, and evaluation of ability tests, has been applied less successfully in the development of personality assessment devices. There are differences between the measurement of ability and personality that make the application of IRT techniques to personality assessment more complex than in the case of ability testing. It can be argued that the item difficulty, discrimination, and guessing indexes, which are important parameters in item-response models, have their counterparts in personality testing. But other problems, such as lack of unidimensionality of whatever the test measures and the greater ambiguity of the items make the application of IRT models to personality assessment more difficult. This is not to say that IRT procedures have not found a place in personality assessment, but only that there are significant problems to overcome and that IRT has not replaced more traditional item-analysis procedures.

■ Sources and Standards for Personality Assessment Instruments

There are many facets to test interpretation and evaluation, and we have just scratched the surface of this important topic. Before continuing with our excursion into psychometrics, however, we shall pause briefly to consider the question of where one can find information about psychological tests, and personality assessment instruments in particular. These sources provide both descriptive and evaluative, verbal and quantitative, information about a wide range of affective and cognitive measuring instruments.

The number of personality assessment devices, both published and unpublished, is truly impressive. The thirteenth edition of *The Mental Measurements Yearbook* (Impara & Plake, 1998), a standard source of descriptive and evaluative information concerning psychological tests and other assessment devices, contains hundreds of entries pertaining to personality tests and assessment. Information and reviews may also be found in *Tests* (Maddox, 1997) and in *Test Critiques* (Keyser & Sweetland, 1984–1994). In general, these reviews contain:
– *A detailed description of the content of the instrument* (title, author, publisher, data and place of publication, forms available, type of instrument, cost, parts

or sections, kinds of items and how selected, theory or conceptual basis of the instrument and the mental operations or characteristics it was designed to measure).
— *Information on administering and scoring the instrument* (instructions, time limits, whole or part scoring, clarity of directions for administration and scoring).
— *A description of norms* (size and composition of the standardization group and how it was selected, kinds of norms reported, overall adequacy of standardization).
— *Reliability data* (kinds of reliability information reported in the manual, nature and sizes of samples on which the reliability information was obtained and whether adequate).
— *Validity data* (kinds of validity information available and whether it is satisfactory in terms of the stated purposes of the instrument).

One of the newest approaches to obtaining information on commonly administered tests is to access the ERIC/AE Test Locator on the internet. This is a joint project of the ERIC Clearinghouse on Assessment and Evaluation at the Catholic University of America, the Library and Reference Services Division of the Educational Testing Service, the Buros Institute of Mental Measurements at the University of Nebraska in Lincoln, the Region III Comprehensive Center at George Washington University and the pro-ed test publishers. The web sites for the ERIC/AE Test Locator are *ericae.net/testcol.htm* and *www.unl.edu/buros*. Six different files—ETS/ERIC Test File, Test Review Locator, BUROS/ERIC Test Publisher Locator, CEEE/ERIC Test Database of tests commonly used with LEP students, Code of Fair Testing Practices, and Test Selection Tips—may be accessed from the Test Locator.

Not only standardized tests, but many questionnaires and rating scales are also administered in applied psychology contexts (see Aiken, 1996, 1997a). *Measures for Clinical Practice: A Sourcebook* (2nd ed., Fischer & Corcoran, 1994) contains descriptive information on dozens of such instruments for clinical and counseling situations.

Information on available computer software and test-scoring services may be obtained from the *Psychware Sourcebook* (Krug, 1993) and *Computer Use in Psychology: A Directory of Software* (Stoloff & Couch, 1992). Among various computer data bases containing information on published tests are the *Mental Measurements Online Database* (Buros Institute of Mental Measurements, Lincoln, NE) and the ETS Test Collection Database of the Educational Testing Service(Internet web site: http://ericae.net/testcol.htm).

Listings and details on unpublished tests and scales can be found in sources such as the *Directory of Unpublished Experimental Mental Measures* (Goldman, Mitchell, & Egelson, 1997, and earlier volumes), *A Consumer's Guide to Tests in Print* (Hammill, Brown, & Bryant, 1992), and *Index to Tests Used in Educational Dissertations* (Fabiano, 1989). Unpublished measures of attitudes are described in the series of volumes produced at the University of Michigan's Institute for Social Research (Robinson, Shaver & Wrightsman, 1991, and earlier volumes). Other useful sources of information on unpublished attitude scales and other psychometric instruments are the HAPI (*Health and Psychosocial Instruments*), PsycINFO, and PsycLIT databases.

Reviews of selected tests are published in professional journals such as *Measurement and Evaluation in Counseling and Development*, *Personnel Psychology*, and *Psychoeducational Assessment*. Articles on the development and evaluation of psychological tests and measures are included in such professional journals as the *Journal of Clinical Psychology*, *Psychological Assessment: A Journal of Consulting and Clinical Psychology*, the *Journal of Counseling Psychology*, and the *Journal of Vocational Behavior*. In addition, entire books and series of books have been written on single psychometric instruments, such as the Minnesota Multiphasic Personality Inventory (MMPI) and the Rorschach Inkblot Test.

As suggested by the list of publishers and distributors of personality assessment instruments in the appendix, the development and marketing of these measures has become a big business. Although not as many personality tests as standardized achievement tests are sold, personality assessment is still a lucrative enterprise. Thousands of customers are in private practice, public mental health clinics, educational institutions, business and industry, government, and other organizations.

Most publishers and distributors of psychological tests require purchasers to have some training or expertise in the use of test materials. One of the best qualification systems for test purchasers is that of The Psychological Corporation. The system consists of three-levels (A, B, and C), from least to most stringent requirements. Tests classified at Level A may be purchased by schools and other organizations and by individuals certified or licensed to administer these tests. Level B tests require a master's degree in psychology or education, equivalent training relevant to assessment, or membership in a professional association that requires appropriate training in assessment of its members. Administering tests at level C, the highest level, requires a Ph.D. in psychology or education, the equivalent in training in assessment, or verification of licensure or certification requiring appropriate training and experience in psychological assessment.

Of course, the requirement of demonstrating one's capabilities and integrity should rest not only on the test purchasers. Many published tests fail to deliver on their promises and are often subject to misleading advertising. One caveat that should be adhered to when make decisions concerning test purchases is not tp be misled by the name of the test. Common errors are the *jingle fallacy* of assuming that tests having similar names necessarily measure the same characteristic, and the *jangle fallacy* of assuming that tests having different names necessarily measure different characteristics.

For purposes of test selection there is often no substitute for direct, hands-on inspection of the test materials. Specimen sets of particular instruments, typically including a copy of the test, an answer sheet, and perhaps a scoring key, can be ordered by professional psychologists and counselors to help them determine whether the instrument is applicable to the individuals and for the purpose that the potential purchaser has in mind. The test manual, which contains a description of how the test was constructed, directions for administration and scoring, and perhaps norms, is usually not included in a specimen set and must be ordered separately. For some instruments, administration and scoring are covered in one manual, and the statistical details of norms, reliability, and validity in a separate technical manual. However, even a technical manual does not necessarily provide comprehensive, up-to-date information on the validity of the test. Much of that information may have to be sought in reports of research investigations published in professional journals and in scholarly books and monographs.

■ Summary

Measurement, the quantification of variables, is a fundamental characteristic of science. As in all scientific enterprises, the measurement of personality involves the classification and measurement of variables. The scale or level of such measurement varies with the mathematical operations that are meaningful with the scores obtained from the tests or other assessment procedure. The measurement of personality characteristics is typically at a somewhat lower level than an interval or ratio scale. On an interval scale, equal numerical differences imply equal differences in the characteristic that is being measured. On a ratio scale, equal numerical ratios imply equal ratios in the assessed characteristic. Scores on most personality assessment instruments represent measurement at an ordinal (rank order) scale or somewhere between an ordinal and an interval scale.

Analysis of personality assessment data involves the application of statistical procedures, including the construction of frequency distributions and the computations of percentiles and percentile ranks, measures of central tendency (arithmetic mean, median, mode), measures of variability (range, semi-interquartile rang, standard deviation), standard scores (z scores and T scores) and measures of correlation (product-moment coefficient, point-biserial coefficient). Product-moment correlations between variables may be used in linear regression equations for predicting scores on a dependent (criterion) variable from scores on an independent (predictor) variable, and in factor analysis to obtain a clearer picture of the basic dimensions underlying a set of correlated variables.

A factor analysis of the scores obtained by a large sample of persons on a group of tests or test items involves extracting the factors, rotating the factor axes, and interpreting the rotated factors. Factors are interpreted by inspecting the loadings of the tests on the factor axes. Computation of the communality (common factor variance) and specificity (specific factor variance) can also assist in interpreting the extracted factors.

Three strategies for constructing rating scales and personality inventories are deductive (content- or theory-based), inductive (internal consistency or factor-analytic), and external (empirical or criterion-group). Each of these strategies has advantages and disadvantages. The deductive approach is perhaps the most straightforward and economical, whereas the external approach is the most predictive of behavior.

The purpose of an item analysis of a test is to determine the extent to which the items comprising the test are functioning as they should: Are the items of the appropriate difficulty, and do they discriminate between high and low scorers on the internal or external criterion measure? Traditional item analysis procedures involve the computation of indexes of item difficulty and discrimination. In recent years these methods have been supplemented or replaced by more complex theoretical models involving the construction and analysis of item response curves.

Sources of information on personality assessment instruments include test publishers' catalogs and specimen sets of tests, articles in professional journals, reviews in *The Mental Measurements Yearbooks*, and many other published books, journals, and newsletters.

■ Questions and Activities

1. The following scores were obtained by 30 students on a personality inventory. Find the arithmetic mean, the variance, and standard deviation of the scores, and then convert the raw scores to z scores.

65	72	79	49	45	70	53	32	53	56	67	70
74	66	45	33	73	54	42	76	51	56	74	66
23	46	48	36	57	29						

2. Construct a frequency distribution of the 30 scores in Exercise 1, using an interval width of 1. Find the mode, median, range, and semi-interquartile range of these scores from the frequency distribution. Is the frequency distribution of these scores fairly symmetrical, or is it skewed positively (more low scores than high scores) or negatively (more high scores than low scores)? Construct a second frequency distribution for these scores with an interval width of 5. In what way does this wider grouping change the shape of the frequency distribution? Draw histograms and frequency polygons of both distributions for comparison purposes.

3. Determine the percentile ranks of the scores in Exercise 1. Interpret these percentile ranks.

4. Compute the product-moment correlation coefficient between the following scores on an Achievement Orientation scale of a personality inventory (X) administered to a group of 30 college freshmen and the grade-point averages (Y) obtained by the students by the end of their freshman year.

X	Y	X	Y	X	Y	X	Y	X	Y	X	Y
65	3.2	53	1.5	74	2.9	42	1.8	23	1.5	72	3.5
32	1.3	66	2.5	76	3.5	46	1.8	79	3.7	53	1.7
45	1.7	51	2.2	48	2.2	49	2.1	56	2.0	33	1.4
56	2.4	36	1.9	45	1.8	67	2.3	73	2.0	74	3.5
57	2.4	70	2.8	70	2.6	54	1.6	66	3.0	29	2.1

What can you say about the relationship of Achievement Orientation scores to grade-point average at the end of the freshman year? Is it positive or negative, high or low? Next determine the linear regression equation for predicting grade-point average (Y) from Achievement Orientation scores. Then find the predicted grade-point average for a student whose Achievement Orientation score is 40 and for a student whose Achievement Orientation score is 70.

6. Twenty students took a ten-item test. Their total test scores are listed on row Y below, and whether they answered a certain item right (1) or wrong (0) is indicated on row X. Compute the point-biserial correlation coefficient between total test scores and whether they answered the item correctly (1) or incorrectly (0). A good item is one that has a high correlation with total test score. Is this item a good one?

Student	Test Score	Item Score	Student	Test Score	Item Score
A	10	1	K	5	0
B	8	0	L	5	1
C	7	1	M	4	1
D	7	1	N	4	0
E	7	1	O	3	0
F	7	0	P	3	1
G	6	1	Q	3	0
H	6	0	R	2	0
I	6	1	S	2	0
J	6	0	T	1	0

7. Is it easier to conduct an item analysis on a test of personality or on a test of cognitive ability? Explain your answer.

■ Sources of Information on Personality Tests

Fischer, J., & Corcoran, K. (1994). *Measures for clinical practice: A sourcebook* (2nd ed., Vols 1–2). New York: Free Press.

Goldman, B.A., Mitchell, D.F., & Egelson, P.E. (Eds.) (1997). *Directory of unpublished experimental mental measurements* (Vol. 7). Washington, DC: American Psychological Association.

Groth-Marnat, G. (1997). *Handbook of psychological assessment* (3rd ed.). New York: Wiley.

Impara, J.C., & Plake, B.S. (Eds.). *The thirteenth mental measurements yearbook*. Lincoln, NE: University of Nebraska and Buros Institute of Mental Measurements.

Keyser, D.J., & Sweetland, R.C. (Eds.). (1984–1994). *Test critiques* (Vols. I–X). Austin, TX: pro.ed.

Maddox, T. (Ed.). (1997). *Tests*. Austin, TX: pro.ed.

Murphy, L.L., Conoley, J.C., & Impara, J.C. (Eds.). (1994). *Tests in print IV*. Lincoln: University of Nebraska and Buros Institute of Mental Measurements.

Newmark, C.S. (Ed.). (1996). *Major psychological assessment instruments* (2nd ed.). Needham Heights, MA: Allyn & Bacon.

Robinson, J.P., Shaver, P.R., & Wrightsman, L.S. (1991). *Measures of personality and social attitudes*. San Diego: Academic Press.

CHAPTER 3

Psychometrics II: Standardization, Reliability, and Validity

Item analysis is an important step in designing and evaluating a psychological test or other assessment device, but it is by no means the final step. Before a test can be used with some assurance that it is an accurate measure of the psychological construct it is supposed to measure, information concerning its reliability and validity must be obtained. Furthermore, it is useful for purposes of score interpretation to have available data on the performance of a large group of people who are representative of the population for which the test is designed. To accomplish this goal, a test, inventory, rating scale, or other psychometric device must be standardized.

■ Standardizing and Equating Tests

A standardized test has standard directions for administration and scoring that should be adhered to closely, leaving little room for personal interpretation or bias. However, standard directions for administration and scoring are necessary but not sufficient for a test to be considered standardized. In addition, the standardization of a personality test or other psychometric instrument requires administering it to a large sample of people (the *standardization sample*) selected as representative of the *target population* for whom the instrument has been designed. But merely because a standardization sample, or *norm group*, is large it does not mean that the sample is necessarily representative of the target population. To be truly representative of the population, a sample must be carefully selected.

The manner in which a standardization sample is selected varies from simple random sampling to more complex sampling strategies such as stratified random sampling and cluster sampling. In *simple random sampling*, every person in the population has an equal chance of being selected. Randomness, however, does not imply representativeness, because a random sample can be biased. Consequently, a more appropriate way to standardize a test is to begin by grouping, or "stratifying," the target population on a set of demographic variables (sex, age, socioeconomic status), geographical region, etc.) presumed to be related to scores on the test. Then the number of individuals selected at random from each group or stratum identified in this way is made proportional to the total number of persons in the target population who fall in that stratum. This strategy, which is referred to as *stratified random sampling*, minimizes the likelihood of selecting an atypical, or biased, sample. Then the obtained norms will provide a sounder basis for interpreting scores on the test than would norms obtained by simple random sampling.

More economical than stratified random sampling and more likely than simple random sampling to yield a sample that is representative of the population is cluster sampling. *Cluster sampling* consists of dividing a designated geographical area or composite population into blocks or clusters. Then a specified percentage of the clusters is selected at random, and within each cluster a certain number of subunits (schools, houses, etc.) is chosen at random. The final step is to question (i. e., test) all individuals within each subunit, or at least a random sample of those having designated characteristics.

Administering all items on a test to a stratified random sample or a cluster sample of people is tedious and time-consuming, so less costly strategies for determining test norms have been devised. One such strategy is to sample test items as well as people. In this *item sampling* strategy, different randomly selected persons answer different sets of items. The process is an efficient one, in that it permits administration of a greater number of items to a large sample of people in a fixed period of time. The results can then be combined to conduct item analyses and determine norms for representative samples of people on a wide range of test content. Research employing item-sampling procedures has shown that the resulting norms are quite similar to those obtained by the traditional but more laborious process of administering the entire test to a large representative sample (see Owens & Stufflebeam, 1969).

Norms

Norms, which serve as a frame of reference for interpreting scores on tests or other psychological assessment instruments, are transformations of the raw scores obtained from a standardization sample. In the case of achievement tests, norms are often expressed as *age equivalents* or *grade equivalents*, which are determined by averaging the scores made by certain age or grade groups. In the case of personality assessment, norms are almost always expressed in terms of percentile ranks or standard scores by age, sex, or other demographic variables.

To serve effectively as a means for interpreting test scores, norms must be appropriate to the group or individual being evaluated. For example, a particular ninth-grader's test score may be higher than that of 80% of seventh graders and higher than that of 40% of college freshmen in the standardization sample. Though it may be of some interest to compare a ninth-grader's score with the scores of seventh graders and college freshmen, of primary concern is the ninth-grader's standing in his or her own grade group. In any case, whenever an examinee's raw score on a test is converted by referring to a table of norms, it is important to indicate the nature of the particular group (age, sex, ethnicity, educational and socioeconomic status, geographical region or area of residence, etc.) from which the norms were obtained. Also important is the time when the norms were collected. Norms obtained in the spring are different from those in the fall, and norms determined during times of rapid social change may be different from those deter mined during more stable periods. Regardless of the type of test—achievement, intelligence, specific aptitude, personality, interest, attitude, norms can become outdated. Consequently, every test should be restandardized periodically so the norms can continue to serve as an appropriate basis for score interpretation.

Percentile Norms. Procedures for determining percentile ranks and standard scores were discussed in Chapter 2. When computed from a frequency distribution, both kinds of norms are based on the midpoints of the score intervals. Determination of the percentile (rank) norm of a given interval midpoint, say the midpoint score of 40 in Table 2–2, consists of computing the percentage of scores falling below the midpoint. The process begins by computing the cumulative frequency (cf) up to the interval containing the midpoint, adding to cf one-half the frequency on the interval ($.5f$), dividing the resulting sum by the total number of scores (n), and multiplying the resulting quotient by 100, i. e., $100(cf + .5f)/n$. For the frequency distribution in Table 2–2, the percentile rank of a raw score of 40 is $100[55 + .5(7)]/90 = 65$, so a score of 40 is the 65th percentile.

Because they are easy to compute and to understand, percentile norms are quite commonly reported for published tests. Tables of percentile norms for different grade, age, gender, occupation, and other demographic groups are

FIG. 3–1   **Cross-scale Variations in the Unit of Measurement of Percentile Ranks.**

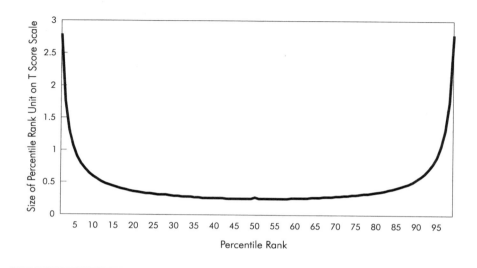

provided for many cognitive and affective instruments. Unfortunately, the unit of measurement is not equal on all parts of the percentile-rank scale. Percentile ranks are ordinal-level rather than interval-level measures; consequently they do not have the same meaning on all parts of the scale. As illustrated in Figure 3–1, the size of the percentile-rank unit becomes progressively smaller toward the center of the scale. Also observe, however, that the unit of measurement is fairly constant between the 20th and 80th percentile ranks.

The tendency for percentile ranks to bunch up in the middle of the scale and to spread out at the extremes may cause difficulty in interpreting changes and differences in percentile norms. For example, the difference between percentile ranks of 5 and 10 (or 90 and 95) is greater, in terms of whatever psychological construct is being measured, than the difference between percentile ranks of 45 and 50 (or 50 and 55). On the percentile-rank scale, the distance from 5 to 10 is greater than the distance from 45 to 50 because the unit of measurement for the first difference is larger than the unit of measurement for the second difference. With practice, however, it is not difficult to interpret percentile norms. One must simply remember to assign greater weight to percentile rank differences at the extremes than to those toward the center of the scale.

Standard Score Norms. In contrast to percentile ranks, standard scores represent measurements on an interval scale. *Standard score norms* are converted scores having a specified mean and standard deviation. Many different types of standard scores—*z* scores, T scores, *stanine scores, sten scores*—are used in scoring and interpreting personality tests. Basically, all of these standard scores are transformations of *z* scores. You will recall from Chapter 2 that *z* scores are computed from the formula $z = (X - \overline{X})/s$, where X is the raw score, $\overline{X}$ the arithmetic mean, and s the standard deviation of the raw scores.

Because half of all *z* scores are negative numbers, which are somewhat troublesome to work with, a further transformation of *z* scores to T scores is often made. T scores are computed as $T = 10z + 50$, rounded to the nearest whole number; they have a mean of 50 and a standard deviation of 10. For example, the T scores corresponding to *z* scores of –1.00 and +1.00 are 10(–1.00) + 50 – 40 and 10(1.00) + 50 = 60, respectively. When determining T scores from a frequency distribution, the T scores corresponding to a given interval midpoint is somewhat more easily computed as $T = 10(\text{Midpoint} - \overline{X})/s + 50$. Computing T score norms in this way changes the mean and standard deviation of the frequency distribution, but it has no effect on the shape of the distribution. If the frequency distribution of raw scores is skewed, the frequency distribution of T scores will be skewed in the same way—either positively or negatively.

Percentile and T score norms corresponding to the frequency distribution of the composite instructor personality ratings in Table 2–2 are given in Table 3–1.

Percentile and T Score Norms for the Distribution of Raw Scores in Table 2–2. **TABLE 3–1**

Raw Score	Percentile Rank	T Score	Raw Score	Percentile Rank	T Score
55	99	76	39	57	51
54	98	74	38	50	50
53	97	73	37	44	48
52	96	71	36	38	47
51	95	70	35	32	45
50	93	68	34	26	44
49	92	67	33	21	42
48	91	65	32	17	41
47	89	63	31	14	39
46	87	62	30	12	38
45	86	60	29	11	36
44	85	59	28	6	35
43	83	57	27	3	33
42	78	56	26	2	32
41	72	54	25	1	30
40	65	53	24	1	29

The average percentile norm, an ordinal-scale number, is 50. The mean T score is also 50, but it is an interval-scale number. In any event, a raw score of 40, which is equivalent to a percentile norm of 65 and a T score of 53, is above average on both scales.

Normalized Standard Scores. Both z and T score norms are simple linear transformations of raw scores. The distribution of converted scores has a different mean and standard deviation than the raw score distribution, but the shapes of the raw and converted score distributions are the same. If the raw score distribution is symmetrical, the distribution of converted scores will also be symmetrical. If one is skewed, the other will be skewed in the same manner.

In order to make the scores on different tests more directly comparable, a score transformation procedure that affects not only the mean and standard deviation but also the shape of the frequency distribution of raw scores to that of a normal distribution can be applied. The conversion of a group of raw scores to these *normalized standard scores* begins with the computation of the percentile ranks of the raw scores. Then, from a table of areas under the normal curve, which can be found in almost any introductory statistics textbook, the z score corresponding to each percentile rank is determined. These normalized z scores may then be transformed to T scores or to a set of scores having any desired mean and standard deviation. One popular scale is the *stanine* ("standard nine") *scale*, which ranges from 1 to 9. The stanine scale has a mean of 5 and a standard deviation of 2, so stanines may be computed from normalized z scores by the formula Stanine = $2z + 5$. Another scale, which is used with the 16 Personality Factor Questionnaire, is the *sten* ("standard ten") *scale*, the scores on which range from 1 to 10 and have a mean of 5.5.

Base Rate Scores. A special type of score transformation procedure is applied to evaluating performance on the Millon Clinical Multiaxial Inventory (MCMI-III). Raw scores on this inventory are weighted and converted to *base rate scores*, which take into account the incidence of a particular characteristic or disorder in the general population. By determining the incidence of a particular personality disorder or trait in a designated population, raw scores on the MCMI-III are transformed in such a way that the ratio of the number of correct classifications (valid positives) to the number of incorrect classifications (false positives) is maximized.

Parallel and Equated Tests

In many situations involving applications and research with psychological tests, more than one form of a test is required. *Parallel forms* of a test are equivalent in the sense that they contain the same kinds of items of equal difficulty and are highly correlated. Therefore, the scores made on one form of the test are very similar to those obtained by the same examinees on a second form at the same age and grade levels as the first form. Construction of parallel tests is, however, a rather expensive and time-consuming process. It begins with the preparation of two tests having the same number and kinds of items and yielding the same means and standard deviations when standardized on the same group of people. The resulting parallel forms are then "equated" by converting the scores on one form to the same units as those on the other form. This may be done, for example, by the *equipercentile method* of changing the scores on each form to percentile ranks. Then a table of equivalent scores on the two forms is prepared by equating the pth percentile on the first form to the pth percentile on the second form.

Tests may also be equated, or rather made comparable, by anchoring them to a common test or pool of items. Item-response theory, which was discussed in the last chapter in connection with item analysis, has also been applied to the task of equating tests. This approach to test equating consists of determining a linear equation that transforms the difficulty and discrimination parameters of one test form to those of a second test form. This procedure, referred to as *linking*, involves the computation of appropriate constants for the transformation equation so that the corresponding parameters on the two tests are equal. Linking one test to another also requires that the two tests have a set of (anchor) items in common, or that some examinees take both tests and a third test that measures the same trait.

The item-response method of test equating is economical in that item sampling, in which randomly selected subsets of items are administered to differently randomly selected groups of people, is employed. Whatever method is used in attempting to equate tests—equipercentile, item-response, linear or nonlinear score transformations, strictly speaking tests that either measure different psychological variables or have different reliabilities cannot be truly equated. In almost every case, about the best that can be done is to make the tests or other psychometric instruments comparable (American Educational Research Association et al., 1985). Consequently, the results of repeated measures or pretest-posttest research involving two or more forms of the same psychometric instrument should be interpreted cautiously.

■ Reliability

No assessment device can be of value unless it measures consistently, or *reliably*. One of the first things that should be ascertained about a newly developed assessment instrument is whether it is sufficiently reliable to measure what it was intended to. If, in the absence of any permanent change in a person due to growth, learning, disease, personal trauma, or the like, a person's score on a given test is unstable across time or situations, then the test is probably unreliable and cannot be used to predict or explain the person's behavior. Note that *reliability* does not mean the same thing as *stability*. In determining the reliability of a measuring instrument, it is assumed that the instrument measures a relatively stable characteristic. Unlike instability of the variable being measured, unreliability is a result of measurement errors produced by temporary internal states (low motivation, temporary indisposition, etc.) or external conditions (distracting or uncomfortable testing environment, etc.).

Classical Reliability Theory

Classical reliability theory makes the assumption that a person's observed score on a test is composed of a true score plus some unsystematic error of measurement. A *true score* is defined as the average of the scores the person would obtain if he or she took the test an infinite number of times. It should be emphasized that true scores can never be measured precisely but must be estimated from observed scores. Classical test theory also assumes that the variance of the observed scores (s_o^2) of a group of examinees is equal to the variance of their true scores (s_t^2) plus the variance of unsystematic errors of measurement (s_e^2):

$$s_o^2 = s_t^2 + s_e^2. \tag{3.1}$$

Then test reliability (r_{11}) is defined as the ratio of true variance to observed variance, or the proportion of observed variance that is accounted for by true variance:

$$r_{11} = s_t^2/s_o^2. \tag{3.2}$$

The proportion of observed variance accounted for by error variance, or unaccounted for by true variance, can be determined from formulas 3.1 and 3.2 to be

$$s_e^2/s_o^2 = 1 - r_{11}. \tag{3.3}$$

The reliability of a test is expressed as a positive decimal number ranging from .00 to 1.00, where 1.00 indicates perfect reliability and .00 indicates the absence of reliability. Because the variance of true scores cannot be computed directly, reliability is usually estimated by analyzing the effects of variations in conditions of administration and test content on observed scores. As noted previously, reliability is not influenced by systematic changes in scores that affect all examinees equally but only by unsystematic changes that have different effects on different examinees. Such unsystematic factors influence the error variance of a test, and hence the test's reliability. Each of the several methods of estimating reliability—test-retest, parallel forms, internal consistency—takes into account somewhat different conditions that may lead to unsystematic changes in test scores and thereby affect the magnitude of the error variance, and consequently the reliability coefficient.

Test-Retest Coefficient

The reliability of a psychometric instrument from one time to another can be estimated by a test-retest coefficient. This procedure consists of finding the correlation between scores made by a group of people on one administration with their scores on a second administration of the instrument. The test-retest procedure takes into account errors of measurement caused by differences in conditions associated with the two occasions on which the test is administered. The same test is administered on both occasions, so errors due to different samples of test items are not reflected in a test-retest coefficient. Because differences between conditions of administration are likely to be greater after a long time interval than after a short one, the magnitude of the reliability coefficient will tend to be larger when the interval between initial test and retest is short (a few days or weeks) rather than long (months or years).

Parallel-Forms Coefficient

When the time interval between initial test and retest is short, on being retested examinees will usually remember many of the responses they gave on the first administration of the test. This will undoubtedly affect their responses on the second administration, a fact that in itself would not change the test's reliability if all examinees remembered equal numbers of responses. However, some examinees recall more responses than other examinees, reducing the correlation between test and retest. What is needed to control for this problem is a parallel form of the test, one consisting of similar items but not the same ones. Then a *parallel-forms coefficient* can be computed as an index of reliability.

The parallel forms idea is reasonable in principle: by administering a parallel form after a suitable time interval following administration of the original form of the test, a reliability coefficient reflecting errors of measurement due to different items *and* different times of administration can be computed. To control for the confounding effect of form with time of administration, Form A should be administered first to half the group and Form B to the other half; then on the next administration the first group takes Form B and the second group takes Form A.

Internal Consistency Coefficients

Although parallel forms are available for a number of tests, particularly tests of ability (achievement, intelligence, special aptitudes), a parallel form is expensive and often quite difficult to construct. Therefore, a less direct method of taking into account the effects of different samples of test items on reliability was devised—the method of *internal consistency*. Errors of measurement caused by different conditions or times of administration are, however, not reflected by an internal consistency coefficient. For this reason internal consistency coefficients are not truly equivalent to either test-retest or parallel forms coefficients. Three procedures for determining the internal consistency of a test are split-half, Kuder-Richardson, and coefficient alpha.

Split-Half Method. It is often convenient to view a single test as consisting of two parts (parallel forms), each of which measures the same thing. Thus, a test can be administered and separate scores assigned to every examinee on two arbitrarily selected halves of the test. For example, an examinee may be given one score on the odd-numbered items and a second score on the even-numbered items on a test. Then the computed correlation (r_{oe}) between the odds and evens scores is a parallel forms reliability coefficient for a test half as long as the original test. Assuming that the two halves are equivalent, having equal means and equal variances, the reliability of the test as a whole can be estimated by the *Spearman-Brown prophecy formula*:

$$r_{11} = 2r_{oe}/(1 + r_{oe}).$$ (3.4)

To illustrate the use of this formula, assume that the correlation between total scores on the odd-numbered items and total scores on the even-numbered items of a test is .80. Then the estimated reliability of the entire test is $r_{11} = 2(.8) / (1 + .8) = .89$.

Kuder-Richardson Method. There are many different ways of dividing a test into two halves. Because each way yields a somewhat different value for r_{11}, it is not clear which halving procedure will result in the best reliability estimate. The *Kuder-Richardson method* solves this problem by determining the average of the reliability coefficients obtained from all possible half-splits as the overall reliability estimate. But even with a test of, say 20 items, a computer is required to calculate and average the resulting 92,378 split-half coefficients!

Under certain conditions the mean of all split-half coefficients can be estimated by one of the following formulas:

$$r_{11} = [k/(k-1)][1 - \Sigma p_i(1 - p_i)/s^2] \tag{3.5}$$

$$r_{11} = [k/(k-1)][1 - \overline{X}(k - \overline{X})/(ks^2)] \tag{3.6}$$

In these formulas k is the number of items on the test, $\overline{X}$ is the mean of total test scores, s^2 is the variance of total test scores, and p_i is the proportion of examinees who gave the keyed response to item i. The summation in formula 3.5 is over all n items. Formulas 3.5 and 3.6 are known as *Kuder-Richardson (K-R) formulas* 20 and 21, respectively. Unlike formula 3.5, formula 3.6 is based on the assumption that all items are of equal difficulty; it also yields a more conservative estimate of reliability and is easier to use than formula 3.5. To demonstrate the application of formula 3.6, assume that a 75-item test has a mean of 50 and a variance of 100. Then $r_{11} = (75/74)\{1 - 50(75 - 50) / [75(100)]\} = .84$.

Coefficient Alpha. Formulas 3.5 and 3.6 are special cases of the more general coefficient alpha (Cronbach, 1951). *Coefficient alpha* is defined as

$$r_{11} = [k/(k-1)][1 - \Sigma s_i^2/s_t^2], \tag{3.7}$$

where s_i^2 is the variance of scores on item i and s_t^2 is the variance of total test scores. Summation of the s_i^2 is over all items on the test. Although the Kuder-Richardson formulas are applicable only when test items are scored 0 or 1, coefficient alpha is a general formula for computing the internal consistency reliability of a test consisting of items on which two or more scoring weights are assigned to answers.

All internal consistency procedures (split-half, Kuder-Richardson, coefficient alpha) overestimate the reliability of speeded tests, that is, tests that most examinees do not finish in the allotted time. Consequently, internal consistency procedures must be modified to provide reasonable estimates of reliability when a test is speeded. One recommendation is to administer two halves of the test on two different occasions but with the same time limits. Then scores on the two separately-timed halves can be correlated and the resulting correlation coefficient corrected by the Spearman-Brown prophecy formula. Test-retest and parallel-forms procedures may also be used to estimate the reliability of a speeded test.

Coefficient alpha determined on the 11 instructor personality items rated by 90 students (see Chapter 2) was computed as .824. This is a modest reliability coefficient, but not unusual for personality rating scales.

The reliability coefficients of affective instruments such as personality and interest inventories are typically lower than those of cognitive tests (achievement, intelligence, and special abilities). However, the reliabilities of personality inventories and other affective measures are sometimes quite respectable, and even cognitive tests can have low reliabilities.

Interscorer Reliability

In scoring projective tests and other types of instruments involving subjective scorer judgment, it is important to know the extent to which different people agree with each other in scoring or rating the responses of different examinees and items. The most common approach to determining this *interscorer* or *interrater reliability* is to have two people score the responses given by a sizable number of examinees and to compute the correlation between the scores assigned by the two scorers; this process yields an interrater or interscorer reliability coefficient. Another approach is to have several people score the test responses of one examine, or better still, have many people score the responses of a number of examinees. The latter approach yields an *intraclass coefficient* or *coefficient of concordance*, which is a generalized interscorer or interrater reliability coefficient. Procedures for computing these indexes are found in many statistics and psychometrics textbooks (e. g., Winer, Brown & Michels, 1991). The author has also provided special methods for computing test-retest and internal-consistency reliability coefficients from rating-scale data and for conducting statistical tests of significance on the coefficients (Aiken, 1985).

Interpreting Reliability Coefficients

Occasionally the reliabilities of objective personality tests and interest inventories are quite high (in the .80s and .90s), but typically they are lower than those of tests of achievement, intelligence, and special abilities. The reason is that responses to personality assessment instruments are generally less stable, or more changeable over time, than responses to tests of cognitive abilities. Whether this instability is due to random fluctuations (error) or to bona fide changes in personality may be debatable, but in any case it tends to depress the measured reliabilities of personality assessment instruments.

How high must a reliability coefficient be in order for a test to be considered useful? The answer depends on what one plans to do with the test scores. If a test is used to determine whether the mean scores of two groups of people are significantly different, then a reliability coefficient as low as .65 may be satisfactory. But if the test is used to compare a person's score with that of another person or with the same person's score on different tests, the test should have a reliability coefficient of at least .85.

Variability and Reliability

As is the case with other measures of relationship, reliability tends to be greater when the variance of the variables (test scores, item scores, ratings, etc.) is larger than when it is small. Because test score variance is related to test length, one common method of increasing reliability is to add more items to the test. The general Spearman-Brown formula is an expression of the effect on reliability of lengthening a test by adding more items of the same general type. This formula, a generalization of formula 3.4, is

$$r_{mm} = mr_{11} / [1 + r_{11}(m - 1)], \qquad (3.8)$$

where m is the factor by which the test is lengthened, r_{11} is the reliability of the original, unlengthened test, and r_{mm} is the estimated reliability of the lengthened test. For example, if a 20-item test having a reliability coefficient of .70 is made three times as long by adding 40 more items to the test, the estimated reliability of the lengthened test will be $3(.7) / [1 + .7(3 - 1)] = .875$. By solving formula 3.8 for m, the factor by which a test with reliability r_{11} must be lengthened in order to obtain a desired reliability (r_{mm}) may also be determined. Increasing the length of a test by adding items has less effect on its reliability when the initial reliability is high than when it is low. In addition, regardless of the test's initial

---

Reliability of a Lengthened Test as a Function of its Initial Reliability and the Lengthening Factor.　　**FIG. 3–2**

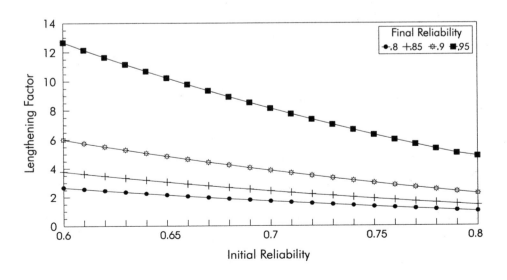

reliability, further increases in a its length beyond doubling produce less and less improvement in reliability.

Figure 3–2 is a graphical plot of the relationship of the reliability of a final (lengthened) test as a function of the initial reliability of the test and the length-ened factor. This chart may be used to determine the (1) expected increase in reliability produced by adding more items of the same general type to the test and (2) the number of items needed to increase a test's reliability by a desired amount. As the reliability of the initial test gets smaller and smaller, it becomes increasingly more difficult to increase its length sufficiently to obtain a high re-liability coefficient.

In addition to being dependent on the number of items comprising a test, the variance and reliability of the test are affected by the degree of heterogeneity of the group of people who take the test. The greater the range of individual differ-ences among a group of people on a certain characteristic, the larger the variance of their scores on a measure of that characteristic. Consequently, the reliability coefficient of a test or other assessment device will be higher in a more hetero-geneous group which has a larger test-score variance, than in a more homogene-ous group, which has a smaller test-score variance. The fact that the reliability of a test varies with the nature of the group that is tested is reflected in the practice of reporting separate reliability coefficients for individuals of different ages, grades, and sexes.

Standard Error of Measurement

Less frequently reported in the context of personality assessment than in ability testing is the *standard error of measurement* (s_e). This statistic is an estimate of the standard deviation of the normal distribution of scores that an examinee would presumably make if he or she took the test an infinite number of times. The mean of this hypothetical frequency distribution is the examinee's true score on the test.

The standard error of measurement is computed as

$$s_e = s_o\sqrt{1 - r_{11}}, \tag{3.9}$$

where s_o is the standard deviation of obtained test scores and r_{11} is the test-retest reliability coefficient.

To illustrate the computation and interpretation of the standard error of mea-surement, assume that the standard deviation of a test is 6.59 and the test-retest reliability coefficient is .85. Then $s_m = 6.59 \sqrt{1 - .85} = 2.55$. Therefore, if a per-son's raw score on the test is 40, it can be concluded with 68% confidence that he or she is one of a group of people with an observed score of 40 whose true scores on the test fall between $40 - 2.55 = 37.45$ and $40 + 2.55 = 42.55$. It can

Standard Errors of Measurement and Estimate as Functions of the   **FIG. 3–3**
Reliability and Validity Coefficients, Respectively.

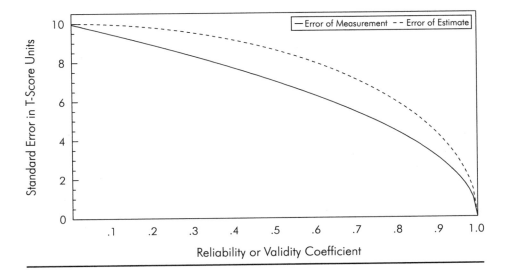

also be concluded with 95% confidence that the person is one of a group of people with observed scores of 40 whose true scores on the test fall between 40 − 1.96(2.55) = 35.00 and 40 + 1.96(2.55) = 45.00.

As can be seen by inspecting formula 3.9 and Figure 3–3, the standard error of measurement increases as the reliability of the test decreases. When r_{11} = 1.00, there is no error at all in estimating a person's true score from his or her observed score; when r_{11} = .00, the error of measurement is a maximum and equal to the standard deviation of observed scores. Of course, a test having a reliability coefficient close to .00 is useless because the correctness of any decisions made on the basis of the scores will be no better than chance.

Percentile Bands

A person's score on certain tests is expressed not as a single number but rather as a score band, or *percentile band*, having a width of one standard error of measurement (or the percentile-rank equivalent of s_e) on either side of the person's observed test score. This practice is an acknowledgment of the fact that a test score is not a fixed, unvarying measure of a characteristic but only an approximation. The standard error of measurement is an estimate of the average error in that approximation.

When a person's scores on several tests are plotted in the form of a profile, it is useful to draw a band having a width of one or two standard errors of measurement around the score points. Then small differences between the scores of the same person on two different tests or the scores of two persons on the same test are less likely to be viewed as significant. In general, the difference between the scores of two people on the same test should not be interpreted as significant unless it is at least twice the standard error of measurement of the test. But the difference between the scores of the same individual on two different tests should be *greater* than twice the standard error of measurement of *either* test before the difference can be interpreted as significant. This is true because the standard error of the difference between the scores on two tests is larger than the standard error of measurement of either test alone.

Reliability and Standard Error of Score Differences

The above rules of thumb for using the standard error of measurement to interpret score differences are helpful, but they are not as revealing as two other statistics for diagnostic purposes. These statistics are the *reliability of score differences* and the *standard error of score differences*. As shown in the following formula, the reliability of differences between scores on two tests depends not only on the reliability of both tests but also on the correlation between them. The reliability of score differences can be estimated from:

$$r_{dd} = (r_{11} + r_{22} - 2r_{12}) \, / \, [2(1 - r_{12})], \qquad (3.10)$$

where r_{11} is the reliability of the first test, r_{22} is the reliability of the second test, and r_{12} is the correlation between the two tests. For example, if the reliability of the first test is .90, the reliability of the second test is .80, and the correlation between the tests is .70, then the reliability of the difference between the scores on the two tests is $[.9 + .8 - 2(.7)] \, / \, [2(1 - .7)] = .50$. In general, unless the tests are uncorrelated, the reliability of the difference between scores on two tests will always be less than the reliability of either test alone.

A second statistic, the *standard error of score differences*, can be used to establish confidence limits for the difference between a person's true scores on two tests. Assuming that the standard deviations of the tests are equal ($s_1 = s_2 = s$), as they will be if scores on the two tests are converted to the same standard-score scale, a simple formula for the standard error of the difference scores is

$$s_{ed} = s\sqrt{2 - r_{11} - r_{22}}. \qquad (3.11)$$

As seen in this formula, the standard error of the difference scores varies inversely with the reliabilities of the two tests. The more reliable the tests, the smaller the standard error of the difference. And the smaller the value of s_{ed}, the greater is the likelihood that the difference between the scores on two tests or part scores on a single test or test composite will be significant and interpretable. A conservative rule of thumb is that the difference between the scores of a person on two tests must be at least two standard errors of the difference in order to be considered significant.

Generalizability Theory

Since the 1950s there has been growing dissatisfaction among specialists in psychometrics with the classical test theory that was developed during the first half of the 20th century. A number of alternative approaches, which are based more securely in modern statistical theory and also influenced by advances in high-speed computing, have been devised. One of these is *generalizability theory*, which views a test score as a single sample from a universe of possible scores. The reliability of a test score is defined as the precision with which it estimates a more generalized universe value (the true score). It is recognized, however, that there may be several universes to which sample findings can be generalized. These universes are defined according to the various conditions *(facets)* which affect the results of psychometric assessments. Examples of such facets are different test forms, different observers or examiners, and different occasions on which people may be observed or examined. Associated with the various facets are different measurement errors, which affect the accuracy of generalizing sample results to an appropriate universe.

In the computations of generalizability theory, the statistical procedures of analysis of variance are applied to determine the generalizability, or dependability, of test scores as a function of changes in the person(s) taking the test, different samples of items comprising the test, the situations or conditions under which the test is administered, and the methods or people involved in scoring the test. A *generalizability coefficient*, which is similar to a traditional reliability coefficient, may then be computed as the ratio of the expected variance of scores in the universe to the variance of scores in the sample. Finally, a *universe value* of the score, which is similar in concept to the true score of classical reliability theory, can be estimated (Cronbach et al., 1972). Despite its greater statistical sophistication, however, generalizability theory has not replaced the classical theory of reliability and validity. The traditional concepts of reliability and validity developed by classical test theory and the procedures derived from them are still applied extensively in psychological assessment (Feldt & Brennan, 1989).

■ Validity

Reliability is a necessary but not a sufficient condition for validity: a measuring instrument can be reliable without being valid, but it cannot be valid without being reliable. A technical limitation on the validity of a test is that it can be no higher than the square root of the parallel-forms reliability of the test. Furthermore, *validity*, the extent to which a psychometric instrument measures what it was designed to measure, is more specific to time and place than reliability. We say that a test is *valid* for such and such a purpose, not *generally valid*.*

Obviously, validity is a more important characteristic of a test than reliability. A valid test is good for something, specifically for helping a psychologist predict and understand behavior and mental functioning. There are three types of validity, or, more precisely, three ways of obtaining information concerning a test's validity: content validity, criterion-related validity, and construct validity.

Content Validity

Sometimes inaccurately referred to as *face validity*, *content validity* is concerned with whether the appearance or content of a measuring instrument supports the assertion that it is a measure of a certain psychological variable. Thus, one would expect a test of mechanical ability to contain mechanical problems and a test of reading achievement to contain reading passages. However, the matter is not quite so simple as merely looking at the test: the content must be examined closely and systematically by experts in the subject-matter of the test in order to arrive at a decision concerning its content validity. The extent to which the content of a test corresponds to a detailed outline or table of specifications of what the test should measure may be used as a criterion of the test's content validity.

Content validity is of major concern on tests of academic achievement and other cognitive skills, but it also has a place in evaluating personality assessment techniques. For example, a personality test such as the Myers-Briggs Type Indicator, which was designed to assess certain constructs of Carl Jung's analytic theory of personality, should obviously contain items related to the theory. And tests designed to measure psychological constructs such as anxiety, depression, or achievement motivation should contain items that appear to be or are otherwise demonstrable indicators of those constructs.

---

* The same can, of course, be said of reliability. Reliability is not a general characteristic of a test: it varies with the group tested and the circumstances of administration.

Criterion-Related Validity

The *criterion-related validity* of a test is determined by correlating test scores with measures of an external criterion of whatever the test is supposed to measure. Scores on the criterion may be obtained at the same time as the test is administered (*concurrent validity*) or at a later time (*predictive validity*). Concurrent validation was one of the approaches used in validating the MMPI: the ability of MMPI items to classify psychiatric patients correctly was evaluated by determining the extent to which the inventory assigned a sample of psychiatric patients to the same diagnostic categories as those to which they were assigned by psychiatrists employing other classification procedures (observation, interviewing, etc.). This is an example of a the *method of contrasting groups*, which is a common technique used in concurrent validation. In this method, two groups of people in different diagnostic, occupational, or other relevant categories are compared with respect to their performance on a personality test or other psychological assessment instrument. Among the criteria that have been used to determine the predictive validity of personality tests are changes in personality and behavior resulting from psychotherapy and other interventions, school or job performance, and other behavioral events (e. g., suicide attempts, violent acts). An example of a predictive validity coefficient is the correlation ($r = .45$) between midterm ratings of instructor personality and end-of-term course ratings that was described in Chapter 2. The use of a linear regression equation for predicting scores on a criterion measure from scores on a predictor (test) variable is an integral part of the predictive validity process.

Standard Error of Estimate. A useful statistic to compute when the predictive validity of a test is of interest is the *standard error of estimate* (s_{est}). This statistic is computed as

$$s_{est} = s_y\sqrt{1 - r^2}, \tag{3.12}$$

where s_y is the standard deviation of the criterion (Y) scores and r is the correlation between predictor (X) and criterion (Y) scores. The standard error of estimate is used to establish a numerical interval within which it can be concluded, with a specified degree of confidence, that the obtained Y score of a person having a given X score is likely to fall.

Using as an example the instructor personality (X) and course evaluation (Y) scores given in Chapter 2, the standard error of estimate for predicting Y from X is $s_{est} = 4.89 \sqrt{1 - .4529^2} = 4.36$.

Assuming that a certain examinee's X score is 50, and substituting X = 40 in the regression equation $Y_{pred} = .3358X + 5.1005$ yields a predicted Y value of 18.53. Therefore, the chances are 95 out of 100 that this examinee is one of a group of people with an X score of 40 whose obtained Y scores fall between $18.53 - 1.96(4.36) = 9.98$ and $18.53 + 1.96(4.36) = 27.08$. As suggested by this example, a person's actual Y score may be quite different from his or her predicted Y score. This is especially likely when the correlation between X and Y is modest. The smaller the correlation coefficient, the larger is the standard error of estimate and hence the less accurate the prediction of Y from X.

As illustrated by the dashed (top) curve in Figure 3–3, the standard error of estimate is inversely related to the validity coefficient. Note that the rate of decrease in the standard error of estimate as a function of the validity coefficient is slower than the rate of decline of the standard error of measurement as a function of the reliability coefficient.

Cross-Validation. Whenever the predictive validity of an assessment instrument is determined for the first time, it is important to *cross-validate* (i. e., re-validate) the results on a second sample of individuals. Because chance factors can spuriously inflate the original validity coefficient, the validity coefficient and regression equation based on a single sample can be misleading. The size of this coefficient may undergo considerable shrinkage when applied to a second sample of people, and it should be corrected for. Cross-validation is also important with regard to concurrent validation. For example, using the method of contrasting groups one may find a set of scores or *signs* on a projective test that appear to differentiate between two psychiatric groups or between mentally disturbed and normal people. Unfortunately, the significance of these indicators may disappear when the instrument is administered to a second sample.

Criterion Contamination. The validity of a test is limited not only by the reliabilities of the test and the criterion but also by the validity of the criterion itself as a measure of the particular variable of interest. Sometimes the criterion is made less valid, or in other words, *contaminated*, by the particular method in which the criterion scores are determined. For example, a clinical psychologist who knows from other information that several examinees have already been diagnosed as psychotic may readily see signs of psychosis in their responses to a projective test. Then the method of contrasting groups, in which the scores of the psychotics are compared with those of normals, will yield false evidence for the validity of the test. Such contamination of the criterion (psychotic vs. normal) can be controlled by *blind analysis*, that is, by making available to the clinician no information about the examinees other than their test scores before attempting to make a diagnosis. Many clinical psychologists maintain, however, that blind analysis is unnatural in that it is not the way in which tests are usually employed in actual practice. Psychodiagnosticians typically possess a great deal of additional information about a client or patient and attempt to find consistencies or congruences among the various test and nontest sources when making a diagnosis or treatment recommendation.

Base Rate. Another factor that affects the magnitude of criterion-related validity coefficients, and hence the identification or prediction of certain behaviors, are the base rates of those behaviors in the target population. The *base rate* is the proportion of people in the population manifesting the characteristic or behavior of interest. A test designed to predict a particular type of behavior is most effective when the base rate is 50% and least effective when it is very high or very low. Thus, characteristics or behaviors such as psychoticism, brain damage, or suicide, which have low base rates in the general population, are much more difficult to assess or diagnose, and hence to predict, that those with higher base rates (e. g., neuroticism, marital discord, spouse or child abuse).

Incremental Validity. In deciding whether the cost of a particular assessment instrument for predictive or diagnostic purposes is justified by its utility, the concept of *incremental validity* should be taken into account. *Incremental validity* is concerned with how much more accurate predictions and/or diagnoses are when a psychometric instrument is administered that when it is not. Other methods of assessment (observation, interview, application blank, etc.) may be less expensive and fulfill the purposes of assessment almost as well without incurring the cost of an additional assessment instrument. Multiple regression analysis, a statistical procedure described briefly in Chapter 2, may be applied to answer the question of a test's incremental validity in a specific situation.

Construct Validity

Predictive validity is of primary interest in situations involving occupational or educational selection and placement. Ability tests of various kinds, and sometimes personality and interest tests, are used for this purpose. Of greater concern with respect to personality tests, however, is construct validity. The *construct validity* of a psychological assessment instrument refers to the extent to which the instrument is an accurate measure of a particular *construct*, or psychological variable, such as anxiety, hostility, achievement motivation, introversion/extroversion, or neuroticism. The construct validity of a test is not determined by one method or by a single investigation. Rather, it involves a network of investigations and procedures designed to determine whether an assessment instrument that was constructed to measure a particular variable does so effectively.

Evidence for Construct Validity. Among the sources of evidence for the construct validity of a test are:

a. Experts' judgments that the content of the test pertains to the construct of interest.
b. Analysis of the internal consistency of the test.
c. Studies of the relationships, in both experimentally contrived and naturally occurring groups, of test scores to other variables on which the groups differ.
d. Correlations of the test with other tests and variables with which it is expected to have certain relationships, and factor analyses of these intercorrelations.
e. Questioning examinees or raters in detail about their responses to a test or rating scale in order to reveal the specific mental processes that played a role in those responses.

As noted in the above list, various kinds of information contribute to the establishment of the construct validity of a psychometric instrument. These involve such procedures as a rational or statistical (e. g., factor analysis) analysis of the variables assessed by the instrument and studies of the ability of the instrument to predict behavior in situations in which the construct is known to operate. Experimental demonstrations such as those in the construct validation of the Taylor Manifest Anxiety Scale (TMAS) (Taylor, 1953) are particularly important in establishing a test's construct validity. In this case, it was predicted that, assuming anxiety is a drive, people with a high level of anxiety would acquire a conditioned eyeblink in a light-airpuff-eyeblink classical conditioning situation more quickly than less anxious people. Then if the TMAS is a valid measure of *anxiety*, high scorers on the scale should be conditioned more readily in this situation than lower scorers. Verification of this prediction contributed significantly to the establishment of the construct validity of the TMAS.

Convergent and Discriminant Validation. To possess construct validity, an assessment instrument should have high correlations with other measures of (or methods of measuring) the same construct *(convergent validity)* and low correlations with measures of different constructs *(discriminant validity)*. Information pertaining to the convergent and discriminant validity of a psychometric instrument can be obtained by comparing correlations between measures of (1) the same construct using the same method, (2) different constructs using the same method, (3) the same construct using different methods, and (4) different constructs using different methods. This *multitrait-multimethod approach* (Campbell & Fiske, 1959) provides evidence for the construct validity of the instrument when correlations between the same construct measured by the same and different methods are significantly higher than correlations between different constructs measured by the same or different methods. Unfortunately, the results are not always as desired: sometimes correlations between different constructs measured by the same method are higher than correlations between the same construct measured by different methods. In this case, the method (paper-and-pencil inventory, projective technique, rating scale, interview, etc.) is more important in determining whatever is measured than the construct or trait that is supposedly being assessed.

■ Summary

A test or other psychometric assessment device that is *standardized* has standard directions for administration and scoring and a set of *norms* based on a representative sample of people for whom the test was designed. Norms serve as a frame of reference for interpreting scores on tests and other psychometric instruments. The types of norms include age- and grade-equivalents, percentiles, and standard scores. Stanine and sten scores are normalized standard scores that not only have different means and standard deviations from the corresponding raw scores but are also normally distributed regardless of the shape of the original raw-score distribution.

The concept of the *reliability* of a test or other assessment technique is concerned with the extent to which the scores are free of errors of measurement. Three procedures for obtaining information on the reliability of a psychometric instrument are test-retest, parallel (equivalent) forms, and internal consistency. Three different types of internal consistency procedures are split-half, Kuder-Richardson, and coefficient alpha. Inversely related to a test's reliability is its standard error of measurement, a numerical index of how accurately a person's obtained score estimates his or her true score on the test. Interpreting differences between the scores of two people on the same test or of one person on two different tests is facilitated by computing the reliability and standard error of measurement of the score differences.

A test can be reliable without being valid, but it cannot be valid without being reliable. *Validity* refers to the extent to which a test measures what it was designed to measure. Depending on the type of test (achievement, aptitude, personality), three types of validity are of interest: content validity, criterion-related validity (concurrent validity, predictive validity), and construct validity. The criterion-related validity of a test is determined by correlating test scores with criterion scores obtained at the same time (*concurrent validity*) or at some future time (*predictive validity*). A linear regression equation for predicting criterion scores from test scores and a measure of the error in this prediction (*standard error of estimate*) can also be determined. The most comprehensive type of validity, and the one of greatest concern on personality assessment instruments, is construct validity. Information on the construct validity of a psychometric instrument may be obtained by various procedures designed to determine the extent to which the instrument is an accurate measure of a specified psychological construct.

■ Questions and Activities

1. Find the percentile ranks, z-score and T-score norms corresponding to the interval midpoints of the following frequency distribution of ratings of the instructor (X) and the course (Y), where $\overline{X} = 38.17$, $s_x = 6.64$, $\overline{Y} = 17.92$, and $s_y = 4.87$.

Instructor Ratings		Course Ratings	
Interval	Frequency	Interval	Frequency
54–56	2	30–31	2
51–53	3	28–29	1
48–50	4	26–27	0
45–47	4	24–25	4
42–44	10	22–23	12
39–41	20	20–21	17
36–38	16	18–19	19
33–35	15	16–17	8
30–32	5	14–15	11
27–29	9	12–13	6
24–26	2	10–11	5
		8– 9	2
		6– 7	3

2. Calculate both Kuder-Richardson reliability coefficients of the following responses of ten examinees on a ten-item test, where 1 indicates the keyed response and 0 a nonkeyed response.

	Examinee									
Item	A	B	C	D	E	F	G	H	I	J
1	1	1	0	1	1	0	1	0	1	0
2	1	0	0	0	0	1	0	0	0	1
3	1	1	1	1	1	0	1	0	0	0
4	1	1	1	0	0	1	0	1	0	0
5	1	0	1	1	0	0	0	0	0	0
6	1	1	1	0	1	1	1	0	0	0
7	1	0	1	1	0	0	1	1	0	1
8	1	1	1	0	1	1	0	0	1	0
9	1	1	0	1	1	1	0	1	0	0
10	1	1	1	1	1	0	0	0	1	0
Total Scores	10	7	7	6	6	5	4	3	3	2

The mean of total scores is 5.30, and variance is 5.21.

3. Compute the standard error of measurement of a test having a standard deviation of 10 and a parallel-forms reliability coefficient of .84. Use the obtained value of the standard error of measurement to find the 95% confidence interval for the true scores corresponding to obtained scores of 40, 50, and 60.

4. What is the standard error of estimate when the standard deviation of the criterion measure is 10 and the correlation between the test and the criterion measure is .60? Within what two values can you be 95% confident that the obtained Y score of a person whose predicted Y score is 30 will fall? Between what two values can you be 99% confident that the obtained Y score of a person whose predicted Y score is 70 will fall?

5. Under what conditions can a test be reliable without being valid? Under what conditions can a test be valid without being reliable?

6. Why do you think that the reliability and validity coefficients of personality tests lower than those of tests of cognitive abilities?

■ Suggested Readings

Angoff, W.H. (1992). Norms and scales. In M.C. Alkin (Ed.), *Encyclopedia of educational research* (6th ed., pp. 909–921). New York: Macmillan.

Felner, R.D. (1994). Reliability of diagnoses. In R.J. Corsini (Ed.), *Encyclopedia of psychology* (2nd ed., pp. 299–300). New York: Wiley.

Green, K.E. (1991). Measurement theory. In K.E. Green (Ed.), *Educational testing: Issues and applications* (pp. 3–25). New York: Garland Publishing.

Messick, S. (1995). Validity of psychological assessment. *American Psychologist, 50,* 741–749.

Shavelson, R.J., & Webb, N.M. (1991). *Generalizability theory: A primer.* Newbury Park, CA: Sage.

Thorndike, R.L., & Thorndike, R.M. (1994). Reliability in educational and psychological measurement. In T. Husén & T.N. Postlethwaite (Eds.), *International encyclopedia of education* (2nd ed., Vol. 9, pp. 4989–4995). Tarrytown, NY: Elsevier.

von Mayrhauser, R.T. (1992). The mental testing community and validity: A prehistory. *American Psychologist, 47,* 244–253.

West, S.G., & Finch, J.F. (1997). Personality measurement: Reliability and validity issues. In R. Hogan, J. Johnson, & S. Briggs (Eds.), *Handbook of personality psychology* (pp. 143–163). San Diego, CA: Academic Press.

Zeller, R.A. (1994). Validity. In T. Husén & T.N. Postlethwaite (Eds.), *International encyclopedia of education* (2nd ed., Vol. 11, pp. 6569–6576). Tarrytown, NY: Elsevier.

CHAPTER 4

Administration, Interpretation, and Reporting

The process of personality assessment does not begin with the administration or even the construction or selection of a personality assessment instrument. It begins with the recognition of a need to know something about human personality in general or about a particular person. This need may result from either a practical goal, such as counseling or other psychological intervention procedures, or a theoretical goal, as in research designed to understand the causes and consequences of human actions. To become operational, the need must be expressed as a question or statement specifying what it is desirable to know about a certain person or group: Why does Bobby have so much trouble getting along with other children? Is Joan so maladjusted that she requires psychological help or perhaps even institutionalization? Does Frank have organic brain damage, or is his problem psychological? What personality variables are related to performance on a particular job? Is this person likely to attempt suicide? Is this person likely to commit rape (or some other violent crime)?

■ Assessment Settings, Goals, and Models

Questions like those listed above, and consequently the need for personality assessment, are not limited to a specific situation. Petzelt and Craddick (1978) delineated a variety of settings in which such assessments are made:

1. Mental health settings (as an aid in diagnosis, treatment, and residential placement)
2. Educational settings (as an aid in formulating proper remedial measures)
3. Legal settings (as an aid in court evaluations, such as sanity hearings, as well as assisting the judicial authorities in planning rehabilitation measures)
4. Medical settings (as an aid in hospital consultation to various clinics in evaluating the psychological aspects of illness)
5. Psychotherapeutic settings (as an aid in planning and evaluating psychotherapy and chemotherapy, and in offering referring therapists better initial understanding of the client's dynamics and important focal issues)

Assessment instruments and procedures also serve as research and teaching tools in the study of human personality, particularly with special populations, such as prisoners and juvenile delinquents. Various psychological evaluations are also required by law, as in cases involving financial compensation, recidivism, custody, competency, and commitment. In many settings, psychological assessments are conducted both before and after some treatment or other intervention is imposed in order to determine its effectiveness. Assessments may also be repeated periodically in order to monitor changes in a person as a result of natural or externally applied conditions.

Once the needs of assessment have been specified, goals can be set and decisions made about the kinds of data required to attain those goals. The general goals of psychological assessments are to provide accurate descriptions of personality and behavior and to make predictions concerning future behaviors. However, the goals in particular cases or settings are usually more specific: to determine the presence or absence of certain characteristics or conditions. Assessment instruments and procedures that are applied in these settings are not limited to standardized tests, inventories, or rating scales. Observations, interviews of the client and other people, application blanks or biographical data forms, ad hoc rating scales, autobiographies, diaries, and other nonstandardized techniques for obtaining information may also be employed.

Other recommendations concerning the collection of personality assessment data are provided by Sundberg (1977):

1. Begin by surveying the examinee's overall life situation and problems, and then obtain more details in areas of particular relevance to the goals of the assessment.
2. Be sensitive to the examinee's sociocultural and ethnic background, as well as his or her age and sex, if relevant.
3. Obtain the *right kind* of information, not merely *more information*, pertaining to the specific situation and purposes of the assessment.

To a great extent, both the goals of personality assessment and the procedures selected to reach those goals vary with the particular assessment theory or model that is followed, whether it is psychodynamic, psychometric, behavioristic, or some other conceptual system. Although clinical assessors of all theoretical persuasions may play a role in deciding what questions require answers and what assessment techniques should be employed, assessors who follow a *psychodynamic* or *psychodiagnostic* model place more emphasis on the subjective judgment of the assessor in collecting, organizing, and summarizing assessment data, as well as making diagnoses and prognoses on the basis of the findings. Psychodynamic assessors most often use interviews and projective techniques to provide an in-depth, multifaceted picture of personality dynamics.

In contrast to psychodynamic models, assessors who follow a *psychometric model* maintain that psychological assessment is valid only when it is objective and that subjective interpretations of personality inventories, rating scales, and other assessment data should be minimized. According to this model, examinees' scores on the traits or factors measured by objectively scored instruments should be interpreted by comparing them with the scores (norms) obtained from representative samples of people. Psychometric assessors are also more likely to advocate a statistical or cookbook approach to combining assessment data and making predictions and classifications.

Assessors who follow a *behavioristic* model emphasize the determination of what people do and where, when, and under what circumstances they do it (Schuldberg & Korchin, 1994). The goal of behavioristic assessment is to discover the antecedent events that elicit or control certain undesirable behaviors, as a prerequisite to designing a behavior modification program to change those behaviors. Traditionally, behavioristic assessors have collected data by means of objective observations of people in naturalistic, contrived, and role-playing situations, in addition to using checklists and rating scales to record and evaluate the objectively observed behavior. However, today's behavioristic assessors, especially those of a *cognitive-behavioral* mold, also interview people to determine not only what they do but also what thoughts, feelings, aspirations, and other internal states they are experiencing.

Whatever theoretical background or conceptual model an assessor may follow, the process of personality assessment begins with an expressed need, after which the goals of assessment should be stated and the instruments or procedures that will provide information relevant to the attainment of those goals are selected or constructed. Although several different instruments and procedures are typically used in collecting data on personality, the shotgun approach of administering every available device in the hope that it will provide significant information and minimize the need for subjective judgment is not advisable. In conducting a comprehensive psychological assessment several procedures and instruments may be required to gain a clear, valid understanding of the examinee. However, it is inadvisable to overwhelm him or her with assessment materials; care should be taken at the outset to select procedures or instruments that can be administered in a reasonable period of time, that take the age and condition of the examinee into consideration, and that provide useful information above and beyond that which is obtained more easily by other means. After deciding what approaches and materials are appropriate, the standardized or nonstandardized data are collected, combined, and reflected upon to arrive at interpretations, diagnoses, predictions, and recommendations.

■ Instrument Selection, Administration, and Scoring

Observations and interviews, which are considered in detail in Chapter 5, are the most popular psychological assessment procedures. Even in making observations and conducting interviews, however, one must be aware of the sociocultural background of the person and be prepared to communicate in words that he or she understands. In a fairly thorough psychological examination of a person, observations, usually uncontrolled and incidental, are made throughout the assessment period. Interviewing, which itself is a kind of observation of the examinee and others who have information about the case, may occur before and/or after the formal testing period, depending on the circumstances and the individual who is being assessed.

Selection of specific personality assessment instruments to be administered depends on the purposes of the assessment, as well as the age, ability, and temperament of the examinee and the skill, time, and theoretical orientation of the examiner. For example, personality inventories and scales require less training and time to administer than projective techniques, and structured interviews are generally easier to conduct that unstructured ones. Preliminary observational and interview data are often helpful, not only in providing information in their own right but also in suggesting what additional techniques or procedures may be appropriate.

The results of a number of surveys of clinical and counseling psychologists (Frauenhoffer et al., 1998; Watkins, Campbell, Nieberding, & Hallmark, 1995) shed some light on which personality assessment instruments are viewed most favorably by professional psychologists. The six personality inventories that are reportedly administered most often by clinical psychologists are the Minnesota Multiphasic Personality Inventory-2, the Beck Depression Inventory, the Millon Clinical Multiaxial Inventory, the Millon Adolescent Personality Inventory, the 16 Personality Factor Questionnaire, and the Personality Inventory for Children (Watkins et al., 1995). Checklists such as the Child Behavior Checklist and the Symptom Checklist-90 R also enjoy fairly extensive usage in clinical situations.

Interest inventories such as the Strong Interest Inventory, the Self-Directed Search, and the Kuder Occupational Interest Survey are administered quite often in educational and counseling contexts.

Although projective tests remain very popular with mental health professionals, and particularly psychologists of a psychodynamic persuasion, because of their greater objectivity and ease of administration and scoring, inventories, rating scales, and checklists are used more frequently. The most popular projective techniques are various sentence completion methods, the Thematic Apperception Test, the Rorschach Inkblot Test, the Bender-Gestalt, various projective drawings tests, and the Children's Apperception Test (Watkins et al., 1995).

Administering Assessment Instruments

Methods of collecting test data and other information concerning personality depend on the type of information desired (oral, written, behavioral, etc.) and the examinee to whom it pertains (child or adult, normal or disabled, etc.). Procedures for obtaining observational and interview data, as well as administering specific objective and projective instruments, are discussed in later chapters. The recommendations in the following sections apply particularly to the administration of standardized psychometric instruments, but they also have implications for other methods of collecting personality assessment data. Because test administration procedures vary with the nature of the test and the examinee, the amount and type of training needed by a psychological examiner also depend on these factors. Formal licensing or certification by an appropriate state agency, or at least supervision by a certified practitioner, is required to administer most individual psychological tests. Such a requirement helps ensure that the examiner has sufficient knowledge and skill in test administration, and it is essential in third-party insurance claims for psychological services.

Assessment Standards and Ethics

Because personality assessment skills cannot be attained without considerable training, in order to conduct formal assessments of personality in most states a psychological examiner is required to be licensed or certified as a clinical psychologist, a counseling psychologist, or a school psychologist. Improper practices, which represent a violation of the ethical codes of the American Psychological Association and a number of other professional organizations, can lead to revocation of a license or certificate.

Realizing that the development, distribution, and use of personality tests and other psychological assessment instruments requires carefully formulated standards and clear ethical controls, some years ago a joint committee of the

American Educational Research Association, the American Psychological Association, and the National Council on Measurement in Education formulated and published a set of *Standards for Educational and Psychological Testing* (American Educational Research Association et al., 1985).* The core of this booklet is a list of 180 standards for constructing, evaluating, administering, scoring, and interpreting psychological assessment instruments. Separate chapters in the booklet describe standards for the application of tests in various contexts and with different groups. Any practicing psychologist (clinical, counseling, school, industrial/organizational) should be thoroughly acquainted with these standards and follow them as closely as possible. The following standards are particularly relevant to test administration:

— *Standard 6.6.* Responsibility for test use should be assumed by or delegated only to those individuals who have the training and experience necessary to handle this responsibility in a professional and technically adequate manner. Any special qualifications for test administration or interpretation noted in the manual should be met.

— *Standard 6.10.* In educational, clinical, and counseling applications, test administrators and users should not attempt to evaluate test takers whose special characteristics—ages, handicapping conditions, or linguistic, generational, or cultural backgrounds—are outside the range of their academic training or supervised experience. A test user faced with a request to evaluate a test whose special characteristics are not within his or her range of professional experience should seek consultation regarding test selection, necessary modifications of testing procedures, and score interpretation from a professional who has had relevant experience.

— *Standard 15.1.* In typical applications, test administrators should follow carefully the standardized procedures for administration and scoring specified by the test publisher. Specifications regarding instructions to test takers, time limits, the form of item presentation or response, and test materials or equipment should be strictly observed. Exceptions should be made only on the basis of carefully considered profession judgment, primarily in clinical applications.

— *Standard 15.2.* The testing environment should be one of reasonable comfort and with minimal distractions. Testing materials should be readable and understandable. In computerized testing, items displayed on a screen should be legible and free from glare, and the terminal should be properly positioned. (pp. 42, 43, 83)

---

* Specialists in psychological assessment should also familiarize themselves with the *General Guidelines for Providers of Psychological Services* (American Psychological Association, 1987), "a set of aspirational statements for psychologists which encourage continual improvement in the quality of practice and service." (p.2)

The ethical use of assessment instruments can be controlled to some extent by a code of ethics to which professional testers and publishers subscribe. Both the American Psychological Association (APA) and the American Personnel and Guidance Association (APGA) have ethical codes pertaining to test administration and other psychological services. These codes cover many of the same matters of test administration, standardization, reliability, and validity as the *Standards for Educational and Psychological Testing* (American Educational Research Association et al., 1985). In particular, they stress the importance of considering the welfare of the examinee or client and guarding against misuses of assessment instruments.

With regard to evaluation and assessment, the "Ethical Principles of Psychologists and Code of Conduct" (American Psychological Association, 1992) emphasizes that evaluation and psychodiagnosis should be provided only in a professional context by trained, competent test users who administer appropriate psychometric instruments. Emphasis is also placed on the applications of scientific procedures for designing and selecting tests and techniques that are appropriate for specified populations, the judicious interpretation of test results, the careful use of test scoring and interpretative services, the clear but careful explanation of assessment findings, and the need for maintaining test security.

The availability of high-quality tests and a set of standards or principles with which test publishers, distributors, and consumers are asked to comply does not guarantee that tests and other psychometric instruments will be administered and interpreted properly. The responsibility for employing tests correctly lies with the test administrators and interpreters themselves, a responsibility that has been increasingly recognized and accepted by professional psychologists. Unfortunately, the skills and knowledge possessed by many counselors, clinicians, and other professionals are inadequate for administering certain tests. Therefore, mental testers must be made aware of the limitations of their professional qualifications, the necessity for further training, and the need to rely on other professionals and up-to-date sources of information for assistance. Furthermore, mental testers must be able to make sound ethical judgments by being sensitive to the needs of examinees, the institutions or organizations by which they are employed, and society as a whole.

Psychological examiners should be thoroughly familiar with the tests they administer and the kinds of individuals for whom the tests are appropriate. On both individual and group tests, directions concerning the method of presenting the test materials, the wording of test questions, and the time limits (if any) for responding must be followed carefully. Differences in the way in which verbal instructions are phrased may affect test performance, even when the differences are subtle. Directions should be read slowly, and they should clearly inform examinees how to indicate their responses but not what responses to make. Written instructions to be read by examinees are usually printed on the front cover of a personality inventory or scale. These instructions tell examinees how and where the questions or items are to be answered.

Repeating or rephrasing a question may be permitted on an individual test, but going beyond the directions printed in the test manual is strictly against the rules. Departures from standard directions, even when they clarify the task to the examinee, may result in a different task being presented than the test designer had in mind. Consequently, if the directions deviate from those given to the standardization (norm) group, the scores may not have the same meaning as those of the norm group. The result will be the loss of a useful frame of reference for interpreting scores.

There are, of course, occasions on which modifications of standard procedure produce better information than strict adherence to the standard conditions of administration. Examples of such modifications are using a different sensory or response modality (auditory rather than visual, oral rather than written), translating the test items into a different language, or increasing the test time limits. Again, however, the examiner must bear in mind that when such modifications in standard testing procedures are made, the resulting information cannot be interpreted with reference to the norms that have been obtained under standard conditions.

Not only must the directions for administration be understood and adhered to; other information in the test manual (reliability, validity, norms, etc.) and the content of the test itself should be familiar to the examiner. To become familiar with the content of the test, it is recommended that, before administering it to anyone else, examiners take the test themselves, score it, and interpret the results.

Physical and Psychological Environments

As with psychological assessment instruments in general, personality tests should be administered under good physical conditions, including appropriate seating, lighting, ventilation, temperature, and noise level. A room familiar to the examinees and free from distractions is preferable for group testing. Individual testing should be conducted in a private room with only the examiner and examinee present, or, if absolutely necessary, one additional person such as a parent or guardian.

In addition to the physical environment, it is important to consider the psychological environment. Except in rare instances, such as stress interviewing, psychological examiners should not purposely attempt to make examinees more uneasy than they already are. In the past, there has been much discussion of the importance of *rapport*—a warm, friendly relationship between examiner and examinee—in encouraging the latter to respond honestly and to do his or her best. A particular examiner, however, is not perceived by all examinees in the same way, and rapport may be difficult to establish or maintain in certain cases. Even examinees who stick closely to the directions for administration may, through differences in their appearance and manner, vary in the amount of encouragement or threat they communicate.

Although the effect of an examiner's actions on the examinee's feelings and behavior varies from person to person, it is recommended that the examiner be neither overly encouraging nor discouraging. Because examinees are typically quite aware of and easily influenced by the examiner's nonverbal behavior, Rosenthal (1966) recommended that the latter maintain a somewhat bland and noncommittal facial expression and tone of voice. Neither approval nor disapproval of particular responses should be shown, lest it serve as a reward or punishment or a sign of correctness or incorrectness for what is the examinee's typical behavior. Be that as it may, the examiner should be alert to the feelings of examinees and respond to their questions without being critical or condescending in voice or manner. The purpose of the examination and how the results will be used should be explained in a way that is appropriate to the examinee's level of ability and need to know.

Psychological examiners are, of course, not robots or creatures encased in stone, and the examination process may create disturbing or mixed feelings in them as well as in those whom they are examining. What intelligence-tester could resist being moved by the tears of a child who realizes that if she doesn't do well on an intelligence test she will be placed in "a dummy class" and other children will make fun of her? Or who can fail to sympathize with an ex-mental patient who admits that he still hears voices but has learned to deny them and give more normal responses to personality test items and interviews so he will not be reinstitutionalized?

There are circumstances in which examiners need to be especially active and encouraging. A testing situation produces a certain amount of tension in almost anyone, and occasionally examinees become quite anxious. In addition, special problems occur in psychological examinations of very young or very old people, mentally disturbed, physically handicapped, or culturally disadvantaged individuals. In such cases, not only must the examiner be thoroughly skilled in administering the test materials, but also quite sensitive, patient, and alert for emergencies. Psychological examiners are seldom prepared to handle every emergency situation that occurs (e. g., an epileptic seizure or violent outburst), but experience in a variety of testing situations is crucial in developing the skills required to cope with these problems. When testing the very young, the elderly, and the handicapped, it may be necessary to use shorter testing periods and to be prepared to devote a longer total amount of time to the process. Awareness of fatigue, anxiety and the presence of sensory-motor deficits is also important.

Deviations from Standard Procedure

Some flexibility is usually permitted in administering nonstandardized instruments and even certain standardized tests, but only on the basis of carefully considered professional judgment and primarily in clinical applications. Whenever such modifications in standard test administration or scoring procedure are made, they should be described in the written or oral report of the test results and cautions concerning interpretation of the results should be stated (American Educational Research Association et al., 1985). In any event, the administration and scoring manual for a test should make clear to what extent deviations from standard procedure are permissible and what effects they may have on the interpretation of scores.

After the Test

Following the examination period, the examiner should make certain that examinees are taken care of, perhaps by providing reassurance, or a small reward or privilege in the case of a child, and returning them to the appropriate place. In individual clinical testing, it is usually important to interview a parent or other person who accompanied the examinee, perhaps briefly both before and after the examination. Some information on what will be done with the test results and how they will be used can be given to the examinee and/or the accompanying party. The examiner should also promise to report the results and interpretations to the appropriate person(s) or agency and to recommend any further action to be taken.

Following administration of a test to a group of people, the examiner collects the answer sheets, test booklets, pencils, scratch paper, and other materials. The booklets and answer sheets are counted, and all other materials are checked to make certain that none are missing. Then the examinees can be dismissed and the tests prepared for scoring.

Administration by Computer

Programming a computer to administer a personality inventory, rating scale, or checklist, or to conduct a structured interview is fairly straightforward. In the case of individual tests and unstructured interviews, however, the process is more complex, and not completely satisfactory.

The *Standards for Educational and Psychological Testing* (American Educational Research Association et al., 1985) has little to say about computer administration of tests. For this reason, a set of *Guidelines for Computer-Based Tests and Interpretations* (American Psychological Association, 1986) was developed to assist practicing psychologists in applying computer-based assessment competently and in the best interest of their clients and to guide test developers in establishing and maintaining the quality of new products. Among the guidelines pertaining to test administration by computer are the following recommendations:

— The environment in which the testing terminal is located should be quiet, comfortable, and free from distraction.
— Test items presented on the display screen should be legible and free from noticeable glare.
— Equipment should be checked routinely and should be maintained in proper working condition.
— Test performance should be monitored, and assistance to the test taker should be provided, as is needed and appropriate.
— Test takers should be trained on proper use of the computer equipment.
— Reasonable accommodations must be made for individuals who may be at an unfair disadvantage in a computer testing situation.
(American Psychological Association, 1986, pp. 11–12)

Test Scoring

Objective tests of personality can be scored either by hand, using special scoring keys—stencil, strip, etc.—or by electronic scanners. Special machines for scoring objective tests have been in use for much of this century, and the increased availability of high-speed computers has made test scoring much more rapid and flexible. Computerized scoring is not limited to group-administered, multiple-choice tests; programs have also been devised to administer, score, and interpret individual tests and even essay tests (see Landauer & Dumais, 1997).

Despite the growing importance of computerized test scoring, most personality inventories, projective techniques, and other instruments are probably still scored by hand. Research studies indicate that even trained clinical personnel make errors in hand scoring objective personality inventories, mistakes that in many instances are serious enough to alter clinical diagnoses (Allard, Butler, Faust, & Shea, 1995). Because errors in scoring can result in a quite different picture of an individual's personality, it is important to double-check the handscoring of paper-and-pencil inventories and other personality assessment devices. Wider use of computerized scoring is also recommended to help prevent errors and improve the accuracy of interpretations based on personality test scores.

Some of the responses to projective techniques and other individual tests can be scored during the examination, but final scoring should wait until the examinee has been dismissed. Scoring during the test should obviously be done as unobtrusively as possible, and at no time should the scores be revealed to the examinee.

The ethical problems of having personality tests scored by clerks who are not trained in psychology and do not always preserve confidentiality should also be mentioned. There is no easy solution to the problem, especially when hundreds or thousands of personality inventories or rating scales must be scored. At the very least, however, clerks who score tests should be made aware of the great importance of accuracy in scoring, for keeping test records securely under lock and key, and not revealing the scores to anyone without authorized permission.

After the raw scores on a personality inventory have been obtained, they can be converted to percentile ranks or standard scores and a profile constructed from these converted scores before beginning the process of interpreting the results. In converting raw scores to standard scores or other norms, it is crucial to use the norms that are appropriate for the examinee's age, sex, and other relevant demographic characteristics. Occasionally a student in one of the author's psychological assessment courses has expressed great concern when the results of a personality inventory that he or she took and scored, and then transformed the raw scores to norms, revealed the student to be extremely high or low on certain variables. After the inventory was rescored and the corrected raw scores converted to norms, the student was usually relieved to discover that the corrected scores were much less extreme than the original ones.

Unfortunately, not all personality assessment instruments can be scored objectively. For example, the procedures for scoring projective tests such as the Rorschach Inkblot Test and the Thematic Apperception Test are quite subjective and impressionistic. Considering the fact that the scoring directions or guidelines for many items on personality tests and even individual tests of intelligence are not always clear, it is not surprising that a wide range of scores may be assigned to the same test responses. One might expect that this would be more likely to occur in the case of individuals who have less experience in using a particular instrument, but even experienced testers and scorers are not immune to inaccurate and biased scoring.

Personality assessments are, of course, rarely conducted blindly, in the sense that the scorer knows nothing about the examinee other than the chronological age, the day on which the test was administered, and the test responses. More commonly, the scorer has enough additional information to form a distinct impression or attitude about the examinee. Knowledge of the examinee's sex, ethnicity, socioeconomic status, occupation, and other personal information may make different impressions on different scorers. But these impressions, which may be positive or negative and lead to different kinds of expectations or degrees of bias, can have an effect on the scoring of less objective tests.

■ Interpreting Assessment Results

A substantial amount of training is needed to interpret the results of a personality assessment or evaluation. Not only must the examiner consider the subscores, the overall scores, and their corresponding norm equivalents on the standardized instrument(s), but this information must be combined with the results of behavioral observations, interviews, and other nonstandardized test and nontest data. Consequently, the examiner should not only be proficient in administering the required assessment instruments but should also be an alert observer, a sensitive interviewer, and a good thinker.

Case Study

A complete case study consists of the collection of information from observations, interviews, psychological tests, and other pertinent sources. A complete case study involves more than a psychological examination, interview, and observational information. A case study may be conducted in a clinical or educational context to determine the cause(s) of a specific problem of behavioral, cognitive, or affective functioning. Details pertaining to background and personal characteristics are obtained both from the individual himself (herself) and from other people who have played important roles in the his or her life; follow-up data are also collected over a period of time. The kinds of information that are important in constructing a detailed picture of personality include:
- family (who is in the home, home attitudes)
- culture (cultural group, cultural deviation and conflict)
- medical examinations and history (medical examination, physical development, physical conditions especially related to adjustment, sex development)
- developmental history (prenatal period and birth, early developmental signs, intellectual development, speech development, emotional development, social development)
- educational history (school progress, educational achievement, school adjustment, educational aspirations and plans)
- economic history in the case of older children and adults (occupation, occupational history, vocational plans and ambitions)
- legal history (delinquencies, arrests)
- the person's life (daily routines, interest, hobbies, recreations, fantasy life, sex, social adjustments).

After the assessment data have been collected and integrated, a summary of the examinee's strengths and weaknesses is prepared and recommendations for clinical, educational, or vocational interventions are made.

When a case study is conducted to determine the cause(s) of a specific psychological problem, conclusions or hypotheses concerning the cause(s) are formulated and specific recommendations are made concerning treatment—psychotherapy, drugs or other medical treatment, special education, etc. A follow-up assessment to evaluate the effectiveness of the prescribed treatment program should also be conducted after an appropriate time interval.

Despite its yield of potentially useful information for forming an overall picture as well as an in-depth understanding of the individual, a clinical case study has some notable weaknesses. These include the retrospective nature of the data (Memories are seldom completely accurate!), the fact that the person who is conducting the study is often biased in selecting and evaluating certain kinds of data or measurements, and the extent to which the findings are generalizable across the situations or circumstances encountered by the person. Employing a variety of assessments in a representative sample of situations and being aware of the likelihood of bias in selection and evaluation can help reduce, if not eliminate, misinterpretations and overgeneralizations.

Psychodiagnosis

The process of examining a person from a psychological viewpoint to determine the nature and extent of a mental or behavioral disorder is called *psychodiagnosis*. In the traditional *medical model* of mental illness, the diagnostician observes,

---

TABLE 4–1 Major Diagnostic Categories of DSM-IV.

Disorders Usually First Diagnosed in Infancy, Childhood, or Adolescence
Delirium, Dementia, and Amnestic and Other Cognitive Disorders
Mental Disorders Due to a General Medical Condition
Substance-Related Disorders
Schizophrenia and Other Psychotic Disorders
Mood Disorders
Anxiety Disorders
Somatoform Disorders
Factitious Disorders
Dissociative Disorders
Sexual and Gender Identity Disorders
Eating Disorders
Sleep Disorders
Impulse-Control Disorders Not Elsewhere Classified
Adjustment Disorders
Personality Disorders
Other Conditions That May Be a Focus of Clinical Attention

Source: American Psychiatric Association (1994).

interviews, and tests the patient to detect the presence or absence of certain psychological and physical symptoms. The patient's symptoms are then compared with standard descriptions of abnormal behavior to determine in which category or categories the patient falls. The end result of this process is a psychiatric classification or succinct description of the patient. In addition to diagnosing the patient's condition, a *prognosis*, or prediction of its likely outcome, is made.

The most popular system of psychodiagnosis, though by no means the only one, is described in the *Diagnostic and Statistical Manual of Mental Disorders*. The first two editions of this manual, which were published in 1952 and 1968, combined the categories of mental disorders proposed by Sigmund Freud, Emil Kraeplin, and other famous psychiatric pioneers. The third edition of the manual (*DSM-III*), which represented a major departure from its predecessors, grouped 200 specific disorders and conditions into 17 major categories. *DSM-III-R*, a revision of DSM-III published in 1987, incorporated further changes in diagnostic criteria (American Psychiatric Association, 1987). Seven years later, a revision of DMS-III-R known as *DSM-IV* was published. This diagnostic system describes nearly 300 mental disorders, grouped into 17 categories (see Table 4–1).

According to its committee of authors:

The purpose of DSM-IV is to provide clear descriptions of diagnostic categories in order to enable clinicians and investigators to diagnose, communicate about, study, and treat people with various mental disorders (American Psychiatric Association, 1994, p. xi)

With its stated goal of improving the reliability of psychodiagnostic judgments, DMS-IV provides explicit criteria and decision-branching sequences for reaching a diagnosis. The approach is purely descriptive, not based on psychoanalytic theory or any other theoretical position. The various disorders are grouped according to very specific behavioral symptoms without specifying their origins or methods of treatment.

Like DMS-III-R, the DMS-IV system is multiaxial, in that a patient may be classified on the following five separate axes, or dimensions:

Axis I: Clinical Disorders; Other Conditions that May Be a Focus of Clinical Attention

Axis II: Personality Disorders; Mental Retardation

Axis III: General Medical Conditions

Axis IV: Psychosocial and Environmental Problems

Axis V: Global Assessment of Functioning

These five axes refer to different kinds of information about the patient. In addition to labeling and numbering each disorder with a five-digit code on Axes I and II, the severity of an existing condition may be specified as mild, moderate, or severe. If the criteria for a diagnosis are no longer met, this may be indicated as in partial remission, in full remission, or by a note on the prior history of the condition. Axis III provides a classification of accompanying physical disorders and conditions, Axis IV provides a classification of the severity of psychosocial stressors, and Axis V gives a global assessment of functioning (GAF) on a numerical scale. DSM-IV also permits multiple diagnoses of a patient's condition on Axes I and II.

It would appear that, by providing more precise psychodiagnostic criteria, DSM-IV would possess greater reliability than previous diagnostic systems. However, questions concerning its validity have been raised. Some authorities have argued that the criteria are too rigid to apply to all patients, whereas other authorities question the appropriateness and possible dangers of any kind of psychiatric labeling. One criticism of DMS-IV is that diagnostic labels such as schizophrenia and depression are not always assigned consistently. In addition to varying with the theoretical orientation and personal biases of the psychodiagnostician and the socioeconomic status and ethnicity of the patient, diagnoses differ from institution to institution, from community to community, and from country to country.

Differences in diagnosing the same disorder are also a product of the special interests and concerns of the diagnostician. In general, clinical psychologists and psychiatrists have tended to be more concerned with detecting signs of abnormality than with denoting indicators of health and coping abilities. Depending on the perceived repercussions or payoffs for making a patient appear more or less disordered, the diagnostician may either exaggerate or minimize the severity of symptoms. For example, if a government agency or private insurance company pays for treatment or awards other forms of compensation to patients who are diagnosed as psychotic or brain-damaged but does not pay for other diagnostic conditions, the result may be a greater number of diagnoses of psychosis and brain damage. In some states, where a patient diagnosed as "psychotic" loses many legal rights, diagnosticians may be reluctant to assign this label.

Advocates of psychodiagnostic classification point out that, by reducing the amount of long-winded explanation, diagnostic terms can actually improve communication among mental health professionals. Furthermore, classifying mental disorders can assist in making diagnostic predictions and in conducting research on abnormal behavior (Meehl, 1962; Woodruff, Goodwin & Guze, 1974; Spitzer, 1976). In any event, precautions must be taken in selecting the appropriate terms or categories to be included in a psychological examination report. Labels such as "psychotic," "neurotic," "psychopathic," and the like too often serve as self-fulfilling prophecies in which the patient becomes, at least in the eyes of others, what he or she is labeled as being (Rosenhan, 1973).

Caution in categorizing or labeling behavior is, or course, not limited to the diagnosis of mental disorders; it applies to descriptions and interpretations of performance on any psychological assessment instrument. As recommended by the *Standards for Educational and Psychological Testing*, "When score reporting includes assigning individuals to categories, the categories chosen should be based on carefully selected criteria. The least stigmatizing labels, consistent with accurate reporting, should always be assigned" (American Educational Research Association et al., 1985, p. 86).

Clinical versus Statistical Prediction

One of the most important reasons for obtaining psychometric data is to make predictions of future behavior. Unfortunately, personality assessments tend to have fairly modest predictive validities, a fact which, coupled with their use in personnel screening and clinical diagnosis, has prompted a great deal of research on methods of improving their forecasting accuracy. The *statistical* (actuarial) approach to collecting behavioral data and making predictions consists of applying a statistical formula, a set of logical rules, or an actuarial table to assessment data. In contrast, the *clinical* (impressionistic) approach involves making intuitive judgments or drawing conclusions on the basis of subjective impressions combined with a theory of personality. The data themselves may be either statistically-based information such as test scores or clinically-based information such as biographical or interview data.

The question of the relative merits of these two approaches—using one's head *(clinical judgment)* versus using a formula *(statistical prediction)* has been debated for many years. The debate has filled numerous pages in psychological journals and books (e. g., Meehl, 1954, 1965; Holt, 1970; Sines, 1970). According to Paul Meehl, a proponent of the statistical approach, "... there are occasions when you should use your head instead of the formula ... But which occasions they are is not, emphatically *not*, clear. What is clear from the available clinical data is that these occasions are much rarer than most clinicians suppose" (Meehl, 1973, p. 235).

Taking a somewhat more middle-of-the-road position, Korchin and Schuldberg (1981) cited evidence that clinicians are superior to standardized assessment instruments in collecting information on personality and behavior. Statistical procedures, on the other hand, are more accurate than clinical impressions in combining or integrating the data in predicting behavior. Arkes (1994) also points out that a clinician is needed to decide what information to look for in the first place. Be that as it may, evidence for the superiority of the statistical, or actuarial, approach continued to be reported and discussed in the 1990s (e. g, Dawes, Faust, & Meehl, 1993). A study by Gardner, Lidz, Mulvey, and Shaw (1996) compared the accuracy of an actuarial procedure with clinicians' ratings in predicting violence by mental patients who were followed up in the community for six months. The actuarial predictions had lower rates of false-positive and false-negative errors than the clinical predictions, but the seriousness of correctly predicted violence was similar for the actuarial and the clinical approaches. In addition, actuarial predictions based on either patients' histories of violence alone or on nonhistory data were more accurate than clinical predictions.

Factors Detracting from Clinical Judgments

Why are clinical judgments apparently so inaccurate, even when compared with simple linear regression equations? Among the factors cited by Arkes (1994) as detracting from clinical judgments are: (1) preconceived notions; (2) failure to give adequate consideration to base rates; (3) hindsight bias; (4) serious overconfidence in one's own judgments.

Preconceived notions detract from clinical judgment in several ways. Memory tends to be distorted by becoming more consistent with preconceived hypotheses. Current information gets distorted toward stereotypes or hypotheses, even tentative ones, and judgment is also warped. One preconceived notion is the *illusory correlation problem* of basing a clinical judgment on the number of times a symptom and a disorder have occurred together and overlooking occasions when they have not occurred together. Illusory correlation occurs when clinicians tend to notice or recall whatever fits their expectations and ignore or forget whatever is contrary to their expectations.

A second factor that detracts from clinical judgments is the *base rate*—the proportion of people in a population who possess a specific characteristic or condition. When the base rate is low, it is much more difficult to identify or diagnose a pathological condition by means of whatever assessment methods are available. Illustrative of conditions having low base rates, and hence difficult to predict, are suicide and homicide. Neurotic behavior, on the other hand, has a much higher base rate and is consequently easier to predict.

A third factor cited by Arkes (1994) as affecting clinical judgment is *hindsight bias*. This is the belief, after an event has occurred, that one could have predicted it if he or she had been asked to do so beforehand. There is, for example, the all-too-human tendency to view an acquaintance who has committed an antisocial or bizarre act as always having been a bit strange or uncontrollable. Clearly, hindsight bias can prevent a clinician from learning as much from the occurrence of an event as might have been learned otherwise.

A fourth factor that impairs clinical judgment is the tendency of those who judge least accurately to be most confident in their judgments (Arkes, 1994). For example merely formulating a rule such as "psychotics are often pale" is sufficient to convince some clinicians that the rule is valid. *Overconfidence* in one's own judgment can lead to the belief that assistance, correction, or remediation from others is unnecessary, thereby solidifying the overconfidence and its false consequences (Lichtenstein, Fischhoff, & Phillips, 1982).

According to Arkes (1994), there are two reasons why these four impediments to accurate judgments are so pervasive. The first reason is that many shortcuts or heuristics used by people in everyday decision-making actually work fairly well. One shortcut that is misleading is to assume that remembered events have occurred more frequently. Thus, a single dramatic occurrence of a rare disorder can create an illusion that it has occurred more often than it actually has. A second reason for the pervasiveness of inaccurate clinical judgments is the fact that people apparently have limited awareness of the bases on which they make judgments. Obviously, improving judgments is difficult when one is unable to remember what factors initially influenced those judgments. Finally, initial assumptions or judgments, even when proved inaccurate in the light of subsequent experience, are typically adjusted somewhat but not changed completely. The decisions of most people, including psychodiagnosticians, are seemingly forever influenced by their initial assumptions concerning the nature and frequency of an event or condition (see Tversky & Kahneman, 1981).

■ Psychological Assessment Reports

Psychological assessment is often prompted by a referral from an agency or person, and as such there is usually an accompanying referral question or questions: Is this person psychotic? Is he or she brain-damaged? What are the chances that the person will be able to succeed in a certain educational, vocation, or therapeutic program? In such instances the primary goal of the report is to answer the referral question. Whether or not there is a formal, specific referral question, the overall goals of a personality assessment may include: diagnosis of mental, behavioral, or organic disorders; determination of the predominant adaptive and maladaptive psychological traits or characteristics of the person; educational or vocational selection, placement, and remediation; research on personality structure and dynamics. Whatever the purposes or goals of the examination may be, some form of written report of the findings is usually required.

The content and style of the report of a psychological examination vary with its purposes, the readers for whom it is intended, and the background and orientation of the report writer. However, the outline given in Form 4–1 is representative. Undoubtedly the most important part of this form is the "Conclusions and Recommendations" section, because it is the end result of describing, evaluating, and diagnosing the individual. If the conclusions and recommendations are not thoughtful and sound, the entire process of psychological evaluation and the time of many people will have been wasted. Report 4–1, which was prepared

FORM 4-1 **Format for a Psychological Examination Report.**

Name of Examinee _____

Age _____ Birth Date _____ Education _____

Referred by _____

Examined by _____

Place of Examination _____

Tests Administered _____

Reason for Referral. Why was the examinee referred for psychological testing? What was the purpose of the referral? What person or facility made it?

Observations and Interview Findings. Describe the appearance and behavior of the examinee during the examination. Give the examinee's own story, as well as that of other observers if available. Describe the examinee's physical and psychological history and characteristics, educational and employment situation. In the case of children in particular, information on the home and family (social status, characteristics of parents, siblings, etc.) is important. Serious sensory of psychomotor handicaps, as well as the presence of emotional disorder, should also be noted.

Results and Interpretations. What were the results of the tests or other instruments administered and how should they be interpreted? If the examiner is interpreting the results according to a particular theory of personality or behavior, make certain that the language and assumptions of that theory are clear. Be as specific and individualized as possible in interpreting the results. Describe the examinee's characteristics, his or her approach to the tasks, level of motivation and emotionality, and any other factors that might have influenced the results.

Conclusions and Recommendations. What conclusions (descriptive, dynamic, diagnostic) can be drawn from the observational, interview and standardized or unstandardized test data? What recommendations are warranted by the results? Include appropriate interpretative cautions, but don't "hedge" or deal in generalities. Additional psychological assessment (be specific), neurological or other medical examinations, counseling or psychotherapy, special class placement and training, vocational rehabilitation and institutionalization are among the recommendations that might be made. If a handicap or disability exists, is it remediable?

Name and Signature of Examiner _____

by a college student for a class project, is an example of such a product. The reader should study this report and note where it fails to meet the requirements discussed in this section.

In preparing a report of a psychological examination, the writer must keep clearly in mind the questions that need to be answered about the cognitive functioning, emotional state, and behavior of the examinee; development, dynamics, and probable outcomes (prognosis) should all be included. The examinee's characteristics and their interrelationships should be considered as fully and specifically as possible, avoiding vague generalizations, stereotypes, and banalities. For example, the following personality description could be true of almost anyone but gives the misleading impression that it is an individualized analysis:

> You have a strong need for other people to like you and for them to admire you. You have a tendency to be critical of yourself. You have a great deal of unused capacity which you have not turned to your advantage. While you have some personality weaknesses, you are generally able to compensate for them. Your sexual adjustment has presented some problems for you. Disciplined and controlled on the outside, you tend to be worrisome and insecure inside. At times you have serious doubts as to whether you have made the right decision or done the right thing. You prefer a certain amount of change and variety and become dissatisfied when hemmed in by restrictions and limitations. You pride yourself on being an independent thinker and do not accept others' opinions without satisfactory proof. You have found it unwise to be too frank in revealing yourself to others. At times you are extroverted, affable, social, while at other times you are introverted, wary, reserved. Some of your aspirations tend to be pretty unrealistic.

Thirty-seven students in a class of 50 who were questioned by the author rated this as a good or excellent description of their personalities. These students were victims of the *Barnum effect* or *Aunt Fanny error* (because the report could even apply to one's "Aunt Fanny") of accepting as correct a personality description replete with generalities, truisms, and other statements that sound specific to a given person but could actually be true of almost anyone. Interestingly enough, students often appear to be more willing to accept the results and interpretations of personality assessments as more self-descriptive than their scores on cognitive ability tests such as the SAT or GRE (Aiken & Romen, 1984). A contributing factor is that academic decisions made on the basis of scores on nationally administered, "high-stakes" tests such as the SAT and the GRE are often crucial to the individual's academic and career success.

A report of psychological findings should be written in a clear, comprehensive style that can be understood by the reader(s) for whom it is intended. Therefore, the report writer should ascertain in advance by whom the report is likely to be read; it may even be necessary to prepare different reports of the same findings for different readers. Unfortunately, many psychological reports are abstruse, ambiguous, overgeneralized, awkward in wording, and go beyond the actual find-

Psychological Assessment Report

Name of Examinee: David C. Lake   Sex: Male
Birth Date: April 14, 1977   Age: 20 years 11 months
Address: 211 Oaks Avenue   Education: College senior
Lawrence, California
Examined by: Dorothy R. Brown   Date: March 19, 1998
Tests Administered: Jackson Personality Inventory
                     Rotter Incomplete Sentences Blank

Observations and Interview Results

David Lake, a somewhat overweight (200 pounds), blond-haired young man of average height (5'10") and a senior major in psychology at Johnson College, volunteered to take the personality tests because of his expressed curiosity about the tests and an interest in "what makes me tick." The tests were administered as an assignment in Psychology 429 (Psychological Assessment) at Johnson College during the Spring of 1998. An interview was conducted prior to administering the tests.

Mr. Lake stated that his health was good, but he regrets that he is not more skilled in athletics. Except for a weight problem, he is a neat, fairly attractive young man who has been married for two years. He admits having been involved in using and selling drugs and to having some marital difficulties. His primary concern at the present time appears to be his occupational future, namely being able to find a job after graduating from college.

Mr. Lake stated that both he and his wife are very religious. His father is a church minister, and the examinee views his childhood as having been warm and loving. He reportedly maintains close ties with his parents. Mr. Lake and his wife attended another church-related college before he enrolled at Johnson College, but he stated that he is happier and making higher grades at Johnson. His wife is currently working as a secretary at the college, but she is anxious to complete her degree and start a family.

Mr. Lake said that he feels that he is "rather hard on myself" for not living up to his potential, but he appears generally optimistic in his outlook and looks forward to a bright future. He stated that he would like to work as a counselor in a church-related context after graduating from college.

Test Results and Interpretations

The examinee worked diligently on the personality test materials, sighing deeply on occasion but persisting in the tasks without interruption. The interview and testing lasted approximately two hours, and it was apparent toward the end of the session that he was getting tired. However, he did not complain and was quite interested in finding out the results.

The standard T score equivalents (male norms) of Mr. Lake's raw scores on the Jackson Personality Inventory scales are as follows:

Anxiety	53	Responsibility	40
Breadth of Interest	39	Risk Taking	57
Complexity	64	Self-Esteem	55
Conformity	56	Social Adroitness	63
Energy Level	49	Social Participation	38
Innovation	49	Tolerance	49
Interpersonal Affect	56	Value Orthodoxy	51
Organization	43	Infrequency	44

All of these scores are within the normal range (30–70), but the pattern of high and low scores points to a conforming, socially adroit individual who is, however, not very socially participative. On the whole he is a conventional, somewhat insecure young man with a fairly narrow range of interests and moderately high self-esteem. He is experiencing problems of organization and responsibility, and prefers deep, more complex explanations and interpretations of events.

Mr. Lake's responses to the Rotter Incomplete Sentences Blank confirm his statements during the interview that he is not applying himself fully, gives up too quickly, and is missing something in life. Fears of not being accepted are also apparent in his responses to the Rotter: he stated that during childhood he often felt like an outsider. He is obviously rather severe on himself, perhaps because of parental pressures toward perfectionism and feelings of guilt concerning his past behavior and failing to live up to his and their expectations. He expressed a lack of self-confidence and a need to achieve his potential more fully. In general, he has feelings of aloneness and of being an outsider. Although optimistic in his expectations of the future, he is self-critical and has rather strong feelings of failure.

Conclusions and Recommendations

The results of the personal interview, the Jackson Personality Inventory, and the Rotter Incomplete Sentences Blank yield a picture of a sensitive, self-critical young man of average to above-average abilities who is not living up to his own expectations and perhaps not those of his parents. He has high moral and personal standards but has violated them on occasion and feels that he may do so again. Although fairly content in his marriage, there are some problems. Financial security (finding a job) is obviously a pressing problem, and success in work may well ease some of the tension and insecurity that he obviously feels. Clearly, he needs to develop closer friendships and to learn to relax a bit more. He might well benefit from personal counseling.

Dorothy R. Brown
Psychology Major, Johnson College

ings. If should be remembered that the report of a psychological examination is of little value if it is too general, unread or not understood by those who are in a position to use the information to help make decisions about the examinee's future and well-being.

The primary aim of psychological report writing is efficient communication of the results of tests and other assessment instruments, as well as observation and interview findings. Thoughtful writers always keep their prospective readers in mind, attempting to bridge the gap between the mind of the writer and the minds of the readers in a straightforward manner. Consequently, wordiness, alliterations, poetic expressions, mixed metaphors, and other circumlocutions or distractions are inappropriate. Colloquialisms, cliches, and vulgar expressions are also bad form, as are scientificisms and similar jargon. A basic rule of professional communication is that if there is more than one way to say something, one should choose the simplest way. This does not mean that only a terse telegraphic style of writing is acceptable. It is possible to write economically but interestingly, avoiding abrupt transitions and choppy wording.

Every well-structured paragraph in an integrated report contains a topic sentence and one or more additional, elaborative statements. The report as a whole is well integrated, the writing flowing or "gliding" from paragraph to paragraph in an organized, goal-oriented manner. The writer knows where he or she is going and communicates this to the reader. Jumping from topic to topic—within or between paragraphs—is avoided, as are misspellings, grammatical errors, and other irregular nonstandard verbal constructions.

Computerized Reports

During recent years computer-generated reports of psychological examinations have increased in popularity. The first computer test-interpretation programs were developed at the Mayo Clinic, the Hartford Institute of Living, and the University of Alabama during the early 1960s (Swenson & Pearson, 1964; Rome et al., 1962; Glueck & Reznikoff, 1965). These programs were designed to score, profile, and interpret responses to the *Minnesota Multiphasic Personality Inventory* (MMPI). Subsequently, more complex programs for the automated interpretation of the MMPI and other measures of personality and cognitive abilities became available.

Today a variety of companies provide computer test scoring and interpretation services and market microcomputer software for interpreting personality tests such as the MMPI-2, the *California Psychological Inventory-Revised*, the *16 Personality Factor Questionnaire* (5th edition), and the *Millon Clinical Multiaxial Inventory-II & III*. A sample excerpt from a computer-generated personality description of the results of administering the Adult Personality Inventory is given

REPORT
4-2

Excerpt from a Computer-Generated Report of Results from the Adult Personality Inventory

She may be described as strongly self-directed, independent, and self-sufficient. Ms. __ likes to do things her own way and make her own decisions. She usually relies on herself, rather than others, and finds it very difficult to accept direction from other people. Her overall level of emotional maturity and adjustment is excellent. Ms. __ shows no evidence of being particularly anxious or distressed at the present time. She describes herself as very stable. She approaches new situations calmly and most probably has the inner resources to cope with every challenge she encounters. Ms. __ is an outward-oriented individual. She prefers to focus on the world around her rather than the world of inner thoughts and feelings. Ms. __ enjoys being with other people. Her profile is that of a person who is above average in creativity. Ms.__ is flexible in her thinking and, on occasion, she can be counted on to generate novel solutions to problems.

With respect to achievement motivation, Ms.__ is about average. Ms.__ shows a good balance of objectivity and sensitivity in the decisions she makes. She usually is logical and rational in her approach to problems, but tries to be sensitive to the feelings of other people and the impact her decisions may have on them. Ms.__ reports being the kind of person who would prefer to see things move along in an orderly way. She would usually be described as more careful and precise than many other people, but she isn't locked into traditional ways of doing things.

in Report 4–2. A computer-based interpretive report of the results of administering another personality inventory—the MMPI-2—is given in Report 8–1. Computer-generated test interpretations are usually not as individualized as the impressionistic interpretations of clinical and counseling psychologists. Many computer programs are designed to take into account the age, sex, and other demographics of the examinee, but no program can consider all of a person's attributes. Consequently, psychological examiners may supplement computer-generated test reports with additional interpretive comments. There are also important ethical issues regarding computer-based testing and interpretation programs. Many of these programs have not been adequately validated and are based on inadequate norms. There is also a tendency for computer-generated test reports to be viewed as accurate even when the validity of such narratives has not been demonstrated. Equally serious is the problem of maintaining the confidentiality of the highly personal information collected and stored by computers. People have a legal right to control the release of their test scores and other personal information, a right that may be jeopardized when such information is stored on a computer data bank.

Informed Consent and Confidentiality

Improper disclosure of psychological assessment information, especially when it is identified by the examinee's name, is a continuing cause of concern in psychological assessment. The expanding use of computers and associated data banks has increased the need for vigilance in ensuring that test scores maintained in electronic files in particular are adequately protected against improper disclosure. Unless otherwise required by law, *informed consent* of the test taker or his or her legal representative is needed to release test results by the name of the examinee to any other person or organization. Informed consent implies that the individual who has agreed to have personal information released is aware of what the information consists of and with whom it is to be shared.

An informed consent form similar to the one in Form 4–2 should be read and signed by the examinee or by a responsible party prior to a psychological examination. As indicated in this form, before any tests or other psychometric procedures are administered, examinees must be told the nature of the examination, why they are being tested, who will have access to the information, and how it will be used.

In addition to the rights of informed consent and confidentiality, the "least stigmatizing label" should be applied in reporting the presence of certain psychological symptoms, disorders, or other conditions. For example, "adolescent adjustment reaction" is a less stigmatizing label than "psychopathic personality." And in the case of intelligence testing, terms such a "mentally retarded," "mentally impaired," or "developmentally disabled" are perhaps less stigmatizing than mentally deficient, and certainly less so than "moron," "imbecile," or "idiot."

From a legal standpoint, data obtained from a psychological examination are considered a *privileged communication* to be shared with other people only on a need-to-know and right-to-know basis. Examinees should be told beforehand why and by whom they are being examined, who will have access to the results, and how they will be used. After the examination, examinees also have a right to know their scores and the interpretations placed on them. Except under unusual circumstances, as when the person is dangerous to himself or others, test information is confidential and should not be released without the necessary informed consent. Even with informed consent, the information may be *privileged* in the sense that, other than the client, and in the case of a minor or legally

Form for Obtaining Informed Consent for a Psychological Examination. FORM 4-2

Informed Consent for a Psychological Examination

I, _____ voluntarily give my consent to serve as a participant in a psychological examination conducted by _____. I have received a clear and complete explanation of the general nature and purposes(s) of the examination and the specific reason(s) why I am being examined. I have also been informed of the kinds of tests and other procedures to be administered and how the results will be used.

I realize that it may not be possible for the examiner to explain all aspects of the examination to me until it has been completed. It is also my understanding that I may terminate my participation in the examination at any time without penalty. I further understand that I will be informed of the results and that the results will be reported to no one else without my permission. At this time, I request that a copy of the results of this examination be sent to:

Examinee's Name and Signature _____

Signature of Examiner _____

---

incompetent person, the parent(s) or guardian, only the client's attorney, physician, or psychologist may have access to it.*

Not only do legally responsible examinees have the right of access to their own test reports, but they can also arrange for transmittal of their test scores to educational, clinical, or counseling agencies for any appropriate use. At the same time, every effort must be made to maintain confidentiality of test scores and other personal information.

Consultations and Conferences

A written report is only one way in which the results of a psychometric evaluation are communicated to those who have a legitimate right to know. Clinical-case conferences or consultations in mental health contexts, and parent-teacher or

---

* The right of privileged communication is not inviolable and has come under scrutiny in a number of court cases dealing with the principle that "protective privilege ends where the public peril begins." Among these cases are Tarasoff v. Regents of University of California (1976), Peck v. Counseling Services of Addison County (1985; Stone, 1986), Jablonski v. United States (1983), White v. United States (1986), Menendez v. The Superior Court of Los Angeles County (1992). In general, these cases were concerned with the legal duty of mental health practitioners to inform appropriate public officials and potential victims when the professional obtains information pertaining to the threat of violence by an individual.

parent-counseling conferences in school settings, may occur both before and after a psychological evaluation. When conducting a post-testing conference with a person who is unsophisticated in psychological jargon and procedures, such as a typical parent, an experienced counselor describes, in language appropriate to the listener, the test results and whatever conclusions can reasonably be drawn from them. In general, qualitative rather than quantitative descriptions and interpretations are employed. The purpose and nature of the tests, why these particular tests were selected, and the limitations of the tests and results are also discussed. Rather than assigning labels, descriptive statements are made; rather than specific scores, score ranges that take into account the standard error of measurement are reported.

When reporting and explaining test results to examinees and/or their parents, facilities for counseling people who become emotionally upset during a consultative session should also be made available. In any event, a case consultation involves the discussion of options and decisions—for treatment, remediation, rehabilitation, or other intervention, and information on referral sources is provided. Following the consultation, the examiner transmits a copy of the examination report to the referral source and other appropriate persons. The examiner also retains a copy of the report and any notes made during the observations and interviews.

■ Summary

Personality assessment begins with a need to know something about the psychology of people in general or about a particular group or individual. Information obtained from personality assessments is useful in a variety of settings: clinical, education, legal, medical, and employment. Following specification of the need(s), the goals of assessment are established and decisions made concerning the kinds of data required to attain those goals.

The goals of personality assessment vary to some extent with the model—psychodynamic (psychodiagnostic), psychometric, or behavioristic—espoused by the assessor. Those who subscribe to a psychodynamic model are more likely to favor projective techniques and other in-depth procedures; those of the psychometric persuasion make greater use of personality inventories and other measures of personality traits; behaviorally-oriented assessors place more emphasis on objectively observed and measured behavior.

The ethical code of the American Psychological Association and the *Standards for Educational and Psychological Testing* are guides for the proper construction, evaluation, administration, and interpretation of psychological assessment instruments. As indicated in the *Standards*, except in highly unusual circumstances examiners should follow the directions for administration, scoring, and interpretation printed in the manual accompanying a standardized test. Care must be taken not only in reading the test directions and presenting the test materials properly, but in arranging the testing environment—both physical and psychological—for the comfort and convenience of examinees.

Computer-based administration of an objective personality inventory or rating scale is a fairly straightforward process, but computer-assisted interviewing and the administration of projective techniques is more difficult. Although test scoring is now conducted routinely with computerized scoring systems, handscoring of answer sheets is still commonplace. The scoring of projective techniques and other nonobjective instruments is a subjective process that can be influenced by the examiner's biases and perceptions of the examinee's demographic and other characteristics.

Interpreting the results of a psychological examination is a fairly subjective process, involving the integration of observational, interview, biographical, test and other data sources to form a coherent picture of the examinee's personality dynamics and areas of strength and weakness. The most comprehensive assessments involve a thorough case study of the individual, frequently for psychodiagnostic or other clinical purposes.

Psychodiagnosis consists of an analysis of psychological and physical symptoms to classify and label an individual as belonging in a particular psychiatric category. In the United States, the most widely applied classification system for mental disorders is the one described in the revision of the fourth edition of the *Diagnostic and Statistical Manual* (*DSM-IV*) of the American Psychiatric Association. Although DSM-IV is probably an improvement over its predecessors, certain psychologists and psychiatrists emphasize the shortcomings and dangers of any sort of psychopathological labeling and the subjectivity of the process.

Numerous studies have shown that statistical (actuarial) prediction of behavior is superior to clinical (impressionistic) prediction. It is recognized that clinicians are needed to make judgments in collecting data on personality, but clinical judgments can be notoriously inaccurate when they are influenced by preconceived, notions, failure to give adequate consideration to base rates, the hindsight bias, and serious overconfidence in one's own judgment.

In preparing a report of personality assessment findings, the writer should avoid vague generalizations, stereotypes, and banalities. The report should address itself to the questions that need to be answered concerning the mental functioning and behavior of the examinee. It should also be as brief as possible, communicating efficiently but comprehensively and following the rules of syntax and good composition style. Computer-generated reports attempt to integrate test and demographic data into a series of descriptive and diagnostic statements about an individual. The information included in these reports is typically supplemented by clinical observations and interview data.

Whether psychological assessment findings are communicated orally or in writing, there are ethical and legal sanctions governing the disclosure of such information. Psychological test data should be kept confidential and, with some exceptions, shared with other people only after the written consent of the examinee or his or her legal guardian or counsel has been obtained. This information may be communicated in a consultative conference, expressed in language that the conferees can understand and with the welfare of the examinee foremost in mind.

■ Questions and Activities

1. At the beginning of this chapter, several settings were described in which personality assessments are conducted. Consider any three of these settings, and obtain as much information as you can on personality assessment instruments that are used to help make decisions about people in the settings and how the instruments are applied.
2. What are the differences between the psychodynamic, psychometric, and behavioristic models of assessing personality? What instruments or procedures are emphasized by each of the three models, and what are their goals of application?
3. Why is it necessary to have an explicit code of ethics for the practice of psychology, considering the fact that psychologists are professional people who are sensitive to the public welfare and also scientists who avoid the exploitation of others in their search for the truth?
4. Examine a copy of the *Diagnostic and Statistical Manual of Mental Disorders (Fourth Edition)* (DSM-IV), and write a brief description of this system for classifying mental disorders. In addition, summarize the descriptions given in DSM-IV of the following disorders: schizophrenia and other psychotic disorders, mood disorders, anxiety disorders, somatoform disorders, factitious disorders, dissociative disorders, adjustment disorders, and personality disorders.
5. To what extent have your own judgments of people been affected by the following four factors? (1) stereotypes and other preconceived notions that you had about the person(s); (2) failure to give adequate consideration to base rates, that is, how common the perceived characteristics are in the general population; (3) the hindsight bias, or believing, in retrospect, that you could have predicted that a person would behave in such a manner; (4) overconfidence in the accuracy of your own judgments. In addition, how influential do you believe these factors are in selecting employees or students, in jury decisions, in the persistence of social prejudice, and in other nonclinical situations? Provide examples from your own observations and experiences.

6. Show the personality description on page 111 to several of your friends. What percent agreed that it is a fairly accurate description of their personalities? How do you explain these findings?

7. Most departments of psychology and education keep on file specimen sets of standardized rating scales, checklists, personality inventories, or other personality assessment instruments, including the instrument itself and associated descriptive and interpretative materials (manual of administration, norms, etc.). Select an available personality assessment instrument, and prepare a review of it by following an outline such as the one given below. Wherever possible, fill in the outline with information obtained from reading the manual and examining the instrument itself. Refrain from consulting a published review of the instrument before completing your own review.

Content. List the title, author(s), publisher, date and place of publication, forms available, type of assessment instrument, and cost. Give a brief description of the sections of the instrument, the kinds of items or materials of which it is composed, and the personality or behavioral characteristics it is supposed to measure. Describe how the instrument was constructed and whether the construction procedure and/or theory on which it is based are clearly described in the manual.

Administration and Scoring. Describe any special instructions, whether the assessment instrument is timed, and if so the time limits. Give details concerning scoring—as a whole, by sections or parts, and so on. Indicate whether the directions for administration and scoring are clear.

Norms. Describe the group(s) (composition, size, etc.) on which the instrument was standardized and how the samples were selected (systematic, stratified random, etc.). What kinds of norms are reported in the administration and scoring manual or in technical supplements? Was the standardization adequate for the recommended uses of the instrument?

Reliability. Describe the kinds of reliability information reported in the manual (internal consistency, parallel forms, test-retest, etc.). Are the nature and sizes of the samples on which reliability information is reported adequate with respect to the stated uses of the instrument?

Validity. Summarize published information on the validity (content, predictive, concurrent, construct) of the instrument reported in the manual. Is the validity information satisfactory in terms of the stated purposes of the instrument?

Summary Comments. Give a summary statement of the design and content of the assessment instrument, and comment briefly on its adequacy as a measure of whatever it was designed to measure. Does the manual include satisfactory descriptions of the design, content, norms, reliability, and validity of the instrument? What further information and/or data are needed to improve the instrument and its uses?

■ Suggested Readings

Airasian, P.W., & Terrasi, S. (1994). Test administration. In T. Husén & T.N. Postlethwaite (Eds.), *International encyclopedia of education* (2nd ed., Vol. 11, pp. 6311–6315). Tarrytown, NY: Elsevier.

Allard, G., Butler, J., Faust, D., & Shea, M.T. (1995). Errors in hand scoring objective personality tests: The case of the Personality Diagnostic Questionnaire. *Professional Psychology: Research and Practice, 26,* 304–308.

American Psychological Association (1992). Ethical principles of psychologists and code of conduct. *American Psychologist, 47,* 1597–1611.

Arkes, H.R. (1994). Clinical judgment. In R.J. Corsini (Ed.), *Encyclopedia of psychology* (2nd ed., pp. 237–238). New York: Wiley.

Booth-Kewley, S., Edwards, J.E., & Rosenfeld, P. (1991). Impression management, social desirability, and computer administration of attitude questionnaires: Does the computer make a difference? *Journal of Applied Psychology, 77,* 562–566.

Butcher, J.N. (1995). How to use computer-based reports. In J.N. Butcher (Ed.), *Clinical personality assessment: Practical approaches* (pp. 78–94). New York: Oxford University Press.

Matarazzo, J.D., & Pankratz, L.D. (1994). Diagnoses. In R.J. Corsini (Ed.), *Encyclopedia of psychology* (2nd ed., Vol. 1, pp. 414–417). New York Wiley.

Spengler, P.M., & Strohmer, D.C. (1994). Clinical judgment biases: The moderating roles of counselor cognitive complexity and counselor client preferences. *Journal of Counseling Psychology, 41,* 8–12.

Weiner, I.B. (1995). How to anticipate ethical and legal challenges in personality assessments. In J.N. Butcher (Ed.), *Clinical personality assessment: Practical approaches* (pp. 95–103). New York: Oxford University Press.

■ PART II

OBSERVING, INTERVIEWING, AND RATING

CHAPTER 5

Observations and Interviews

Observations and interviews, whether formal or informal, are the two oldest methods of psychological assessment. Long before the invention of writing, people made judgments and evaluations of others by observing their behavior and talking with them. For example, oral examinations, during which both the examinee's statements and behavior were recorded, were used to evaluate governmental employees in ancient China and to test students in the Middle Ages at institutions such as Oxford University and the University of Bologna. Not until the nineteenth century did uniform testing with written essay examinations become the principal method of evaluating academic achievement. And despite the progress made in mental measurement during the last century, observing and interviewing have retained their popularity in educational, employment, and clinical situations.

Observing and interviewing are, of course, similar in that both procedures involve looking at and listening to nonverbal and verbal behavior and drawing conclusions from the findings. The difference is that in interviewing the interviewer interacts with the person being observed (the interviewee), focusing primarily on the verbal responses made by the interviewee to a series of questions. By their very nature, interviews are typically more obtrusive than noninteractive observations because interviewees are aware of being observed. The potential price to pay for the obtrusiveness of interviews is that interviewees may behave less naturally or be more inclined to role-play than if they did not know that they were being observed. On the other hand, interviewing offers a greater opportunity than simply observing to obtain details on a person's thoughts aspirations, attitudes, and other internal states, as well as information about the person's past behavior. It is also more efficient than simple observation in that an interviewer can prompt and direct the individual's behavior in specific directions rather than merely waiting for it to occur. Both observations and interviews may, however, impose less structure on the process of obtaining information and hence greater subjectivity in recording and interpreting responses than more standardized paper-and-pencil techniques.

■ Observations

Certainly the most widely employed and probably the most generally understood and accepted method of personality assessment is some form of observation. When using the method of observation, which is basic to all science, one takes note of events and perhaps makes a written record of what is seen or heard. Whether or not it is done consciously or unconsciously, everyone engages in casual or informal observation of other people and events. Some perceptive individuals are better than others at noting and describing other people and in drawing conclusions and making predictions from what they observe. The following quotation from the short story "Four Meetings", by Henry James, illustrates the perceptiveness of an acute observer and an eloquent writer.

> I saw her but four times, though I remember them vividly. She made an impression on me. Close upon thirty, by every presumption, she was made almost like a little girl and had the complexion of a child. She was artistic, I suspected. Her eyes were perhaps too round and too inveterately surprised, but her lips had a mild decision, and her teeth, when she showed them, were charming. (Fadiman, 1945, pp. 3–4 passim)

Painstaking observation is also a tool or characteristic of individuals whose profession necessitates an in-depth understand of other people, whether for the purpose of assisting or exploiting them.

Uncontrolled and Controlled Observation

Psychological researchers and psychodiagnosticians tend to be more systematic observers than the average layperson, but they also obtain information about other people by informal, *uncontrolled observation* of behavior with no attempt to restrict it to a contrived situation or controlled conditions. Observing the activities of children on a playground and the behavior of people in a waiting line are examples of uncontrolled, naturalistic observation.

Observations can be uncontrolled and yet systematic and objective. For example, teachers can be trained to make objective observations of the behavior of schoolchildren and accurate *anecdotal recordings* of whatever behavior seems significant. A well-trained teacher-observer realizes that pulling Mary's hair is not invariably an act of hostility on the part of Johnny, and an accurate anecdotal record of the event indicates precisely what was observed and distinguishes between the observed act and the interpretation placed upon it.

An illustration of uncontrolled observation in the world of work is the *critical incidents technique* (Flanagan, 1954). Supervisors and others who are familiar with a particular job are asked to identify specific behaviors that are critical to job performance or that distinguish between good and poor workers. These behaviors or incidents are critical because they have either highly positive or highly negative consequences. Examples are "secures machinery and tidies up work place when finished" and "follows up customers' requests promptly." Identification of a large number of such incidents supplies valuable information on the nature of the job and the requirements for effective performance.

In contrast to uncontrolled observation, *controlled observation* consists of observations made in prearranged, or contrived situations; the goal is to determine how specific people typically behave in those situations. For example, a developmental psychologist may arrange or structure a situation beforehand to determine if a child will act honestly or dishonestly under a certain set of circumstances. Or a psychological researcher may use a one-way mirror or closed-circuit television to observe the interaction between an adult and a child in a certain prearranged situation. In this way the researcher can see the interaction of the adult and child without them seeing him. This precaution reduces the effects of the observer's presence on the behavior of the performers.

People often find it difficult to behave naturally when they know they are being observed. They tend to behave as if they were on stage, engaging in role-playing to some extent, and to monitor what they say and do more carefully. This reaction may be referred to as the *guinea pig effect*: the person perceives herself or himself as a kind of guinea pig in an experiment.

Participant Observation

People who are aware of being observed may tend, at least initially, to behave atypically, but sometimes it is advantageous to have the observer interact with those who are being observed. In such *participant observation*, the observer becomes a part of the situation and can make observations at first hand while experiencing what it is like to be in the situation itself. Participant observation has been used extensively by cultural anthropologists, so much so that at one time it was quipped that a typical aborigine family consisted of a mother, a father, two children, and a cultural anthropologist! Realizing that they must take into account the likelihood that the observer's own behavior will affect the responses of other people, proponents of participant observation maintain that active involvement in a real-life situation can provide insights that are unobtainable by other methods.

Both clinical interviewing and psychotherapy involve participant observation, in that the interviewer or therapist is not an impassive, inactive recorder of the interviewee's (patient's or client's) behavior, but is dynamically involved in influencing the behavior of the interviewee. Much of what is known about the dynamics of personality and mental disorders is the result of observations made by people in clinical settings. Obviously, this *clinical method* is not completely objective. Not only does the therapist-observer affect the patient's behavior, but the patient also affects the reactions of the therapist. Consequently, the accuracy of clinical observations and the interpretations placed upon them should be carefully checked by other observers and procedures. For example, to what extent does the following description provide a valid, specific picture of a child's behavior during an examination rather than reflecting the observer's own personality and preconceptions?

> Michael is an attractive child, with long, straight brown hair and freckles. He seemed somewhat anxious during the examination, squirming around in his chair, but not excessively. He tended to give up easily on more difficult tasks, and showed other signs of low frustration tolerance (sighing deeply, reluctance to attempt certain tasks). He was fairly cooperative and seemed mildly interested in the tasks, but he showed signs of fatigue toward the end of the examination. In general, he was attentive and energetic, answering questions briefly, but was not especially talkative. He did not smile during the entire time, and responded in a brief, occasionally uncertain manner.

Notice that even the "Four Meetings" description by Henry James, cited previously in the chapter, contains as many elements of interpretation as objective observation, and it is not entirely clear where one ends and the other begins. Compare these two descriptions with the following, more objective behavioral observations of a child referred for possible emotional disturbance:

> Mrs. Cash and I observed and recorded Terry's classroom behavior for 1 week. Mrs. Cash kept a frequency count of disruptive behavior for 5 days. Terry averaged 50 disruptive acts a day. I observed Terry for six randomly chosen intervals of 10 minutes' duration over a period of 2 days. My observations validated those of Mrs. Cash. Using a 20-second interval recording pace, Terry was observed to engage in disruptive behavior in 25% of the intervals. In addition, I recorded disruptive acts by other classmates. The total amount of disruption from others amounted to only 5% of recorded intervals. Other school personnel were asked to observe and record any instances of the following behaviors: conversing with adults, cooperative play with other students, initiating social interactions with peers or adults. They observed for 1 week in the cafeteria, play areas, and during recess. Terry was never observed conversing with adults, playing cooperatively with other students for more than 10% of the time, or initiating any social interactions. (Keller, 1986, p. 386)

Situational Testing and Leaderless Group Discussion

A classic research study that used a controlled observation procedure known as *situational testing* was the Character Education Inquiry of Hartshorne and May (1928). In this series of investigations, children were surreptitiously provided with opportunities to demonstrate their honesty, altruism, and other character traits. To test the children's honesty, the investigators placed them in a situation where they could copy test answers, seemingly without being detected. Among the findings of the study were that older children, less intelligent children, children of lower socioeconomic status, and more emotionally unstable children tended to be less honest in all of the situations. Perhaps the most important outcome of this research study was that honesty and other traits of character varied as much with the situation as with the individual. In other words, a child's honesty, altruism, and other character traits were typically highly dependent on the situation in which the child was placed.

Situational testing for military uses was introduced by the Germans and subsequently adapted by the British and American armed forces during World War II. A series of simulated situational tests administered by the U.S. Office of Strategic Services (OSS) was designed to select espionage agents, and, as in the Hartshorne and May (1928) studies, entailed deceiving the examinees. For example, in the "wall problem," a group of men was assigned the task of crossing a "canyon." Unknown to the real candidate, the men assigned to assist him were accomplices of the examiners; in other words, they were "plants." One of the plants acted obstructively by making unrealistic suggestions and insulting or worrisome remarks; another plant pretended not to understand the task and passively resisted directions from the examinee. Most examinees did not realize that those assigned to assist them were accomplices of the examiners. The examinee's efforts to complete the task in the face of these frustrating circumstances was observed and evaluated by the examiners.

One interesting variety of situational testing is the *leaderless group discussion* (*LGD*) test, which has been used extensively in the *assessment center approach* for selecting executive personnel. In the LGD test, a small group of examinees (typically 12 or fewer) is asked to discuss an assigned topic—say a specific administrative, political, or social problem—for a period of time (30 minutes to one hour). The performances of individual members of the group are rated by observers and other examinees. Reliable ratings in an LGD situation are usually made in terms of the degree of ascendance, task facilitation, and sociability shown by the examinees.

Despite their real-life quality, it has proven difficult to determine the effectiveness of situational testing procedures for selection purposes. Even in the OSS assessment program, examinees frequently realized that the test situations were contrived. For this reason and others, the reliabilities and predictive validities of situational tests have usually been rather low in comparison with their expense. In another assessment context—the selection of clinical psychology students—situational testing was found to be of questionable validity (Kelly & Fiske, 1951).

Self-Observation and Content Analysis

Self-observation, which most people engage in to some extent, is an appealing data-collection method in both research and clinical contexts. The appeal of the method lies in both its economy and the fact that it is the only direct way to get at private mental events such as thoughts and feelings. A problem with self-observations is that they are likely to be even more biased that observations made by others; very seldom are people entirely objective in describing their own thoughts and behavior. However, as with observations by others, people can be trained to make more objective, systematic observations of themselves. Thus, they can learn to distinguish what they are actually feeling, thinking, or doing from what they should or would like to feel, think, or do.

By keeping a continuous written record of one's thoughts, feelings, and actions, a wealth of self-observational data can be accumulated. Unfortunately, it is not always clear what to do with such an abundance of data. How should it be analyzed and interpreted? As seen in the *content analysis* of diaries, autobiographies, letters, drawings, and other personal documents, important insights into personality and behavior can be gained from interpreting self-observational data (Allport, 1965). But the complexity and laboriousness of content analysis have kept this interpretative approach from being applied routinely in clinical or other applied contexts. Wrightsman (1994) reviewed the uses and shortcomings for psychodiagnostic purposes of content analyses of autobiographical and other personal documents.

Nonverbal Behavior

Because information on personality dynamics is communicated not only by words but also by actions, effective observers of human behavior take note of the apparel, grooming, general demeanor, and modes of expression of those whom they are observing. How the person shakes hands, looks at the observer and other people, sits, stands, and walks, as well as characteristic facial expressions, body movements, and voice tones may are all noted. When properly recorded and interpreted, such nonverbal behaviors can provide useful insights into personality dynamics and problems.

Most people realize that interpersonal communication is not entirely verbal, but they are usually unaware of the extent to which movements of the hands, feet, eyes, and mouth, as well as body posture and tone of voice, are interpreted as messages. As seen in the following quotation from Sigmund Freud, the founder of psychoanalysis was quite aware of these nonverbal cues:

> He that has eyes to see and ears to hear may convince himself that no mortal can keep a secret. If his lips are silent, he chatters with his fingertips; betrayal oozes out of him at every pore. (Freud, 1905, p.9 4)

During the past several decades, a great deal of research interest has been shown in *nonverbal behavior*. According to the findings of one investigation (Mehrabian & Weiner, 1967), 65–90 percent of the meaning of interpersonal communications comes from nonverbal cues. Studies of both expert and nonexpert evaluators of behavior reveal that interpretations of nonverbal messages are often quite reliable (Dittman, 1962; Ekman, 1965a, 1965b). For example, the following body movements have been found to be reliably associated with the corresponding emotions (Mahl, 1968; Ekman & Friesen, 1984):

— Moderate scratching and rubbing of the nose: depression
— Playing with one's wedding ring: feelings of marital conflict
— Movements of the hands: feelings about the self
— Movements of the feet: anger, annoyance, and irritation

Kinesics. Certain kinds of nonverbal cues are more important than others in message transmission. Particularly significant are *kinesics*, which are movements of small (*microkinesics*) or large (*macrokinesics*) body parts. Also of interest are the kinesic cues obtained from eye contact and gaze. Among the findings on this topic are:

— Eye contact may be used by dependent individuals to communicate positive attitudes to, and to elicit positive attitudes from, others. Eye contact almost can establish an obligation to interact.
— Individuals who are looked at most tend to be perceived and tend to perceive themselves as possessing group power and status.
— Dominant people speak more and look less. Long gazers, however, tend to be seen as more dominant than senders of short glances.
— Extroverts look more frequently. Their percentage of gaze is greater and their glances are longer.
— People tend to maximize eye contact with communicants of moderately high social status. They respond to high status with a moderate amount of looking, and they spend the shortest time of all with those of low social status.
— Eye contact may increase or decrease with psychological distance. That is, when people are too close, they look less. When they are farther away (i. e., from three to ten feet), they look more.
— Amount of gaze varies with degree of topic intimacy. The more intimate the topic, the less gaze.
— When persons communicate to deceive others, they usually look less.

Box 5-1 | **Fifty-Two Ways That Women Flirt**

Monica Moore (1985) and teams of graduate students spent hundreds of hours in bars and student centers covertly watching women and men court. The following is a list of 52 gestures they found that women use to signal their interest in men:

Facial/Head Patterns

Coy smile	Laugh
Eyebrow flash	Lip lick
Face to face	Lipstick application
Fixed gaze	Neck presentation
Giggle	Pout
Hair flip	Room-encompassing glance
Head toss	Short, darting glance
Head nod	Smile
Kiss	Whisper

Posture Patterns

Aid solicitation	Lateral body contact
Approach	Lean
Breast touch	Parade
Brush	Placement
Dance (acceptance)	Play
Foot to foot	Point
Frontal body contact	Request dance
Hang	Shoulder hug
Hug	Solitary dance
Knee touch	Thigh touch

Gestures

Arm flexion	Caress (torso)
Buttock pat	Gesticulation
Caress (arm)	Hand hold
Caress (back)	Hike skirt
Caress (face/hair)	Palm
Caress (leg)	Primp
Caress (object)	Tap

— Glances are used for synchronizing conversation. If the speaker does not look at the listener when about to conclude an utterance, the latter lacks permission to speak. When the listener looks away, the speaker is notified that he or she has talked long enough and that the listener is getting ready for his or her turn. (Bernard & Huckins, 1978, pp. 420–421)

As documented by Moore's (1985, 1995) observations of flirting behavior in women, facial/head patterns, posture, and gestures are all important in communicating sexual messages (see Box 5–1). Such messages can, however, be misinterpreted: a myopic stare or a smile can be misconstrued as an invitation or promise. Movements of the eyes and eyebrows ("eyebrow flash") are also not always clear as to their meaning. Depending on the situation, an eyebrow flash may be interpreted as flirting, agreement, surprise, fear, disbelief, disapproval, or a silent greeting. The way in which it is interpreted may also vary with culture: it connotes disagreement among Greeks but disapproval among other Europeans and Americans. Because the upper part of the face is under less control than the lower part, an eyebrow flash is considered to be more authentically expressive of one's feelings than a smile (Kelleher, 1996).

Proximics. Another class of nonverbals is *proximics*, which refers to the distance zone between communicators (personal space or territoriality). Hall (1969) grouped communication distances into four categories: intimate distance (0 to 18 inches), personal distance (18 inches to 4 feet), social distance (4 to 12 feet), and public distance (12 feet and over). Being situated at an *intimate distance* from another person facilitates touching and other kinds of contact. Verbalization is relatively unimportant at this distance because messages can be sent and received by all the senses. *Personal distance* is approximately the same as *personal space*, the kind of invisible territorial bubble that an individual carries around from place to place. The extremes of this distance are too great for discussing personal topics and becoming mutually involved. However, people spend most of their time and are usually most comfortable at a *social distance* of 4 to 12 feet. At this distance it is easy to keep from becoming personally involved and to get away. Of course, social distance varies with culture, social relationships, sex, age, and other factors. Personal involvement does not occur at all at the *public distance* of 12 feet or more. The topics discussed at a public distance are usually formal or impersonal, being limited to what can be seen and heard.

Paralinguistics. A third class of nonverbal message transmitters is *paralinguistics*, which includes tone of voice, rate of speaking, and other nonverbal aspects of speech. Five categories of paralinguistic cues and the emotions reportedly communicated by each cue dimension are as follows (Scherer, 1974):
— Amplitude variation (moderate to extreme): pleasantness, activity, happiness, fear
— Pitch variation (moderate to extreme): anger, boredom, disgust, fear, pleasantness, activity, happiness, surprise
— Pitch contour (down to up): pleasantness, boredom, sadness, potency, anger, fear, surprise
— Pitch level (low to high): pleasantness, boredom, sadness, activity, potency, anger, fear, surprise

— Tempo (slow to fast): boredom, disgust, sadness, pleasantness, activity, potency, anger, fear, happiness, surprise

The relationship of culture and proximics, for example, the fact that people in
certain cultures stand closer when conversing than people in other cultures, was
referred to earlier. When two individuals from different cultures are interacting,
this tendency may result in a kind of dance in which one person moves closer
and the other moves away. Culture also affects mode of dress, eating habits, postures, and a wealth of other nonverbal behaviors that convey specific messages
to those who are familiar with the cultures. These habits or behaviors are collectively referred to as *culturics.*

Western visitors to non-Western countries might save themselves considerable
grief and embarrassment by becoming familiar not only with the culturics of the
country they are visiting but also with the kinesic, proximic, and paralinguistic
communications characteristics of the culture. For example, the gesture made by
joining the forefinger with the thumb means "OK" in the United States, "okane"
(money) in Japan, and a dirty name in Mexico!

Interpretive Accuracy. Although most people probably succeed more often than
not in interpreting nonverbal messages in their own culture correctly, mistakes
do occur. The poker-faced gambler and the glad-handed sales representative or
politician are renowned for their ability to deceive others with nonverbal behavior. The author once interviewed a mental patient who refused to speak to him
at first. I was determined to remain silent until he answered my previous questions, so for a time both of us sat quietly and refrained from speaking. After a
while he unexpectedly demanded, "Why do you want to kick me out of here?"
Somewhat surprised, I looked at my crossed legs and observed that my right foot
was moving back and forth. The patient had interpreted my foot movement as
a desire to get rid of him. Reflecting on this incident, I revised his interpretation
by concluding that my moving foot was indicative of anxiety (an implicit walking
out of the room on my part?). In any event, such nonverbal behavior is often a
more valid indicator than a verbal report of how a person is feeling. It is usually
easier to lie or distort one's true feelings by moving the the vocal apparatus than
the rest of the body.

The PONS. To assess individual differences in the ability to interpret nonverbal
communications, Rosenthal et al. (1979) devised a test, the Profile of Nonverbal
Sensitivity (PONS). The PONS consists of a 45-minute film in which viewers are
presented with a series of scenes such as facial expressions or spoken phrases
heard as tones or sounds, but not as words. After each scene is presented, the
viewer selects one of two labels as an appropriate description of the actor's feelings. The authors of the PONS reported that men and women who scored high

tended to have fewer friends, but warmer, more honest, and more satisfying sexual relationships than those who scored low on the test.

Reasoning that sensitivity to nonverbal messages is an important ability for diplomats, David McClelland used the PONS in an applicant screening program for the U.S. Information Agency (USIA). Short taped segments from the test were played to USIA applicants, who were then asked to indicate what emotion was being expressed. It was discovered that applicants who scored high on the PONS were considered significantly more competent by their colleagues than those who scored low (Rosenthal et al., 1979, pp. 304–306). The PONS has subsequently been used in a variety of research settings in the United States and other countries, and with both adults and children (e. g., Evans, Coman, & Stanley, 1988; Hodgins & Koestner, 1993).

Unmasking the Face. Another contribution to the assessment of nonverbal behavior is the Facial Action Coding System (FACS). Designed by Paul Ekman and Wallace Friesen (1984), the FACS material consists of 135 photographs of various facial expressions for training observers in scoring dozens of *facial action units*. Also, useful in training observers to judge emotion from facial expressions are Friesen and Ekman's Pictures of Facial Affect. These are 110 black-and-white pictures expressing fear, anger, happiness, sadness, surprise, or disgust (plus a neutral expression).

Observations for Behavior Modification

Behavior modification is a term applied to a set of psychotherapeutic procedures based on learning theory and research and designed to change inappropriate behavior to more personally and/or socially acceptable behavior. Inappropriate behaviors may consist of excesses, deficits, or other inadequacies of action that are correctable through behavioral techniques such as systematic desensitization, counterconditioning, and extinction. To assess the effectiveness of any of these techniques in modifying the behavior in question, a *baseline* (operant) level of the frequency and/or intensity of the behavior is determined before the technique is applied. The incidence or strength of the behavior after the technique has been applied may then be compared with the baseline level to determine whether there has been any improvement.

Among the maladaptive behaviors that have received special attention by behavior modifiers are specific fears (or phobias), smoking, overeating, alcoholism, drug addiction, underassertiveness, bedwetting, chronic tension and pain, and sexual inadequacies of various kinds. Whatever the *target behaviors* or responses may be, they should be defined precisely and occur with sufficient frequency to be recordable and modifiable. Although target behaviors have typically been rather narrowly defined, behavior therapists of a more cognitive persuasion have also tackled less specific problems such as a negative self-concept or an identity crisis. Furthermore, the target behaviors consist not only of nonverbal movements but also of verbal reports of thoughts and feelings.

Behavior therapists attempt to understand behavior by studying not only its antecedents, which include both the social learning history and current environment of the person, but also the results or consequences of the behavior. A basic tenet of *behavior modification*, adopted from operant learning theory, is that behavior is controlled by its consequences. So in designing a program for correcting problem behavior, the reinforcing consequences that sustain the behavior, in addition to the conditions that precede and trigger it, must be identified. In summary, the process of behavior modification begins with a *functional analysis* of the problem behavior(s), consisting of an A-B-C sequence in which A stands for the *antecedent* conditions, B the problem *behavior*, and C the *consequences* of that behavior. Then B is modified by controlling for A and changing C. The antecedents and consequences of the target behavior may be either overt, objectively observable conditions or covert mental events reported by the person whose behavior is to be modified.

A variety of procedures may be used to analyze or assess the antecedents and consequences of target behaviors. These procedures, which vary with the specific therapeutic methods and goals, include observations, interviews, checklists, rating scales, and questionnaires completed by the patient and/or a person who is closely connected with him or her. On occasion behavior modifiers have even used projective techniques by employing the responses as samples of behavior.

The observational procedures applied in a behavioral analysis involve taking note of the frequency and duration of the target behaviors and the particular contingencies (antecedents and consequences) of their occurrence. Depending on the context and the age of the patient, behavior observations can be made and recorded by teachers, parents, nurses, nursing assistants, or anyone who is acquainted with the patient (Hartmann & Wood, 1990). For example, diagnoses of psychopathology can be facilitated by observations made by nurses and psychiatric aides of the behavior of patients on hospital wards. Rating scales such as the Nurses' Observation Scale for Inpatient Evaluation (NOSIE-30) (Honigfeld & Klett, 1965) and the Ward Behavior Inventory (Burdock et al., 1968) are useful devices for assessing patients' aggressive, communicative, and cooperative behaviors as well as other behaviors and appearance.

Several other procedures for behavioral assessment have been proposed (see Bellack & Hersen, 1998; Ciminero, Calhoun, & Adams, 1986; Haynes, 1990, 1991; O'Brien & Haynes, 1993; Ollendick & Green, 1990). The specific assessment procedures and instruments used vary with the therapeutic techniques and goals. A representative approach begins with the determination of the frequency and intensity of the target behavior(s), what triggers the behavior (antecedents), and what effects the behavior has (consequences). These antecedents and consequences, both motor and mental, are identified by observing and interviewing the person, as well as significant other people, and administering various questionnaires, rating scales, and inventories.

Many questionnaires, checklists, and inventories, some of which are commercially available, may be employed in behavior analysis. Examples are the Revised Fear Survey Schedule for Children (Ollendick, 1983), the Beck Depression Inventory (BDI) (Beck & Steer, 1993), and the Alcohol Use Inventory (Horn, Wanberg, & Foster, 1990). There is no standard, generally recommended battery of assessment instruments for this purpose, and the great majority of psychometric instruments administered in behavior analysis are somewhat makeshift devices that are inadequately standardized and frequently fail to meet the reliability and validity requirements of good psychological assessment instruments.

Perhaps the easiest and most economical way of determining how frequently and under what circumstances a particular target behavior occurs is self-observation. As noted earlier in the chapter, although self-observation is not always reliable, people can be trained to make accurate and valid observations of their own behavior (Kendall & Norton-Ford, 1982). In self-observation, for purposes of behavior analysis and modification, patients are instructed to carry with them at all times materials such as index cards, a notepad, a wrist counter, and a timer to keep a record of occurrences of the target behaviors and the time, place, and circumstances under which they occur. The self-observational procedure, referred to as *self-monitoring*, can be fairly reliable when patients are carefully trained. Interestingly enough, the very process of monitoring oneself, that is, observing and tabulating occurrences of specific behaviors in which one engages, can affect the occurrences of these behaviors, sometimes in a therapeutic way (Ciminero, Nelson, & Lipinski, 1977). For example, a heavy smoker may find himself smoking less when he has to keep track of how often and how long he smokes. Other assessment procedures and instruments used in analyzing behavior for purposes of behavior modification are discussed in the next section and the next chapter.

Improving the Accuracy of Observations

A chronic problem of observational methods is that of subjectivity. Consequently, a number of special procedures have been devised to improve the objectivity and accuracy of observations. Because time frequently plays tricks on memory, it is better to record observed events immediately rather than retrospectively. Immediate recording can be facilitated by the use of a standard observational form or schedule. Video and or audio recordings are also helpful when they are not obtrusive. A more recent technique, computer-assisted observation, can help not only in recording and transcribing observational events, but, with the proper equipment, transferring the observed data from coding sheets into computer storage, cleaning up the data, analyzing it, and interpreting the results. Also available are portable microcomputer systems that facilitate the collection and analysis of observational data, and thereby increase its reliability (Kratchowill, Doll, & Dickson, 1991; Repp & Felce, 1990).

In addition to forms and machines for recording observations, methodological procedures such as subject sampling, time sampling, and incident (event) sampling can make observations more objective and efficient. Before beginning a clinical or research investigation involving observational procedures, the investigator must make a number of decisions, including what, how, when, and where the observations are to be made, and who is to be observed. With respect to the last question, that of *subject sampling*, it is obviously impractical to observe everyone who might possess the characteristics in which one is interested. Consequently, a representative sample of the pool of potential subjects must be selected. However, even a relatively small sample of subjects cannot be observed all the time. Continuous observation of the behavior of a single person yields a voluminous amount of data, not all of which is significant or pertinent to the clinical or research questions. For this reason, it is usually wise to focus on a limited number of specific, predetermined incidents or *target behaviors*. Then a manageable but representative number of those behaviors is observed. For example, a certain target behavior may consist of incidents of aggression. Then the frequency and duration of objectively defined occurrences of aggression are recorded. In addition to this *incident sampling* procedure, the efficiency of observations may be improved by *time sampling*, that is, making a series of observations lasting for an interval of a few minutes each over a period of a day or so.

Training Observers

Special procedures and devices are helpful in improving the accuracy of observations, but perhaps even more critical is the training of observers to be as perceptive and objective as possible. People typically filter their observations through their own personal biases and desires. Consequently, untrained observers usually have a great deal of difficulty making accurate observations and separating observation from interpretation or fact from opinion.

The training of observers begins by describing the form or schedule on which the observations are to be made, going over the objective definition of each target behavior and how its occurrence and duration are to be recorded. Emphasis is placed on common errors made in recording behaviors and the importance of not letting one's own biases, expectancies, personality, attitudes, or desires interfere with what is being observed. Observers must be aware of the effects of their own biases, backgrounds, and behaviors on what they see and hear, and the tendency to confuse fact with interpretation.

Because previous knowledge about certain people may lead to assumptions or expectations that they should behave in a certain way, only information that it is absolutely necessary to have about the persons to be observed should be provided to the observer. In addition, to minimize the bias in observations created by a desire to provide the researcher or supervisor with supporting data, observers should be given minimal information concerning the purposes of the research project and no details on the specific hypotheses or expected outcomes. Whenever observers are visible to the persons being observed, the former should be cautioned to remain as inconspicuous and unobtrusive as possible, remaining in the background and recording what is seen and heard without any undue display of emotion, approval or disapproval. Observer-trainees should also be provided with an opportunity to practice or role-play their observational activities and have their performance critiqued before going into the field or laboratory to make *bona fide* observations. Finally, in the interest of greater reliability, two or more observers are better than one, and defining the behaviors to be observed as specifically as possible is better than using general descriptive observational categories.

■ Interviews

Interviewing is one of the oldest and most widely used methods of assessment. Not only does it yield much of the same kind of behavioral information as observation, but information on what a person says as well as what he or she does is obtained. The interviewee's nonverbal behavior, including body postures and poses, gestures, eye movements, and the quality and pattern of speech, are important and should be noted. The major emphasis in interviewing is, however, on the content of verbal statements made by the interviewee. For this reason, an interview may be defined as a "face-to-face verbal interchange in which one person, the interviewer, attempts to elicit information or expressions of opinion or belief from another person or persons" (Maccoby & Maccoby, 1954, p. 449). Information obtained in interviews consists of details of the interviewee's background or life-history, in addition to data on feelings, attitudes, perceptions, and expectations that are not usually observable.

Successful interviewing is not an easy task; it requires skill and sensitivity and may be quite time consuming and laborious. It is as much of an art as a science: some interviewers are naturally more effective than other in putting interviewees at ease or establishing rapport and in other ways eliciting personal information. The approach of the interviewer varies with the purpose and context of the interview, but, as in any interpersonal situation, the personality and actions of both participants influence the outcomes. Thus, an interview is not a oneway, master-slave situation in which the interviewer remains unaffected; almost always it is a dynamic, two-way interchange in which the participants mutually influence one another. Not only do the actions of the interviewer affect the behavior of the interviewee, but the latter's own responses alter the responses of the former.

An interview can be an end it itself, but it may also function as a way to get acquainted or warm up, a lead-in to other assessment procedures. Most clinical and counseling psychologists like the face-to-face closeness of an interview because it enables them to acquire a "feel" for the patient or client and his or her problems and coping abilities. Personnel psychologists, employment counselors, and other interviewers usually justify the time and expense of the interview with the belief that private information of this sort cannot be obtained in any other way. Patients, counselees, and applicants usually express feelings of being more involved when interviewed that when they are merely asked to fill out paper-and-pencil questionnaires or applications and are not provided with an opportunity to communicate their problems, needs, opinions, and circumstances in person.

Interviewing Technique and Structure

A personal interview can take place anywhere, but it is usually conducted more effectively in a quiet room that is free from distractions. Both the interviewer and the interviewee should be comfortably seated, facing each other. Because interviewing is a complex interpersonal skill that is to some extent a function of the interviewer's personality, effective interviewing is not easily taught. Attention to the following recommendations, however, can improve one's interviewing skills.

Professional interviewers are usually friendly but neutral, interested but not prying in their reactions to interviewees; they are warm and open, accepting interviewees for what they are without showing approval or disapproval. They do not begin with leading questions of the "How often do you beat your wife?" sort, or ask questions that imply a certain answer (e. g., "You still do that don't you?"). By properly timing the questions and varying their content with the situation, effective interviewers are able to develop a conversation that flows from topic to topic. But they are also comfortable with silences, allowing the interviewee sufficient time to answer a question completely, and listening to the answer without interrupting. In addition, they pay attention not only to what the interviewee says but also the manner in which it is said. Realizing that the interviewer's behavior (activity level, amount and speed of talking, etc.) tends to be imitated by the interviewee, a trained interviewer is patient and comfortable and does not hurry the interviewee. Skilled interviewers also check their understandings, impressions, and perceptions of interviewees' statements by asking for clarification or repetition. They may rephrase an interviewee's answers to clarify them, making certain that they do not misunderstand, or ask direct questions to fill in gaps. They are, however, not voyeurs who unremittingly probe or relish the discussion of certain topics and consciously or unconsciously reinforce an interviewee's statements pertaining to those matters.

Although the techniques described above are generally applicable in an effective interview, the specific techniques that are applied vary with the theoretical orientation (behavioral, client-centered, psychoanalytic, etc.) of the interviewer, as well as the goals and stage of the interviewing process. Most interviewers outside of clinical contexts, as well as many clinicians, are fairly eclectic in their orientation, following no particular theory of personality but applying relevant concepts from a variety of theories.

Structured and Unstructured Interviews. The degree to which an interview is *structured* should depend primarily on the goals of the interview, but it is also important to consider the characteristics of the interviewee and the interviewer. Some interviewees respond more readily to a relatively unstructured, open-ended approach; others provide more relevant information when the interviewer follows an *interviewing guide* in deciding what questions to ask. In addition, certain interviewers feel more comfortable and accomplish more when using the highly structured procedure of asking a series of questions similar to those found on an application blank or personal history form. Less experienced interviewers typically find it easier to handle a structured interview, the results of which can be more easily quantified for purposes of analysis (see Hodges & Zeman, 1993). On the other hand, many experienced interviewers prefer greater flexibility in the content and timing of interview questions, in other words, less structure.

It requires more skill and time to conduct an interview in an unstructured or open-ended manner. but the interviewer can follow up interesting leads or concentrate on details of greater significance. To accomplish this the interviewer encourages the interviewee to feel free to discuss his or her problems, interests, behaviors, or whatever else is relevant to the goals of the interview. When answers to a large number of specific questions are needed, as in an employment selection situation, a fairly structured interview is appropriate. When the goal is to obtain an in-depth picture of a personality or to define the nature of certain personal problems and their causes, a more unstructured interview is desirable. Whether highly structured or relatively open-ended, the sequence of questions in an interview should usually proceed from general to specific and from less personal to more personal topics. Most professional interviewers are able to vary their approach with the personality of the interviewee and the objectives of the interview.

They begin by asking a series of nonthreatening, open-ended questions to establish rapport and get the conversation going, and then become more specific and personal in their questioning as the interview progresses.

Interview Topics and Questions. The specific questions asked depend on the purposes of the interview, but it is helpful to prepare beforehand by outlining the topics to be covered if not the exact questions. A general topical outline for an interview designed for a comprehensive psychological assessment is given in Table 5–1. A complete life-history interview, whether conducted in a clinical, social service, employment, or research context, requires obtaining the kinds of information listed in this table. Not all of the topics need to be covered in a given situation; the interviewer can concentrate on those areas that are consid-

---

TABLE 5–1 Information to Obtain in an Assessment Interview.

Identifying Data: Name, age, sex, education, ethnic group, nationality, address, date of birth, marital status, date of interview, and so forth.

Purpose(s) of Interview: Employment, psychiatric intake, psychodiagnostic, problem solving or troubleshooting, performance evaluation, termination or exit.

Physical Appearance: Clothing, grooming, physical description (attractiveness, unusual features, etc.), obvious or apparent physical disorders or disabilities.

Behavior: Attitudes and emotions (cooperative, outgoing or reserved, friendly or hostile, defensive, etc.); motoric behavior (active versus passive, posture, gait, carriage); level of intellectual functioning (bright, average, retarded—estimated from vocabulary, immediate and long-term memory, judgment, abstract thinking); signs of mental disorder (distorted thought processes—bizarre constructions, thought blocking, etc; distorted perceptions—delusions, hallucinations, disorientation in time or space, etc; inappropriate or extreme emotional reactions—depression, mania; unusual mannerisms, postures, or facial expressions).

Family: Parents, siblings, other family members; sociocultural group; attitude(s) toward family members.

Medical History: Present health, health history, physical problems.

Developmental History: Physical, intellectual, language, emotional, and social development; irregularities or problem of development.

Education and Training: Schools attended, performance level, adjustment to school, plans for further education and training.

Employment: Nature and number of jobs or positions held, military service (rank and duties), job performance level(s), job problems.

Legal Problems: Arrests and convictions, nature of misdemeanors or felonies.

Sexual and Marital History: Sexual activities and problems, marriages, marital problems, separations and divorce(s), children.

Interests and Attitudes: Hobbies, recreational activities, social activities and attitude(s) toward others, level of self-acceptance and satisfaction, aspirations or goals.

Current Problems: Details of current problems and plans for solving them.

ered most important. In any event, the specific interview questions, expressed in words with which the interviewer is familiar and comfortable, can be developed from the outline.

Clinical Interviewing

Interviews are conducted in various contexts and for a wide range of purposes. In research contexts, they are used for polling, for surveys, and for obtaining in-depth information on personality and behavior to test some hypothesis or theoretical proposition. In employment situations, interviews are used for selection and screening, evaluation or appraisal, troubleshooting, and termination. In clinical contexts, intake or diagnostic interviews of patients and their relatives are essential for obtaining case histories for making medical and/or psychological diagnoses. Therapeutic interviews are part of the psychological treatment process and exit interviews are designed to determine whether a person is ready for release from a treatment center or institution.

In clinical interviews conducted for intake purposes at a social agency or mental hospital, in diagnostic interviews to determine the causes and correlates of an person's problems, and in therapeutic interviews (counseling, psychotherapy) it is recommended that, among other things, the interviewer:
— Assure the interviewee of confidentiality of the interview.
— Convey a feeling of interest and warmth (rapport).
— Try to put the interviewee at ease.
— Try to "get in touch" with how the interviewee feels (empathy).
— Be courteous, patient, and accepting.
— Encourage the interviewee to express his or her thoughts and feelings freely.
— Adjust the questions to the cultural and educational background of the interviewee.
— Avoid psychiatric or psychological jargon.
— Avoid leading questions.
— Share personal information and experiences with the interviewee (self-disclosure) if appropriate and accurately timed.
— Use humor sparingly, and only if appropriate and not insulting.
— Listen without overreacting emotionally.
— Attend not only to what is said but also to how it is said.
— Take notes or make a recording as inconspicuously as possible.

Many of these recommendations are, of course, not restricted to clinical interviews.

When properly conducted, a diagnostic or therapeutic interview can provide a great deal of information about a person, including: the nature, duration, and severity of his or her problems; how the problems are manifested (inwardly or outwardly); what past influences are related to present difficulties;* the person's resources and limitations for coping with the problems; the kinds of psychological assistance the person has had in the past; what kinds of assistance are expected and might be of help now.

In many instances, structured diagnostic interviewing can be made less difficult, as well as more objective and efficient, by using a standard form such as the Psychiatric Diagnostic Interview–Revised (PDI-R) by E. Othmer and his coauthors (from Western Psychological Services). Based on the clinical criteria of *Diagnostic and Statistical Manual* of the American Psychiatric Association (1987), the PDI-R can be administered by a psychologist, a psychiatrist, or a trained and supervised paraprofessional to a person 18 years or older. From the interviewee's "yes" or "no" responses to a series of questions pertaining to basic psychiatric syndromes, the PDI-R reveals whether the interviewee has, or has every had, any of 17 basic psychiatric syndromes or four derived syndromes. Another useful standardized psychodiagnostic interviewing instrument is the Structured Clinical Interview for DSM-III-R (SCID) (Spitzer, Williams, Gibbon, & First, 1992).

Useful in the diagnosis of of emotional disorders in which anxiety is a prominent component are the interview schedules and clinician manuals of the Anxiety Disorders Interview Schedule for DSM-IV (from The Psychological Corporation). Both Child and Adult & Lifetime versions of this schedule are available. The questions on the Child Version are concerned with assisting in the diagnosis of anxiety-related conditions such as school refusal behavior, separation anxiety, school phobia, specific phobia, panic disorder, agoraphobia, obsessive-compulsive disorder, post-traumatic stress disorder, and attention-deficit/hyperactivity disorder. In addition to anxiety disorders, questions on the Adult & Lifetime Version can facilitate identification and understanding of mood disorders, substance abuse disorders, and somatoform disorders.

Mental Status Interview. A special type of diagnostic interview known as a *mental status interview* is used in both clinical and legal contexts to determine the mental competence of an individual for legal and psychiatric purposes. A mental status interview is designed to obtain in-depth information about a person's:
— Emotional state (affect and mood)
— Intellectual and perceptual functioning (attention, concentration, memory, intelligence, judgment)

* A recent approach devised in Germany for research on the retrospective assessment of premorbid personality traits of psychiatric patients is the Biographical Personality Interview (BPI). The procedure requires two independent, specially trained investigators—one who conducts the clinical interview, and the other who rates the personality traits in the resulting interview protocol. Acceptance and inter-rater reliabilities of the BPI procedure are satisfactory, and scores on the six personality types statistically differentiated between diagnostic groups (von Zerssen et al., 1998a, 1998b).

- Style and content of thought processes and speech
- Level of insight into his or her mental status and personality problems
- Psychomotor activity
- General appearance
- Attitude
- Insight into his or her condition

The categories that are covered and examples from a report of a mental status interview of a patient are given in Table 5-2.

A number of interview and observation schedules for use in mental status examinations are available. An example is the Schedule for Affective Disorders and Schizophrenia (3rd ed.) (SADS),* which provides information consistent with the various categories of the American Psychiatric Association's *Diagnostic and Statistical Manual* (DSM-III-R). Each of the three forms of SADS consists of two parts. Part 1 contains a series of open-ended questions and rating scales concerning the occurrence and severity of certain symptoms during the previous week. Part 2, which focuses primarily on information about the patient's psychiatric history, consists of a series of checklists to be answered Yes, No, or No information. Not all of the questions need to be asked; a branching procedure allows the

---

Categories and Examples from Report of a Mental Status Interview. **TABLE 5-2**

General Appearance, Attitude, and Behavior: He is friendly and cooperative. He has made no complaints about ward restrictions. He smiles in a somewhat exaggerated and grotesque manner.
Discourse: He answers in a deep, loud voice, speaking in a slow, precise, and somewhat condescending manner. His responses are relevant but vague.
Mood and Affective Fluctuations: His facial expressions, although not totally inappropriate, are poorly correlated with the subject of discourse or events in his environment.
Sensorium and Intellect: The patient's orientation to place, person, and time is normal. His remote and recent memory also are normal. Two brief intelligence measures indicate about average intelligence.
Mental Content and Specific Preoccupations: He readily discusses what he calls his "nervous trouble." He complains of "bad thoughts" and a "conspiracy." He reports hearing voices saying, "Hello, Bill, you're a dirty dog."
Insight: The patient readily accepts the idea that he should be in the hospital. He feels that hospitalization will help him get rid of these "bad" thoughts. He is not in the least defensive about admitting to auditory and visual hallucinations or to the idea that everyone on earth is his enemy.

Source: Kleinmuntz, 1982, 1985. Reprinted by permission of Robert Krieger Publishing Company.

---

* Available from Department of Research Assessment and Training, New York State Psychiatric Institute, 722 West 168th Street, New York, NY 10032.

interviewer to skip certain questions, depending on the interviewee's answers to other questions. After completing the schedule, the interviewer makes a diagnostic decision depending on the specific answers given.

A review by Arbisi (1995) concluded that SADS appears to have realized its goal as a research tool and not as an aid for clinicians in making diagnoses. It has good diagnostic reliability but requires a highly trained administrator in order to attain an acceptable level of reliability. Arbisi recommends that if a reliable DSM-III-R diagnosis is needed and resources required to achieve such expertise are not available, then the structured interview provided by SCID (Spitzer et al., 1992) is preferable to SADS.

Computer-Based Interviewing. Psychodiagnostic interviewing can be automated by storing in a computer a set of questions and instructions so the computer asks a questions, receives an answer, and decides ("conditionally branches") what question to ask next. Such branching strategies have been applied effectively in patient data systems at numerous psychiatric hospitals.

Representative of available computer software packages for psychodiagnostic interviewing and report preparation are the Diagnostic Interview for Children and Adolescents (from Multi-Health Systems), the Giannetti On-Line Psychosocial History (GOLPH) (Giannetti, 1987; from National Computer Systems), and the Quickview Social History (from National Computer Systems). Software that enables clinicians to develop their own interviews or to modify existing interviews is also available.

As with other psychometric applications of computers, the advantages of interviewing by computer are efficiency, flexibility, and reliability. Computerized interviews save professional time, permit a broader coverage of topics, are more flexible than most questionnaires, and have greater reliability than person-to-person interviews. There is generally a high degree of agreement between information obtained by computer interviewing and that elicited from standard psychiatric interviews and questionnaires. Furthermore, being interviewed by a computer is not objectionable to most people. Patients are often more willing to divulge personal information, particularly of a sensitive nature, to an impersonal, nonjudgmental computer than to a human interviewer (Farrell, 1993; Rosenfeld et al., 1989). Computers are, however, limited in their ability to deal with anything other than highly structured information (Erdman, Klein, & Greist, 1985). They also have limited utility in crisis cases and with children and adults of low mentality, and they may not be flexible enough for use with the wide range of problems and symptoms found in psychiatric patients.

Behavioral Interviews. A *behavioral interview* is a type of clinical interview that focuses on obtaining information to plan a program of behavior modification. As discussed earlier in the chapter, this entails describing, in objective behavioral terms, the problem behaviors of the person as well as the antecedent conditions and reinforcing consequences. In order for such an interview to be conducted successfully, the interviewee must be encouraged (and taught if necessary) to respond in specific behavioral terms rather than in the more customary language of motives and traits. After the information needed to develop a behavior modification program has been obtained, the patient must then be familiarized with the program and motivated to follow it.

Stress Interviewing. The usual rule of cordiality toward the interviewee is suspended in a *stress interview*. A goal of stress interviewing, which is employed in clinical, selection, and interrogation contexts, is to determine the interviewee's ability to cope with or solve a specific problem under conditions of emotional stress. Stress interviewing may also be appropriate when time is short or when the interviewee is very repetitious, emotionally unresponsive, or quite defensive. The following excerpt from a case study by Butcher (personal communication) is illustrative of the defensiveness and resistance offered by some patients:

> During the intake interview, Mr. D was sullen, argumentative, and difficult for the examiner to relate to. He took a long time to answer questions that were asked, was reluctant to discuss his present legal problems, and tended to change the subject when his charges were discussed with him.*

In stress interviewing, an attempt is made to produce a valid emotional response—to get beneath the superficial social mask of the interviewee—by asking probing, challenging questions in a kind of police interrogation atmosphere. A great deal of professional expertise is obviously required to make such an approach appear realistic and to keep the situation from getting out of control.

Methode Clinique and Morality Research. The clinical method of interviewing, in which the interviewer asks probing questions to test the limits or elicit in-depth information about a person, was employed extensively by Sigmund Freud, Jean Piaget, and many other famous psychologists. The use of clinical interviewing in research, referred to as the *methode clinique*, requires considerable skill.

An example of a research instrument that involves the *methode clinique* is Lawrence Kohlberg's Moral Judgment Scale. Kohlberg (1969, 1974) maintained that the development of moral judgment in a person progresses through three ascending levels, consisting of two stages each. At the lowest level (*premoral level*), moral judgments are guided either by punishment and obedience or by a kind of naive pleasure-pain philosophy. At an intermediate level (*morality of conventional rule conformity*), morality depends either on the approval of other people ("good boy-good girl") morality or adherence to the precepts of authority.

* Courtesy of James N. Butcher, personal communication.

In the first stage of the highest level (*morality of self-accepted moral principles*), morality is viewed in terms of acceptance of a contract or democratically determined agreement. In the second stage of the highest level, an internal set of principles and a conscience that directs the person's judgment and behavior develops.

The Moral Judgment Scale is administered by presenting to the examinee nine hypothetical moral dilemmas and obtaining judgments and reasons for the judgment associated with each dilemma. One such dilemma, that of Heinz and the druggist, is as follows:

> In Europe, a woman was near death from a special kind of cancer. There was one drug that the doctors thought might save her. It was a form of radium that a druggist in the same town had recently discovered. The drug was expensive to make, but the druggist was charging ten times what the drug cost him to make. He paid $200 for the radium and charged $2000 for a small does of the drug. The sick woman's husband, Heinz, went to everyone he knew to borrow the money, but he could only get together about $1000 which is half of what it cost. He told the druggist that his wife was dying, and asked him to sell it cheaper or let him pay later. But the druggist said, "No, I discovered the drug and I'm going to make money from it." So Heinz got desperate and broke into the man's store to steal the drug for his wife. (From Kohlberg & Elfenbein, 1975. Reprinted, with permission, from the *American Journal of Orthopsychiatry*. Copyright 1975 by the American Orthopsychiatric Association, Inc.).

Scoring responses to stories such as this one in terms of the levels or stages described by Kohlberg obviously involves making subjective evaluations of the examinee's responses.

Employment Interviews

Production and service organizations of all types make use of interviews for purposes of selecting, classifying, and placing employees, as well as for counseling, troubleshooting, termination (exit interview), and research. Interviewing is an expensive and time consuming process, so it is reasonable to wonder if it is the most efficient procedure for obtaining data on job applicants. Structured interviewing is the preferred approach in most employment settings, but much of the information produced in this way can be obtained more easily from an application blank or questionnaire. Job applicants are, however, usually more willing to reveal matters of significance in the personal atmosphere of an interview than in writing. In any case, a personal interview is the final step in selecting employees for all but the lowest-level jobs in most organizational settings.

Employment interviewers usually have available a variety of other information concerning applicants, including that supplied by application blanks, letters of recommendation, test scores, and the like. The task of an employment interviewer is to integrate data from all of these sources with that obtained from a personal interview to make job recommendations or decisions about applicants.

Employment interviewers must be careful in asking questions pertaining to private, personal matters. Such questions may not only place interviewees under a great deal of emotional stress, but they may also be illegal. According to the Equal Employment Opportunity Commission, it is permissible to ask the following questions in an employment interview ("Interview Questions," 1980, p. 8):
- How many years experience do you have?
- (To a housewife) Why do you want to return to work?
- What are your career goals?
- Who have been your prior employers?
- Why did you leave your last job?
- Are you a veteran? Did the military provide you with job-related experience?
- If you have no phone, where can we reach you?
- What languages do you speak fluently?
- Can you do extensive traveling?
- Who recommended you to us?
- What did you like or dislike about your previous jobs?
- What is your educational background? What schools did you attend?
- What are your strong points? Weaknesses?
- Do you have any objection if we check with your former employer for references?

On the other hand, it is illegal to ask the following questions:
- What is your age?
- What is your date of birth?
- Do you have children? If so, how old are they?
- What is your race?
- What church do you attend?
- Are you married, divorced, separated, widowed, or single?
- Have you ever been arrested?
- What kind of military discharge do you have?
- What clubs or organizations do you belong to?
- Do you rent or own your own home?
- What does your wife (husband) do?
- Who lives in your household?
- Have your wages ever been attached or garnished?
- What was your maiden name (female applicants)?

Reliability and Validity of Interviews

Interviewing is an important psychological assessment tool, but it has problems of reliability and validity similar to those of the observational method. In order to be reliable, responses must show some consistency across time and situation.

But in the case of the interview, the measuring instrument—the interviewer—may vary in appearance, approach and style. Because these factors affect the impressions made on interviewees, a particular interviewer may appear friendly, outgoing, and approachable to one interviewee but hostile and remote to another. The interviewer's perceptions of an interviewee can also be affected by the experiences and personality of the former.

A common procedure for determining the reliability of an interview is to compare the ratings assigned to interviewee responses by two or more interviewers. The resulting interrater reliability coefficient varies with the sample of interviewees and interviewers, the specificity of the questions asked, and the behaviors being rated. Reliability is higher for structured and semistructured interviews than for unstructured ones, and higher when the interviewer-raters are carefully trained. But even when the interview questions are fairly specific and objective, the reliability coefficients are rarely higher than .80 (Bradley & Caldwell, 1977; Disbrow, Doerr, & Caulfield, 1977).

The interviewer is the assessment instrument in an interview, so many of the reliability problems of interviews are related to his or her characteristics and behavior. The interviewer is almost always in charge in an interviewing situation, and his or her personality and biases are usually more significant than those of the interviewee in determining what kinds of information are obtained. The interviewer's appearance and behavior are typically more influential than those of the interviewee in establishing the socioemotional tone of the interview. The interviewer usually talks more, and the length of the interviewee's answers is directly related to the length of the questions asked. In addition to being overly dominant, an interviewer may ask the wrong questions, not encourage or permit enough time for complete answers, and not record the responses correctly, thereby failing to obtain complete, accurate information.

Among the other shortcomings of interviewers are the tendency to assign more weight to first impressions and to be influenced more by unfavorable than favorable information about an interviewee. Errors affecting ratings also occur in interviewers' judgments. The *halo effect* of making judgments, both favorable and unfavorable, on the basis of a "general impression" or a single prominent characteristic of the interviewee is an example of such an error. This effect occurs when a person who is actually above average or below average on only one or two characteristics is given an overall above average or below average evaluation. Another example is the *contrast error* of judging an average interviewee as below average when the preceding interviewee received an above average evaluation or as above average when the preceding interview was judged as below average.

An interviewer's impressions are influenced by the neatness, posture, and other nonverbal behaviors of an interviewee, as well as the interviewee's verbal responses. Consequently, prospective interviewees would do well to prepare themselves, both mentally and physically, for interviews. Applicants for employment should have some knowledge of the organization and its philosophy, and be prepared to give a synopsis of their background and aspirations. They should refrain from controversial comments or engaging in bad habits such as smoking or nailbiting during an interview.

Regarding the validity of the interview as an employment selection or clinical diagnostic technique, a consistent research finding is that it is overrated (Arvey, 1979; Reilly & Chao, 1982). Interviews can be made more valid, but they must be carefully planned or structured and interviewers must receive extensive training. Interview findings are also more valid when the interviewer focuses on specific information (job or clinical) and when answers are evaluated question by question, preferably by at least two evaluators, rather than as a whole. This process can be facilitated by recording the entire interview on audiotape or videotape for later playback and evaluation. Then the task of interpreting an interviewee's responses can be separated more effectively from the actual process of interviewing. It can be argued, however, that even a videotape recording, and especially an audiotape recording, of an interview is inadequate in that pictures and words are not always clear and the emotional tone and contextual variables are often missed in an electronic recording. Consequently, a keen human observer who takes good notes is usually needed to supplement an electronic recording of an interview.

■ Application Blanks and Biographical Inventories

Interviewing is the most common procedure for obtaining biographical or life-history information, but demographic and experiential information about an individual is also available in personal documents and various data bases. Much of this information can be obtained more efficiently from an application blank or a biographical inventory.

Employment Application Blank

Although the information provided by completed application blanks and other life-history forms is useful in clinical, educational, and other contexts, the most systematic use of biographical data obtained in this manner has occurred in employment contexts. A sizable portion of the data (applicant's name, birthdate, marital status, number of dependents, employment history, etc.) is highly factual and verifiable from other sources. A substantial amount of information may also be derived from the applicant's self-observations and impressions (e.g., past experiences, interests, attitudes, aspirations).

A completed application blank is both a formal request for employment and a brief description of the applicant's fitness for a job. It provides a personnel department with an efficient, inexpensive way to determine whether an applicant meets the minimum requirements for a job. Following a series of questions to identify the applicant (name, address, employment desired, etc.), detailed background information (education, physical handicaps, military record, previous employment, and experience) is requested. If the completed application is not filed away and forgotten, it can also serve as a foundation for any subsequent interviews. Furthermore, the demographic and descriptive information obtained from a completed application blank may be numerically weighted to predict work quality, absenteeism, turnover, and other job performance criteria.

Biographical Inventories

Formal biographical inventories, or biodata forms, which consist of a variety of items pertaining to the life history of an applicant (family relationships, friendships, extracurricular activities, interests, etc.), have been constructed and used by many different organizations. A great deal of research on these longer forms of the weighted application blank has been conducted with employees at all levels of an organization (Schoenfeldt & Mendoza, 1994; Stokes, Mumford, & Owens, 1994).

Not only do biographical inventories have a great deal of content validity; they are also effective predictors of performance in a variety of job contexts ranging from unskilled work to high-level executive responsibilities (Childs & Klimoski, 1986; Drakeley, Herriot, & Jones, 1988). Furthermore, the validity of these inventories is often generalizable from one context to another (Rothstein, Schmidt, Erwin, Owens, & Sparks, 1990). Despite these advantages, biographical inventories are not widely used for personnel selection purposes (Hammer & Kleiman, 1988). One explanation is the seeming conflict between research findings and practical applications is that legal problems are associated with requests for certain kinds of information (e. g., age, sex, ethnicity, religion, marital status, number of children) on application blanks and biographical inventories. Applicants may object to certain items (personal finances, family background, and other intimate details) as being too personal or otherwise offensive (Rosenbaum, 1973). In a sense this is unfortunate because responses to these items are frequently good predictors of on-the-job performance.

References and Recommendations

A section of a typical application blank is usually provided for the names, addresses, and telephone numbers of former employers or other associates of the applicant who can be contacted for additional details and recommendations.

Information from an applicant's listed references, whether obtained from letters, telephone calls, interviews, or questionnaires, can be useful despite some obvious limitations. Letters of recommendation are probably the most limited in providing an accurate picture of an applicant's abilities and limitations. Because former employers or other reference sources are often reluctant to make negative comments about a person in writing, one telephone call is sometimes worth a dozen letters of recommendation. In fact, laudatory letters of recommendation are so common that personnel administrators and other selection officials may become overly sensitive to anything less than very positive written statements about an applicant. There is also a tendency to interpret short letters as indicative of disapproval of the applicant and longer letters as more complimentary.

■ Summary

Observations of behavior and personal interviews are the oldest, if not the most accurate, methods of personality assessment. Depending on their purpose and the situation in which they take place, observations may be formal or informal, and controlled or uncontrolled. Uncontrolled, or naturalistic, observations occur in situations in which the individuals who are being observed are unaware of the observers. Examples are observing a group of children on a playground, a crowd at a sporting event, or people walking, working, or just "hanging out" in the street. This is the most common and least expensive form of observation. However, it is usually not as objective nor as scientifically useful as controlled observations of individual behavior or interactions among people in a prearranged, contrived situation.

Special types of observational procedures include *participant observation*, in which the observer is a part of the situation where the observations take place; *situational testing*, in which the participants are given a task to solve in a seemingly realistic but actually prearranged situation under frustrating conditions; and *self-observation*, in which a person makes a detailed record of his or her own behavior. Self-observations, recorded in diaries and other personal documents, are sometimes interpreted by content analysis procedures.

The objectivity and efficiency of observations can be improved by methodological procedures such as subject-, time-, and incident-sampling; electronic recording and analysis; and careful training of observers. Observers should be trained to attend to both the verbal and nonverbal (kinesics, proximics, paralinguistics, culturics) of the individuals whom they are observing.

Although the procedures employed in collecting observational data for purposes of behavior modification are not radically different from those used to collect observations for other purposes, the behavioral model emphasizes careful specifications of the target behavior (B), the antecedent condition (A), and the consequences (C) of the behavior. The observer records the occurrence and duration of the target behavior to establish an operant level or baseline and changes in the rate and duration of the behavior after the behavior modification program is instituted. A common approach in behavior modification is to have the patient record his or her own target behaviors, a procedure referred to as self-monitoring.

An interview is a face-to-face verbal interchange in which one person attempts to elicit information or expressions of opinion or belief from another person. The obtained information is usually concerned with the background or life-history of the interviewee, in addition to the feelings, perceptions, and attitudes of the interviewee. Although anyone who enjoys conversing with other people can conduct an interview of sorts, certain individuals, usually those who have been trained extensively, are more effective interviewers than others.

A professional interviewer begins by establishing rapport with the interviewee and then, depending on whether the interview is structured, semistructured, or unstructured, asks both general and specific questions to derive a psychological portrait of the interviewee. Variations from a standard format are characteristic of unstructured interviewing, in which the interviewer feels free to follow up interesting leads by asking additional questions. The interviewer must be cautious about asking certain questions, not only because they may embarrass the interviewee but because they are illegal in certain (e. g., employment) contexts.

Structured interviews, in which a sequence of objective, preplanned questions is asked, are simpler to conduct and usually more reliable than unstructured interviews. However, they lack the flexibility of less structured interviews, which are more likely to reveal in-depth information about the interviewee. The particular approach of the interviewer varies with the context and purposes of the interview. In personnel or employment contexts, greater emphasis is placed on whether the interviewee can perform, can learn to perform, or is effectively performing a certain job. In clinical contexts, the emphasis is more on determining the nature and causes of a person's psychological problems and whether or not the person is competent.

Special types of clinical interviews include: mental status interview, which is conducted for psychiatric and legal purposes to determine the mental competence of an interviewee; computer interview, which entails programming a computer to ask a series of questions in a structured or semistructured format; behavior interview, which is designed to obtain information for planning a program of behavior modification; and stress interview, designed to break down an individual's defenses by treating him or her in a confrontational manner and asking stress-provoking questions.

The reliability of an interview is usually determined by correlating the judgments or ratings given by two or more interviewers to the same person. The resulting interrater reliability coefficients are typically quite modest. The reliabilities are higher for structured than for unstructured interviews, and higher with trained than with untrained interviewers. The training of interviewers emphasizes efforts to minimize the effects of the biases, expectations, and personality of the interviewer on the responses given by the interviewee and making an objective recording of the interview.

Much of the objective data concerning a person's life-history or background can be obtained more efficiently from an application blank or biographical inventory than from an interview. Information from the first two sources is also useful for interviewers to have on hand to guide their questioning of interviewees in an attempt to verify the data and obtain supplementary or in-depth information. Additional information about applicants in personnel contexts can be obtained from letters of recommendation and telephone calls to former employers or other individuals who are acquainted with the applicant. Letters and telephone calls to relatives, physicians, and others who have come in contact with a patient are also helpful in making diagnoses and prescribing treatments in clinical contexts.

■ Questions and Activities

1. Make a series of careful observations of a student in one of your courses, preferably someone whom you don't know and toward whom you have neutral feelings. Unobtrusively watch the person over a period of three or four class meetings, inconspicuously recording what he or she does and says. Try to be as objective as possible, looking for consistent, typical behaviors, as well as noting responses that occur infrequently. At the end of the observation period, write a two- to three-page description of what you have seen and heard. Without having access to any other information about his person (what other students say about the person, how well he or she does in college, and the like), how would you describe his or her personality and characteristic behavior? Finally, check your observations against those of other people who are acquainted with or have observed this person carefully. After this experience of close observation using a time sampling technique, how do you feel about objective observation as a method of assessing personality? Do you consider it a valid and useful method of obtaining data on personality?

2. Ask six people, one at a time, to make facial expressions indicative of each of the following emotions: anger, disgust, fear, happiness, sadness, surprise. Make notes on the facial expressions that differentiate among the various emotions. Did your "actors" find the task difficult? Was there a reasonable degree of consistency from person to person in the expressions characterizing a

particular emotion? Were certain emotions easier to express and were they expressed more consistently than other emotions?

3. Referring to the outline on pages and other interviewing guidelines that are available to you, conduct a structured personal interview of someone whom you do not know well. Write up the results as a formal report providing identifying information, a summary of the interview findings, and recommendations pertaining to treatment of the interviewee.

4. Conduct a simulated employment interview with an acquaintance. A fairly structured interview is most appropriate if you are a beginning interviewer. A list of questions to be asked during the interview should be prepared beforehand. However, you should feel free to deviate from the interview schedule if you later think of questions that are more pertinent to the applicant's job performance. Make certain that all questions you ask are job-related and legally acceptable.

5. Compare observational and interview methods of personality assessment in terms of their simplicity, objectivity, reliability, validity, and any other advantages or disadvantages that they may possess. For what kinds of assessment situations are observations most appropriate? For what situations are they least appropriate?

6. Differentiate between planned and unplanned, controlled and uncontrolled observations. Between structured and unstructured interviews. What are the relative advantages and disadvantages of observational and interviewing approaches to personality assessment?

7. What is participant observation, in what contexts is it most useful, and what are its benefits and shortcomings? Similarly, could there be such a thing as participant interviewing in which two or more people simultaneously interview each other? In what situations or contexts might such *participant interviewing* be a useful personality assessment method?

■ Suggested Readings

Beutler, L.E. (1995). The clinical interview. In L.E. Beutler & M.R. Berren (Eds.), *Integrative assessment of adult personality* (pp. 94–120). New York: Guilford Press.

Edelbrock, C., & Costello, A.J. (1990). Structured interviews for children and adolescents. In G. Goldstein & M. Hersen (Eds.), *Handbook of psychological assessment* (2nd ed., pp. 308–323). New York: Pergamon.

Hartmann, D.P., & Wood, D.D. (1990). Observational methods. In A.S. Bellack, M. Hersen, & A.E. Kazdin (Eds.), *International handbook of behavior modification and therapy* (2nd ed., pp. 107–138). New York: Plenum.

Haynes, S.N. (1990). Behavioral assessment of adults. In G. Goldstein & M. Hersen

(Eds.), *Handbook of psychological assessment* (2nd ed., pp. 423–463). New York: Pergamon.

Hersen, M., & Van Hasselt, V.B. (Eds.). (1998). *Basic interviewing: A practical guide for counselors and clinicians*. Mahwah, NJ: Erlbaum.

Hodges, K., & Zeman, J. (1993). Interviewing. In T.H. Ollendick & M. Hersen (Eds.), *Handbook of child and adolescent assessment* (pp. 65–81). Boston: Allyn & Bacon.

Leichtman, M. (1995). Behavioral observations. In J.N. Butcher (Ed.), *Clinical personality assessment: Practical approaches* (pp. 251–266). New York: Oxford University Press.

Ollendick, T.H., & Green, R. (1990). Behavioral assessment of children. In G. Goldstein & M. Hersen (Eds.), *Handbook of psychological assessment* (2nd ed., pp. 403–422). New York: Pergamon.

Phares, E.J. (1992). The assessment interview. In *Clinical psychology: Concepts, methods, & profession* (4th ed., pp. 150–178). Belmont, CA: Wadsworth.

Rogers, R. (1995). *Diagnostic and structured interviewing: A handbook for psychologists*. Odessa, FL: Psychological Assessment Resources.

Wiens, A.N. (1990). Structured clinical interviews for adults. In G. Goldstein & M. Hersen (Eds.), *Handbook of psychological assessment* (2nd ed., pp. 324–344). New York: Pergamon.

Chapter 6

Checklists and Rating Scales

Information obtained from controlled and uncontrolled observations or structured and unstructured interviews may be recorded and analyzed in a variety of ways. Because of the large quantity of data yielded by a lengthy observational session or by a comprehensive interview, the findings must be summarized and interpreted in a form suitable for a report to a referring agency or an individual. People to whom psychological examination reports are transmitted are typically quite busy and not always patient with tedious, rambling descriptions of insignificant or irrelevant behavior. Therefore, such reports should contain only enough information to provide a clear picture of the observational or interview results and what they seem to indicate.

Simplifying and summarizing the findings of a lengthy observational session or a comprehensive, in-depth interview can be facilitated by the use of a properly constructed checklist or rating scale. A checklist consists of a set of descriptive terms, phrases, or statements pertaining to actions and thoughts that the checker endorses, that is, checks, underlines, or in some other way indicates acceptance of. The person to whom the checklist items pertain may be the checker himself (herself) or someone else about whom the checker has sufficient information to make the required judgments. Unlike the items on a checklist, which require dichotomous judgments, responses to rating scales are made on multiple categories or on continua (straight lines). Different categories, or different points on the continuum, of a rating scale correspond to different frequencies or intensities of the particular behavior or characteristic that is being rated.

Although checklists and rating scales have been in use since the last century, during recent years interest in constructing standardized instruments of these kinds and conducting both theoretical and applied research with them has been rekindled. One reason for this renewed interest is the recognition that the effectiveness of mental health, educational, and other social intervention programs cannot be taken for granted but must be periodically reevaluated. The need to determine whether such programs, which are frequently supported by governmental and private grants, produce appropriate changes in behavior, cognition, attitudes, and feelings has led to the construction of more carefully designed and standardized evaluation instruments. In many instances, particularly when the programs call for repeated, periodic evaluations, multiple forms of the same instrument are required. To meet this need, checklists and rating scales have been constructed in large numbers.

■ Checklists

A *checklist* is a relatively simple, highly cost-effective, and fairly reliable method of describing or evaluating a person. More easily constructed than rating scales and personality inventories, but frequently just as valid, checklists can be administered as self-report or observer-report instruments. A checklist may be filled out by the person who is being evaluated or by a parent, teacher, supervisor, spouse, or peer. In completing a checklist, the respondent marks the words or phrases in a list that he or she views as descriptive of the individual who is being evaluated. Responses to checklists are usually scored dichotomously (1 point for checking and 0 points for not checking an item, or +1 for a checked item and −1 point for an unchecked item). Other numerical weights are occasionally used in scoring, but differential item weighting makes little difference in the reliability and validity of a checklist when the number of items is large. When a number of judges or checkers evaluate a person on the same items of a checklist, the person's score on each item can be set equal to the number of judges who checked it and perhaps converted to a percentage figure.

In scoring checklists, the so-called *frequency response set*—the tendency of some individuals to check more items than other individuals, no matter whom they are evaluating—must be handled in some way. One procedure is to use some form of statistical control for this response set before scoring the content variables or scales. For example, in standardizing the Adjective Check List, the frequency distribution of the number of items checked by respondents in the standardization sample was divided into five categories and standard scores on the other (content) variables were computed separately for each of the categories. Thus, converting an examinee's scores on the various content scales of the Adjective Check List begins by computing the number of adjectives checked by the examinee and then using this number to refer to the appropriate norms tables for the particular category in which the number falls. Other statistical possibilities for controlling for the frequency response set in scoring checklists are described by Aiken (1996).

Despite their simplicity of construction, checklists are usually fairly reliable. Furthermore, assuming that a checklist is not the only instrument that is being administered in a personality or clinical assessment, the flexibility and efficiency of a checklist may outweigh its disadvantages.

An example of a checklist that can be employed repeatedly, in this case to record the presence of behaviors indicative of anxiety, is shown in Form 6–1. Used in connection with the application of *desensitization*, a behavior modification procedure for treating anxieties and fears, the form allows one to check relevant behaviors over several time periods. In this way, it serves as a reliably recorded source of information on changes produced by treatment and other intervening events.

A Behavioral Checklist for Performance Anxiety.   **FORM 6–1**

Behavior Observed	Time Period							
	1	2	3	4	5	6	7	8
1. Paces								
2. Sways								
3. Shuffles feet								
4. Knees tremble								
5. Extraneous arm and hand movement (swings, scratches, toys, etc.)								
6. Arms rigid								
7. Hands restrained (in pockets, behind back, clasped)								
8. Hand tremors								
9. No eye contact								
10. Face muscles tense (drawn, tics, grimaces)								
11. Face "deadpan"								
12. Face pale								
13. Face flushed (blushes)								
14. Moistens lips								
15. Swallows								
16. Clears throat								
17. Breathes heavily								
18. Perspires (face, hands, armpits)								
19. Voice quivers								
20. Speech blocks or stammers								

Adapted from *Insight vs. Desensitization in Psychotherapy*, by Gordon L. Paul, with the permission of the publishers, Stanford University Press. © 1966 by the Board of Trustees of the Leland Stanford Junior University.

Ad hoc checklists can be prepared for specific purposes in clinical, educational, industrial/organizations, and other contexts. The problem with such "home-grown" instruments is that rarely are they adequately validated or standardized. The norms (if any) have often been obtained on unrepresentative samples, and the reliability and validity data are meager. For these reasons, it is uncertain whether the checklist is serving its intended purpose. These criticisms may also apply to standardized checklists, but hopefully not as often.

Some standardized checklists are designed for a specific purpose or to assess a specific characteristic, symptom, or group of people. Among the many conditions and circumstances for which standardized checklists are commercially available are:

adaptive behavior	moods
anxiety	multiple affects
autism	neuropsychiatric disorders
behavior disturbances	occupational preferences
career problems	parent behavior
child behavior	performance appraisal
classroom communication skills	preschool behavior
coping mechanisms	psychopathy
depression	reading readiness
developmental observation	sales attitudes
health problems	school behavior
hostility	school readiness
interests	sexual desires/activities
interpersonal relations	stress
learning disabilities	student performance
life experiences	substance abuse
listening and speaking	teacher performance
marital relations	test behavior

Of particular relevance to research and applications in the field of personality are adjective checklists, behavior and problem checklists, checklists of clinical symptoms, and personal history checklists. Examples of standardized check lists in these categories are given in Table 6–1. For example, in the personal history category are checklists that facilitate taking a patient's personal history (medical, family, educational, occupational, etc.) during intake at a treatment facility.

Adjective Checklists

Among the most widely-administered checklists for research on personality and in some clinical contexts are those that consist of a list of adjectives. Two popular representatives of this class of instruments are the Adjective Check List and the Multiple Affect Adjective Check List. Both of these are omnibus checklists, in that they can be scored on a number of variables rather than being restricted to a single variable such as anxiety, depression, or hostility.

The Adjective Check List (ACL). The Adjective Check List (Gough & Heilbrun, 1983) consists of 300 adjectives, arranged alphabetically from *absent-minded* to *zany*. The examinee takes 15–20 minutes to mark those adjectives that he or she considers self-descriptive. Responses may then be scored on the thirty-seven scales described in the 1983 manual: four modus operandi scales, fifteen need scales, nine topical scales, five transactional analysis scales, and four origence-intellectence (creativity and intelligence) scales. Scores on the modus operandi scales (total number of adjectives checked, number of favorable adjectives checked, number of unfavorable adjectives checked, communality) pertain to the manner in which the respondent has dealt with the checklist. The need scales are based on Edwards's (1954) descriptions of 15 needs in Murray's (1938) need-press theory of personality, and each of the topical scales assesses a different topic or component of interpersonal behavior (counseling readiness, personal adjustment, creative personality, masculine attributes, etc.). The transactional analysis scales are measures of the five ego functions in Berne's (1966) transactional analysis theory, and the origence-intellectence scales are measures of Welsh's origence-intellectence (creativity and intelligence) dimensions of personality.

Raw scores on the ACL scales may be converted to standard T scores for purposes of interpretation and counseling. The T scores are interpreted with reference to norms, based on 5,238 males and 4,144 females. Profiles and associated interpretations for several sample cases are also provided. As listed in the 1983 manual, the test-retest reliability coefficients of the separate scales are quite modest, ranging from .34 for the high-origence/low-intellectence scale to .77 for the aggression scale (median of .65). The internal consistency reliability coefficients of the majority of the 37 scales are higher. The ACL scales are significantly intercorrelated, and therefore should not be interpreted as independent factors. A factor analysis conducted by the author on the 15 need scales (scales 5–19) revealed three factors: Self-Confidence or Ego Strength, Goal Orientation, and Social Interaction or Friendliness.

Despite the seeming simplicity of the instrument and the low to modest reliabilities of the scales, reviews of the Adjective Check List have been fairly positive (Teeter, 1985; Zarske, 1985). The instrument is considered to be well-developed and has been particularly useful in studies of self-concept. The ACL has been used principally with normal people, but its validity in psychodiagnosis and treatment planning has not been determined.

Multiple Affect Adjective Check List-Revised (MAACL-R). The MAACL-R (Zuckerman & Lubin, 1985) consists of 132 adjectives describing feelings;

TABLE 6–1   **Checklists for Evaluating Personality Characteristics and Problems.**

Adjective Checklists

Adjective Check List (H. G. Gough & A. B. Heilbrun; CPP; high school students and older; designed to identify personal character istics of individuals; reviews MMYB 9:52 & TC 1:34)

Multiple Affect Adjective Check List–Revised (M. Zuckerman & B. Lubin, EdITS; ages 20–79; measures positive and negative affects as traits or states; reviews MMYB 10:205 & TC IV:449)

Personality Adjective Checklist (S. Strack; 21st Century Assessment; ages 16-adult; self-report measure of personality in normal adults; review MMYB 12:289)

State-Trait Depression Adjective Check Lists (B. Lubin; PAR; ages 14 and older; measures depressed mood and feelings in a form that neither implies pathology nor is judgmental; review MMYB 13:297)

Behavior & Problem Checklists

Child Behavior Checklist (T. M. Achenbach & C. Edelbrock; Thomas M. Achenbach; ages 4–18; problem behavior checklist completed on child by parent or teacher; review MMYB 11:64)

Emotional Behavioral Checklist (J. G. Dial, C. Mezger, T. Masey, & L. T. McCarron; McCarron-Dial; ages 16 and over; assesses overt emotional behavior; review MMYB 11:130)

Jesness Behavior Checklist (C. F. Jesness; MHS; ages 13–20; used by self and others to measure individuals at risk for antisocial behavior; reviews MMYB 8:594 & TC V:226)

Kohn Problem Checklist (J. Kohn; Psychological Corporation; ages 3–6; designed to assess the social and emotional functioning of preschool and kindergarten children through the systematic observation of classroom behavior; review MMYB 13:171)

Louisville Behavior Checklist (L. C. Miller; WPS; children and adolescents; screens children and adolescents for psychopathology; gives clinicians a quick, systematic, and standardized assessment of children's behavior; reviews MMYB 10:176 & TC II:430)

Mooney Problem Check Lists (R. L. Mooney & L. V. Gordon; Psychological Corporation; designed to help individuals express their personal problems; reviews MMYB 6:145 & TC II:495)

Personal Problems Checklists—Children's, Adolescent, Adult (by J. A. Schinka; PAR; designed to facilitate the rapid assessment of an individual's problems as seen from that person's point of view; reviews MMYB 10:278 & TC X:531)

Pre-School Behavior Checklist (J. McGuire & N. Richman; WPS; 2–5 year olds; screening instrument for behavioral and emotional difficulties in preschoolers; review MMYB 11:299)

Problem Experiences Checklist—Adolescent & Adult Versions (by L. Silverton; WPS; adolescents and adults; used prior to the initial intake interview to identify potential problems for further discussion; review MMYB 12:309)

Revised Behavior Problem Checklist (H. C. Quay & D. R. Peterson; PAR; grades K-12; developed as a screening measurement of dimensions of behavior problems; reviews MMYB 9:1043 & TC V:371)

TABLE 6–1 cont.

School Behavior Checklist (L. C. Miller; WPS; ages 4–13 years; teachers rate a wide range of school behaviors, from social competence to moderate social deviance that may indicate psychopathology; reviews MMYB 9:1076 & TC IV:565)
Time-Sample Behavioral Checklist (G. L. Paul, M. H. Licht, M. J. Mariotto, C. T. Power, & K. L. Engel; Research Press; adults in residential treatment settings; measures level and nature of functioning of adult residential patients and documents how and where residents and staff spend their time; review MMYB 12:401)

Clinical Symptoms Checklists
Checklist for Child Abuse Evaluation (J. Petty; PAR; children and adolescents; for investigating and evaluating children and adolescents who may have been abused or neglected)
DSM-IV Symptom Checklist Computer Program (M. First; MHS; adults, adolescents, and children; clinician clicks on the patient's symptoms in the checklist and the program suggest a potential DSM-IV differential diagnosis)
Hare Psychopathy Checklist-Revised & Screening Version (R. D. Hare; PAR; MHS; prison inmates; identifies psychopathic (antisocial) personality disorders in forensic populations; review MMYB 12:177)
Mental Status Checklist Series—Adolescent & Adult (J. A. Schinka, PAR; adult and adolescents; surveys items that are commonly included in a comprehensive mental status examination; review MMYB 10:187)
S-D Proneness Checklist (W. T. Martin; Psychologists & Educators; depressed or suicidal clients; a measure of depression and suicide-proneness; reviews MMYB 8:664 & TC 1:568)
Symptom Checklist-90-Revised (SCL-90-R) (by L. R. Derogatis; NCS Assessments; adults and adolescents aged 13 and older; identifies psychological symptoms patterns in psychiatric and medical patients and nonpatients; reviews MMYB 9:1082 & TC III:583)
Trauma Symptom Checklist for Children (by J. Briere; The Psychological Corporation; ages 8–16 years; self-report measure of posttraumatic stress and related psychological symptomatology in children who have experienced traumatic events (physical or sexual abuse, major loss, natural disaster, witnessing violence, etc.)

Personal History
Personal History Checklist-Adolescent (J. A. Schinka; PAR; ages 13–17 years; covers 8 areas commonly addressed in completing an adolescent's clinical history)
Personal History Checklist-Adult (J. A. Schinka; PAR; adult clients of mental health services; covers 8 areas commonly addressed in completing an adult's clinical history; review MMYB 11:285)

CPP = Consulting Psychologists Press; MHS = Multi-Health Systems; PAR = Psychological Assessment Resources; WPS = Western Psychological Services.
MMYB = *Mental Measurements Yearbook*; TC = *Test Critiques*

examinees check those adjectives that indicate how they generally feel (on the trait form) or how they feel today or at present (on the state form). Standard T scores on both the trait and state forms are obtained on five basic scales: Anxiety (A), Depression (D), Hostility (H), Positive Affect (PA), and Sensation Seeking (SS). Two summary standard scores—Dysphoria (Dys = A + D + H) and Positive Affect and Sensation Seeking (PASS = PA + SS)—may also be computed. Norms for the trait form of the MAACL-R are based on a representative, nationwide sample of 1,491 individuals aged 18 years and over; norms for the state form are based on a (nonrepresentative) sample of 538 students at a midwestern college. With the exception of the Sensation Seeking scale, the internal-consistency reliability coefficients for both the trait and state scales are adequate. The test-retest reliabilities are satisfactory for the trait scales but, as might be expected from momentary fluctuations in attitudes and behavior, low for the state scales. The results of validity studies on various populations, including normal adolescents and adults, counseling clients, and patients from clinics and state hospitals, are reported in the MAACL-R manual (Zuckerman & Lubin, 1985). Scores on the MAACL-R correlate in the expected direction with other measures of personality (e. g., the Minnesota Multiphasic Personality Inventory, the Profile of Mood States, peer ratings, self-ratings, and psychiatric diagnoses).

In his review of the MAACL-R, Templer (1985) concluded that it is definitely superior to its predecessor, the MAACL, and listed a number of advantages: brevity and ease of administration, provision of both state and trait measures, assessment of five affect dimensions, sensitivity to changes over time, good reliability, relatively independent of response sets, commendable construct validity, and a wide range of research applications with normal and abnormal populations, especially in assessing temporal changes.

Checklists of Behavior Problems and Clinical Symptoms

Problem behaviors of various kinds (interpersonal, education al, health, emotional, financial, religion, etc.) may also be noted during the taking of a personal history, but checklists of special problems are also widely administered. Although checklists containing "behavior" in their titles are also concerned with personal problems or problem behaviors, "behavior" in the title of a checklist often means *adaptive behavior*. Adaptive behavior does not refer specifically to personality, but rather to abilities or deficiencies in coping with the demands of everyday living. Instruments for assessing adaptive behavior are designed primarily to determine the extent to which children with physical, mental, and emotional disabilities are able to function independently in their environments.

Mooney Problem Checklists. The most time-honored of the published instruments listed in Table 6–1 is the Mooney Problem Checklists (MPC). Designed for individuals ranging from junior-high to adulthood, the four forms of the MPC consist of 210 to 330 problems concerned with health and physical development, home and family, boy and girl relations, morals and religion, courtship and marriage, economic security, school or occupation, and social and recreational matters. The examinee begins by underlining problems that are of some concern to him or her. Next, the problems of greatest concern are circled. Finally, the examinee writes a summary of his or her problems. The Mooney checklists can be scored for the number of problems in each area, but no national norms have been published. Responses are either interpreted impressionistically or compared with locally obtained norms. The test-retest reliability of the rank orders of importance of the problem areas in different groups of respondents appears satisfactory, but the validity of the Mooney instruments is made, as is the case with most problem checklists, on the basis of content.

In contrast to *narrow-band instruments* designed for an in-depth examination of specific disorders or problem areas, the Mooney Problem Checklists are *broad-band instruments*: they provide a fairly comprehensive overview of social, behavioral, and emotional functioning. Other examples of broad-band checklists are the Child Behavior Checklist and the Revised Behavior Problem Checklist. Unlike the Mooney, which is a *self-report instrument*, the last two instruments are *informant instruments* completed by a parent or teacher. Strictly speaking they are rating scales rather than checklists, in that responses are made on multiple categories.

Child Behavior Checklist (CBCL). The CBCL (Achenbach & Edelbrock, 1983) is a broad-band instrument designed to assess the behavioral problems and competencies of children as reported by their parents or others who know the child well. One of the most popular checklists used in child-clinical contexts, the parent version of the CBCL, consists of 118 Behavior Problem items to be rated on a scale of 0 (behavior "not true" of child), 1 (behavior "sometimes or somewhat true" of child), and 2 (behavior "very true or often true" of child). Scores on the social competency items are summed as Activities, Social, and School subscores.

The CBCL was standardized in 1981 on 1300 students in the Washington, D.C. area, and separate norms by gender and three age levels (4–5, 6–11, 12–16 years) on 8–9 factors are provided in the manual. The norms yield six different Child Behavior Profiles on 8–9 factors; they are grouped into Externalizing, Internalizing, and Mixed Syndromes. Test-retest reliability coefficients on the behavior problems and social competence variables are moderate to high; indexes of parental agreement are mixed. A substantial amount of validity data has been collected on the CBCL. For example CBCL scores are significantly correlated with scores on similar instruments such as the Conners' Parent Rating Scale and the Revised Behavior Problem Checklist (Conners, 1973, 1985; Quay & Peterson, 1983).

A parallel version of the Child Behavior Checklist, the Teacher's Report Form (TRF) (Achenbach & Edelbrock, 1986), is completed by teachers or teacher aides. The TRF provides a picture of the problem and adaptive behaviors of children in school settings. Respondents indicate, on a three-point scale (not true, somewhat or sometimes true, very often true), how frequently specific behaviors have occurred during the past two months. The child's academic performance is rated on a five-point scale ("far below grade" through "far above grade"), and four items concerned with adaptive behavioral functioning are rated on a seven point scale ("much less" through "much more"). The TRF was initially standardized on a sample of 6–11 year-old boys, but norms on other groups of children are also been obtained. Reported reliability and validity data appear to be satisfactory (Edelbrock & Achenbach, 1984). For example, comparisons between the TRF scores of clinical and nonclinical groups of children, in addition to comparison of children in regular classes with those in special education, have yielded significant results. Correlations of children's TRF scores with their observed behaviors have also been found to be significant (Edelbrock, 1988). A Youth Self-Report form (YSR) of the CBCL, designed for 11–18 year-old boys and girls, is also available (Achenbach & Edelbrock, 1987). Both the TRF and the YSR have received high marks from reviewers as instruments for documenting the problem behaviors of children and adolescents (Christenson, 1992; Elliott & Busse, 1992). Users of these instruments should note, however, that although they can contribute to the processes of clinical interviewing and clinical decision-making, they are not adequate, stand-alone instruments for diagnostic or classification purposes.

Revised Behavior Problem Checklist (RBPC). Similar to the Mooney checklists, this 89-item instrument was designed to identify problem behaviors in individuals aged 5–18 years (Quay & Peterson, 1983). It has been used for a variety of purposes: to screen for behavior disorders in schools, as an aid in clinical diagnosis, to measure behavior change associated with psychological or pharmacological interventions, as part of a battery to classify juvenile offenders, and to select samples for research on behavior disorders in children and adolescents. The RBPC can be completed by a teacher, a parent, or another observer in approximately 20 minutes and scored on six subscales: conduct disorder, socialized aggression, attention problems—immaturity, anxiety-withdrawal, psychotic behavior, and motor tension-excess. T score norms based on teachers' ratings are available for grades K-12. The interrater reliability coefficients for the six subscales are moderate to high, but the test-retest reliabilities are somewhat lower. Analysis of the construct validity of the RBPC indicate that it represents a consensus of what is known about maladaptive child behavior. Research findings show that the subscale scores are significantly related to various criteria of behavior problems.

Symptom Checklists. Even more analytic or diagnostic in their orientation than the above instruments are symptom checklists such as the Mental Status Checklist Series (Adult and Adolescent) and the Derogatis Symptom Checklist Series. Each of the two Mental Status Checklists (from Psychological Assessment Resources) consists of 120 items pertaining to matters typically included in a comprehensive mental status examination of an adult (presenting problem, referral data, demographics, mental status, personality function and symptoms, diagnosis, disposition). With respect to the Derogatis Symptom Checklist Series, the most popular clinical instrument in this series is the Symptom Checklist-90-Revised (SCL-90-R) (Derogatis, 1994). The SCL-90-R can be administered by mental health professionals in 12–15 minutes to evaluate adolescent or adult psychiatric patients at intake, to screen for psychological problems, to monitor patient progress or changes during treatment, and to assess post-treatment outcomes. Scores are provided on nine primary symptom dimensions: Somatization, Obsessive Compulsive, Interpersonal Sensitivity, Depression, Anxiety, Hostility, Phobic Anxiety, Paranoid Ideation, and Psychoticism. The level or depth of a disorder, the intensity of the symptoms, and the number of patient-reported symptoms are also indicated by three measures of stress. Norms are provided for nonpatient adults, nonpatient adolescents, psychiatric outpatients, and psychiatric inpatients.

■ Rating Scales

Since their introduction by Francis Galton during the latter part of the nineteenth century as scientific research tools, rating scales have become popular assessment devices in clinical, educational, and industrial/organizational contexts. Rating scales are fairly easy to construct and quite versatile in their applications. Self-ratings may be made by the person being rated (the "ratee"), or other-ratings may be made by someone else (the rater) who has knowledge of the behavior, abilities, temperament, and other characteristics of the ratee.

A rating scale requires that judgments concerning the behavior or personality of the rater be made on an ordered scale containing enough categories or points, usually 5 to 7, to provide sufficient response variability to differentiate among people. Consequently, the numbers obtained when scoring rating scales represent measurement on at least an ordinal scale.

Like checklists of behaviors, rating scales may be used to record observational data or as accessories to interviews. Rating scales are generally considered superior to checklists but less precise than personality inventories and more superficial than projective techniques. Their superiority to checklists is particularly apparent when the number of raters or judges is small. However, when the number of raters is large, a well-constructed checklist may discriminate just as accurately as a rating scale.

Types of Rating Scales

Rating scales may be unipolar or bipolar. On a *unipolar scale*, a single term or phrase refers to a specific behavior or trait; the rater indicates the extent to which the ratee possesses that behavior or trait. For example, degree of dominance may be rated on a scale of 1 to 7, where 1 is the lowest and 7 the greatest degree of dominance. This unipolar scale can be converted to a *bipolar scale* by using two adjectives—submissive and dominant—to designate the two extreme categories; the middle category represents equal amounts of dominance and submission.

Rating scales may be classified in ways other than unipolar or bipolar. For example, there are numerical rating scales, semantic-differential scales, graphic rating scales, standard rating scales, behaviorally anchored scales, and forced-choice scales.

Numerical Rating Scale. On a *numerical rating scale*, the ratee is assigned one of several numbers corresponding to particular descriptions of the characteristic to be rated, such as "sociability" or "studiousness." All that is required is for the ratings to be made on a series of ordered categories, with different numerical values being assigned to different categories. For example, in rating a person on "sociability," five categories, ranging from very unsociable (1) to very sociable (5), may be used.

Or in making self-ratings on a clinical symptom such as anxiety, the following numerical scale may be employed:

Not anxious	0	1	2	3	4	5	6	7	8	9	10	As anxious as I can be

Semantic-Differential Scale. A special kind of a numerical rating scale is a *semantic-differential scale*. This type of scale was employed initially in research concerned with the connotative (personal) meanings of concepts such as "father," "mother," "sickness," "sin," "hatred," and "love" (Osgood, Suci & Tannenbaum, 1957). The assessment procedure begins by having a person rate a series of concepts on several seven-point, bipolar adjectival scales. For example, the concept of "mother" might be rated on the following seven-point scales:

MOTHER

Bad __ __ __ __ __ __ __ Good

Weak __ __ __ __ __ __ __ Strong

Slow __ __ __ __ __ __ __ Fast

A semantic differential instrument typically consists of ten or more bipolar scales of this sort.

After all concepts of interest have been rated on the various scales, the rater's response to each concept is scaled on several semantic dimensions and compared with his or her responses to the remaining concepts. The principal connotative meaning (semantic) dimensions that have been determined by factor analyses of ratings given by different raters to a series of concepts on many different bipolar adjectival scales are "evaluation," "potency," and "activity." A *semantic space* may be constructed by plotting, on these three dimensions, the rater's scores on the rated concepts. Concepts falling close to each other in the semantic space presumably have similar connotative meanings for the rater.

Graphic Rating Scale. Another popular type of rating scale is a *graphic rating scale*, which contains graphic descriptions of the end points and perhaps various intermediate points on a scale continuum. An example is:

What is the likelihood that the person will be able to maintain his (her) self-control in frustrating circumstances?

Will lose control all of the time	Will lose control most of the time	Will retain control about half the time	Will retain control most of the time	Will retain control all of the time

The rater makes a mark on each of a series of lines such as this one containing descriptive terms or phrases pertaining to a certain behavior or characteristic. The verbal description at the left end of the line usually represents the lowest amount or lowest frequency of occurrence, and the description at the right end represents the highest amount or highest frequency of occurrence. Two variations of the graphic rating scale format are the following *visual analogue scales* for measuring the intensity of the subjective experience of anxiety (see Wewers & Lowe, 1990). The patient indicates (by pointing or marking) the place on the line corresponding to the intensity of his or her anxiety level:

Not anxious	MILD MODERATE SEVERE _____	As anxious as I could be

Not anxious	LIGHTMODERATESEVERE _____	As anxious as I could be

Standard Rating Scale. On a *standard rating scale*, the rater supplies, or is supplied with, a set of standards against which the ratees are to be compared. An example of a standard rating scale is the *man-to-man (person-to-person) scale* for rating people on a specified characteristic or behavior. Raters begin by thinking of five people who fall at different points along a hypothetical continuum of the characteristic. Then they compare each person to be rated with these five individuals and indicate which one the ratee is most like with respect to the characteristic.

Behaviorally Anchored Scales. Based on the critical incidents technique, *behaviorally anchored rating scales (BARS)* represent attempts to make the terminology of ratings scales more descriptive of actual behavior and therefore more objective. Understandably, the meanings of concepts such as "anxiety," "self-confidence," and "aggressiveness," which are rated in traditional trait-oriented scales, may be interpreted somewhat differently by different raters. This is particularly true when the raters have received little or no training in what these terms mean in the assessment context.

Constructing a behaviorally anchored rating scale begins by convening a group of people who possess expert knowledge of a particular job or other situation of interest. Through discussion and painstaking deliberation, the group attempts to reach a consensus on a series of behaviorally descriptive, critical incidents from which an objective, highly reliable rating scale can be constructed. Behavioral descriptions that survive repeated reevaluation by the group, or other groups, may then be prepared as a series of items to be rated.

One might expect that the emphasis on objectively observable behavior and the concentrated group effort, which are features of behaviorally anchored scales, would make these scales psychometrically superior to other rating methods. In addition, the fact that the technique requires group involvement and consensus in constructing the scale, and hence a greater likelihood of group acceptance, would seem to be an advantage. After reviewing the research literature on the topic, Murphy and Constans (1987) concluded, however, that behaviorally anchored scales are not necessarily an improvement over other types of rating scales.

Behavioral Observation Scales. Behavioral observation scales (BOS) are similar to behaviorally anchored scales, in that ratings are on critical incidents. However, unlike the BARS approach, BOS ratings are in terms of the frequency of occurrence ("never, seldom, sometimes, generally, always") of critical behaviors during a specified time period. Some research studies have found that the BOS method is preferred over the BARS method in employment contexts (Wiersma & Latham, 1986).

Forced-Choice Rating Scale. On the simplest type of *forced-choice rating scale*, the rater is provided with two descriptive words, phrases, or statements that are closely matched in desirability. The rater is told to indicate which description best applies to the ratee. When the rating scale contains three or more descrip-

tions, the rater is asked to indicate which is most applicable and which is least applicable to the ratee. In the case of a scale containing four descriptions, say an item consisting of two equally desirable and two equally undesirable descriptions, the rater is instructed to mark the one that is most applicable and the one that is least applicable to the ratee. Only one desirable and one undesirable statement discriminate between high and low ratees on the criterion (behavioral adjustment, etc.), but the rater presumably does not know which of the four statements these are. A hypothetical example of a four-statement, forced-choice item that might be useful in evaluating supervisors or other leaders is:
— Accepts responsibility for his (her) actions.
— Doesn't know how or when to consider others' feelings.
— Is generally willing to let others have their say.
— Doesn't listen to other people when they make suggestions.

Notice that the first and third statements are positive, and the second and fourth statements are negative. Which statement is most positive and which is least negative? Presumably, only the scale designer knows for sure.

When the forced-choice rating method was first introduced, it was viewed as a way of controlling for deliberate distortion and personal biases such as *response sets* (the tendency of raters to respond on the basis of the form rather than the content of items on assessment instruments). But because the method is often cumbersome in practice, some people who were initially enthusiastic about the forced-choice format eventually returned to the man-to-man format or other types of evaluation. Bowmas and Bernardin (1991) found that the forced-choice method has several disadvantages and is not a popular technique among raters.

Errors in Rating

Cumbersome as it may be to select one of four descriptions that is most characteristic and one that is least characteristic of a person, forced-choice ratings have the advantage of controlling for certain errors in rating, such as the *constant error*, the *halo effect*, the *contrast error*, and the *proximity error*. Not all raters are equally prone to these errors, and, as with any other evaluation method that relies on observations, the background and personality of the rater affect his or her perception, judgment, and style of responding. One type of error to which all raters are susceptible, however, is the *ambiguity error* caused by poor descriptions of the various locations (*anchors*) on the scales and by scales consisting of items about which the rater has insufficient information. Other types of errors made in ratings are described below.

Constant Errors. These errors occur when the assigned ratings are higher (*leniency* or *generosity error*) lower (*severity error*), or are in the average category (*central tendency error*) more often than warranted. Transforming ratings to standard scores or other convenient units can assist in coping with constant errors, but making raters aware of the various types of errors that can occur in rating is probably more effective.

Halo Effect. The *halo effect* is the tendency of raters to respond to the general impression made by the ratee or to overgeneralize by assigning favorable ratings on all traits merely because the ratee is outstanding on one or two traits. A negative halo effect, in which one bad characteristic spoils the ratings on all other characteristics, can also occur. Similar to the halo effect is the *logical error* of assigning similar ratings on characteristics that the rater believes to be logically related.

Contrast Error. This term has been used in at least two different senses. In one sense the *contrast error* refers to the tendency to assign a higher rating than justified when an immediately preceding person received a very low rating, or to assign a lower rating than justified when the preceding person received a very high rating. In a second sense, the contrast error refers to the tendency for a rater to compare or contrast the ratee with the rater himself (herself) in assigning ratings on certain behaviors or traits.

Proximity Error. The actual location of a particular rating item on a printed page may affect the ratings assigned to it. In the *proximity error*, the rater tends to assign similar ratings to a person on items that are closer together on the printed page. Likewise, if a person is consistently rated high, low, or average on the majority of a set of items located close together, other items that are situated near those items may be rated in the same way—a kind of spread of response or response set.

Improving Ratings

It is not easy to make reliable and valid ratings of people under any circumstances and particularly so when the behaviors or personality characteristics are poorly defined or highly subjective. In addition, the meanings of the scale units may be unclear and hence interpreted differently by different raters.

Personal biases can obviously affect ratings: if you like someone you will probably assign higher ratings to him or her, and if you dislike the person you will tend to assign lower ratings than to someone whom you neither like nor dislike. Furthermore, raters frequently lack sufficient familiarity with the person being rated to make accurate ratings, or they may be familiar with the person's behavior in certain situations but not in others. Training in how to make ratings more objective—by being aware of the various kinds of errors that can occur, by becoming more familiar with the person and the characteristics being rated by the instrument, and by omitting items that the rater feels unqualified to judge, can improve the accuracy of ratings (Stamoulis & Hauenstein, 1993; Sulsky & Day, 1994). Not only training raters but also selecting them is important. Some individuals are simply not interested, are clearly too biased, or are unwilling to invest the necessary time and effort to become objective, unbiased raters. Such people should not be used as raters if they cannot be motivated and trained to be conscientious in what they are required to do.

Another way to improve ratings is to balance out the biases of individual raters by combining the responses of several raters. In addition, careful attention to the design of rating scale items can result in greater reliability and validity. Both the behaviors or traits being rated and the scale points should be designated in precise behavioral terms that will be interpreted in the same way by different raters. Matters of format are also important in providing accurate, meaningful results. Good format consists of arranging items on the rating sheets so they can be easily completed and scored, making certain that bipolar scales are not all in the same direction, placing items so they are not too close together (one per page is preferable but probably impossible), and making certain that the rating form is not unnecessarily long,

Scoring Ratings

The appropriate procedure for scoring ratings depends, among other things, on whether they are unipolar or bipolar. The simplest way to score a unipolar scale is to assign a score of 0 to responses falling in the category corresponding to the lowest amount of the rated characteristic and a score of c–1, where c is the number of rating categories, to responses falling in the category representing the highest amount of the characteristic. Composite scores on different sections or variables may then be determined as the sum of scores on the various items.

Scoring responses to bipolar scales is a bit more involved, but the following procedure is straightforward:
1. Assign the same integers (0 to c–1) to successive rating categories as in the case of a unipolar scale.
2. Subtract (c – 1) / 2 from each of these integers.

For example, if c = 5 the values 0, 1, 2, 3, and 4 are assigned to the five successive categories at step 1. Then (5 – 1) / 2 = 2 is subtracted from each of these values, yielding –2, –1, 0, 1, and 2 as the numerical scores corresponding to the five categories of the bipolar scale.

Reliability and Validity of Ratings

Because of the many sources of possible errors, the reliabilities and validities of various ratings are often marginal. The reliabilities of ratings may be improved, however, by careful training of the raters. Ratings may be made by subordinates, superiors, or peers (colleagues) of the ratee, or by the ratees themselves. Among these, the most reliable ratings are those given by the ratee's peers (Imada, 1982; Wexley & Klimoski, 1984). Ratings made by subordinates, superiors, peers, and self are not always consistent with each other, but combining ratings from these four sources may result in greater reliability and validity than any of the sources by itself (Harris & Schaubroeck, 1988).

Standardized Rating Scales

The great majority of rating scales are non-standardized, special purpose instruments designed for particular research investigations. Nevertheless, many standardized scales for rating the behavior and personality traits of children and adults are commercially available. Researchers in the fields of child development, special education (e. g., autism, ADHD, speech and language impairments, mental retardation), and school psychology, in particular, have constructed dozens of rating instruments for assessing behavioral changes resulting from specific educational, therapeutic, and other intervention programs. Many of these instruments are oriented toward behavioral assessments, whereas others have a trait-factor orientation, and still others were developed in a psychodynamic, psychiatric context. Furthermore, many standardized interview and observation instruments involve ratings of behavior and personality and hence consist in part of rating scales. Descriptions of a representative sample of standardized rating scales are given in Table 6–2.

   Three of the most widely administered series of rating scales are the Conners' Rating Scales, the Hamilton Scales, and the Derogatis Scales. The two Conners' scales—the Conners' Teacher Rating Scale and the Conners' Parent Rating Scale—have been used primarily to identify hyperactivity, but they are also useful in evaluating other behavior problems and signs of adjustment disorders in children and adolescents.

Hamilton Scales. Considering the significance of anxiety and depression as symptoms of mental disorders, it is not surprising that many checklists, rating scales, and personality inventories have been designed to assess these variables. Two popular rating scales for assessing depression and anxiety are the Hamilton Anxiety Scale and the Hamilton Depression Scale (from Psychological Assessment Resources). A revised version of the latter instrument, which has become a kind of standard for identifying clinically depressed patients, consists of a Clinician

Some Commercially Distributed Rating Scales for the Assessment of Personality Characteristics and Problems.   TABLE 6-2

Behavioral and Emotional Rating Scale: A Strength-Based Approach to Assessment (M.H. Epstein & J.M. Sharma; Psychological Assessment Resources; children and adolescents ages 5–18.11 years; designed to assess the behavioral and emotional strengths of children instead of their problems and deficits)

Brief Derogatis Psychiatric Rating Scale (L.R. Derogatis; NCS Assessments; adult and adolescent psychiatric and medical patients; for obtaining clinical observers' ratings on nine personality dimensions)

Clinical Rating Scale (D.H. Olson; Family Social Science; couples & families; to type marital and family systems and identify intervention targets; review MMYB 12:81)

Conners' Rating Scales (by C.K. Conners; Multi-Health Systems; consist of the Conners' Teacher Rating Scales and the Conners' Parent Rating Scales for identifying hyperactivity and a number of other symptoms and behavioral problems in children; reviews MMYB 11:87 & TC X:172)

Dementia Rating Scale (S. Mattis; Psychological Assessment Resources; individuals aged 65–81 suffering from brain dysfunction; measures the cognitive status of individuals with known cortical impairment; reviews MMYB 11:107 & TC X:199)

Derogatis Psychiatric Rating Scale (L.R. Derogatis; NCS Assessments; adults and adolescents; multidimensional psychiatric rating scale for use by clinicians to assist in validating patient-reported results; review MMYB 13:92)

Devereaux Behavior Rating Scales—School Form (by J.A. Naglieri, P.A. LeBuffe, & S.J. Pfeiffer; Psychological Corporation; for identifying behaviors that may indicate severe emotional disturbance in children and adolescents; review MMYB 13:96)

Disruptive Behavior Rating Scale (by B.T. Erford; Slosson; for identifying children "at risk" for attention deficient disorder, oppositional disorders, and antisocial conduct problems)

Global Assessment Scale (by R.L. Spitzer, M. Gibbon & J. Endicott; Dept. of Research Assessment & Training, N.Y. State Psychiatric Institute; psychiatric patients and possible psychiatric patients; ratings of Mental health-Illness on scale of 1–100; for evaluating the overall functioning of a person during a specified time period on a continuum ranging from psychological or psychiatric illness to health; review MMYB 11:147)

Revised Hamilton Rating Scale for Depression (W.L. Warren; Western Psychological Services; depressed adults; designed as a clinician-rated scale for evaluating individuals already diagnosed with depressive illness; review MMYB 13:263)

SCL-90 Analogue (L.R. Derogatis; NCS Assessments; adults and adolescents; a brief rating scale for collecting observer data on a patient's psychological symptomatic distress)

MMYB = *Mental Measurements Yearbook*; TC = *Test Critiques*

Rating Form and a Self-Report Problem Inventory; information concerning 22 clusters of depressive symptoms is provided by both forms. For the most part, reviews of this instrument have been positive (Burnett, 1998; Kaplan, 1998), although the standardization sample for the revision was small and more research on the validity of the scores in different populations is needed.

Derogatis Scales. Of the five instruments in this series, one—the SCL-90-R—was described earlier in the chapter. Like the SCL-90-R, the Brief Symptom Inventory (BSI) (Derogatis & Lazarus, 1994) is a self-report inventory for screening psychiatric patients on intake, to record the progress of patients, and to serve as an indicator of the effectiveness of treatment. The same variables as those for the SCL-90-R and the BSI are assessed by the remaining three instruments in the Derogatis series—the Derogatis Psychiatric Rating Scales (DPRS), the Brief Derogatis Psychiatric Rating Scale (B-DPRS), and the SCL-90 Analogue, but they are completed by an observer rather than by the patient. The observer, who is a clinician, or, in the case of the SCL-Analogue, a health professional who may lack in-depth training or knowledge of psychopathology, rates his or her observations of the patient on nine dimensions: Somatization, Obsessive Compulsive, Interpersonal Sensitivity, Depression, Anxiety, Hostility, Phobic Anxiety, Paranoid Ideation, and Psychoticism. The DPRS also yields scores on eight additional dimensions and a global index. The briefness of the DPRS is an advantage to the busy clinician, but an unfortunate consequence is that many scales contain few items. For this reason, plus poor documentation, the DPRS has not been well-received by reviewers (Juni, 1998; Retzlaff, 1998a).

Q-Sort Technique

Introduced by William Stephenson (1953), a special type of rating scale known as a *Q sort* has been used extensively in research in clinical and social psychology. The Q sort technique requires the respondent, who may be the person being described or someone else (e. g., an acquaintance or expert observer), to sort a set of 100 statements that are descriptive of personality into a series of nine categories (piles) varying from "most descriptive" to "least descriptive" of the person. Each card in a Q sort deck contains a statement such as these:
— Has a wide range of interest.
— Is productive; gets things done.
— Is self-dramatizing; is histrionic.
— Is overreactive to minor frustrations; is irritable.
— Seeks reassurance form others.
— Appears to have a high degree of intellectual capacity.
— Is basically anxious. (Block, 1961, pp. 132–136 passim)

In sorting the cards in a Q sort deck, the respondent is directed to make his or her choices so that a certain number of cards fall in each category and the resulting frequency distribution of statements across categories has a predetermined shape, usually normal. To approximate a normal distribution for a Q sort of 100 statements, Block (1961) recommended that sorters be instructed to place the following numbers of statements into categories 1 through 9: 5, 8, 12, 16, 18,

16, 12, 8, 5. The response to each statement on a Q sort instrument is assigned an integer ranging from 1 to 9, depending on the category assigned to the statement by the respondent. The results obtained from different sorters can then be correlated by using the product-moment correlation formula and factor analysis or cluster analysis procedures.

Q sorts were initially used to assess changes in clients' self-concepts resulting from psychotherapy (Rogers & Dymond, 1954). In this research investigation, clients made before-and-after Q-sorts of a series of statements describing their feelings and attitudes. Every client was directed to make separate Q-sorts according to his or her "real self" and "ideal self." The results showed that, compared with "no-therapy" control groups, differences between the "real" and "ideal" self-sorts of clients who had undergone client-centered therapy decreased. This was interpreted as meaning that the therapy produced a greater congruence between clients' real and ideal selves.

Q sort statements are usually written specifically for particular applications or investigations, but sets of statements, such as the California Q-Sort Revised (Adult Set; Block, 1978), have also been published. The California Q-Sort, which consists of 100 cards containing statements descriptive of personality, has been administered for psychodiagnostic purposes in numerous research studies (e. g., Reise & Oliver, 1994; Wink, 1992). A set of cards for children, the California Q-Sort Child Set, is also available. Although the Q sort represents a versatile method of personality assessment, it appears to have declined in popularity since the 1960s. Other Q-sort procedures, for example, the Affect Regulation and Experience Q-Sort (AREQ; Westen et al., 1997) have also been applied in clinical research and psychodiagnosis.

Sorting and Selecting People

Instead of sorting cards containing statements, one can sort or select people according to certain criteria. Examples of this approach are the *sociometric* or peer nomination technique, the *guess-who technique*, and the Rep Test.

Sociometric Technique. In this technique, the respondent is asked to select two subsets of people from a large group: those with whom he or she would like to engage in a certain activity and those with whom he or she would dislike or prefer not to engage in the activity. Alternatively, only acceptances (choices) may be requested. For example, the individuals in a school class, a place of worship, a military unit, or any other organization may be asked to select individuals with whom they would like to study, work, serve, or engage in any other activity. The resulting acceptances (and rejections) of each person can then be listed and analyzed, revealing which group members need assistance or attention and whether the physical arrangement of the group members is satisfactory in terms of efficiency and morale.

The sociometric process can be facilitated by depicting the results as a *sociogram*. In a sociogram, each person is represented by a circle; choices are indicated by arrows drawn from one circle (one person) to another circle (another person). People chosen most frequently are designated as *stars*, and people chosen by no one are called *isolates*. Two people who choose each other are known as *mutual admiration societies*, and groups of people who choose each other but no one else are referred to as *cliques*.

Guess-Who Technique. Another example of selecting people, based on a guessing game for children, is known as the guess-who technique. Children in a classroom, or any other group of acquaintances, are given a list of behavioral descriptions, such as, "Someone who always seems rather sad, worried, or unhappy" and "Someone who is very friendly, who is nice to everybody." The children are asked to write down the names of persons whom they think fit each description. As is the case with the sociometric technique, the results of the guess-who technique can help to identify children who have problems and need help.

Role Construct Repertory Test. A final example of an assessment procedure in which people are selected (and compared) is the Role Construct Repertory (Rep) Test. According to George Kelly's (1955) theory of personal constructs, people are scientists, albeit not necessarily good ones. Like scientists, they conceptualize or categorize their experiences in what appears to them to be a logical way. But many people, particularly those who are considered neurotic, perceive or construe the world incorrectly and develop faulty systems of constructs. Consequently, Kelly believed that a psychotherapist who wants to help a neurotic individual must begin by identifying the system of constructs used by the person in interpreting those people who are important to her or him.

One procedure devised by Kelly to identify a person's system of personal constructs is the Rep Test. The first step in administering the Rep Test is to ask the examinee to list the names of the 22 people in his or her life who fill each of the following roles:
1. yourself
2. your mother
3. your father
4. brother nearest to you in age (or person most like a brother)
5. sister nearest to you in age (or person most like a sister)
6. your spouse (or closest friend of opposite sex)
7. friend of opposite sex after person in 6
8. closest friend of same sex as you
9. person once a close friend but no longer

10. religious leader with whom you could discuss feelings about religion
11. your medical doctor
12. neighbor you know best
13. person you know who dislikes you
14. person for whom you feel sorry and would like to help
15. person with whom you feel uncomfortable
16. recent acquaintance you would like to know better
17. most influential teacher when you were in your teens
18. teacher you disagreed with most
19. employer or supervisor under whom you worked while experiencing stress
20. most successful person you know
21. happiest person you know
22. most ethical person you know

Typical Form Used for the Role Construct Repertory Test.   **FORM 6–2**

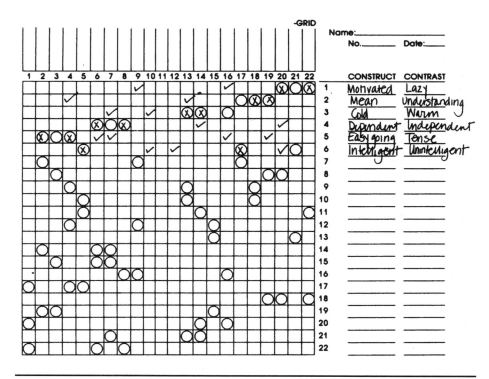

After designating the 22 people, the examinee is instructed to compare them in groups of three corresponding to the three circles on each row of Form 6–2. In this example, the first comparison is among persons 20, 21, and 22, and the second comparison is among persons 17, 18, and 19. Then on the appropriate row under the column headed "Construct," the examinee writes a word or phrase, for example, "motivated," describing how two of the three people are alike; under "Contrast" the examinee also writes a word or phrase, for example, "lazy," describing how the third person is different from the other two. Next the examinee writes an X in the circles corresponding to the two people on that row who are alike. For the remaining 19 people on the row, the appropriate box is checked if the "Construct" part applies to them and is left blank if it does not apply. This process is continued for the remaining 21 constructs, or for as many or as few constructs as the examinee wishes to list. Six construct-contrast examples are included in Form 6–2.

A person's performance on the Rep Test is analyzed by noting how many constructs are used and what they are, what aspects of people are emphasized in the constructs (physical, social, etc.), and which people are most similar to or different from the person. Interpreting the results of the Rep Test is a laborious, subjective process because the Rep Test as much of a projective technique as it is a rating scale. In the absence of an objective scoring system it should not be surprising that, although the grid responses appear fairly reliable, the Rep Test has not been widely used for either clinical or research purposes. Its validity is largely unknown.

■ Summary

Checklists and rating scales serve many different purposes, among which are to provide an objective record of the results of observations and interviews. Checklists are similar to rating scales in that they require decisions concerning the presence or absence of particular behaviors or characteristics. Unlike rating scales, which demand responding on a multicategory continuum, checklists necessitate making only a Yes-No decision or other dichotomous response. Both checklists and ratings scales are useful in determining whether individuals possess certain behaviors or traits, and if changes occur in these variables as a result of a particular treatment regimen, educational program, or other intervention process.

A checklist can usually be constructed quite simply, but it is more behaviorally based, and hence more objective, when the items deal with critical incidents; these are specific behaviors that are necessary for effective performance on some criterion. Commercially available checklists of problems, adaptive behavior, psychiatric symptoms, and adjectives have been used extensively for diagnostic and research purposes in educational, clinical, and industrial/organizational contexts. Although checklists are not usually considered to be as precise as rating scales, summing the responses of a large number of people to a checklist can produce fairly stable results.

The effective use of rating scales requires that judgments (ratings) concerning behaviors, personality traits, or other characteristics of individuals (ratees) be made by objective, unbiased raters. A rating scale may be unipolar or bipolar, depending on the nature of the concept that is being rated. Depending on whether it is a numerical, graphic, or behaviorally anchored scale, points on a rating scale may consist of numerical designations, verbal descriptions, or objective behavioral descriptions, A semantic differential is a special form of numerical scale used to assess the connotative meanings of specific concepts to the rater. Another type of rating scale is the standard rating scale, such as the man-to-man scale, on which ratees are compared against a set of standards.

Different kinds of errors that occur in making ratings include the ambiguity error, constant errors (leniency, severity, and central tendency errors), the contrast error, the logical error, the proximity error, and the halo effect. The forced-choice rating procedure, on which the rater is required to choose between two equally desirable descriptions and perhaps between two equally undesirable descriptions as well, controls for some of these errors, but it is cumbersome to use and is disliked by many raters. Ratings may be transformed to standard scores as a statistical control for constant errors, but perhaps the most effective procedure for reducing the effects of all types of errors in rating is to train raters carefully and familiarize them with the various kinds of errors than can be made.

Although standardized rating scales tend to be more reliable than unstandardized scales, ratings are not typically as reliable as scores on personality inventories or cognitive tests. However, when a rating scale is constructed as carefully and as objectively as possible and the raters are extensively trained, reliability coefficients in the .80s or even the .90s can be attained. Averaging the ratings of several raters also improves the reliability coefficient of a rating scale.

Q sorts are modified rating scales on which respondents sort a set of a 100 or so cards containing personality descriptions into nine piles to form a normal distribution of statements across piles. The Q sort procedure has been used in studies concerned with the effectiveness of psychological counseling and in other research and applied contexts.

Personality assessment approaches similar to checklists and ratings are the sociometric technique, the guess-who technique, and the Role Construct Repertory (Rep) Test. All three procedures involve selecting and comparing people according to various criteria or on several dimensions. The results of applying the sociometric and guess-who techniques can be used to identify individuals in a group who have personal and social problems. The Rep Test is a complex procedure based on George Kelly's theory of personal constructs.

■ Questions and Activities

1. Make a copy of the Behavioral Checklist for Performance Anxiety (Form 6–1) and use it to record your observations of a person over eight time periods of ten minutes each. Put a check mark after the behavior in the appropriate time period column if it occurred during that time. Make multiple check marks if the same behavior was observed more than once during the time period. How consistent was each of the behaviors across the eight time periods, and how many times did each behavior occur? Would you characterize the person whom you observed as "anxious?" Do you believe that all of the 20 behaviors listed in Form 6–1 are indicative of "anxiety?" Why or why not?

2. Consult a dictionary or thesaurus, and select 50 adjectives referring to traits or characteristics of personality. Try to choose a mixture of positive and negative adjectives that are not synonyms or antonyms of each other. Make multiple copies of the alphabetized list of adjectives. Leave a short blank line after each adjective, and administer the list to a sample of people. Ask the respondents to check each adjective that they feel is generally descriptive of themselves. Summarize the results, comparing them with what you already know about the individuals from other reports and observations.

3. One problem with the research literature on Type A behavior is that different assessment methods—for example, interview and questionnaire—do not yield the same results. Although questionnaires such as the Jenkins Activity Survey are more efficient than interviews, Rosenman (1986) and other have rejected such self-report measures because Type A personalities presumably have little insight into their own behavior. One way of testing this hypothesis is to compare self-ratings of behavior with ratings of behavior made by unbiased observers. With this in mind, select a few individuals who seem to fit the following description of the Type A personality:

   A personality pattern characterized by a combination of behaviors, including aggressivity, competitiveness, hostility, quick actions, and constant striving.

   Administer the following checklist to each person, and then have someone who knows the person well fill out the same checklist to describe that person. Use an appropriate statistical procedure to compare the self-ratings and the other-ratings.

   Checklist
   Directions: Check each of the following terms or phrases that is descriptive of you.
   ___ 1. achievement-oriented
   ___ 2. aggressive

___ 3. ambitious
___ 4. competitive
___ 5. constant worker
___ 6. dislikes wasting time
___ 7. easily angered
___ 8. easily aroused to action
___ 9. easily frustrated
___ 10. efficient
___ 11. emotionally explosive
___ 12. fast worker
___ 13. hard worker
___ 14. highly motivated
___ 15. impatient
___ 16. likes challenges
___ 17. likes to lead
___ 18. likes responsibility
___ 19. restless
___ 20. tries hard to succeed

4. Construct a ten-item checklist of symptoms of depression and a second check-list of symptoms of anxiety. Administer your two checklists to a dozen people and compute the correlation coefficient between the number of items that they check on each list. Interpret the correlation.

5. Rate yourself on each of the following characteristics on a scale of 1 ("Considerably well below average") to 10 ("Considerably well above average").
___ 1. ability to get along with others
___ 2. athletic ability
___ 3. cooperativeness
___ 4. creativeness
___ 5. energy level
___ 6. helpfulness
___ 7. intelligence
___ 8. leadership ability
___ 9. patience
___ 10. reasonableness
___ 11. responsibility
___ 12. sincerity
___ 13. thoughtfulness
___ 14. tolerance
___ 15. trustworthiness

Use the following procedure to evaluate your responses:
Add your ratings on all 15 characteristics and divide the sum by 15 to give your average rating. An "Average" mean rating is 5.5, but if you are like most

students your average will be higher than this. This "better-than-average" phenomenon, which is related to the "social desirability" response set, is a tendency for most people to see themselves as better than average.

6. On a scale of 1 to 10, where 1 is the lowest rating and 10 is the highest rating, rate each of the following adjectives according to how descriptive it is of: (a) your *real self* (the way you actually are), (b) your *ideal self* (the way you would like to be), and (c) *people in general* of your chronological age and sex.

	Your Real Self	Your Ideal Self	Other People in General
brave	____	____	____
careful	____	____	____
cheerful	____	____	____
conscientious	____	____	____
considerate	____	____	____
courteous	____	____	____
creative	____	____	____
dependable	____	____	____
energetic	____	____	____
friendly	____	____	____
good looking	____	____	____
helpful	____	____	____
honest	____	____	____
humorous	____	____	____
intelligent	____	____	____
organized	____	____	____
patient	____	____	____
strong	____	____	____
studious	____	____	____
trusting	____	____	____

Evaluate your responses by the following procedure:
Compute the sum of the absolute values of the differences between the ratings assigned to your: (a) real self and ideal self, (b) real self and others' selves, (c) ideal selves and others' selves. Compute the "Percent Congruency" coefficient for each of the three comparisons by dividing the sum by 180 and subtracting the resulting quotient from 1. The closer the congruency coefficient is to 1.00, the more similar the two selves are. Interpret your results in terms of Rogers' self theory or social learning theory.

■ Suggested Readings

Aiken, L.R. (1996). *Rating scales and checklists* (pp. 191–253). New York: Wiley.

Bech, P. (1993). *Rating scales for psychopathology, health status and quality of life.* New York: Springer-Verlag.

Lachar, D. (1993). Symptom checklists and personality inventories. In T.R. Kratchowill & R.J. Morris (Eds.), *Handbook of psychotherapy with children and adolescents* (pp. 28–57). Boston: Allyn & Bacon.

McReynolds, P., & Ludwig, K. (1987). On the history of rating scales. *Personality and Industrial Differences, 8,* 281–283.

Piacentini, J. (1993). Checklists and rating scales. In T.H. Ollendick & M. Hersen (Eds.), *Handbook of child and adolescent assessment* (pp. 82–97). Boston: Allyn & Bacon.

Witt, J.C., Heffer, R.W., & Pfeiffer, J. (1990). Structured rating scales: A review of self-report and informant rating processes, procedures, and issues. In C.R. Reynolds & R.W. Kamphaus (Eds.), *Handbook of psychological & educational assessment of children: Personality, behavior, & context* (pp. 364–394). New York: Guilford.

PART III

PERSONALITY INVENTORIES

CHAPTER 7

Rational-Theoretical and Factor-Analyzed Inventories

Like a personality rating scale or checklist, a *personality inventory* consists of items concerning personal characteristics, thoughts, feelings, and behavior. Personality inventories, however, typically measure a broader range of variables and are usually more carefully constructed and standardized than rating scales and checklists. They are frequently designed to yield scores on several personality variables, but many single score or single-purpose inventories are also available. Personality inventories have been used, with mixed success, for a variety of purposes, including research on personality development and change, psychiatric diagnosis, personality counseling, educational and vocational counseling, occupational selection and placement, and premarital, marital, and family counseling.

Historically, the initial focus of personality assessment was on the development of instruments to serve a very practical purpose—that of identifying and diagnosing maladjustment or mental disorders. As seen in the popularity of tests used in clinical and counseling situations to detect mental illness, behavioral disorders, and delinquency, and to predict various kinds of personally and socially destructive behaviors, the emphasis in personality assessment continues to be on the pathological. Nevertheless, personality inventories designed for so-called "normal" individuals and inventories that focus on more positive features and effective coping behaviors are used extensively—primarily in research, but also in guidance, self-exploration, personal development, and applicant selection. The use of these inventories is not limited to mental hospitals and mental health clinics; they are also administered in schools, colleges, business-industrial contexts, and other organizational situations.

Despite decades of criticism of personality assessment methods, an increase in research and development in personality assessment during the past three decades has given rise to many new instruments. A number of these are special-purpose devices designed for particular research programs concerned with anxiety, depression, substance abuse, suicide, cardiovascular disease, criminal behavior, and other problems or disabilities. Other inventories are general-purpose devices designed with greater psychometric sophistication than their predecessors to measure a host of personality variables. Table 7–1 is a representative list of commercially available, multiscore inventories of personality. Of these, the most popular by far is the Minnesota Multiphasic Personality Inventory (MMPI). Inventories for assessing specific clinical symptoms are also available, among which are those listed in Table 7–2.

TABLE 7–1 Representative Multiscore Personality Inventories.

- *Adult Personality Inventory* (by S.E. Krug; Metritech; reviews MMYB 12:20 & TC VI:21)
- *Basic Personality Inventory* (by D.N. Jackson; Sigma Assessment Systems; reviews MMYB 12:42 & TC VIII:38)
- *Children's Personality Questionnaire, 1985 Edition* (by R.B. Cattell; IPAT; review MMYB 13:60)
- *Comrey Personality Scales* (by A.L. Comrey; available from EdITS).
- *Early School Personality Questionnaire* (by R.B. Cattell & R.W. Coan; IPAT; reviews MMYB 8:540 & TC III:246)
- *Edwards Personal Preference Schedule* (by A.L. Edwards; Psychological Corporation; reviews MMYB 9:378 & TC I:252)
- *Eysenck Personality Inventory—Revised* (by H.J. Eysenck & S.B.G. Eysenck; EdITS; review MMYB 9:405)
- *Eysenck Personality Questionnaire* (by H.J. & S.B.G. Eysenck; EdITS; reviews MMYB 9:406 & TC I:27)
- *Guilford-Zimmerman Temperament Survey* (by J.P. Guilford, J.S. Guilford, & W.S. Zimmerman; Consulting Psychologists Press; reviews MMYB 9:460 & TC VIII:251)
- *Hogan Personality Inventory* (by R. Hogan & J. Hogan; Hogan Assessment Systems; review MMYB 13:138)
- Inwald Personality Inventory-Revised (by R. Inwald; Hilson Research; review MMYB 12:194)
- *Jackson Personality Inventory—Revised* (by D.N. Jackson; Sigma Assessment Systems; review MMYB 13:162)
- *Junior Eysenck Personality Inventory* (by H.J. Eysenck & S.B.G. Eysenck; EdITS; review MMYB 9:561)
- *Jr.-Sr. High School Personality Questionnaire* (by R.B. Cattell, M.D. Cattell, & E. Johns; IPAT;review MMYB 11:18)
- *Maudsley Personality Inventory* (by H.J. Eysenck; EdITS; reviews MMYB 9:668 & TC IV:387)
- Millon Adolescent Clinical Inventory (by T. Millon, C. Millon, & R. Davis; NCS Assessments; review MMYB 12:236)

- *Millon Adolescent Personality Inventory* (by T. Millon, C.J. Green & R.B. Meagher; NCS Assessments; reviews MMYB 9:707 & TC IV:425)
- *Millon Clinical Multiaxial Inventory—II & III* (by T. Millon; NCS Assessments; reviews MMYB 11: 11:239 and MMYB 13:201)
- *Millon Index of Personality Styles* (by T. Millon; Psychological Corporation; review MMYB 13:202)
- *Minnesota Multiphasic Personality Inventory—Adolescent* (by J.N. Butcher et al.; NCS Assessments; reviews MMYB 12:238)
- *Minnesota Multiphasic Personality Inventory-2* (by J.N. Butcher, W.G. Dahlstrom, J.R. Graham, & A. Tellegen; based on original work by S.R. Hathaway & C. McKinley; NCS Assessments; reviews MMYB 11:244 & TC VIII:485 & TC X:424)
- *Myers-Briggs Type Indicator* (by I.B. Myers & K.C. Briggs; Consulting Psychologists Press; reviews MMYB 10:206 & TC I:482)
- *NEO Five-Factor Inventory* (by P.T. Costa & R.R. McCrae; Psychological Assessment Resources).
- *NEO Personality Inventory—Revised* (by P.T. Costa & R.R. McCrae; Psychological Assessment Resources; reviews MMYB 12:330 & TC X:443)
- *Personality Assessment Inventory* (by L.C. Morey; Psychological Assessment Resources; review MMYB 12:290)
- *Personality Inventory for Children—Revised Format* (by R.D. Wirt, D. Lachar, J.K. Klinedinst, P.D. Seat, & W.E. Broen; Western Psychological Services; reviews MMYB 10:281 & TC II:570)
- *Personality Inventory for Youth* (by D. Lachar & C.P. Gruber; Western Psychological Services; review MMYB 13:231)
- *Personality Research Form* (by D.N. Jackson; Sigma Assessment Systems; reviews MMYB 10:282 & TC III:499)
- *Profile of Mood States* (by M. McNair, M. Lorr, & L. Droppelman; EdITS; reviews MMYB 9:998 & TC I:522).
- *Singer-Loomis Inventory of Personality* (by J. Singer & M. Loomis; Consulting Psychologists Press; review MMYB 10:334)
- *Sixteen Personality Factor Questionnaire, Fifth Edition* (by R.B. Cattell; IPAT; review MMYB 12:354).
- *Taylor-Johnson Temperament Analysis* (by R.M. Taylor & L.P. Morrison; Consulting Psychologists Press; review MMYB 13:315)
- *Western Personality Inventory* (by M.P. Manson; Western Psychological Services; reviews MMYB 11:468 & TC II:826)

MMYB = *Mental Measurements Yearbook*; TC = *Test Critiques*

The assessment instruments discussed in this chapter and the following one are objective measures, in that they consist of dichotomous, multiple-choice, or other types of items that can be scored objectively. Respondents are required to select a response from a dichotomy (true-false, yes-no, agree-disagree, etc.) or from a list of three or more alternatives (e. g., completely false, mostly false, partly false and partly true, mostly true, or completely true; strongly disagree, disagree, neutral, agree, or strongly disagree) A trained psychologist or other mental health professional is not needed to score a personality inventory; it can be done by a

TABLE 7–2 **Representative Personality Inventories for Assessing a Specific Clinical Symptom or Disorder.**

Alcoholism
- *Adolescent Drinking Index* (by A. V. Harrell, & P. W. Wirtz, Sigma Assessment Systems; review MMYB 12:17)
- *Alcohol Use Inventory* (by J. L. Horn, K. W. Wanberg, & F. M. Foster; NCS Assessments; review MMYB 12:25)

Anxiety
- *Anxiety Scale for Children and Adults* (by J. Battle; pro-ed; review MMYB 12:30).
- *Beck Anxiety Inventory* (by A. T. Beck; Psychological Corporation; review MMYB 13:30)
- *Child Anxiety Scale* (by J. S. Gillis; IPAT; reviews MMYB 9:212 & TC III:139)
- *IPAT Anxiety Scale* (by R. B. Cattell & I. H. Scheier; IPAT; reviews MMYB 9:537 & TC II:357)

Depression
- *Beck Depression Inventory* (by A. T. Beck; Psychological Corporation; reviews MMYB 11:31 and MMYB 13:31)
- *Children's Depression Inventory* (by M. Kovacs; Western Psychiatric Institute; reviews MMYB 11:66 & TC V:65)
- Children's Depression Scale, Second Research Edition (by M. Lang & M. Tisher; Consulting Psychologists Press; review MMYB 12:77)
- *Depression and Anxiety in Youth Scale* (by P. L. Newcomer, E. M. Barenbaum, & B. R. Bryant; pro-ed; review MMYB 13:91)
- *Reynolds Adolescent Depression Scale* (by W. M. Reynolds; Psychological Assessment Resources; reviews MMYB 11:333 & TC VII:485)
- *Reynolds Child Depression Scale* (by W. M. Reynolds; Psychological Assessment Resources; reviews MMYB 11:334 & TC X:601).

Eating Disorders
- *Eating Inventory* (by A. J. Stunkard & S. Messick; Psychological Corporation; reviews MMYB 13:111 & TC VIII:158)
- *Eating Disorder Inventory–2* (by D. M. Garner; Psychological Assessment Resources; reviews MMYB 12:130 & TC X:226)

Stress
- *Coping Inventory for Stressful Situations* (by N. Endler & J. Parker; Multi-Health Systems, North Tonawanda, NY)
- *Coping Resources Inventory, Form D* (by A. L. Hammer & M. S. Marting; Consulting Psychologists Press; review MMYB 12:95)
- *Daily Stress Inventory* (by P. J. Brantley & G. N. Jones; Sigma Assessment Systems; review MMYB 11:101)
- *Life Stressors and Social Resources Inventory* (by R. H. Moos & B. S. Moos; Psychological Assessment Resources; review of Adult Form in MMYB 13:184; review of Youth Form in MMYB 13:185)

- *NPF* (by R. B. Cattell, J. E. King, & A. K. Schuettler; MetriTech; review MMYB 12:261).
- *Occupational Stress Inventory* (by S. H. Osipow & A. R. Spoken; Sigma Assessment Systems; reviews MMYB 11:269 & TC X:498)

Suicidal Ideation
- *Adult Suicidal Ideation Questionnaire* (by W. M. Reynolds; Psychological Assessment Resources; review MMYB 12:2)
- *Beck Scale for Suicide Ideation* (by A. T. Beck; Psychological Corporation; review MMYB 12:21, 13:33)
- *Inventory of Suicide Orientation-30* (by B. Kowalchuk & J. D. King; NCS Assessments; review in MMYB 13:158)
- *Suicidal Ideation Questionnaire* (by W. M. Reynolds; Psychological Assessment Resources; reviews MMYB 11:393 & TC VIII:663)

MMYB = *Mental Measurements Yearbook*; TC = *Test Critiques*

clerk or a scoring machine. Another advantage of personality inventories is that a large number of items, covering a wide range of topics, can be answered in a relatively short period of time to provide a comprehensive description of various features of personality.

■ Construction Strategies

Strategies for constructing personality inventories, rating scales, and checklists were discussed briefly in Chapter 2. Although the terms differ somewhat depending on who is doing the describing, most authorities agree that three approaches or strategies may be followed in developing a personality inventory.

Rational-Theoretical Strategy

The first strategy has been referred to as content-based, rational, intuitive, judgmental, logical-content, face-valid, common-sense, or theoretical. We shall use Lanyon and Goodstein's (1997) term *rational-theoretical strategy*, which emphasizes its origins in both reasoning and theory.

In the rational-theoretical strategy, the design of a personality inventory begins with a conception of personality derived from a variety of sources—common sense, professional judgment, research findings, and perhaps one or more theories of personality. Illustrative of this approach are inventories and rating scales derived from the work of the trait theorists Gordon Allport and Henry Murray. Murray's needs-press theory, in particular, stimulated the development of a number of personality assessment instruments, including the Thematic Apperception Test, the Adjective Check List, the Edwards Personal Preference Schedule, and the Personality Research Form. Other theories of personality that have played a role in the development of assessment instruments are the psychodynamic theories of Sigmund Freud and Carl Jung, George Kelly's theory of personal constructs, Julian Rotter's social learning theory, and various theories of single concepts such as anxiety, depression, repression-sensitization, and self-esteem. The Myers-Briggs Type Indicator, which is based on concepts from Carl Jung's analytic theory, is a good example of a *theory-based inventory*.

Factor-Analytic Strategy

A second approach to constructing personality tests has been referred to as the inductive, internal consistency, clustering, itemetric, or factor analytic strategy. This strategy, which we shall refer to as *factor-analytic*, emphasizes the development of a set of internally consistent scales consisting of a group of highly intercorrelated items. In order to measure different personality variables, the correlations among scores on the various scales must be low. The construction of such scales, in which the items within scales are highly intercorrelated but total scores on the scales themselves have low correlations with each other, relies on the methods of factor analysis. Illustrative of personality inventories constructed by the factor-analytic strategy are the Guilford-Zimmerman Temperament Survey, the 16 Personality Factor Questionnaire, and the Eysenck Personality Inventory.

Criterion-Keying Strategy

A third strategy for developing personality assessment instruments is variously referred to as the external, empirical, group-contrast, criterion group, criterion-validated, or criterion-keying strategy. These labels emphasize the fact that the selection of items by this approach consists of determining the extent to which the items and scores on specific scales differentiate between specified criterion groups. Depending on the purpose of the inventory, the two criterion groups may be dichotomies such as physicians versus men in general, psychiatric patients versus normal people, delinquents versus nondelinquents, or high-anxious versus low-anxious people. The criterion-keying strategy, which was used initially in selecting items for the Strong Vocational Interest Blank for Men, was subsequently applied in the development of the Minnesota Multiphasic Personality Inventory, the California Psychological Inventory, the Jesness Inventory, and a number of other psychometric instruments.

There are advantages and disadvantages to each of the above strategies. For example, inventories developed by using a rational-theoretical approach have greater face validity and can be constructed more easily than criterion-keyed inventories, but they are more easily faked than the latter (Burisch, 1984). In terms of their effectiveness in predicting external criteria, Goldberg (1972) found that scales produced by the three strategies were equally effective. He noted that criterion-keyed inventories possess certain advantages over rational-theoretical and factor-analyzed inventories, but these advantages are not impressive.

The various strategies for developing personality assessment instruments are not mutually exclusive, and psychologists who devise such instruments frequently try to capitalize on the merits of several approaches. Construction of a scale to measure a specific personality variable or concept typically begins with a careful definition of the concept based on reasoning and theory, followed by preparation of a large pool of items designed to measure the construct. The items may consist of terms, phrases, statements, or questions. Then the item pool is administered to a sample of subjects (a pilot group) representative of the target population, and the responses of the pilot group are analyzed to identify items that should be edited or discarded. Items answered (or not answered) in a certain direction by an excessive number of respondents and items having low correlations with total scores on the scale are particularly suspect. Statistical analyses of the items involving internal consistency checks and perhaps factor analysis are also conducted. Next, the revised items are administered to a new sample of people, and the results are analyzed to determine their psychometric properties (reliability, validity, norms, etc.). Of special interest is the ability of the scale to differentiate between criterion groups, that is, groups of people who, from independent evidence, are known to possess a high degree of the variable or construct and a group known to possess a low amount of it. This process may continue, of course, including additional research on the reliability and validity of the scale and any other scales comprising the inventory.

■ Response Sets and Psychometric Characteristics

Early developers of personality inventories assumed that respondents were aware of their own characteristics and would answer the questions honestly and accurately, interpreting the words and phrases of the items in the same way as other people. Unfortunately, these assumptions were not always justified, and response validity has continued to be a serious problem with personality inventories. Not only may respondents be unwilling to tell the truth about themselves as they know it, but they may not even know the truth and unintentionally give false responses.

Psychodynamic psychologists and other critics of self-report questionnaires have long alleged that these instruments tap only surface or conscious aspects of personality and can easily be faked. According to these critics, projective tests are more valid than personality inventories because they get at deeper layers of personality and are less subject to faking. These criticisms are not without merit: research findings demonstrate that people can distort their responses to personality inventories (Jacobs & Barron, 1968; Radcliffe, 1966; Stricker, 1969; Wiggins, 1966). Outright lying or faking on self-report measures of personality administered in counseling and job placement situations is, however, probably not as common as one might suspect (Abrahams, Neumann, & Gilthens, 1971; Schwab & Packard, 1973). In any event, faking is usually more of a problem on personality inventories than on ability tests, and it can contribute to the lower reliabilities of the former instruments.

Response Sets

Malingering (faking bad) and faking good are not the only response tendencies that affect the validity of personality test scores; acquiescence, social desirability, overcautiousness, extremeness, oppositionalism, deviancy, and other *response sets* or response styles also contribute to a distorted picture of personality. Faking "good," in which respondents given what they consider socially desirable responses, is undoubtedly more common than faking "bad." However, when financial or other compensation is contingent upon the presence of certain pathological or maladaptive symptoms, the respondent may "fake bad" by pretending to be worse than he or she actually is.

All of the above response sets are tendencies to answer items in a particular way, regardless of their content. The two most common, and the ones on which the greatest amount of research has been done, are acquiescence and social desirability. *Acquiescence* (yea-saying), which causes particular problems on true-false items, is the tendency to agree (answer *true*) rather than disagree (answer *false*) when in doubt (Couch & Keniston, 1960). The *social desirability* response set is the tendency to respond in a more socially acceptable manner, giving the answer that the examinee believes will create a favorable impression.

Designed specifically to measure the social desirability response set are the Edwards Social Desirability (SD) Scale (Edwards, 1957), the Crowne-Marlowe Social Desirability Scale (Crowne & Marlowe, 1964), and Wiggins's (1959) SD Scale. Edwards's SD scale consists of 39 true-false items on which a group of people (judges) showed perfect agreement when directed to respond in a socially desirable manner. Scores on this instrument have been shown to correlate positively with personality scales that measure socially desirable traits (agreeableness, cooperativeness, responsibility, objectivity, etc.) and negatively with personality scales that measure socially undesirable traits (anxiety, hostility, insecurity, neuroticism, etc.) (Edwards, 1970). These findings prompted a debate within psychology as to whether personality inventories merely assess the ability to detect responses that are socially acceptable or unacceptable (Block, 1965; Heilbrun, 1964; Rorer, 1965).

The controversy as to whether personality inventories and scales measure something other than the ability to perceive what is socially desirable has not been completely resolved. It has led, however, to greater awareness of the effects of perceived socially desirable behavior and other response sets, or *response styles*, on responses to personality test items and a need to take them into consideration in evaluating the responses to content scales. Efforts to control for the social desirability response set have taken various forms, among which are developing separate social desirability scales or multiscore inventories and designing inventories in such a way that either the item format controls for social desirability or the items are neutral in terms of their social desirability.

The response sets of acquiescence and social desirability have been of particular concern because the items on so many personality inventories are of the true-false variety and therefore seemingly more susceptible to these response sets. The meanings of the other response sets referred to above should be fairly obvious: *overcautiousness* means being excessively careful in answering; *extremeness* means tending to give more extreme responses than even mentally disordered people might give; and *oppositionalism* is the tendency to answer in the opposite direction to what one believes to be true. Research has also been conducted on these three variables, but not nearly as extensively as research on acquiescence and social desirability.

It may have occurred to the reader that response sets themselves are personality characteristics of a sort. Some people appear to be naturally acquiescent, while others are preoccupied with presenting themselves in the most favorable light (social desirability). A case can be made for viewing response sets as personality characteristics (Jackson & Messick, 1958, 1962), but in general they have been seen as a source of difficulty in getting examinees to respond to the content rather than the form of an item and thereby revealing their true personality. Edwards (1957) argued that the social desirability response set, in particular, is so strong in responding to true-false items such as those on the MMPI that it interferes significantly with a correct analysis or psychodiagnosis of the examinee. Still, the great response set (style) issue remains unresolved. While most authorities point to the fact that all kinds of response sets and malingering interfere with realistic self-portrayal on personality inventories, others view the use of special scales and other methods for detecting and controlling for response sets as having a depressing effect on the validity of the content scales of these inventories with certain populations (Costa & McCrae, 1992). Nevertheless, on many popular inventories scores on such specific verification (validity) scales are examined before interpreting scores on the content scales of the inventory.

Checks and Controls for Truthfulness in Responding

Various methods have been applied at the instrument-design stage to control for dissimulation (faking), misunderstanding of directions, and carelessness in responding. For example, to reduce the acquiescence response set on true-false questionnaires one should make the number of items keyed that are *true* approximately equal to the number keyed *false*. To control for the social desirability response set, some inventories are designed with a forced-choice item format in which each item consists of two or more phrases or statements designed to be equal in social desirability; examinees select one of the phrases as being more characteristic or descriptive of themselves. Items can also be rated on social desirability, and those with extremely high social desirability ratings can be eliminated. Another technique is to repeat items in the same or a different form later in the inventory, and then compute an index of consistency in responding to them. Other procedures for evaluating the truthfulness of responses to items on personality inventories are:

1. Count the number of items omitted by the examinee. If this number is quite different from the average number of omissions in the norm group, the examinee has probably responded incorrectly.
2. Count the number of items that the normative sample rarely answered in the same way as the examinee. If this number is quite large, doubt may be cast on the validity of the examinee's responses. *Infrequency scales* on various inventories consist of a set of items that were endorsed by a relatively small number of people in the normative sample.
3. Compute the examinee's scores on special validity scales designed to detect faking, failure to follow the directions, carelessness in responding, or response sets. If these scores are significantly larger than expected, the validity of the examinee's responses should be questioned. Illustrative of this approach are the TRIN (True Response Inconsistency) and VRIN (Variable Response Inconsistency) scales of the MMPI-2. Scores on both of these scales reflect the tendency to disregard item content in responding, either by giving mostly true (or false) answers (TRIN) or by giving inconsistent or contradictory responses to items that are either similar or opposite in content (VRIN).

In constructing special validity scales, trial administrations are often conducted in which the inventory is administered with special instructions: to fake good, to fake bad, to answer in the socially desirable direction, to answer like a mentally ill person, and so on. The item responses of examinees who were given the special directions are then compared with the responses of examinees who received the standard directions, and the significance of the differences are determined. Items showing significant response differences are then formed into a special validity scale, which is cross-validated and standardized. Finally, the obtained norms on the special scale are used to detect faking or the given response set.

It would be misleading to give the impression that all responses to personality inventories bear the taint of response sets and that it is impossible to count on these inventories to reveal anything of value concerning an individual's personality. Although the possibility of response sets should never be over looked, the great majority of people probably tell the truth *as they see it* on a personality inventory when it is not against their own best interests to do so.

Norms, Reliability, and Validity

Unlike many checklists and rating scales, most personality inventories have norms. Be that as it may, the norms are frequently based on small and perhaps unrepresentative samples and must therefore be interpreted with caution. A special problem exists with respect to the norms on forced-choice inventories in that they are *ipsative*: scores on the various scales comprising the inventory are related to or affect each other. Consequently, one cannot interpret a score on a given ipsative scale in any absolute sense, but only with respect to scores on other ipsative scales. This lack of independence of scores on the various scales causes problems in comparing a person's scores with those of other people.

The reliability coefficients of personality inventories, as with measures of all affective characteristics, are almost always smaller than those of ability tests. This is understandable when one considers that responses to personality test items are, on the whole, more variable across time and situation than responses to questions on tests of ability. This does not necessarily mean that personality traits are less stable than cognitive abilities, though responses to measures of personality do tend be more influenced by temporary changes in mood or attitude. Personality test items are also typically less objective or universal in meaning than ability test items, and hence the manner in which they are answered is more affected by differences in perception and interpretation.

For the most part, personality inventories are also quite limited in their validities. One factor that is related to validity is the tendency of the user of a personality inventory to believe that scales having similar names necessarily measure the same variable (the *jingle fallacy*) or that scales have different names measure different variables (the *jangle fallacy*). Thus, the anxiety scales on two different inventories may have a lower correlation with each other than the anxiety scale on one inventory and the depression or hostility scale on the other. Furthermore, even when similarly named scales on two different inventories are highly correlated one must consider the possibility of a common response set.

■ Early Personality Inventories

Recently published personality inventories are far from perfect, but they are psychometrically superior to early inventories such as the Personal Data Sheet, the A-S Reaction Study, and the Bell Adjustment Inventory. Early inventories were rather crude according to today's standards, though in their time they were employed fairly extensively in research, counseling and selection.

Single-Score Inventories

The Personal Data Sheet, which was constructed by R.S. Woodworth (1919) to identify U.S. Army recruits who were most likely to break down under the stress of military combat, was the first personality inventory of any significance. Some years previously, Heymans and Wiersma (1906) had constructed a list of symptoms indicative of psychopathology, a list that was revised by Hoch and Amsden (1913) and by Wells (1914). However, the Personal Data Sheet was the first personality inventory to be administered on a mass basis. Designed to detect emotional disorders, this paper-and-pencil inventory consisted of 116 yes/no questions reduced from an original group of 200 questions concerning physical symptoms, abnormal fears and worries, social and environmental adjustment, unhappiness, obsessions, compulsions, tics, nightmares, fantasies, and other feelings and behaviors. The questions, similar to those asked in psychiatric screening interviews, were based on common neurotic symptoms, as well as feelings and behaviors described and observed in soldiers who had not been able to adjust to the stress of military life. These neurotic symptoms were included as items only if they occurred at least twice as frequently in normal people as in people who had already been diagnosed by psychiatrists as neurotics.* Some illustrative items from the Personal Data Sheet are (Hollingworth, 1920, pp. 120– 126):

- Do you feel sad and low-spirited most of the time?
- Are you often frightened in the middle of the night?
- Do you think you have hurt yourself by going too much with women?
- Have you ever lost your memory for a time?
- Do you usually feel well and strong?
- Do you ever walk in your sleep?
- Do you ever feel an awful pressure in or about your head?
- Are you troubled with the idea that people are watching you on the street?
- Do you make friends easily?
- Are your troubled by shyness?

---

* This item selection procedure was a forerunner of the empirical approach employed in constructing the MMPI and other criterion-keyed inventories.

— Did you have a happy childhood?
— Are you ever bothered by feeling that things are not real?

The Personal Data Sheet yielded a single-score—the total number of items answered by the examinee in the direction judged to be indicative of maladjustment or neurosis. Only items that were answered in the keyed direction by less than 25% of a sample of normal individuals were included in the final form of the inventory (Woodworth, 1920). Construction of the Personal Data Sheet was completed too late to be of use in selecting military personnel during World War I, but in its final form, known as the Woodworth Psychoneurotic Inventory, it served as a basis for the development of other paper-and-pencil inventories of personality during the postwar period.

Other pioneering personality inventories of the single-score variety were the X-O Test (Pressey & Pressey, 1919) and the A-S Reaction Study (Allport & Allport, 1928). On the X-O Test, examinees were told to cross out (X) each of 600 words that they considered unpleasant, activities they considered to be wrong (e. g., smoking, spitting in public), or things that they worried about or made them anxious (e. g., money, pain). The A-S Reaction Study, a multiple choice inventory used in a number of social-psychological investigations, was designed to measure a person's disposition to be ascendant (A) or submissive (S) in everyday social relationships.

Multiscore Inventories

The first *multiscore inventory* to become commercially available was the Bernreuter Personality Inventory (1931). It consisted of 125 items to be answered *yes, no,* or *?* in 25 minutes or so by high school and college students or adults (age 13 or over). Different numerical weights were assigned to items to yield scores on six variables: Neurotic Tendency, Self-Sufficiency, Introversion-Extroversion, Dominance-Submission, Sociability, and Confidence.

Another multiscore inventory, the Bell Adjustment Inventory, was published initially in the 1930s but remained in use until fairly recently (Bell, 1939). Like the Personal Data Sheet, the A–S Reaction Study, and the Bernreuter Personality Inventory, the Bell Adjustment Inventory was developed by rational or content-validation procedures. However, the six scales on which the inventory was scored (Home, Health, Submissiveness, Emotionality, Hostility, Masculinity) were refined by internal-consistency procedures and validated against various external criteria. Separate forms were provided for high school students and adults. Another widely administered multiscore inventory during the years 1939– 1953 was the California Test of Personality (Thorpe, Clarke & Tiegs, 1953).

■ Contemporary Rational-Theoretical Inventories

Items on the earliest personality inventories were all derived by logical reasoning and judgment concerning the nature of personality and psychological disorders. Many of the questions, such as those on the Personal Data Sheet, were of the same kind as a clinical psychologist or psychiatrist might ask in trying to obtain a diagnostic picture of a patient. Similar psychiatrically oriented inventories, which provide several scores rather than a single maladjustment index, are popular today.

Although the primary purpose of early multiscore inventories such as the Bernreuter Personality Inventory and the Bell Adjustment Inventory was to identify problems of personality adjustment, the focus was more on milder problems than on severe psychological disorders. The items on subsequent *rational-theoretical* or *content-validated inventories*, like those on the early inventories, were selected because the developers considered them to be indicators of significant personality characteristics or constructs. As noted previously, this *a priori* approach is flawed, but it is still applied in the development of other inventories.

Rational or Content-Validated Inventories

Many multiscore personality inventories were constructed during the 1940s and 1950s, after which a number continued to be used for a time and then declined in popularity. Examples are the California Test of Personality, which was widely administered in the schools, and the Omnibus Personality Inventory for college students. Revisions and new editions kept some of these inventories from going out of print, but the majority have been discontinued. A notable exception is the Taylor-Johnson Temperament Analysis.

Published originally in 1941, the current edition of the Taylor-Johnson Temperament Analysis (T-JTA) (from Psychological Publications) was prepared by R. M. Taylor and L. P. Morrison. This 180-question inventory, which takes about 30 minutes to complete, was designed especially for premarital, marital, and family counseling. It can be taken in "criss-cross" fashion, in which a couple or various family members each take the test and also describe the other person(s). The latest normative data, based on males and females ranging in age from 12 through 74 were published in 1992. The T-JTA can be scored on nine bipolar traits: nervous versus composed, depressive versus light-hearted, active-social versus quiet, expressive-responsive versus inhibited, sympathetic versus indifferent, subjective versus objective, dominant versus submissive, hostile versus tolerant, and self-disciplined versus impulsive. The T-JTA is still widely used and has received high marks from reviewers for its design and scoring and its use in youth work and

| **Self-Concept Scales.** | **TABLE 7–3** |

- *Behavioral Academic Self-Esteem* (by S. Coopersmith & R. Gilberts; Consulting Psychologists Press; reviews MMYB 9:132 & TC III:35)
- *Coopersmith Self-Esteem Inventories* (by S. Coopersmith; Consulting Psychol- ogists Press; reviews MMYB 9:267 & TC I:226)
- *Culture-Free Self-Esteem Inventories, Second Edition* (by J. Battle; pro-ed; review MMYB 12:100)
- *Dimensions of Self-Concept* (by W. B. Michael & R. A. Smith; EdITS; review MMYB 11:113)
- *Multidimensional Self-Concept Scale* (by B. Bracken; pro-ed; review MMYB 12:246).
- *Offer Self-Image Questionnaire for Adolescents-Revised* (by D. Offer, E. Ostrov, K. I. Howard & S. Dolan; Western Psychological Services; review MMYB 12:268).
- *Piers-Harris Children's Self-Concept Scale* (by E. V. Piers & D. B. Harris; Western Psychological Services; reviews MMYB 9:960 & TC I:511).
- *Student Self-Concept Scale* (by F. M. Gresham, S. N. Elliott & S. Evans- Fernandez; American Guidance Service; review MMYB 13:303)
- *Self-Esteem Index* (by L. Brown & J. Alexander; pro-ed; reviews MMYB 11:354 & TC X:644).
- *Tennessee Self-Concept Scale, Second Edition* (by W. H. Fitts & W. L. Warren; Western Psychological Services; reviews MMYB 11:424 and MMYB 13:320).

MMYB = *Mental Measurements Yearbook*; TC = *Test Critiques*

relationship counseling (Stahmann, 1978; Small, 1984). It is available in five languages and also comes in a special edition for the blind.

A number of the personality inventories listed in Table 7–2 focus on a single clinical construct, such as alcoholism, anxiety, depression, stress, or suicidal ideation. Other single-construct inventories deal with less pathological constructs such as self-concept and self-esteem (see Table 7–3). Among the most popular of the single-construct measures are the Beck inventories and various measures of self-concept.

The Beck Inventories

The four instruments in this group—the Beck Depression Inventory, the Beck Hopelessness Scale, the Beck Anxiety Scale, and the Beck Scale for Suicide Ideation—are all clinically-based inventory. Reviews of all four inventories have been quite positive with respect to content, administration, and scoring (Carlson, 1998; Dowd, 1998a; Fernandez, 1998; Hanes, 1998a; Stewart, 1998; Waller, 1998a, 1998b). Each of the inventories consists of 20–21 items and can be completed in 5–10 minutes. The most widely used of the of the four inventories is the Beck Depression Inventory (BDI) or its revision, the BDI-II (Beck & Steer, 1993). The 21 sets of items on the BDI-II were designed to assess the intensity of depression in normal and psychiatric patients and were written in compliance with the DSM-

IV guidelines for the diagnosis of depression. The items, which focus on symptoms present during the preceding two weeks, are comprised of four statements arranged in order of increasing severity with respect to a particular symptoms of depression. Scores on two BDI-II subscales (cognitive-affective and somatic-performance), as well as a total score, may be determined. Total scores of 0 to 9 are designated as "normal," scores of 10–18 as "mild-moderate depression", scores of 19–29 as "moderate-severe depression" and scores of 30 and above as "extremely severe depression." Norms for various psychodiagnostic and normal groups are reported in the manual, and internal consistency reliabilities of the scores reach as high as .92. Evidence of the validity of the BDI and BDI-II, including high correlations with clinical ratings of depression, are given in the manual and in the hundreds of studies that have been conducted with these instruments.

Similar in format to the BDI is the 20-item Beck Hopelessness Scale (BHS). The BHS was designed to measure three major aspects of hopelessness—feelings about the future, loss of motivation, and expectations. BHS scores are moderately correlated with those on the BDI, but the former instrument is considered to be a better predictor of suicide intention and behavior than the latter. The internal consistency reliabilities reported in the 1988 BHS manual are reasonably high (.82 to .93 in seven norm groups). The test-retest reliability coefficients are, however, quite modest (.69 after 1 week and .66 after 6 weeks). Reviewing the BHS, Dowd (1992) concluded that it is "a well-constructed and validated instrument, with adequate reliability" (p.82). Owen's (1992) review of the BHS was also positive but less enthusiastic than Dowd's.

Two other Beck scales similar in format to the BDI and BHS are the Beck Anxiety Inventory (BAI) and the Beck Scale for Suicide Ideation (BSI). Like the other Beck scales, these newer instruments were designed for adults from 17–80 years and are available in both English and Spanish. The BAI was designed to measure the severity of anxiety in adolescents and adults, and has been found to discriminate between anxious and nonanxious diagnostic groups. The anxious groups included patients with agoraphobia, panic disorder, social phobia, obsessive-compulsive disorder, and generalized anxiety. The BSI was designed to evaluate suicidal thinking and attitudes and thereby to identify individuals at risk for suicide. The internal consistency reliabilities of the BAI and the BSI are high, but the test-retest reliabilities are more modest. Studies of the clinical validity of the two instruments are reported in the BAI (1990) and BSI (1991) manuals.

Measures of Self-Concept and Self-Esteem

The *self-concept*, which consists of how a person views herself, depends on the person's comparisons of her physical characteristics, abilities, and temperament, as compared with those of other people. The self-concept also includes the attitudes, aspirations, and social roles of the person. Whereas self-concept refers to the ideas or beliefs that an individual has about himself or herself, *self-esteem* consists of how the self is evaluated by the person. People may come to evaluate themselves highly (high self-esteem) or lowly (low self-esteem).

Q-Sorts, which were discussed in Chapter 6, are measures of self-concept based on a rating or sorting technique. Other measures of self-concept and self-esteem, those that have an inventory format, are listed in Table 7–3. Three of the most popular of these instruments—the Tennessee Self-Concept Scale, the Piers-Harris Self-Concept Scale, and the Coopersmith Self-Esteem Inventories—will be discussed in some detail.

Tennessee Self-Concept Scale, Second Edition (TSCS:2). This inventory is a re-standardized, streamlined and updated version of a widely used measure of self-concept (Fitts, 1965). The self-descriptive statements can be answered in a total of 10–20 minutes on a scale ranging from 1 (completely false) to 5 (completely true). Items on the Adult Form of the TSCS:2 (ages 13 +) are written at a third-grade reading level, and items on the Child Form (ages 7–14 years) at a second-grade level. A Short Form (20 items) is also available. The Adult Form of the TSCS:2 can be scored by computer or by hand on the following 15 variables: Self-Concept Scores—Physical, Moral, Personal, Family, Social, Academic/Work; Summary Scores—Total Self-Conflict, Conflict; Supplementary Scores—Identity, Satisfaction, Behavior; Validity Scores—Inconsistent Respondent, Self-Criticism, Faking Good, Response Distribution.

Piers-Harris Self-Concept Scale. This inventory, also known as The Way I Feel About Myself, consists of 80 yes-no statements written at a third grade level (Piers, 1969). It is used with children in grades 4 through 12. Percentile and sta-nine scores, based on a standardization group of 1,183 Pennsylvania schoolchil-dren in grades 3 through 11, are obtained on a total Self-Concept scale and six subscales (Physical Appearance Attributes, Anxiety, Intellectual and School Sta-tus, Behavior, Happiness and Satisfaction, Popularity). The six subscales have high internal-consistency reliabilities, and low to high test-retest reliabilities. Among the limitations of the Piers-Harris are the fact that it was standardized on small groups of people and has only moderate correlations with other mea-sures of self-concept. The scores are also substantially influenced by the tendency to fake good or fake bad and other response sets (Cosden, 1984).

Coopersmith Self-Esteem Inventories (CSEI). This instrument consists of three forms: School Form (50 self-esteem items and 8 Lie Scale items) for ages 8 through 15, a School Short Form (50 self-esteem items) for ages 8 through 15, and Adult Form (25 items) for ages 16 and above (Coopersmith, 1981). The items on all three forms are dichotomous (Like Me, Unlike Me). The CSEI can be scored for General Self, Social Self-Peers, Home-Parents, School Academic, Total Self, and

Lie Scale. It has been widely-used, the School Form being especially popular. The CSEI manual, which is based on Stanley Coopersmith's (1981) book, *The Antecedents of Self-Esteem*, goes beyond the usual test manual in providing specific suggestions for counselors and teachers on how to improve students' self esteem. However, the reliability, validity and standardization data, as reported in the manual and in other publications, are inadequate (Adair, 1984). Furthermore, no exact criteria for evaluating self-esteem, which is categorized as low, medium, or high, are provided.

Health-Related Inventories

The number of commercially available checklists, ratings scales, and other questionnaires concerned with health-related matters has increased markedly during recent years. Included among these are instrument designed to inventory health problems in general and specific health areas, opinions and beliefs pertaining to health, measures of stress and ways of coping with stress, measures of pain perception and control, and measures of anxiety, depression, and addictive behavior (alcohol and drugs). Use of these kinds of instruments is indicative of the growing interest in the field of health psychology. Illustrative of health-related personality inventories are the Eating Disorder Inventory for assessing behavior traits associated with anorexia nervous and bulimia and the Millon Behavioral Health Inventory for assisting in formulating a comprehensive treatment plan for adult medical patients.

Eating Disorder Inventory-2 (EDI-2). This revised edition of the Eating Disorder Inventory (Garner, 1984) consists of 91 forced choice items (64 original items plus 27 additional items). The respondent (age 12 and over) rates each item on a six-point scale ranging from "always" to "never," and then completes a four-page symptom checklist. Designed to assess a broad range of psychological features of eating disorders such as anorexia nervosa and bulimia nervous, EDI-2 is scored on eight original subscales (Drive for Thinness, Ineffectiveness, Body Dissatisfaction, Interpersonal Distrust, Bulimia, Perfectionism, Maturity Fear, Interoceptive Awareness) and three provisional subscales (Impulse Regulation, Social Insecurity, and Asceticism). However, the significant positive correlations among the majority of the scales show that they do not represent independent dimensions. The majority of the correlations of the EDI and EDI-2 scales with scores on several personality inventories and clinicians' ratings are modest but significant. Sample cases and a few research studies employing the EDI-2 and the EDI are also described in the manual. From these data, it can be tentatively concluded that the EDI-2 has promise as a clinical screening tool, an outcome measure, and an adjunct to clinical judgments of patients with eating disorders. It has received positive reviews as a clinical tool in dealing with anorexia nervosa, bulimia, and other eating disorders (e. g., Ash, 1995; Schinke, 1995).

Millon Behavioral Health Inventory (MBHI). Unlike the Eating Disorder Inventory-2, which focuses on a specific disorder, the MBHI is more general in its relationship to health (Millon, Green, & Meagher, 1982). Designed to assist clinicians (physicians, nurses, psychologists) in formulating a comprehensive treatment plan for physically ill and behavioral-medicine adult medical patients, the MBHI consists of 150 true-false, problem-descriptive statements and can be completed by an adult in 20 minutes or so. It is scored on scales grouped into four broad categories: eight Basic Coping Styles (likely style of dealing with health care personnel and medical regimens), six Psychogenic Attitudes (problematic psychological attitudes and stressors), six Psychosomatic Correlates (similarity to patients with psychosomatic complications), and Prognostic Indexes (possible treatment difficulties). A computer-generated interpretive report for the MBHI, prepared by NCS Assessments, is based on norms obtained on clinical (medical) and nonclinical samples of adults 18 years and older. The report indicates how the patient will probably relate to health care personnel, what psychosocial attitudes and stressors are likely to cause problems, and the patient's similarity to people with psychosomatic complications or those who respond poorly to medical treatment. The test-retest and internal-consistency reliabilities of the MBHI are comparable to those of other multivariable inventories (median correlation of .80). A variety of psychometric and empirical research data pertaining to the construct validity of the instrument are described in the manual. In a review of the MBHI, Allen (1985) maintained that the manual does not adequately describe the test construction, standardization, and interpretation procedures. He pointed out that the reliabilities of the 20 MBHI clinical scales are modest in a nonpatient sample and unknown among patients; the scales also have rather high correlations with each other, making profile analysis difficult. Allen also concluded that evidence for the validity of the computer narrative interpretations of the MBHI scores is inadequate.

Theory-Based Inventories

Construction of the personality inventories described previously in this chapter was not guided by a specific theory of personality, though informal theories or constructs played a role in the development of some of them. For example, theories pertaining to the self presumably influenced the construction of the Tennessee Self-Concept Scale and the Coopersmith Self-Esteem Inventories.

Two theories that have been particularly influential in the design of personality inventories are Henry Murray's needs/press theory and Carl Jung's analytic theory. Among the instruments that have employed concepts from Murray's theory are the Adjective Check List, the Edwards Personal Preference Schedule, the Personality Research Form, and the Thematic Apperception Test. Two inventories that are based on Jung's typology are the Myers-Briggs Type Indicator and the Singer-Loomis Inventory of Personality.

Edwards Personal Preference Schedule (EPPS). The EPPS, which consists of 225 pairs of statements pertaining to likes and feelings, is one of the most widely researched of all personality inventories (Edwards, 1959). Each pair of forced-choice statements pits two psychological needs against each other. Examinees are instructed to indicate which statement is more descriptive or characteristic of themselves. In an effort to control for the social desirability response set, the two statements comprising each item were selected to be approximately equal in social desirability. An example of such a pair of statements is

A. I like to do things by myself.
B. I like to help others do things.

The 15 needs on which the EPPS is scored are achievement, deference, order, exhibition, autonomy, affiliation, intraception, succorance, dominance, abasement, nurturance, change, endurance, heterosexuality, and aggression; consistency and profile stability scores are also computed. Percentile and T score norms for each scale are based on over 1,500 students in 29 colleges and approximately 9,000 adults in 48 states; separate norms for high school students are also available. Split-half reliabilities of the scores range from .60 to .87, and test-retest reliabilities range from .74 to .88.

As with other forced-choice inventories, scores on the EPPS are *ipsative* rather than *normative*, and must be interpreted accordingly. By endorsing statements pertaining to certain needs, the respondent *ipso facto* rejects statements pertaining to other needs. Consequently, the person's score on one need is relative to his or her scores on the other needs. This means that scores on the various need scales are not statistically independent, a circumstance that creates problems in interpreting the scores.

The forced-choice format of the EPPS controls to some extent for the social desirability response set, but many examinees find the format awkward and difficult. The validity of the EPPS scales as measures of psychological needs is also questionable. For example, the scores do not correlate very highly with other measures of similar variables.

Edwards reportedly designed the EPPS as an exercise in personality test construction rather than as a serious competitor with other inventories. The EPPS has stimulated a great deal of research, but it remains, even after more than 40 years, an interesting research and instructional tool rather than a diagnostic device that is applicable to clinical situations. In a survey of assessment procedures used by clinical psychologists, 13% of the same ($n = 355$) reported using the EPPS at least occasionally (Watkins et al., 1995).

Myers-Briggs Type Indicator. One of the most widely-used personality inventories, particularly in business/industrial contexts, is the Myers-Briggs Type Indicator (MBTI; Myers & McCaulley, 1985). Items on the two forms of this inventory—Form G (Standard) with 126 two-choice items and Form K (Advanced) with 131 items, are concerned with preferences or inclinations in feelings and behavior in individuals aged 14 and above. Following Carl Jung's theory of personality types, the MBTI can be scored on four bipolar scales: Extraversion-Introversion, Sensing-Intuition, Thinking-Feeling, and Judging-Perceiving. The Extraversion-Introversion scale measures the extent to which examinees relate to the outer world of people and things (Extraversion) or to the inner world of ideas (Introversion). The Sensing-Intuition scale measure the extent to which examinees prefer to work with known facts (Sensing) or to look for possibilities and relationships (Intuition). The Thinking-Feeling scale measures the extent to which examinees base their judgments more on impersonal analysis and logic (Thinking) or on personal values (Feeling). The Judging-Perceiving scale measure the extent to which people prefer a planned, orderly way of life (Judging) or a flexible, spontaneous way of life (Perceiving). Combinations of scores on the four two-part categories result in 16 possible personality types. For example, an ENFP type is a person whose predominant modes are Extraversion, Intuition, Feeling, and Perceiving. An ISTJ type, on the other hand, is a person whose predominant modes are Introversion, Sensing, Thinking, and Judging. Unfortunately, no measures of test-taking attitude are provided, a shortcoming that could lead to errors in diagnosis and screening (Willis, 1984).

Percentile norms for the four MBTI indicator scores, based on small samples of high school and college students, are provided in the manual (Myers & McCaulley, 1985). The split-half reliabilities of the four scores are reported as in the .70s and .80s, and a number of small-scale validity studies are also described. Although the conceptualization of personality in terms of types is not favorably viewed by most American psychologists, an impressive array of materials on the Myers-Briggs Type Indicator has been published by Consulting Psychologists Press. These materials include profiles, books, computer software, and various kinds of narrative reports (individual, team, career, relationship, leadership, entrepreneur). The materials should be studied extensively by anyone wishing to obtain the necessary background information and skills for administering and interpreting the MBTI.

Millon Index of Personality Styles (MIPS). This inventory is an extension of the Millon Clinical Multiaxial Inventory (see Chapter 8) to "normal" people (Millon,

1994). It is based on Theodore Millon's biopsychosocial taxonomic theory of personality and personality pathology. The MIPS consists of 180 true-false items designed for individuals aged 18 years and above, and requires about 30 minutes to complete. Scores are computed on three pairs of Motivating Aims scales (Enhancing/Preserving, Modifying/Accommodating, Individuating/Nurturing), four Cognitive Modes scales (Extraversing/Introversing, Sensing/Intuiting, Thinking/Feeling, Systematizing/Innovating), and five Interpersonal Behaviors scales (Retiring/Outgoing, Hesitating/Asserting, Dissenting/Conforming, Yielding/Controlling, Complaining/Agreeing). The Cognitive Modes scales, which assess information processing styles, are based on the four Jungian-type variables on which the Myers-Briggs Type Indicator is also scored. The Motivating Aims scales of the MIPS assess orientation toward obtaining reinforcement from the environment, and the Interpersonal Behaviors scales assess the respondent's style of relating to other people. Scores on three validating measures (Positive Impression, Negative Impression, Consistency), plus an Overall Adjustment Index, can also be determined. Raw scores on the various MIPS scales are converted to Prevalence Scale (PS) values ranging from 0 to 100. These prevalence scores take into account the frequency of occurrence of a particular characteristic in the population of interest.

Two separate national samples were used in standardizing the MIPS: 1000 adults stratified by age, race/ethnicity, and geographical region; and 1600 college students. Split-half reliabilities of scores were in the low .80s for both groups, while test-retest reliabilities for the adult sample averaged .85. Research reported in the MIPS manual includes the screening of military recruits for general adjustment, selection and training of law enforcement officers, identification of management talent, and vocational guidance and career decision making. Reviews of the MIPS (e. g., Aiken, 1997b; Choca, 1998; Zachar, 1998b) have been positive for the most part, but the reliability coefficients are fairly modest and the validity data presented in the manual are interesting but not impressive. The MIPS receives higher marks on its theoretical underpinnings rather than on practical applications.

Factor-Analyzed Inventories

A common goal of researchers who apply factor-analytic techniques to the analysis of personality has been to identify a relatively small number of personality factors or traits to account for variations in scores on different inventories and then to construct a measure of each factor. The first published application of factor analysis to the study of personality was made by Webb (1915), who had large groups of males in schools and colleges rate 40 or more qualities that they considered to have "a general and fundamental bearing on the total personality."

Treatment of the data by an early form of factor analysis led Webb to conclude that "consistency of action resulting from deliberate volition, or 'will,' is the most basic characteristic of personality."

J.P. Guilford, whose research and development work began in the late 1930s and early 1940s (Guilford, 1940; Guilford & Martin, 1943), deserves credit for being the first person to construct a multivariable personality inventory by factor-analytic techniques. Guilford's initial inventories were the Inventory of Factors STDCR (Guilford, 1940), the Personnel Inventory (Guilford & Martin, 1943a), and the Inventory of Factors GAMIN (Guilford & Martin, 1943b). Construction of these inventories, which was influenced by Carl Jung's introversion-extroversion typology, involved correlating scores on a large number of existing personality tests. Guilford's tests were carefully reviewed by Louis and Thelma Thurstone, who then devised their own personality inventory, the Thurstone Temperament Schedule (Thurstone, 1949). This 140-item inventory was scored on seven traits (Active, Vigorous, Impulsive, Dominant, Stable, Sociable, Reflective), but the reliabilities of the trait measures were not high.

Guilford-Zimmerman Temperament Survey. Following the Thurstones' analysis of Guilford's data, the latter reanalyzed his earlier results and published a ten-factor composite of his three earlier inventories. Known as the Guilford-Zimmerman Temperament Survey (GZTS) (Guilford & Zimmerman, 1949), this inventory was designed for high school through adult levels and is scored on ten trait scales: General Activity, Restraint, Ascendance, Sociability, Emotional Stability, Objectivity, Friendliness, Thoughtfulness, Personal Relations, and Masculinity. Three verification keys for detecting false and careless responding have also been provided. Percentile and standard score norms for the ten scales, which have moderate reliabilities, are based mainly on samples of college students. Though still in print (Consulting Psychologists Press), the GZTS has never been as popular as the more clinically-oriented Minnesota Multiphasic Personality Inventory.

Cattell's Questionnaires. Perhaps the most comprehensive series of inventories for assessing personality in both children and adults was designed by R.B. Cattell. Cattell began his personality research with a list of 17,953 personality-descriptive adjectives, which Allport and Odbert (1936) had gleaned from the dictionary. By combining terms having similar meanings, the list was first reduced to 4,504 "real" traits and then to 171 trait names; subsequent factor analyses of scores on these trait dimensions produced 31 surface traits and 12 source traits of personality. Cattell devised a number of measures of these traits and four others isolated in his later work, but his major product was the 16 Personality Factor Questionnaire (16PF).

The fifth edition of the 16PF (Cattell, Cattell, & Cattell, 1993) contains 185 three-choice items (the middle choice is always "?"), including 10–15 items for each of the 16 primary factor scales (Russell & Karol, 1994). The items were written to reflect modern language usage, and they have been screened for ambiguity as well as gender, race, and cultural bias. Overall readability of the inventory is at the fifth-grade level, and total testing time is 35–50 minutes. In addition to the 16 primary factors, the inventory can be scored (by hand or by computer) on five global (second-order) factors and three validity indices (see Figure 7–1). These indices—Impression Management, Infrequency, and Acquiescence—provide a preliminary check on the validity of the responses, but they are not used to adjust the factor scores. In addition to score profiles like the one in Figure 7–1, a Comprehensive Personality Interpretation analyzes the results in terms of the three validity indices, global perspective, cognitive and perceptual functioning, interpersonal style, intimate relationships, occupational considerations, personality dynamics, and therapeutic and counseling issues. The normative data on the fifth edition are based on the 1990 U.S. Census, and combined gender norms are available. In addition to improvements in the construction and norms, the reliabilities of the 16PF scales are higher than those of its predecessors. Internal consistency reliabilities range from .64 to .85, with an average of .74. Test-retest reliabilities average about .80 over a two-week interval and .70 over a two-month interval.

Four inventories designed by Cattell as downward extensions of the 16PF are the High School Personality Questionnaire (for ages 12 through 18), the Children's Personality Questionnaire (for ages 8 through 12), the Early School Personality Questionnaire (for ages 6 through 8), and the Preschool Personality Questionnaire (for ages 4 through 6). Like the 16PF, these questionnaires have some problems with reliability, but they are generally well-constructed and have proved useful in educational and research contexts. Cattell also designed several single-score instruments (for example, the IPAT Anxiety Scale and the IPAT Depression Scale) as measures of more general factors of personality. By factor analyzing 16PF items related to psychological disorders, 12 new factors were obtained, and a new inventory, the Clinical Analysis Questionnaire, was then constructed to assess scores on these 12 factors in clinical populations.

Adult Personality Inventory. Related to the 16PF is the Adult Personality Inventory (API), a 324-item self-report inventory for assessing personality in normal adults. In addition to four validity scales, the API can be scored on 21 content scales. These consist of seven personality characteristics (Extroverted, Adjusted, Tough-minded, Independent, Disciplined, Creative, Enterprising), eight interpersonal styles (Caring, Adapting, Withdrawn, Submissive, Uncaring, Non-Conforming, Sociable, Assertive), and six career/lifestyle factors (Practical, Scientific, Aesthetic, Social, Competitive, Structured). The API was standardized on 1000 adults, and separate norms for men and women are available. The norms, however, have been criticized as unrepresentative (D'Amato, 1995). The reliability

Score Profile for 16PF Fifth Edition.
(From the 16PF Fifth Edition Basic Interpretive Report. Copyright © 1994
by the Institute for Personality and Ability Testing, Inc. Reproduced by
permission. 16PF is a trademark of IPAT, Inc.)

FIG. 7-1

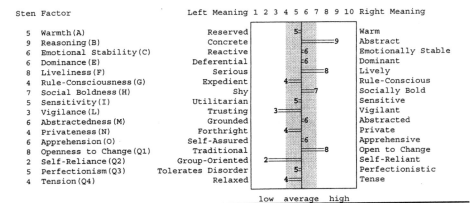

Basic Score Report   NAME: Mark Sample
Profile   DATE: August 10, 1998

                                                      Norms: Combined


```
            ┌────────────────────────────────────────────────────────────┐
            │              Response Style Indices                          │
            │                                                              │
            │  Index                    RS                                 │
            │  Impression Management    14    within expected range        │
            │  Infrequency               0    within expected range        │
            │  Acquiescence             56    within expected range        │
            │                                                              │
            │  All response style indices are within the normal range.     │
            └────────────────────────────────────────────────────────────┘
```


                              Global Factors

Sten Factor   Left Meaning 1 2 3 4 5 6 7 8 9 10 Right Meaning

  8 Extraversion   Introverted   8   Extraverted
  4 Anxiety   Low Anxiety   4   High Anxiety
  5 Tough-Mindedness   Receptive   5   Tough-Minded
  7 Independence   Accommodating   7.   Independent
  4 Self-Control   Unrestrained   4   Self-Controlled

                          low average high

                               16PF Profile

Sten Factor   Left Meaning 1 2 3 4 5 6 7 8 9 10 Right Meaning

  5 Warmth(A)   Reserved   5   Warm
  9 Reasoning(B)   Concrete   9   Abstract
  6 Emotional Stability(C)   Reactive   6   Emotionally Stable
  6 Dominance(E)   Deferential   6   Dominant
  8 Liveliness(F)   Serious   8   Lively
  4 Rule-Consciousness(G)   Expedient   4   Rule-Conscious
  7 Social Boldness(H)   Shy   7   Socially Bold
  5 Sensitivity(I)   Utilitarian   5   Sensitive
  3 Vigilance(L)   Trusting   3   Vigilant
  6 Abstractedness(M)   Grounded   6   Abstracted
  4 Privateness(N)   Forthright   4   Private
  6 Apprehension(O)   Self-Assured   6   Apprehensive
  8 Openness to Change(Q1)   Traditional   8   Open to Change
  2 Self-Reliance(Q2)   Group-Oriented 2   Self-Reliant
  5 Perfectionism(Q3)   Tolerates Disorder   5   Perfectionistic
  4 Tension(Q4)   Relaxed   4   Tense

                          low average high

and construct validity information reported in the manual are quite limited; the internal consistency and test-retest reliability coefficients average around .75. Despite these shortcomings, the API has been used in various counseling and personnel contexts. The availability of accompanying Career Profile computer software has contributed to the attractiveness of this inventory to many practitioners and researchers (see Report 4–2 on page 115).

Eysenck Personality Questionnaire–Revised (EPQ-R). This revision of the Eysenck Personality Inventory and the Junior Eysenck Personality Inventory represents a more parsimonious conception of personality than the inventories of Guilford and Cattell (Eysenck & Eysenck, 1975). Hans Eysenck's earlier inventories (Maudsley Personality Inventory and Eysenck Personality Inventory) were scored for two basic dimensions, Neuroticism or Emotionality (N) and Extraversion (versus Introversion) (E), that had emerged from his factor-analytic research. A measure of a third dimension, Psychoticism or Tough-mindedness (P), and a Lie Scale (L) were added in constructing the EPQ. The EPQ-R was designed for college students and adults in general, and takes only 10 to 15 minutes to complete. The test-retest reliabilities for the N, E, P, and L scales are in the .70s and .80s.

The EPQ-R and its predecessors have been used extensively in personality research, but less frequently in clinical and other applied contexts. Eysenck (1965, 1981) used scores on the introversion-extraversion and neuroticism factors in particular to predict how individuals will react in certain experimental situations (see Chapter 13, pp. 407–409).

Profile of Mood States. Requiring even less testing time (3–5 minutes) than the Eysenck Personality Questionnaire is the Profile of Mood States (POMS; McNair, Lorr, & Droppleman, 1971/1981). Designed for ages 18 through adult, the POMS consists of 65 adjectives describing feelings and mood. For each adjective, examinees are instructed to fill in the circle corresponding to the term or phrase that best describes how they have been feeling during the "past week including today." Possible responses on the five-point scale are *Not at all, A little, Moderately, Quite a bit, Extremely.* In the sense that it aspires to measure short-term or transitory conditions, the POMS is similar to the State Scale of the State-Trait Anxiety Inventory, the Multiple Affect Adjective Check List (see Chapter 6), and Bergner and Gilson's (1981) Sickness Impact Profile.

The POMS is scored on six factors derived from repeated factor analyses: Tension-Anxiety (T), Depression-Dejection (D), Anger-Hostility (A), Vigor-Activity (V), Fatigue-Inertia (F), and Confusion-Bewilderment (C). Scores on the six factors may also be summed to yield a Total Mood Disturbance (TMD) score. Internal-consistency reliability coefficients for the six factors range from .84 to .95. As might be expected with transitory moods, the test-retest coefficients are quite low (.43 to .52). A variety of studies pertaining to the validity of the POMS are described in the manual, including short term psychotherapy studies, controlled outpatient drug trials, and studies of emotion-inducing conditions. Normative data are based on several hundred psychiatric outpatients and college students, but they are probably not representative.

Peterson and Headen (1984) gave the POMS a fairly positive review. It was judged to be a relatively valid measure of momentary mood states, particularly in psychiatric outpatients and for use in research on the effects of medical or psychological interventions. There are problems concerning the appropriateness of the norms and the factor structure of the POMS, but it is convenient and easy to administer and score and has been employed fairly extensively as a research instrument (see Chapter 13, p. 418)

■ Factor Analysis and the Five-Factor Model

Many other personality inventories have been constructed using factor-analytic methodologies. Most specialists in this field, however, do not claim that factor analysis, regardless of how mathematically sophisticated it may be, reveals true dimensions of personality. Rather, by revealing internal consistencies and differences among test items and scales, factor analysis helps clarify the relationships among personality constructs or variables. Personality assessment instruments constructed from the results of factor analyses of the responses of large samples of people to a wide assortment of items do not rest on a solid theoretical foundation but rather are a reflection of lexical, or language-related, consistencies in the meanings of psychological trait names (Cohen, Swerdlik, & Phillips, 1996). Combining items into relatively homogeneous, independent factors may improve the prediction of empirical criteria from such variables and enhance understanding of the constructs purportedly measured by instruments scored on these factors, but it would be a mistake to conclude that the scores can account for the complexity of human personality. The factors may be heuristic indicators of personality, and measures of them may serve as effective predictors of various behavioral criteria, but they are in no way construable as the "stuff" of personality itself.

The criterion-related validities of personality inventories constructed by factor analysis tend to be either low or unknown. The result is that these inventories are generally less helpful in making behavioral predictions and decisions (diagnostic, intervention, training, and the like) in clinical and other applied psychological contexts than content-validated and criterion-keyed inventories.

Five-Factor Model

Despite the limitations of factor analysis, applications of factor analytic procedures to the construction of personality inventories and to even more basic research on the nature of human personality remain appealing to many psychologists. There is fairly general agreement that a large number of personality inventories measure at least two of the factors described by Eysenck—extraversion-introversion and neuroticism (emotionality). In addition, recently there has been some consensus that personality can be efficiently described in terms of five factors. As listed by Goldberg (1980), these five factors are extraversion or surgency, agreeableness, conscientiousness, emotional stability, and culture. Costa and McCrae (1986) prefer the terms neuroticism, extraversion, openness, agreeableness, and conscientiousness, which they defined as follows:

Neuroticism is characterized as being worrying rather than calm, insecure rather than secure, and self-pitying rather that self-satisfied. High scorers on this factor feel generally anxious, cope poorly with stress, have unrealistic self-assessments, and readily experience negative emotions.

Extraversion is characterized as being sociable rather than retiring, fun-loving rather than sober, and affectionate rather than reserved. High scorers on this factor are active, assertive, cheerful, optimistic people who enjoy social gatherings. Low scorers (introverts) possess the opposite characteristics.

Openness is characterized as being imaginative rather than down to earth, preferring variety rather than routine, and independent rather than conforming. High scorers on this factor feel emotions keenly, are intellectually sensitive, and are attuned to external sights and sounds and internal experiences. Low scorers are conventional, down-to-earth people who have narrow interests and low aesthetic appreciation.

Agreeableness is characterized as being soft-hearted rather than ruthless, trusting rather than suspicious, and helpful rather than uncooperative. High scorers on this factor are eager to help other people and expect to be treated similarly. Low scorers are cynical, suspicious, and uncooperative.

Conscientiousness is characterized as being well-organized rather than disorganized, careful rather than careless, and self-disciplined rather than weak willed. High scorers on this factor are persistent, consistent, reliable, and frequently puritanical in their attitudes. Low scorers are aimless, lax, and unreliable.

After reviewing research on the structural validity of the five-factor model in several languages and cultures, Ostendorf and Angleitner (1994) concluded that these five factors are highly consistent across various groups of people in different situations (see also Goldberg, 1994; McCrae & Costa, 1987). However, Block (1995) questioned the conceptual and methodological assumptions underlying the five-factor model and concluded that there are serious uncertainties with respect to the model and the meanings of the five factors on which it is based.

Butcher and Rouse (1996) also maintained that the five-factor model is an inadequate conceptualization of personality, for the following reasons:

1. The failure of empirical research to support the hypothesized relationships between the five-factor model and the disorders on Axis II of DSM-IV. Although the factors of the model may be related to psychopathology, the relationships are not high enough to validly differentiate between diagnostic categories.

2. The underrepresentation of many important concepts in personality assessment in the five-factor model.

3. The possibility that the five-factor model is a result of an analysis of common linguistic structure rather than basic dimensions of personality or behavior.

NEO-PI-R and NEO-FFI

An assessment of personality in terms of the five-factor model is provided by the NEO Personality Inventory—Revised (NEO-PI-R) and an abbreviated version, the NEO Five-Factor Inventory (NEO-FFI) (Costa & McCrae, 1992). The NEO-PI-R consists of 243 items rated on a five-point scale and takes about 30 minutes to complete. The NEO-FFI contains 60 items and requires 10–15 minutes to complete. Both inventories are scored for the three N-E-O domains (factors) of Neuroticism (N), Extroversion (E), and Openness to Experience (O), as well as Agreeableness (A), and Conscientiousness (C). Each of the five domains is further divided into six facets:

- Neuroticism: Anxiety, Hostility, Depression, Self-Consciousness, Impulsiveness, Vulnerability
- Extraversion: Warmth, Gregariousness, Assertiveness, Activity, Excitement-Seeking, Positive Emotions
- Openness to Experience: Fantasy, Aesthetics, Feeling, Actions, Ideas, Values
- Agreeableness: Trust, Modesty, Compliance, Altruism, Straightforwardness, Tender-Mindedness
- Consciousness: Competence, Self-Discipline, Achievement Striving, Dutifulness, Order, Deliberation

Internal consistency reliability coefficients for the domain scales range from .86 to .95 for NEO-PI-R and from .74 to .89 for NEO-FFI, but are lower for the facet scales (.56 to .90 for NEO-PI-R). Test-retest reliabilities computed over a six-month period range from .86 to .91 for the domain scales and from .66 to .92 for the facet scales on the original NEO-PI. Evidence for the validity of these inventories is rather meager, but significant correlations with other personality inventories, experts' ratings, and sentence-completion test scores are reported in the manual.

Hogan Personality Inventory

Another example of a personality inventory based on factor analysis and consistent with a five-factor model, as well as with Robert Hogan's (1983) theory relating basic human motivation to social behavior and personal development, is the Hogan Personality Inventory (Hogan & Hogan, 1992). This measure of normal personality was designed for use in personnel selection, individualized assessment, and career-related decision making. The 206 true/false items are written at a fourth grade reading level and can be answered in about 20 minutes. Responses are scored on seven personality scales (Adjustment, Ambition, Sociability, Likability, Prudence, Intellectance, School Success) and six occupational scales (Service Orientation, Stress Tolerance, Reliability, Clerical Potential, Sales Potential, Managerial Potential). The seven personality scales represent an extension of the five-factor model, in that the factors of extraversion and openness have been broken down into two factors each; ambition and sociability for extraversion, intellectance and school success for openness. The Hogan Personality Inventory was standardized on over 30,000 working adults in a wide variety of industries and validated on dozens of work-related occupations.

■ Summary

Personality inventories were originally designed to identify and diagnose maladjustment and psychiatric disorders, but they were expanded to include the assessment of a wide range of normal and abnormal characteristics. These inventories are objective, in the sense that they can be scored reliably by individuals having no special psychological training. They can also tap a variety of personality variables in a fairly short period of time.

Three strategies that have been applied to the construction of personality inventories are the rational-theoretical strategy, the factor-analytic strategy, and the criterion-keying strategy. Inventories devised by the first two strategies are described in this chapter, and those designed by the third strategy are examined in Chapter 8. No single strategy is uniformly superior to the others; each has it advantages and disadvantages, and a combination is usually best.

The problem of truthfulness in responding to items on personality inventories, including faking good, faking bad, and response sets such as acquiescence and social desirability, has been dealt with in a number of ways. The number of items omitted by the examinee, the number of items that the examinee answered differently from the normative sample, and the use of special validity scales are three ways of detecting faking (good or bad) and response sets on personality inventories. The use of special response formats, such as the forced-choice technique, can also help to control for response sets.

Norms on personality inventories are typically not as representative of the target population as those on tests of achievement and intelligence. Special problems also occur in interpreting the results of ipsative scales, in which the responses to items on one scale affect responses to items on other scales. Furthermore, the reliabilities of personality inventories tend to be lower than those of cognitive abilities tests. Personality inventories are also limited in their ability to diagnose and predict behavior, and the uses of many of these instruments should be restricted to research.

The first personality inventory to be administered on a mass basis was the Woodworth Personal Data Sheet, for identifying soldiers likely to break down in combat. Other early single-score inventories included the X-O Test and the A-S Reaction Study. Two of the first multiscore personality inventories were the Bernreuter Personality Inventory and the Bell Adjustment Inventory. Among the most popular rational or content-validated, multiscore inventories published initially in the 1940s and 1950s were the California Test of Personality and the Omnibus Personality Inventory. Widely administered, special-purpose inventories such as measures of anxiety and self-concept also made their debut during the 1960s.

Personality, as expressed in reactions to stress and mechanism used in coping with it, have an influence on physical health. Consequently, the relationships of scores on personality inventories to health and health-related behaviors have been of interest to psychological researchers. Illustrative of questionnaires and inventories employed in this research are the Eating Disorder Inventory-2 for identifying anorexia nervosa, bulimia, and related eating problems with psychological bases, and the Millon Behavioral Health Inventory for assistance in formulating comprehensive treatment plans for adult medical patients.

Two theories that have greatly influenced the development of personality inventories are Henry Murray's need-press theory and Carl Jung's analytic theory. Instruments designed to measure the psychological needs posited by Murray include the Edwards Personal Preference Schedule, the Personality Research Form, the Jackson Personality Inventory, and the Adjective Check List. The Myers-Briggs Type Indicator and the Singer-Loomis Inventory of Personality are examples of instruments designed to assess an individual's standing on the various Jungian types.

The use of factor analysis in the development of personality inventories dates back to the pioneering work of J.P. Guilford and L.L. Thurstone. Prominent instruments in this category include the Guilford-Zimmerman Temperament Survey, the 16 Personality Factor Questionnaire, and the Eysenck Personality Questionnaire. Also noteworthy are the Adult Personality Inventory, the Profile of Mood States, the NEO Personality Inventory, the NEO Five-Factor Inventory, and the Hogan Personality Inventory. Factor analysis cannot be said to reveal the true structure of personality, though it can assist in the understanding of personality structure and what is being measured by various inventories and tests.

■ Questions and Activities

1. With respect to the issue of dissimulation or faking on personality inventories, write five true-false items that you think would be answered "true" more often by fakers than nonfakers. Then write five items that you believe would be answered "false" more often than "true" by fakers than nonfakers.

2. Construct an inventory consisting of ten true-false statements that you consider to be effective measures of the social desirability response set. Phrase the statements in such a way that for five of them the keyed response is true and for the other five the keyed response is false.

3. Construct a ten-item self-concept inventory, using a Likert-type item format (SA = Strongly Agree, A = Agree, U = Undecided, D = Disagree, SD = Strongly Disagree). Write five of the statements in the positive direction (positive self-concept) and the remaining five statements in the negative direction (negative self-concept). Mix up the positive and negative statements in the final form of your inventory. An example of a "Positive" statement is "I believe I can accomplish almost anything that I want to." An example of a "negative" statement is "There are times when I have serious doubts about my abilities." Administer your Self-Concept Inventory to several people, and compute their total scores according to the following key:

   Positive self-concept statements—SA = 4, A = 3, U = 2, D = 1, SD = 0.
   Negative self-concept statements—SA = 0, A = 1, U = 2, D = 3, SD = 4.

   Compute the mean, median, range, and standard deviation of the total scores. On the basis of these results, what can you say about the average self-concept score of these people? What can you say about the range of individual differences in self-concept in this group? What evidence can you provide that your ten-item inventory is a valid measure of self-concept?

4. Consult *The Twelfth Mental Measurements Yearbook* (Conoley & Impara, 1995) and *The Thirteenth Mental Measurements Yearbook* (Impara & Plake, 1998) for reviews of any three personality inventories. Are the reviews generally positive or negative? What are the most common sources of criticism of the inventories?

5. Make multiple copies of the following personality inventory and administer them to several other people.

Directions: For each statement, circle the number that indicates how true the statement is of you.

	Hardly				A Lot
1. I make friends easily.	1	2	3	4	5
2. I tend to be shy.	1	2	3	4	5
3. I like to be with others.	1	2	3	4	5
4. I like to be independent of people.	1	2	3	4	5
5. I usually prefer to do things alone.	1	2	3	4	5
6. I am always on the go.	1	2	3	4	5
7. I like to be off and running as soon as I wake up in the morning.	1	2	3	4	5
8. I like to keep busy all of the time.	1	2	3	4	5
9. I am very energetic	1	2	3	4	5
10. I prefer quiet, inactive pastimes to more active ones.	1	2	3	4	5
11. I tend to cry easily.	1	2	3	4	5
12. I am easily frightened.	1	2	3	4	5
13. I tend to be somewhat emotional.	1	2	3	4	5
14. I get upset easily.	1	2	3	4	5
15. I tend to be easily irritated.	1	2	3	4	5

(From *Individual and Group Differences*, by L. Willerman, New York: Harper's College Press, 1975. Reprinted with permission.)

Scoring: For all items except numbers 2, 4, 5, and 10, the score is simply the number circled; for items 2, 4, 5, and 10, reverse the numbers before scoring (1 = 5, 2 = 4, 3 = 3, 4 = 2, 5 = 1). Add the scores on items 1 through 5 to yield an index of Sociability; add the scores on items 6 through 10 to yield an index of Activity Level; add the scores on items 11 through 15 to yield an index of Emotionality. Interpret your scores and those of the other people to whom you administered the inventory with respect to the following "norms." These are the ranges within which 68% of samples of men and women students at a large university scored on the three scales:

Index	Average Range for Men	Average Range for Women
Sociability	13–19	15–20
Activity Level	13–19	13–20
Emotionality	11–18	9–16

Scores outside these ranges can be interpreted as high or low on the particular characteristic. Why is it important for you to be cautious in your interpretations of scores on this inventory?

6. On each of the following scales, check the number which corresponds to your perceived standing on the characteristic.

1.	affectionate	1 — 2 — 3 — 4 — 5 — 6 — 7	reserved
2.	calm	1 — 2 — 3 — 4 — 5 — 6 — 7	worrying
3.	careful	1 — 2 — 3 — 4 — 5 — 6 — 7	careless
4.	conforming	1 — 2 — 3 — 4 — 5 — 6 — 7	independent
5.	disorganized	1 — 2 — 3 — 4 — 5 — 6 — 7	well–organized
6.	down–to–earth	1 — 2 — 3 — 4 — 5 — 6 — 7	imaginative
7.	fun–loving	1 — 2 — 3 — 4 — 5 — 6 — 7	sober
8.	helpful	1 — 2 — 3 — 4 — 5 — 6 — 7	uncooperative
9.	insecure	1 — 2 — 3 — 4 — 5 — 6 — 7	secure
10.	prefer routine	1 — 2 — 3 — 4 — 5 — 6 — 7	prefer variety
11.	retiring	1 — 2 — 3 — 4 — 5 — 6 — 7	sociable
12.	ruthless	1 — 2 — 3 — 4 — 5 — 6 — 7	soft–hearted
13.	self–disciplined	1 — 2 — 3 — 4 — 5 — 6 — 7	weak–willed
14.	self–pitying	1 — 2 — 3 — 4 — 5 — 6 — 7	self–satisfied
15.	suspicious	1 — 2 — 3 — 4 — 5 — 6 — 7	trusting

Score your responses according to the procedure:

Subtract the numbers corresponding to your responses to items 1 and 7 from the number corresponding to your response to item 11; add 13 to the result. This is your raw "Extraversion" score.

Subtract the numbers corresponding to your responses to items 9 and 14 from the number corresponding to your response to item 2; add 13 to the result. This is your raw "Neuroticism" score.

Subtract the numbers corresponding to your responses to items 3 and 13 from the sum of your response to item 5; add "13" to the result. This is your raw "Conscientiousness" score.

Add the numbers corresponding to your responses to items 4, 6, and 10; subtract "3" from the result. This is your raw "Openness" score.

Add the numbers corresponding to your responses to items 12 and 15; subtract the number corresponding to your response to item 8, and add "5" to the result. This is you raw "Agreeableness" score.

Graph and rank-order your scores on the five scales of this "Five-Factor Questionnaire." Are your highest and lowest scores consistent with your subjective evaluation of your personality characteristics?

■ Suggested Readings

Allport, G.W., & Odbert, H.S. (1936). Trait-names, a psycholexical study. *Psychological Monographs, 47*(1).

Allport, F.H., & Allport, G.W. (1921). Personality traits: Their classification and measurement. *Journal of Abnormal and Social Psychology, 16,* 6–40.

Briggs, S.R. (1992). Assessing the five-factor model of personality description. *Journal of Personality, 60,* 253–293.

Burisch, M. (1986). Methods of personality inventory development—a comparative analysis. In A. Angleitner & J.S. Wiggins (Eds.), *Personality assessment via questionnaires* (pp. 109–123). New York: Springer.

Goldberg, L.R. (1993). The structure of phenotypic personality traits. *American Psychologist, 48,* 26–34.

Loevinger, J. (1993). Measurement of personality: True or false? *Psychological Inquiry, 4,* 1–16.

McAdams, D.P. (1992). The five-factor model of personality: A critical appraisal. *Journal of Personality, 60,* 329–361.

CHAPTER 8

Criterion-Keyed Inventories

Rather than relying on rational-theoretical or factor-analytic strategies to determine the items to be included on an inventory to assess affective characteristics, certain psychologists decided quite early to adopt the empirical strategy of letting the items speak for themselves. One of the first psychologists to employ this approach was E. K. Strong. Each item on the Strong Vocational Interest Blank for Men was keyed (scored) on a particular occupational scale only if the item significantly differentiated between the responses of men in that occupation and the responses of men in general. In this *criterion-keyed*, or group-contrast, approach to inventory construction, items are given a numerical scoring weight (keyed) for a designated group if they discriminate between members of that group (the contrast group) and a control group. When constructing a vocational interest inventory by this method, the contrast groups may be salespersons, physicians, engineers, or practitioners of other occupations. In developing a personality inventory by the criterion-keyed approach, the contrast group may consist of anxious people, depressed people, delinquents, schizophrenics, or any other diagnostic group that the inventory is supposed to identify.

Although theoretical in its orientation, the empirical or criterion-keyed approach to inventory construction is not *devoid of* rational forethought: reason, based on common sense and psychological experience, is involved in the initial selection or construction of the items on which the contrast and control groups are to be compared. Nevertheless, the items on a criterion-keyed inventory are typically rather heterogeneous and may not appear to be as face-valid as the items on inventories constructed by rational-theoretical or factor-analytic methods. For example, one of the items keyed for the Banker scale of the original Strong Vocational Interest Blank for Men was concerned with whether the respondent liked men with gold teeth. Items such as this one, which may seem perplexing when they appear on personality inventories, have been the subject of quips by social satirists and others who are critical of personality assessment. Consider the following 14-item, true-false personality inventory devised by the humorist Art Buchwald ("I Was An Imaginary Playmate," 1965, p.9 90):

— When I was young, I used to tease vegetables.
— Sometimes I am unable to prevent clean thoughts from entering my mind.
— I am not unwilling to work for a jackass.
— I would enjoy the work of a chicken flicker.
— I think beavers work too hard.
— It is important to wash your hands before washing your hands.
— It is hard for me to say the right thing when I find myself in a room full of mice.
— I use shoe polish to excess.
— The sight of blood no longer excites me.
— It makes me furious to see an innocent man escape the chair.
— As a child, I used to wet the ceiling.
— I am aroused by persons of the opposite sexes.
— I believe I smell as good as most people.
— When I was a child, I was an imaginary playmate.

It is doubtful that many, if any, of these "rationally constructed" items would differentiate between two diagnostic groups, but they may discriminate between less deceptive persons and those who delight in poking fun at psychologists or parodying their efforts!

■ Minnesota Multiphasic Personality Inventory

By far the most famous, but by no means the first, criterion-keyed inventory of personality was the Minnesota Multiphasic Personality Inventory (MMPI). An earlier instrument of this type was the A-S Reaction Study by G. W. and F. H. Allport (1929–1938); items were included on this inventory only if they differentiated between groups of individuals who were rated by their peers as ascendent or submissive. In addition, experience with earlier inventories such as the Humm-Wadsworth Temperament Scale (Humm & Wadsworth, 1935) provided psychologist S. R. Hathaway and psychiatrist J. C. McKinley with a basis for the development in 1940 of the MMPI. The original purpose of the MMPI was, like that of the Personal Data Sheet constructed by R. S. Woodworth more than two decades earlier, to distinguish between psychologically normal and abnormal people. The MMPI was subsequently employed extensively for diagnostic and research purposes in clinics and mental hospitals, where examinees' scores on the several clinical scales were analyzed for evidence of psychological problems and disorders.

Constructing the MMPI

Hathaway and McKinley (1943) began by assembling hundreds of statements concerning psychological symptoms from psychological reports, textbooks, and other sources. After eliminating ambiguous and similar statements, 504 items remained. These statements were then administered to groups of psychiatric patients who had been diagnosed as hypochondriacal, depressed, hysterical, psychopathic, paranoid, psychasthenic, schizophrenic, or hypomanic, and their responses were compared with those of approximately 700 persons having no history of psychiatric disorders. Comparisons were also made between the responses of each diagnostic group and those of all other diagnostic groups combined. The resulting eight diagnostic scales were then cross-validated by comparing the scores of new groups of patients having each diagnosis with the scores of (1) a new normal group and (2) patients in all other diagnostic groups combined.

Later, the original pool of 504 items was expanded to 566 by including a Masculinity-Femininity scale that was originally designed to identify homosexuals but succeeded only in differentiating between males and females. In addition, a scale for measuring Social Introversion (Si) was constructed. Items on the Si scale were selected to contrast college women who were highly involved in extracurricular activities with those who were less involved (Drake, 1946). This brought the number of scales on the standard MMPI to 14, including four validity scales, nine clinical scales, and the Si scale.

Description of the MMPI

Designed for persons 16 years and older with a minimum of a sixth-grade education, the statement items on the MMPI are to be answered *true or mostly true (T)* versus *false or not usually true (F)*. Statements that do not apply or that the examinee does not know about can be left unanswered (?), but respondents are encouraged to answer them all. The statements are concerned with attitudes toward education, marriage, family, and occupation, as well as emotions, motor disturbances, psychosomatic symptoms, sexual values, political values, religions values, obsessive compulsive behaviors, phobic behaviors, delusions, hallucinations, sadomasochistic thoughts and behaviors, and other thoughts, feelings, and behaviors indicative of psychological problems or disorders. Some examples are
− I am happy most of the time.
− I enjoy social gatherings just to be with people.
− I have never had a fainting spell.
− I believe I am a condemned person.

Sixteen out of a total of 566 statements are repeated. Only 399 items are actually scored for the basic scales, each of which is composed of 15 to 78 items. Because many items appear on more than one scale, the scales are not independent and certain scales have substantial correlations with each other.

MMPI Scales

The nine clinical scales, together with the Si scale and the four validity scales (?, L, F, K) are described in Table 8–1. Many special scales have been developed from the MMPI item pool during the course of literally thousands of research investigations conducted during the past half-century. However, the majority of these special scales, which were designed to measure such variables as accident proneness, alcoholism, anxiety, caudality (frontal vs. nonfrontal cortical damage), control, dependency, dominance, ego strength, low back pain, originality, prejudice, repression, social responsibility, and social status, are seldom used. Among the most commonly used scales are the Taylor Manifest Anxiety Scale, the Welsh A (Anxiety) Scale, the R (Repression) Scale, the Es (Ego Strength) scale, and the Mac (MacAndrew Alcoholism) scale.

TABLE 8–1   **Descriptions of Validity and Clinical Scales on the Original MMPI.**

Validity (Test-taking Attitude) Scales

? (Cannot Say) Number of items left unanswered

L (Lie) Fifteen items of overly good self-report, such as "I smile at everyone I meet." (Answered True)

F (Frequency or Infrequency) Sixty-four items answered in the scored direction by 10 percent or less of normals, such as, "There is an international plot against me." (True)

K (Correction) Thirty items reflecting defensiveness in admitting to problems, such as, "I feel bad when others criticize me." (False)

Clinical Scales

---

1 or Hs (Hypochondriasis) Thirty-three items derived from patients showing abnormal concern with bodily functions, such as, "I have chest pains several times a week." (True)

2 or D (Depression) Sixty items derived from patients showing extreme pessimism, feelings of hopelessness, and slowing of thought and action, such as, "I usually feel that life is interesting and worthwhile." (False)

3 or Hy (Conversion Hysteria) Sixty items from neurotic patients using physical or mental symptoms as a way of unconsciously avoiding difficult conflicts and responsibilities, such as, "My heart frequently pounds so hard I can feel it." (True)

4 or Pd (Psychopathic Deviate) Fifty items from patients who show a repeated and flagrant disregard for social customs, an emotional shallowness and an inability to learn from punishing experiences, such as, "My activities and interests are often criticized by others." (True)

Table 8-1 continued

5 or *Mf (Masculinity-Femininity)* Sixty items from patients showing homoeroticism and items differentiating between men and women, such as, "I like to arrange flowers." (True, scored for femininity.)

6 or *Pa (Paranoia)* Forty items from patients showing abnormal suspiciousness and delusions of grandeur or persecution, such as, "There are evil people trying to influence my mind." (True)

7 or *Pt (Psychasthenia)* Forty-eight items based on neurotic patients showing obsessions, compulsions, abnormal fears, and guilt and indecisiveness, such as, "I save nearly everything I buy, even after I have no use for it." (True)

8 or *Sc (Schizophrenia)* Seventy-eight items from patients showing bizarre or unusual thoughts or behavior, who are often withdrawn and experiencing delusions and hallucinations, such as, "Things around me do not seem real" (True) and "It makes me uncomfortable to have people close to me." (True)

9 or *Ma (Hypomania)* Forty-six items from patients characterized by emotional excitement, overactivity, and flight of ideas, such as, "At times I feel very 'high' or very 'low' for no apparent reason." (True)

0 or *Si (Social Introversion)* Seventy items from persons showing shyness, little interest in people, and insecurity, such as, "I have the time of my life at parties." (False)

Source: After Sundberg (1977). The items quoted are simulated MMPI items. The MMPI scale names and abbreviations are from Minnesota Multiphasic Personality Inventory. Copyright © by the Regents of the University of Minnesota, 1942, 1943 (renewed 1970). Reproduced by permission of the University of Minnesota Press. ("Minnesota Multiphasic Personality Inventory" and "MMPI" are registered trademarks of the University of Minnesota, Minneapolis, Minnesota.)

Examining Scores on the Validity Scales

Before attempting to interpret scores on the clinical or special scales of the MMPI, attention should be directed to scores on the four validity scales—the "?" (*Cannot Say*) scale the L (*Lie*) scale, the F (*Frequency* or *Infrequency*) scale, and the K (*Correction*) scale. A person's score on the "?" scale is the number of items left unanswered. A high "?" score can be interpreted as "defensiveness" or "uncertainty," and, if it is quite high, it may invalidate scales on which many items are not answered. Although there is no set maximum "?" score that invalidates an MMPI profile, omitting 10% or more of the items casts serious doubt on the validity of the profile as a whole. For this reason, examinees are encouraged to respond to every statement even when they are uncertain.

The L (raw lie) or "fake good" score, is the number of items out of 15 special statements that the examinee answers in such a way as to place himself or herself in a favorable light. For example, people who answer true to many statements of the sort "I always tell the truth, never get mad, read every editorial in the newspaper every day, and have as good manners at home as when out in company" tend to obtain high *L* scores. An *L* score of 10 or more, which is at least two standard deviations above the mean, is indicative of an invalid profile.

The *F*, or "fake bad," score ("F" originally stood for "feeblemindedness") is a measure of random or highly deviant responding. Examples of the 64 items on the *F* scale that are rarely endorsed by the general population are "Everything tastes the same" and "I see things, animals, or people around me that others do not see." A high *F* score of, say, 16 or more, suggests that the examinee is trying to appear very emotionally disturbed, has not read the items carefully, or does not understand them. Failure to comply with the test directions, for whatever reason, is also associated with high *scores on the F* scale.

The *K* score is a measure of overcriticalness or overgenerosity in evaluating oneself; high *K* scores indicate defensiveness in responding and are related to the social desirability response set. Examples of the 30 items on the *K* scale are "At times I feel like swearing." and "At times I feel like smashing things." High *K* scorers tend to deny personal inadequacies and deficiencies in self-control, whereas low *K* scorers are willing to say socially undesirable things about themselves. The authors of the MMPI maintained that subtracting a portion of *K* from certain clinical scales improves the discriminatory power of these scales. Consequently, fractions of the *K* score may also be applied as correction factors to the raw scores on clinical scales 1, 4, 7, 8, and 9. However, the value of these corrections has been questioned, and they are not always made. The *F* and *K* scores can also be used in combination, as an *F* minus *K* index, to detect the tendency to fake good or bad. When F-K is greater than 11, the examinee is probably trying to fake bad, when F-K is less than -11, the examinee is probably trying to fake good.

Interpreting Scores on the MMPI Clinical Scales

Although a generally high profile on the nine clinical scales of the MMPI suggests serious psychological problems, a T score of 70 or above on a given clinical scale is not necessarily indicative of the disorder with which that scale is labeled. For this and other reasons, the nine clinical scales are usually referred to by their numerical designations rather than by diagnostic categories. In addition, a psychiatric diagnosis or personality analysis is not made on the basis of a single score but rather from a consideration of score combinations.

One popular approach to MMPI interpretation, proposed some years ago by Paul Meehl (1951), is to examine pairs of scales having T scores of 70 or above. A subsequently developed approach bases the interpretation and psychiatric diagnosis on the pattern displayed by the entire group of scores on the clinical scales. First, the scores are coded according to one of several systems, after which the score profile is interpreted. In addition to placing the examinee into one or more diagnostic categories, behaviors typically associated with various high scores are also described. Several coding systems for analyzing MMPI score profiles have been devised, those of Hathaway and Welsh being the most popular (Duckworth & Anderson, 1986). The coding and profile interpretation processes are described below in connection with MMPI-2.

Reliability, Norms, and Group Differences

Reported test-retest reliability coefficients for the MMPI clinical scales are based on data obtained many years ago from relatively small samples of normal people and psychiatric patients. The coefficients, which are not atypical for instruments of this kind, range from .50 to .90 over relatively short time intervals (days and weeks). After an interval of a year or more, the test-retest coefficients drop to a median of .30 to .40. The substantial decline in reliabilities over longer time periods is not surprising. The extent of psychological disturbance registered by the MMPI fluctuates over time as the examinee receives psychological help, experiences personal crises or changes in stress level, or develops more effective coping skills. Also not surprising is the fact that the internal-consistency coefficients of the MMPI scales are higher than their test-retest correlations. The average internal consistency reliability is around .70 and as high as .90 for some scales.

■ MMPI-2

The MMPI was first published in the early 1940s, so by the 1980s the norms and some of the item content were out-of-date. A revision of the inventory was undertaken for several reasons: to provide new norms; to broaden the item pool by including content not represented in the original version; to revise and reword the language of some of the existing items that were dated, awkward, or sexist; and to provide separate forms of the inventory for adults and adolescents. All 550 of the original MMPI items were retained in the Adult and Adolescent revised versions, but 14 percent of the original items were changed because of antiquated language or awkward wording. Words or phrases more characteristic of the 1940s (for example, "streetcar", "sleeping powder", and "drop the handkerchief") were omitted, and other modifications were made to update statements (for example, "I like to take a bath" became "I like to take a bath or shower"). Included in the Adult Version (MMPI-2) (Butcher et al., 1989) are 154 new experimental items designed to assess certain areas of psychopathology (e.g, eating disorders, Type A personality, drug abuse) not well represented on the original MMPI. The Adolescent Version (MMPI-A) (Butcher et al., 1992) contains 104 new items concerned specifically with the problems of adolescents. In addition,

TABLE 8–2 Scoring Scales for the MMPI-2.

BASIC VALIDITY AND CLINICAL SCALES

Validity:
L Lie
F Infrequency
K Defensiveness
? Cannot Say

Clinical:
(1) Hs Hypochondriasis
(2) D Depression
(3) Hy Conversion Hysteria
(4) Pd Psychopathic Deviate
(5) Mf Masculinity-Femininity
(6) Pa Paranoia
(7) Pt Psychasthenia
(8) Sc Schizophrenia
(9) Ma Hypomania
(0) Si Social Introversion

Content Scales

ANX	Anxiety
FRS	Fears
OBS	Obsessiveness
DEP	Depression
HEA	Health Concerns
BIZ	Bizarre Mentation
ANG	Anger
CYN	Cynicism
ASP	Antisocial Practices
TPA	Type A
LSE	Low Self-Esteem
SOD	Social Discomfort
FAM	Family Problems
WRK	Work Interference
TRT	Negative Treatment Indicators

CONTENT COMPONENT SCALES
Experimental
Fears Subscale

FRS1	Generalized Fearfulness
FRS2	Multiple Fears

Depression Subscales

DEP1	Lack of Drive
DEP2	Dysphoria
DEP3	Self-Depreciation
DEP4	Suicidal Ideation

Health Concerns Subscales

HEA1	Gastrointestinal Symptoms
HEA2	Neurological Symptoms
HEA3	General Health Concerns

Bizarre Mentation Subscales

BIZ1	Psychotic Symptomatology
BIZ2	Schizotypal Characteristics

Anger Subscales

ANG1	Explosive Behavior
ANG2	Irritability

Cynicism Subscales

CYN1	Misanthropic Beliefs
CYN2	Interpersonal Suspiciousness

Antisocial Practices Subscales

ASP1	Antisocial Attitudes
ASP2	Antisocial Behavior

Type A Subscales

TPA1	Impatience
TPA2	Competitive Drive

Low Self-Esteem Subscales

LSE1	Self-Doubt
LSE2	Submissiveness

Social Discomfort

SOD1	Introversion
SOD2	Shyness

Family Problems

FAM1	Family Discord
FAM2	Familial Alienation

Negative Treatment Indicators

TRT1	Low Motivation
TRT2	Inability to Disclose

Table 8-2 continued

Supplementary Scales
TRIN True Response Inconsistency
VRIN Variable Response Inconsistency
FB Back F
A Anxiety
R Repression
Es Ego Strength
MAC-R MacAndrew Alcoholism-Revised
O-H Overcontrolled Hostility
Do Dominance
Re Social Responsibility
Mt College Maladjustment
GM Gender Role Masculine
GF Gender Role-Feminine
PK Post-Traumatic Stress Disorder
    —Keane
PS Post-Traumatic Stress Disorder
    —Schlenger
MDS Marital Distress Scale
APS Addiction Potential Scale
AAS Addiction Admission Scale

Social Introversion Subscales
Si_1 Shyness/Self-Consciousness
Si_2 Social Avoidance
Si_3 Alienation-Self and Others

Harris-Lingoes Subscales
D_1 Subjective Depression
D_2 Psychomotor Retardation
D_3 Physical Malfunctioning
D_4 Mental Dullness
D_5 Brooding
Hy_1 Denial of Social Anxiety
Hy_2 Need for Affection
Hy_3 Lassitude-Malaise
Hy_4 Somatic Complaints
Hy_5 Inhibition of Aggression
Pd_1 Familial Discord
Pd_2 Authority Problems
Pd_3 Social Imperturbability
Pd_4 Social Alienation

Pd_5 Self-Alienation

Pa_1 Persecutory Ideas
Pa_2 Poignancy
Pa_3 Naivete
Sc_1 Social Alienation
Sc_2 Emotional Alienation
Sc_3 Lack of Ego Mastery, Cognitive
Sc_4 Lack of Ego Mastery, Conative
Sc_5 Lack of Ego Mastery, Defective
    Inhibition
Sc_6 Bizarre Sensory Experiences
Ma_1 Amorality
Ma_2 Psychomotor Acceleration
Ma_3 Imperturbability
Ma_4 Ego Inflation

Wiener-Harmon Subtle-Obvious Subscales
D-O Depression, Obvious
D-S Depression, Subtle
Hy-O Hysteria, Obvious
Hy-S Hysteria, Subtle
Pd-O Psychopathic Deviate, Obvious
Pd-S Psychopathic Deviate, Subtle
Pa-O Paranoia, Obvious
Pa-S Paranoia, Subtle
Ma-O Hypomania, Obvious
Ma-S Hypomania, Subtle

SPECIAL INDICES
Welsh Codes (based on MMPI-2
and MMPI norms)
F-K Dissimulation Index
Percentage True and False
Average Profile Elevation

SETTING-SPECIFIC INDICES
Megargee Classification
Pain Classification
Henrichs Rules
Goldberg Index
Cooke's Disturbance Index

Source: Minnesota Multiphasic Personality Inventory-2 (MMPI-2). Copyright © by the University of Minnesota 1942, 1943 (renewed 1970), 1989. Reproduced by permission of the publisher. ("MMPI-2" and "Minnesota Multiphasic Personality Inventory 2" are registered trademarks of the University of Minnesota, Minneapolis, Minnesota).

the tendency for normal adolescents in a temporary state of turmoil to score like adult psychopaths on the original MMPI has been corrected.

Designed to be suitable for nonclinical as well as clinical uses, MMPI-2 consists of 567 true-false questions written at an eighth-grade level and takes approximately 90 minutes to complete. The four validity scales and the ten basic clinical scales are scored from the first 370 items, whereas the supplementary content and research scales are scored on items 371 to 567 (see Table 8–2). Many of the content and research scales are holdovers from the original MMPI.

As shown in Table 8–2, the MMPI-2 is scored on the same clinical scales as its predecessor. However, the T scores for eight of the clinical and other (content) scales have been made uniform so that a given T score is now comparable from scale to scale. The uniform T scores were devised because, due to differences in score distributions, the traditional T scores on different scales were not strictly comparable. Not only do uniform T scores remove these differences, but, unlike normalized T scores, they preserve the general shape of the original distribution of T scores.

To provide a more representative sample of the U.S. adult population than that on which the original MMPI norms were determined, MMPI-2 was standardized on a sample of 2600 U.S. residents aged 18 to 90 (1138 males and 1462 females) based on statistics from geographical distribution, ethnic and racial composition, age and educational levels, and marital status data in the 1980 census. Reliability data reported in the MMPI-2 manual (Hathaway & McKinley, 1989) are based on relatively small samples (82 men and 111 women); test-retest coefficients of the basic scales range from .58 to .92. Some of the low reliability coefficients, coupled with the fairly sizable standard errors of measurement, indicate that differences in scores on the various scales should be interpreted cautiously.

Profile Interpretation

Figure 8–1 is a profile of scores on the MMPI-2 obtained by the 60-year-old businessman described in Report 8–1. Although a generally high profile on the clinical scales suggests serious psychological problems, a high T score on a given clinical scale is not necessarily indicative of the disorder with which the scale is labeled. Rather than being dictated by a single score, a psychiatric diagnosis or personality analysis is made on the basis of the pattern displayed by the entire group of scores. Therefore, the process of profile interpretation starts with profile coding.

The profile coding process is begun by arranging the numerical designations of the nine clinical scales and the Social Introversion scale (scale 0), from left to right, in descending order of their T scores. Performing this ranking process for

Sample Profile of Scores on MMPI-2. See Report 8-1. **FIG. 8-1**

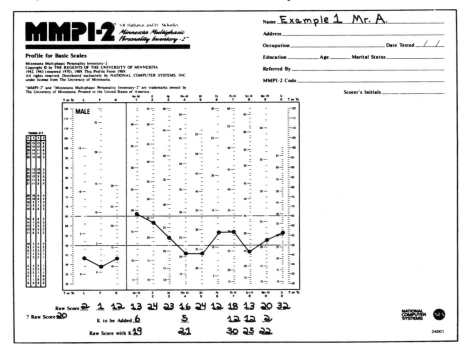

Mr. A. 60-year-old businessman.
Code: 12-670 39/845 /LK:F

the profile in Figure 8–1 yields 1267039845. Both Hathaway's and Welsh's profile coding systems require placing a prime (') after the number of the last scale having a T score of 70 or greater and a dash (-) after the number of the last scale having a T score of 60 or greater. The numerical designations of scales having T score values within 1 point of each other are underlined, and scores on the L, F, and K scales are ranked after the profile code. The complete Welsh code for the profile in Figure 8–1 is 12–670 39/845/LK:F.

A number of interpretive computer programs based on rules for configural or pattern analysis of MMPI and MMPI-2 scores have been developed. Despite the seeming expertness and plausibility of many of these computer-based interpretations, one must be careful not to overmechanize the process of profile interpretation. Machines, as well as people, make mistakes, but the former are often incorrectly perceived as more trustworthy than the latter.

Interpretative Report of Scores on MMPI-2 Profile in Figure 8–1

Mr. A was seen in a medical outpatient service complaining of a variety of abdominal pains and distress. He is a sixty-year-old businessman, white, married, with two years of college. Little evidence could be found for an organic basis for his complaints, and he was referred for psychological assessment.

The profile he obtained on the MMPI-2 is shown in Figure 8–1; the code is 12–670 39/845/LK:F. All the traditional validity indicators are below the mean and suggest that he was very cooperative with the test. There is no evidence of defensiveness or of intention to distort his self-presentation on the inventory. His L and K scores fell in the ranges that raise the possibility that he was deliberately faking a poor adjustment, but his score on the F scale does not indicate that this is true. The correlates of these validity indicators suggest that this man is open, conventional, likely to display his problems, but is not in the midst of a serious emotional crisis.

On scale 1, his highest clinical score, he earned a T score of 66. A score in the high range on this scale suggests that he is rather self-centered and demanding, pessimistic and defeatist in his view of the future, and is likely to overreact to any real problems. It is likely Mr. A will have numerous physical complaints that will shift to different places on his body.

His second highest score is on scale 2 and it falls in the moderate range. This score also suggests that he is pessimistic and discouraged about the future. He is dissatisfied with himself or the world, is worrying and moody. His temperament is introverted, but he is a responsible and modest individual.

Three other scores fall within the moderate range: scales 6, 7, and 0. These scores also characterize Mr. A as responsible, hard-working, and reserved.

Individuals with 12/21 profiles show an exaggerated reaction to physical disorders, are prone to fatigue, and are often shy, irritable, seclusive, and depressed. Visceral pain, overconcern with bodily functions, and lack of insight are prominent features.

The scale-by-scale analysis of this man's profile highlights some hypochondriacal and depressive trends in an introverted, moody, and hard-working man. The code type characteristics are present but only to a moderate degree, as would be expected for profile elevations of this magnitude.

These characterizations are clearly borne out in the background information about Mr. A. He was married at the age of 25 to his present wife;

there have been no marital difficulties. However, Mrs. A has recently quit her job, which resulted in a loss in the family income. They have one child, a son age 25, who is living away from home.

Mr. A has consulted his family physician very frequently in the last year and has made three visits to a Veterans Administration outpatient clinic in the last few months. In addition to his abdominal symptoms, Mr. A has had problems sleeping, complains of chronic fatigue, a loss of interest in sex, and recurring fears of death. He has also lost considerable weight and has had difficulty concentrating in his work. Sedatives have not been helpful. The present diagnostic impression is that Mr. A is suffering from dysthymia (moderate depression) with hypochondriacal features.

In interpreting an MMPI or MMPI-2 profile, special attention is given to scales having T scores above 65 or 70. Scale 2 is considered to be a measure of depression and scale 7 a measure of anxiety, tension, or alertness to unknown danger. Since depression and anxiety are the most common symptoms of mental disorder, psychiatric patients typically have high scores on scale 2, scale 7, or both. High scores on both scales 2 and 7 are indicative of a combination of anxiety and depression, whereas other patterns of high scores point to other symptoms. For example, high scores on scales 4 and 9 suggest impulsiveness, low frustration tolerance, rebelliousness, and hostile aggression. High scores on scales 6 and 8 indicate withdrawal, apathy, and paranoid delusions.

Special terms have become associated with certain patterns of high scores on the MMPI clinical scales. Scales 1, 2, and 3 are referred to as the "neurotic triad," because high scores on these scales are so often associated with psychoneurotic problems. When the T scores on all three scales are above 70 but scale 2 is lower than scales 1 and 3, the picture is referred to as a "conversion V" and suggestive of a diagnosis of conversion hysteria. At the other end of the profile, scales 6, 7, 8, and 9 have been designated as the "psychotic tetrad"; high scores on these four scales are associated with psychotic problems. When the T scores on these four scales are all above 70, but the T scores on scales 7 and 9 are lower than those on scales 6 and 8, the picture is referred to as a "paranoid valley" and suggests a diagnosis of paranoid schizophrenia.

Problems and Prospects

The original MMPI was referred to by one writer as a "psychometric nightmare" (Rodgers, 1972) and by another as ". . . matchless as the objective instrument for the assessment of psychopathology" (King, 1978, p.9 38). The apparent conflict between these assertions might lead one to conclude that this is merely an example of beauty being in the eye of the beholder. Strange as it may seem, both characterizations may be appropriate. The older MMPI certainly had a host of problems: the true-false keying of items on many scales (e. g., L, K, 7, 8, 9) was lopsided, that is, many more items were keyed "true" than "false"; different scales contained many of the same items (as many as six items overlapping between scales); the use of extreme groups in constructing the scales made applications of the MMPI with less extreme groups questionable; and the use of groups of normal people in the criterion-keying procedure by which the scales were developed did not seem appropriate for purposes of differentiating among various psychiatric groups.

Faced with these and other psychometric difficulties, it may seem miraculous that the MMPI has not been replaced by an instrument constructed by a more sophisticated methodology. Starke Hathaway, one of the authors of the original MMPI, reportedly remarked during his later years that he was puzzled why the MMPI had not been made obsolete by new developments in testing (Megargee & Spielberger, 1992). Yet the MMPI has remained the objective personality inventory of choice by over 90% of clinical psychologists. It is difficult to know whether this popularity is a cause or an effect of the thousands of research investigations that have been conducted with this inventory, its translation into dozens of languages, and the determination of norms on a variety of populations. Since it appears unlikely that the MMPI or MMPI-2 will be replaced any time soon, it is hoped that the new norms, the computer interpretations, and the hundreds of recent investigations with MMPI-2 will result in improvements in the validity and manner in which this instrument is used.

■ The CPI and Other MMPI-Related Inventories

The MMPI has been a parent instrument for a number of other personality inventories. Of the many empirically validated, MMPI-like inventories that have been devised for "normal" people, the most popular and extensively researched is the California Psychological Inventory.

California Psychological Inventory

Designed by Harrison Gough (1957, 1975) and published by Consulting Psychologists Press, the California Psychological Inventory (CPI) is a measure of adolescent and adult personality. Half of the 480 true-false statements on the original version of this inventory were taken from the MMPI and the remaining statements were new. Unlike the MMPI clinical scales, which emphasize maladjustment and psychiatric disorders, the CPI scales stress more positive, normal aspects of personality.

Basic Scales on the California Psychological Inventory, Revised Edition and Meanings of Scores.   **TABLE 8–3**

Interpersonal Style and Manner of Dealing with Others
Dominance: degree of dominance and persistence, leadership ability.
Capacity for Status: extent of personal qualities that underlie and lead to status
Sociability: degree of outgoingness, sociability, and participativeness
Social Presence: degree of poise, spontaneity, and self-confidence in social situations
Self-acceptance: degree of self-acceptance and sense of personal worth
Independence: sense of personal independence and resistance to outside influence
Empathy: capacity to empathize with other people

Internalization and Endorsement of Normative Conventions
Responsibility: degree of conscientiousness, responsibility, and dependability
Socialization: strength of social maturity and integrity
Self-Control: self-control, extent of freedom from impulsivity and self-centeredness
Good Impression: degree of concern with respect to creating a good impression
Communality: validity and thoughtfulness of response pattern
Tolerance: degree of permissiveness, acceptance, and freedom from judgmental social beliefs
Well-Being: extent of freedom from worrying, complaining, or self-doubt

Cognitive and Intellectual Functioning
Achievement via Conformance: achievement in settings in which conformity is required
Achievement via Independence: achievement in settings in which independence is necessary
Intellectual Efficiency: degree of personal and intellectual efficiency

Thinking and Behavior
Psychological-Mindedness: interest in and responsiveness to the inner needs, motives, and experiences of other people
Flexibility: degree of flexibility and adaptability in thought and social behavior
Femininity-Masculinity: degree of feminine interests

---

*Scales on original version of California Psychological Inventory.
Source: Based on Gough, N. G. (1987). *California Psychological Inventory Administrator's Guide*. Palo Alto, CA: Consulting Psychologists Press.

CPI Scales. The original CPI is scored for the starred (*) scales listed in Table 8–3. Three of these scales—Well-being, Good Impression, and Communality—are validity scales. The first two validity scales were constructed from items that tended to be responded to in a certain way by normal people who were either asked to fake bad (Well-being) or to fake good (Good Impression), whereas the Communality score is simply a count of highly popular responses. Eleven of the remaining 15 scales, like those of the MMPI, were selected by comparing the responses of different groups of people; the other four scales (Social Presence, Self-acceptance, Self-control, and Flexibility) were content-validated.

Norms, Reliability, and Validity. The CPI was more extensively standardized than any other criterion-keyed inventory and, with the exception of the MMPI, is the most thoroughly researched. Its standard score norms were based on the responses of 6000 males and 7000 females of varying ages and socioeconomic status. The test-retest reliability coefficients for all scales except Psychological Mindedness and Communality range from .57 to .77 for high school students over a period of one year. Coupled with the fact that the correlations among CPI scales are rather high, the relatively low reliabilities point to problems of differentiating among a person's scores on different scales.

    The CPI fared much better in differentiating between the mean scale scores of different groups of people. The majority of the validity coefficients for single scales are low, but the usefulness of the inventory as a predictor of grades, delinquency, dropouts, parole violations, and other criteria was improved by combining scores on several scales by means of multiple-regression equations. Among the areas in which the CPI proved helpful were in predicting high-school and college achievement, the effectiveness of student teachers, grade point averages in medical school, the effectiveness of police and military personnel, and leadership and executive success (see Groth-Marnat, 1990, 1997; Hargrave & Hiatt, 1989).

Revised CPI. The first revision of the CPI consisted of 462 items retained or reworded from the original 480-item CPI, and a second revision—the CPI, Third Edition—reduced the number of items to 434. In addition to item editing, legally objectionable items were omitted (Gough & Bradley, 1996). The scales on the third addition of the CPI are grouped into three clusters: 20 Folk Scales, consisting of the 18 original scales plus the Empathy and Independence scales; three Vector Scales; and 13 Special Purpose Scales. The second group of measures represents a theoretical model containing three major themes: role, character, and competence. Vectors 1, 2, and 3 (v.1, v.2, v.3) assess these three themes. The role of interpersonal orientation (internality versus externality) theme, which is the interpersonal presentation of self inherent in the Capacity for Status, Dominance, Self-acceptance, Sociability, and Social Presence scales, is measured by the structural scale v.1. The character (norm favoring versus norm questioning) theme, involving intrapersonal values of the sort assessed by the Responsibility, Socialization, and Self-control scales, is measured by the structural scale v.2. The competence or realization theme, involving the Achievement via Conformance, Achievement via Independence, Intellectual Efficiency, Well-being, and Tolerance scales, is measured by the structural scale v.3. The three structural scales are uncorrelated with each other, but are significantly related to the folk-concept scales.

Scores on v.1 and v.2 were classified separately to create a fourfold typology—alpha, beta, gamma, delta. *Alphas* are described as externally-oriented and norm-favoring, *betas* as internally oriented and norm-favoring, *gammas* as externally oriented and norm-doubting, and *deltas* as internally oriented and norm-doubting. In a word, alphas are "manipulative," betas "conventional," gammas "alienated," and deltas "conflicted." The third structural scale (v.3) is divided into seven competence levels. Level 1 is described as poor ego integration, with minimal realization of the positive potential of the type. Level 4 is described as average ego integration, with moderate realization of the positive potential of the type. Level 7 is described as superior ego integration, with good realization of the positive potential of the type. The descriptions of levels 2 and 3 are between those of levels 1 and 4, and the descriptions of levels 5 and 6 are between those of levels 4 and 7. Scores on v.1, v.2, and v.3 can be combined to produce a total of 4 types X 7 levels = 28 different personality configurations (Gough & Bradley, 1996).

With respect to the psychometric characteristics of the CPI, the reported reliability coefficients are acceptable, but the norms on the first two editions were not completely adequate and certain technical information was omitted from the manual. However, the three editions of the CPI have been favorably reviewed as research and instructional instruments, as well as for their provision of useful information for personal counseling (e. g., Bolton, 1992; Engelhard, 1992). The publisher, Consulting Psychologists Press, has emphasized uses of the CPI in business, including finding and developing successful employees, developing leaders, creating efficient and productive organizations, and promoting teamwork.

The fourfold typology of the CPI is apparently an attractive feature of the inventory to industrial/organizational users, but Engelhard (1992) is critical of the classification of examinees into four dichotomous types.

Personality Inventory for Children

Because of the low reading comprehension of most children, self-report personality inventories tend to be less reliable and valid when used with children. There are any number of inventories on which children rate themselves, for example, the Children's Personality Questionnaire (by R. B. Porter & R. B. Cattell; from

IPAT). However, instruments on which adults rate children are perhaps more valid. One of the most widely used diagnostic instruments of this kind is the Personality Inventory for Children–Revised Format (PIC) (Wirt & Lachar, 1981; Wirt, Lachar, Klinedinst, & Seat, 1991). The original form of this MMPI-based inventory consisted of 600 true-false statements of the following type to be completed by a parent or caregiver of the child:
− My child finds it difficult to fall asleep.
− My child is a finicky eater.
− My child has threatened to kill himself (herself).
− Sometimes my child swears at other adults.

The revised version of the PIC (PIC-R), for children aged 3–16, consists of 420 items that can be administered in three different ways. The usual procedure is for the parent or caregiver to complete the first 280 items in 25–30 minutes. The respondent is asked to indicate whether each statement describes the child. Alternatively, all 420 items can be administered if a longer critical item analysis is desired in the computer report.

Scores on the 20 PIC-R scales listed in Table 8–4 are derived from the first or second administrative options. The third administrative option is to have the parent answer only the first 131 items, yielding scores on the four Broad-Band Factor Scales and the Lie Scale (see Table 8–4).

Prior to profiling and score interpretation, the raw scores are converted to standard T scores. Computer-based scoring and interpretation of the PIC scores is provided by Western Psychological Services. The report covers symptoms,

TABLE 8–4 Scales on the Personality Inventory for Children.

Clinical Scales	Broad-Band Factor Scales
Intellectual Screening	Undisciplined/Poor Self-Control
Social Skills	Social Incompetence
Delinquency	Internalization/Somatic
Family Relations	Symptoms
Achievement	Cognitive Development
Withdrawal	
Hyperactivity	Validity/Screening Scales
Development	Lie
Psychosis	Frequency
Somatic Concern	Defensiveness
Depression	Adjustment
Anxiety	

Material from the *Personality Inventory for Children-Revised,* © 1977, 1984, 1990 by Western Psychological Services. Reprinted by permission of the publisher, Western Psychological Services, 12031 Wilshire Boulevard, Los Angeles, California 90025.

behavior at home, behavior at school, family interaction, typical preadolescent educational placement, ability and achievement estimates, possible DSM-III-R diagnoses, and profile comparisons to 12 clinical types to aid in differential diagnosis. It also examines the appropriateness of seven different classroom settings for the child.

The construction process for the PIC-R was quite sophisticated, and the reliabilities of the scale scores are mostly in the high .80s (Wirt, Lachar, Klinedinst, & Seat, 1984). The norms, which are based on over 2000 children and adolescents (primarily from the Minneapolis area), are, however, rather limited. Among the validity studies conducted with this inventory is one by Keenan and Lachar (1988), which found the PIC to be successful in identifying preschool children who needed special education services.

Reviewers of the PIC have been mixed in their evaluations. Achenbach (1981) faulted the PIC scales for being constructed from old personality theories. Reynolds (1985) concluded that there were serious deficiencies in the standardization, norming, and reliability of the inventory. Reviews by Dreger (1982), Rothermel and Lovell (1985) and Tuma (1985) were more positive. However, Tuma decried the lack of a straightforward, integrated, user-oriented manual that might increase the clinical usefulness and decrease confusion and misuse of the PIC.

Personality Inventory for Youth

The Personality Inventory for Youth (PIY), an extension of the Personality Inventory for Children, is a self-report measure designed for 9–18 year olds (Lachar & Gruber, 1995a, 1995b). The 270 items on this inventory are written at a fourth-grade level and take about 40 minutes to complete. When time is short, the first 80 items may be administered for the purpose of screening adolescents who can be expected to reveal significant problems on the total scale.

The PIY can be scored on nine clinical scales: Cognitive Impairment, Impulsivity/Distractibility, Delinquency, Family Dysfunction, Reality Distortion, Somatic Concern, Psychological Discomfort, Social Withdrawal, Social Skills. More specific clinical content (depression, anxiety, feelings of alienation, social introversion, conflict with peers, noncompliance, etc.) may be obtained from 24 subscales. It can also be scored on several validity scales to detect lying, exaggerating, or defensive responding. The norms are based on a standardization sample of 2300 students in grades 4 through 12 and a clinical sample of 1100 individuals.

For the most part, reviews of the Personality Inventory for Youth have been positive. It is generally regarded as a well-developed measure of personality, with acceptable internal consistency and test-retest reliability coefficients and a substantial amount of empirical support for the validity of the score profiles (DeStefino, 1998; Marchant, 1998). DeStefano (1998) points out, however, that the technical limitations of some of the PIY subscales preclude their use as a basis for interpretative and reporting purposes.

■ The MCMI and Other Millon Inventories

The descriptions given previously of the original and revised versions of the California Psychological Inventory (CPI) should make clear that it is not merely an extension of the MMPI to normal adolescents and adults—a sane person's MMPI so to speak. Instruments such as the CPI have expanded and supplemented the MMPI rather than replacing it. Several inventories, however, have been suggested as potential successors or replacements for the MMPI. One of the most prominent of these is the Millon Clinical Multiaxial Inventory (MCMI).

Millon Clinical Multiaxial Inventory

The MCMI and the two revisions, the MCMI-II and MCMI-III, consist of 175 brief, self-descriptive statements to be answered "true" or false." Written at an eighth-grade level, these inventories were designed for clinical patients aged 17 and older and can be taken in 25–30 minutes.

The designations of the diagnostic scales on the MCMI followed the personality theory described in Theodore Millon's *Modern Psychopathology* (1969) text, a theory that played an important role in the development of the *Diagnostic and Statistical Manual of Mental Disorders* (American Psychiatric Association, 1980, 1987, 1994). Similarly, the MCMI-II was designed to coordinate with the categories of personality disorders and clinical syndromes incorporated in the revised version of DSM-III (DSM-III-R). Like the two previous editions, the latest edition of the MCMI (MCMI-III) is based on Millon's theory of personality and psychopathology (Millon, Millon, & Davis, 1994; Millon et al., 1996). In revising the MCMI-II to produce MCMI-III, 95 of the items were reworded or replaced to align them more closely with DSM-IV. The scope of the inventory was also broadened by two new scales: Scale 2B. Depressive (related to DMS-IV, Axis II Depressive Personality Disorder) and Scale R. Post Traumatic Stress Disorder.

Of the 24 diagnostic scales of the MCMI-III, 14 are personality patterns scales and 10 coordinate with disorders on Axis I of DSM-IV. The five categories and 24 diagnostic scales grouped under them, in addition to three modifier indices, are listed in Table 8–5. The three modifier indices and a validity index were designed to detect careless, confused, or random responding.

Administration and Scoring. The MCMI-III was designed for administration to adults 18 years and older in clinical situations where people are evaluated for

MCMI-III Scales.   **TABLE 8–5**

1.	Modifier Indices (Correction Scales)
Scale X	Disclosure
Scale Y	Desirability
Scale Z	Debasement
2.	**Clinical Personality Pattern Scales (DSM-IV, Axis II)**
Scale 1	Schizoid
Scale 2A	Avoidant
Scale 2B	Depressive
Scale 3	Dependent
Scale 4	Histrionic
Scale 5	Narcissistic
Scale 6A	Antisocial
Scale 6B	Aggressive/Sadistic
Scale 7	Compulsive
Scale 8A	Negativistic (Passive-Aggressive)
Scale 8B	Self-Defeating
3.	**Severe Personality Pathology Scales**
Scale S	Schizotypal
Scale C	Borderline
Scale P	Paranoid
4.	**Clinical Syndrome Scales (DSM-IV, Axis I)**
Scale A	Anxiety
Scale H	Somatoform
Scale N	Mania
Scale D	Dysthymic
Scale B	Alcohol Dependence
Scale T	Drug Dependence
Scale R	Post-Traumatic Stress Disorder
5.	**Severe Clinical Syndrome Scales**
Scale SS	Thought Disorder
Scale CC	Major Depression
Scale PP	Delusional Disorder

emotional, behavioral, or personality problems. It can be scored with a set of hand-scoring templates or by means of MICROTEST Q System computer software available from NCS Assessments. Raw scores on the various scales are weighted and converted to *base rate scores*, which take into account the incidence of a certain characteristic or disorder. By determining the incidence of a particular personality disorder or trait in a specified population, raw scores can be transformed in such a way that the ratio of the number of correct classifications (valid positives) to the number of incorrect classifications (false positives) is minimized.

Responses are scored and interpreted by NCS Assessments on the 24 diagnostic scales and the three correction scales of the MCMI-III; the scores are listed and a score profile is provided. The narrative portion of the report makes a statement concerning the validity of the responses, provides interpretations for both DSM-IV Axis I and Axis II disorders, and lists statements involving noteworthy responses made by the examinees, parallel DSM-IV multiaxial diagnoses, and therapeutic implications. A capsule summary section of the report reviews the severity of the symptoms and briefly describes indications on DSM-IV Axis I and Axis II in and related treatment considerations. Score profiles and interpretative guidelines for various DSM-IV diagnostic groups are provided in the *Manual for the MCMI-III* (Millon, Millon, & Davis, 1994).

Norms, Reliability, and Validity. The MCMI-III manual describes standardization data from various samples. The average test-retest and internal consistency reliabilities of the MCMI-III scales are quite good for a personality inventory. Alpha coefficients range from .66 to .89 for the personality scales (Scales 1 through P) and .71 to .90 for the clinical syndrome scales (Scales A through PP); test-retest reliabilities range from .84 to .96 for the clinical syndrome scales.

Reviews(e. g., Haladyna, 1992; Reynolds, 1992) have been generally positive regarding the theoretical foundation, construction methodology, and research agenda of the MCMI-II. The MCMI-III has also received some positive reviews (e. g., Retzlaff, 1998b), but at least one reviewer (Hess, 1998) was quite negative in his evaluation of the inventory. As on the MMPI and the CPI, there is some item overlap among the scales on both the MCMI-II and MCMI-III. The scale overlap decreases the reliability of differences among scale scores and hence increases the difficulty of interpreting profiles of scores on the inventory. Furthermore, the fact that substantially more items are keyed "true" than "false" increases the susceptibility of the scores to an acquiescence response set.

Millon Adolescent Personality Inventory

Similar to the MCMI-I in the coordination of its scoring with DSM-III is the 150-item Millon Adolescent Personality Inventory MAPI) (Millon, Green, & Meagher, 1982). Item selection and scale development for the MAPI, which was designed for individuals aged 13 through 18, involved a three-stage process: theoretical-substantive, internal-structural, and external-criterion. After passing each of the three stages, the items were cross-validated on additional samples.

Scales, Scoring, and Interpretation. Also similar to the MCMI-I is the fact that the eight Personality Styles scales (Introversive, Inhibited, Cooperative, Sociable, Confident, Forceful, Respectful, Sensitive) of the MAPI are based on Millon's theory of personality (Millon, 1969, 1981). The MAPI can be scored on these eight Personality Styles scales, eight Expressed Concerns scales (Self-Concept, Personal Esteem, Body Comfort, Sexual Acceptance, Peer Security, Social Tolerance, Family Rapport, Academic Confidence), four Behavior Correlates scales (Impulsive Control, Societal Conformity, Scholastic Achievement, Attendance Consistency), and on reliability and validity indexes for identifying poor test-taking attitudes and confused or random responding. Computer-based scoring and interpretation of the MAPI, which is provided by NCS Assessments, yields a score profile and narrative report of personality patterns, expressed concerns, behavioral correlates, noteworthy responses, and therapeutic implications. Descriptive case illustrations are also given in the manual (Millon, 1982).

Reliability and Validity. Test-retest reliabilities of the 20 MAPI clinical scales range from .53 to .82 over five months and .45 to .75 over one year; internal-consistency coefficients range from .67 to .84. The manual also presents the results of a principal components, varimax-rotation factor analysis of the 20 scales from which four factors were extracted. Correlations with the CPI, 16PF, and the EPPS are also listed in the manual.

Evaluation. Reviews of the MAPI, like those of the PIC, have been mixed. On the positive side, Brown (1985) referred to the MAPI as an excellent addition to the list of personality assessment instruments that are available for adolescents; its use of modern statistical procedures in standardization and its well-written manual are also noted. Widiger (1985) concluded that the MAPI is potentially useful for describing adolescent personality, but both of these reviewers maintained that the personality theory underlying the instrument is weak and the interpretation of MAPI scores is complex and tentative; the language of the computer-generated report is said to be too adult and too pathologically-oriented for young teenagers. Widiger (1985) claimed that the MAPI scales have little empirical foundation, that the cutoff points for the scales were chosen on the basis of unspecified base rates, and that the percentages of correct decisions were not cross-validated. Brown (1985) and Widiger (1985)concluded that the MAPI needs additional empirical support before being relied on extensively in the personality assessment of adolescents.

Millon Adolescent Clinical Inventory

The Millon Adolescent Clinical Inventory (MACI) (Millon, Millon, & Davis, 1993) is a brief, self-report personality inventory designed with a strong clinical focus and standardized on a large sample of adolescents in various clinical treatment settings. Most of the 160 true-false items on the MACI are new or rewritten from the Millon Adolescent Personality Inventory and are aligned with Axes I and II of DSM-III-R and the new clinical scales of DSM-IV. The MACI is scored, profiled, and interpreted by the NCS Assessments computer service on the scales listed in Table 8–6). In general, the MACI has received positive reviews (Retzlaff, 1995; Stuart, 1995). Some of the many tests on the inventory contain too few

---

TABLE 8–6 **Scales on the Millon Adolescent Clinical Inventory.**

Modifying Indices
Disclosure
Desirability
Debasement

1. Personality Patterns
Introversive (Schizoid personality features)
Inhibited (Avoidant personality features)
Doleful (Depressive personality features)
Submissive (Dependent personality features)
Dramatizing (Histrionic personality features)
Egotistic (Narcissistic personality features)
Unruly (Antisocial personality features)
Forceful (Sadistic personality features)
Conforming (Compulsive personality features)
Oppositional (Passive-Aggressive personality features)
Self-Demeaning (Self-Defeating personality features)
Borderline Tendency (Borderline personality features)

2. Expressed Concerns
Identity Diffusion
Self-Devaluation
Body Disapproval
Sexual Discomfort
Peer Insecurity
Social Insensitivity
Family Discord
Childhood Abuse

3. Clinical Syndromes
Eating Dysfunctions
Substance Abuse Proneness
Delinquent Predisposition
Impulsive Propensity
Anxious Feelings
Depressive Affect
Suicidal Tendency

---

items, but the overall evaluation is that it works well as a screening and diagnostic instrument for behaviorally disordered adolescents.

■ Inventories Based on Combined Strategies

Recent efforts to construct personality inventories have taken place in an atmosphere of renewed interest in research on personality and a greater appreciation of its complexity. Rather than relying on a single strategy—content (rational), theoretical, factor analytic, or empirical—the development of certain inventories has involved a combination of approaches. Representative of this new level of sophistication in personality test construction are the inventories designed by D.N. Jackson and available from Sigma Assessment Systems.

Jackson's overall approach began with detailed descriptions of the characteristics to be measured. Next a large pool of items was prepared and administered to a sizable, representative sample of people. Using the trait descriptions prepared at the outset, judges' ratings of the examinees on these traits were also obtained. In analyzing the data, the item responses of separate samples of examinees were subjected to different item analyses. A statistical, computer-based procedure was employed to ensure that the correlations among the items constituting a given scale were high but that the correlations among different scales were low. Realization of this goal resulted in the reliabilities of subtest score differences being high, thereby facilitating effective differentiation among scores on different subtests.

Personality Research Form

The Personality Research Form (PRF) is a true-false personality inventory designed for grade 6 through adulthood. It takes 45 to 75 minutes to administer, depending on the form. There are five forms: Form E, the most popular form, consists of 352 items; parallel Forms AA and BB of 440 items each, and parallel Forms A and B of 300 items each. Based on Henry Murray's (1938) trait theory of personality, each of the 15 scales of Forms A and B and the 22 scales of Forms AA, BB, and E consists of 20 items. Many of these scales bear the same names as those listed in the description of the Edwards Personal Preference Schedule (see page 210). In addition to the content scales, all forms are scored on an Infrequency scale consisting of rarely marked items; Forms AA, BB, and E are also scored on a Social Desirability scale.

Forms A, B, AA, and BB of the PRF were originally standardized on 1,000 men and 1,000 women in 30 North American colleges and universities. The latest manual for Form E (Jackson, 1989b) provides separate general norms for stratified samples of males and females in 31 U.S. colleges and two Canadian universities. The test-retest reliabilities of the 14 content scales common to all five forms cluster around .80, but the reliabilities of the six additional content scales on Forms AA, BB, and E fall into the .50s. Validity coefficients obtained by correlating the content scales with behavior ratings and scores on a specially devised trait rating form are in the .50s. Evidence for convergent and discriminant validity is also reported in the manual.

One might assume from the psychometric sophistication with which the PRF was constructed that it would escape much criticism. However, as seen in Tinsley's (1985) review this is not the case. Tinsley faults the PRF for the impoverished conceptualization of personality underlying its development, its inadequate reliabilities, its lack of adequate norms, and difficulties in interpreting the scores because of insufficient information in the manual as to what the scores mean. In addition, little validity information concerning the relationships between PRF scores and real-life criteria is provided. Finally, even the removal of variation due to the social desirability response set from PRF scores is viewed by Tinsley as a mistake that probably leads to a loss of information. He recommends that the PRF not be used in practical or applied settings and that the Jackson Personality Inventory is a more appropriate instrument for research purposes.

Jackson Personality Inventory

Like the PRF, the Jackson Personality Inventory (JPI) was designed for adolescents and adults. A revision of the JPI, the JPI-R, consists of 300 true-false items and takes about 45 minutes to complete (Jackson, 1994). The JPI-R has a more social or interpersonal orientation than the PRF, providing a method for predicting behavior in a variety of practical settings (business industrial, education, recreational) as well as in clinical and counseling situations. The construction methodology for the JPI and JPI-R was even more sophisticated than that for the PRF. Separate item analyses of a large item pool administered to two samples of people were conducted to maximize content variances in relation to social desirability variance, to maximize item variance, and to minimize the overlap among scales. The subscales were renamed and reorganized, the Infrequency scale of the JPI was removed to facilitate use in employment screening, updated college norms and new norms based on samples of blue and white collar workers were provided, and the accompanying manual was updated in various ways.

The JPI-R can be scored on the following 15 subscales grouped into the following clusters and subscales:

Analytical   **Extroverted**
Complexity   Sociability
Breadth of Interest   Social Confidence
Innovation   Energy Level
Tolerance
                            Opportunistic
Emotional   Social Astuteness
Empathy   Risk Taking
Anxiety
Cooperativeness   **Dependable**
                            Organization
                            Traditional Values
                            Responsibility

Median internal consistency reliability coefficients (Bentler's Theta) for the JPI subscales are in the low .90s. Because the items on the JPI-R are mostly the same as those on the JPI, it can be argued that the hundreds of correlations of JPI scales with various criteria are also applicable to the JPI-R. With respect to reviews of the JPI and JPI-R, Dyer (1985) concluded that use of the JPI should be limited to research contexts, particularly research on personality correlates of occupational criteria and specific teacher-learning situations or styles.

Basic Personality Inventory

Somewhat different in orientation than Personality Research Form and the Jackson Personality Inventory, which were designed to assess "normal" personalities, is the Basic Personality Inventory (BPI) (Jackson, 1989a). The BPI is intended to be used with both clinical and normal populations to identify sources of maladjustment and personal strengths in juveniles and adults. It consists of 240 true/false items at a fifth-grade reading level and can be completed in approximately 35 minutes. As seen in the following list of 11 substantive clinical scales and one critical item scale (Deviation), the BPI emphasizes dimensions of psychopathology:

Alienation   Deviation   Persecutory Ideas
Anxiety   Hypochondriasis   Self Depreciation
Denial   Impulse Expression   Social Introversion
Depression   Interpersonal Problems   Thinking Disorder

The maladjustment orientation of the BPI has made it more applicable to juvenile and adult correctional facilities, psychological, psychiatric and counseling practices, and other institutions concerned with behavioral or conduct disorders. Separate BPI profiles for groups of psychiatric patients with symptoms ranging from anorexia to suicidal behavior and hallucinations are given in the manual (Jackson et al., 1989). The norms used for the adult profiles described in the manual were obtained from mail surveys or interviews of 709 men and 710 women selected at random from telephone directories and voters' records in the U.S. and Canada. The internal-consistency and test-retest reliabilities of the BPI scales are moderate to high in both nonclinical and clinical samples (Holden et al., 1988; Jackson et al., 1989). The validity data on the BPI are not as adequate as one might wish, but it holds promise for clinical use in the fields of health psychology and juvenile delinquency in particular. Reviews by Urbina (1995) and Yelland (1995) praise the BPI for its brevity, psychometric sophistication, and ease of administration and scoring. However, the reviewers underscored the need for more representative norms for adults and non-white ethnic groups, and more research on use of the inventory with clinical populations.

Personality Assessment Inventory

Similar to the BPI in its reliance on a combined rational/empirical strategy of instrument development is the Personality Assessment Inventory (PAI) (Morey, 1991). This self-report inventory consists of 344 four-point (F = False, Not At All True; ST = Slightly True; MT = Mainly True; VT = Very True) items written at a fourth-grade level. As a multidimensional alternative to the MMPI, the PAI was designed to provide information relevant to clinical diagnoses, treatment planning, and screening for psychopathology in adults aged 18 and older. It can be scored on four validity scales (Inconsistency, Infrequency, Negative Impression, Positive Impression), 11 clinical scales (Somatic Complaints, Anxiety, Anxiety-Related Disorders, Depression, Mania, Paranoia, Schizophrenia, Borderline Features, Antisocial Features, Alcohol Problems, Drug Problems), five treatment scales (Aggression, Suicidal Ideation, Stress, Nonsupport, Treatment Rejection) and two interpersonal scales (Dominance, Warmth). Ten scales are subdivided into 31 conceptually distinct subscales.

The U.S. norms for the PAI are based on a normative sample of American adults aged 18 years and older, stratified by gender, race, and age according to 1995 U.S. Census projections. Norms are also available on large samples of adult clinical patients and college students.

Reviews of the PAI have been encouraging (Boyle, 1995; Kavan, 1995; White, 1996), and an extensive amount of research has been conducted with the it in various countries and ethnic groups, particularly in clinical and forensic contexts (e. g., Alterman et al., 1995; Fals-Stewart & Lucente, 1997; Hays, 1997; Herrington-Wang & Taylor, 1997; Rogers, Ustad, & Salekin, 1998; Schinka, 1995). The number of research citations of the PAI in PsycINFO since 1995 has been greater than that for any other personality inventory, greater even than the MMPI-2, a statistic indicative of the interest in this inventory as a clinical instrument.

■ Summary

This chapter discusses personality inventories that were developed, in whole or in part, through criterion-keying procedures. The most widely used of these inventories is the Minnesota Multiphasic Personality Inventory (MMPI). It is also the most time-tested of all personality inventories in this category, the original edition having been constructed during the early 1940s at the University of Minnesota. The MMPI was designed to differentiate among various groups by analyzing differences in scores on nine clinical scales obtained by normal adults and patients having specific psychiatric diagnoses. The MMPI may be scored on several other scales as well, including four validating scales (?, L, F, K). The validating scales are scored to determine whether the examinee has completed the inventory according to the directions and to adjust content scores for faking and response sets. The MMPI was updated and restandardized in the 1980s, and a revised version, the MMPI-2, was published in 1986.

Second only to the MMPI in popularity among practicing psychologists is the California Psychological Inventory (CPI). The CPI was constructed from a combination of items borrowed from the MMPI and new items to provide an empirically keyed inventory for the assessment of personality in normal high school and college students and adults. A revised version of the CPI consisting of 462 items and employing even more sophisticated scoring and interpretation procedures than its predecessor was published in 1986. Like the MMPI-2, the revised CPI is scored and interpreted by a computer-based service.

One of the most popular criterion-keyed inventories for children is the Personality Inventory for Children (PIC). The revised version (PIC-R) consists of 420 true-false items designed for children aged 6 through 16. The PIC-R is somewhat unique among personality inventories in that it is completed by a parent or other caretaker who is acquainted with the child's behavior. In addition to three validity scales (Lie, Frequency, and Defensiveness), the PIC-R is scored on 17 clinical scales and three validity scales. A recent extension of the PIC designed for adolescents is the Personality Inventory for Youth (PIY).

One of the most psychometrically sophisticated and carefully constructed of all personality inventories is the Millon Clinical Multiaxial Inventory (MCMI-I, MCMI-II, and MCMI-III). Based on Theodore Millon's theory of psychopathology, which contributed to the preparation of the *Diagnostic and Statistical Manual of the American Psychiatric Association*, this true-false inventory was designed for clinical patients aged 18 years and older. Included among the scales on which MCMI-III is scored are three modifier indices, 11 personality patterns scales, 3 severe personality pathology scales, 7 clinical syndrome scales, and 3 severe clinical syndrome scales. Inclusion of items on particular scales was based on a combination of rational, empirical, and cross-validation procedures.

The scoring procedure for the MCMI-III is unique, in that it takes into account the base rate of a particular psychopathological disorder or personality type. The test-retest and internal consistency reliabilities of the various scales are as high as those of most personality inventories, and the validity of the inventory is attested to by correlational evidence presented in the manual (Millon, Millon, & Davis, 1994). Despite its developmental sophistication and brevity, however, the MCMI-III has not replaced the MMPI.

The Millon Adolescent Personality Inventory (MAPI), a 150-item true-false inventory of adolescent personality, has received mixed reviews from critics. The three-stage strategy by which MAPI was designed is similar to that of the MCMI, but the MAPI has a weak theoretical foundation, and the results of administering it are sometimes difficult to interpret. More recently, the MAPI evolved into the Millon Adolescent Clinical Inventory (MACI), which focuses on clinical cases. The MACI was designed to assess personality and diagnose personality disorders in adolescents and can be scored on 3 modifying indices, 12 personality patterns, 8 expressed concerns, and 7 clinical syndromes.

Perhaps the best examples, from a psychometric viewpoint, of personality inventories constructed by a combination of rational-theoretical, factor-analytic, and criterion-keyed construction strategies are the Personality Research Form, the Jackson Personality Inventory, and the Basic Personality Inventory. Like the inventories designed by Theodore Millon, D. M. Jackson's personality inventories are products of sophisticated statistical methodology.

■ Questions and Activities

1. Compare the MCMI-III with the MMPI-2 on the variables assessed by each, sophistication of design, ease of administration, psychometric characteristics (norms, reliability, validity, etc.) and usefulness of diagnostic information obtained. Why do you think the MCMI-III has not replaced the MMPI-2 as the diagnostic paper-and-pencil inventory of choice by clinical psychologists?
2. Read reviews of any two of the personality inventories described in this chapter in the *Mental Measurements Yearbooks*, *Test Critiques*, or other authoritative sources. Summarize the good and bad features of the two inventories according to the reviewers.
3. Compare the criterion-keyed approach discussed in this chapter with the rational-theoretical and factor-analytic approaches to personality inventory construction that were discussed in Chapter 7. What are the advantages and disadvantages of each approach?
4. Arrange to take the latest version of the California Psychological Inventory (CPI), and have your scores interpreted by your instructor or another qualified

person. (For a small fee, Consulting Psychologists Press (P.O. Box 10096, Palo Alto, CA 94303) provides a computer-scoring and interpretation service for CPI users.) Were your CPI scores consistent with your own subjective assessment of your personality? After taking it, what criticisms of this personality inventory do you have to offer?

5. Following the procedure outlined in exercise 7 of Chapter 4, prepare a critical review of the any of the personality inventories listed in this chapter.

6. As a class exercise in criterion-keying of a personality inventory, administer the following altruism questionnaire to equal numbers of men and women. Then score the responses according to the following key: score items 1, 3, 6, 7, 9, 11, 14, and 16 as SD = 0, D = 1, U = 2, A = 3, and SA = 4; score items 2, 4, 5, 8, 10, 12, 13, and 15 as SD = 4, D = 4, U = 2, A = 1, SA = 0.

Next determine the mean and standard deviation of the scores on each of the 15 statements separately for the men and women. Finally, conduct appropriate statistical tests on the difference between the pairs of means for each statement. On which statements was the mean score of women students significantly higher than the mean score of men students? Can it be concluded that this subset of statements constitutes a better measure of altruism than the entire set of 15 statements? Why or why not?

Questionnaire

Sex: _____ Grade-point average: _____ Religion: _____
Directions: For each of the numbered statements listed below write the appropriate letters in the marginal dash to indicate your degree or agreement or disagreement with the statement:

SA = Strongly Agree
A = Agree
U = Undecided
D = Disagree
SD = Strongly Disagree

_____ 1. I want to live a life that is filled with caring for other people and service to them.

_____ 2. Admittedly I'm a rather self-centered person, but that's only natural.

_____ 3. I have a great deal of respect for anyone who devotes his or her life to helping unfortunate people.

_____ 4. In this life a person should look after his or her own affairs first and worry about helping other people second.

_____ 5. Most of the time people resent it when someone tries to help them, so it's usually not worth the trouble.

_____ 6. There is nothing finer and nobler than a person who goes out of the way to render assistance to another human being.

_____ 7. People should be more concerned with the feelings and welfare of others than with how everything affects them personally.

_____ 8. Enlightened self-interest is a very realistic and appropriate philosophy of life.

_____ 9. I am willing to devote my life to helping people who are less fortunate than I.

_____ 10. Like most people I'm primarily interested in my own life and how things affect me personally.

_____ 11. I would sacrifice my life for a friend or relative whom I loved or respected.

_____ 12. Intelligent people stick to their own affairs and let others take care of themselves.

_____ 13. It is usually wise not to become involved or interfere when someone whom you don't know has a problem or is in trouble.

_____ 14. I am quite willing to give money and time to charitable causes or organizations that provide help to needy people.

_____ 15. I wouldn't donate one of my kidneys or any other duplicate but important body organ to someone while I'm still alive.

_____ 16. If given half a chance, anyone can be generous and considerate to other people.

■ Suggested Readings

Butcher, J.N. (1995). Interpretation of the MMPI-2. IN L.E. Beutler & M.R. Berren (Eds.), *Integrative assessment of adult personality* (pp. 206–239). New York: Guilford Press.

Finn, S.E., & Butcher, J.N. (1991). Clinical objective personality assessment. In M. Hersen, A.E. Kasdin, & A.S. Bellack (Eds.), *The clinical psychology handbook* (2nd ed., pp. 362–373). New York: Pergamon.

Keller, L.S., Butcher, J.N., & Slutske, W.S. (1990). Objective personality assessment. In G. Goldstein & M. Hersen (Eds.), *Handbook of psychological assessment* (2nd ed., pp. 345–386). New York: Pergamon Press.

Kline, R.B., Lachar, D., & Gdowski, C.L. (1992). Clinical validity of a Personality Inventory for Children (PIC) profile typology. *Journal of Personality Assessment*, *58*, 591–605.

Meyer, P., & Davis, S. (1992). *The CPI applications guide: An essential tool for individual, group, and organizational development*. Palo Alto: Consulting Psychologists Press.

Millon, T. (Ed.). (1996). *The Millon inventories*. New York: Guilford.

Chapter 9

Interests, Values, and Attitudes

Interests, values, and attitudes are related but not identical concepts. *Interests* are feelings or preferences for certain activities, ideas, or objects. *Values* are concerned with the importance or worth attached to particular things, and *attitudes* are tendencies to respond positively or negatively to specific objects, persons, or situations. Unlike personality inventories, which were originally designed to detect and diagnose maladjustment or mental disorder, measures of interests developed primarily within vocational counseling contexts. As such, they have made important practical contributions educational and employment selection and placement. Measures of values and attitudes, on the other hand, stemmed mainly from research in social psychology, and only secondarily have they contributed to vocational psychology.

Interests, values, and attitudes are related not only to each other but to beliefs, opinions, sentiments, personal orientations, and many other psychological variables. Attitudes, beliefs, and opinions involve judgments or acceptances of propositions as facts, but the factual supports for attitudes and opinions are usually weaker than those for beliefs. In terms of the extent to which their formation is based on factual information, attitudes are in lowest place, opinions next, and beliefs at the top of the list. However, opinions and beliefs are less pervasive and less resistant to change than attitudes. Attitudes are expressed in a wider range of situations and are more easily influenced.

■ Development of Interests

Where do interests come from? Are they inborn or do they develop through interactions with other people and situations? If interests stem from the interactions of innate abilities and temperaments with experience, how do the interaction take place and what conditions support or inhibit them? Research designed to answer these questions has not been especially systematic, but a number of theorists have attempted to provide guides for such research by means of speculations and reasoning about the development of vocational interests. For example, developmental theorists such as Eli Ginzberg and Donald Super maintain that vocational interests develop in a series of three or four stages.

Ginzberg's Developmental Theory

Ginzberg, Ginsburg, Axelrad, and Herma (1951) maintained that there are three major developmental periods in the process of making vocational choices: fantasy, tentative, and realistic. During the *fantasy period* of early and middle childhood, occupational choices are arbitrary and unrealistic. During the four substages of the *tentative period* (interest, capacity, value, and transition), which starts at about age 11 and ends by about age 18, adolescents begin considering possible vocations by asking themselves what they most like to do and think about. As they progress through the four substages of the tentative period, children begin to realize that not only do certain vocations require more ability than others but that some vocations are more valued by society. The final, or *realistic*, developmental period in vocational decision-making begins with an exploratory stage and progresses through a crystallization stage occurring between the ages of 19 and 21. During this stage the successes and failures experienced during the exploratory stage lead to a clear vocational pattern, and finally to the selection of a position or professional specialty.

The adequacy of an adolescent's vocational choice process depends, according to Ginzberg et al. (1951), on the extent to which he or she is able to test reality, develop a suitable time perspective, defer gratification, accept and implement compromises in vocational plans, and identity suitable vocational role models at the appropriate time. These factors and other intrinsic characteristics are important in determining whether the individual learns to delay gratification and becomes primarily work-oriented or is unable to delay gratification and becomes primarily pleasure-oriented. Another personality variable that influences vocational choice is whether the person is an active problem solver who attacks problems and attempts to solve them or a passive problem solver who merely waits for things to happen (Osipow, 1983).

Super's Developmental Theory

Another stage theory of interest development is Donald Super's (1957, 1972) multistage conception of changes in self-concept and interests. The theory stresses the importance of identification and role playing in the development of interests. According to Super, the search for identity and vocational maturity occurs in a sequence of three stages. First is an *exploratory stage* with three substages: tentative, transition, and uncommitted trial. Next in order is an *establishment stage,* consisting of a committed trial substage and an advancement substage. Career choices are reinforced and continued during the third, or *maintenance*, stage. Progress through these three stages of vocational maturation involves five developmental tasks occurring during specific chronological age periods: crystallization of a vocational preference (ages 14–18), specification of a vocational preference (ages 18–21), implementation of the preference (ages 21–24); stabilization of the preference (ages 25–35), and consolidation of status and advancement (late-30s to mid-40s). A final stage for many people—*disengagement—occurs* during later life. At this time the pattern of career interests that characterized young and middle adulthood is gradually phased out.

As expressed in the following quotation, Super (1970) viewed interests and values as related not only to each other but also to needs and traits:

> Traits, values, and interests derive from needs. The need . . . leads to action, and action leads to modes of behavior or traits that seek objectives formulated in generic terms (values) or in specific terms (interests). Traits are ways (styles) of acting to meet a need in a given situation. Values are objectives that one seeks to attain a need. Interests are the specific activities and objectives through which values can be attained and needs met. (pp. 189–190)

Super maintained that *needs* are more characteristic of a person than values, and values are more general than interests. Needs, values, and interests can all be satisfied by various types of activities, but the relationship to goal-oriented activities is closer for interests than for values and closer for values than for needs. Both values (the objectives or goals of behavior) and interests (the activities in which values are pursued or sought) are more closely related than needs to the actual vocational decisions or choices made by an individual.

■ Interests and Personality

Super's description of the relationships among interests, values, and needs underscores the fact that what are called interests (vocational, educational, recreational, social, etc.) and values are actually personality variables that induce people to behave in certain ways. Certain activities and goals are selected by a person because they are seen as having the potential for satisfying his or her needs. However, not only do specific personality characteristics result in behavior that shapes or determines a person's environment, but that environment also affects personality. People with similar personality characteristics tend to select similar occupations, and after being exposed to a particular occupation for an extended period of time an individual becomes more like other people in that occupation (Osipow, 1983).

The conception of interests as dynamic characteristics that form a part of a the self-concept and direct a person's choice of a career was proposed initially by Carter (1940). Other psychologists (e. g., Bordin, 1943; Forer, 1948; Super, 1957; and more recently, Betz, 1992, 1994) elaborated on this idea. Forer appears to have been the first to construct a personality inventory composed of items concerned with interests and activities, and he also demonstrated how an interest inventory could be used to differentiate between medical and psychiatric groups ranging from asthmatics to schizophrenics. Betz (1994) not only accepted Super's (1957, 1972) emphasis on the importance of the self-concept in determining preferences for particular occupations, but also incorporated Bandura's (1977) self-efficacy model into the theory and practice of vocational counseling.

Darley and Hagenah (1955) and Super (1972) emphasized the fact that interests become differentiated in the process of personality development, and consequently that interest inventories are actually measures of personality. However, they were preceded by psychoanalytic writings on the psychodynamics of career choice.

Psychoanalytic Theories

Since Freud's time, psychoanalysts have maintained that personality traits influence the selection of particular vocations. Freud and other psychoanalysts emphasized the roles of sublimation (the channeling of frustrated sexual or aggressive drives into substitute activities) and identification in the formation of interests. With respect to sublimation, a person with strong sadistic impulses might become interested in being a surgeon and a person whose sexual impulses were frustrated might write romantic poetry or enter an occupation concerned with decoration, display, and other emphasis on the body (modeling, acting, sports, etc.).

Although evidence for the operation of sublimation in determining interests and vocational choice is far from clear-cut, data pertaining to the role of identification with parents and significant other people in one's life is more impressive. Consistent with the role of identification in occupational choice are Nachmann's (1960) findings of differences in the acceptance of aggressive impulses, the emphasis on fairness and obedience to authority, and the relative dominance of the mother and father in families of lawyers, dentists, and social workers. The influence of parents was also underscored by Steimel and Suziedelis's (1963) finding that college students who were influenced more by their fathers were more likely to major in the exact sciences but students influenced more by their mothers tended toward the liberal arts. Additional research on the role of identification with parents in determining vocational interests is reported by Stewart (1959), Crites (1969), and Heilbrun (1969).

Correlations of Interests and Personality Traits

Related but not restricted to a psychoanalytic perspective on interests is research linking vocational and educational interests to specific needs and other personality characteristics. For example, significant correlations have been found between scores on interest inventories and personality inventories (Utz & Korben, 1976). Introversion has been found to be more common among people with scientific interests, aggressiveness to interest in selling, and the incidence of psychoneurosis to strong literary and aesthetic interests (Darley & Hagenah, 1955; Osipow, 1983; Super & Bohn, 1970). Other researchers (Sternberg, 1955; Siegelman & Peck, 1960) have delineated specific patterns of personality characteristics associated with the choice of college major or career. Siegelman and Peck (1960) described chemists as curious, imaginative, intellectual, creative, relating to objects, and emotionally involved in their work; ministers were described as nurturant, personally insecure, and more likely to feel vocationally inadequate; military officers were characterized as valuing security and variety in associations and living quarters, dedicated to country, accepting of responsibility and authority, and concerned with loyalty and honesty.

Roe's Person-Environment Theory

Based to some extent on psychoanalytic theory and Maslow's (1954) hierarchy of needs, coupled with the results of her own research, is Anne Roe's dimensional model of career choice (Roe & Siegelman, 1964). Findings from her initial research on the personalities of physical, biological, and social scientists led Roe to conclude that these individuals could be distinguished by the extent of their interest in people versus their interest in things. A strong interest in *people* stimulates entry into more person-oriented vocational environments, including general cultural, arts, entertainment, services, and business contact occupations. A strong interest in *things*, on the other hand, leads to more non-person-oriented vocations (e. g., scientific, outdoor, technological, organizational activities). Roe theorized that these differences in orientation result from childhood experiences, in particular the rewards and punishments administered for various activities and the psychological climate of the home (warm or accepting versus cold or avoiding). She maintained that a warm family environment promotes an interest in people and a cold environment an interest in things.

Although environment undoubtedly has an effect on what people are interested in, the findings of a study by Grotevant, Scarr, and Weinberg (1977) suggest that children are born with a hereditary predisposition toward certain interests. Rather than trying to lead children into particular interest areas, these researchers recommended that parents provide them with a variety of experiences. Then children will have a better opportunity to develop whatever pattern of interests they may have inherited. Rather than having a direct effect on interests, however, it can be argued that heredity affects interests by way of abilities, temperament, and physical structure. For example, a person with a genetically based high level of activity but a modest level of intelligence would probably have little interest in becoming a theoretical physicist who spends most of the time indoors thinking about complex scientific problems. And a temperamentally energetic individual with a strong physique might show a greater interest in becoming a professional athlete.

Roe and Klos (1969) subsequently extended their theory of career choice to the three-dimensional conical model depicted in Figure 9–1. The left to right line on this figure depicts the dimension of Orientation to Personal Relations versus Orientation to Natural Phenomena, while the near to far line depicts the dimension of Orientation to Resource Utilization versus Orientation to Purposeful Communication. The third or vertical dimension, Low Level versus High Level, refers to the skill level (professional, skilled, unskilled) required by the occupation; lower-level (unskilled) occupations are closer to the pointed end of the cone, and higher-level (professional) occupations are closer to the broader end. The cross-sectional circles are larger near the broad end than near the narrow end of the cone, consistent with Roe's belief that variability on the first two (horizontal) dimensions is greater among professional occupations than among the lower-skilled occupations located further toward the tip of the cone.

The specifics of Roe's theoretical model have not been well supported by research (Osipow, 1983). One difficulty is that various orientations are possible within a single career, and different careers may involve similar orientations. For example, both scientists and artists may work with people *and* things in various contexts. Furthermore, differences among the interests of people in low-level occupations may be as great as those in high-level occupations. Osipow (1983) concluded that even the assertion that individuals are either person- or nonperson-oriented in their interests and that this orientation influences vocational choice cannot be stated categorically. However, Roe's model has been applied to the construction of several vocational interest inventories, include Ramak (Meir & Barak, 1974), the COPS Interest Inventory, the Hall Occupational Orientation Inventory, and the Vocational Interest Inventory.

Roe's Three-Dimensional Conical Model of Career Choice.   **FIG. 9–1**

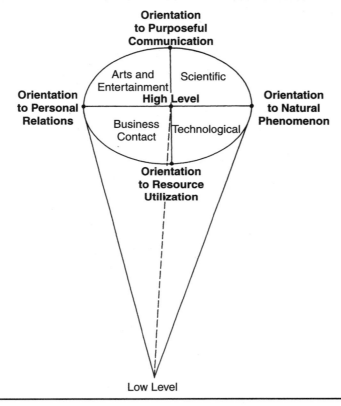

COPS Interest Inventory. This interest inventory is designed for seventh grade through college and adult and takes 30 to 40 minutes to answer and self-score. The items are in Likert-type format (L = like very much, l = like moderately, d = dislike moderately, D = dislike very much). Based on factor analyses of items reflecting Roe's (1956) classification of occupations into clusters and levels within each cluster, the COPS Interest Inventory is scored on the eight major clusters depicted in Figure 9–2. As shown in the figure, the Communication, Clerical, and Outdoor level have only one level—skilled. The Arts, Service, Science, and Business scales have two levels each—Professional and Skilled, and the Technology scale also has three levels—Professional, Skilled, and Consumer Economics. The clusters are keyed both to curriculum choices and to detailed job information sources such as the *Dictionary of Occupational Titles* and the *Occupational Outlook Handbook*.

Three additional forms of the COPS are the professional level COPS-P for

FIG. 9-2   **Model of Variables Measured by the COPS Interest Inventory
(see text for explanation).**

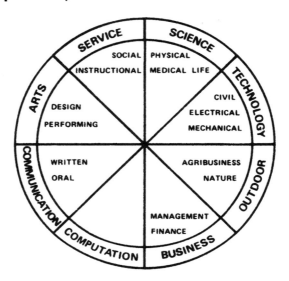

(From *COPSystem Technical Manual* (p. 4) by R. R. Knapp, L. Knapp, & L. Knapp-Lee, 1990, San Diego, CA: EdITS. Copyright 1990 EdITS. Reprinted with permission.

senior high school and college students as well as adult professionals, an intermediate level COPS II for elementary and high school students, and the COPS-R for sixth grade through high school.* The COPS-R is written in simplified language and uses a single norms profile. All of the COPS inventories may be used, in conjunction with measures of abilities (CAPS) and work values (COPES), for purposes of career counseling.

Bauerfeind's (1986) review of the COPS noted that there are weaknesses in regard to the norms and predictive validities, and that there are some problems with regard to clarity of the manual. He concluded, however, that the items are well written and highly relevant to real-life job activities and that the answer sheets are convenient to use and easily scored. Students seem to enjoy taking the COPS, and it has served as an effective stimulus for career exploration.

Vocational Interest Inventory-Revised. This inventory, which consists of 112 forced-choice items, is appropriate for grade through adulthood and takes 20–30

---

* Also available is a COPSystem Picture Inventory of Careers (COPS-PIC), a nonverbal form designed to measure the interests of elementary through high school students and adults with motivational or language difficulties.

minutes to complete. It was designed to measure relative interest in the eight occupational areas designated in Figure 9–2. An effort was made to control for gender bias in constructing the items, and mixed-sex norms are provided to encourage respondents to explore nontraditional careers and interests. Norms for the revised edition of the Vocational Interest Inventory are based on the responses obtained in 1987 on over 27,000 high school juniors.

Holland's Vocational Personalities-Work Environments Theory

Even more influential than Roe's theoretical model has been J. L. Holland's theory of vocational personalities and work environments. Holland (1985) maintained that the complementary match between personality type and psychological environment determines the behavior of a person in that environment. People who receive sufficient reinforcement and satisfaction in their environments tend to remain in them; otherwise they either change the environment or themselves.

According to Holland's RIASEC model (see Figure 9–3), there are six types of vocational personalities and six work environments: Realistic (R), Investigative (I), Artistic (A), Social (S), Enterprising (E), and Conventional (C). A *realistic type* of person likes to manipulate tools, machines, and other objects, and to be outdoors and work with plants and animals, but dislikes educational and therapeutic activities. Such a person tends to possess athletic, mechanical, and technical competencies but is deficient in social and educational skills. He or she is characterized as a practical, conforming, and natural person who is likely to avoid situations requiring verbal and interpersonal skills and to seek jobs such as automobile mechanic, farmer, or electrician.

An *investigative type* of person prefers activities that demand a great deal of thinking and understanding, for example, scientific enterprises. He or she likes to observe, learn, investigate, analyze, evaluate, and solve problems, but tends to avoid situations requiring interpersonal and persuasive skills. Such a person is characterized as rational, cautious, curious, independent, introversive, and more likely to be found in fields such as chemistry, physics, biology, geology, and other sciences.

An *artistic type* of person is imaginative, introspective, complicated, emotional, expressive, impulsive, nonconforming, and disorderly. He or she tends to prefer unstructured situations in which creativity or imagination can be expressed. Consequently, jobs such as actor, musician, or writer are likely to appeal to people in this category.

A *social type* of person verbally and interpersonally skilled and likes to work with people—developing, enlightening, informing, training, curing, and helping or supporting them in various ways. People in this category tend to be humanistic,

FIG. 9–3   **Holland's Hexagonal Model of Interests.**

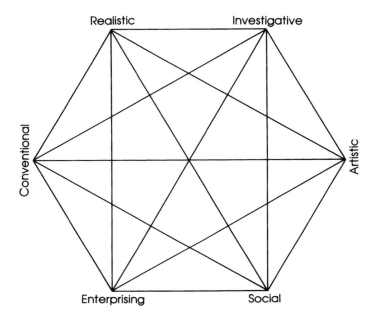

empathic, and to have good teaching abilities, but minimal mechanical and scientific abilities. Such individuals are viewed as cooperative, friendly, helpful, persuasive, tactful, and understanding, and are likely to be found in clinical or counseling psychology, speech therapy, teaching, and related fields.

An *enterprising type of person*, described as aggressive, ambitious, energetic domineering, pleasure seeking, self-confident, and sociable, tends to have high verbal and leadership abilities. Such a person likes to influence and persuade others, and to lead or manage organizations for economic gain. Jobs such as manager, business executive, or salesperson are preferred by these individuals.

A *conventional type* of person is described as conscientious, efficient, inflexible, obedient, orderly, persistent, and self-controlled. People of this type tend to have good arithmetic and clerical abilities, and to be adept at filing, record keeping, and data processing. These skills are congruent with an emphasis on business and economic achievement, leading to jobs such as banker, bookkeeper, and tax expert.

Corresponding to the six personality types are six model environments—realistic, investigative, artistic, social, enterprising, and conventional. Each environment is sought by persons having corresponding skills, abilities, attitudes, values and personality traits. Behavior in a particular environment is, according to Holland, determined by the interaction between the individual's personality and the type of environment. People tend to seek environments that are congruent with their personalities and are generally happier, more satisfied, and more productive in such environments than in those that are incongruent with their personalities. However, both the personality types and the environmental types are idealizations; a given individual or environment is typically a composite of more than one ideal type.

As depicted by their proximity in the model (Figure 9–3), according to Holland some of the 15 pairs of personality types are more closely related to each other, and hence more consistent. *Consistency* refers to the degree to which personality types or environmental types (models) are related; the consistency of a person's interest pattern is indicated by the extent to which he or she scores high on types of interests that are close to each other on the hexagonal model. As shown in Figure 9–3, the investigative and conventional types are closer to, and hence more consistent, with the realistic type, whereas the artistic and enterprising types are more consistent with the social type.

Other important concepts in Holland's theory are differentiation, identity, congruence, and calculus. A person who has only one or two high scores has a greater degree of *differentiation* than a person with several high scores. Holland maintains that high consistency and differentiation of personality types are characteristic of people who cope effectively with their vocational problems. A second concept, *identity*, may be either personal or environmental. An individual with a sense of *personal identity* has a clear and stable picture of his or her goals, interests, and talents; this condition is associated with having a small number of vocational goals in a few major categories. *Environmental identity* is concerned with whether the goals, tasks, and rewards of the environment are stable over time. A third concept, *congruence*, refers to the fact that different personality types function best in different environments: Does the environment provide opportunities and rewards that are congruent with the person's abilities and preferences? Finally, the concept of *calculus* refers to the fact that personality types or environments are orderable according to a hexagonal model in which the distances between personality types or environments are consistent with the theoretical relationships between them.

Although Osipow (1983) maintained that Holland's theory is limited in its ability to explain the process of personality development and its role in vocational selection, he concluded that "with respect to the research testing it, the record of Holland's theory is extremely good. The research program has been broad, varied, and comprehensive." (p. 112) Holland's vocational personalities model has served as a stimulus for research on career interests and choices throughout the world for many years, and, when complemented by measures of vocational aspiration, has achieved notable successes. In addition, the variables in the RI-

ASEC model have been shown to be closely related to four of the Big Five personality variables (Tokar & Swanson, 1995). Holland (1996) has recently maintained, however, that the model should be revised to include the idea that different belief systems are characteristic of different personality types and are promoted by different environments. He proposed to increase the explanatory power of the model by selectively incorporating into it the concepts of career beliefs and strategies.

Self-Directed Search. One of the most prominent inventories stemming from Holland's research and theorizing is the Self-Directed Search (SDS). This inventory consists of questions concerning aspirations, activities, competencies, occupations, and self estimates that add up to scores on the six RIASEC themes in Figure 9–3. The scores are converted to a three-letter code designating the three personality types that the examinee resembles most closely. The code is then used in consulting the *Career Options Finder* to determine the match between the examinee's personality type and a list of 1321 occupations. In addition to English, Spanish, French-Canadian, Vietnamese, and computer versions, a host of materials to facilitate the exploration of career options, college majors, and leisure activities is available in the SDS program.

The 1995 revision of the SDS (Form E) represents an improvement over the previous version. The reading level of the items is lower (fourth grade), questionable items have been edited or eliminated, the items are less complicated, and the scoring system has been simplified to a two-letter system. In addition, the accompanying resource materials are appealing and helpful to both examinees and counselors (Ciechalski, 1998).

Vocational Preference Inventory. The Vocational Preference Inventory (VPI) is a supplement to the Self-Directed Search and certain other interest inventories. Examinees indicate whether they like or dislike each of 160 or more different occupations, and their responses are scored on the six RIASEC themes and five other scales (Self-Control, Status, Masculinity-Femininity, Infrequency, and Acquiescence). The first six scores can be used with the SDS *Career Options Finder* for purposes of career exploration and vocational guidance. Different patterns of high scores on these six types result in the examinee being assigned to different vocational categories. For example, a person who scores high on the C, E, and S scales falls in the same category as advertising agents and sales representatives.

In a review of a previous (seventh) edition of the VPI, Rounds (1985) concluded that this inventory cannot be recommended because of "unsubstantiated clinical and personality interpretations that might easily mislead the unwary user" (p. 1684) and its failure to provide adequate reliability, validity, and normative data. The situation improved somewhat with the 1985 edition and the new manual, but the psychometric characteristics of the VPI still leave something to be desired.

Personality Inventories as Measures of Interests

Personality inventories like those described in chapters 7 and 8 typically contain a number of questions concerning interests, values, attitudes, and other aspects of personality. Consequently, scores on many of these inventories may be useful in vocational counseling and guidance. An example is the 16 Personality Factor Questionnaire, which can be scored and interpreted by computer in terms of occupational variables corresponding to Holland's RIASEC themes. An examinee's profile of scores on these variables (see Report 9–1) can then be compared with the profiles of several dozen occupations to determine the similarity of the examinee's interests to those of people in each occupation.

One of the most favorably reviewed of personality inventories that can serve as measures of interests is the Self-Description Inventory (SDI) (by C. B. Johansson, from NCS Assessments). Designed for grades nine and over, the SDI yields scores on 11 personal description scales (Caution/Adventurous, Nonscientific/Analytical, Tense/Relaxed, Insecure/Confident, Conventional/Imaginative, Impatient/Patient, Unconcerned/Altruistic, Reserved/Outgoing, Soft-spoken/Forceful, Lackadaisical/ Industrious, Unorganized/Orderly) and six vocationally oriented scales based on Holland's RIASEC themes. Five Administrative Indices —Total Response, Pattern of Response (% yes,% no,% sometimes), and a Response Check—may also be computed to provide a check on validity biases. Scoring and narrative interpretation of responses to the SDI are done by computer.

The 17 scales of the SDI were standardized on six separate samples of males and females between the ages of 15 and 55 (three age groups for each sex), and its reliability and validity appear fairly satisfactory. Test-retest reliabilities range from .70 to .94 for the personality scales and from .76 to .91 for the vocationally oriented scales. Moderate correlations with other personality inventories are reported in the manual, and additional validity data confirm the ability of SDI scores to differentiate among people in varying occupational groups who are experienced and satisfied with their work.

**REPORT
9–1**

Vocational Interests Interpreted from the Report for Figure 7–1

Basic Interpretive Report   NAME: Mark Sample
Vocational Activities   DATE: August 10, 1998

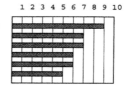

Holland Themes

Sten		1 2 3 4 5 6 7 8 9 10
9	Investigative	
7	Artistic	
7	Realistic	
6	Social	
6	Enterprising	
5	Conventional	

Investigative = 9
Mr. Sample shows personality characteristics similar to Investigative persons. Such persons typically have good reasoning ability and enjoy the challenge of problem-solving. They tend to have critical minds, are curious, and are open to new ideas and solutions. Investigative persons tend to be reserved and somewhat impersonal; they may prefer working independently. They tend to be concerned with the function and purpose of materials rather than aesthetic principles. Mr. Sample may enjoy working with ideas and theories, especially in the scientific realm. It may be worthwhile to explore whether Mr. Sample enjoys doing research, reading technical articles, or solving challenging problems.

          Occupational Fields: Science
                               Math
                               Research
                               Medicine and Health
                               Computer Science

Artistic = 7
Mr. Sample shows personality characteristics similar to Artistic persons, who are self-expressive, typically through a particular mode such as art, music, design, writing, acting, composing, etc. Like Artistic persons, Mr. Sample may be venturesome and open to different views and experiences. Sometimes he may be preoccupied with thoughts and ideas, which may relate to the overall creative process. He may do his best work in an unstructured, flexible environment. It may be worthwhile to explore whether Mr. Sample appreciates aesthetics and possesses artistic, design, or musical talents.

          Occupational Fields: Art
                               Music
                               Design
                               Theater
                               Writing

Report 9-1 continued

Basic Interpretive Report   NAME: Mark Sample
Vocational Activities (continued)   DATE: August 10, 1998

Realistic = 7
Mr. Sample shows personality characteristics similar to Realistic persons. Persons
who score high on this theme indicate a preference for physical activity and for
working with tools and machinery. They tend to be reserved and somewhat aloof with
others and may not like extensive social interaction. Activities which can be
pursued independently may be more to their liking. Realistic persons show interest
in the function and purpose of objects. They are also self-assured and tend not to
worry about what others think. Many Realistic persons indicate a proclivity for
activities such as repairing electronic, mechanical, or automotive products, or a
willingness to take coursework in those areas. It may be worthwhile to explore
whether Mr. Sample's interests include activities involving physical exertion,
knowledge of mechanical principles, or manual dexterity.

        Occupational Fields: Machine Trades
                             Skilled Trades
                             Protective Service
                             Outdoor Occupations
                             Construction Work

Degree of compatibility between top two themes:
The first two themes are highly compatible, and jobs that involve both areas should
be common.

From the 16 PF® Fifth Edition Basic Interpretive Report. Copyright © by the Institute
for Personality and Ability Testing, Inc. Reprinted by permission. 16 PF is a trademark
of IPAT, Inc.

■ Criterion- and Content-Validated Interest Inventories

Unlike psychometric instruments based on the theories of Roe and Holland, the
majority of interest inventories have not been constructed according to a specific
theoretical framework. Contemporary versions of the Strong Vocational Interest
Blank and related psychometric instruments have incorporated certain concepts
from interest theories such as Holland's thematic categories into their interpretive
structure. However, the items comprising these inventories were originally selected only if responses to the items were significantly related to a specified external
or internal criterion or on the basis of common and psychological sense.

The research by James Miner marks the beginnings of systematic efforts to
develop criterion- and content-validated measures of interests. The interest questionnaire constructed by Miner in 1915 led to a seminar on interest measurement
at Carnegie Institute of Technology in 1919. One outcome of that seminar was

a research program on interest measurement undertaken by E. K. Strong, Jr. and development and refinement of the first standardized interest inventory—the Strong Vocational Interest Blank for Men. Other noteworthy events in the history of interest measurement were the publication by G. F. Kuder in 1939 of the Kuder Preference Record and the research on objective interest measurement conducted by the U.S. Army Air Corps psychologists during World War II. Many interest inventories have been published since that time, but modifications of the inventories developed originally by Strong and Kuder continue to be among the most popular.

The Strong Inventories

As a result of research conducted during the 1920s, Strong discovered consistent, significant differences in people's reports of what they liked and disliked. To construct an inventory for assessing these individual differences, he administered a variety of items concerning preferences for specific occupations, school subjects, amusements, activities, and types of people, in addition to a scale for rating their own abilities and characteristics, to groups of men employed in specific occupations. By comparing the responses of these occupational groups with the responses of men in general, a series of occupational scales consisting of items that were answered differently by men in specific occupations than by men in general were developed. Several dozen occupational scales for men were devised, and a separate women's blank that could be scored on over two dozen occupational scales was constructed a few years later.

For various reasons, including the desire to comply with Title IX of the Civil Rights Act of 1964 and to meet allegations of sexism, in 1974 the separate men's and women's forms of the Strong Vocational Interest Blank were combined into a single instrument—the Strong-Campbell Interest Inventory (SCII). An attempt was made to remove gender bias in the content of the items and the occupational labels and to create a more unisex inventory. Consequently, gender bias was reduced, if not entirely eliminated, in the SCII.

Format of the Strong Interest Inventory. The latest (1994) edition of the instrument originated by Strong is the Strong Interest Inventory (SII). It consists of 317 items grouped into the following eight sections:

    I. *Occupations.* Each of 135 occupational titles is responded to with like (L), indifferent (I), or dislike (D).

    II. *School Subjects.* Each of 39 school subjects is responded to with like (L), i ndifferent (I), or dislike (D).

    III. *Activities.* Each of 46 general occupational activities is responded to with like (L), indifferent (I), or dislike (D).

IV. *Amusements*. Each of 29 amusements or hobbies is responded to with like (L), indifferent (I), or dislike (D).

V. *Types of People*. Each of 20 types of people is responded to with like (L), indifferent (I), or dislike (D).

VI. *Preference Between Two Activities*. For each of 30 pairs of activities, preference between the activity on the left (L) and the activity on the right (R) or no preference (=) is indicated.

VII. *Your Characteristics*. Each of 12 characteristics is responded to with Yes, ?, or No, depending on whether or not they are self-descriptive.

VIII. *Preference for the World of Work*. For each of six pairs of ideas, data, and things, preference between the item on the left (L) and the item on the right (R), or no preference (=), is indicated.

The items, format, and administration procedure of the Strong Interest Inventory were essentially unchanged from the preceding edition, but the profile was expanded to include 211 occupational scales, including 102 pairs of separate scales for men and women and 7 scales for occupations represented by only one gender.

Scoring the SII. The SII can be scored only by computer, and the item scoring weights and scoring procedure are a trade secret. Completed inventories must be sent to Consulting Psychologists Press for computerized scoring, profiling, and interpretation, and the results are printed as a Strong Profile Report and/or a Strong Interpretive Report. The former report displays the examinee's scores on hundreds of scales, whereas the latter provides detailed graphic information on the examinee's occupational interests and tailored descriptions of the best occupations for him or her.

The SII is scored on five groups of measures: Administrative Indexes, General Occupational Themes, Basic Interest Scales, Occupational Scales, and Special Scales. Before attempting to interpret a person's scores on the last four groups of measures, scores on three Administrative Indexes—Total Responses, Infrequent Responses, and the percentages of "Like," "Indifferent," and "Dislike" responses should be inspected. Total Responses must be 300 or above; the Infrequent Responses Index must be 0 or greater; and the Like, Indifferent, and Dislike percentages must be between 14 and 60; (Harmon, Hansen, Borgen, & Hammer, 1994).

The six General Occupational Themes are based on the six categories of Holland's (1985) RIASEC model. Listed under each of these six themes are scores on three to five Basic Interest Scales. These scores are indicative of the strength and consistency of special interest areas, such as Agriculture, Science, Music/Dramatics, Teaching, Public Speaking, and Data Management. The corresponding T scores are interpreted as "Very Little Interest, Little Interest, Average Interest, High Interest, or Very High Interest." Scores on the Occupational Scales are indicative of the extent to which the examinee's responses to the items on a particular scale are similar to those of men or women employed in a particular occupation. The corresponding T scores are designated as "Dissimilar Interests," "Mid-Range," or "Similar Interests."

Finally, scores on the four Personal Style Scales are the ratings given by the respondent on the following four bipolar scales:
- Work Style: "Works with ideas/data/things" versus "Works with people"
- Learning Environment: "Practical" versus "Academic"
- Leadership Style: "Leads by example" versus "Directs others"
- Risk Taking/Adventure: "Plays it safe" versus "Takes chances"

Like scores on the other SII scales, scores on this scale are useful in vocational counseling and career exploration.

Reliability and Validity. Coefficient alpha reliabilities for scores on the General Occupational Themes of the SII are in the low .90s, and test-retest coefficients over 3–6 months are in the high .80s and low .90s. Alpha and test-retest coefficients for the Basic Interest Scales and the Personal Style Scales are somewhat lower. Various types of evidence for the content, concurrent, predictive and construct validity of the SII is presented in the manual (Harmon et al., 1994). An analysis of the composition of the SII attests to its content validity. The ranks of mean scores on the General Occupational Themes, the Basic Interest Scales, the Occupational Scales, and the Personal Style Scales in 109 occupational groups, as well as correlations of these scales with other measures of interest, attest to the concurrent and construct validity of the SII. Additional evidence for the validity of the Personal Style Scales is found in the differences in the mean scores on these scales by educational level, educational major, and occupation. With regard to the predictive validity of the SII, the results of studies conducted with previous editions of the inventory have been extrapolated to the current edition; further prediction studies have also been conducted.

Kuder Interest Inventories

Rather than the varied item format of the Strong Interest Inventory, G. F. Kuder applied a forced-choice item format in devising the items on his interest inventories. In constructing his first inventory, the Kuder Vocational Preference Record, Kuder administered a list of statements concerning activities to college students and determined which items clustered together in terms of responses to them. Following this procedure yielded ten scales of items having low correlations across scales but high correlations within scales. Triads of items, with each member of a triad belonging to a different interest scale, were then formed and ad-

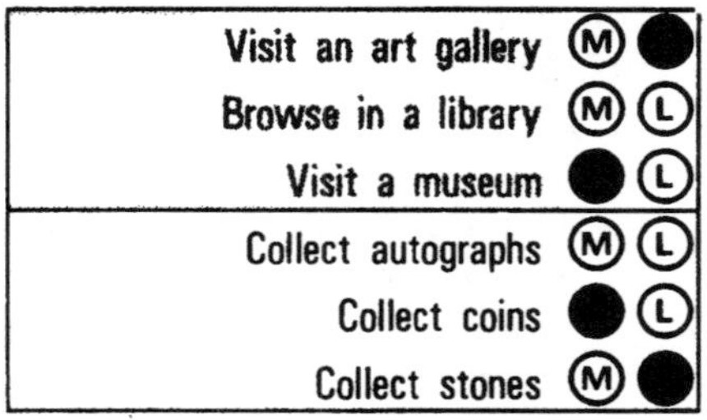

Visit an art gallery Ⓜ ●	
Browse in a library Ⓜ Ⓛ	
Visit a museum ● Ⓛ	
Collect autographs Ⓜ Ⓛ	
Collect coins ● Ⓛ	
Collect stones Ⓜ ●	

Two examples of items on the Kuder General Interest Survey.

FIG. 9–4

Reproduced from *Kuder General Interest Survey*, Form E by permission of the publisher, CTB/McGraw-Hill. Copyright © 1966 by G. Frederic Kuder.

ministered in forced-choice format. This procedure resulted in interests in different areas being pitted against each other.

All items on the Kuder inventories are composed of three statements of activities; respondents are told to indicate which of the three activities they *most* prefer and which they *least* prefer. To illustrate, answers to the first item triad in Figure 9–4 indicate that the respondent would most like to visit a museum and least like to visit an art gallery. Responses to the second item triad indicate that the examinee would most like to collect coins and least like to collect stones.

There are both advantages and disadvantages to the forced-choice item format selected by Kuder. Although this format tends to minimize certain response sets (acquiescence, social desirability, and so forth), examinees sometimes find that responding to forced-choice items is awkward. Another problem is the ipsative nature of responses to forced-choice items. By accepting or rejecting an activity on one scale, the respondent does not select or reject an activity falling on another scale. Because a person's scores on a particular scale are affected by his or her responses to items on other scales, it is impossible to obtain uniformly high or uniformly low scores across all scales. A typical score pattern consists of high scores on one or more scales, low scores on one or more scales, and average scores on the remaining scales.

Kuder General Interest Survey. Two of Kuder's inventories that are currently commercially available are the Kuder General Interest Survey (KGIS) and the Kuder Occupational Interest Survey (KOIS). The KGIS, which was designed for grades 6–12 and takes 45–60 minutes to complete, consists of 168 triads of statements describing various activities; one activity in each triad is to be marked "Most Preferred" and one "Least Preferred." The KGIS is scored on ten general interest areas: Outdoor, Mechanical, Computational, Scientific, Persuasive, Artistic, Literary, Musical, Social Service, and Clerical. Separate percentile norms for four groups (males and females in grades 6–8 and males and females in grades 9–12) were obtained in 1987. The availability of separate sex norms permits examinees to compare their KGIS scores with those of both boys and girls. The score report provides a rank-order listing of percentiles in the ten interest areas, as well as the three areas in Holland's RIASEC system on which the examinee ranks highest with respect to other males and with respect to other females. Although the provision of separate sex norms helps to control for gender bias resulting from combined norms, differences in the interests of males and females can be seen in the fact that, on the average, boys score higher on the mechanical, computational, scientific, and persuasive scales, while girls score higher on the artistic, literary, musical, social service, and clerical scales. Reviews of the KGIS (Pope, 1995; Thompson, 1995) are supportive of its use for career exploration in junior and senior high students or with adults of low reading ability. Thompson (1995) cautions, however, that, because of a scarcity of evidence of its effectiveness as a predictor of occupational success and satisfaction, the KGIS should not be used in making specific career choices.

Kuder Occupational Interest Survey. The KOIS, which was designed for grade 11 to adult and takes 30–40 minutes to complete, consists of 100 triads of statements describing various activities; one activity in each triad is to be marked "Most Preferred" and one "Least Preferred." In scoring the KOIS, the examinee's responses are compared with those of people who were reportedly satisfied with their occupational choices and with those of college students majoring in particular fields of study. A person's score on any of the KOIS occupational or college-major scales is a modified biserial correlation coefficient *(lambda coefficient)* between his or her responses to the items and the proportion of individuals in the specified occupational or college major group who endorsed each item. The higher the lambda coefficient, the more closely the person's score resembles the interest pattern of the corresponding occupational group or major. The report of scores on the KOIS lists the lambda coefficients, by sex, in the norm group, for occupational and college-major scales. In interpreting a person's lambda coefficients, the highest coefficients are emphasized; the associated occupations or majors are those in which the examinee's interests are greatest. However, occupations or majors falling within .06 units of the highest coefficients should also be considered.

The short-term test-retest reliability coefficients of the KGIS and KOIS scales are in the .80s and .90s, and the scores have been found to be fairly stable over a decade or more (Zytowski, 1976). In general, the evidence points to adequate content validity for both interest inventories. With respect to the predictive validity of the KOIS, Zytowski (1976) found that over half the individuals who had taken the KOIS 12–19 years earlier had entered occupations on which they had scored within .07-.12 points of their highest lambda coefficients.

■ Other General Interest and Special Purpose Interest Inventories

Along with the Self-Directed Search, the Strong and Kuder inventories are in the top three among all standardized psychometric instruments for the assessment of vocational interests (Watkins, Campbell, & Nieberding, 1994). However, many other general and special-purpose interest measures have been devised since the 1920s (see Table 9–1). Most of these instruments have focused on vocational interests, but some of them were designed primarily to measure school-related interests. Many special-purpose inventories for measuring the interests of children, the disadvantaged, and people planning to enter nonprofessional occupations have also been published. Two of the most carefully designed and validated are the Jackson Vocational Interest Survey and the Career Assessment Inventory.

Jackson Vocational Interest Survey (JVIS). Based on the results of an extensive research program directed by D.N. Jackson (1977), the JVIS consists of 289 forced-choice pairs of statements descriptive of job-related activities. The statements comprising an item pair refer to two equally popular interests, and examinees are told to indicate a preference between them. Designed for high school age and beyond, the JVIS takes 45–60 minutes to complete. Initial scoring is on 34 basic interest scales representing 26 work-role and eight work-style dimensions. The definitions of these dimensions were refined by referring to job descriptions in the *Dictionary of Occupational Titles.* Another approach to scoring the JVIS is in terms of ten occupational themes (Expressive, Logical, Inquiring, Practical, Assertive, Socialized, Helping, Conventional, Enterprising, Communication). These themes are based on the six RIASEC themes and a factor analysis of responses to the JVIS. Scores on the ten themes are highly reliable (test-retest coefficients between .82 and .92), as are scores on the 34 basic interest scales (median r = .84). With respect to the validity of the JVIS, a large study conducted at Pennsylvania State University found that JVIS profiles did a better job of predicting choice of academic major than any previously reported combination of interest and aptitude measures (Jackson, 1977).

Reviewers of the JVIS have praised its careful construction and factorially pure scales, but it has been noted that more evidence for its validity is needed (Davidshofer, 1985; Thomas, 1985). The JVIS is also a rather long inventory, taking more time to complete than an inventory with a similar format—the Kuder Occupational Interest Survey.

Career Assessment Inventory. Certain scales on the Strong Interest Inventory, the Kuder Occupational Interest Survey, and other general-interest inventories pertain to interests in nonprofessional occupations, but none of these inventories

TABLE 9–1 Vocational Interest Inventories.

- *Campbell Interest and Skill Survey;* by D. Campbell; from NCS Assessments; ages 15 years to adult; review MMYB 13:43.
- *Career Assessment Inventory, Second Edition* (Vocational Version); by C.B. Johansson; from NCS Assessments; grade 10 through adult; reviews MMYB 11:59 & TC II:128.
- *Career Interest Inventory;* grades 7–9, grades 10–12, and adults; from Psychological Corporation; review MMYB 13:51.
- *COPS Interest Inventory;* by L. Knapp-Lee, R.R. Knapp, & L.F. Knapp; from EdITS; grade 7 through high school, college, and adults; review TC V:76.
- *The Guilford-Zimmerman Interest Inventory;* by J.S. Guilford & W.S. Zimmerman; from Consulting Psychologists Press; college and adults; review MMYB 12:174.
- *Hall Occupational Orientation Inventory;* by L.G. Hall, R.B. Tarier, & D.L. Shappel; from Scholastic Testing Service; grades 3–7, 8–16 and adults, low-literature adults, junior high students-adults; review MMYB 12:175.
- *The Harrington-O'Shea Career Decision-Making System Revised;* by T.F. Harrington & A.J. O'Shea; from American Guidance Service; grade 7 and over; review MMYB 12:178.
- *IDEAS: Interest Determination, Exploration and Assessment System;* by C.B. Johansson; from NCS Assessments; grades 7–12 and adults; review MMYB 11:172.
- *Jackson Vocational Interest Survey;* by D.N. Jackson; from Sigma Assessment Systems; high school and college students; reviews MMYB 9:542 & TC IX:308.
- *Kuder General Interest Survey, Form E;* by G.F. Kuder; from CTB/McGraw-Hill; grades 6–12; review MMYB 12:209.
- *Kuder Occupational Interest Survey,* Form DD; by G.F. Kuder; CTB/McGraw-Hill; reviews MMYB 10:167 & TC X:488.
- *MDS Vocational Interest Exploration System;* high school-adults; from McCarron-Dial Systems; review MMYB 13:194.
- *Occupational Aptitude Survey and Interest Schedule, Second Edition—Interest Schedule;* by R.B. Parker; from pro.ed; grades 8–12; review MMYB 12:264.
- *Occupational Interests Card Sort;* adults; review MMYB 13:213.
- *Reading-Free Vocational Interest Inventory-Revised;* by R.L. Becker; from The Psychological Corporation; adolescents and adults; reviews MMYB 9:1035 & TC II:627.
- *Self-Description Inventory;* by C.B. Johansson; NCS Assessments; adults and students 15 years and older; reviews MMYB 9:1096 & TC VI:491.
- *The Self-Directed Search Form E—1990 Revision* (by J. Holland; from Psychological Assessment Resources; high school, college, and adults; reviews MMYB 13:281.
- *Strong Interest Inventory* (Fourth Edition); by E.K. Strong, Jr., D.P. Campbell, & J.C. Hansen; from Consulting Psychologists Press; ages 16 and over; review MMYB 12:374.
- *Vocational Interest Inventory—Revised;* by P.W. Lunneborg; from Western Psychological Services; high school juniors and seniors; review MMYB 13:357.
- *Vocational Preference Inventory;* by J.L. Holland; from Psychological Assessment Resources; adults and older adolescents; reviews MMYB 9:1342 & TC V:545.

was designed specifically with this purpose in mind. Since the 1950s, a number of inventories focusing on the skilled trades and somewhat simpler in content and vocabulary than the Strong and Kuder instruments have been constructed. One such instrument is the Career Assessment Inventory (CAI).

The Vocational Version of the CAI was modeled after the Strong inventories and has sometimes been referred to as "the workingman's Strong Interest Inventory." Responses to the 305 items on the CAI are on a five-point scale (L = like very much, l = like somewhat, I = indifferent, d = dislike somewhat, and D = dislike very much). The items, which were written at a sixth-grade level and cover activities, school subjects, and occupational titles, can be answered in 30–45 minutes. The computer-based report of T-scores on the CAI consists of four sections: I. Administrative Indices (Total Responses, Response Consistency, Response Percentages on Activities, School Subjects, Occupations); II General Themes (Realistic, Investigative, Artistic, Social, Enterprising, Conventional); III. Basic Interest Area Scales; and IV. Occupational Scales. The 25 Basic Interest Area Scales and the 111 Occupational scales are grouped under the six RIASEC themes. Scores on four special Scales (Fine Arts-Mechanical, Occupational Extroversion-Introversion, Educational Orientation, and Variability of Interests), a computer-generated narrative report, and a counselor's summary are provided. From a psychometric viewpoint the CAI is well-designed and has good reliability. On the negative side, McCabe (1985) noted that no predictive validity information is reported in the manual and that the CAI is relatively expensive to score. Overall, however, he rates it as a very important test that fills a significant need and is well developed and engineered to be easily and appropriately used (for another review, see Kehoe, 1992). A 370-item Enhanced Version of the CAI, which can be scored on more professional occupations than the Vocational Version, was published in 1986. Both the Vocational and Enhanced Versions can also be scored on General Occupational Themes based on Holland's RIASEC model.

Gender and Ethnic Differences in Interests

As noted in the discussions of the Self-Directed Search and the Kuder General Interest Survey, significant gender differences have been found on many measures of interests. Data from the general reference sample in the standardization of the 1994 Strong Interest Inventory indicate, for example, that the mean scores obtained by women on the General Occupational Themes are lower than those of men on Realistic and Investigative, but higher on the Artistic, and Social themes (Harmon et al., 1994). Gender differences in scores on the Basic Interest and Personal Style Scales of the SII were also found. For example, men scored higher than women on the Risk Taking/Adventure scale, while women scored higher than men on the Work Style scale. These results are similar to those reported two decades earlier (Gottfredson, Holland, & Gottfredson, 1975; Prediger & Hanson, 1976). Gender differences in vocational interests have persisted despite social, political, and professional efforts to equalize educational and occupational opportunities for the sexes (Hackett & Lonberg, 1994).

It has been alleged, perhaps with some justification, that earlier versions of the Strong and other interest inventories contributed to gender discrimination by directing young women into traditional women's occupations such as teaching, nursing, and clerical work (Diamond, 1979). Responding to the allegation of gender bias, the developers of the Strong Interest Inventory decided to prepare a combined version of the men's and women's form. Furthermore, combined sex norms, as well as the traditional separate-sex norms, were provided. To eliminate gender differences in responses, certain instruments, such as the revised version of the Vocational Interest Inventory and the UNIACT Interest Inventory, contain sex-balanced items endorsed by approximately equal percentages of men and women. Perhaps an even more effective way of reducing or eliminating sex differences in scores on interest inventories is to provide equal opportunities, encouragement, and experiences for both sexes in a variety of activities, both traditionally male and traditionally female.

Standardization data on the 1994 edition of the SII also provided an opportunity to compare the responses of groups of four ethnic minorities—African-Americans, American Indians, Asian, and Latino(a)/Hispanic—with each other and with the general reference sample. Analysis of responses to specific items found that, compared with the general reference sample: African-Americans and American Indians scored higher on religious items; except for American Indians, all groups liked to communicate with people from other cultures and liked living in a city; American Indians had a greater liking for the outdoors; Latinos/Hispanics, and to a lesser extent Asians, were more interested in language (Harmon et al., 1994). Significant differences between the mean scores of the four ethnic groups, when compared with those of the general reference sample and with each other, were also found on the General Occupational Themes, the Basic Interest Scales, the Occupational Scales, and the Personal Style Scales.

In another investigation of the relationships of interests to ethnicity, Kaufman, Ford-Richards, and McLean (1998) found the following differences between the mean scores of 756 Whites and 85 Blacks aged 16–65 years on the Occupational Themes scores of the SII: Whites scored higher than Blacks on the Realistic and Investigative themes, but Blacks scored higher than Whites on the Social, Enterprising, and Conventional themes.

Despite the existence of ethnic and gender group differences in responses to vocational interest inventories, research supports the assumption that traditional ways of measuring interest are valid for different minorities and for both sexes. Day and Rounds (1998) concluded that people of different ethnic and gender groups hold the same cognitive map of the world of work, responding to activities in the same patterns and expressing their likes and dislikes for pursuits grouped according to the RIASEC model and the People-Things and Data-Ideas dimensions (also see Lippa, 1998; Ryan, Tracey, & Rounds, 1996)

Using Interest Inventories in Counseling

Young men and women are frequently unrealistic in making academic and vocational plans. Many more high school students expect to graduate from college than actually do, and the career aspirations of college students and graduates are often inconsistent with their career possibilities. On the other hand, many young people, women and minorities in particular, experience feelings of low self-efficacy with respect to certain traditionally male or traditionally white middle-class occupations, and consequently are reluctant to explore those occupations and the possibilities of entering them. Changing political and social circumstances have opened up many vocations or professions in which blacks, women, disabled persons, and other groups previously experienced discrimination and may continue to view as inaccessible or beyond their capacities. For this reason, teachers and counselors need to encourage all students to explore a wide-range of vocational opportunities and occupations, but with a realistic appreciation of their own personal interests, abilities, and financial resources, as well as the nature and duties of the occupations and the rewards offered by them.

Career aims and decisions are affected not only by environmental factors such as the economic situation and the kinds of jobs that are available, but also by psychosocial variables such as sex, socioeconomic status, physical and mental abilities, interests, and knowledge of particular occupations. For these reasons, high school and college counselors should be well-informed about the world of work, including what particular jobs entail—and whether the abilities, interests, and resources of students are appropriate for entering or preparing for certain occupations.

Properly trained vocational counselors are prepared to obtain personal data from counselees and to supply them with information on various training programs and occupations. However, vocational counseling must be done with caution. Both jobs and people are multifaceted and dynamic: they possess many different characteristics which may change with time. The job of psychologist, for example, involves different activities in different situations, and the nature of the job has changed over the years. But even in the same situational context and time frame, many jobs have enough diversity so that people with different abilities and interests can adjust and perform satisfactorily.

Despite the need for a flexible, realistic approach to vocational counseling in which advice and predictions are couched in terms of likelihoods rather than certainties, counselors must make some interpretation of scores on psychological tests and inventories. Furthermore, in interpreting the results of an interest inventory it should be made clear that *interest* is not the same as *ability*. It is not uncommon for a person to conclude from the results of an interest inventory that he or she has the ability to succeed in a particular occupation when all that has actually been shown is that the person's interests are similar to those of people in the occupation. For this and other reasons, it is unwise to leave the task of interpreting a self-administered inventory to the examinee, especially a young examinee. In any case, scores on interest inventories should be employed in counseling in the light of other information about the counselee—test scores, accomplishments (grades, awards, extracurricular activities), work experiences, and interests. Also helpful to experienced vocational counselors are books such as the *Dictionary of Occupational Titles*, the *Occupational Outlook Handbook*, the *Occupational Outlook for College Students*, and *The Guide for Occupational Exploration*. Various career exploration and development materials published by commercial testing companies are also useful in vocational counseling.

■ Values

As noted earlier in the chapter, *values* are more general or abstract than *interests*; they are concerned with the utility, importance, or worth attached to particular activities or objects. Milton Rokeach (1973) who conducted extensive international and cross-cultural research on the topic, defined a value as "an enduring belief that a specific mode of conduct or end-state of existence is personally or socially preferable to an opposite or converse mode of conduct or end-state of existence" (p. 5). This definition implies that values are of two kinds—those concerned with modes of conduct (*instrumental values*) and those concerned with end-states (*terminal values*). Although vocational psychologists have in large measure limited their attention to terminal values, Rokeach defined subcategories of both instrumental and terminal values and designed an instrument to measure them.

Rokeach Value Survey

Rokeach classified instrumental values as being of two kinds—*moral values* and *competence values*. The former category is concerned with interpersonal modes of conduct, which produce guilt feelings when violated. The latter category, competence values, has to do with intrapersonal, self-actualizing modes of conduct, the violation of which leads to feelings of inadequacy. Terminal values can also be further divided into *personal values* and *social values*. Personal values, which include such end-states as peace of mind and salvation, are self-centered; social values, including end-states such as equality and world peace, are society-centered.

The Rokeach Value Survey consists of a series of 18 instrument and 18 terminal value terms or phrases for assessing the relative importance of these values to people. Respondents are directed to rank order the 18 items in each list according to their importance to them. No other instrument attempts to measure as many values, a fact which, coupled with the speed of its administration and scoring and its inexpensiveness, may account for the popularity of the Rokeach Value Survey. The reliability with which it serves to compare different groups of people, a purpose for which it has been used in hundreds of investigations, is adequate. People of different nationalities and in different walks of life rank the items on the survey differently. For example, Rokeach (1973) reported that Israeli students assigned highest rankings to the terminal values of "a world at peace" and "national security", whereas American students assigned the highest ranks to the terminal value of "a comfortable life" and the instrumental value of "ambitious"

Representative Measures of Values.   **TABLE 9–2**

- *Career Anchors: Discovering Your Real Values, Revised Edition*; by E.H. Schein; Pfeiffer and Company International Publishers; review MMYB 13:46.
- *Career Values Card Sort*; from Career Research and Testing, San Jose, CA; review MMYB 13:53.
- *Hall-Tonna Inventory of Values (The)*; by B.P. Hall & B. Tonna; from Behaviordyne, Palo Alto, CA; review MMYB 11:153.
- *Maferr Inventory of Feminine Values*; by A.G. Steinmann, D.J. Fox, & M. Toro; from Maferr Foundation, New York, NY; review MMYB 9:641.
- *Maferr Inventory of Masculine Values*; by A.G. Steinmann, D.J. Fox, & M. Toro; from Maferr Foundation, New York, NY; review MMYB 9:642.
- *Personal Values Questionnaire*; review MMYB 13:230.
- Rokeach Value Survey; by M. Rokeach; from Consulting Psychologists Press; review MMYB 12:334.
- *Survey of Interpersonal Values*; by L.V. Gordon; from McGraw-Hill/London House; reviews MMYB 8:688 & TC II:759.
- *Survey of Personal Values*; by L.V. Gordon; from McGraw-Hill/London House; reviews MMYB 10:354 & TC II:773.
- *Survey of Work Values, Revised, Form U*; authored and published by Bowling Green State University review MMYB 12:383.
- *Temperament and Values Inventory*; by C.B. Johansson & P.L. Webber; from NCS Assessments; reviews MMYB 9:1233 & TC I:660.
- *Values Inventory*; W.J. Reddin & K. Rowell; from Organizational Tests Ltd. (Canada); review MMYB 9:1308.
- *The Values Scale*, Second Edition; by D.E. Super & D.D. Nevitt; Consulting Psychologists Press; review MMYB 13:355.
- *Work Values Inventory*; by D.E. Super; review MMYB 8:1030 & TC II: 835.

(Rokeach, 1973, 1979). Reviews of the Rokeach Value Survey (e. g., Brookhart, 1995; Sanford, 1995) support its use in research, but moderate reliabilities and out-of-date norms make it unsuitable for individual counseling.

Many other standardized and nonstandardized measures of values have been devised and used to study such topics as vocational values, masculine/feminine values, personal/interpersonal values, religious values, political values (liberalism-conservatism), and, of course, "family values." Table 9–2 is a representative list of published inventories of values.

Vocational Values

It is possible to administer the Rokeach Value Survey and the Study of Values in vocational counseling situations, but these inventories were not designed specifically for that purpose. More closely related to career and work choices and satisfactions are instruments such as the Work Values Inventory, the Values Scale, and the Temperament and Values Inventory. The *vocational values* measured by such instruments vary with the person and the situation. For example, Super (1973) found that people in upper-level occupations were more motivated by the need for self-actualization, an intrinsic goal, whereas extrinsic values are more likely to be subscribed to by people in lower-level occupations.

Work Values Inventory. This inventory consists of 45 Likert-type items designed to assess 15 values considered important in vocational success and satisfaction. Examples of these values, each of which is measured by only three items, are achievement, supervisory relations, independence, aesthetics, and creativity. For each statement, respondents indicate, on a five-point scale, the degree of importance attached to the value represented by the statement. Percentile norms by grade (7–12) for each of the 15 values are based on data collected in 1968 on a representative national sample of approximately 9,000 high school boys and girls. Test-retest reliability coefficients, obtained from retesting 99 tenth graders after two weeks, range from .74 to .88 for the 15 scales. Evidence for the content, concurrent, and construct validity of the Work Values Inventory is described in the manual. The Work Values Inventory has been praised for its excellent psychometric foundations and its continuing research uses (Bolton, 1985), but it has not gone uncriticized. The manual needs to be revised and brought up to date by incorporating the findings of research conducted since 1970, in particular occupational validity studies based on the current form of the inventory. In addition, reliability data based on college students and adults, not just tenth graders, and new normative data are needed.

The Values Scale. Developed by the Work Importance Study, an international consortium of vocational psychologists from America, Asia, and Europe, this instrument possesses characteristics of both the Work Values Inventory and the Rokeach Value Survey. The purpose of the consortium and the Values Scale was to understand values that individuals seek or hope to find in various life roles and to assess the relative importance of the work role as a means of value realization in the context of other life roles. The scale, which consists of 106 items and takes 30–45 minutes to complete, is scored for the following 21 values (five items per value):

Ability utilization	Creativity	Social Interaction
Achievement	Economic rewards	Social Relations
Advancement	Life Style	Variety
Esthetics	Personal development	Working conditions
Altruism	Physical activity	Cultural identity
Authority	Prestige	Physical prowess
Autonomy	Risk	Economic security

The reliabilities of all 21 values are adequate for individual assessment at the adult level; the reliabilities of ten scales are high enough for individual assessment at the college level, and the reliabilities of eight scales are adequate at the high school level. The means and standard deviations for three samples (high school, college, and adult), as well as data on the construct validity of the instrument, are given in the manual. The Values Scale appears to have good potential for research on vocational counseling and selection, and particularly for cross-cultural or cross-national comparisons.

Temperament and Values Inventory (TVI). This carefully constructed inventory was designed to complement information obtained from ability tests and vocational interest inventories. It is administered to high school students and adults and takes approximately 30 minutes to complete. The 230 items are divided into two sections: 133 true-false items scored on seven Temperament Scales (Personal Characteristics) and 97 Likert-type items scored on seven Values Scales (Reward Values). The seven bipolar Temperament Scales are Routine-Flexible, Quiet-Active, Attentive-Distractible, Serious-Cheerful, Consistent-Changeable, Reserved-Social, and Reticent-Persuasive. The seven Values Scales are Social Recognition, Managerial-Sales Benefits, Leadership, Social Services, Task Specificity, Philosophical Curiosity, and Work Independence.

The TVI scales were developed on an initial sample of 802 males and females and verified on a separate sample of 456 high school students. The standard T-score scale norms are based on males and females in three age groups (15–19, 20–25, and 26–53 years). Test-retest reliabilities, computed on small samples retested over 1 to 2 weeks, are fairly satisfactory (.79-.93). Comparisons with other related inventories support the construct validity of the inventory, and data on its ability to differentiate between relatively small samples of individuals in a rather narrow range of occupations is reported in support of the claim of concurrent validity.

The TVI has received fairly positive evaluations (Wheeler, 1985; Zuckerman, 1985), especially for its careful construction and well-designed manual. Among its psychometric shortcomings are a lack of long-term reliability data, a lack of convergent and discriminant validity studies, and norms that are based on fairly small and nonrepresentative samples.

■ Personal Orientations and Attitudes

Personal Orientations

Similar to inventories of interests and values are measures of *personal orientations*, which cut across a wide range of personality variables and are related to the cognitive and perceptual styles discussed in Chapter 13, as well as the concept of *lifestyle*. One example of a personal orientation is the extent to which an individual tries "to be all that he can be"—to fulfill his or her potential or become "self-actualized." Another personal orientation that has received a great deal of research attention is sex role. The masculinity/femininity variable has been included in many inventories of interests and personality characteristics. In fact, differences between the preferences and activities of males and females are so commonplace that it has been routine procedure to standardize psychological tests separately by sex.

Bem Sex-Role Inventory. Concern over sex discrimination and an interest in the nature and origin of sex differences in psychological characteristics prompted the development of a number of measures of sex-role during the past 25 years. The most prominent of these is the Bem Sex Role Inventory (BSRI; Bem, 1974). The short form of the Bem Sex-Role Inventory (Short BSRI), which was designed to classify individuals according to their sex-role orientation, consists of 60 words or phrases to be rated on a seven-point scale on which 1 means *never or almost never true* and 7 means *always or almost always true*. Twenty of the items refer to characteristics considered significantly more desirable in men than in women (e. g., aggressive, ambitious), 20 items refer to characteristics considered significantly more desirable in women than in men (e. g., affectionate, cheerful), and 20 items are presumably sex-neutral (e. g., adapt able, conscientious). Scores on three scales—Masculinity (M), Femininity (F), and Androgyny (A)—are determined first. Next the examinee is placed in one of the following four categories according to his or her scores on the M, F, and A scales. Masculine (above median on M and below median on F), Feminine (above median on F and below median on M), Androgynous (above median on both M and F), or Undifferentiated (below median on both M and F).

Payne (1985) concluded that the short form of the Bem Sex-Role Inventory (Short BSRI) provides promising indices of stereotypically sex-linked descriptions, which have significant correlations with various indices of adjustment. The test-retest and internal-consistency reliabilities of the short form are generally satisfactory, but the validity data are meager. In addition, researchers are cautioned not to rely on the norms reported in the manual because they are based solely on samples of Stanford University undergraduates and cannot be considered representative of college or university students in general.

Similar in content and scoring to the BSRI, but not perfectly correlated with it, is the Personal Attributes Questionnaire (PAQ) (Spence & Helmreich, 1978). Like the BSRI, data obtained from the PAQ support a dualistic rather than a bipolar conception of masculinity and femininity in that the two constructs are viewed as different dimensions rather than simply opposite ends of the same continuum.

Sex-Role Egalitarianism Scale (SRES). Another inventory concerned with psychological and behavioral differences between the sexes is the Sex-Role Egalitarianism Scale (SRES) (by L. A. King & D. W. King; from Sigma Assessment Systems). Designed to measure attitudes toward the equality of men and women, the SRES contains 95 attitudinal statements to be answered on five-point scales. The items are written at a 6th or 7th grade level, and require approximately 25 minutes to answer. The five 19-item scales on the SRES cover the following domains: Marital Roles, Parental Roles, Employment Roles, Social-Interpersonal-Heterosexual Roles, Educational Roles.

The internal-consistency, test-retest, and alternate forms reliabilities of the SRES are fairly high. With respect to its validity, relationships between the SRES and other variables, as well as group differences in the scores, support convergent, discriminant, and construct validity of this instrument (King & King, 1993).

Personal Orientation Inventory (POI). This widely used inventory (by E. L. Shostrom; from EdITS) was designed to measure values and behaviors that are important in the development of self-actualizing people. Such people develop and use all of their potentials and are free of the inhibitions and emotional turmoil that characterize less self-actualized people. The POI consists of 150 forced-choice items appropriate for high school students, college students, and adults. The inventory is scored first for two majority orientation ratios: Time Ratio (Time Incompetence/Time Competence), which indicates whether time orientation is primarily in the present or past and/or the future; and Support Ratio (Other/Inner, which indicates whether a person's reactions are basically toward others or the self). Secondly, the POI is scored on the following ten scales: Self-Actualizing Value, Existentiality, Feeling Reactivity, Spontaneity, Self-Regard, Self-Acceptance, Nature of Man, Synergy, Acceptance of Aggression, and Capacity for Intimate Contact. Percentile norms based on a sample of 2,607 western and Midwestern college freshmen (1,514 males and 1.093 females), in addition to mean scores and profiles based on a smaller sample of adults, are given in the manual. Test-retest reliabilities of the individual scales, computed on a sample of 48 college students, are moderate (mostly in the .60s and .70s). Correlations with other personality scales and other evidence from the validity of the POI are also given in the POI manual.

Attitudes

Attitude, defined as a learned predisposition to respond positively or negatively to certain objects, situations, institutions, or persons, consist of cognitive (knowledge of intellect), affect (emotion and motivation), and performance (behavior or action components. Attitudes are a reflection of personality, and attitude-type items are often found on personality assessment instruments. Cattell (1965) viewed attitudes, which he defined as "readinesses to act," as being at a lower level than other personality variables. Attitudes are the starting point in Cattell's dynamic lattice model of personality, and they are subservient to *sentiments*. Sentiments, in turn, are subservient to *ergs*—biologically based needs or drives that are satisfied by means of attitudes and sentiments. For example, a liking for plays and films (attitude level) may stem from an involvement with photography (sentiment level), which in turn may satisfy various needs (sex, gregariousness, curiosity) at the ergic level.

Various methods may be used to obtain information on attitudes, including direct observations of behavior, indirect methods such as projective techniques, and the administration of attitude questionnaires or scales. Direct observations of behavior consists of noting what a person actually does or says in situations in which the attitude object or event is present. Willingness to do a favor, sign a petition, or make a donation to some cause are examples of direct behavioral measures of attitudes.

Direct observation of behavior is informative, particularly with certain individuals (e. g., young children) or when other methods are considered obtrusive. However, obtaining a representative sample of behavior observations in various situations is very time consuming and expensive. In addition, behavioral measures of attitudes often yield results that are different from those obtained from projective techniques and attitude questionnaires.

An example of a projective technique for assessing attitudes is to ask people to make up a story about each of a set of ambiguous pictures. Because the pictures can be interpreted in various ways, the stories that are told by the respondents should reveal something about their attitudes toward the characters, scenes, or situations in the pictures.

The most popular method of measuring attitudes for purposes of research and individual evaluation is to administer an attitude scale. An *attitude scale*, which consists of a set of positive and negative statements concerning a subject of interest (a group of people, an institution, a concept, etc.), can be constructed in a number of different ways. One of the first attitude scales was the Bogardus Social Distance Scale (Bogardus, 1925). On this instrument respondents were asked to indicate their degree of acceptance of various racial and religious groups by ranking them. The Bogardus scale proved useful in research on regional differences and other variables associated with racial prejudice, but it permitted attitude measurement on only an ordinal scale and was somewhat crude by today's standards. More precise measures of attitudes were subsequently made possible by the work of Louis Thurstone, Rensis Likert, Louis Guttman, and other psychometricians. Other attitude-scaling procedures include the semantic-differential technique, Q sorts, and facet analysis. Multivariate statistical procedures, such as factor analysis, multidimensional scaling, latent-structure analysis, latent-partition analysis, and the repertory grid technique, have also been applied to the scaling of attitudes (see Ostrom, Bond, Krosnick, & Sedikides, 1994; Procter, 1993).

Judging by the variety of attitude instruments that have been devised, an individual can have an attitude toward almost anything—any school subject, any vocation, any defined group, any institution, any proposed social action, any practice. A series of volumes published by the Institute for Social Research at the University of Michigan describes many different scales for assessing social attitudes (Robinson, Shaver, & Wrightsman, 1991), political attitudes (Robinson, Rush, & Head, 1973), and occupational attitudes (Robinson, Athanasiou, & Head, 1974). Several dozen attitude measures in a wide range of areas are also listed in *Tests in Microfiche* and can be ordered from Educational Testing Service. A number of publishers and distributors of psychological assessment instruments market attitude questionnaires and scales. These instruments are concerned with attitudes toward such things as aging, jobs, medical and health practices, physical attractiveness, safety, school subjects (mathematics, science, etc.), teachers, tests, violence, and women. However, the majority of attitude instruments are home-grown or ad hoc devices constructed for a particular research study or other purpose.

■ Summary

Theories relating interests to personality and behavior have been proposed by researchers of various persuasions and emphases—psychoanalytic, developmental, trait-factor, and social learning. Psychoanalysts have emphasized the roles of sublimation and identification (modeling) in the development of vocational interests and career choice. Illustrative of developmental theories of vocational interests and maturation are the stage conceptions of E. Ginzberg and Donald Super. Ginzberg and his colleagues viewed vocational decision making as a three-stage process beginning with a fantasy period, progressing through a tentative period, and ending with a realistic period; the last two stages consist of four and two substages, respectively. Emphasizing developmental changes in self-concept and interests, the stage theory of Super and his collaborators begins with an exploratory stage comprised of three substages and ends with an establishment stage having two substages.

Two other theories that have greatly influenced both research and the construction of psychometric instruments concerned with vocational interests are Anne Roe's person-environment theory and J. L. Holland's theory of vocational personalities and work environments. Roe's three-dimensional conical model of career choice consists of Orientation to Personal Relations versus Orientation to Natural Phenomena, Orientation to Resource Utilization versus Orientation to Purposeful Communication, and level of skill (professional, skilled, unskilled) involved in the occupation. Interest inventories based on Roe's theory include the COPS Interest Inventory, the Hall Occupational Orientation Inventory and the Vocational Interest Inventory.

Among all theories of interests and career choices, the most influence on the development of interest inventories has been exerted by J. L. Holland's hexagonal model and the associated concepts. According to this model there are six types of vocational personalities—realistic, investigative, artistic, social, enterprising, and conventional; six kinds of vocational environments corresponding to the personality types are also described. The concepts of consistency (the degree to which personality types or environmental types are related to each other), differentiation (making high scores on only one or two dimensions), identity (personal or environmental), congruence (the fit between personality types and environments), and calculus (ordering the personality types or environments according to the hexagonal model) are also employed in the theory. The major career-planning instruments designed on the basis of Holland's theory are the Self-Directed Search and the Vocational Preference Inventory, but the development and scoring of a number of other interest inventories have also been influenced by the theory.

Not only can interest inventories be construed as measures of personality, but personality inventories can also be scored on interest categories and used in career planning. Two personality inventories that have been employed in career counseling and decision making are the 16 Personality Factor Questionnaire and the Self-Description Inventory.

Historically, the most popular interest inventories, such as the Strong Vocational Interest Blanks and the various inventories constructed by G. F. Kuder, were designed not on the basis of a particular theory but either by criterion-keyed or content-validated procedures. Over the years, the Strong and Kuder inventories have moved closer together in their use of a combination of criterion-keying and content-validation. For example, the occupational scales of the Strong Interest Inventory are criterion-keyed, but the basic interest scales are content validated. Similarly, scales on the Kuder General Interest Survey are content-validated, whereas the occupational and college-major scales of the Kuder Occupational Interest Survey were developed by criterion-keying procedures.

Although the Strong Interest Inventory, the Kuder General Interest Survey, the Self-Directed Search, and the Kuder Occupational Interest Survey are the most popular of all interest inventories, many other measures of vocational interests have been developed. Two of the most carefully designed instruments of this type are the Jackson Vocational Interest Survey and the Career Assessment Inventory. The Vocational Edition of the Career Assessment Inventory was designed by criterion-keying procedures to assess interests in nonprofessional occupations. Special purpose instruments to measure the interests of children as well as disadvantaged and handicapped individuals are also available. As is the case with all vocational interest inventories, these instruments are useful in career counseling when applied in conjunction with information on the aptitudes, experiences, motivations, and other characteristics of counselees.

Values are generally viewed as being on a higher, more abstract conceptual plane and less directly related to behavior than interests. Measures of values have been employed mostly in research and less often than interest inventories in vocational counseling and career decision-making. Milton Rokeach differentiated between instrumental values and terminal values and devised a checklist, the Rokeach Value Survey, to measure two kinds of instrumental values (moral and competence) and two kinds of terminal values (personal and social).

More frequently administered for vocational counseling purposes than the Rokeach Value Survey are the Work Values Inventory, the Values Scale, and the Temperament and Values Inventory. The first two inventories, which measure 15 and 21 values, respectively, are products of the research of Donald Super and his colleagues on the values that people seek in various life roles and the work role in particular. The third inventory, which is scored on seven bipolar temperament scales and seven values scales, is a carefully designed instrument developed and scored by NCS Assessments.

Personal orientations, such as self-actualization and sex-role identification, cut across a somewhat wider range of personality variables than either interests or values. The most influential researcher in the field of sex-role identification has been Sandra Bem, whose Bem Sex-Role Inventory has been used in numerous investigations to differentiate between the masculine, feminine, and androgynous roles. Results of research with the Bem Sex-Role Inventory, the Personal Attributes Questionnaire, and similar instruments indicate that masculinity and femininity are two different psychological constructs and not simply polar opposites on a single dimension. Two other multiscale measures of personal orientations are the Sex-Role Egalitarianism Scale and the Personal Orientation Inventory.

The former instrument measures attitudes toward the equality of men and women, and the latter instrument measures various aspects of self-actualization.

Attitudes are learned predispositions to respond positively or negatively to some object, situation, or person. As such, attitudes are personality characteristics, although at a more superficial level than temperaments and traits. Attitudes can be assessed in a number of ways, the most popular being an attitude scale. The procedures devised by Thurstone, Likert, and Guttman for scaling attitudes have been applied extensively in the construction of attitude scales. More statistically complex methods have also been developed for scaling attitudes.

The great majority of the hundreds of attitude scales and questionnaires listed in various reference sources are unstandardized instruments designed for a particular research investigation or application. However, a number of standardized instruments for assessing attitudes, especially attitudes toward school and work situations, are commercially available.

■ Questions and Activities

1. Compare the Strong Interest Inventory with the Kuder Occupational Interest Survey (Form DD) in terms of design, scoring, and interpretation.
2. Defend the thesis that interests are characteristics of personality and consequently that interest inventories are measures of personality. Cite specific theories, research findings, and specific instruments to support your position.
3. Write the letter corresponding to the interest area in the right column to the personality characteristic in the left two columns. You may put more than one letter from the right column opposite the adjective in the columns at the left.

1. active	16. methodical	a. artistic
2. aggressive	17. organized	b. clerical
3. attractive	18. original	c. computational
4. charming	19. outgoing	d. literary
5. conservative	20. pleasant	e. mechanical
6. conscientious	21. practical	f. musical
7. conventional	22. precise	g. outdoor
8. cooperative	23. robust	h. persuasive
9. courageous	24. serious	i. scientific
10. dependable	25. sociable	j. social service
11. friendly	26. strong	
12. hard-headed	27. sympathetic	
13. intelligent	28. tactful	
14. inventive	29. thoughtful	
15. logical	30. thrifty	

Compare your responses with those of your classmates and friends. Was there any consistency in the way that different people matched the items in the left column with those in the right column? What do the results tell you about the relationships of personality to vocational interests? Are some personality characteristics associated with interests in a wide variety of occupations, whereas others are associated with a more narrow range of occupations?

4. In J. L. Holland's theory of interests and personality, certain interest clusters are characteristic of people with certain personality traits and point to certain vocations or careers. Complete the first two parts of six statements listed below and determine how closely your responses predict the occupations in which you believe you are truly interested.

Part I: Interests

Which one of the following descriptions fits you best: A, B, C, D, E, or F?

A. You like and are good at manipulating tools, machines, and other objects, and working outdoors with plants and animals.

B. You like and are good at observing, learning, investigating, analyzing, evaluating, and solving problems.

C. You like and do well in unstructured situations in which your creativity or imagination can be expressed.

D. You like and are good at working with people—developing, enlightening, informing, training, curing, and helping or supporting them in various ways.

E. You like and are good at influencing and persuading other people, and you would like to lead or manage an organization.

F. You like and are good at arithmetic and clerical activities such as filing, record keeping, and data processing.

Part II. Personality Characteristics

Which one of the following descriptions fits you best: A, B, C, D, E, or F?

A. You are a realistic, practical, conforming, and natural person.

B. You are a rational, cautious, curious, independent, and introversive person.

C. You are an imaginative, introspective, complicated, emotional, expressive, impulsive, nonconforming, and disorderly person.

D. You are a cooperative, friendly, helpful, persuasive, tactful, and understanding person.

E. You are an aggressive, ambitious, energetic, domineering, pleasure-seeking, self-confident, sociable, and talkative person.

F. You are a conscientious, efficient, inflexible, obedient, orderly, persistent, and self–controlled person.

Part III. Suggested Vocations

The following statements corresponding to the letter(s) you selected in Parts I and II are jobs that are most likely to appeal to you.

A.   Jobs such as automobile mechanic, farmer, or electrician.

B.   Jobs in fields such as chemistry, physics, biology, geology, and other sciences.

C.   Jobs such as actor, musician, or writer.

D.   Jobs in clinical or counseling psychology, speech therapy, teaching, and related fields.

E.   Jobs such as manager, business executive, or salesperson.

F.   Jobs such as banker, bookkeeper, and tax expert.

Did your answers in Parts I and II point to the same vocations in Part III? Are these suggested vocations consistent with the ones you feel you are truly interested in and have the abilities and personality to be successful in?

5. Administer the following Educational Values Inventory (EVI) to several students of various backgrounds and compute their scores. Construct and compare the profiles of scores of the students on the six values scales. Responses to each item on the EVI are scored on a scale of 1 to 5 from left (U or N) to right (Ed), respectively. The sum of the scores on items 2, 7, 18, and 21 is the Aesthetic Value score. The sum of the scores on items 1, 8, 13, and 24 is the Leadership Value score. The sum of the scores on items 4, 9, 15, and 23 is the Philosophical Value Score. The sum of the scores on items 5, 12, 16, and 19 is the Social Value score. The sum of the scores on items 6, 11, 17, and 22 is the Scientific Value score. The sum of scores on items 3, 10, 14, and 20 is the Vocational Value score.

Educational Values Inventory

Part I. Each of the items in this section refers to a possible goal or emphasis of higher education. Check the appropriate letter after each of the following statements to indicate how important you believe the corresponding goal should be. Use this key: U = unimportant, S = somewhat important, I = important, V = very important, E = extremely important.

1. Ability to lead or direct other people.	U	S	I	V	E
2. Appreciation of the beautiful and harmonious things in life.	U	S	I	V	E
3. Preparation for a vocation or profession of one's choice.	U	S	I	V	E
4. Gaining insight into the meaning and purpose of life.	U	S	I	V	E
5. Understanding social problems and their possible solutions.	U	S	I	V	E
6. Understanding scientific theories and the laws of nature.	U	S	I	V	E
7. Acquiring the ability to express oneself artistically.	U	S	I	V	E
8. Understanding how to direct others in the accomplishment of some goal.	U	S	I	V	E
9. Development of a personal philosophy of life.	U	S	I	V	E

10. Learning how to succeed in a chosen occupation or field.   U S I V E
11. Learning about scientific problems and their solutions.   U S I V E
12. Understanding people of different social classes and cultures.   U S I V E

Part II. Check the appropriate letter after each of the following items to indicate your estimate of how valuable the particular kinds of college courses are to students in general. Use this key: N = not at all valuable, S = somewhat valuable, V = valuable, Q = quite valuable, E = extremely valuable.

13. Courses concerned with how to direct and organize people.   N S V Q E
14. Courses in one's chosen vocation or professional field.   N S V Q E
15. Courses dealing with philosophical and/or religious ideas.   N S V Q E
16. Courses concerned with understanding and helping people.   N S V Q E
17. Courses in science and mathematics.   N S V Q E
18. Courses in music, art, and literature.   N S V Q E

Part III. Check the appropriate letter after each of the following items to indicate how much attention you feel should be given to each kind of college course in the education of most college students. Use this key: N = no attention at all, L = little attention, M = a moderate degree of attention, A = above average attention, E = an extensive amount of attention.

19. Courses concerned with how to understand and be of help to other people.   N L M A E
20. Courses in the vocational or professional field of your choice.   N L M A E
21. Courses in art, literature, and music.   N L M A E
22. Courses in scientific and mathematical fields.   N L M A E
23. Courses concerned with philosophy and religion.   N L M A E
24. Courses concerned with organizing and directing people.   N L M A E

6. How is sex-role orientation related to sexual orientation? Would you expect men who score high on the "Femininity" scale of a personality or interest inventory to be gay and women who score high on a "Masculinity" scale to be lesbians? Why or why not?

7. During the past decade, the terms "family values" and "Christian values" have been used extensively by politicians, social reformers, and by the media in general. What are *family values*, and how are they similar to and different from *Christian values*? Try your hand at constructing a scale consisting of a set of items to measure family values. What kinds of people would you expect to score high and what kinds of people would you expect to score low on your scale?

■ Suggested Readings

Ashmore, R.D. (1990). Sex, gender, and the individual. In L.A. Pervin (Ed.), *Handbook of personality theory and research* (pp. 486–526). New York: Guilford Press.

Betz, N.E. (1994). Self-concept theory in career development and counseling. *Career Development Quarterly, 43*(1), 32–42.

Donnay, D.A.C. (1997). E.K. Strong's legacy and beyond: 70 years of the Strong Interest Inventory. *Career Development Quarterly, 46*(1), 2–22.

Hansen, J.C. (1990). Interest inventories. In G. Goldstein & M. Hersen (Eds.), *Handbook of psychological assessment* (2nd ed., pp. 173–196). New York: Pergamon Press.

Procter, M. (1993). Measuring attitudes. In N. Gilbert (Ed.), *Researching social life* (pp. 116–134). London: Sage.

Rokeach, M. (1979). *Understanding human values: Individual and societal.* New York: Free Press/Macmillan.

Tavris, C. (1992). *The mismeasure of woman.* New York: Simon & Schuster.

Watkins, C.E., Campbell, V.L., & Nieberding, R. (1994). The practice of vocational assessment by counseling psychologists. *The Counseling Psychologist, 22*, 115–128.

Weinrach, S.G., & Srebalus, D.J. (1990). Holland's theory of careers. In D. Brown & L. Brooks (Eds.), *Career choice and development: Applying contemporary theories to practice* (2nd ed., pp. 37–67). San Francisco: Jossey-Bass.

■ PART IV
PROJECTIVE TECHNIQUES

CHAPTER 10

Associations, Completions, and Drawings

Since time immemorial people have looked at clouds and imagined seeing all sorts of objects and persons in these changing forms. Shakespeare did, as well as Wilhelm Stern, whose Cloud Picture Test was one of the first projective techniques. Credit for introducing the projective technique in personality assessment actually belongs to Sir Francis Galton (1879), whose word association procedure was subsequently adapted by Emil Kraepelin and C. G. Jung as a psychodiagnostic and therapeutic tool. Other pioneers in projective techniques were H. Ebbinghaus (sentence completion test) and A. Binet (verbal responses to pictures), both of whom initially used these methods as measures of intelligence.

The term *projective technique* appeared initially in an article by Horowitz and Murphy (1938), but they attributed it to Lawrence K. Frank. Frank (1948) defined a projective technique as "a method of studying the personality by confronting the subject with a situation to which he will respond according to what the situation means to him and how he feels when so responding" (p. 46). The essential feature of a projective technique was described as evoking from a person "... what is in various ways expressed in his private world and personality processes" (Frank, 1948, p. 42). Frank maintained that projective techniques could reveal the conscious and unconscious conflicts, desires, fears, and needs of a person, as well as his or her overall way of perceiving and responding to the world.

■ Concepts and Examples

Projective techniques are composed of relatively unstructured stimuli that people are asked to describe, tell a story about, complete, or respond to in some other way. In contrast to the more structured personality inventories and rating scales, projective techniques are usually less obvious in their intent. There are no right or wrong answers on projective tests, so they are presumably less subject to faking and response sets. Because projectives are relatively unstructured in content and usually open-ended in terms of the responses required, it is assumed that whatever structure is imposed on the stimulus material represents a projection of the respondent's own perceptions of the world. It is also maintained that the more unstructured the task, the more likely are the responses to reveal important features of personality.

The use of projective techniques such as word associations, early memories, inkblots, and picture stories goes back to the late nineteenth and early twentieth centuries. However, the period from the late 1930s through the 1950s may be characterized as the zenith of these assessment methods. In particular, the decade following World War II, which witnessed the rapid growth of clinical psychology, was a time of extensive development, administration, and investigation of projective techniques. It was also during this period that personality inventories such as the MMPI became increasingly influential, and projectives acted to some extent as a counterweight to the reportedly more superficial personality analyses and psychodiagnoses provided by inventories and ratings scales.

The Influence of Psychoanalysis

From the time of their first clinical application during the early 1900s, projective devices have been associated with psychoanalytic theory and accompanying efforts to reveal and analyze deeper, unconscious aspects of personality. The psychoanalytic concept of *projection* holds that individuals, both defensively and nondefensively, project their own motives, desires, problems, and conflicts onto external situations or stimuli. In theory, the same unconscious forces that are revealed in distorted, symbolic form in dreams, hypnotic or drug-induced states, slips of the tongue and pen, free verbal associations, and other external manifestations can also elude the mental censor and be expressed in responses to relatively amorphous, unstructured test situations. Unconscious forces lead the person to structure ambiguous material in ways that express the operation of these forces. Consequently, an understanding of the dynamics of individual personality should be obtainable by analyzing how the person perceives, organizes, relates to, or otherwise responds to projective test materials. These responses are thought to provide *signs* of underlying personality structure and functioning, revealing the nature of unconscious forces and conflicts.

In addition to being influenced by psychoanalysis and other psychodynamic theories of personality, psychologists who interpret projective test protocols usually try to form an overall impression of the respondent's personality by searching for consistencies and outstanding features in the pattern of responses. As a consequence, administering, scoring, and interpreting a typical projective test instrument usually demands greater sensitivity and more clinical experience than that required for a self-report inventory. But even psychologists who are well-trained in the use of projectives frequently disagree in their interpretations of responses. Furthermore, responses to projectives vary with the method of administration, the situation or context, the personality of the examiner, and the mood or attitude of the respondent. If such responses are highly unstable, the ability of projectives to reflect deeper, more persisting features of personality structure and dynamics should be questioned.

Detractors and Supporters

Opponents of projective techniques view these instruments as little more than an opportunity for the imagination and intuition of the interpreter to have free rein and even run riot (e. g., Eysenck, 1960). Even proponents of the techniques admit that projectives: (1) are highly fakable in either a good or bad direction (Albert, Fox, & Kahn, 1980; Exner, 1978); (2) are very susceptible to the conditions under which they are administered (phrasing of directions and questions, personality of examiner, degree of encouragement given to the respondent, etc.) (Klopfer & Taulbee, 1976); (3) are scored and interpreted differently by examiners with different theoretical orientations and personality dynamics (Hamilton & Robertson, 1966); (4) have inadequate, unrepresentative norms or no norms at all (Anastasi & Urbina, 1997); (5) are poorly validated and cross-validated (Kinslinger, 1966). The tendency for users of projective techniques to take note of findings that are consistent with their own expectations and beliefs and remember them but to overlook or forget contrary findings often results in *illusory correlations* between projective signs and psychopathological symptoms (Chapman & Chapman, 1967, 1969; Golding & Rorer, 1972) Despite repeated criticisms and some decline in their popularity during recent years, however, projective techniques continue to be used not only by clinical and developmental psychologists and psychiatrists but by anthropologists, market researchers, and other investigators of human behavior.

Consistent with the decline of research on projective techniques during the past several years are the negative attitudes toward projectives expressed by many clinical psychology faculty. Be that as it may, projective techniques continue to be popular (Watkins et al., 1995), a phenomenon that is attributable in part to refinements in scoring and interpretation systems such as that of Exner (1993). A survey conducted during the early 1990s of directors of doctoral programs in clinical psychology found that at least some coursework in projective techniques was required in a large majority of clinical psychology programs (Piotrowski & Zalewski, 1993).

Advocates of projective techniques claim that these procedures get at deeper layers of personality of which even the respondent may be unaware. But Frank's (1948) unfortunate analogy that projective techniques provide a kind of X-ray of the mind should not be interpreted as meaning that they are an open sesame to the unconscious. The lack of structure in projectives is also a double-edged sword in that it makes for scoring difficulties. Subjectivity of scoring results in most projective techniques failing to meet conventional standards of reliability and validity. The validity coefficients, as determined against various criteria, are generally low, reflecting both situational factors and subjectivity of scoring and interpretation (Anastasi & Urbina, 1997).

Types of Projective Techniques

Projective techniques may be grouped into five categories, according to the type of response required: *association* (to words or inkblots), *construction* (of stories, sequences, etc.), *completions* (of sentences or stories), *arrangement* or *selection* (of pictures or verbal options), and *expression* (through drawings, play, etc.) (Lindzey, 1959). Examples of association techniques are word associations, early memories, and the Rorschach Inkblot Test. Construction techniques include such instruments as the Thematic Apperception Test, the Blacky Pictures, the House-Tree-Person Technique, and the Make-a-Picture-Story Test. Illustrative of completion techniques are various sentence completion tests and the Rosenzweig Picture Frustration Study. Arrangement or selection techniques include the Szondi Test, the Tomkins-Horn Picture Arrangement Test, and the Kahn Test of Symbol Arrangement. The Draw-a-Person Test, handwriting analysis, finger painting, play activities, and psychodrama—the last three of which are also psychotherapeutic methods—are examples of expression techniques. The most popular projectives in use in clinical situations, as indicated by the reported frequency with which they are administered by clinical psychologists (Watkins et al., 1995), are:
1. Sentence Completion Methods
2. Thematic Apperception Test
3. Rorschach
4. Bender-Gestalt
5. Projective Drawings
6. Children's Apperception Test

A representative list of projective instruments of various types that are commercially available is given in Table 10–1.

Illustrative Memory, Sentence Completion, and Drawing Tests.   **TABLE 10–1**

Memory Techniques
- *Early Memories Procedure* (A. R. Bruhn; from Psychological Corporation; for ages 10 and over with at least a fourth-grade reading level; method of exploring personality organization, especially life currents, based on the respondent's memory of the past; no scores; review MMYB 13:109)
- *Wilson-Barber Inventory of Childhood Memories and Imaginings: Children's Form* (S. A. Myers; for ages 8–18; measure of imaginative and fantasy ability and how they affect interests, experiences, and functioning; see *Journal of Mental Imagery*, 7(1), 83–94, 1983)

Sentence-Completion Tests
- *Activity Completion Technique* (J. M. Sacks; Psychological Assessment Resources; high school and over; 60 sentence stems covering the areas of Family, Interpersonal, Affect, and Self-Concept; review MMYB 10:8).
- *Bloom Sentence Completion Attitude Survey* (W. Bloom; Stoelting; for students aged 6–21 and adults; designed to reveal subject's attitudes (positive, neutral, or negative) toward important factors in everyday living; review MMYB 9:153).
- *Columbus Sentence Completion for Children* (by J. A. Shaffer & A. S. Tamkin; Educational Testing Service; for ages 4–17; covers the following topics: self concept, self concept (problems), picture of self, wishes and plays, family, social, and school)
- *Curtis Completion Form* (J. W. Curtis; Western Psychological Services; for grades 11–15 and adults; sentence completion test designed to evaluate emotional maturity and adjusted; reviews MMYB 6:208 & TC V:83)
- *EPS Sentence Completion Technique* (D. C. Strohmer & H. T. Prout; Psychological Assessment Resources; for mildly mentally handicapped ages 14 and over; 4 levels of scores; semi-projective instrument designed specifically for use with individuals in the mildly retarded and borderline intelligence ranges; review MMYB 13:121)
- *The Forer Structured Sentence Completion Test* (B. R. Forer; Western Psychological Services; for ages 16–18 and adults; designed to measure personality variables and attitudes that may be of some value in treatment planning; review MMYB 5:134 and TC IV:300)
- *Geriatric Sentence Completion Form* (P. LeBray; Psychological Assessment Resources; adults aged 60 and over; 30 items; scored for 4 content domains—physical, psychological, social, and temporal orientation; review MMYB 9:436)
- *Miner Sentence Completion Scale* (J. B. Miner; Organizational Measurement Systems; for workers and prospective workers in management, professional, and entrepreneurial or task-oriented occupations; review MMYB 11:241)
- *Politte Sentence Completion Test* (A. J. Politte; Psychologists & Educators, Inc.; for grades 1–8, 7–12, and adults; designed to elicit information from individuals concerning their immediate environment, especially the people in the environment; review TC V:323)

Table 10–1 continued

■ *Rotter Incomplete Sentences Blank, Second Edition* (J.B. Rotter, M.I. Lah, & J.E. Rafferty; from Psychological Corporation; for highschool and college students, adults; used primarily as a screening instrument of overall adjustment; reviewed in MMYB 12:335).

■ *Sentence Completion Series* (L.H. Brown & M.A. Unger; Psychological Assessment Resources; for adolescents and adults; consists of 8 self-report forms, each with 50 content-valid sentence stems pertaining to a specific area of concern: adult, adolescent, family, marriage, parenting, work, illness, aging.

■ *Sentence Completion Test* (F.S. Irvin; Psychologists and Educators; high school and college students; designed to assess feelings, urges, beliefs, attitudes, and desires; 35 item scores in six areas)

■ *Sentence Completion Tests* (A. Roe; Diagnostic Specialists; ten sentence completion tests, eight of which (General Incomplete Sentence Test, Short Incomplete Sentences, Full Incomplete Sentences Test, Full I Am Test, Marriage Incomplete Sentences Test, Relationship Incomplete Sentences Test, Full Length Alcohol Sentence Completion, and Drug Inquiry Sentence Completion) are appropriate for adults)

■ *Washington University Sentence Completion Test for Measuring Ego Development—Revised* (J. Loevinger; see Loevinger, Wessler, & Redmore, 1970; designed to assess ego development of girls and women; seven alternate forms are available including some for men and boys, but scoring procedures have only been developed for girls and women)

Drawing Tests

■ *Draw-a-Story: Screening for Depression and Age or Gender Difference* (R.A. Silver; Ablin Press; Sarasota, FL; used as a semi-projective interview technique and as a measure for assessing depression; review MMYB 13:103)

■ *Draw A Person: Screening Procedure for Emotional Disturbance* (J.A. Naglieri, T.J. McNeish, & A.N. Bardos; pro.ed; screening measure for identifying children and adolescents having emotional or behavioral disorders; review MMYB 12:124)

■ *Draw-A-Person Questionnaire* (by S.A. Karp; International Diagnostic Services, Worthington, OH; children and adults; uses projective assessment to measure mastery, feels accepted, basic trust, denial, extreme thinking, antisocial behavior, mood, alienation, demeaning, body image, and helplessness; 52 items using a Likert scale to describe the male and female figures drawn by the test taker)

■ *H-T-P House-Tree-Person Projective Technique* (J.N. Buck & W.L. Warren; Western Psychological Services; for ages 3 and over; total score only; designed to provide diagnostically and prognostically significant data concerning a person's total personality; review of earlier edition in MMYB 6:215, TC II:436 and TC IX:358)

■ *The Kinetic Drawing System for Family and School*; by H.M. Knoff & H.T. Prout; from Western Psychological Services; ages 5–17 and adults; a combination of the Kinetic Family Drawing and Kinetic School Drawing into a single procedure for evaluating the interactions of children and adolescents with other people in the family and school; review of handbook in MMYB 10:66.

■ Association Techniques

Inkblots, pictures, words, and other stimuli designed to elicit a variety of associations were employed by Binet, Dearborn, Sharp, Wundt, and other psychologists during the late nineteenth century to study imagination, memory, and other cognitive abilities. However, the systematic analysis of personality and the diagnosis of mental disorders by the use of such stimulus material was not undertaken until sometime later. Following the emphasis of nineteenth-century psychology on the structure and functioning of the mind, American and British psychologists of the time were more interested in individual differences in intelligence than personality. Furthermore, greater attention was devoted to pure, theoretical science than to applying scientific findings and techniques in clinical or other practical situations.

Early Memories

Ruth Munroe (1955) described Alfred Adler's use of *early recollections* as the first truly projective test to be used in a clinical context.* In keeping with the psychoanalytic emphasis on the importance of early experiences in the formation of personality, the technique involves instructing the respondent to "Tell me your earliest memory," with the further condition that the memory should be a specific, concrete, single one. The requirement that the memory be specific rather than general is what differentiated this early recollection procedure from a report. In any case, three to six distinct memories are usually obtained so that common themes can be determined (Armstrong, 1994).

The following quotations from Corsini and Marsella (1983) are examples of earliest memories:

> I remember being on a train seated between my parents and I was bored and restless. I was looking through the window and all I saw was telephone poles and I wanted to get away but I was hemmed in and so I began to inch my way down without my parents knowing and I finally got to the floor and began to look around and I noticed the legs

---

* In recent years, a number of court cases have involved the recovery by adults of memories that have supposedly been "hidden" for many years because they involved incest and/or other abusive acts when the victim was a child. There have also been countersuits in which the therapist, who presumably encouraged the revival of those memories, was sued in turn by the defendant ("Dubious Memories," 1994). To what extent these "recovered memories" represent events that actually happened or whether they are the results of fantasy or therapists' persuasiveness and suggestions is unclear in many cases. Young children often confuse fantasy with reality, and consequently their communications and stories cannot always be taken at face value. Suggestions made by a prestigious or powerful person, in addition to the imperfections of recollections, may lead people, both children and adults, to believe that something actually happened when it did not.

of people and I remember the smell of the floor and the dust there. And I began to move forward being careful not to let anyone know I was there. And I came upon an oil can; it was brass and shiny. And I picked it up and began to squirt oil on the shoes of a man. Suddenly the man cried out and he reached down and pulled me out. And the conductor came and picked me up while I was screaming and I was brought to my father who began to spank me.

I was about ten years of age and I wanted to build a wooden automobile using tires from any old baby carriage. And I announced this to everyone. But most kids who made one of these used two strings to steer the wagon, but I wanted a steering wheel. My father wanted to help me but I said I would do it alone. However, when I came to making the steering wheel, I couldn't figure out how to do it. So, I secretly got rid of the car, how much I had done and I reported to everyone that someone had stolen my car, and that was the end of it. However, I felt that my father had known what I had done. (pp. 605–607)

Interpreting an earliest memory is an impressionistic, subjective process, entailing good common sense and some conceptual or theoretical guidelines. Each early recollection given by the respondent is analyzed for its cognitive and behavioral patterns, and an effort is made to determine the broad themes underlying the early recollections and the frame of reference reflected in them. The characteristic outlook and attitude revealed by the behavior rather than the behavior itself is what is important. Manaster and Perryman (1974) devised a scoring manual for categorizing the content of early recollections into seven categories: characteristics, themes, concern with detail, setting, activity level, source of control, and emotion. Using their scheme, the two memories listed above were interpreted as follows (Corsini & Marsella, 1983):

You are a wanderer, and you move not only from place to place but also from person to person, a kind of Don Juan. You are easily bored and always restless, and on the go, and you want excitement and will do things in a mischievous manner to get excitement. However, you know you won't succeed in getting away with your mischief and you expect to be caught and to be punished.

He is overambitious, trying to do better and bigger things that others, but he goes over his head and can't complete what he starts out doing; eventually he gives up but will not admit that he tried to do more than he could. (pp. 605–607)

A Comprehensive Early Memories Scoring System, based on psychoanalytic theory, was developed by Last and Bruhn (1991). A commercial adaptation of this research, the Early Memories Procedure (EMP), was prepared by A. R. Bruhn (1992, 1995) and published by The Psychological Corporation. On the EMP, respondents, who may be ten years or older, are asked to reveal and relate both their general and specific memories in writing according to the directions in a 32-page booklet. On part I, the respondent is directed to relate his or her earliest memory and the next four memories that come to mind. The respondent then rates the five memories on a scale of 1 to 7 according to a set of criteria. In Part II the respondent is asked to produce 15 directed memories of various kinds. The responses may be tape-recorded if the respondent is unable to write. The administrator interprets the produced memories by following a Cognitive-Perceptual model described in the manual. Among the systems that have been developed for scoring the EMP are those for predicting proneness to delinquency and violence (Tobey & Bruhn, 1992). Because of questions concerning the objectivity of the scoring, a lack of reliability and validity data, and the fact that it has not been standardized on representative samples, reviewers (e. g., Hanes, 1998b; Phelps, 1998) view it as an exploratory procedure and not recommended for general use.

The EMP and related procedures are typically interesting and appealing tasks and thereby particularly useful in getting started and establishing rapport during initial or intake interviews.

Reports of early recollections or memories can assist clinicians in formulating a general picture of the respondent's needs, interests, major attitudes and beliefs, self-perceptions, and views of other people and the world. In addition to revealing something about the experiences, problems, and personality of the individual, the early memories procedure can provide information on the respondent's abilities, interests, social relationships, and world view.

Research on early memories, which was still being pursued during the late 1990s, has provided some support for Adler's view that they reflect the respondent's frame of reference (Mosak, 1969). Other psychologists have successfully identified homosexuality and predicted occupational choice (Friedberg, 1975; Manaster & Perryman, 1974) from early recollections. Findings from a study conducted in Israel of personality predictions made from earliest memories provided empirical support for the hypothesis that earliest memories reflect a wide range of basic needs, affective states, coping and defense mechanisms, ego functioning, and object relations (Rosenheim & Mane, 1984). Although research has failed to demonstrate that psychodiagnoses can be made solely on the basis of early memories (Armstrong, 1994), Anastasi and Urbina (1997) concluded that the technique has potential as a personality assessment tool, especially in psychotherapeutic contexts (Ritzler, 1993). The early recollections technique has also been shown to be helpful to school counselors in the identification of themes and issues in a student's life and assisting in treatment-planning and counseling (Clark, 1994).

Word Associations

The method of *word associations* was introduced by Francis Galton (1879), and later used in association experiments in Wilhelm Wundt's psychological laboratory. Precise methods for recording the responses and the number of seconds elapsing between the time the stimulus word was presented and the response was made were developed by Trautscholdt (1883) and Cattell (1887). A few years later the technique was applied by Emil Kraepelin (1892) and Carl Jung (1910) in clinical situations.

It was Jung who first employed word associations to detect mental complexes and neurotic conflicts. His procedure was to read to a patient a list of 100 words representing common emotional problems (anger, fear, death, etc.). Signs of emotional disturbance revealed in the patient's associations to the words included abnormal response content, long response times, and emotional reactions. Of some interest is the fact that the pioneering work of Carl Jung on word association tests is related to the development of the polygraph ("lie detector" test).

In administering a word association test today, the examiner reads a list of words aloud, one at a time, to a person who has been instructed to respond to each word with the first word that comes to mind. The examiner begins by making a statement such as: "I am going to read a list of words, one at a time. After I read a word, please respond with the first word that comes into your mind." Individualized clinical application of the word association technique involves interspersing certain emotionally loaded words, or words of special significant to the respondent, among a list of neutral words. Long response times or unusual associations may be symptomatic of emotional disturbance. The form or part of speech represented by the response may also be significant. For example, a general principle guiding the psychoanalytic interpretation of language is that nouns are more likely than verbs to be disguised expressions of needs and conflicts. This is so because, according to Freudian theory, it is easier to alter the object of a desire (a noun) than its direction (a verb).

Many clinical psychologists prefer to construct their own word lists, but standardized lists are available. An illustration is the Kent-Rosanoff Free Association Test, a standard list of 100 nouns, adjectives, and verbs first published in 1910 and one of the oldest psychological tests still in use (Isaacs & Chen, 1990). Unlike Jung's word list, the words on the Kent-Rosanoff list are neutral rather than emotionally loaded. Also unlike Jung, Kent-Rosanoff determined norms by obtaining the associations of 1,000 normal people to the list of words. Responses were classified as common or individual reactions. Individual reactions included categories such as juvenile responses, neologisms, repetitions, parts of speech, associations to a previous stimulus or response, and word complements. Twenty-five types of associative disturbances and six reproduction disturbances are included in the system. Appelbaum's (1960) addition to the Kent-Rosanoff scoring system includes repetitions, blockings, multi-words, self-references, perseverations, and repetitions of stimulus words; this system is used primarily with brain-damaged individuals.

Another standard word list was provided by Rapaport, Gill and Schafer (1946) (see Table 10–2) and first used at the Menninger Clinic. Twenty of the 60 nouns

Revised Word List from Rapaport, Gill and Schafer.		**TABLE 10-2**
1. rat	21. suicide	41. cut
2. lamp	22. mountain	42. movies
3. love	23. smoke	43. cockroach
4. book	24. house	44. bite
5. father	25. vagina	45. dog
6. paper	26. tobacco	46. dance
7. breast	27. mouth	47. gun
8. curtain	28. horse	48. water
9. trunk	29. masturbation	49. husband
10. drink	30. wife	50. mud
11. party	31. table	51. woman
12. spring	32. fight	52. fire
13. bowel movement	33. beef	53. such
14. rug	34. stomach	54. money
15. boy friend	35. farm	55. mother
16. chair	36. man	56. hospital
17. screen	37. taxes	57. girl friend
18. penis	38. nipple	58. taxi
19. radiator	39. doctor	59. intercourse
20. frame	40. dirt	60. hunger

From Rapaport, Gill, and Schafer, *Diagnostic Psychological Testing, Vol. 2.* Chicago: Year Book Publishers, 1946, p. 84. Reproduced with permission of the publisher.

in the list are traumatic (they have aggressive, excretory, or sexual connotations), and 40 are nontraumatic. A complex system of scoring responses focuses on the stimulus words that produce disturbances in the associative process and behavior of the respondent. Rapaport, Gill and Schafer (1968) proposed a three-stage process in eliciting responses to words and provided numerous diagnostic hypotheses concerning word associations. Among these hypotheses are that: (1) Inability to provide an association (blocking) is typical of deteriorated schizophrenics and certain preschizophrenic persons; (2) Long delays before providing an association may be indicative of depression; (3) Bizarre or distant associations (e. g., *breast*—"frankness") suggest that the word is a topic of conflict for the respondent. Unfortunately, research support for these hypotheses has not been impressive.

Despite their shortcomings, word associations are an economical and sometimes enlightening psychodiagnostic procedure. Infrequent or unusual responses to standard or specially prepared word lists are considered indicative of emotional disturbance, though this conclusion has not been found to be consistently valid.

Associations to specific words may be indicative not only of personality and psychopathology, but also vary with linguistic ability, speech disorders, and other individual differences (Merten, 1995). They may also vary with the situation and with temporary emotional states or moods. Furthermore, limiting responses to one word on word association tests usually provides insufficient information for a useful content analysis. The response time pressure experienced by respondents also tends to result in mechanical, stimulus-bound responses. For these reasons, along with the decline of the psychoanalytic model that inspired their usage in clinical contexts, word associations are not as popular as they once were. In the main, they have been replaced by techniques such as sentence completions and apperception tests that elicit richer, more detailed associations.

Various modifications in the technique of word associations have been introduced over the years. Siipola, Walker, and Kolb (1955) required the respondent to delay responding until he or she found a response that was personally satisfying. According to the findings of Dunn, Bliss, and Siipola (1958), associations obtained under this delayed condition are related to the degree of impulsivity and the values of the respondent.

Sutherland and Gill (1970) proposed an approach that combines word associations with sentence completions A list of 100 stimulus words is prepared, and the respondent is directed to respond to each word with a complete sentence. A response to the stimulus word "garden," for example, might be "I hate working in a garden" or "Gardening is a good hobby." Sutherland and Gill claimed that requiring complete sentences in responding makes possible a more thorough quantitative analysis of ego functioning in a variety of situations. They advocated scoring responses on six dimensions: (1) form of expression, (2) syntactical use of the stimulus word, (3) self and other references, (4) mode of communication (generations and personal statements), (5) affective tone, and (6) affective reference in four key areas. However, this combined technique has rarely been used for purposes of clinical diagnosis.

■ Completion Techniques

Completion techniques in which the respondent is told to finish an incomplete sentence, a story, a picture, or in other ways construct a whole from a part are more structured than many other projective instruments. Because of their greater structure, it is maintained that completion techniques produce more superficial, less psychodynamic information concerning the respondent's personality and conflicts. Despite the fact that they presumably tap more conscious or superficial aspects of personality than inkblots, the three completion techniques discussed in this section—sentence completions, story completions, and the Rosenzweig Picture Frustration Study—still provide clues to the respondent's attitudes, conflicts, and problems. Responses to completion techniques that have been standardized on representative samples can be interpreted by comparing them with normative data obtained from various normal and pathological groups of people.

Sentence Completions

Asking a person to complete specially written incomplete sentences is a flexible, easily administered, and nonthreatening semiprojective technique that can identify a broad range of psychological concerns in a relatively short period of time. *Sentence completion* is appropriately labeled "semi-projective" because sentence stems are more structured, more apparent in their intention, and thus more fakable than the Rorschach Inkblot Test, the Thematic Apperception Test, and many other proactive instruments. As with other projectives, however, it is assumed that the completed sentences reflect the respondent's underlying needs, fears, and conflicts.

Because the purpose of sentence completion tests is not disguised well and people can more easily censor their responses, Phares (1994) concluded that the technique often yields little information that is not obtained from an intensive interview. However, many psychologists have been impressed with the utility of the technique, which Murstein (1965) considered "probably the most valid of all projective techniques" (p. 777). Concurring with this evaluation, Goldberg (1965) deemed sentence completions to be one of the most valid of all projectives for diagnostic and research purposes.

Historical Background. Sentence completions were used originally by Ebbinghaus (1897) as an intelligence test, and more subsequently by Copple (1956) as a creative-response measure of intelligence. Two of the first psychologists to use the technique in personality assessment were Payne (1928) and Tendler (1930). Sentence completions were employed in a variety of military settings during World War II, for example, in the psychological evaluation and selection of pilots, army officers, and OSS (Office of Strategic Service) candidates. They have also been used for personnel selection in business and industry. During the decade immediately following World War II standardized sentence completion instruments were developed by Rotter (1946), Rohde (1947), Sacks and Levy (1950), Forer (1950), and Holsopple and Miale (1954). More recent entries include the Bloom Sentence Completion Attitude Survey, the Sentence Completion Series, and the Rotter Incomplete Sentences Blank, Second Edition.

Responses to sentence fragments are usually written, but they may be expressed orally. The form may be administered either individually, in which case hesitations, emotional reactions, and other overt behaviors can be observed, or simultaneously to a group of people. The number of sentence fragments on a form ranges from about 20 to 100, sufficient space being provided after each fragment for the individual to write his or her response.

Content and Scoring. A variety of sentence fragments relating to attitudes, emotions, and conflicts can be constructed, for example:

My greatest fear is _____

I only wish my mother had _____

The thing that bothers me most is _____

Other examples of incomplete sentences are given in Form 10–1, which was designed by the author for use with school-age children. Typically, respondents are instructed to finish each item by making a complete statement expressing their true feelings. Stems are usually written in the first person, and there is no time limit. It has been maintained, however, that responses are less likely to be censored when the stems are written in the third person and the test is speeded up (Hanfmann & Getzels, 1953).

Most clinicians evaluate and interpret the responses to incomplete sentences impressionistically and in the light of other information about the respondent. The accuracy of impressionistic evaluations and predictions made from sentence completions varies, of course, with the skill of the evaluator in making such subjective judgments. In addition to possessing high interpersonal sensitivity and clinical judgment, an effective evaluator understands the limitations of the sentence completion technique and takes into account information obtained from behavioral observations, interviews, and other tests, as well as the situation in which the sentences are completed.

FORM 10–1 A Sentence Completion Test for Children.

Directions: Complete these sentences to show your real feelings.

1. I like ...
2. The best time ...
3. My mother ...
4. I feel ...
5. I can't ...
6. Other children ...
7. I need ...
8. My father ...
9. This school ...
10. I want ...
11. I don't like ...
12. I am very ...
13. My teacher ...
14. I worry about ...
15. I am sorry that ...

In interpreting responses, affective tone (negative or positive), the respondent's role (active or passive), the form of the response (specific or qualified, imperative or declarative), temporal orientation (past, present, future), degree of commitment (wholehearted vs. hedging), degree of definiteness from one response to another (definite vs. vague), and variation in verbalization from one response to another should be kept in mind (Rabin & Zlotogorski, 1981). Objective scoring systems that can be followed by nonprofessionals have been provided for several published instruments in this category. For example, the Rohde Sentence Completions, one of the oldest blanks, is scored on 38 variables, among which are inner integrates, emotional stage, and general traits. In addition to content scoring, noncontent properties of responses may be evaluated. Among the noncontent properties scored in such a formal analysis are length of completion, use of personal pronouns, response time, verb/adjective ratio, range of words used, grammatical errors, and first word used (Benton, Windle, & Erdice, 1957).

Sentence completions do not easily lend themselves to computer scoring, but computer programs for scoring limited or restricted responses are available. An example is the program for scoring the One-Word Sentence Completion Test (Veldman, Menaker, & Peck, 1969). Interscorer and test-retest reliabilities of certain sentence completion tests are in the .80s and .90s, high enough for making diagnostic differentiations among individuals. However, relatively few sentence completion tests meet accepted standards for test construction and standardization.

The majority of sentence completion tests are unpublished and unstandardized instruments designed for a specific purpose in a given situation. For example, a set of sentence fragments pertaining to a patient's problems can be constructed to break through the resistance or opposition of the patient to further exploration of the causes of his or her psychopathological behavior and thoughts.

Other sentence completion tests have been constructed to detect malingering during examinations for disability (Timmons, Lanyon, Almer, & Curran, 1993), to predict managerial effectiveness (Carson & Gilliard, 1993), and to identify defense mechanisms (Johnson & Gold, 1995).

In addition to unpublished sentence completion instruments, a number of forms dealing with general or specific problems and characteristics are commercially available. Sentence completion tests have been designed for individuals of all ages and for various groups and purposes. For example, the EPS Sentence Completion Technique was designed specifically for use with mildly retarded or intellectually borderline individuals; the Geriatric Sentence Completion Form for geriatric patients or older adults (age 60 and above); the DOLE Vocational Sentence Completion Blank for assessing the concerns, general emphases, and specific vocational preferences of students; and the Williams Awareness Sentence Completion for identifying feelings of racial conflict in blacks and racial prejudice in whites. Two standardized instruments with a more general focus—the Rotter

Incomplete Sentences Blank and the Bloom Sentence Completion Attitude Survey—are discussed in more detail below.

The Rotter Incomplete Sentences Blank, Second Edition. One of the most carefully constructed and standardized of sentence completion tests is the Rotter Incomplete Sentences Blank (RISB). Each of the three forms (high school, college, adult) consists of 40 sentence fragments written mostly in the first person and takes 20–40 minutes to complete. The RISB is scored for conflict (C) or unhealthy response (e. g., "I hate ... almost everyone."); positive response (P) (e.g, "The best ... is yet to come."), and neutral responses (N) (e. g., "Most girls ... are females"). Failing to respond or making a response that is too short to be meaningful is counted as an omission. Scoring weights for C responses are C1 = 4, C2 = 5, and C3 = 6, from lowest to highest degree of conflict expressed. Scoring weights for P responses are P1 = 2, P2 = 1, and P3 = 0, from least to most positive response. N responses receive no numerical weight. After scoring each responses, an overall adjustment score is obtained by adding the weighted ratings in the conflict and positive categories. The overall adjustment score ranges from 0 to 240, higher scores being associated with greater maladjustment. The second (1992) edition of the RISB manual contains a number of case examples to demonstrate the scoring of the blank.

Research has shown that the RISB correctly classifies most respondents into adjusted and maladjusted categories and hence can be used in screening for overall maladjustment. The newer (1992) norms provide cutoff scores based on adjusted and non-adjusted samples. The 1992 manual also contains an updated review of the literature of studies that substantiate the reliability, validity, and clinical utility of the RISB (Rotter, Lah, & Rafferty, 1992).

Bloom Sentence Completion Attitude Survey. Peterson's (1985a) review of the Bloom Sentence Completion Attitude Survey (BSCS) begins with the question: "What has forty stems but only one Bloom and smells like a rose?" (p. 204). This question reveals something of the generally favorable evaluation given by Peterson (1985a) to the BSCS. The BSCS has two levels (student and adult), and is designed to assess attitudes toward important factors in everyday living. Both levels reveal positive, neutral, and negative attitudes of the respondent toward important factors in everyday life.

Referred to as both an objective and a projective test, the BSCS can be scored for eight factors: age mates (student version) or people (adult version), physical self, family, psychological self, self-directedness, education (student version) or work (adult version), accomplishment, and irritants. The first stems are arranged in groups of eight items representing each of the eight factors, repeated at equal intervals through the survey. This format facilitates scoring the first items in each area. Item responses are scored + (positive, favorable, or well disposed), – (negative, unfavorable, or ill-disposed), or 0 (concrete or objective description, a response that does not fit the dichotomy or a completely tangential one). Scores on each of the five items constituting an area are added to yield a total area score having an 11-point range (–5 to + 5).

Evidence for the reliability of the BSCS is fairly meager: interrater reliability coefficients are reported to be over .90 for technicians having a high school education. Validation data indicate that the BSCS differentiated better than chance between individuals retained in the U. S. Air Force and those who were discharged for psychological reasons. Statistically significant negative correlations between the eight scores and scores on measures of anxiety are also reported in the manual. Apparently less anxious people tend to make higher scores on this instrument, which is one bit of evidence for its construct validity.

Play Techniques

As indicated above, sentence completions have been used in the personality assessment of all age groups. However, because of the limited ability of most children to express their feelings in writing, the technique may not be as revealing as other approaches with younger examinees. Techniques involving the use of materials and activities that are more appropriate or characteristic of children usually yield richer, more meaningful responses. For example, observing how children play with dolls, puppets, and other constructions can provide useful insights into their thoughts and behavior. An example of a commercially available test consisting of toys of various kinds (animals, dolls, bathroom and kitchen figures, furniture, and other household furnishings) is the Scenotest (Staabs, 1991). In theory, by noting which items the child chooses, what he or she does with them, and his or her comments, expressions, and other behaviors during play, the examiner/observer obtains information on the child's attitudes toward family, sibling rivalry, fears, aggression, and conflicts. As in other diagnostic settings with children, the examiner makes a note of the objects selected by the child, what he or she does with them, and other behaviors (emotional expressions, verbalizations, etc.).

Story Completions

Children are active creatures who enjoy playing, but they also like to listen to stories and tell them. Consequently, presenting a child with the beginning of a story, that is, at least one complete sentence representing the start of a plot, and asking him or her to complete the story can be motivating to the child and informative to the examiner. Such story fragments, as with sentence fragments, can be tailor-made for the particular child and for the purposes of the assessment, but standard sets of incomplete stories are also available. Among these are the Madeline Thomas Stories and the Duss (Despert) Fables. The following are two of the 15 incomplete stories in the former series (Zlotogorski & Wiggs, 1986):

— A boy (or girl) goes to school. During recess he (she) does not play with other children; he (she) stays by himself (herself) in a corner. Why?
— A boy fights with his brother. Mother comes. What is going to happen? (p. 196)

Two of the incomplete stories or fables from the Duss (Despert) series are as follows (Rabin & Zlotogorski, 1981):

— A boy (or girl) took a very nice walk in the woods alone with his mother (or her father, for the girl). They had lots of fun together. When he returned home the boy found that his father did not look as he usually did. Why? (Similarly, upon returning the girl finds that the mother does not look the same as usual.)
— A child comes home from school. Mother says to him (her), "Don't start your homework right away—I have something to tell you." What is the mother going to say to the child? (p. 141)

The purpose of the first Madeline Thomas story is to give the child an opportunity to explain reasons for withdrawal from the group (fears, shame, guilt etc.), whereas the second story involves sibling rivalry. Equally obvious is the Oedipal theme in the first Duss (Despert) fable; the last story is designed to reveal some of the fears and desires of the child.*

Story completions are interpreted impressionistically and in the light of other diagnostic information. As with sentence completions, however, it is possible to classify and quantify the responses according to a predetermined conceptual or theoretical scheme. The examiner may also structure or direct the individual's responses to the incomplete stores by presenting stories that encourage a particular class of responses, by providing the individual with a sample completed story, and by asking specific questions pertaining to the story after it has been completed.

The story completion technique is, of course, not limited to children; it can also be applied in clinical and research settings with adolescents and adults. For example, Moore, Gullone, and Kostanski (1997) used a story-completion task to examine risk-taking in adolescents, and Kitzinger and Powell (1995) explored representations of heterosexual infidelity in the stories of young men and women.

---

* Court-appointed psychologists and other child psychodiagnosticians and therapists must be very careful that the techniques that they use (story-telling, doll-play, games, etc.) to obtain information from children concerning abusive or unlawful acts perpetrated against them or other people do not suggest to the child that certain events took place when they actually did not.

Although story completions would seem to possess face validity, there is little psychometric evidence for the reliability and validity of the technique. According to certain critics of this method, the concept of "face validity" should be modified to "faith validity" as far as story completions are concerned.

Rosenzweig Picture-Frustration Study

Another projective (or semi-projective) device that requires respondents to make verbal completion responses to verbal (and pictorial) stimuli is the Rosenzweig Picture-Frustration Study (RPFS). Each of the three forms—Children (ages 4–13; Rosenzweig, 1981b, 1988), Adolescent (ages 12–18; Rosenzweig, 1981a), and Adult (ages 18 and over; Rosenzweig, 1978)—of this instrument consists of 24 comic-strip pictures in an eight-page booklet. Every picture contains two people; the person on the left is depicted as saying words that are frustrating to the person on the right or words describing the frustrating situation. The examiner is instructed to indicate, by writing in the balloon above the frustrated character's head, the first verbal response that comes to mind as being made by this anonymous person (see Figure 10–1). After the examinee has responded to all items, the examiner conducts a post-test interrogation or inquiry to assist in interpreting and classifying the responses. This task is facilitated by an extensive list of scored examples included in the manual.

Psychoanalytic in its rationale, the RPFS focuses on the characteristic manner in which a person responds to ego- or super-ego blocking situations. Based on the assumption that a typical response to frustration involves aggression, the RPFS is scored according to the direction and type of aggression expressed in the responses. Included under Direction of Aggression are: *extraggression* or E-A (outwardly, or toward the environment); *intraggression* or I-A (inwardly, toward oneself); *imaggression* or M-A (avoidance or nonexpression of aggression).* Type of Aggression includes: obstacle-dominance or O-D (the frustrating object stands out); etho-defense or E-D (the respondent's ego predominates to defend itself); need-persistence or N-P (the goal is pursued despite the frustration).

Scores on the six variables listed above are combined to yield nine factors, making a total of 15 scores. In addition to these 15 scores, a Group Conformity Rating (GCR) indicating how closely the responses correspond to those given most frequently by a norm group, and a trends score designed to reflect changes in responses to frustration in the first and second halves of the RPFS, may be determined. The fact that responses to the 24 pictures are assigned to specific categories results in ipsative scoring, in which high and low scores in the various

---

* The terms used for extraggression, intraggression, and imaggression in the older research literature on the Rosenzweig Picture Frustration Study are extrapunitive, intrapunitive, and impunitive, respectively.

FIG. 10–1 **Item from the Rosenzweig Picture-Frustration Study.**

Reproduced by permission of the author,
S. Rosenzweig. © Psychological Assessment
Resources

categories balance out. Finally, Rosenzweig (1978) emphasized that, in addition to quantitative scoring, responses to the RPFS should be evaluated impressionistically.

The RPFS is typically administered individually as part of a battery of psychological assessment instruments. With some loss of scoring accuracy, it can be administered simultaneously to a group of people. It is also possible to give it orally to handicapped individuals and to young children by reading aloud the comments of the figure on the left and then recording the response.

Like sentence completion tests, the RPFS is a semi-projective technique that can be scored quantitatively and more reliably than most projectives. Agreement in scoring the nine factors is reported to be approximately 85%. However, the test-retest reliabilities of the three forms are fairly modest (.50s and .60s for E-A, M-A, E-D, and N-P, and even lower for other variables). Norms on many special groups are reported in the manuals (Rosenzweig, 1978, 1981a, 1981b, 1988). The most recent norms, however, are over two decades old and based on fairly small samples that are not truly representative of the general population.

The RPFS has been administered throughout the world in a large number of research investigations concerned with the nature of frustration and its correlates, but has declined in popularity in recent years. Significant relationships have been found between RPFS scores and age trends, cultural differences, hypnotizability, scores on other personality tests, psychiatric reports, sex differences, and various physiological measures. Wagner's (1985) review points out a number of flaws in the RPFS, in particular the low split-half reliabilities, but nevertheless views it as "the premier test for investigating frustration" and "a versatile instrument for studying the dynamics of frustration and rounding out a personality appraisal" (Wagner, 1985, p. 1061).

■ Projective Drawings

Instruments requiring oral or written responses to words and sentences represent only one of many types of tests in the category of projective techniques. Among the materials that have been employed in both psychodiagnosis and psychotherapy are clay, paints, building materials, colored chips, and other objects for eliciting self-expression. Although it has not received wide acceptance among professional psychologists, handwriting analysis (graphology), which was discussed briefly in Chapter 1, also has advocates (e. g., Holt, 1974) as a psychodiagnostic technique. Graphologists use either an analytic or a pattern approach to interpreting handwriting. In the analytic approach, characteristics of individual letters (e.g, angularity, curvature, slant, width) presumably indicate certain traits of personality and character. In the pattern approach, the writer's script is analyzed for consistent patterns composed of various elements.

More widely respected than handwriting analysis are *projective drawings* of people (alone or doing something together) and objects. Three examples of instruments in this category—the Draw-a-Person Test, the House-Tree-Person Technique, and the Bender Visual-Motor Gestalt Test—are described below.

Draw-a-Person Test

The first person to use drawings in formal psychological assessment was Florence Goodenough (1926). Goodenough's Draw-a-Man Test was originally designed as a performance test of intelligence, but it became apparent that various features in the drawings made by various people (e. g., facial expression, size, boldness, and position of the drawing on the page) reflected other psychological characteristics. Subsequently, Karen Machover (1949, 1951) developed a Draw-a-Person Test (DAP) specifically to assess personality structure and functioning. On this test, the respondent is presented with a blank sheet of paper and instructed to "draw a person." Following completion of the figure, the respondent is usually told to draw, on the other side or on a separate sheet, a picture of a person of the opposite sex from that of the first figure. Finally, the respondent is asked to indicate the age, educational level, occupation, fears, ambitions, and other facts about the person, and perhaps tell a story about him or her.

The DAP is interpreted in terms of the placement of various features in the drawings (e. g., size, body details, position, clothing), Machover (1949) maintained that there is a tendency for people to project impulses that are acceptable to them onto the same-sex figure and impulses that are unacceptable to them onto the opposite-sex figure. The relative sizes of the male and female figures reportedly reveal clues concerning the sexual identification of the respondent. Other details of the drawings that are considered to be indicative of certain personality characteristics or psychopathological conditions are: large eyelashes are associated with hysteria; exaggerated eyes and/or ears are indicative of suspiciousness, ideas of reference, or other paranoid characteristics; many clothing details suggest neurosis; large drawings suggest acting out impulses; dark, heavy shading suggests strong aggressive impulses; small drawings, few facial features, or a dejected facial expression point to depression; few body periphery details reveal suicidal tendencies; few physical features suggest psychosis or organic brain damage. Other features that are noted and interpreted include disproportionate body parts, missing parts, erasures, and symmetry or asymmetry.

To Machover, a disproportionately large or small head—the center of intellectual power, control of body impulses, and social balance—indicated functional difficulties in these areas. She made a number of sweeping generalizations about heads, such as "Disproportionately large heads will often be given by individuals suffering from organic brain disease." and "The sex given the proportionately larger head is the sex that is accorded more intellectual and social authority."

Although many of the interpretative signs and generalizations proposed by Machover on the basis of her clinical experience make psychoanalytic and even common sense, they have not held up under close scrutiny. Swensen (1957, 1968) criticized Machover's system of interpreting the DAP and urged caution in applying her hypotheses concerning the psychological meanings revealed by the drawings. Some evidence has been found for a positive relationship between the judged quality of the drawings and overall psychological adjustment (Lewinsohn, 1965; Roback, 1968), but most of Machover's interpretative hypotheses have not been supported by research. More recently, Naglieri, McNeish, and Bardos (1991) developed a Draw A Person: Screening Procedure for Emotional Disturbance to be used as a screening test for children suspected of behavior disorder and emotional disturbance. This approach to scoring the DAP has met with some success in the diagnosis of problem children (Naglieri & Pfeiffer, 1992)

A number of variations on the DAP Test, such as having the respondent draw pictures of several objects, a group of people, or a story, have been published. Several of these instruments are listed in Table 10–1, two of which—the House-Tree-Person Technique and the Kinetic Drawing System for Family and School—will be considered in more detail.

House-Tree-Person Technique

The most popular variation of the DAP Test is the House-Tree-Person Technique(H-T-P) (Buck, 1948, 1992). Along with the DAP and several other projectives, the H-T-P has been listed among the top ten tests in terms of usage by clinical and counseling psychologists (Craig & Horowitz, 1990; Frauenhoffer, Ross, Gfeller, Searight, & Piotrowski, 1998). In administering the H-T-P, the respondent is given a pencil and sheets of white paper, and instructed to make freehand drawings of a house, a tree, and a person. The house drawing is made with the longer axis of the paper placed horizontally; the tree and person drawings are made on separate sides with the longer axis of the sheet vertical. After the drawings are completed in pencil, they are taken away and the respondent is given crayons to make drawings of a house, a tree, and a person. Lastly, he or she is asked some 20 questions about each drawing; the questions involve descriptions and interpretations of the drawings and their backgrounds.

The drawings may be scored quantitatively on a number of variables: drive (level and control), primary needs and assets, psychosexual concerns (satisfaction and conflicts), interpersonal relationships, and interenvironmental matters (reality level, and extratensive-intratensive) (Siipola, 1994). However, the drawings are usually interpreted impressionistically and holistically.

According to the theory, the drawing of the house represents the respondent's home, presumably arousing associations or perceptions concerning his or her home-life and familial relationships. The tree drawing is said to reflect the respondent's deeper, more *unconscious* feelings about the self. The condition of the tree is related to the respondent's vivacity or attitude toward life: a dead tree points to emotional emptiness, a full-blown tree to liveliness, a weeping willow to weakness, and a spiky tree to aggressiveness. The drawing of the person, which represents the self and is interpreted similarly as on the DAP test, is said to reflect a more conscious view of the respondent's self and his or her relationship with the environment.

The H-T-P has been used extensively in clinical practice as well as in many research investigations involving assorted groups, but it has not been standardized on a specific population. The reliability and validity of the H-T-P vary with the scoring criteria and the nature of the individuals tested. Swensen (1968) concluded that global ratings of the H-T-P are more reliable than ratings of the details of the drawings. In any case, the reliability coefficients are typically quite modest. Buck (1948) reported that the H-T-P was validated by comparing personality evaluations made from H-T-P responses with diagnoses by staff psychiatrists, intimate friends, and the Rorschach Inkblot Test. However, evidence for the reliability and validity of the instrument is, like that of most projectives, rather skimpy (Killian, 1987). In fact, the author of the technique maintained that, because of the variability and multiplicity of the meanings of the diagnostic signs on the H-T-P from person to person and situation to situation, it is not possible to conduct validation research with the instrument (Buck, 1981)! This may be one reason why reviews of the H-T-P have generally been negative (Killian, 1987).

A recent addition to the DAP and the H-T-P is a book entitled *House-Tree-Person and Draw-A-Person as Measures of Abuse in Children: A Quantitative Scoring System* (Van Hutton, 1996). The book gives a detailed description of a procedure for scoring and analyzing children's drawings in terms of four areas:

Sexually Relevant Concepts, Aggression and Hostility, Withdrawal and Guarded Accessibility, Alertness for Danger/Suspiciousness and Lack of Trust. Each area is further divided into four categories: Behavioral, General, House, Tree, and Person. The scorer looks for specific items, such as elongated feet, the omission of arms, or a very small door, in each of the drawing categories; these items are described throughout the book. The book also contains two interpreted cases, in addition to information on research directions, norms, reliability, and validity. Samples of normal, sexually abused, and emotionally disturbed served as the standardization group. Despite these efforts, which Dowd (1998b) views as commendable, the question of the validity of the procedure has not been laid to rest. In fact, an extensive review by Knoff (1998b) concludes that not only are significant improvements in norms, validity, and reliability needed, but there is a serious question whether this or any other psychometric instrument "can ever be sensitive and efficacious enough to be useful as a diagnostic tool in an area as complex as child abuse" (p. 490). In light of the mistakes made both by psychological examiners and law enforcement officers during the 1980s with regard to the legal prosecution of suspected child molesters, Knoff's conclusion should give cause for pause to those who attempt to determine whether children have been physically or psychological abused.

Kinetic Drawing System for Family and School

This instrument is a combination of the Kinetic Family Drawing and the Kinetic School Drawing tests (Burns, 1982; Burns & Kaufman,1970, 1972). On the family drawing portion, the child or adolescent respondent is asked to draw a picture of his or her family doing something. After the drawing is completed, the respondent is asked to identify each of the family members in the drawing, what they are doing in the picture and why, and to talk about their relationships with each other. A similar procedure is followed in administering the school portion: the child or adolescent is asked to draw a picture of himself (herself) interacting with relevant persons at school, and the examiner asks several questions about the drawing. On both the family and school segments of the test, the examiner attempts to clarify the meanings of the drawings and to determine what covert processes may have affected their construction. Two of the most psychologically important features of the drawings are the degree of interaction between the figures in the drawings and the extent of interaction among them (Anastasi & Urbina, 1997). In addition to its use as a diagnostic projective test for assessing a child's perceptions of his or her relationships with peers, family, school, and other significant persons, it is a good "ice breaker technique" for facilitating rapport between the child and the examiner. Furthermore, the technique may serve a combined diagnostic/therapeutic function with respect to family or school problems. In a review of research on the Kinetic Family Drawing test, the first part of the combined instrument, Handler and Habenicht (1994) point out that many of the findings with the procedure are promising and deserve to be pursued and extended.

Bender Visual-Motor Gestalt Test and Hutt Adaptation

More a measure of cognitive and psychomotor abilities than personality, but also frequently included in a battery of tests for diagnosing mental disorders, is the Bender Visual-Motor Gestalt Test. This test (Bender, 1938, 1970) consists of nine geometric designs borrowed from Wertheimer (1923). The respondent is directed to copy the designs, which are presented individually on 4" × 6" white cards (see Figure 10–2); afterwards, the respondent may also be asked to reproduce the designs from memory. The Bender-Gestalt was introduced as a measure of visual-motor coordination, but its primary clinical application has been in the detection of central nervous system impairment (brain damage or organicity) in

The Bender Visual-Motor Gestalt Test Figures.   **FIG. 10–2**

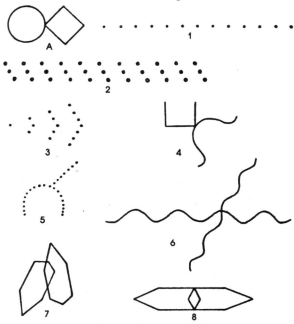

Reprinted with permission from *Bender® Motor Gestalt Test Cards and Manual of Instructions* by Loretta Bender, MD. Copyright © 1938 and 1965 by the American Orthopsychiatric Association, Inc.

persons aged 4 years through adulthood. It can be completed in a few minutes or so, and is frequently administered as part of a battery of tests to assess perceptual/cognitive functioning and learning disabilities. Many clinicians administer a brief projective test such as the Bender-Gestalt or the H-T-P at the beginning of the testing period to establish rapport with the respondent.

Evaluating the Drawings. Scoring the Bender-Gestalt to detect neurological impairment focuses on the number and types of reproduction errors that are made. Children eight years or older and of normal intelligence usually make no more than two errors. Errors that suggest organic brain damage are: shape distortions; rotating the design; problems in integrating the design; disproportionate, overlapping, or fragmented drawings; and perseverations. A restandardization of the Bender-Gestalt, including norms for ages five through ten years, was published in 1975; the scores are highly correlated with intelligence quotients up to ages nine through ten (Koppitz, 1975). The drawings can also be evaluated as projective responses. For example, figure reversals suggest negativism (Hutt, 1969), and exact reproductions point to obsessive-compulsive personality traits (Tolor & Schulberg, 1963).

Hutt Adaptation of the Bender-Gestalt. A number of modifications of the Bender-Gestalt materials and procedure have been published, including the Bender Visual-Motor Gestalt Test for Children, the Watkins-Bender Test Scoring System (to detect learning disabilities), the Canter Background Interference Procedure for the Bender-Gestalt (the designs must be reproduced on a background of intersecting sinusoidal lines), and the Hutt Adaptation of the Bender-Gestalt Test (Hutt, 1977).

Responses in the Hutt Adaptation, which uses nine designs similar to those of the original Bender-Gestalt but more uniform in size, can be evaluated by an objective approach, a projective approach, or a configurational analysis approach. In the objective approach, the designs are scored on a Psychopathology Scale and a Scale for Perceptual Adience-Abience. The Psychopathology Scale consists of 17 factors, almost all of which are weighted one to ten points. The norms on this scale are based on relatively small samples of normal and mentally disordered groups of people, and the test-retest reliability coefficients over two weeks are in the .80s. With respect to its validity, scores on the Psychopathology Scale have been found to differentiate significantly between normal people and psychotics but not between brain-damaged and chronic schizophrenic individuals (Hutt, 1977).

The Scale of Perceptual Adience-Abience was designed to assess the respondent's perceptual orientation or style—openness (approach) versus closedness (avoidance). There are 12 factors on this scale, which is significantly correlated ($r = .69$) with the Psychopathology Scale. Like those for the Psychopathology scale, norms for the Scale of Perceptual Adience-Abience are based on limited samples. Some evidence for the construct validity of the latter scale is reported by Hutt (1977), but the validity data are actually rather meager.

In the projective approach to evaluating responses to the Hutt Adaptation, evidence is sought in the drawings for the individual's style of adaptation, cognition, affect, areas of conflict, defensive methods, and maturational characteristics. To provide the required data for the projective approach, the respondent begins by copying the designs, then redraws them to make them more pleasing, and finally indicates what the originally copied and redrawn designs look like or suggest.

A third approach to scoring the Hutt Adaptation—configurational analysis—consists of determining the presence or absence of specific signs that are characteristic of five clinical syndromes: brain damage, depression, mental retardation, psychoneuroses, and schizophrenia. Cutting scores on various measures are used to differentiate among psychiatric groups. However, as with the projective approach, configurational analysis of responses is not sufficiently valid to make good diagnostic decisions. Although the objective approach to scoring the Hutt Adaptation of the Bender-Gestalt warrants higher marks than the other two approaches, Sattler (1985) concluded in his review of this instrument that extreme caution should be exercised in using it as a projective assessment technique.

Postscript on Projective Drawings

After reviewing the psychometric problems with the Draw-a-Person Test and related construction techniques, the reader may well wonder why many practicing clinicians continue using them. Is it possible that they are unaware of the low reliabilities and validities of the majority of these instruments, or are they simply deceiving themselves by believing that the instruments are diagnostically useful? Several of the factors detracting from clinical judgments, which were discussed in Chapter 4, may operate to protect one's beliefs in the diagnostic utility of a particular psychometric instrument. One of these is the illusory correlation between certain *signs* on a given instrument and the actual presence of a psychopathological disorder. Popular stereotypes, such as the notion that strange eyes are indicative of suspiciousness, that large heads are associated with intelligence, that erasures in the genital or buttocks regions indicate conflicts concerning those areas, and the like are also commonplace, even among highly-trained professionals. Another factor that may lead clinicians to misjudge the effectiveness of a diagnostic instrument or procedure is failure to consider the base rates, or frequencies of occurrences, of particular diagnostic conditions in the target population. Whatever the explanation may be, psychodiagnosticians and psychotherapists will undoubtedly continue to use figure drawings to help them understand and be of assistance to patients. In interpreting these drawings, most clinical psychologists place less credence on formal scoring systems than on their own

| BOX 10-1 | **Combining Projective Drawings with an Interview** |

During the Vietnam War, a Veteran's Administration psychologist tested a young soldier who had accidentally shot himself in the leg with a .45 caliber pistol while practicing quick draw in the jungle. Surgeons found it necessary to amputate the soldier's leg from the knee down. He was quite depressed, and everyone assumed that he suffered from grief and guilt over his great personal tragedy. He was virtually mute and nearly untestable. However, we did persuade him to complete a series of figure drawings. In one drawing he depicted himself as a helicopter gunner, spraying bullets indiscriminately into the jungle below. When questioned about this drawing, he became quite animated and confessed that he relished combat. Guided by the possible implications of the morbid drawing, the psychologist sought to learn more about the veteran's attitudes toward combat. In the course of several interviews, the veteran revealed that he particularly enjoyed firing upon moving objects—animals, soldiers, civilians—it made no difference to him. Gradually, it became clear that the young veteran was an incipient war criminal who was depressed because his injury would prevent him from returning to the front lines. Needless to say, this information had quite an impact on the tenor of the psychological report.

From Gregory, R.L., *Psychological Testing: History, Principles, and Applications* (p. 528). Copyright © 1996 by Allyn & Bacon. Reprinted by permission.

impressionistic understanding. The down side of this process is that it permits biases and stereotypes to run rampant; the up side is that the clinician may actually be more sensitive than a formal scoring system to subtle cues or signs. Furthermore, clinicians do not generally use projective techniques in isolation; a number of other methods, including observations, in-depth interviewing, and more objective measures are also employed. Rather than leading to a definitive diagnosis, the results of projective tests may suggest hypotheses. These hypotheses may then be confirmed or disconfirmed by other methods (see Box 10–1).

■ Summary

Surveys of clinical and counseling psychologists indicate that sentence completion methods, projective drawings, and the Bender-Gestalt, along with the Rorschach and the Thematic Apperception Test, are among the top ten psychological tests administered in mental health settings. Thus, despite continuing criticisms of projectives, they have not been totally replaced by personality inventories, rating scales, or other objective personality assessment techniques.

With the possible exception of completely unstructured interviews, projectives are the most open-ended of all personality assessment techniques. Projectives have been classified as association, completion, construction, arrangement or selection, and expression techniques. Examples of instruments in these categories are given in this chapter and in Chapters 11 and 12. Included in the present chapter are descriptions of: association techniques such as early memories and word associations; completion techniques such as sentence completions, story completions, and the Rosenzweig Picture-Frustration Study; projective drawings (expression techniques) such as the Draw-a-Person Test, the House-Tree Person Technique, the Kinetic Drawing System for Family and School, and the Bender Visual-Motor Gestalt Test.

In the early memories procedure, respondents are asked to recall their earliest memories and provide associations to them. Typical directions to respondents are to recall three to six specific, concrete, single memories, from which common themes are determined. Interpretation of the memories is typically impressionistic, but systems for categorizing memories have been devised.

The method of word associations requires respondents to listen to each of a set of individually presented words and report the first associated word that comes to mind. Clinical psychologists and psychiatrists have used this procedure to detect conflicts, complexes, and other sources of emotional stress. Standard word lists, such as the Kent-Rosanoff Free Association Test and the Rapaport-Gill-Schafer word lists, are available, but in most cases the words are selected by the examiner for a particular clinical or research purpose. Responses to the words on these lists may be compared to norms and content-analyzed. Modifications of the word association technique, such as requiring that sentences be given in response to stimulus words, have been proposed. Because of its poor information yield, word association is not one of the most popular projective techniques.

More popular and reliable than word associations and many other projectives are sentence completion tests. In this procedure, respondents complete a series of sentence fragments in any way they choose. Although unstandardized incomplete sentence tests are frequently devised by clinicians for specific purposes, a number of published standardized instruments are available. Examples are the Rotter Incomplete Sentences Blank and the Bloom Sentence Completion Attitude Survey. The former, in particular, is a highly reliable instrument that can be scored for conflict or unhealthy responses, positive responses, neutral responses, and an overall adjustment score.

Story completions are an infrequently used technique in which the respondent, who is typically a child, is told the beginning of a story and asked to complete it. Standard sets of incomplete stories include the Madeline Thomas Stories and The Duss (Despert) Fables. Responses are interpreted impressionistically and by referring to other diagnostic information concerning the respondent.

The Rosenzweig Picture-Frustration Study consists of 24 comic-strip pictures, each of which depicts an individual in a frustrating situation; the respondent indicates what the frustrated person's response to the situation is likely to be. Responses are scored according to the direction of aggression (extraggression, intraggression, imaggression) and type of aggression (obstacle-dominance, etho-defense, need-persistence) manifested in the respondent's responses. In addition to these six categories, separate scores on nine combinations of direction and type of aggression, a group conformity rating, and a trends score may be obtained. Like sentence completion tests, the Rosenzweig is considered to be a semi-projective instrument.

The personalities of both children and adults are frequently revealed through expressive behavior, as in drawing a person or an object. The most popular projective drawing tests are the Draw-a-Person Test, the House-Tree-Person Technique, and the Kinetic Drawing System for Family and School. On the Draw-a-Person Test, the respondent is asked to draw a person on a sheet of white paper and then draw on another sheet a person of the opposite sex from the first drawing. The drawings are analyzed impressionistically in terms of various signs revealed by the drawings. On the House-Tree-Person Technique, the respondent constructs pencil and crayon drawings of a house, a tree, and a person. In the impressionistic interpretation of the drawings, the house is considered to arouse associations or perceptions concerning home life, the tree is presumed to reflect unconscious feelings about the self, and the person is interpreted as reflecting a more conscious view of the self. On the Kinetic Drawing System for Family and School, respondents draw and provide details concerning family and school groups, and the social interactions among the group members are analyzed.

Another projective technique of the drawing type is the Hutt Adaptation of the Bender Visual-Motor Gestalt Test, in which the respondent copies a series of nine, individually-presented geometrical designs. Responses to the Hutt may be evaluated objectively, projectively, or by configurational analysis. The objective approach, which yields scores on a Psychopathology Scale and a Scale of Perceptual Adience-Abience, is considered to be more reliable and valid than the projective and configurational analysis approaches to evaluating the drawings.

■ Questions and Activities

1. What are the principal advantages and limitations of projective techniques? What factors have led to the decline in their use in clinical diagnosis, and why do they remain popular among clinical psychologists?
2. Ask several of your friends or relatives to relate to you two or three of their earliest memories, and see what reasonable interpretations you can make of

the memories. In addition, it might be interesting to obtain such recollections from individuals who are fairly unknowledgeable about psychology and presumably less likely than psychology majors to interpret and perhaps censor or embellish their psychologically significant memories. Whether viewed from a common sense, psychodynamic, or other theoretical perspective, do the memories lend themselves to unambiguous interpretations? Do the interpretations make sense, and are they consistent with what you know about the individual from other sources?

3. What are "recovered memories," and how can you tell if the remembered events actually occurred or are simply the results of fantasy or suggestion?

4. Construct an alphabetized list of 25 nouns pertaining to subjects of interest to people in your age group (college, grades, graduation, failure, sex, marriage, religion, mother, father, career, health, and so on). Read your list to twelve acquaintances and ask each person to respond to each work on the list as quickly as possible with the first word that comes to mind. Record the response to each word and the response time (in seconds). Summarize the results in terms of the number of responses of a given kind made to each stimulus word, average response times, and insights provided into the personalities of the respondents. Review the section on "Word Associations" in this chapter before drawing any conclusions.

5. Complete each of the sentence fragments in Form 10–1 to show your true feelings. What consistent themes, problems, and sources of conflict are revealed in the way that you completed these sentences? Were you subjectively aware of any physical or mental tension in responding to any of the items? Did you take longer to complete some sentences than others? Did you give any strange or unusual responses? If so, what could they mean? What do you think of this sentence completion technique as a method for analyzing personality? Do you think that you revealed anything that an expert psychodiagnostician could detect?

6. Construct two incomplete stories that you believe will reveal something about the respondent's personality when he or she is asked to complete the stories. Have several of your classmates or friends finish the stories. Does the content of the completed stories suggest anything significant about the respondent's personality? Do you consider this technique of personality assessment to be reliable and valid? What or why not?

7. Have each of several people draw a picture of a person on a clean sheet of paper. Then have them turn the sheet over and draw a picture of a person of the opposite sex. Collect the drawings, and tell the participants that you are going to have the drawings interpreted by an expert personality analyst and that you will give them the interpretations later. Some time later, present the following personality description (Forer, 1949) to each participant:

You have a strong need for other people to like you and for them to admire you. You have a tendency to be critical of yourself. You have a great deal of unused capacity, which you have not turned to your advantage. While you have some personality weaknesses, you are generally able to compensate for them. Your sexual adjustment has presented some problems for you. Disciplined and controlled on the outside, you tend to be worrisome and insecure inside. At times you have serious doubts as to whether you have made the right decision or done the right thing. You prefer a certain amount of change and variety, and become dissatisfied when hemmed in by restrictions and limitations. You pride yourself on being an independent thinker and do not accept others' opinions without satisfactory proof. You have found it unwise to be too frank in revealing yourself to others. At times you are extroverted, affable, social, while at other times you are introverted, wary, reserved. Some of your aspirations tend to be pretty unrealistic.

Be sure to scramble the sentences in the interpretation so the order will be different for different people. Ask each person to read the description and tell you whether it is (a) a highly accurate description, (b) an accurate description, (c) a somewhat accurate and somewhat inaccurate description, (d) an inaccurate description, or (e) a very inaccurate description of his or her personality. Tabulate the results, interpret them as well as you can, and report them to your course instructor. After the exercise has been completed, you should tell the participants that you have deceived them, and hope that they react to the information with good humor!

■ Suggested Readings

Bruhn, A. R. (1995). Early memories in personality assessment. In J. N. Butcher (Ed.), *Clinical personality assessment: Practical approaches* (pp. 278–301). New York: Oxford University Press.

Canter, A. (1996). The Bender-Gestalt Test (BGT). In C. S. Newmark (Ed.), *Major psychological assessment instruments* (2nd ed., pp. 400–430). Boston: Allyn & Bacon.

Groth-Marnat, G. (1997). Projective drawings. In *Handbook of psychological assessment* (3rd ed., pp. 499–533). New York: Wiley.

Haak, R. A. (1990). Using the sentence completion to assess emotional disturbance. In C. R. Reynolds & R. W. Kamphaus (Eds.), *Handbook of psychological & educational assessment of children: Personality, behavior, & context* (pp. 147–167). Norwood, NJ: Ablex.

Handler, L. (1996). The clinical use of figure drawings. In C. S. Newmark (Ed), *Major psychological assessment instruments* (2nd ed., pp. 206–293). Boston: Allyn & Bacon.

Knoff, H. M. (1990). Evaluation of projective drawings. In C. R. Reynolds & R. W. Kamphaus (Eds.), *Handbook of psychological & educational assessment of children: Personality, behavior, & context* (pp. 89–146). Norwood, NJ: Ablex.

Worchel, F. F., & Dupree, J. L. (1990). Projective story-telling techniques. In C. R. Reynolds & R. W. Kamphaus (Eds.), *Handbook of psychological & educational assessment of children: Personality, behavior, & context* (pp. 70–88). Norwood, NJ: Ablex.

CHAPTER 11

The Rorschach Inkblot Technique*

In all probability, the Swiss psychiatrist Hermann Rorschach did not realize when he unexpectedly died in 1922 that the ten inkblots which were to bear his name would become the most popular of the psychodiagnostic methods known as projective techniques. Few personality assessment instruments provide broad band idiographic information yielding such dynamic formulations and descriptions as the Rorschach. Clinical users of the technique view it as a real-life sample of behavior that provides data from which description, explanation, and, it is hoped, prediction of a person's thoughts and actions can be made.

The question of whether the Rorschach is actually a projective technique, a problem-solving strategy, a perceptual-cognitive task, an apperceptive process, a structured interview, or an X-ray of the mind continues to be debated. Nevertheless, the basic hypothesis that lies at the heart of the interpretive foundation of the Rorschach is considered by many practitioners to be as true today as it was over a half-century ago (Frank, 1948):

> What is of major significance for understanding the individual personality is that the individual organizes experiences as he warps, twists, distorts, and otherwise fits every situation, event, and person into the framework of his private world, giving them the affective significance which they must have for him in his private world. (p. 15).

---

* The original version of this chapter in the first edition of this book was written by Chris Piotrowski of the University of West Florida. The present chapter is an updating that retains the structure and much of the content of the original version.

■ Format and Foundations

The Rorschach consists of ten inkblots, almost all of which are bilaterally symmetrical and placed on a white 5½ inch by 9½ inch card. Cards I, IV, V, VI, and VII, which are noncolored or achromatic, are printed in varying shades of black and gray. Cards II and III are printed in black and red, whereas the remaining cards, VIII, IX, and X, are multicolored and somewhat more elaborate than the others. These ten inkblots, which are reproduced from those originally published by Hermann Rorschach, have been standardized worldwide and are published by Hans Huber in Bern, Switzerland. In the United States, they are available from The Psychological Corporation, Psychological Assessment Resources, NCS Assessments, and Western Psychological Services. An inkblot similar to those on the Rorschach test is shown in Figure 11–1.

FIG. 11-1 **An inkblot figure similar to those on the Rorschach.**

Rationale and Administration Procedure

The theoretical rationale underlying the Rorschach is that an ambiguous, unstructured stimulus such as an inkblot presents an organizational, perceptual, or problem-solving task, to which a person responds in a unique manner. The person's idiosyncratic motives, desires, needs, and ways of relating to the animate and inanimate world are presumably reflected in his or her reactions to the inkblots.

In administering the Rorschach, each card is presented individually, in order, and viewed at no greater than arm's length; the examinee is permitted to turn the card in viewing it. To minimize the effects of his or her body language on the examinee's responses, the examiner typically sits alongside rather than across from the examinee. Administration of all ten inkblots usually takes 45 to 55 minutes, involving two phases and sometimes a third phase referred to as the *testing the limits*. During the first, or *free association*, phase, the examiner, who is usually a psychologist, presents one card at a time and makes a verbatim record of the examinee's responses to it. Also recorded for each card are the response time and the position(s) of the card while the examinee is holding it. Upon completion of the free association phase, the *inquiry phase* begins. In this phase the examiner attempts to discover how the examinee arrived at each response. Through nondirective questioning or probing, the examiner determines what characteristics of the inkblot prompted each response. The examinee's reported perceptions of the characteristics of the inkblots, such as form, color, shading, and animate or inanimate movement seen in the blots, are known as *determinants*. They are critical features of formal Rorschach scoring and protocol interpretation.

Historical Background

Although people have long been fascinated by their own responses, as well as those of others, to ambiguous visual stimuli such as clouds, it was not until the early 1900s that inkblots were used in a systematic manner to investigate mental phenomena. Early investigators of the technique, for example, Alfred Binet, T. Rybakow, and Stella Sharp, used inkblots to test and investigate imagination, but their efforts were not directed toward the assessment of personality as such. In 1911 the Swiss psychiatrist Hermann Rorschach began working on what was to develop into the *psychodiagnostic method*. Rorschach and his mentor Konrad Gehring, employed inkblots in their experiments with Swiss school children. Not until 1917 did Rorschach begin to synthesize his observations of normal adults and psychiatric patients into a clinical and theoretical framework, an effort which culminated in a monograph entitled *Psychodiagnostik* (Rorschach, 1921). Rorschach was quite interested in applying psychoanalytic concepts to his research, but his interpretation of responses to the inkblots focused on the *formal* aspects of percept formation rather than content.

Rorschach's efforts were interrupted by his untimely death in the year following publication of *Psychodiagnostik*, but a small group of followers continued his work in Switzerland. One of these individuals, Emil Oberholzer, taught the Rorschach method to David Levy and Samuel Beck, who were instrumental in bringing credibility to the technique in the United States. The efforts of many other psychologists and psychiatrists who emigrated from Europe to the United States during the 1930s encouraged acceptance and development of the

Rorschach method. The major proponents of the technique were Samuel Beck, Marguerite Hertz, Bruno Klopfer, Zygmunt Piotrowski, and David Rapaport. All of these individuals developed their own formulations and methodology, and eventually five distinct Rorschach systems evolved.

Samuel Beck was the first student to fulfill a dissertation requirement by investigating the Rorschach, and several years later he developed the first American Rorschach scoring system. In 1937 Beck presented his novel approach to the Rorschach in his book, *Introduction to the Rorschach Method*. About this same time, Marguerite Hertz completed her dissertation on the Rorschach and developed a Rorschach system. Hertz's scholarly publications described a distinct Rorschach System that evolved during the 1940s.

Bruno Klopfer was introduced to the Rorschach in Zurich, having completed his Ph.D. some ten years earlier. Upon immigrating to the United States, Klopfer accepted an academic position at Columbia University, where he conducted graduate seminars on the Rorschach. In 1937, he founded the periodical *Rorschach Research Exchange* to provide a research outlet and network of communication among the ever-increasing number of adherents to the Rorschach technique. It was subsequently renamed the *Journal of Projective Techniques and Personality Assessment* and is currently known as the *Journal of Personality Assessment*. Serving as the official journal of the Society for Personality Assessment, this journal continues to publish research on projective techniques in general and the Rorschach in particular.

Zygmunt Piotrowski received his doctorate in 1927, having been trained in the European experimental tradition in Poland. Several years later, while involved in postdoctoral work at Columbia University, Piotrowski participated in Klopfer's seminars on the Rorschach and became interested in how neurologically impaired patients respond to the ambiguity of the inkblots. During the 1940s Piotrowski gradually drifted away from the Klopfer and Beck Systems and created his own scoring and interpretive approach. He emphasized the use of signs, which are single characteristics (formal or content) used by the examiner to draw certain clinical conclusions. In his popular text *Percept Analysis* (Piotrowski, 1957), Piotrowski expounded on the intricacies of his scoring system. Some years later, he developed a computerized scoring method based on some 1,000 rules, referred to as the Piotrowski Automated Rorschach.

The fifth major Rorschach system was developed by David Rapaport during his many years at the Menninger Foundation in Topeka, Kansas. Since Rapaport had a keen interest in psychoanalytic theory and particularly psychopathological thinking, clinical data obtained from Rorschach responses provided a useful tool in his clinical work and research. The results of a collaborate research project on the Rorschach were subsequently described in an influential book entitled *Diagnostic Psychological Testing* (Rapaport, Gill, & Schafer, 1946, 1968). Rapaport's system, which deviated from the other four well-established Rorschach systems and adopted a psychoanalytic approach, attracted many adherents at the time. Rapaport's approach did not have a dramatic impact, but his colleague Roy Schafer was quite influential in keeping the approach alive for many years.

As this brief history indicates, the development of the Rorschach was not very consistent or uniform. By the mid-1950s five Rorschach systems were in use, and debate among the major innovators became rather heated. At times, it appeared that the Rorschach itself was in the midst of a family feud. Nevertheless, the inkblot test survived the internal struggles of its proponents, as well as many criticisms and attacks from opponents.

For three decades following publication of *Psychodiagnostik* (Rorschach, 1921), several trends became evident in clinical psychology in the United States. The spirit of the times in clinical psychology and psychiatry was strongly psychoanalytic. Due to the projective nature of the inkblots, clinicians and researchers found in the Rorschach a measurement tool for the study of unconscious processes and responses which could be interpreted in Freudian terms. Furthermore, the role of the clinician during this time was largely that of a diagnostician, and psychologists were hard pressed to find sound diagnostic tests or instruments. There was dissatisfaction with objective (paper-and-pencil) tests in the evolving special area of clinical psychology, and the inkblot method was intriguing and captured the imagination of many clinicians. The Rorschach stimulated much theoretical speculation and diagnostic insight, and it appeared to be a rational approach to understanding the workings of the human mind.

Despite these strong influences that seemed to sway opinion in favor of the Rorschach, the technique had a number of drawbacks. One of these was the lack of a standard system for evaluating interpretations and theoretical suppositions. In fact, all five Rorschach systems had idiosyncrasies of their own and were for all practical purposes five distinct methods. Moreover, the five systems were not based on any one systematic theory. The Rorschach survived for several decades in this precarious state until the mid-1970s and the systematic efforts of John Exner.

Popularity of the Rorschach

Despite the seemingly equivocal status of the Rorschach in clinical circles, it has withstood the attacks of critics (some of which have been justified) for over a half century. The earliest research paper on the Rorschach cited in PsycINFO was published in 1925 (Loepfe, 1925), but no papers on the technique were published in 1926, and only three in 1927. As Figure 11–2 illustrate, however, research on the Rorschach then gathered momentum. As demonstrated by the number of research citations in PsycINFO and other abstract and index services, the Rorschach is not as popular as it was in the 1950s and 1960s (see Figure 11–2).

FIG. 11–2   **Frequency of Citations of Rorschach Inkblot Test and Thematic Apperception Test in PsycINFO by 10-Year Interval.**

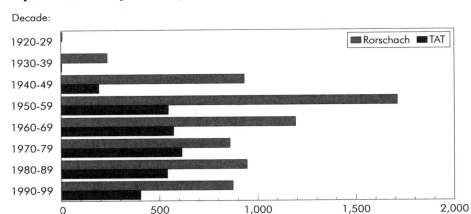

However, it remains a widely administered instrument in both academic and clinical settings.

In recent surveys of psychological practitioners (e. g., Watkins, Campbell, Nieberding, & Hallmark, 1995; Frauenhoffer, Ross, Gfeller, Searight, & Piotrowski, 1998), the Rorschach placed fifth or sixth among all tests in frequency of usage by clinical psychologists. It is also fifth in order of frequency among personality tests cited in *Tests in Print IV* (Murphy, Conoley, & Impara, 1994). Because of the changing nature of clinical psychology, with less emphasis on in-depth, psychodynamic assessment, in addition to the publication of competing assessment psychodiagnostic instruments, research and clinical use of the Rorschach have declined since the 1960s. Still, it remains one of the foremost assessment tools of practicing clinical psychologists.

In summary, the Rorschach technique has been dethroned from its previous high status, but it is still considered a worthwhile tool in the hands of highly trained psychodiagnostic clinicians. Since the introduction of Exner's work in the mid-1970s, renewed interest has occurred among adherents to the Rorschach and increased respect has been observed among many opponents of projective testing.

■ Five Major Systems and Content Analysis

By the late 1950s there were five distinct Rorschach systems, as well as many varied approaches differing in their administrative, scoring, and interpretive features. This state of affairs led to much disagreement among proponents of the major systems, and critics were quick to seize the opportunity to refer to the chaos and disunity as unscientific. Surprisingly, the Beck, Klopfer, Hertz, Piotrowski, and Rapaport-Schafer systems survived side-by-side with little consensus among them, each system having a unique approach to the Rorschach inkblots.

Beck's System

The approach of Samuel Beck, a dedicated follower of Hermann Rorschach, was highly empirical and experimental. But Beck welcomed evidence from clinically validated data. He emphasized standardized procedures and in many ways viewed his approach as a "continuing experiment in perception," with an emphasis on objectivity (Beck, 1944). At the same time, Beck was criticized for not providing enough information on the nature of the clinical population and procedures by which his samples had been selected.

Klopfer's System

Probably due to the influence of his European training, Bruno Klopfer's approach was based largely on phenomenology and as such contrasted with a behavioral-empiricistic perspective. His methodology involved little statistical analysis but emphasized the subjective, experiential view of the examiner. Klopfer's qualitative approach was obviously at odds with the scientific-empirical traditional evident in the United States. He developed a rather elaborate scoring system, but was criticized for his subjective, unsystematic guidelines.

Hertz's System

The system proposed by Marguerite Hertz followed the tenets originally prescribed by Rorschach and was consistent with the empirical-statistical emphasis prevalent in American psychology. Originally, Hertz sided with Beck's objective approach, but later developed her own method with a focus on standardization.

Rapaport-Schafer System

The popularity of this system is probably attributable to the fact that it is heavily slanted toward psychoanalytic theory. In addition, *Diagnostic Psychological Testing* (Rapaport, Gill, & Schafer, 1946) and *Psychoanalytic Interpretation in Rorschach Testing* (Schafer, 1954) proved to be popular references and textbooks in psychodiagnostic training. But because of its strong psychoanalytic emphasis and unacceptability to behavioral-empiricists, the Rapaport-Schafer system had few adherents and was never formalized into a true major system.

Piotrowski's System

Of the five major Rorschach systems, the final one was developed by Zygmunt Piotrowski. Piotrowski's system was based on clinical observation and the application of a sign approach to diagnostic formulations (Piotrowski, 1957). One of his adaptations, which was far removed from Rorschach's original work, was concerned with the meaning and importance of the *movement response*. Although clinicians were attracted to some of Piotrowski's ideas regarding the inkblots, his system has had few adherents and the approach is rarely used today.

Content Analysis

A rather novel alternative method of scoring Rorschach responses is the focus on *content* rather than on structural variables and formal percept analysis, that is, an emphasis on *what* is perceived as opposed to *where* and *how*. The focus on *content analysis* and its relationship to the psychological characteristics of the individual is clinical in nature, in that interpretations are based on the attributed meaning of responses for an individual. Aronow, Reznikoff, and Moreland (1994, 1995), for example, treat the Rorschach as a standardized clinical interview that provides a sample of the examinee's perceptual operations. But rather than relying on methods of scoring according to content, which they consider too undependable for diagnostic purposes, Aronow et al. (1995) concentrate on the impressionistic analysis of idiosyncratic responses to the Rorschach cards. Following principles derived from psychodynamic theories of personality, they interpret as significant in understanding the individual such things as responses that are uncommon or deviate markedly from the actual stimulus properties of the blot. Relationships between particular responses and their clinical significance are, however, difficult to substantiate even within the context of a person's own experience.

Clinicians and researchers have also developed numerous scoring methods based on developmental level, hostility, anxiety, and body image, in addition to signs or indicators of homosexuality, suicide ideation, neurotic tendencies, and schizophrenia (see Goldfried, Stricker, & Weiner, 1971). For example, hostility responses may include animals fighting, a killed animal, an angry face, people arguing, a squashed bug, or a wolf devouring its prey. The content approach to Rorschach analysis is employed largely in conjunction with one of the major systems. However, many clinicians use the content approach as an adjunct to interviewing when conducting a clinical assessment of an individual.

Another alternative approach to the Rorschach is Lerner's (1991) psychoanalytically-based system. This approach focuses on the responses as providing a window to the examinee's internal world and a means of assessing such psychodynamic constructs as object representations and defensive maneuvers. Also of interest is a variation known as the *consensus Rorschach* (Blanchard, 1968; Cutter & Farberow, 1970) for analyzing interpersonal relationships and other social behaviors. In this technique, the blots are interpreted jointly by small natural groups of people, such as married couples or members of juvenile gangs. Group members are told to discuss their perceptions and thoughts pertaining to each blot and to achieve consensus on a set of responses.

■ Exner's Comprehensive System

Quite early it became apparent that clinicians and academicians were using the Rorschach in unstandardized ways, and even those who espoused one of the major Rorschach systems personalized the administration, scoring and interpretation of the test. A survey of college professors conducted during the 1960s found that Rorschach courses were frequently being taught by inexperienced, unmotivated faculty members. In fact, few instructors had any clinical experience at all with the technique (Jackson & Wohl, 1966). Subsequent investigations in academic settings found that junior faculty members, who were often inexperienced and uninterested in the Rorschach, were assigned to teach courses on projective techniques.* With such poor role models, it is not surprising that exposure to the Rorschach was rather cursory and that instruction in the various systems was inadequate. Over several decades, this superficial indoctrination of students, coupled with a lack of cohesiveness among Rorschach's followers, led to gross misuse and improper adaptations of the technique. Exner and Exner (1972) found that the majority of clinicians were using idiosyncratic methods of scoring the Rorschach and actually combining features of the major systems. It was obvious that someone with patience, fortitude, and ability was needed to bring order out of the chaos.

In 1974, after many years of painstaking work, John Exner introduced the *Comprehensive System* to the Rorschach community. According to Exner, even in the 1960s none of the Rorschach systematizers was reconciled to synthesis or compromise. A project was undertaken to examine each system carefully and select from it those features that yielded valid and substantive data. Exner found

---

* Contrasting markedly with this situation is the recommendation of Hilsenroth and Handler (1995) that two full-semester courses devoted exclusively to the Rorschach be required to attain competence in administering, scoring, and interpreting it.

many disparities among the systems, even with respect to such fundamental issues as seating arrangement and instructions for administration. Furthermore,

> differences in scoring led to many differences concerning interpretation. They differed significantly about which scores should be calculated in a quantitative summary of the record and what relationships between scores would be important to interpretation. They differed concerning the meaningfulness of many variables and which configurations of variables might be interpretively important. In spite of their substantial differences, several interpretive postulates appeared in each of the Systems that were the same or similar. For the most part these were drawn from Rorschach's original work, but to the casual observer that common thread could easily convey the impression that the Systems were much more similar than was actually the case. Major differences existed across the Systems on issues about which Rorschach was not definitive or had offered no procedures or postulates. (Exner, 1993, p. 19)

Exner performed an extensive analysis of the Rorschach literature and selected 700 research reports that he considered to be methodologically sound. This collection served as a data base from which various elements of each of the five systems could be carefully studied, and the features from all the systems that could be empirically validated were subsequently integrated. Thus, the Comprehensive System represents a combination of the psychometrically credible aspects of all the major Rorschach systematizers.

Administration Procedures in the Comprehensive System

The seating arrangement is usually side-by-side, and after a brief introduction concerning the purpose of the test the examiner hands Card I to the examinee and asks: "What might this be?" If the examinee gives only one response to Card I, the examiner may prompt him or her with "If you take your time and look some more, I think that you will find something else too." No further prompting is encouraged and if questions arise, the examiner answers in a neutral and judicious manner. Responses to all ten inkblots are recorded verbatim during this association phase; the position in which the examinee holds the card is also noted. An *inquiry phase* is conducted after responses to all ten inkblots have been obtained. The intent of the inquiry is to obtain sufficient information to score each response accurately, that is, what was perceived that formed the subject's response? Exner (1993) recommends that the examiner introduce the inquiry with:

> O.K., we've done them all. Now we are going to go back through them. It won't take long. I want you to help me see what you saw. I'm going to read what you said, and then I want you to show me where on the blot you saw it and what there is there that makes it look like that, so that I can see it too. I'd like to see it just like you did, so help me now. Do you understand? (p. 75)

Information obtained from the inquiry should permit scoring and coding of all responses according to location (where on the blot the percept was seen), determinant (what made it look or appear like that), and content (what it actually represents). Responses are also noted on the location sheet, a one-page chart with miniature versions of all ten inkblots; the examinee's responses to each inkblot are outlined on this sheet.

Scoring in the Comprehensive System

Location. The first scoring category is *location*, that is, the area or part of the blot used by the examinee or with which each response is associated. If the entire blot is involved, it is scored as a whole response and designated by the symbol W. Responses to major segments of the blot are scored D (common detail), or Dd (uncommon detail), depending on the frequency with which a normative group used the area in responding. The notation for any white space area used in the response is WS, DS, or DdS, depending on the area of the percept. Location responses are then scored for degree of organization or differentiation, such as v (vague response) denoting a diffuse impression of the percept without an attribution to structural features.

Determinants. In the second scoring category, *determinants*, the examiner notes the features or characteristics of each inkblot that contributed to the response process. Those features encompass three major classifications: form and movement, color, and shading. According to Exner (1993), the symbols and criteria selected for determinant scoring in the Comprehensive System involve 24 symbols representing nine categories. These symbols and the associated criteria are given in Table 11–1.

The form (F) response describes the perceived object, based on its form features. For example, on Card IV the examinee may attribute seeing a "giant monster" to "there's the head with its arms and legs here, the center forms the body." Clearly, form characteristics have determined this percept. According to Exner, form features are the most frequently used determinant category and are included in about 95% of the total responses.

Some empirical evidence has supported the notion that the three types of movement responses (human, animal, inanimate) actually reflect different psychological processes. The symbol M denotes human activity, both active and passive movement; examples are "two Indians fighting" or "a girl sitting and thinking." Animal movement is denoted by FM, such as "a bat flying." However, if animals are involved in human-type activities such as "two elephants laughing," the percept should be scored M. The symbol m denotes nonhuman/animal motion; some common responses include rocks falling, explosions, and objects floating. All

TAB. 11-1 Symbols and Criteria for Determinant Coding.

- ■ **Form [F].** To be used separately for responses based exclusively on form features of the blot, or in combination with other determinant symbols (*except* **M** and **m**) when the form features have contributed to the formulation of the answer.
- ■ **Human movement [M].** To be used for responses involving the kinesthetic activity of a human, or of an animal or fictional character in human-like activity.
- ■ **Animal movement [FM].** To be used for responses involving a kinesthetic activity of an animal. The movement perceived must be congruent to the species identified in the content. Animals reported in movement not common to their species should be coded as *M*.
- ■ **Inanimate movement [m].** To be used for responses involving the movement of inanimate, inorganic, or insensate objects.
- ■ **Pure color [C].** To be used for answers based exclusively on the chromatic color features of the blot. *No* form is involved.
- ■ **Color-form [CF].** To be used for answers that are formulated primarily because of the chromatic color features of the blot. Form features are used, but are of secondary importance.
- ■ **Form-color (FC).** To be used for answers that are created mainly because of form features. Chromatic color is also used, but is of secondary importance.
- ■ **Color naming [Cn].** To be used when the colors of the blot or blot areas are identified by *name*, with the intention of giving a response.
- ■ **Pure achromatic color [C'].** To be used when the response is based exclusively on the gray, black or white features of the blot, when they are clearly used as color. *No* form is involved.
- ■ **Achromatic color-form [C'F].** To be used for responses that are formulated *mainly* because of the black, white, or gray features, clearly used as color. Form features *are* used, but are of secondary importance.
- ■ **Form-achromatic color [FC'].** To be used for answers that are based *mainly* on the form features. The achromatic features, clearly used as color, are also included, but are of secondary importance.
- ■ **Pure texture [T].** To be used for answers in which the shading components of the blot are translated to represent a tactual phenomenon, with no consideration to the form features.
- ■ **Texture-form [TF].** To be used for responses in which the shading features of the blot are interpreted as tactual, and form is used secondarily, for purposes of elaboration and/or clarification.
- ■ **Form-texture [FT].** To be used for responses that are based *mainly* on the form features. Shading features of the blot are translated as tactual, but are of secondary importance.
- ■ **Pure vista [V].** To be used for answers in which the shading features are interpreted as depth or dimensionality. No form is involved.
- ■ **Vista-form [VF].** To be used for responses in which the shading features are interpreted as depth or dimensionality. Form features are included, but are of secondary importance.

Table 11–1 continued

- **Form-vista [FV]**. To be used for answers that are based *mainly* on the form features of the blot. Shading features are also interpreted to note depth and/or dimensionality, but are of secondary importance to the formulation of the answer.
- **Pure shading [Y]**. To be used for responses that are based exclusively on the light-dark features of the blot that are completely formless and do not involve reference to either texture or dimension.
- **Shading-form [YF]**. To be used for responses based primarily on the light-dark features of the blot. Form features are included, but are of secondary importance.
- **Form-shading [FY]**. To be used for responses that are based *mainly* on the form features of the blot. The light-dark features of the blot are included as elaboration and/or clarification and are secondary to the use of form.
- **Form based dimension [FD]**. To be used for answers in which the impression of depth, distance, or dimensionality is created by using the elements of size and/or shape of contours. No use of shading is involved in creating this impression.
- **Pair [(2)]**. To be used for answers in which two identical objects are reported, based on the symmetry of the blot. The objects must be equivalent in all respects, but must *not* be identified as being reflected or as mirror images.
- **Reflection-form [rF]**. To be used for answers in which the blot or blot area is reported as a reflection or mirror image, because of the symmetry of the blot. The object or content reported has no specific form requirements, as in clouds, landscape, shadows, etc.
- **Form-reflection [Fr]**. To be used for answer in which the blot or blot area is identified as reflected or a mirror image, based on the symmetry of the blot. The substance of the response is based on form features, and the object report has a specific form demand.

Adapted with permission from Exner, 1993, pp. 104–105.

movement responses are also labeled as either *active* or *passive*, although there is disagreement on the precise criteria for various response (see Exner, 1993, pp. 106–113).

Chromatic color responses (C, CF, FC) are indicated when the percept involves the spectrum of hues other than black, white, or gray. At times, these classifications are difficult and the examiner must determine whether the primary criterion for the percept is color-form (CF), form-color (FC), or color alone (C). The response "sun" followed by "it's all yellow and the rays are shining outward, plus there's some sunspots" would be coded CF. The primary emphasis is on color with some secondary form features. Obviously, at times it is difficult to determine whether color is primary, secondary, or the sole characteristic of a percept; however, a thorough inquiry should facilitate the decision. *Achromatic color* determinants, which were discussed initially by Klopfer and Kelley (1942) are responses in which gray, black, and white parts of the inkblot are used as color and represented by *C'*, *C'F*, or *F'C*. The response "a black bat" to Card V denotes the use of achromatic color as a secondary features and is therefore scored *F'C*. A critical factor for both the chromatic and achromatic color responses is whether form is primary or secondary for clarification or elaboration of the percept or not involved at all in the percept.

The *texture* determinant represents tactual features such as furry, rough, grainy, and silky. A response of actually rubbing the color confirms either a pure texture (*T*), texture-form (*TF*), or form-texture (*FT*) response. Although a pure texture response is rare, a *TF* response such as "some fur" is quite common. In short, a *TF* response should indicate shaded features as texture with elaboration based on form characteristics. Conversely, an *FT* response primarily involves form with texture as secondary. Many of the common animal skin responses to Card VI are coded *FT*.

The use of the light-dark features of the inkblots usually indicates a *shading* determinant. The shading response could include variations in hue or a diffusion of light-dark tones. *FY* refers to percepts that are based primarily on form with shading features used for elaboration, such as "a light from a lighthouse with some dark and light areas." Shading-form (*YF*) and pure shading (*Y*) responses occur infrequently. Shading determinants have been one of the most unsettled and controversial aspects of Rorschach testing, involving various methods of coding from all five major systems. Responses that use shading with a percept of depth or dimension are coded as vista-form (*VF*), form-vista (*FV*), or pure vista (*V*). These shading dimension responses usually signify depth or contour in the percept.

Several determinants specific to the Comprehensive System have been incorporated into the scoring in recent years; they are referred to as form-dimension and pairs and reflections (see Table 11–1). In addition, three other elements— blend, organizational activity, and form quality – have critical significance in the Rorschach record and should be evaluated carefully. A *blend* response occurs when more than one determinant is attributed to a percept. Exner (1993) states that approximately 20% of the responses in a given protocol are scored as blends and that each response to a percept must be scored separately. The response "rows of trees on both sides of a mountain" qualifies as a blend response. *Organizational activity* (*Z*) refers to responses that integrate two or more detail areas in a meaningful, organized fashion. Form must always be involved in the percept, for example, "two elephants dancing around a drum trying to push each other away." *Z* scores reveal the level of cognitive activity and possibly the individual's intellectual efficiency. Third, *form quality* is the level of perceptual accuracy or "goodness of fit" of each response in the protocol. In other words, does the examinee's use of form correspond well with the actual inkblot percept? Whereas most of previous Rorschach systems used "good form/poor form," the Comprehensive System involves a four-category coding system that permits

Symbols and Criteria Used in Scoring for Content. **TAB. 11–2**

- **Whole human [H].** Whole human form. If the percept involves real historical figures, such as Napoleon, Joan of Arc, etc., the content coded *Ay* should be added as a secondary code.
- **Whole human (fictional or mythological) [(H)].** Whole human form that is fictional or mythological, such as clowns, fairies, giants, witches, fairy tale characters, ghosts, dwarfs, devils, angels, science fictional creatures that are humanoid, human-like monsters.
- **Human detail [Hd].** Incomplete human form, such as an arm, leg, fingers, feet, the lower part of a person, a person without a head.
- **Human detail (fictional or mythological) [(Hd)].** Incomplete human form that is fictional or mythological such as the head of the devil, the arm of a witch, the eyes of an angel, parts of science-fiction creatures that are humanoid, and all masks.
- **Human experience [Hx].** Human emotion or sensory experience such as love, hate, depression, happiness, sound, smell, fear, etc. Most answers in which **Hx** is coded will also include the use of **AB** as a special score.
- **Whole animal [A].** Whole animal form.
- **Whole animal (fictional or mythological [(A)].** A whole animal that is fictional or mythological such as a unicorn, dragon, magic frog, flying horse, Black Beauty, Jonathan Livingston Seagull.
- **Animal detail [Ad].** An incomplete animal form such as the hoof of a horse, claw of a lobster, head of a dog, animal skin.
- **Animal detail (fictional or mythological) [(Ad)].** An incomplete animal form that is fictional or mythological such as the wing of Pegasus, the head of Peter Rabbit, the leg of Pooh Bear.
- **Anatomy [An].** Skeletal, muscular, or internal anatomy such as bone structure, rib cage, heart, lungs, stomach, liver, muscle fiber, vertebrae, brain. If the response involves a tissue slide, the code **Art** should be added as secondary.
- **Art [Art].** Paintings, drawings, or illustrations, either abstract or definitive, art objects such as statues, jewelry, chandelier, candelabra, crests, badges, seals, and decorations.
- **Anthropology [Ay].** Objects with a specific cultural or historical connotation such as a totem, Roman helmet, Magna Carta, Santa Maria, Napoleon's hat, Cleopatra's crown, arrowhead, prehistoric axe.
- **Blood [Bl].** Blood, either human or animal.
- **Botany [Bt].** Any plant life such as bushes, flowers, seaweed, trees, or parts of plant life such as leaves, petals, tree trunk, roots.
- **Clothing [Cg].** Any article of clothing such as hat, boots, belt, necktie, jacket, trousers, scarf.
- **Clouds [Cl].** Used specifically for the content cloud. Variations of this category, such as fog or mist are coded *Na*.
- **Explosion [Ex].** A blast or explosion, including fireworks.
- **Fire [Fi].** Fire or smoke.
- **Food [Fd].** Any edible such as fried chicken, ice cream, fried shrimp, vegetables, cotton candy, chewing gum, steak, a filet of fish.
- **Geography [Ge].** A map, specified or unspecified.

Table 11–2 continued

■ **Household [Hh].** Household items such as bed, chair, lamp, silverware, plate, cup, glass, cooking utensil, carving knife, lawn chair, garden hose, rug (excluding animal skin rug, which is coded **Ad**).

■ **Landscape [Ls].** Landscape such as mountain, mountain range, hill, island, cave, rocks, desert, swamp, or seascapes such as coral reef or underwater scene.

■ **Nature [Na].** Used for a broad variety of contents from the natural environment, that are not coded as **Bt** or **Ls** such as sun, moon, planet, sky, water, ocean, river, ice, snow, rain, fog, mist, rainbow, storm, tornado, night, raindrop.

■ **Science [Sc].** Percepts that are associated with, or are the products of science or science fiction such as microscope, telescope, weapons, rocket ships, motors, space ships, ray guns, airplane, ship, train, car, motorcycle, light bulb, TV aerial, radar station.

■ **Sex [Sx].** Sex organs or activity of a sexual nature such as penis, vagina, buttocks, breast (except if used to delineate a female figure), testes, menstruation, abortion, intercourse. **Sx** is usually scored as a secondary content. Primary contents are typically **H, Hd,** or **An**.

■ **X-ray [Xy].** Used specifically for the content of X-ray and may include either skeletal or organs. When **Xy** is coded, **An** is not included as a secondary code.

Adapted with permission from Exner, 1993, pp. 158–159.

differentiation of form quality. The four categories are: superior-elaborated (+), ordinary (o), unusual (u), and minus (–).

Content. The third scoring category is the coding of response content. Originally, Rorschach included only six distinct scoring categories for content: human, human detail, animal, animal detail, landscape, and inanimate objects. To permit finer discriminations of responses, Exner selected a list of 26 categories for the scoring of content. Table 11–2 summarizes the criteria for each of the content categories used in the Comprehensive System.

Popular responses are common percepts given quite frequently by normative samples. Exner (1993) reports that in a sample of 7,500 protocols, 13 popular responses were produced at least 2,500 times. The criteria for these responses, which are based on the frequency of occurrence of at least once in every three protocols of nonpatient adults and nonschizophrenic adult patients, are given in Table 11–3.

Because of their peculiar nature, some responses require a *special score*. The current version of the Comprehensive System includes 14 special scores, which, with subdivisions, comprise 18 categories. Six of the basic 14 special scores deal with unusual verbalizations: *deviant verbalizations* (*DV* and *DR*), *inappropriate combinations* (*INCOM, FABCOM, CONTAM*), and *inappropriate logic*

| **Popular Responses in the Comprehensive System.** | **TAB. 11–3** |

Card I.	Bat or butterfly; always involves the whole blot.
Card II.	Animal forms, usually heads of dogs, bears, elephants, or lambs.
Card III.	Two human figures, or representations thereof, such as dolls and caricatures.
Card IV.	Human or human-like figure such as a giant, monster, science fiction creature, etc.
Card V.	Butterfly or bat, including the whole blot; the apex of the card upright or inverted.
Card VI.	Animal skin, hide, rug, or pelt.
Card VII.	Human head or face, specifically identified as female, child, Indian, or with gender not identified.
Card VIII.	Whole animal figure. The content varies considerably, such as a bear, dog, rodent, fox, wolf, and coyote.
Card IX.	Human or human-like figures such as witches, giants, science fiction creatures, monsters, etc.
Card X.	Spider or crab with all appendages restricted to a specified area (D1). Other variations of multilegged animals are not coded as **P** (popular responses).

Adapted with permission from Exner, 1993, p. 162.

(*ALOG*). Responses scored as unusual verbalizations typically signal the presence of cognitive disarray or a thought disorder. Two other categories are for perseverations and integration failure (confabulation). *Perseveration (PSV)* occurs when redundant responses are given to the same percept or to a number of inkblot cards throughout the protocol. *Confabulation (CONFAB)* occurs when the examinee generalizes a response from one detail of the blot to a larger area or to the entire blot. Both perseverations and confabulations are cognitive distortions that usually indicate the presence of psychopathology. Another group of three special scores involve special characteristics of content: *aggressive movement (AG), cooperative movement (COP), morbid content (MOR)*. A final group of three special scores—*abstractions (AB), personalized answers (PER), color projection (CP)*—involve responses that are reflective of defensive psychological activity.

Structural Summary

The *structural summary* includes Rorschach elements such as location features, determinants, form quality, contents, organizational activity, populars, pairs and reflections, and special scoring. Various ratios, percentages, and derivations are computed and listed in the seven sections of the structural summary (see Table 11–4). In addition, several special indices, including *Schizophrenic Index (SCZI)*,

TAB. 11–4   Ratios, Percentages, and Derivations Listed in the Structural Summary.

Core Section: *Lambda, Erlebnistypus (EB), Experience Actual (EA), EB Pervasive (EBPer), Experience Base (eb), Experienced Stimulation (es), The D Score (D), Adjusted es (Adj es), Adjusted D Score (Adj D)*

Ideation Section: *Active:Passive Ratio (a:p), M Active:Passive Ratio (M^a:M^p), The Intellectualization Index—2AB + (Art + Ay)*

Affect Section: *Form-Color Ratio (FC:CF + C), Affective Ratio (Afr), Complexity Index (Blends:R)*

Mediation Section: *Conventional Form (X+%), Conventional Pure Form (F+%), Distorted Form (X–%), White Space Distortion (S–%), Unusual Form (Xu%)*

Processing Section: *Economy Index (W:D:Dd), Aspirational Ratio (W:M), Processing Efficiency (Zd)*

Interpersonal Section: *Isolation Index (Isolate/R), Interpersonal Interest—(HH) + Hd + (Hd), (H) + (Hd):(A) + (Ad), H + A:Hd + Ad*

Self-Perception Section: *Egocentricity Index (3r + (2)/R)*

From Exner, 1993, pp. 183–188.

Depression Index (DEPI), Coping Deficit Index (CDI), Suicide Constellation (S-CON), Hypervigilance Index (HVI), and *Obsessive Style Index (OBS)* may be computed.

For an in-depth discussion of the structural summary computations listed in Table 11–4, the reader should refer to Exner (1993, pp. 175–190). Another useful source is chapter 9 of Groth-Marnat (1997). Among these ratios, percentages, and derivations, of particular importance is the *experience balance* or *erlebnistypus (EB)*. EB, computed as the ratio of all human movement (M) responses to the weighted sum of the chromatic color responses (.5FC + CF + 1.5C), reflects a preferential response style referred to as *introversive* and *extratensive;* high EBs are introversive, and low EBs are extratensive. *Introversive* designates a person who utilizes inner resources for basic gratification, whereas an *extratensive* individual is more likely to allow emotion to permeate his or her life experiences. Introversive individuals tend to subdue their feelings when involved in cognitive tasks such as decision-making, but the cognitive activities of extratensive persons are more likely to be affected by their feelings and emotions.

Another index, the *form-color ratio* [FC:(CF + C)], denotes the balance or modulation of affect. A higher number on the *color* side of the ratio suggests heightened emotional experiences and possibly impulsiveness. Related to this proportion is the *affective ratio* (*Afr*), which compares response frequency between the last three inkblots, which contain a variety of colors, and the first seven blots. The *Afr* indicates an individual's receptivity to emotionally charged stimulation. *Lambda* (*L*) refers to the judicious use of rational resources, and compares the frequency of all pure form (*F*) responses with all other responses in a record. A very high *Lambda* points to a pragmatic, somewhat conventional approach to the environment.

Interpreting Rorschach Responses

As in other methods of personality assessment, formulating interpretive conclusions from Rorschach data is an arduous process. Sound knowledge and extensive experience in personality theory and psychopathology are required, and clinical data from other assessment sources must be considered before worthwhile conclusions regarding the functioning of an individual's personality can be drawn. Exner (1993) emphasizes that in Rorschach assessment all aspects of the structural summary—accuracy in scoring, verbalizations, and content of response sequence—must be evaluated together to form "working hypotheses" and interpretive postulates. Only through a "global" approach can valid data be interpreted to provide a meaningful psychological portrait of a unique person.

Several critical areas of personality functioning are paramount in attempting to understand and describe a person's psychological processes,. For example, does a person use cognitive/intellectual resources or emotional reactivity in dealing with the demands of the real world? How does a person select an active or passive coping strategy? What defensive styles are used in times of stress? Can the person maintain a rational approach during the process of decision making? Is the person self-focused, task-oriented, conventional, or so unique that the consequence is extreme anxiety and interpersonal conflict? Does the person have an inclination toward depressive symptoms, psychopathic acting-out, or schizophrenic ideation?

An intensive and comprehensive appraisal of an individual's Rorschach performance can provide promising clues in attempting to answer the above questions. A synthesis of all Rorschach data should yield a number of preliminary hypotheses, and, when integrated with other clinical information, provide a systematic framework for understanding personality functioning.

■ Computer-Based Scoring and Interpretation

Piotrowski's CPR

Zygmunt Piotrowski (1964) developed the first computer-based scoring and interpretation system, the Piotrowski Automated Rorschach (PAR), for this test. Based on clinical observations, Piotrowski provided about 1,000 descriptive personality statements. These interpretive comments and statements focused on problem-solving strategies, cognitive abilities, and interpersonal effectiveness. Later, the name of this computer-interpretive program was changed to Computerized Perceptanalytic Rorschach (CPR). In applying the procedure, interpretive statements were matched to all Rorschach responses. Unfortunately, Piotrowski offered no standardization or normative data and no documentation pertaining to the validity of the statements. Because of the idiographic approach favored by Piotrowski, the CPR was criticized for its disregard of psychometric criteria and has few proponents today.

Miller's and Perline's Programs

Other attempts have been made to take advantage of the speed and flexibility of computers in Rorschach administration, scoring, and interpretation. For example, Franklin Miller (1986) developed an online computer-assisted interview program for Rorschach administration that was designed to bring some standardization to the test setting. With the advent of this program, interactive computer administration of the Rorschach appeared to have a promising future.

A Computer Interpreted Rorschach program, developed by Irvin H. Perline, became commercially available in 1979 from Century Diagnostics. In using this program, which is based on the Klopfer system, the clinician tallies Rorschach scores on a tabulation sheet and mails them to Century Diagnostics for interpretation.* Percentages and ratios are calculated by the computer and recorded in the Data Summary. The Interpretive Analysis, which is atheoretical, yields interpretive statements based on research with the Rorschach. A Keyword Summary quantifying the occurrence of ego strength and six areas of pathological functioning, in addition to a Narrative Summary, is contained in the report.

The Exner Report

Another computer-based Rorschach interpretation program was developed for Exner's Comprehensive System at the Rorschach Research Foundation in New

---

* Address: Century Diagnostics, 2101 E. Broadway, Suite 22, Tempe, AZ 85282.

York. The program follows a logical progression of decision-tree rules yielding a composite of findings that lead to interpretive hypotheses. A scoring and interpretation service for the Rorschach Comprehensive System was made commercially available by National Computer Systems in 1983. Computer software for the most recent version of the Rorschach Interpretation Assistance Program (RIAP3 Plus) is provided by The Psychological Corporation and Psychological Assessment Resources. Scoring of Rorschach responses prior to interpretation may be facilitated by use of Exner's Rorschach Scoring Program Version 3(RSP3), also available from The Psychological Corporation and Psychological Assessment Resources.

RIAP3 Plus calculates a Structural Summary, scanning all the structural data included in the test, by considering over 30 critical clusters derived from several hundred scores and derivations of scores. Two categories are represented by the clusters: those related to the examinee's basic personality characteristics (e. g., coping styles, emotional controls, self-esteem, stress tolerance, and perceptual accuracy), and those dealing with psychopathology (e. g., depression proneness, schizophrenia, stress reaction, suicide potential).

A synopsis of a typical computer printout for the Exner Report is shown in Report 11–1. The report consists of a series of interpretive narrative statements, suggesting hypotheses concerning the personality and behavioral tendencies of the patient.

Because scoring, organizing, and interpreting Rorschach data are time consuming activities, a computer program that assists in scanning a large pool of variables and combinations of derived scores can be an asset in terms of speed and reliability of computations. As with the Century Diagnostics program, validity and outcome studies are needed to enable clinicians to evaluate the usefulness and credibility of Exner's RIAP3 Plus program.

Illustrative Synopsis of a Rorschach Interpretation Assistance Program Report

REPORT 11–1

Client: John Jones *Gender*: Male *Date of Birth*: 11/12/59
Age: 35 *Education*: 16 *Marital Status*: Married *Test Date*: 8/10/95

Ideation
His protocol contains many features similar to those found among schizophrenics. It appears likely that his thinking is seriously disturbed. He lacks a marked stylistic approach to decision making or problem solving. Apparently, he does not react very much to subtle ideational stimuli, that is, those not in the focus of attention, as is common in people. He tends to react hastily to demands created by such stimuli.

Report 11–1 continued

Cognitive Mediation
He has some chronic and pervasive problems that promote perceptual inaccuracy and/or mediational distortion. His peculiarities in thinking often lead to considerable perceptual inaccuracy which, in turn, creates an impairment in reality testing.

Information Processing
He is hypervigilant, investing considerable energy to maintain a state of hyperalertness. His processing activity includes an overincorporative style. Some of his processing is not very thorough and seems to reflect a conservative motivation. The quality of his processing generally appears to be similar to that of most others. However, the quality of his processing activity falters significantly at times to an unsophisticated, less mature level. His processing habits tend to be regular and predictable.

Capacity for Control and Tolerance for Stress
This person has a sturdier tolerance for stress and is far less likely to experience problems in control than the average person.

Affect
His emotions are not consistent in the way in which they influence his thinking, problem solving, and decision making behaviors. he has a marked tendency to avoid emotional stimuli. He is very lax about modulating or controlling his emotions. His level of psychological complexity is not unlike that of others of this age who have a similar approach to decision making.

Self Perception
His estimate of his personal worth tends to be more negative than should be the case. He appears to engage in self inspection more often than most people. His self image and/or self value tend to be based largely on imaginary rather than real experience.

Interpersonal Perception and Relations
He has a hypervigilant style, which is a core element of his psychological structure. It is likely that he will manifest many more dependency behaviors than usually is expected. His interest in, and expectations concerning needs for closeness are dissimilar to those of most people. He appears to be as interested in others as much as most people. He is apparently quite insecure about his personal integrity and tends to be overly authoritarian or argumentative when interpersonal situations appear to pose challenges to the self. It is likely that much of his interpersonal behavior will be marked by forcefulness and/or aggressiveness that is usually obvious to the frequent observer.

Report 11-1 continued

General Summary

He has serious problems in thinking and perceptual accuracy. This composite is markedly similar to that found among schizophrenics. The likelihood that a schizophrenic picture has been produced by some alternative condition is remote, but could occur if he is currently suffering from toxicity or is actively psychotic due to some other condition. In that he is also hypervigilant, the schizophrenic, toxic, or psychotic state will be marked by noticeable paranoid features.

He is very lax about controlling his emotional displays. He is not very consistent in his problem solving or decision making behaviors. This lack of consistency makes him less efficient in his everyday life and more prone to make judgmental errors. He tends to regard himself less favorably when he compares himself to others. His conception of himself is not well developed and is probably rather distorted. A hypervigilant style forms a core element of his personality. He uses considerable energy to maintain a state of preparedness. This hyperalert state has its origins in a very negative or mistrusting attitude toward people. He is cautious about interpersonal relations and does not usually anticipate being close to others. He seems to be reasonably interested in people. He probably is more aggressive or forceful than most people in his relations with others.

■ Psychometric Issues and Future Prospects

Inadequate validation is a crucial issue with respect to the majority of personality assessment instruments, and the Rorschach is no exception. Satisfactory validity is especially difficult to achieve when the variables are as complex as those comprising the human mind, including cognitive processes, personality traits, defensive structure, emotional life, and predispositions to behavioral reactivity. To make matters worse, the Rorschach inkblots are not amenable to certain psychometric procedures, for example, determining split-half reliability. Variability in response frequency, unsystematic scoring and administration, and interpreting statements without reference to normative samples are problems that have plagued the Rorschach since its inception. Regardless of such difficulties, it is incumbent upon Rorschach psychodiagnosticians and researchers to verify the psychometric qualities of the test. For many decades, this was difficult to accomplish because of inconsistencies among the five major systems, In fact, reliability and validity studies of the instrument were rare and the findings disappointing.

Reliability

Because the Rorschach is not a homogeneous test in which different cards or items measure the same variable, internal-consistency coefficients computed across cards are not appropriate and generally quite low. One complicating factor in determining reliability and validity is that the total number of responses may vary substantially from person to person. The numbers of responses in different scoring categories (form, color, shading, movement, etc.) are also too small to yield reliable percentages or other stable indices. Furthermore, examinees do not respond independently to different cards; this very interdependence is used by clinicians to assess trends in responses over cards. For these and other reasons, such as temporal changes in examinees, traditional methods of determining reliability (test-retest, parallel-forms, internal consistency) have not proved feasible for the Rorschach and most other projective tests.

Whatever earlier studies may have revealed, some encouraging results have been obtained in a series of investigations of the temporal stability of Rorschach scores (test-retest reliability). In a nonpatient adult sample, correlational analyses of 19 Rorschach variables and elements and directional analyses of five ratios indicated that scores based on the Comprehensive System scoring categories are fairly stable over a three-year interval. Four of the five ratios were consistent in direction over the time span, whereas nine of the 19 variables yielded test-retest correlations greater than .80 (Exner, Armbruster, & Viglione, 1978). These findings are not particularly surprising because preferred response styles are usually fairly crystallized by the time a normal person reaches adulthood.

Response consistency, however, is not yet apparent in the developing child, and findings concerning the temporal stability of children's Rorschach scores have been equivocal. Exner and Weiner (1982) found low to moderate test-retest coefficients over a 24 to 30 month time period in children's Rorschach scores. A subsequent study of fourth graders who were retested after an interval of three weeks yielded test-retest coefficients in the .70 to .80 range for many Rorschach variable and ratios (Thomas, Alinsky, & Exner, 1982). However, longitudinal research on the temporal reliability of Rorschach variables reveals poor score consistency up to age 14 (Exner, Thomas, & Mason, 1985). Perhaps these results are a reflection of inconsistency of response styles, which is expected during the developmental years. Thus the empirical findings seem to suggest that the Comprehensive System's elements and indices are reliable only for adult samples. In regard to the reliability of the Rorschach with other than normal populations, a study by Haller and Exner (1985) obtained promising results in a group of psychiatric patients.

Another approach to determining the reliability of Rorschach scores and interpretations is interscorer or interrater agreement. To what extent do two or more scorers or interpreters of the same protocols agree on the scores assigned and the interpretations made? A decision by the editors of the *Journal of*

Personality Assessment to require at least 80% interscorer agreement on a Rorschach scoring category improved the reliability of published articles involving the Rorschach (Weiner, 1991).

With respect to the basic scoring categories of the Comprehensive System, different scorers show fairly good agreement in the scores assigned to the responses of different examinees (Ames, Learned, Metraux, & Walker, 1974). Interrater agreement percentages from 87% to 99% for form, movement, color, and shading determinants were reported by Exner (1986), and interrater reliabilities averaging .90 for simple responses and .81 for complex responses were reported by DeCato (1994). On the other hand, studies of interscorer agreement in protocol interpretation have not fared so well: In earlier studies, the degree of agreement in interpretations made by expert Rorschach users was found to be around 30% (Datel & Gengerelli, 1955; Lisansky, 1956). The accuracy of predictions of future behavior from Rorschach responses was also not very high, regardless of the degree of experience with the Rorschach (Rogers, Knauss, & Hammond, 1951; Turner, 1966). However, the results of more recent investigations (e. g., Coleman et al., 1993; Stricker & Healey, 1990) have demonstrated that raters can agree on their interpretations of such conditions as thought disorder when using appropriate Rorschach indices as guides.

Validity

As might be expected, the issue of validity has been a thorny one for the Rorschach. At best, the literature points to inconsistent, ambiguous findings concerning validity. However, several studies have obtained evidence of some empirical validity for response frequency, movement perceptions, use of color, and form level. Rorschach content analysis has been more amenable to validity studies, and the findings of certain investigations in this area are encouraging but not uniformly positive (Goldfried, Stricker, & Weiner, 1971; Reznikoff, Aronow, & Rauchway, 1982; Zubin, Eron, & Schumer, 1965). Although Tamkin (1980) obtained little evidence of a relationship between experience balance and measures of introversion and extroversion derived from personality inventories, Hermann Rorschach had originally noted that the two constructs are not necessarily synonymous. And in a longitudinal study of children undergoing residential treatment (Tuber, 1983), Rorschach object relationships and thought organization scores proved to be significant predictors of rehospitalization.

During the past several years interest has been high in validating Exner's Comprehensive System on psychiatric populations. For example, research with antisocial personalities, homosexuals, and depressed patients suggests that the Egocentricity Index is related to self-esteem. One study utilizing the MMPI Ego Strength Scale as a criterion found no relationship between this variable and the

Egocentricity Index on the Rorschach (Barley, Dorr, & Reid, 1985). In addition, scores on the Comprehensive System variables and ratios have been factor analyzed for schizophrenics, depressives, and nonpatient groups. The results reveal distinct personality organizations for the three groups, a finding that supports the discriminatory power of the Comprehensive System variables.

Faking

Related to the question of validity is that of the susceptibility of the Rorschach to faking. Because of the unstructured nature of its stimulus material, the Rorschach has been touted as being highly resistant to faking. Although the findings of some investigations support this assertion (e. g., Exner & Wylie, 1975), mixed results were obtained by Albert, Fox, and Kahn (1980). The latter study involved an analysis of the Rorschach protocols from six individuals in each of four groups: paranoid schizophrenics, uninformed fakers, informed fakers, and normal controls. Evaluation of the protocols by 6–9 judges revealed that both the informed and uninformed fakers did a good job of faking psychotic responses to the Rorschach. A subsequent study conducted by Netter and Viglione (1994) substantiated the conclusion that the Rorschach can be faked. But another study found that the Rorschach responses of patients who were malingering posttraumatic stress disorder were overdramatic, relatively unrestrained, and imbued with an exaggerated sense of impaired reality testing (Frueh & Kinder, 1994).

Future Prospects

A resurgence of interest in the Rorschach Inkblot Test occurred during the 1980s, a phenomenon attributable in large measure to the development and application of Exner's Comprehensive System. This framework for administering, scoring, and interpreting the Rorschach has had positive effects, not only on practitioners of the technique but also on more psychometrically-oriented academics and researchers. In fact, a study by Piotrowski, Sherry, and Keller (1985) found that by the mid-1980s Exner's system was being used by 35% of the practicing clinicians who responded to a survey questionnaire. Some staunch supporters continue to adhere to one of the original major systems, but even they have been influenced by the work of Exner and his associates.

Alternative approaches to Rorschach administration and scoring, such as content-interview analysis, continue to be popular. Also noteworthy are the consensus Rorschach for couples and family therapy (Klopfer, 1984), the Rorschach Prognostic Rating Scale in psychotherapy outcome studies (Garwood, 1977; Shields, 1978), and other non-traditional approaches (e. g., Blatt & Berman,

1984). It appears, however, that Exner's Comprehensive System has led the way in both practice and research.

Despite the fact that the Rorschach has not been a popular assessment instrument in research with adolescents (LeUnes, Evans, Karnei, & Lowry, 1980), increased interest in the Rorschach assessment of children and adolescents has been observed (Exner & Weiner, 1994; Ornberg & Zalewski, 1994). The resurgence of projective testing is ascribable in part to the changing roles of psychodiagnostics in general and to the specialty areas of neuropsychological, forensic, and health assessment in particular. Does the Rorschach really have a bright future? As suggested by the discussion in this chapter, apparently so. But the future of Rorschach's ten inkblots lies in the continued scrutiny of research data, practical applications, and empirical investigations of reliability and validity. Questions concerning the ethics of assessment and fakability will also play an important role in the future well-being of this assessment instrument. If it is to maintain its position against new competitors, continued examination and evaluation of the Rorschach Inkblot Technique should not be feared but welcomed. Herman Rorschach would undoubtedly have wanted it that way.

■ Holtzman Inkblot Technique

Although the Rorschach test has had a few competitors, such as instruments utilizing inkblots different from Rorschach's, most of these have received little attention in the literature and are of interest today only for their historical significance. The single instrument that has captured the attention of empirically-conscious clinicians is the Holtzman Inkblot Technique (HIT), but it has been used much less extensively than the Rorschach.

According to Holtzman (1981), the HIT was designed to overcome psychometric limitations in the Rorschach. Unlike the Rorschach, the HIT consists of two parallel forms (A and B) of 45 inkblots each. Some blots are asymmetrical, some in one color other than black, and some with visual textures. The blots are more varied in color, form, and shading that those on the Rorschach, and only one response is permitted per card. Restricting the number of responses is said to sharpen the discriminating power of the content, determinants, and other comparisons used in interpreting the responses. Like the Rorschach, the HIT is usually administered individually, but group administration by means of a projector is possible. Following each response, the examinee is asked where in the blot the percept is represented and what features of the blot suggests that percept.

The HIT is scored on the following variables:

Reaction Time (Form A only)	Pathognomic Verbalization
rejection	Integration
Location	Content (human, animal,
Space	anatomy, sex, abstract)
Form Definiteness	Anxiety
Form Appropriateness	Hostility
Color	Barrier
Shading	Penetration
Movement	Balance (Form A only)
	Popular

A scoring guide, based on computer analysis of hundreds of HIT protocols, has produced highly consistent scoring by different scorers.

The HIT was originally standardized on over 1400 individuals ranging in age from five years to adulthood. The sample consisted of normal, schizophrenic, depressive, and mentally retarded individuals. Separate percentile norms are available for college students, average adults, seventh graders, and elementary school children, five-year olds, chronic schizophrenics, depressed patients, and mentally retarded persons.

The results of reliability and validity studies of the HIT have generally been satisfactory. Interscorer reliabilities for most scoring categories are in the high .90s, and split-half coefficients are in the .70s and .80s. Test-retest coefficients are, however, only fair. The findings of hundreds of research studies have revealed modest but significant relationships between HIT scores and other measures of personality and psychopathology, supporting claims for the HIT as a psychodiagnostic instrument (e.g, Hill, 1972; Holtzman, 1988; Swartz, Reinehr, & Holtzman, 1983).

Although the HIT has experienced problems in being accepted by clinical practitioners, it represents a noteworthy attempt to provide an inkblot technique with appropriate psychometric characteristics. Be that as it may, the HIT will almost certainly never attract as wide a following as the Rorschach (Cundick, 1985). In the late 1980s, the HIT 25, which requires two responses to each of 25 cards selected from Form A, was published (Holtzman, 1988). This variant of the HIT has demonstrated promise in the diagnosis of schizophrenia, in that it correctly classified 26 of 30 schizophrenics and 28 of 30 normal college students (Holtzman, 1988; also see Swartz, 1992).

■ Summary

This chapter began by tracing the development of the Rorschach Inkblot Technique from the publication of Hermann Rorschach's *Psychodiagnostic* in 1921 through its early growth and eventual divergence into five major systems. Over the past several decades the Rorschach has encountered extensive criticism, particularly from academic clinicians and psychometricians. Due in some measure to decreased interest in psychoanalysis and the rise of more objective personality testing, the Rorschach has declined in popularity since the 1960s. However, John Exner's efforts at synthesizing empirically sound aspects of the five major systems and the provision of a systematic framework for testing hypotheses concerning personality resulted in new credibility for the Rorschach technique. Since the mid-1970s Exner's Comprehensive System has been the most popular Rorschach method, not only among clinical practitioners but also among psychometricians and others concerned with research involving projective methods.

The Rorschach Inkblot Technique is best conceptualized as a perceptual-cognitive task, a broad-band instrument, and a method for assessing and understanding personality functioning. Despite advances in research and practical applications, the Rorschach continues to experience problems of reliability and validity. Nevertheless, research employing this instrument is continuing.

Many variations in methods of administering, scoring, and interpreting the Rorschach have been proposed. Included among these are content-interview analysis, the consensus Rorschach, and the Rorschach Prognostic Rating Scale, and even a multiple-choice Rorschach. More than a variation, and psychometrically sounder than the Rorschach, is the Holtzman Inkblot Technique (HIT). Research studies conducted on the HIT have found it to be useful in psychodiagnosis, but it has been nowhere nearly as popular among clinicians as the Rorschach.

■ Questions and Activities

1. Construct an inkblot picture by putting a large drop of black ink in the middle of an 8 1/2 inch by 11 inch sheet of white paper. Fold the sheet in half so the ink is inside, crease the sheet in the middle and press it flat. Then open up the sheet and let the blot dry. Repeat the process with other sheets of paper until you obtain five fairly detailed, preferably symmetrical inkblots. Then administer your inkblot test to several people. Direct them to tell you what they see in each blot, where on the blot they see it, and what it was about the blot (shape, color, texture, or other quality) that caused them to give that response. Record the response(s) made by each person to each inkblot, and then see if you can tell anything about the various personalities from their responses to the five inkblots. Compare the results with your personal knowledge of the individual and any other test results that are available. Summarize your findings in a report.

2. What are the major characteristics of the Rorschach scoring and interpretive systems devised by Beck, Klopfer, Hertz, Rapaport-Schafer, and Piotrowski? How do these five major systems differ from Exner's Comprehensive System?

3. Do you believe that the form of the responses to Rorschach cards is more revealing of unconscious processes than the content of those responses? Why or why not?

4. Read reviews of the Rorschach Inkblot Technique and the Holtzman Inkblot Technique in *The Mental Measurements Yearbook* and *Test Critiques*. Then write a comparative summary of the major characteristics of the two instruments.

5. What improvements in the five traditional Rorschach Systems are represented by Exner's Comprehensive System?

6. Why do you believe that the Rorschach has remained relatively popular among clinical psychologists even though it psychometric properties (validity, reliability, norms) leave much to be desired?

7. Compare the Rorschach with the MMPI in terms of the (a) psychometric qualities, (b) interest to examinees, and (c) richness of information obtained from the two instruments. See Atkinson (1986) and Polyson, Peterson and Marshall (1986).

■ Suggested Readings

Allen, J. C., & Hollifield, J. (1990). Using the Rorschach with children and adolescents: The Exner. In C. R. Reynolds & R. W. Kamphaus (Eds.), *Handbook of psychological & educational assessment of children: Personality, behavior, & context* (pp. 168–186). Norwood, NJ: Ablex.

Beck, S. J. (1972). How the Rorschach came to America. *Journal of Personality Assessment, 36,* 105–108.

Blatt, S. J. (1990). The Rorschach: A test of perception or an evaluation of representation. *Journal of Personality Assessment, 55,* 394–416.

Erdberg, P. (1996). The Rorschach. In C. S. Newmark (Ed.), *Major psychological assessment instruments* (pp. 148–165). Needham Heights, MA: Allyn & Bacon.

Exner, J. E. (1997). The future of the Rorschach in personality assessment. *Journal of Personality Assessment, 68*(1), 37–46.

Giacono, C. B., & Meloy, J. R. (1994). *The Rorschach assessment of aggressive and psychopathic personalities.* Hillsdale, NJ: Erlbaum.

Groth-Marnat, G. (1997). The Rorschach. In *Handbook of psychological assessment* (3rd ed., pp. 393–457). New York: Wiley.

Hertz, M. R. (1986). Rorschachbound: A 50-year memoir. *Journal of Personality Assessment, 50,* 396–416.

Holtzman, W. H., & Swartz, J. D. (1990). Use of the Holtzman Inkblot Technique (HIT) with children. In C. R. Reynolds & R. W. Kamphaus (Eds.), *Handbook of psychological*

& educational assessment of children: Personality, behavior, & context (pp. 187–203). Norwood, NJ: Ablex.

Weiner, I. B. (1995). Methodological considerations in Rorschach research. *Psychological Assessment, 7,* 330–337.

Weiner, I. B. (1996). Some observations on the validity of the Rorschach Inkblot Method. *Psychological Assessment, 8,* 206–213.

CHAPTER 12

The TAT and Other Apperception Techniques*

Second only to the Rorschach in terms of the number of research investigations and clinical usage during the past half century is the Thematic Apperception Test (TAT). One of the early psychometric precursors of the TAT was Binet and Simon's (1905) use of children's verbal responses to pictures as a measure of intellectual development. In a similar manner, Brittain (1907) asked children aged 13 to 20 years to write stories about a series of nine pictures that he showed to them. Qualitative analysis of the responses included degree of imagination and creativity, coherence, length, use of picture details, and use of moral, religious, and social content. Differences were found between the stories told by boys and girls: boys' stories were concerned more with the consumption of food, whereas girls' stories had more emotional, moral, religious, and social content. In a related investigation, Libby (1908) examined the relationship between imagination and feelings in adolescents. Significant differences were found between the stories of thirteen- and fourteen-year-olds: the stories told by 13-year-olds were more objective and those told by 14-year-olds were more subjective.

One of the earliest uses of picture story tests in psychodiagnosis was Schwartz's (1932) Social Situation Test, which consisted of eight pictures and was used in psychiatric interviews of delinquent boys. The technique facilitated the establishment of rapport and assisted in initiating interviews. Another relative of the TAT

---

* This chapter is based on a draft prepared in cooperation with Floyd G. Jackson for the first edition of the book.

TAB. 12–1 Descriptions of TAT Pictures.

Picture 1	A young boy is contemplating a violin which rests on a table in front of him..
Picture 2	Country scene: In the foreground is a young woman with books in her hand; in the background a man is working in the fields and an older woman is looking on.
Picture 3BM	On the floor against a couch is the huddled form of a boy with his head bowed on his right arm. Beside him on the floor is a revolver.
Picture 3GF	A young woman is standing with downcast head, her face covered with her right hand. Her left arm is stretched forward against a wooden door.
Picture 4	A woman is clutching the shoulders of a man whose face and body are averted as if he were trying to pull away from her.
Picture 5	A middle-aged women is standing on the threshold of a half-opened door looking into a room.
Picture 6BM	A short elderly women stands with her back turned to a tall young man. The latter is looking downward with a perplexed expression.
Picture 6GF	A young women sitting on the edge of a sofa looks back over her shoulder at an older man with a pipe in his mouth who seems to be addressing her.
Picture 7BM	A gray-haired man is looking at a younger man who is sullenly staring into space.
Picture 7GF	An older woman is sitting on a sofa close beside a girl, speaking or reading to her. The girl, who holds a doll in her lap, is looking away.
Picture 8BM	An adolescent boy looks straight out of the picture. The barrel of a rifle is visible at one side, and in the background is the dim scene of a surgical operation, like a reverie-image.
Picture 8GF	A woman sits with her chin in her hand looking off into space.
Picture 9BM	Four men in overalls are lying on the grass taking it easy.
Picture 9GF	A young woman with a magazine and a purse in her hand looks from behind a tree at another young woman in a party dress running along a beach.
Picture 10	A young woman's head against a man's shoulder.
Picture 11	A road skirting a deep chasm between high cliffs. On the road in the distance are obscure figures. Protruding from the rocky wall on one side are the long head and neck of a dragon.
Picture 12M	A young man is lying on a couch with his eyes closed. Learning over him is the gaunt form of an elderly man, his hand stretched out above the face of the reclining figure.
Picture 12F	The portrait of a young woman. A weird old woman with a shawl over her head is grimacing in the background.
Picture 12BG	A rowboat is drawn up on the bank of a woodland stream. There are no human figures in the picture.
Picture 13MF	A young man is standing with downcast head buried in his arm. Behind him is the figure of a woman lying in bed.
Picture 13B	A little boy is sitting on the doorstep of a log cabin.
Picture 13G	A little girl is climbing a winding flight of stairs.

Table 12-1 continued

Picture 14	The silhouette of a man (or woman) against a bright window. The rest of the picture is totally black.
Picture 15	A gaunt man with clenched hands is standing among gravestones.
Picture 16	Blank.
Picture 17BM	A naked man is clinging to a rope. He is in the act of climbing up or down.
Picture 17GF	A bridge over water. A female figure leans over the railing. In the background are tall buildings and small figures of men.
Picture 18BM	A man is clutched from behind by three hands. The figures of his antagonists are invisible.
Picture 18GF	A woman has her hands squeezed around the throat of another woman whom she appears to be pushing backward across the banister of a stairway.
Picture 19	A weird picture of cloud formations overhanging a snow-covered cabin in the country.
Picture 20	The dimly illuminated figure of a man (or woman) in the dead of night leaning against a lamppost.

Bellak (1993). Reprinted by permission of the publisher, Allyn & Bacon.

was the Four Picture Test, which its author, Van Lennep (1951), traced back to 1930.

An initial version of the Thematic Apperception Test (TAT) was published by Christina Morgan and Henry Murray in 1935, but the current version is the second revision (Murray, 1943). The TAT consists of a set of 31 pictures—30 black-and-white picture cards depicting people in various ambiguous situations, plus one blank card. The 31 cards, which are described in Table 12–1, can be arranged as four overlapping sets of 19 picture cards and the blank card for administration to boys, girls, men, and women. However, a full set of 20 cards is seldom administered. Depending on the special purposes of the test administrator, as few as one card may be sufficient.

The following story, told by a young women in response to Picture 12F (see Table 12–1) is illustrative, but not necessarily typical, of the kinds of stories prompted by TAT pictures:

> This is a woman who has been quite troubled by memories of a mother she was resentful toward. She has feelings of sorrow for the way she treated her mother; her memories of her mother plague her. These feelings seem to be increasing as she grows older and sees her children treating her in the same way she treated her mother. She tries to convey this feeling to her own children, but does not succeed in changing their attitudes. She is living her past in the present, because the feeling of sorrow and guilt is reinforced by the way her children are treating her.

Although it still widely administered, the TAT has declined in popularity as both a clinical and research instrument during recent years. As shown in Figure 11–2, the number of research citations of the TAT reached a peak during the 1970s and declined after then. Interestingly, the peak decade for TAT research was approximately 20 years later than that for the Rorschach. With respect to clinical application of the TAT, a sample of psychologists surveyed during the early 1980s ranked the TAT seventh in usage by this group (Lubin, Larsen, Matarazzo, & Seever, 1986). A subsequent survey of directors of doctoral programs in clinical psychology found that among the respondents the TAT was ranked second only to the Rorschach in response to the question of which five projective tests clinical Ph.D. candidates should be familiar with (Piotrowski & Zalewski, 1993). In an even more recent survey, 39 of 50, or 78%, of the training directors of doctoral programs in clinical psychology who responded indicated that training in TAT interpretation formed at least a modest part of their programs (Rossini & Moretti, 1997). Unfortunately, the response rate in this survey was only 39% (50 returns out of 130 posted surveys forms). Because it might be expected that directors of programs of which the TAT was a part would be more likely to respond, 78% is undoubtedly too high. Findings from other surveys of psychologists and other mental health practitioners, however, point to a continuing interest in the TAT as a psychodiagnostic instrument (Watkins et al., 1995; Frauenhoffer et al., 1998).

According to Henry Murray (1943), the TAT reveals underlying tendencies that a person may not be willing to acknowledge or cannot express because the impulses are unconscious. Advocates of the TAT also claim that it assists the psychodiagnostician in determining an individual's dominant needs, emotions, sentiments, complexes, and conflicts, and the perceived external pressures (*press*) impinging on him or her. It is felt to be particularly helpful in understanding the examinee's relations and difficulties with his or her parents and is often included in a psychological assessment battery in which a variety of other tests such as the Rorschach, the MMPI, the Rotter Incomplete Sentences Blank, the Bender Visual-Motor Gestalt Test, and the Wechsler Adult Intelligence Scale are administered.

■ Administering the TAT

The procedure for administering the TAT varies somewhat with whether it is administered by another person, self-administered, or administered to a group of people simultaneously.

Individual Administration

In administering the TAT to one person, it is important to establish good rapport and then situate oneself at a 45 degree angle alongside the person so his or her facial expressions can be seen clearly. This position minimizes the examinee's view of the examiner and simultaneously provides the latter with a full view of the former. The examiner can then write down or tape-record the stories and related information unobtrusively.

Two forms of the TAT are available for individual administration (A and B). Form A is suitable for adolescents and adults of average intelligence and sophistication; Form B is for children, adults of below average education and/or intelligence, and psychotics. Murray (1943) recommended that the following instructions be given when administering Form A:

> This is a test of imagination, one form of intelligence. I am going to show you some pictures, one at a time, and your task will be to make up as dramatic a story as you can for each. Tell what has led up to the event shown in the picture, describe what is happening at the moment, what the characters are feeling and thinking; and then give the outcome. Speak your thoughts as they come to your mind. Do you understand? Since you have fifty minutes for ten pictures, you can devote about five minutes to each story. Here is the first picture. (p. 3)

The following instructions are recommended for Form B:

> This is a storytelling test. I have some pictures here that I am going to show you, and for each picture I want you to make up a story. Tell what has happened before and what is happening now. Say what the people are feeling and thinking and how it will come out. You can make up any kind of story your please. Do you understand? Well, then, here's the first picture. You have five minutes to make up a story. See how well you can do. (p. 3)

And the following instructions are recommended for children:

> I have some pictures here that I am going to show you, and for each picture I want you to make up a story. Tell what has happened before and what is happening now. Say what the people are feeling and thinking and how it will come out. You can make up any kind of story you please. Do you understand? Well, then, here is the first picture. You have five minutes to make up a story. See how well you can do. (p. 4)

Bellak (1993) criticized Murray's opening sentence in the instructions for Form A, claiming that it makes the examinee suspicious and thus impairs his or her performance. Not only is the opening sentence in the instructions for Form A often omitted, but the instructions are frequently adapted to the age, intelligence, personality, and circumstances of the examinee. Karon (1981) maintained that standard instructions are less important than making certain that the examinee tells good stories. He found the following instructions to be adequate:

I'm going to show you a set of ten pictures, one at a time. I want you to tell me what is going on, what the characters might be feeling and thinking, what led up to it, and what the outcome might be. In other words, tell me a good story.

When the examinee has finished the first story, the examiner says, "O.K., that was pretty good. Now let's see what you can do with this one."

Self-Administration

The following instructions are usually presented to people who administer the test to themselves, that is, they simply look at each card and write down a story (Bellak, 1993):

1. Please write a story about each picture in this folder.
2. Do not look at the pictures before you are ready to write.
3. Look at one picture at a time only, in the order given, and write as dramatic a story as you can about each. Tell what has led up to the event shown in the picture, describe what is happening at the moment, what the characters are thinking and feeling; and then give the outcome. Write your thoughts as they come to your mind.
4. It should not be necessary to spend more than about seven minutes per story, although you may spend more time if you wish.
5. Write about 300 words per story, or about one typing page if you write in long hand. If at all possible, please type the long hand story later, without changes, in duplicate, double-spaced, one story per page.
6. Please number the stories as you go along, and then put your name on the front sheet. (p. 47)

One advantage of this method is that it saves time for the examiner, but it also has several disadvantages. For example, the examinee's emotional response are not observed and recorded by the examiner. The opportunity for the examiner to intervene if the examinee becomes discouraged and the ability of the examiner to control the length of the story are also lost. Finally, the examinee's spontaneity may be affected; shorter, less elaborate stories are usually obtained when examinees write their own responses to the TAT pictures. An alternative is to have the examinee record his or her responses on audio tape, but in most cases the recorded stories will still have to be transcribed for scoring and interpretation purposes.

Group Administration

Projecting TAT pictures onto a screen by means of an overhead or slide projector makes it possible to administer the test to a large number of examinees simultaneously. In group administration, the instructions for self-administration are presented to the entire group, and everyone is expected to write down his or her own story as each picture is projected on the screen. Although it is an efficient procedure, group administration poses the same problems as those described above for self-administration.

The results of empirical comparisons between individual- and group-administered TATs indicate that the two procedures are not necessarily equivalent. In a study of 30 university students, Eron and Ritter (1951) found that the stories obtained in oral individual administration were longer, less happy, and less flippant, but essentially the same in thematic content as stories obtained in group administration. Even fewer differences between individual and group administration were found by Clark (1944) in a study of 50 university students. When the results of administering the TAT to these students as a group were compared with the results of individual administration of a portion of the test to the same students, the differences were negligible. The standard clinical, or individual, procedure proved to be only slightly better than the group procedure. This finding led Clark to conclude that the group-administered TAT can serve as an effective screening test when individual administration is not feasible.

Follow-Up Inquiry

Further inquiry into the TAT stories of examinees can serve several functions. For example, it can ensure that the examinee has followed the instructions and that the stories include the three A's—action, antecedents, and aftermath—along with the characters' thoughts and feelings. Associations or thoughts obtained during the inquiry concerning the proper names of people, places, dates, or any unusual information can be crucial for accurate interpretation of the stories.

Rapaport, Gill and Schafer (1968) recommended that an inquiry be conducted after each story has been told. Other clinicians (e. g., Bellak, 1993) maintain that an inquiry should be conducted only after all stories have been told, a procedure that may facilitate the movement of unconscious or preconscious material to consciousness. On the other hand, by conducting an inquiry after each story one can stay with the manifest content and ensure that each story is complete in accordance with Murray's basic instructions.

After the examinee has provided stories for all the pictures that are presented, and perhaps in subsequent sessions, the inquiry can be continued to determine the latent, or less apparent, meaning of the stories. Such an inquiry can also serve as an important tool in psychotherapy.

Shortened TAT Card Sets

Not only may recording TAT stories by hand result in writer's cramp but it can also take a great deal of time. This is especially true when an entire set of 20 cards is administered. Bellak (1993) indicates that an optimum amount of information is obtained from responses to ten TAT pictures, which can be administered in about an hour. He advocates administering pictures 1, 2, 3BM, 4, 6BM, 7BM, 11, 12M, and 13MF for testing any male and pictures 1, 2, 3BM, 4, 6GF, 7GF, 9GF, 11, and 13MF for testing any female. Bellak includes 3BM in the list of picture stimuli for females because clinically it works well for both males and females and is more effective than its counterpart, 3GF. The specific problem of the examinee is also an important factor in selecting TAT cards for administration. Cards 12M and 15, for example, are particularly appropriate for patients with reactive depression or acute grief reaction due to the death of loved ones. And cards 9BM, 10, 17BM, and 18BM are considered important in the psychological assessment of individuals with sexual orientation disturbances or fears of being homosexual.

Other recommendations for shortened TAT card sets have been made. From rankings by 170 highly-experienced psychologists of the ten TAT cards judged most valuable for a basic set, Hartman (1970) proposed that cards 1, 2, 3BM, 4, 6BM, 7BM, 8BM, and 13MF be administered for purposes of clinical research and teaching. For assessing adolescent males, Cooper (1981) recommended using cards 4, 6BM, 3BM, 8BM, 10, 18BM, 15, 7BM, 1, and 13B.

■ An Illustration: Testing Juvenile Delinquents

In diagnostic workups for a juvenile court system, Jackson (personal communication) reports that cards 1, 3BM, 4, 6BM, 7BM, 9BM, 10, 13MF, 13B, 14, 17BM, and 18BM are the most useful. The following response is typical of the stories told by juvenile delinquents to card 1: *The boy is wondering how much money he can get for this violin if he steals it from the school and then sells it on the street.* Another frequent plot is that this boy is just sitting there and thinking about how boring it is to play the violin. Bellak (1993) maintains that card 1 is probably the most useful card with adolescents. It is often descriptive of how individuals at this age level deal with impulse control, especially with respect to personal dictates versus environmental demands. Stories given to card 1 may provide information on parent-child relationships as well as the nature, intensity, and mechanism for the resolution of achievement needs. The most frequently occurring stories given by delinquents to this picture tend to be characterized by the absence of comments on relationships with parents; such children rarely comment on their relationships with their parent(s), or when made the comments tend to be negative. This fact can be attributed to the emotional impoverishment suffered by delinquents, whose parents are often absent or who provide little emotional warmth. Achievement needs are often present and strong in responses to card 1, but their direction is usually counter to what is considered socially desirable. Narcissism and obsession with elaborate methods of crime are also displayed in stories given to this card.

A typical response to card 3BM is: *This guy just killed himself. No one liked him, and he didn't like himself.* Another frequently occurring plot among delinquents is: *This kid has been in a fight. He got hurt pretty bad, but he was able to hurt a lot of other people.* Bellak (1993) states that this highly useful picture elicits themes of guilt, depression, impulse control, and aggression. Guilt is often absent in delinquent protocols, but aggression is strongly expressed. This aggression can be internally directed or, at other times, externally directed. The gun on the floor in the lower left portion of card 3BM is usually significant; it can be used to do harm to oneself or to others. Depression, aggression, suicidal and homicidal ideation, gesturing, and intent may be elicited by this potently useful scene. The themes that seem to be present most often in the protocols of delinquents are those of loneliness, isolation, alienation, depression, aggression, and a lack of adequate impulse control. If guilt were to arise, it might be a good sign since it can easily be linked to remorse, an indicator of residual strength and health.

Characteristic of the responses of delinquents to card 4 is: *This guy is about to beat up a man who just made a pass at his girl friend. His girl friend is trying to stop him, but he breaks away from her and he creams him.* Another frequently occurring plot among delinquents is: *This is Burt Reynolds and his lady. Burt is getting ready to make a drug bust, but his lady friend wants him to stay with her so that they can get high together and have a good time.*

Card 4 also serves as a barometer in appraising the quality of male-female relationships and various feelings, thoughts, attitudes, and beliefs about sex roles. Themes of betrayal and infidelity are common. The man may be depicted as aggressive, distracted, destructive, or fed up. The woman is often depicted as luring, protective, detaining, or controlling. The woman's seductive look and revealing dress elicit sexual commentary. A third person in the picture easily suggests a theme of triangular jealousy in which betrayal or infidelity has occurred. Delinquents are often pulled into this theme, expressing dramatic hostility and aggression toward the third party. The picture also stimulates memories of films such as *Gone With the Wind* and the like. Teenagers often idolize Hollywood heroes, identifying with them and introjecting many of their characteristics. The woman symbolizes control that is strongly rebelled against and overcome; she ineffectually attempts to control the man; he does as he pleases. The issues of impulse control and autonomy versus dependency, which are manifested in these kinds of stories, are serious problems for juvenile delinquents—and to some extent for normal adolescents.

Delinquent teenagers tend to respond to card 6BM with stories similar to the following: *This guy is saying goodbye to his aunt before going off to jail.* Another frequently occurring theme is that this guy was called to the principal's office because he missed so many days of school. She tells him he is not going to graduate from high school. Bellak (1993) suggests that card 6BM is indispensable when testing males because it elicits mother-son relationship problems and similar problems such as those relating to wives and women in general. *Oedipal themes* often emerge. Most juvenile delinquents, however, defend against the recognition of the woman as mother, substituting an aunt, a teacher, or some other woman who is a significant authority figure. She often exerts control, which is usually resisted.

A typical story told by delinquents to card 7BM is as follows: *This is a guy and his lawyer, and from the look on his face he is not going to be getting out any time soon.* Or, *This is a guy and his lawyer. They are talking about his case because they have to go to court.* In response to this card, an adolescent often defends against the father figure, substituting a lawyer. The seriousness of the picture is seldom underestimated, and the outcome is often pessimistic. Bellak (1993) claims that card 7BM is essential in bringing out the father-son relationship and related themes. Attitudes toward authority figures, as seen in boss/employee relationships, for example, are evoked and frequently included in the commentary.

One delinquent responded to card 9BM with: *These guys have just smoked a whole lot of marijuana and have gotten all high and mellow. These guys don't have anything better to do.* According to Bellak (1993), this picture is instrumental in disclosing contemporary man-to-man relationships and insight into social relationships in general. It could be important to determine with whom the examinee identifies. Is he the center of the group, or is he outside the group looking suspiciously at them?

Social prejudices and homosexual issues may also be brought to the surface via card 9BM. Some delinquents tend to relate to the relative inactivity of the men rather than to group cohesiveness and closeness, a fact that may reflect the high degree of idleness of many delinquent children. A large percentage are truant, unemployed, and consequently idle.

A distinction can be made between the responses of socialized and unsocialized delinquents. The child with a socialized conduct disorder tends to associate with the group theme in the picture, whereas the unsocialized child tends to comment on nongroup dimensions. The picture also elicits comments regarding drug abuse, for example, marijuana. As many teenage delinquents have stated, "These men look wasted." Stories concerned with homosexuality and fears of being homosexual can also be expected in response to card 9BM, but in this author's experience juvenile delinquents tend to refrain from comments about homosexuality. Exceptions occur more frequently in borderline, and sometimes psychotic, patients, where ego boundaries and defenses are weak and grossly dysfunctional.

Card 10 tends to elicit stories such as, *These people are slow dancing now and later they will be making love,* or *This man is whispering sweet nothings into his girl friend's ear, and she falls for it.* This card is designed to bring out feelings, attitudes, and beliefs concerning the relationships between men and women (Bellak, 1993). The arrival versus departure theme may be noteworthy and revealing of dependency, autonomy, and even hostility needs. Bellak (1993) indicates that a description of two men embracing or kissing may be indicative of homosexuality or homosexual tendencies.

Dominance and arrogance are typical among juvenile delinquents. Teenage boys are particularly fond of boasting about their own sexual prowess, and sometimes even fonder of boasting about the sexual prowess of another male. Consequently, in responding to card 10 they note the overwhelming power that the man has over the woman, partly because he is so "cool" and partly because the woman is so gullible and "easy." In fantasy and probably in reality, juvenile delinquents see intimacy as a power struggle where at all costs they need to be in control. Manipulation is a powerful technique in achieving such control.

A teenage delinquent gave the following response to card 13MF: *This man has just raped and killed this woman, and now he is wiping the sweat from his forehead.* Another typical response obtained from delinquents is that this man has just raped his girl friend because she wouldn't give it to him. Bellak (1993) states that card 13MF helps disclose sexual conflicts in both men and women. Groth-Marnat (1997) maintains that it provides information on a person's attitudes and feelings toward his sexual partner, especially those experienced immediately before and after sexual intercourse. The relationship between the patient's aggressive and sexual feelings is often woven into the story. In a sample of juvenile delinquents tested by the author, the respondents expressed sex and aggression in their plots. In fact, rape is such a common theme in the responses of teenage delinquents that card 13MF has sometimes been referred to as the "rape card." The intertwined display of sex and aggression in the form of rape is indicative of sexual immaturity. The lack of remorse suggests inadequate superego (conscience) development, which is typical among delinquents. The importance of power and lack of impulse control—taking what one desires when one desires it—are also evident in the stories.

Here is a response given by a juvenile delinquent to card 13B: *This is Jimmy Carter. When he was a boy he hardly had a house to live in. He hardly had shoes on his feet, or a mother or a father to take care of him. He hardly had food to eat, or kids to play with. When he grew up he became President of the United States, and now we hardly have the United States.* Another typical response from a teenage delinquent is that this little boy is lonely. He has no father, and his mother is always busy.

Among juvenile delinquents, card 13B can be a powerful look into earlier childhood experiences. Issues of loneliness, emotional impoverishment, emptiness, pessimism, sadness, and identity confusion (Who am I, and what is life all about?) are drawn out. Emotional impoverishment almost always underlies delinquency, and this card can serve as an effective means of therapeutic communication. In adults, this card similarly evokes childhood experiences that may be dynamically significant for psychotherapy.

A typical delinquent response to card 14 is: *This guy is going to commit suicide. He is about to jump from a high building.* Another common response from juvenile delinquents is that this man is committing a B & E (breaking-in-and entry) and is getting away with the loot. Still another common response is that the man is looking out on the smoggy city and wondering what's the sense of it all. Bellak (1993) says that it is essential to administer card 14 when one suspects suicidal tendencies, which may be expressed in a story of jumping out of the window. Contemplation, philosophical thought, and wish-fulfillment stories are also expressed in responses to this card. In a sample of delinquents, stories range from suicide to B & E to philosophical contemplation.

A delinquent response to card 17BM: *This guy has climbed up a rope so he can get a free view of the concert.* Another common response is that the man is showing off in front of his friends; they dared him to climb to the top and he did it. Bellak (1993) maintains that this picture is useful in revealing fears, as expressed in stories of flight or escape from fire, another person, or some unknown physical trauma. Oedipal fears (repressed feelings of romantic attraction for the parent of the opposite sex and repressed feelings of threat from the parent of the same sex) or homosexual feelings may also be evoked. Active outgoing people who are achievement oriented often tell stories of a man climbing up a rope (McClelland, 1961; Mira, 1940). Several juvenile delinquents in one sample expressed an underlying fear of being left out in responding to card 17BM.

A typical delinquent response to card 18BM is: *This man is about to be mugged.* Groth-Marnat (1997) poses some interesting questions regarding the apparent anxiety depicted in this picture. Consider the following: Does the respondent see himself as a victim of circumstances in which he is completely helpless? How does he resolve his feelings? Is helplessness a trait or a state? Juvenile delinquents tend to agree that the man in the picture is about to be mugged. The stories usually vary in details such as, *He was walking where he shouldn't have been.* or *Serves him right for being such a whimp.* Delinquents virtually never admit to fantasizing themselves as the victim; they are much more apt to be innocent bystanders or even the aggressor.

■ Scoring and Interpreting TAT Stories

A variety of scoring and interpreting systems exist for analyzing TAT stories. As with other projective techniques, it is assumed that examinees project their own needs, desires, and emotional conflicts into the story and its characters, and the stories should be interpreted with this in mind. Pictures containing more than one human figure are particularly helpful in revealing needs, conflicts, and desires related to familial and other social or interpersonal matters.

Although the usual methods of scoring and interpreting the TAT are highly impressionistic, scores determined by one of the more systematic scoring procedures are fairly reliable and can be interpreted in terms of norms based on standardization studies.

The interpretative process may be facilitated by a TAT analysis sheets published by C.P.S., Inc. and Psychologists and Educators, Inc.. Murray (1938) quantified the needs expressed in TAT stories in the context of his theory of personality, which is outlined in Chapter 1.

Clinical Interpretation

A basic ground rule in the clinical interpretation of TAT stories is that the interpersonal scenario that is described cannot be taken at face value as reflecting the examinee's actual current or former relationships. The analysis is an analysis of fantasy, and waking fantasy has about as much relationship to reality as dreams do. To understand, and therefore to correctly interpret, the fantasies expressed in TAT stories the clinician must consider them against a background of psychiatric interview findings, the results of a mental status examination, observational and historical data, and other psychological test information. The most important guideline to follow in interpreting a series of TAT stories is to search for recurrent themes and to determine how the TAT responses fit into the context of interview data and other psychometric findings.

In using TAT stories to diagnose psychological disorders, clinicians often look for certain *signs*. For example, slowness or delays in responding may indicate depression. Overcautiousness and preoccupation with details suggest obsessive-compulsive disorders, and stories by males that include negative comments about women or affection for other men may point to homosexuality. However, these interpretations should be viewed as hypotheses, to be confirmed or disconfirmed by other information, rather than as conclusive diagnoses.

Interpretation is an activity that is common to all sciences, but a certain artistic ability is required for good psychodiagnostic work. Karon (1981) maintained that a fundamental principle in interpreting the TAT is to consider the stories one at a time, sentence by sentence, while asking oneself: Out of all the possibilities that exist, why would a human being say that? Murray (1943) talked about having a certain flair for the task of interpretation, possessing rigorously trained critical intuition, and having an extensive background of clinical experience. In addition, thorough training in the use of the test instrument, the TAT, is required. Thus, Murray recommended that the interpreter have considerable practice in analyzing stories in contexts where the conclusions can be checked against known facts about thoroughly studied personalities.

Murray's Interpretative System

Six elements are incorporated into Murray's (1943) system of analyzing the content of TAT stories:
- The main character(s) or *hero(es)*.
- The motives, trends, and feelings of the hero(es).
- The environmental forces (*press*) in the hero(es)'s environment (which may be benign or inimical).
- The *outcomes* (happy or unhappy? results of actions by hero or environmental forces?).
- The *themas*.
- The *interests* and *sentiments* expressed.

The first step in the analysis is to determine in which character the storyteller is most interested. This hero character is the one who is most integrally involved in the outcome and plays a leading role in the plot. He or she is often the character who most resembles the storyteller in age, goals, sentiments, sex, status, and perhaps other areas. The story is frequently told from the main character's perspective, and his or her feelings and motives are most intimately portrayed. The main character may, of course, be a heroine, or there may be two main characters—a hero and a heroine, or any combination of the sexes.

The second step in TAT interpretation is to examine the personalities of the heroes. What do they feel? What are their motives and unusual or unique characteristics? Most importantly, what are their needs and how are they satisfied? (see Table 12–2) In quantifying the needs of the hero, Murray (1943) recommended using a five-point scale on which 1 indicates the slightest hint of a need and 5 a potent form of the need or a repeated occurrence of a milder form. The strength of the need, and hence the rating assigned to it, is determined by its duration, frequency, and relevance or relative importance in the plot.

An assessment of the hero's environment constitutes the third step in interpretation. What are the physical and interpersonal environments, in other words the *press* on the heros(es)? (see Table 12–3) Similar to those of needs, ratings of press are made on a 1 to 5 scale with 5 being the most intense press. The criteria for strength of a press are intensity, duration, frequency, and general significance in the plot. The basic difference between needs and press is that needs are forces originating within the person whereas press are forces originating from the environment.

The fourth step in Murray's interpretative system involves a comparative analysis of the strength of the hero versus press forces. Do needs dominate press or vice versa Is the hero's path to achievement difficult or easy? When confronted with obstacles, does the hero get stronger, overcoming his adversity, or succumb? Is the hero active, making things happen, or merely reactive, allowing things to

Murray's List of Psychogenic Needs.

TAB. 12–2

Needs concerned with power, prestige or knowledge

Achievement	Construction	Exposition
Acquisition	Counteraction	Recognition
Aggression	Dominance	Understanding

Needs concerned with love, praise, sympathy, and dependence

Affiliation	Nurturance	Succorance
Deference	Sex	

Needs concerned with change, excitement, freedom, and play

Autonomy	Excitance
Change, travel, adventure	Playmirth

Other needs

Abasement	Harm avoidance	Retention
Blame avoidance	Passivity	Sentience
Cognizance	Rejection	

Adapted from Murray 1938, pp. 152–226.

Murray's List of Press.

TAB. 12–3

Press of deprivation:

Acquisition	Retention

Press of emptiness and rejection

Lack	Rejection
Loss	Uncongenial environment

Press of force and restraint

Dominance	Imposed duty, task, and training

Press of aggression

Aggression

Press of danger, death, and injury

Affliction	Physical danger
Death of a hero	Physical injury

Press of love, respect, friendliness, and dependence

Affiliation	Sex
Deference	Succorance
Nurturance	

Other press

Birth of offspring	Example
Claustrum	Exposition
Cognizance	Luck

Adapted from Murray, 1938, pp. 292–292.

happen? Is the hero more dependent or autonomous? Does the hero succeed when others help or when he/she strives alone? After a misdeed, does the hero get rewarded or punished? How much energy does the hero direct against himself How does the hero react to failure? Under what conditions does the hero fail? What role do others play in the hero's failure? What is the ratio of failures to successes? And finally, what is the ratio of happy to unhappy endings?

The fifth step in Murray's system is a consideration of simple and complex themas. A *simple thema* is an interaction of the hero's need(s), press, or fusion of press with the outcome (e. g., the success or failure of the hero). *Complex themas* are combinations and networks of simple themas. Common themas focus on issues such as conflict of desires, love, punishment, war, achievement, and the like. Murray notes that the interpreter need not score separate variables in order to make a thematic analysis. Although the test interpreter may obtain useful information from the story told to each picture, the overall pattern of themes emerging from all the stories is of greatest importance in determining the final interpretive impression. Some of the common themes or themes elicit by the 31 TAT pictures are given in Table 12–4.

The sixth and last step in Murray's interpretative scheme is an evaluation of interests and sentiments. What characteristic interests and sentiments does the storyteller attribute to the hero or heroes? What is the nature of these interests and sentiments? How and why does the narrator choose them? In what manner does the narrator deal with these interests and sentiments? What are the men and women, young and old, attracted to? How are they related to their "loved object(s)?" How do the men relate to men and the women to women? What is the mechanism of their relationship formation and maintenance?

Among the alternatives to Murray's (1938) procedure of scoring stories by rating needs and press on a five-point scale are the systems developed by Wyatt (1947), Eron (1950), Dana (1955), McClelland (1971), and Bellak (1993). Bellak's (1993) approach follows a ten-category outline consisting of:

1–3. Unconscious structure and drives of the subject (derived from scoring categories 1–3: Main Theme, Main Hero, and Main Needs and Drives of the Hero).
4. Conception of environment (world).
5. Relationships to others.
6. Significant conflicts.
7. Nature of anxieties.
8. Main defenses against conflicts and fears.
9. Adequacy of superego.
10. Integration and strength of the ego.

An analysis sheet consisting of these ten categories and a set of descriptive items listed under each that can be checked or completed by the interpreter is available

| **Typical Themes Elicited by TAT Pictures.** | **TAB. 12-4** |

Picture 1.   Relationship toward parental figures; achievement; symbolic sexual responses; aggression, anxiety, body image or self-image; obsessive preoccupations; sexual activity.

Picture 2.   Family relations; autonomy versus compliance; pregnancy; compulsive tendencies; role of the sexes.

Picture 3BM.   Latent homosexuality; aggression.

Picture 3GF.   Depressive feelings.

Picture 4.   Male-female relationships; triangular jealousy.

Picture 5.   Mother who may be watching; masturbation; voyeurism; primal scene; fear of attack; rescue fantasies.

Picture 6BM.   Mother-son relationships.

Picture 6GF.   Relationship of females to father.

Picture 7BM.   Father-son relationships.

Picture 7GF.   Relationship between mother and child in females; attitude toward expectancy of children.

Picture 8BM.   Aggression, ambition; Oedipal relationship.

Picture 8GF.   Almost any theme. Rarely a useful picture.

Picture 9BM.   Contemporary man-to-man relationships; homosexual drives and fears; social prejudices.

Picture 9GF.   Depression and suicidal tendencies; paranoia.

Picture 10.   Relation of men to women; latent homosexuality.

Picture 11.   Infantile or primitive fears; fears of attack; oral aggression.

Picture 12M.   Relationship of a younger man to an older man; passive homosexual fears.

Picture 12F.   Conceptions of mother figures.

Picture 12BG. Suicidal tendencies; depression.

Picture 13MF. Sexual conflicts in both men and women; economic deprivation; oral tendencies; obsessive-compulsive trends.

Picture 13B.   Stories of childhood.

Picture 13G.   Not a very useful picture.

Picture 14.   Sexual identification; fears in relation to darkness; suicidal tendencies; esthetic interests.

Picture 15.   Death in the immediate family; fears of death; depressive tendencies.

Picture 16.   May be extremely valuable with verbally gifted subjects.

Picture 17BM. Oedipal fears; homosexual feelings; body image.

Picture 17GF. Suicidal tendencies in women.

Picture 18BM. Anxiety in males.

Picture 18GF. How aggression is handled by women; mother-daughter conflicts.

Picture 19.   Sometimes useful with children, but otherwise not notable.

Picture 20.   Fear of the dark (females).

Bellak (1993). Reprinted by permission of the publisher, Allyn & Bacon.

from C.P.S., Inc. This sheet, in addition to a form for recording information obtained from the assessment of ego functioning on the TAT and further details on the use of these two forms, is included in a chapter by Groth-Marnat (1997, pp. 488–498).

Alternative Scoring Procedures

A variety of derived scores on variables have been devised and applied in research investigations. Among these variables are communication deviance (Wynne & Singer, 1963), pathogenesis (Karon, 1981; Pam & Rivera, 1995), affect maturity (Thompson, 1986), affect tone (Barends et al., 1990), defense mechanisms (Cramer & Blatt, 1990; Hibbard et al., 1994; Hibbard & Porcerelli, 1998), ego development (Sutton & Swensen, 1983), interpersonal affect (Thomas & Dudek, 1985), motives or needs (achievement, affiliation, power, etc.) (McClelland, 1985; Winter, 1998), object relations (Alvarado, 1994; Freedenfeld, Ornduff, & Kelsey, 1995; Rosenberg et al., 1994; Westen et al., 1990; Westen, 1991), and personal problem-solving process (Ronan, Colavito, & Hammontree, 1993; Ronan, Date, & Weisbrod, 1995) Of particular interest are Westen's (1991) Social Cognition and Object Relations Scales—Complexity of Representations of People, Affect-Tone of Relationship Paradigm, Capacity for Emotional Investment and Moral Standards, and Understanding of Social Causality. Scores on these four scales have been shown to differentiate between normal and borderline patients (Westen et al., 1990) and between physically abused and non-abused children (Freedenfeld, Ornduff, & Kelsey, 1995). Many other scoring and interpretative systems for the TAT have been developed, nearly two dozen of which are reviewed by Bellak (1993).

■ Psychometric Issues and Research

The decline in TAT research during the past two decades (see Figure 11–2) can be attributed to a combination of factors: the dated quality of the TAT pictures; a lack of standardization in card selection, administration, and scoring procedures; and relatively unimpressive or undetermined reliability and validity.

Reliability

As is the case with most open-ended, free-response techniques such as projectives, the reliability of the TAT has been difficult to establish by conventional psychometric methods. Various sources of error contribute to the low reliabilities of these assessments. Not only must one account for differences in the stories told by the same person on different occasions, but also differences in the scoring and interpretation of those stories. For example, Wade and Baker (1977) determined that approximately 82 percent of users of the TAT and other projective techniques employ "personalized" procedures for interpreting the responses. A majority of these procedures are based on strategies of low or unknown reliability and validity (Gregory, 1996).

For the most part, the results of older studies indicated that the reliabilities of scores on the TAT are rather modest (Tomkins, 1947; Sanford, 1943; Harrison & Rotter, 1945). The results of more recent studies that have focused on objectively scored variables have been more encouraging. Thomas and Dudek (1985) obtained inter-rater reliability coefficients between .93 and .97 for evaluations of the affective content of TAT stories. And Stricker and Healey (1990) reported inter-rater reliabilities of .75 to .95 for several psychodynamic characteristics assessed from TAT responses. Finally, Leigh et al. (1992) obtained inter-rater coefficients ranging from .89 to .93 in their analysis of the complexity of representations of people in TAT protocols.

With respect to the stability of TAT scores, older studies generally found low test-retest reliability coefficients for TAT protocols scored according to Murray's need/press system (e. g., Tomkins, 1947). Winter and Stewart (1977) computed the median test-retest reliabilities from various studies as .28, much lower than required for group differentiation, much less intra- or interindividual differentiation.

The relatively unstructured nature of the test task and the lack of objectivity in scoring are important contributors to the low test-retest reliability coefficients obtained in many investigations of the psychometric characteristics of the TAT. Situational variables, transient internal need states, and intentional faking (dissimulation) can also lower reliability. The examinee's emotional state and experiences prior to the examination, the conditions under which the test is administered, the personality of the examiner and the comments made by him/her during the examination, and the specific instructions for the test can all affect responses to the TAT pictures and the reliability of the test. For example, Bellak (1942) found a significant elevation of expressed aggression in the content of TAT stories when examinees' initial stories were sharply criticized. Subsequent research has demonstrated that the age of the examiner (Mussen & Scodel, 1955), whether the examiner stays in the testing room or leaves (Bernstein, 1956), whether the examinee was frustrated (Lindzey, 1950) or insulted (Feshbach, 1961) prior to the test, and the physical needs of the examinee (hunger, sleep, etc.) (McClelland & Atkinson, 1948; Atkinson, 1958) can influence the content of TAT stories. Other possible sources of error leading to unreliability are discussed by Kraiger, Hakel, and Cornelius (1984).

In conducting diagnostic workups for court hearings on juvenile delinquents, which requires testing and retesting defendants accused of repeated offenses, the author frequently encountered the problem of relatively low test-retest reliability coefficients of the TAT. The high degree of plasticity in the personalities of children and adolescents contribute to the low reliabilities of scores obtained with these age groups. Furthermore, children (and adults) often remember the stories they told the first time and want to create something different, leading to low test-retest coefficients (White, 1943; Sanford, 1943).

Validity

In view of the fact that the TAT is an instrument for analyzing fantasy, which may or may not reflect actual behavior, the problem of determining the validity of this test is extremely complex. Worchel and Dupree (1990) maintain that the validity of the interpretations of TAT stories depends as much on the skills of the interpreter as on the psychometric characteristics of the instrument itself. The validity of the TAT has usually been investigated consensually, or by a construct validation approach, by determining its relationships to performance on other projective techniques, case history material, and other fantasy material such as dreams. As is the case with most projective techniques, a wide range of validity coefficients has been obtained with the TAT.

A fundamental point that should be kept in mind in analyzing the validity of the TAT is that the measurement of any variable (e. g., aggression, affect tone, dangerousness, defense mechanisms, depression, needs or motives, object relations, sexual pathology) by this technique, or any other projective technique for that matter, is accompanied by errors of measurement that tend to lower both reliability and validity coefficients. The validity of the TAT is also limited by its internal consistency, that is, the extent to which different pictures tap the same variables.

With respect to diagnostic validity, the TAT has been found to discriminate among normals, neurotics, and psychotics on measures of story organization, popular references, and superfluous commentary (Dana, 1955, 1959) and on measures of emotional tone, story outcome, and activity level (Eron, 1950; Ritter & Effron, 1952; Barends et al., 1990; Westen et al., 1990). The test has also been applied with some success to the task of differentiating between adolescent psychiatric patients and controls (Tripathi & Pillai, 1981), as a measure of change in defense mechanisms following intensive psychotherapy (Cramer & Blatt, 1990), and as a measure of ego development (Sutton & Swenson, 1983). Other studies have found, however, that depressives cannot be differentiated from normals in terms of the emotional tone of their stories (Eron, 1950; Sharkey & Ritzler, 1985).

The validity of evaluating ethnic minorities and other groups such as the aged and the disabled by means of the TAT has also been questioned. Furthermore, the TAT has been criticized because of the negative, sad tone of many of the pictures, which too easily induce pessimistic and depressive reactions or at least exert a negative stimulus pull on the storyteller (Eron, Terry, & Callahan, 1950; Goldfried & Zax, 1965). Consequently, many modifications and new apperceptive projectives have been developed—instruments that present clinicians and researchers with new psychometric problems.

■ TAT Modifications and Other Apperception Tests

Despite a number of worthy competitors, the TAT remains the most widely administered of all apperception tests. Its use as a method for obtaining information concerning needs, conflicts, and coping mechanisms or styles, in particular those related to family relationships and other interpersonal or social interactions, coupled with its flexibility or adaptability, is quite appealing to many clinicians. But its limitations with respect to different age, cultural, and disabled groups, in addition to specificity of the clinical problems for which it is an appropriate assessment tool, have prompted efforts to develop apperception tests having greater reliability, validity, and utility. For example, reported misdiagnoses of black and Hispanic children encouraged the production of more culturally appropriate apperception techniques (Thompson, 1949; Malgady, Costantino, & Rogler, 1984). Other modifications have been made for children, older adults, and the physically disabled (Bellak & Bellak, 1973; Wolk & Wolk, 1971). Criticisms regarding the dated quality of the TAT pictures, the limited range of human experience depicted in them (Ritzler, Sharkey, & Chudy, 1980), the predominant sadness in most scenes (Eron, Terry, & Callahan, 1950; Goldfried & Zax, 1965), the relative lack of specificity in the instructions for administration (McClelland, 1971), the low test-retest reliabilities (Entwisle, 1972; Winter & Stewart, 1977), and the decline in TAT research (Polyson, Norris, & Ott, 1985) prompted additional changes.

Picture Projective Test

One alternative to the TAT, the Picture Projective Test (PPT), was designed by Ritzler, Sharkey, and Chudy (1980; Sharkey & Ritzler, 1985). Employing a more rigorous methodology and a wider range of picture materials than the TAT, and consequently evoking a broader range of fantasy responses, the PPT consists of 30 pictures selected from the *Family of Man* photographic collection of the Museum of Modern Art (1955). Interpersonal involvement is stressed throughout the set of pictures, and unlike the primarily negative themes elicited by the TAT, the PPT pictures incorporate a balance of positive and negative stimulus cues. Approximately half of the pictures show people displaying positive affect—smiling, embracing, and dancing—whereas people in the remaining pictures reveal more negative feelings. In most of the pictures in the first half of the test the main characters are involved in high energy activities, whereas those in the second half display more subdued energy and activity levels. Sharkey and Ritzler (1985) compared the TAT and PPT stories produced by 10 adults in each of five groups (normals, nonhospitalized depressive, hospitalized depressives, hospitalized psychotics with good premorbid histories, and hospitalized psychotics with poor premorbid histories). The two tests were essentially equal in differentiating between the normal and depressed groups, but the PPT did a better job of differentiating psychotic from normal and depressed groups. Despite its promise as an alternative to the TAT, the PPT has not been widely used or reviewed.

Apperceptive Personality Test

Also contrasting with the negative or gloomy tone of the TAT pictures and the unreal or fantastic scenes depicted in them is the Apperceptive Personality Test (APT). This eight-card set of pictures depicts everyday people in familiar settings, including males and females of different ages and ethnic groups (Karp, Holmstrom, & Silber, 1990). Examinees tell a story about each picture and then answer a series of multiple-choice questions designed to provide further details about stories that are brief or cryptic. Responses are scored on 16 personality measures: active hostile feelings; passive hostile feelings; total hostile feelings; active hostile actions; passive hostile actions; total hostile actions; passivity; mastery; trust; mood, body image; denial; demeaning; emotional immaturity; outlook, and character distinction. A Brief Adult version of the APT and a Children's version (Children's Apperceptive Personality Test) for 4–12 year olds are also available. A related test for mentally retarded children and adults (Apperceptive Personality Test: Mental Retardation), consists of a set of picture cards for tapping psychological themes of damage and isolation from a group. The Apperceptive Personality Test was standardized on 517 male and 689 female college undergraduates, 60 male and 71 female adolescents, and 20 male and 45 female older adults. Like the Picture Projective Test, however, it has not been widely administered or reviewed.

Apperception Tests for Minority Groups

An unfortunate history of abuse and misuse has characterized the use of projective techniques with minority children (Anderson & Anderson, 1955), but the need to develop reliable and valid tests for the personality assessment of ethnic, racial, and linguistic minority groups cannot be overestimated (Padilla, 1979).*

Thompson TAT. On the assumption that blacks identify more closely with pictures of other blacks than with those of whites, Thompson (1949) redrew 21 of the original TAT pictures with black (and white) figures. The pictures on the resulting Thompson Modification of the TAT (T-TAT) were designed to be similar to those on the standard TAT, but they are not completely comparable in facial expression or situation to those on the latter instrument (Murstein, 1959; Cowan & Goldberg, 1967).

Thompson (1949) believed that identification with the figures in the pictures is greatest when the picture stimuli reflect the culture of the storyteller. He found that blacks told longer stories to the T-TAT than to the standard TAT pictures, a result confirmed by several other researchers (Cowan & Goldberg, 1967; Cowan, 1971; Bailey & Green, 1977). Entwisle (1972) suggested that the number of words used in telling a TAT story is an indicator of verbal achievement and academic socialization, and consequently there should be a positive relationship between achievement motivation and the length of stories told. Bailey and Green (1977) found that black youths do not necessarily obtain higher need achievement scores on the T-TAT than on the standard TAT, but that white youths obtain higher need achievement scores on the standard TAT than matched black youths.

Another thematic test designed expressly for African-Americans (adolescents and adults) is Themes Concerning Blacks (by R. L. Williams), consisting of 15 pictures designed to elicit themes of achievement, pride, and awareness, as well as hate, aggression, and depression, from respondents. Also noteworthy in this context is the Projective Prejudice Test, a picture-story test for measuring racial attitudes in children. A number of other apperception tests, including the Adolescent Apperception Cards and the Roberts Apperception Test for Children, have separate forms for blacks and whites.

TEMAS. Special TAT-like tests have also been developed for other minority groups in the United States. One such apperception instrument is the TEMAS (Spanish for "themes" and an acronym for "tell me a story"; Costantino, 1978; Costantino, Malgady, & Rogler, 1988). TEMAS was designed for use with urban Hispanic children aged 5–18, but it can be administered to both minority and nonminority children. The 23 chromatic pictures depict Hispanic characters interacting in urban settings and represent negative and positive emotions, cognitions, and interpersonal activities. Malgady, Costantino and Rogler (1984)

---

* A Chinese version of the Thematic Apperception Test, the TATC, has been prepared and normed in China and subjected to extensive psychometric analysis (Zhang et al., 1993)

reported that TEMAS discriminates between Puerto Rican clinical samples of children and matched non-patient samples of school children. These investigators also found the reliability and validity of TEMAS to be respectable, supporting the diagnostic and clinical usefulness of the instrument. In another study, Costantino, Malgady, and Vazquez (1981) found that Hispanic children were more verbally fluent in telling stories about the TEMAS pictures than about the TAT cards. Nevertheless, Lang (1992) concluded that the TEMAS "has not yet established criterion-related validity and has yet to show that it is better than the TAT or similar measures in assessing the personality characteristics of minority children" (p. 926). For an additional review, see Ritzler (1993).

Picture Tests for Children

Among the criticisms of the TAT and modifications of it are the lack of representativeness and variety in the stimulus material, the lack of psychometric rigor in design, standardization, and validation, and the inappropriateness of the test for certain age groups. Illustrative of TAT-like instruments constructed specifically for younger age groups are the Picture Story Test (Symonds, 1949) and lesser-known instruments such as the Education Apperception Test (Thompson & Sones, 1973) and the School Apperception Method (Solomon & Starr, 1968). Each of the 22 pictures on the Picture Story Test was designed to be more appropriate for adolescents than the TAT pictures. Stories that are more pertinent to the adolescent years, such as coming home later, leaving home, and planning for the future are elicited by the Picture Story Test. The purpose of the Education Apperception Test and the School Apperception Method is more specific, in that these instruments were designed to elicit stories revealing children's attitudes toward school and learning. But of all picture-story projectives for children, the most widely administered has been the Children's Apperception Test.

Children's Apperception Test. Bellak and Bellak (1949) constructed the Children's Apperception Test (CAT) because they considered the TAT to be inappropriate for young children. Based on the assumption that children identify more readily with animals than humans and will tell more elaborate stories about them, the CAT consists of ten pictures of animals in various situations (see Table 12–5).* The ten CAT cards, which were selected from an original set of 18 and designed for children from three to ten years old, depict animal figures involved in human activities suggestive of common childhood conflicts. Rather than being

---

* A variation on the TAT known as the Animal Apperception Test (ATAT) was constructed for adults. The results of research with the ATAT indicate that it is useful in evaluating people's perceptions of animals and for analyzing ethnic group differences in this regard (Friedman & Lockwood, 1991).

Descriptions of the CAT Pictures.   **TAB. 12-5**

Picture 1.	Chicks seated around a table on which is a large bowl of food. Off to one side is a large chicken, dimly outlined.
Picture 2.	One bear pulling a rope on one side while another bear and a baby bear pull on the other side.
Picture 3.	A lion with pipe and cane, sitting in a chair; in the lower right corner a little mouse appears in a hole.
Picture 4.	A kangaroo with a bonnet on her head, carrying a basket with a milk bottle; in her pouch is a baby kangaroo with a balloon; on a bicycle, a larger kangaroo child.
Picture 5.	A darkened room with a large bed in the background; a crib in the foreground in which are two baby bears.
Picture 6.	A darkened cave with two dimly outlined bear figures in the background; a baby bear lying in the foreground.
Picture 7.	A tiger with bared fangs and claws leaping at a monkey which is also leaping through the air.
Picture 8.	Two adult monkeys sitting on a sofa drinking from tea cups. One adult monkey in foreground sitting on a hassock talking to a baby monkey.
Picture 9.	A darkened room seen through an open door from a lighted room. In the darkened room there is a child's bed in which a rabbit sits up looking through the door.
Picture 10.	A baby dog lying across the knees of an adult dog; both figures with a minimum of expression in their features. The figures are set in the foreground of a bathroom.

Bellak (1993). Reprinted by permission of the publisher, Allyn & Bacon.

scored in a formal sense, the story told on each of the ten cards is described in terms of the ten variables listed on page 380 for the TAT (Bellak, 1993).

Considerable training is required to administer, score, and interpret the CAT. Stories given in response to both the CAT and the CAT-H cards are interpreted from the viewpoint of psychodynamic theory, specifically in terms of conflicts, anxiety, and guilt. Scores may be determined on: level of reality testing and judgment, control and regulation of drives, object relations, thought processing, ego functioning, defense mechanisms, stimulus sensitivity, and degree of autonomy. Because of developmental changes in children, analysis of the CAT differs from that of the TAT. Allowances must be made for a child's relative immaturity, a different quality of defensiveness, a greater frequency of primary process (wishful) thinking, in addition to confabulated (confused or mixed) and perseverative (repetitive) responses. A checklist, the Haworth Schedule of Adaptive Mechanisms, is available (from The Psychological Corporation) to assist in interpreting CAT and CAT-H stories.

Bellak also designed an additional series of ten irregularly shaped picture cards, the CAT Supplement (CAT-S) for further exploration of sources of tension in children. An extension of the CAT to older children, the CAT-H, which is composed of pictures of humans in situations paralleling those of the CAT animal pictures, is also available (from The Psychological Corporation).

Despite its wide usage, the psychometric characteristics of the CAT leave much to be desired. The inter-rater, internal-consistency, and test-retest reliabilities of the CAT are low, the validity data are inconclusive, and the norms are inadequate. Bellak (1993) does not consider the lack of norms for the CAT as an overwhelming shortcoming. He maintains that norms are not essential for projective techniques because each record is an adequate sample of the examinee's needs and behavior.

Be that as it may, the CAT has not fared well with reviewers. Hatt (1985) concluded that it is a useful clinical tool with children, but that the unstandardized administration and scoring of the test permits considerable subjectivity. If anything, reviews of the 1991 revision of the CAT are even more negative than those of its predecessor. Summing up his review, Knoff (1998a) concluded that "A great deal of test development and research demonstrating the CAT's reliability and validity is needed before this instrument can even approach the claims made by the authors." (p. 233) In a similar vein, Reinehr (1998) maintained that "The use of the technique as a method of developing a personality description is entirely unjustified by any scientific standard." (p. 234)

Four other story-telling projectives for children that have experienced some popularity are the Blacky Pictures, the Michigan Picture Test-Revised (MPT-R), the Roberts Apperception Test for Children, and the Children's Apperceptive Story-Telling Test. The first two of these are rather old and are no longer administered to any great degree. Interested readers will find descriptions of them in the previous two editions of this book.

Roberts Apperception Test for Children. Another attempt to meet the psychometric standards of a good test with a projective technique is represented by the Roberts Apperception Test for Children (RATC; McArthur & Roberts, 1982). Designed for children aged 6 to 15 years, the RATC is also usable with families. The 27 stimulus cards (line drawings of adults and children in modern clothing) on the test emphasize everyday interpersonal situations, including family confrontation, parental conflict, parental affection, observation of nudity, school and peer interpersonal events, in addition to situations of the sort found on the TAT and the CAT. The RATC test is administered in two overlapping sets of 16 cards each, one set for boys and one for girls. Explicit guidelines are provided for scoring the stories with respect to adaptive and maladaptive functioning on the following scales: Reliance on Others, Support-Other, Problem Identification, Unresolved Problems, Anxiety, Support-Child, Limit Setting, Resolution, Aggression,

Depression, Rejection. Three other dimensions—Atypical Response, Maladaptive Outcome, and Referral—serve as critical indicators. Raw scores on each area are converted to standard scores based on norms, by age and sex, obtained on 200 Caucasian children. A supplementary set of pictures designed specifically for black children is also available.

The RATC has met with mixed reviews. Friedrich (1984) concluded that it is a promising test that generates stories having many different themes and has a well-documented, easy-to-learn scoring system. However, the 16-card series is rather long for younger children and leads to briefer, more stereotyped stories. Sines (1985) viewed the RATC as a serious attempt to combine the flexibility of a projective approach and the quantification possible with a more objective scoring system and norms. He noted, however, that users of the RATC may choose to abandon the objective scoring approach and apply a more global and clinical scoring method.

Children's Apperceptive Story-Telling Test (CAST). This test is based on Adlerian theory and designed to assess the social, emotional, and behavioral functioning of children and young adolescents (ages 6–13). It consists of 31 colorful pictures, including separate male and female cards, to which children make up stories (Schneider, 1989; Schneider & Perney, 1990). CAST was constructed to be racially sensitive, and different ethnic groups are represented in the pictures. The following 19 scores and nine indicators are obtained:
- Adaptive Thematic: Instrumentality, Interpersonal Cooperation, Affiliation, Positive Affect
- Nonadaptive Thematic: Inadequacy, Alienation, Interpersonal Conflict, Limits, Negative Affect
- Adaptive Problem-Solving: Positive Preoperational, Positive Operational
- Nonadaptive Problem-Solving: Refusal, Unresolved, Negative Preoperational, Negative Operational
- Factor Profile: Adaptive, Nonadaptive, Immature, Uninvented
- Thematic Indicators: Sexual Abuse, Substance Abuse, Divorce, Hypothetical Thought, Emotionality, Self-Validation
- Life Tasks: Family, Peer, School

CAST was standardized on a presumably representative sample of 876 typical children (ages 6–13) in 16 states, in addition to 322 behavior-disordered children. The internal consistency and test-retest reliability coefficients of the factor scores are reported as being in the .80s and .90s. Some evidence for the content, criterion-related, and construct validity, including score profiles for several clinical groups of children (attention deficit disorder, conduct disorder, anxiety disorder, oppositional disorder, and childhood depression) are reported in the CAST manual.

Reviews of CAST by Aronow (1995) and Wiese (1995) are quite positive. Because of the neutrality of the stimulus pictures, the objectivity of scoring, and the representative standardization of the test, CAST is preferred to the CAT for both psychodiagnostic and research purposes. When used clinically, however, it is anticipated that, as in the case of the RATC, CAST stories will be evaluated idiographically and impressionistically rather than with respect to the norms.

Apperception Tests for Older Adults

The 16 pictures on the Senior Apperception Technique (SAT; Bellak & Bellak, 1973), which were designed specifically for older adults, depict older people in a wide range of human circumstances. The situations shown in the pictures were designed to reflect the themes of helplessness, illness, loneliness, uselessness, family difficulties, dependence, and lowered self-esteem; happier, more positive situations are also depicted in certain pictures. As on a similar instrument, the Gerontological Apperception Test (GAT; Wolk & Wolk, 1971),* responses to the pictures on the SAT reflect serious concerns about health, getting along with other people, and being placed in a nursing or retirement home. In interpreting these tests allowances must be made for changes in personality and behavior due to aging.

Both the SAT and the GAT have been criticized for inadequate norms, stereotyping of older adults, and possessing no advantage over the TAT in testing older age groups (J. P. Schaie, 1978; K. W. Schaie, 1978). According to Klopfer and Taulbee (1976), the SAT and GAT portray older adults in such a way as to discourage active responding and tend to reveal only superficial aspects of personality. Reviews of the 1985 Revision of the SAT (Arbisi, 1998; Kavan, 1998) fault it for its poor psychometric characteristics. The reviewers conclude that the pictures may serve to facilitate communication between elderly patients and therapists, but that the test should not otherwise be employed in clinical and research settings. Arbisi (1998) also concurred with other reviewers (e. g., Foote & Kahn, 1979) that the TAT is more age-relevant than the SAT, and boasts of greater research support for its use with the elderly. The same can has been said of another geriatric apperception test—the Projective Assessment of Aging Method (Peterson, 1985b).

Other Pictorial/Story Techniques

In addition to the tests described above, many other projectives involving responses to pictures have been developed over the years. Most apperception tests

---

* The Gerontological Apperception Test is no longer in print.

consist of pictures of people or animals, but one employs pictures of hands (The Hand Test) and another uses ambiguous stick drawings (Group Personality Projective Test). In addition, there is a Family Apperception Test and a Pain Apperception Test. Some apperception tests, such as the Four Picture Test, the Tomkins-Horn Picture Arrangement Test, the Szondi Test (see Chapter 1), and the Make-a-Picture Story Test have enjoyed popularity for a time but are now largely defunct. A fairly comprehensive list of apperception tests that are still commercially available is given in Appendix 12–1.

Certain projective tests have employed a combination of constructions and stories. Thus, a child may be asked to arrange dolls or other play materials in any way that he or she desires and then explain or tell a story about the arrangement. In such situations, the dolls, miniatures, or game materials may be used for therapeutic as well as diagnostic purposes. A psychologist or other clinical observer notes the child's behavior with respect to the test materials and interacts verbally with the child as considered appropriate.*

The use of miniatures or doll-like materials for psychodiagnostic purposes is seen in the Make a Picture Story (MAPS) test (Shneidman, 1952). The test material for the MAPS, which is designed for children aged 6 years and older, consists of 22 pictorial backgrounds and 67 cutout figures of people and animals. The child selects a background, places figures in it as they are presented by the examiner, and either tells a story about the arrangement or merely acts out a story with the figures. An assumption underlying the MAPS is that the child will become personally involved in creating the scenes and, by the number and types of figures selected and the interactions among them, reveal certain covert aspects of his or her personality. Though the MAPS is an interesting test, standardization and reliability are poor and the test has been used infrequently in comparison with other story techniques.

Another combination projective technique involving picture stories is the Draw-a-Story: Screening for Depression and Emotional Needs (DAS; Silver, 1988). The examinee selects two pictures out of 14, tells a story about each of the two, and then writes out the stories. The themes of the stories are evaluated on a seven-point scale ranging from "strongly negative" (e. g., "sad, dead/ dying, helpless, and isolated" story characters and "hopeless" futures) to "strongly positive." Norms on the DAS are based on 350 people (5 groups of children and two adult groups), and the interscorer reliability coefficients range from .75 to .82. Reviewers of the DAS (Katkovsky, 1992; Lachar, 1992) concur that available data do not support its use for early identification and screening of depressives but that the test warrants further development and research.

---

* This technique is often employed with children who are suspected victims of child abuse or molestation.

■ Summary

The Thematic Apperception Test (TAT), designed by Christina Morgan and Henry Murray, consists of 30 picture cards and a blank card. Depending on the examinee's age, sex, and circumstances, the examiner usually selects 10 of the cards for administration. The pictures are designed to elicit stories that reveal the conflicts, desires, feelings, and life themes of the examinee. The examinee is instructed to tell a complete story about each card, including what happened before, what's going on now, and how it will turn out. The TAT is typically administered to one individual at a time by another person, but it can also be self-administered or administered simultaneously to a group of people. The stories obtained from self- or group-administration, however, tend to be less elaborate than those obtained from individual administration of the test.

In testing psychiatric patients or other individuals with serious problems, a set of TAT pictures is selected that are most likely to reveal the dynamics of the particular disorder. Typical stories obtained from a sample of juvenile delinquents to an appropriate selection of TAT pictures (1, 3BM, 4, 6BM, 7BM, 9BM, 10, 13B, 13MF, 14, 17BM, 18BM) are described in this chapter as an illustration of the kinds of responses that are obtained and what they may mean.

Various methods of scoring and interpreting TAT stories, some of which are more objective or structured than others, have been applied. The traditional method of interpretation, as proposed by Henry Murray, is a rather subjective, impressionistic process that centers on an analysis of the needs and personality of the main character (the hero), who frequently represents the examinee, and the environmental forces (press) impinging on him or her. The frequency, intensity, and duration of the stories are taken into account in the interpretation. The interpreter also seeks to establish consensual validation by noting overlapping elements and themes in the various stories and their relationships to personality and behavioral data obtained by other methods (interview, other tests, etc.). Although the usual procedure of scoring and interpreting the TAT is highly impressionistic, scores determined by one of the more systematic scoring procedures are moderately reliable and can be interpreted in terms of norms based on standardization studies.

Asking a person to tell stories about pictures would appear to be a more valid approach to personality assessment than asking for responses to inkblots, but TAT stories are affected by the particular context in which the test is administered, the personality and comments of the person who administers it, and the physical and mental state of the test-taker. Consequently, the stories told in response to the pictures are not always significantly different in normal persons and those with psychological disorders. Furthermore, many psychologists maintain that less structured stimuli such as inkblots are more effective than picture stories in getting at unconscious conflicts and repressed desires. For these and other reasons the TAT has not been as popular as the Rorschach for psychodiagnostic purposes.

Other apperception techniques have been developed in response to questions concerning the datedness and lack of psychometric rigor of the TAT. Examples are the Picture Projective Test and the Apperceptive Personality Test. The pictures on the former test, which were taken from the *Family of Man* photographic collection of the Museum of Modern Art, have a more uniform balance of positive and negative themes and a more contemporary appeal in terms of characters and settings than those on the TAT. The Apperceptive Personality Test, which incorporates picture stories with multiple-choice questions, possesses many of the same features as the Picture Projective Test, in addition to four separate forms (Adult, Brief Adult, Children's, and Mental Retardation).

The TAT has been criticized with respect to its inappropriateness for non-white ethnic and non-adult age groups. The Thompson Modification of the TAT attempts to appeal to blacks by using black figures in the cards, and it has been successful in eliciting more articulate responses from some blacks. Another ethnically-oriented picture-story test is TEMAS, which was designed for Hispanic persons. A number of other TAT-like tests designed for different ethnic groups and nationalities have also been devised, and separate forms of some apperception tests are available for blacks and whites.

The Children's Apperception Test (CAT) is available in two forms—one consisting of pictures of animals in various human-like situations, and a second form with pictures of humans. Both forms have been successful in evoking psychologically meaningful stories from children, but the CAT is not considered to be a psychometrically sound instrument. The Michigan Picture Test, the Roberts Apperception Test for Children, and the Children's Apperceptive Story-Telling Test are the products of efforts to combine the flexibility of projectives with the psychometric qualities of a good test (objective scoring, reliability, representative standardization, etc.), but they are not as popular with clinicians as the CAT.

The Senior Apperception Test and the Gerontological Apperception Technique were designed for older adults, but they have not proved to be as successful in eliciting meaningful material from this age group as their designers desired. The same is undoubtedly true of the many of the other projective tests that use pictures as stimulus material.

■ Questions and Activities

1. Look through several popular magazines and either cut out or photocopy five pictures of people in ambiguous situations. That is, it should not be obvious

what the people in the pictures are doing or thinking. Present the pictures, one at a time, to several people, and ask them to tell a story about each picture. Tell them that they should include in their stories (a) what is going on now, (b) what led up to it (what happened before), and (c) how it will turn out. Try your hand at interpreting the stories in terms of common themes, the actions and feelings of the main characters, the pressures and frustrations occurring in the stories, whether the stories are generally pleasant or unpleasant, and whether the endings are upbeat or downbeat (comedic or tragic). Are there common elements in all the stories? What can you tell from these stories about the personality, attitudes, and feelings of the storyteller?

2. Read and summarize reviews of five of the apperception tests listed in Appendix 12–1. Locations of reviews in the *Mental Measurements Yearbook* and/or *Test Critiques* are provided with the brief descriptions of the tests in Appendix 12–1.

3. What are the differences in the procedures used in individual administration, group administration, and self-administration of the TAT? What are the relative advantages and disadvantages of each of these three procedures?

4. With respect to Lindzey's (1959) classification of projective techniques into association, construction, completion, arrangement /selection, and expression categories (Chapter 10), in which category or categories do picture-story tests fall? Explain.

5. Evaluate the psychometric characteristics (standardization or norms, reliability, validity, etc.) of the TAT. Compare your evaluation with those of reviews of the TAT in the *Mental Measurements Yearbook* (MMYB 8:697 and 9:1287) and *Test Critiques* (II:799).

6. What procedures have been used to evaluate the reliability and validity of picture-story tests such as the TAT? What have these procedures revealed concerning the reliability and validity of these psychometric instruments?

7. How might you use a test such as the TAT as a measure of (1) attitudes toward school, (2) racial or gender prejudice, (3) group cohesiveness, (4) vocational interests, (5) job satisfaction, (6) self-concept? What kinds of pictures would you select for each measurement purpose, and what would you look for in the stories told by the examinees?

8. List some of the advantages and disadvantages of the projective techniques discussed in Chapters 10–12 as compared with the more objective procedures described in Chapters 6–9. Consider the viewpoints of both clinicians and specialists in psychometrics.

Apperception Tests.

Adolescent Apperception Cards, White Version (by L. Silverton; from Western Psychological Services; 11 cards suggesting themes important to adolescents, such as relationships with parents, siblings, and peers; must be interpreted by an experienced clinician)

Adolescent Apperception Cards, Black Version (by L. Silverton; from Western Psychological Services; 11 cards suggesting themes important to adolescents; pictures evoke narratives concerning abuse and neglect, and relationships with parents, siblings, and peers)

Apperceptive Personality Test (by S. A. Karp et al.; from IDS Publishing; for adolescents or adults; eight stimulus cards and a multiple-chooice questionnaire that provides further details when the initial telling of the story is brief or cryptic; scored on 13 personality measures; also Adult Brief version)

Apperceptive Personality Test (by S. Reiss et al.; from IDS Publishing; for mentally retarded children and adults; stimulus cards tap psychological themes of damage and isolation from a group; post-story inquiry phase uses multiple-choice questionnaire to obtain consistent and comprehensive information; 16 scores)

Children's Apperception Test-Revised (by L. & S.S. Bellak; from C.P.S, Inc.; for ages 3–10; ten drawings of animals in various social situations, designed to aid in understanding a child's relationships to important figures and drives; review MMYB 13:58)

Children's Apperceptive Story-Telling Test (CAST) (by M. F. Schneider; from pro-ed; for ages 6–13; a set of cards depicting scenes concerning family, peers, and school, about which the child tells a separate story; designed to assess social, emotional, and behavior adjustment of children and early adolescents; reviews MMYB 12:73 & TC IX:66)

Draw-a-Story: Screening for Depression and Age or Gender Differences (by R. A. Silver; from Ablin Press Distributors; for 5 years to adult; two sets of stimulus drawings that prompt negative fantasies (Form A) or offset the negativity (Form B); respondents choose two subjects from the drawings, imagine something happening begtween the subjects they choose, then show what is happening by making drawings of their own; review MMYB 13:103)

Draw-a-Story: Screening for Depression and Emotional Needs (by R.A. Silver; from Ablin Press; for ages 5–17 & adults; designed to promote early identification of depressed individuals, opportunities for therapeutic dialogue, and increases in understanding of depressive illnees; 14 pictorial stimuli, from which the subject chooses any two, relates them in a story, and makes a drawing to tell what is happening; review MMYB 11:115)

Education Apperception Test (by J. M. Thompson & R. A. Sones; from Thompson Patrick Association; for ages 4–6; 18 pictures depicting middle elementary school students in school and school related activities for assessing children's percepitons of school and the educational process; review TC IV:

The Facial Interpersonal Perception Inventory (by J. J. Luciani & R. E. Carney; from Timao Foundation for Research and Development; for ages 5 and over; designed to evaluate real versus ideal perceptions of self and others by soliciting responses to simplified line drawings of faces displaying different emotional expressions; review MMYB 9-I:407)

Family Apperception Test (by A. Julian III, W. M. Sotile, S. Henry, & M. O. Sotile; from Western Psychological Services; for ages 6 and over; 35–40 scores; designed to assess family system variables; review TC X:251)

Four Picture Test, Third Revised Edition (by D. J. Van Lennep; from Swets Test Services; for ages 10 and over; a projective test of the TAT-type, requiring written rather than verbal responses; earlier edition reviews MMYB 6:213 & TC III:288).

The Group Personality Projective Test (by R. N. Cassel & T. C. Kahn; from Psychological Test Specialists; for ages 12 and over; test of personality concerned with assessing personal, social, and emotional need projections; the examinee is given a choice among alternative interpretations of a set of ambiguous "stick" drawings; review MMYB 7-I:167)

The Hand Test, Revised 1983 (by E. E. Wagner; from Western Psychological Services; for ages 5 and over; a diagnostic technique utilizing nine drawings of hands in various ambiguous poses; examinee "projects" by telling what the hand is doing; reviews MMYB 10:134 & TC I:315)

Michigan Picture Test Revised (by G. Andrew; for grade 1 through high school; consists of 15 picture cards depicting social and emotional situations and one blank card; scored on Tension Index, Direction of Force, Verb Tense, and overall Maladjustment Index; reviews MMYB 9:701 & TC III:447)

Pain Apperception Test (by D. V. Petrovich; from Western Psychological Services; for adults functioning at an elementary school level; to assess and evaluate psychological variables involved in the experience of pain; 3 area scores and total; reviews MMYB 8:639 & TC VII:404)

Picture Projective Test (by B. A. Ritzler, K. J. Sharkey, & J. Chudy; for adults; 30 pictures from Family of Man collection of Museum of Modern Art; emphasizes interpersonal rather than intrapersonal themes)

Projective Assessment of Aging Method (by B. D. Starr, M. B. Weiner, & M. Rabetz; from Springer Publishing Co.; for older adults; designed as a projective method for exploring thoughts and feelings about significant themes and problems of aging; reviews MMYB 9:1008 & TC III:539)

Roberts Apperception Test for Children (RATC) (by G. E. Roberts & D. McArthur; from Western Psychological Services; for ages 6–15; designed to assess children's perceptions of common interpersonal situations as an aid in general personality description and clinical decision making; review MMYB 9:1054)

School Apperception Method (by I. L. Solomon & B. D. Starr; from Springer Publishing Company; for ages 2–17; designed to assess student attitudes toward school and school personnel; respondent describes events preceding and following school situations depicted in each of 12 pictures; review TC III:564)

The Senior Apperception Technique, Revised (by L. Bellak; from C.P.S., Inc.; for older adults; projective instrument for gathering information on forms of depression, loneliness, or rage in the elderly; reviews MMYB 13:283 & TC III:604)

Tell-Me-A-Story (TEMAS) (by G. Costantino et al.; from Western Psychological Services; age 5–18 & adults; individually administered multicultural thematic apperception test for use with minority and nonminority children and adolescents; includes two sets of parallel pictorial stimuli, one for minorities and the other set for nonminorities; review MMYB 11:422)

Thematic Apperception Test (H. A. Murray; Psychological Corporation; for ages 4 and over; a method of revealing to the trained interpreter some of the dominant drives, emotions, sentiments, complexes, and conflicts of personality; total score only; reviews MMYB 8:697, 9:1287 & TC II:799).

■ Suggested Readings

Bellak, L. (1992). Projective techniques in the computer age. *Journal of Personality Assessment, 58,* 445–453.

Cramer, P. (1996). *Storytelling, narrative, and the Thematic Apperception Test.* New York: Guilford.

Dana, R. H. (1993). *Multicultural assessment perspectives for professional psychology.* Needham Heights, MA: Allyn & Bacon.

Dana, R. H. (1996). The Thematic Apperception Test. In C. S. Newmark (Ed.), *Major psychological assessment instruments* (2nd ed., pp. 166–205). Needham Heights, MA: Allyn & Bacon.

Elms, A. C. (1987). The personalities of Henry A. Murray. In R. Hogan & W. H. Jones (Eds.), *Perspectives in personality.* Greenwich, CT: JAI Press.

Groth-Marnat, G. (1997). The Thematic Apperception Test. In *Handbook of psychological assessment* (3rd ed., pp. 458–498). New York: Wiley.

Haworth, M. R. (1986). Children's Apperception Test. In A. Rabin (Ed.), *Projective techniques with children and adolescents* (pp. 73–84). New York: Springer-Verlag.

Teglasi, H. (1993). *Clinical use of story telling: Emphasizing the TAT with children and adolescents.* Boston: Allyn & Bacon.

Worchel, F. F., & Dupree, J. L. (1990). Projective story-telling techniques. In C. R. Reynolds & R. W. Kamphaus (Eds.), *Handbook of psychological and educational assessment of children: Personality, behavior, and context* (pp. 70–88). New York: Guilford Press.

PART V

PERSONALITY ASSESSMENT TODAY AND TOMORROW

CHAPTER 13

Other Measures, Applications, and Issues

As demonstrated by the number of citations of *personality assessment* and *personality testing* in the psychological literature, interest in the topic has increased steadily since mid-century (see Figure 13–1 next page). However, not all of the procedures that have been applied in the assessment of personality are discussed in the preceding chapters. New rating scales, personality inventories, and projective tests have appeared every year, as well as other types of instruments and procedures that have not been considered so far in this book. Many of these devices have been developed and validated in connection with particular research programs to measure an assortment of variables in both the affective and cognitive domains. The first part of this chapter considers some of these measures of personality, in particular those related to physiological and cognitive processes.

The specific purposes for which personality assessments are conducted most often have been referred to in previous chapters, but detailed discussions of the clinical, educational, organizational, and other contexts in which specific instruments are administered have not been provided. The second part of the chapter attempts to correct that deficiency to some extent.

Standards for psychological assessment and issues such as clinical versus statistical prediction are also considered in previous chapters, but there are many other issues and controversies regarding personality assessment. The last part of the chapter considers several of these issues and how research and practice in psychological assessment has dealt with them.

FIG. 13-1 **Frequency of Citations of Intelligence and Personality Testing in Psyc-INFO by Five-Year Periods since 1950.**

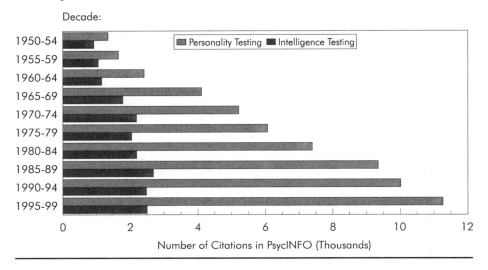

■ Physiological, Perceptual, and Cognitive Measures

Research and practice concerned with personality variables have employed many other devices for measuring a wide range of personality variables. In addition to the observations, interviews, biographical methods, paper-and-pencil instruments, and projective techniques, research and application have focused on physiological and chemical techniques for analyzing arousal, stress, emotions, psychopathology, and other devices associated with the measurement of affective variables. For example, bioelectric indicators of muscle tension, blood pressure, pulse rate, respiration rate, and the galvanic skin response have been employed extensively in research and in the polygraph ("lie detector") test for many years. Various types of apparatus, including the electromyograph for measuring muscle tension, the sphygmomanometer for blood pressure, the psychogalvanometer for skin resistance, the plethysmograph for measuring finger volume, the pupillometer for measuring pupillary diameter, and the voice-stress analyzer have been applied in studies of emotion and personality. But despite hundreds of investigations designed to discover links between specific emotions or personality traits and specific physiological response patterns, the evidence remains weak (Levenson, 1992).

Introversion/Extraversion and Physiology

Two personality variables that have been the topics of continuing investigation in psychophysiology are introversion/extraversion and sensation seeking. Eysenck (1967, 1990) hypothesized that extraverts have lower cortical excitation levels and higher sensory thresholds than introverts, causing extraverts to seek external stimulation in order to elevate their excitation levels and thereby to be conditioned more rapidly than introverts. On the other hand, the level of autonomic nervous system activity is greater in neurotics than in normals, regardless of whether they are extraverts or introverts.

Eysenck also maintained that there is an interaction between introversion/extraversion and normal/neurotic characteristics in their relationships to cortical activation level. Neurotic introverts (anxiety, phobic, and obsessive-compulsive neurotics) presumably have higher cortical excitation levels than normal introverts, whereas the cortical excitation levels of neurotic extraverts are higher than in normal extraverts but lower than in normal introverts. Consequently, Eysenck argues, neurotic extraverts (e. g., antisocial or psychopathic personalities) experience insufficient fear to inhibit the expression of their impulses and thereby are more likely to act out those impulses.

Eysenck devised various personality inventories, e. g., the Eysenck Personality Questionnaire and the Eysenck Personality Inventory, to differentiate between introverts and extraverts, but perhaps his most novel approach is the lemon juice test in which the amount of salivation is measured when drops of natural lemon juice are placed on the tongue. On this test, introverts tend to salivate more than extraverts. Other research has demonstrated that introverts are also more readily aroused than extraverts to stimulants such as caffeine but less readily aroused by depressants such as alcohol (Stelmack, 1990). In addition, the finding that introverts show a greater cortical response than extraverts to simple auditory and visual stimuli is consistent with Eysenck's distinction between these two groups (De Pascalis & Montirosso, 1988; Stenberg, Rosen, & Risberg, 1988, 1990).

Related to the research of Eysenck and others on introversion and extraversion is Zuckerman's (1983, 1989) concept of sensation seeking. Box 13–1 is a list of the ten items on Zuckerman's Disinhibition Scale, on which extraverts score significantly higher than introverts. High scorers on this scale have also been shown to have lower blood levels of monamine oxidase (MAO), an enzyme which regulates the concentration of two heredity-based neurotransmitters that are believed to play important roles in motivation and emotion. Also of interest in this context is the finding by Jerome Kagan and his coresearchers (Kagan, Reznick, & Snidman, 1988; Kagan, 1994) of significantly higher blood levels of MAO in shy than in outgoing children. Finally, Zuckerman (1995) reported that the level of testosterone in the blood is related to sensation seeking, as well as to extraversion, dominance, and heterosexual activity.

BOX 13-1 | **Disinhibition Scale.**

1. A. I like "wild" uninhibited parties.
   B. I prefer quiet parties with good conversation.

2. A. I dislike "swingers" (people who are uninhibited and free about sex).
   B. I enjoy the company of real "swingers."

3. A. I find that stimulants make me uncomfortable.
   B. I often like to get high (drinking liquor or smoking marijuana).

4. A. I am not interested in experience for its own sake.
   B. I like to have new and exciting experiences and sensations even if they are a little frightening, unconventional or illegal.

5. A. I like to date members of the opposite sex who are physically exciting.
   B. I like to date members of the opposite sex who share my values.

6. A. Heavy drinking usually ruins a party because some people get loud and boisterous.
   B. Keeping the drinks full is the key to a good party.

7. A. A person should have considerable sexual experience before marriage.
   B. It's better if two married persons begin their sexual experience with each other.

8. A. Even if I had the money I would not care to associate with flighty rich persons like those in the "jet set."
   B. I could conceive of myself seeking pleasures around the world with the "jet set."

9. A. There is altogether too much portrayal of sex in movies.
   B. I enjoy watching many of the "sexy" scenes in movies.

10. A. I feel best after taking a couple of drinks.
    B. Something is wrong with people who need liquor to feel good.

This constitutes one of the four subscales on Zuckerman's 40-item Sensation Seeking Scale. Scores are computed by giving one point to each response corresponding to the following key: 1-A, 2-B, 3-B, 4-B, 5-A, 6-B, 7-A, 8-B, 9-B, 10-A.

(From Zuckerman, M. (1994). *Behavioral expressions and biosocial bases of sensa- tion seeking*. New York: Cambridge University Press. Reprinted by permission of M. Zuckerman)

Another physiological measure associated with the personality dimension of introversion/extraversion is the P300 brain wave, which occurs about 300 milliseconds following the presentation of a meaningful, momentary stimulus. Research has demonstrated that the P300 waves of introverts produced by novel stimuli are larger than those of extraverts (Polich & Martin, 1992; Wilson & Languis, 1990), and that the amplitudes of P300 waves are smaller in psychotics than in normals (Stelmack, Houlihan, & McGarry-Roberts, 1993). Other research has found shorter P300 latencies in neurotics than in normals matched on extraversion (Pritchard, 1989). The latencies of auditory potentials evoked from the brain stem are also shorter in introverts than in extraverts (Stelmack & Houlihan, 1995).

The very large number of neurotransmitters and associated receptor sites in the human body has prompted interest in determining whether there are significant relationships between neurotransmitter receptors and personality. Useful in this regard are behavioral genetics techniques employing DNA markers to identify genes that are associated with complex behaviors. An example of this type of research are studies of genes that control the development of dopamine type 2 (D2) and dopamine type 4 (D4) receptors. According to the notion of a "reward deficiency syndrome," people with the D2 form of the receptor are unable to obtain a normal amount of reinforcement in everyday life and consequently are more likely to seek more adventurous, pleasurable methods of stimulating their D2 receptors. This is presumably what happens in alcoholism, drug abuse, obesity, and habitual gambling (Blum, Cull, Braverman, & Comings, 1996). On the other hand, people who inherit a gene that controls the development of the D4 receptor are more likely to exhibit a so-called "novelty-seeking" behavioral syndrome characterized by impulsivity, exploratory behavior, and quick-temperedness (Benjamin et al., 1996; Ebstein et al., 1996).

Perception and Personality

The assumption that personality affects one's perception and interpretation of his or her experiences is, of course, inherent in projective tests such as the Rorschach and the TAT. Experimental research on the relationships of personality and emotion on perception goes back at least to the middle of the twentieth century (e. g., McGinnies, 1949; Bruner, 1957). Since then, a host of perceptual variables (vigilance, pain sensitivity, word recognition, identifying incomplete figures, dark adaptation, conditioning, etc.) have been found to be related to personality variables such as introversion/extraversion (Eysenck, 1962; Eysenck & Rachman, 1965; Wilson, 1978). Also of interest is Witkin's long-running research program on field independence/dependence (e. g., Witkin, 1973; Witkin & Berry, 1975; Witkin & Goodenough, 1977). The three tests—Body Adjustment Test,

FIG. 13-2 **Sample item on the Embedded Figures Test. Field-dependent people have difficulty locating the figures at the left in the complex patterns at the right.**

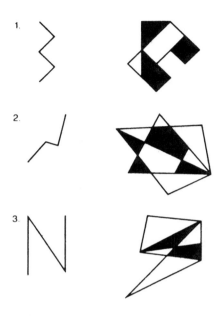

(From Witkin et al. (1977). Field dependent and field independent cognitive styles and their educational adaptations. *Review of Educational Research, 47,* 1–64. Reprinted with permission of the publisher.)

Rod and Frame Test, Embedded Figures Test (see Figure 13–2)—devised for these investigations are measures of the extent to which people are able to differentiate aspect or parts of a complex confusing whole (see Figure 13–2). Persons who can easily determine the true vertical position of his/her body or a luminous rod in the first two tests or quickly locates the embedded figures in the second test are characterized as *field independents,* while those who experience difficulties in determining the upright position and locating the embedded figures are *field dependents.*

Witkin found that field independents are typically secure, independent, more psychologically mature, self-accepting, active in dealing with the environment, more aware of their inner experiences, and tend to use intellectualization as a defense mechanism. Field dependents, in contrast, are less secure, psychologically immature, passive, less attuned to inner experiences, and likely to use repression and denial as defense mechanisms. In general, males are more field-independent than females, and people in hunting and foraging cultures are more independent than those in sedentary, agricultural societies. With respect to child rearing practices, field independents typically have less restrictive and less authoritarian parents than field-dependents.

Cognitive Styles

From a holistic viewpoint, perception, cognition, affect, and behavior are all an integral part of human personality. In particular, stylistic behaviors, modes of thinking, approaches to problems, and ways of coping are all viewed as personality variables in a broader sense. For example, some people are more concrete in their thinking, whereas others are more abstract; some are more analytic, whereas others are more synthetic or global in their approach to problems; and some prefer a rational strategy, whereas others rely more on intuition.

A holistic definition of personality considers *cognitive styles*—the various strategies or approaches that people use in trying to understand and deal with

---

Sample Item on the Matching Familiar Figures (MFF) Test. Examinees are told to select the picture in the second or third row that is identical to the picture at the top.   **FIG. 13-3**

From Jerome Kagan (1966). Reflection-impulsivity: The generality and dynamics of conceptual tempo. *Journal of Abnormal Psychology, 71*, 17–24. Copyright 1966 by the American Psychological Association. Reprinted by permission of the author.)

their experiences—as characteristics of personality. In addition to field independence/dependence, an extensive amount of research has been conducted on cognitive styles such as impulsive vs. reflective, leveling vs. sharpening, scanning vs. focusing, broad vs. narrow categorizing, cognitive complexity vs.simplicity, and automatization vs. restructuring (Bostic & Tallent-Runnels, 1991). Specific tests have been designed to measure each of these cognitive styles. For example, the Matching Familiar Figures Test (see Figure 13–3) is a popular measure of the reflective versus impulsive style (Kagan, 1966). The items on this test consist of a stimulus figure and several response figures, only one of which matches the former. The child's time and accuracy in identifying the correct match determines whether he she is designated as "reflective" or "impulsive." Faster and accurate responses are more characteristic of reflective than of impulsive children. Other personality characteristics that affect performance on cognitive tasks are constricted vs. flexible control, internal vs. external locus of control, tolerance vs. intolerance for incongruous or unrealistic experiences, and internal vs. external attributions (see Aiken, 1997c, pp. 180–186).

Though research on cognitive styles is several decades old, according to Sternberg and Grigorenko (1997), it is still in style, and many of the associated measures are useful in predicting performance in school and employment contexts. Indicative of the continuing interest in this area are investigations by Epstein et al. (1996), Jones (1997), Riding & Read (1996), Sorrentino et al. (1995), and Wooten, Barner, and Silver (1994).

■ Applications of Personality Assessment

Personality assessment instruments and procedures are used extensively in clinical and counseling, business and industrial, governmental and military, and educational and school contexts. Clinical usage, for purposes of psychodiagnosis, prognosis, and treatment planning, accounts for a large percentage of the total number of personality assessments, but schools and colleges, as well as business and other work organizations, also conduct large numbers of personality evaluations. Business usage of personality tests consists primarily of the administration of self-report inventories such as the Inwald Personality Inventory-Revised (from Hilson Research) and the Hogan Personality Inventory (from Hogan Assessment Systems), but screening applicants for sensitive jobs and selecting managerial personnel who possess the traits of leadership and coping abilities demanded by particular job situations often entails assessment in greater depth. Many schools and higher learning institutions have traditionally administered some sort of standardized personality test at the beginning of the school year to identify students who are or can be expected to experience personal problems during the ensuing term, but the growing number of students and the shortage of funds has curtailed this practice to some extent. Federal and state governments and military organizations also continue to conduct personality assessments, but concerns over civil rights, efficiency, and other selection methods have led to a reduction in the use of standardized personality tests in these institutions as well.

Despite economic and social changes that have produced constraints on the applications of psychological assessment and treatment, there are a number of areas in which the demand for psychological services has increased during the past two or three decades. Five of these are the health professions, the forensic (legal) professions, marriage and family counseling, amateur and professional sports, and marketing (consumer behavior). All five areas have attracted some of the best students of psychology, and a number of universities have instituted graduate degree programs in these areas.

Assessment in Health Contexts

Health psychology has been defined as the "educational, scientific, and professional contributions of the discipline of psychology to the promotion and maintenance of health, the prevention and treatment if illness, and the identification of etiological and diagnostic correlates of health, illness, and related dysfunction" (Matarazzo, 1980, p. 815). Interest in the role of attitudes, self efficacy, and other psychological factors or personality variables in health is not limited to so-called psychosomatic disorders such as duodenal ulcers and migraine headaches, but includes cardiovascular disorders, cancer, and other life-threatening illnesses. Psychologists are called upon not only to identify psychological factors that are related to various medical conditions and to help diagnose specific disorders but also to assist in planning intervention or treatments.

The number of commercially available checklists, rating scales, and inventories concerned with health-related matters has increased markedly in recent years (see Streiner & Norman, 1995). Included among these are instruments designed to identify health problems in general and specific health areas, questionnaires of opinions and beliefs pertaining to health, measures of stress and ways of coping with it, measures of pain perception and control, and measures of anxiety, depression, substance abuse, violence and suicide potential. As defined by certain instruments, *health* connotes more than the absence of disease; it means *positive wellness* and a focus on attaining a good *quality of life*.

Illustrative of health-related personality inventories are the Substance Abuse Subtle Screening Inventory for identifying alcoholic and drug-dependent individuals, the Jenkins Activity Survey for identifying coronary-prone Type A personalities, the Eating Disorders Inventory-2 and the Eating Inventory for assessing attitudes and behaviors associated with eating disorders, the TMJ Scale for measuring pain perception and control, the Imagery and Disease and the Imagery of Cancer for coping with cancer, and the Millon Behavioral Health Inventory for assisting in the formulation of comprehensive treatment plans for adult medical patients.

A variable that has played a central role in the field of health psychology is *stress*. Among the commercially available instruments with the word *stress* in the title are the Daily Stress Inventory (from Sigma Assessment Systems) and the Parenting Stress Index (from Psychological Assessment Resources). Other stress-related instruments are the Coping Resources Inventory and the Hassles and Uplifts Scale, both of which are available from Consulting Psychologists Press, and the Health Attribution Test (from Institute for Personality and Ability Testing).

Managed Care in Mental Health

The rising cost of health care in recent years and the emphasis on fiscal responsibility, third-party payers, and managed care have increased concern about the value of psychological testing for psychodiagnostic purposes. Changes made in diagnostic procedures, and the necessity of justifying all diagnostic procedures fiscally and from the standpoint of real changes in behavioral and mental health, has led to a decline in the frequency of psychological testing in health contexts in recent years (Acklin, 1996; Piotrowski, Belter, & Keller, 1998). Managed-care companies and third-party payers tend to prefer that clinicians base their plans on interviews and short, brief self-report measures targeting specific symptoms or problem areas rather than comprehensive, time-consuming tests (Ben-Porath, 1997; Piotrowski, Belter, & Keller, 1998). Test designers have, however, not been idle in the face of the managed care revolution. Brief psychometric instruments such as the Butcher Treatment Planning Inventory (from The Psychological Corporation), which helps clinicians determine whether their clients possess the characteristics that will aid or impede their progress in psychological treatment, are being marketed. Assessment is beginning to focus on the acuity, risk, and potential destructiveness of psychological problems, such as mood disorders, psychosis, and anger control, to both the patient and other people. In addition, as pointed out by Acklin (1996), the language in which psychological assessors talk to case managers who make decisions regarding medical necessity is becoming more medicalized.

Assessment in Forensic Contexts

Psychologists employed in law enforcement and other legal contexts perform a variety of tasks. They serve as human relations experts and staff developers. They use tests, questionnaires, and interviews to assist in selecting personnel and evaluating staff development programs. They counsel police offers and their families in crisis situations. They conduct research on the training and treatment of law enforcement personnel. In court cases, psychologists may be asked by either the prosecution or the defense to examine the plaintiff for signs of mental disorder, dangerous or violent behavior, incompetency to stand trial or to handle his (her) own affairs, inability to serve as a suitable parent in a child custody hearing, or for a number of other reasons.

Among the questions that may be asked of psychologists by legal representatives and officials in court cases are (Lanyon, 1986);

- Is this person insane?
- What is the likelihood that this person will engage in dangerous or violent behavior?
- Who should assume custody of this child?
- Why did this person commit homicide?
- What are the personal characteristics of a particular murderer who has not been apprehended?
- How can sex offenders be identified from psychological evaluations, and can their future behavior be predicted?
- How can one tell whether a particular client will be defensive or honest in testifying?

Not only the defendant but also other persons (witnesses, etc.) associated with a legal dispute may require examination by a psychologist. The psychologist may be asked for an opinion concerning an unknown or apprehended criminal, whether a child will be better off if placed with one of the parents or with another person, and even how potential jurors are likely to respond to the evidence and the participants in the trial. For example, an expert in personality analysis may be called upon to assist is the process of jury selection in criminal or civil trials. Many attorneys consider the *voir dire*, or questioning of the jury to decide whether to accept or dismiss a potential juror, to be one of the most important phases of a trial. Although both the defense and prosecution attorneys in a legal dispute presumably desire to see justice done, to the prosecution *justice* usually means a guilty verdict, and to the defense it means a not guilty verdict. The makeup of the jury, as much as the actual evidence presented in the trial, affects which of these verdicts is handed down. Generally speaking, prosecutors in criminal trials are inclined to select jurors who, from their dress, manner, hobbies, or occupation, appear to be conservative in their political and legal views. Defense attorneys, on the other hand, are more likely to select jurors who appear liberal in their thoughts and behavior. Nordic-appearing types with crew cuts tend to be favored by prosecutors and long-haired Latins by defenders. Sometimes whether a potential juror is prosecution-oriented or defense-oriented can be determined from his or her occupation. Bankers and engineers, for example, are said to be prosecution-oriented, whereas teachers and social workers tend to be defense-oriented. But even the most conservative-appearing professional may harbor liberal sentiments. Who would have guessed that the most prosecution-oriented of all occupational groups are secretaries? (Bugliosi, 1991)

The most frequently administered of all psychometric instruments in legal settings is the Minnesota Multiphasic Personality Inventory. The MMPI and MMPI-2 have been used to predict dangerous or violent behavior, defensiveness (willingness to tell the truth), and many other matters of concern in court trials. The Rorschach is another work horse in legal settings, but neither the MMPI nor the Rorschach permits unqualified answers and opinions concerning legal matters.

Because recidivism is common in violent crimes, parole board, personnel departments, and other organizations or persons with whom violent offenders come into contact need the best information they can get regarding the probability of repeat offenses. No single psychometric instrument is foolproof in predicting violence, although The Hare Psychopathy Checklist-Revised (from Psychological Assessment Resources) has been particularly helpful. Behavioral predictors of violence include a recent history of violence, substance abuse, breakup of a marital or love relationship, being disciplined or terminated on a job, and having access to guns or other weapons (Hall, 1987). With respect to sexual offenses, the Clarke Sex History Questionnaire for Males (Langevin, 1983), which reportedly assesses types and strength of sexually anomalous behavior, may be of help to the forensic psychologist.

Among the psychological measures used by psychodiagnosticians in assessing competency to stand trial are the Competency Screening Test (Lipsitt, Lelos, & McGarry, 1971), the Georgetown Screening Interview for Competency to Stand Trial (Bukatman, Foy, & De Grazia, 1971), the Competency Assessment Instrument (McGarry et al., 1973), and the Georgia Court Competency Test (Wildman et al., 1980). The Rogers Criminal Responsibility Scales (Rogers, 1984, 1986) may be administered to determine criminal responsibility according to the degree of impairment on psychological variables significant to the determination of insanity under the American Law Institute (ALI) standard.* The five scales on this instrument assess Patient Reliability, Organicity, Psychopathology, Cognitive Control, and Behavioral Control at the time of the crime the patient is alleged to have committed. Neuropsychological tests may also be administered to defendants in insanity pleas. Unfortunately, none of these instruments is perfectly valid,

---

* As cited by Smith and Meyer (1987), the ALI definition of insanity states that "A person is not responsible for criminal conduct, i.e., insane if, at the time of such conduct, as a result of a mental disease or defect, he lacks substantial capacity either to appreciate the criminality (wrongfulness) of his conduct, or to conform his conduct to the requirements of the law." (American Law Institute, 1956)

and there is a need for psychodiagnostic measures that provide more accurate answers to legal questions than currently available instruments.

Child custody evaluations may include administration of the Bricklin Perceptual Scales (Bricklin, 1984) in an effort to understand the child's perceptions of his or her parents in four areas (competence, supportiveness, follow-up consistency, possession of admirable personality). In addition, measures of the parents' knowledge and attitudes concerning child rearing practices could contribute to decision making in child custody cases. Gordon and Peck's (1989) Custody Quotient, which yields ratings on ten parenting factors, is helpful in this regard. Even more comprehensive is the Uniform Child Custody Evaluation System, which consists of ten general data and administrative forms, nine parent forms, and six child forms.

Marital and Family Assessment

Growth in the adult population and rises in the incidence of marital discord, separation, and divorce during recent years have led to an increase in the number of persons certified as marriage, family, and child counselors. The need and availability of these counseling services has been accompanied by the publication of numerous paper-and-pencil scales and tests for the assessment of caring relationships, marital and family communication, marriage expectations, and marital and family conflicts and distress.

Instruments are available for premarital advising, identifying the sources and possible solutions for family disagreements and problems, and helping victims of divorce, either parents or children, to pick up the pieces and get on with their lives. Traditional inventories and projectives such as the MMPI, the 16PF, the Rorschach, and the TAT are frequently administered to analyze marital and family problems. Also useful in analyzing marital relations are checklists such as the Marital Evaluation Checklist (from Psychological Assessment Resources) and inventories such as the Marital Attitude Evaluation (from Consulting Psychologists Press), which and the Marital Satisfaction Inventory (from Western Psychological Services). The last of these is a self-report measure of marital interaction and distress for couples beginning marriage counseling. Separate scores are provided on conventionalism, global distress, affective communication, problem-solving communication, time together, disagreement about finances, sexual dissatisfaction, role orientation, family history of distress, dissatisfaction with children, and conflict over child rearing.

Also available for family counseling purposes are special projectives such as the Family Relations Test: Children's Version (from Psychological Assessment Resources) and the Family Apperception Test (from Western Psychological Services). Another useful psychometric instrument, the Family Environment Scale (from Consulting Psychologists Press), which was designed to assess the social climate of family systems and how the characteristics of the family interact, can be used to identify family strengths and problems and important issues for family treatment. Administration of all of these instruments should, of course, be supplemented by sensitive interviewing and observations of couples and family members in face-to-face social interaction.

Psychological Assessments in Sports

The psychology of sport is a broad field of research, theory, and application that deals not only with optimizing the performance of elite athletes but also with the physical activities of all age groups and all levels of athletic competence (see Butt, 1987; LeUnes & Nation, 1989). Numerous studies concerned with the selection of potentially winning athletes have used personality assessment instruments such as the Athletic Motivation Inventory, the Minnesota Multiphasic Personality Inventory, the 16 Personality Factor Questionnaire, the Eysenck Personality Inventory, and the Edwards Personality Inventory. None of these instruments has proven to be a very valid predictor of athletic performance, but somewhat more encouraging results have been obtained with the Profile of Mood States (POMS). Morgan (1980) compared the POMS scores of Olympic rowers, wrestlers, and distance runners with the scores of unsuccessful candidates in these sports. In all three sports, successful candidates scored lower than unsuccessful candidates on the tension (TEN), depression (DEP), anger (ANG), fatigue (FAT), and confusion (CON) scales, but higher on the vigor (VIG) scale of the POMS. This so-called iceberg profile has also been reported by other investigators (e. g., Furst & Hardman, 1988; Mastro, Sherrill, Gench, & French, 1987; Ungeleiter & Golding, 1980), but a review of studies of across many different sports and levels of performance provided little support for it (Rowley, Landers, Kyllo, & Etnier, 1995).

With respect to the variables of extraversion discussed earlier in the chapter, a number of investigations have shown that men and women who engage in sports activities are more extraverted than non-exercisers (Egloff & Gruhn, 1996; Furnham, 1990; Kerr & Cox, 1991; Kirkcaldy & Furnham, 1991; Newcombe & Boyle, 1995).

Studies involving endurance sports have discovered a tendency for extraversion to be higher among participants in team sports than those in individual sports, and higher in sprinters than in marathon runners (Dowd & Innes, 1981; Svebak & Kerr, 1989). Other research has shown that sensation seekers prefer high risk sports (Brevik, 1996; Canton & Mayor, 1994; Schroth, 1995), and that athletes tend to be lower on anxiety-neuroticism than non-athletes (Brevik, 1996; Newcombe & Boyle, 1995; O'Sullivan, Zuckerman, & Kraft, 1998).

Another kind of investigation of the relationships of personality variables to athletic performance and exercise has been concerned with the effects of exercise on mood and other affective variables. The results of such studies indicate that, in general, physical exercise has a significant effect on anxiety, depression, self-esteem, and other indices of mental well-being (Kerr & Van Den Wollenberg, 1997; Ransford & Bartolomeo, 1996; Yeung, 1996).

Consumer Behavior

Consumer psychology is concerned with identifying attitudes, interests, opinions, values, personality traits, and life-styles that are associated with preferences for and purchases of certain products and services. A particular focus of consumer psychology is *psychographics*, which attempts through research to describe the characteristic patterns of temperament, cognition, and behavior that differentiate between diverse human components of the marketplace. The results of psychographic research may contribute to segmenting a particular market according to consumer personality and behavioral characteristics and then designing advertising, packaging, and promotional efforts to appeal to that market. Two popular approaches in psychographic studies are AIO inventories and VALS (values and life-styles).

AIO Inventories. An *AIO inventory* consists of a set of statements concerning the activities, interests, and opinions of specified groups of people. Illustrative of this approach are the following items on an AIO inventory administered to a sample of 18-24-year-old men who both drank and drove (Lastovicka, Murray, Joachimsthaler, Bhalla, & Scheurich, 1987):
- It seems like no matter what my friends and I do on a weekend, we almost always end up at a bar getting smashed.
- A party wouldn't be a party without some liquor.
- I've been drunk at least five times this month.
- Being drunk is fun.
- The chances of an accident or losing a driver's license from drinking and driving are low.
- Drinking helps me to have fun and do better with girls.
- A few drinks will have no noticeable effect on my coordination and self-control.

VALS Approach. *VALS™2** is based on the dimensional concepts of self-orientation and resources. Consumers are seen as motivated by one of three *self-*

---

* VALS™2 is a trademark of Business Intelligence Center, Values and Lifestyles Program, 333 Ravenswood Ave., Menlo Park, CA 94025-3493.

FIG. 13–4 **VALS™2 Two-Dimensional Psychographics Model.**

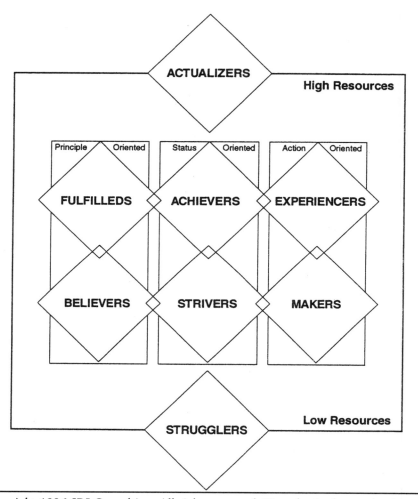

orientations: principle, status, and action. The choices of *principle-oriented* consumers are guided by abstract, idealized criteria, rather than by feelings, events, or the behaviors or opinions of other people. *Status-oriented* consumers, on the other hand, are interested in products and services that indicate success to their peers. Finally, *action-oriented* consumers are motivated toward social or physical activity, variety, and risk-taking.

The *resources* dimension of the VALS™ 2 system refers to the psychological, physical, demographic, and material means and capacities that are available to consumers. These resources include education, income, self-confidence, health, eagerness to buy, intelligence, and energy level. Resources are on a continuum from low to high, generally increasing from adolescence to middle age but decreasing with old age, depression, financial reverses, and physical or psychological impairment.

The three self-orientations and the low to high resources dimensions define eight segments of adult behavior and decision making (see diamond-shaped boxes in Figure 13–4). Approximately equal proportions of the population are represented by each segment, which is a viable marketing target. *Actualizers*, who have abundant resources and are a combination of the principle-, status-, and action-orientations, are at the top of the VALS™2 hierarchical segmentation system. Of the two segments with the greatest amount of principle-orientation, *fulfilleds* have more abundant resources than *believers*. Of the two primarily status-oriented segments, *achievers* have more resources than *strivers*. Of the two primarily action-oriented segments, *experiencers* have more abundant resources than *makers*. At the bottom of the resources hierarchy are the *strugglers,* whose lives are constricted and difficult and who are therefore cautious consumers.

The relationships of personality to consumer behavior have also been studied with other theories and instruments. For example, the five-factor model discussed in Chapter 7 has served as a starting point for studies of shopping motives (Mooradian, 1996) and "brand personality" (Aaker, 1997)

■ Issues in Personality Assessment

It would be reassuring to conclude in the last section of the last chapter of this book that all of the issues and controversies debated since the early years of personality assessment have been resolved by compromise among the various disputants. Though some of the issues of yesteryear have been muted by time, they have not disappeared and new controversies have arisen to replace those that have grown stale. Arguments over idiographic versus nomothetic assessment, clinical versus statistical (actuarial) prediction and interpretation, response sets (styles), and the relative importance of traits and situations as determinants of behavior may not be debated as vociferously as they once were, but to some extent they are still with us. Questions concerning the ethics and legalities of personality assessment, computer-based test administration and interpretation, and the fairness and validity of assessment instruments for particular cultural, ethnic, and gender groups and in specific contexts also continue to be of concern.

Continuing Controversies

Many of the older disputes in personality assessment and research have become less strident with time. For example, the idiographic versus nomothetic controversy and the clinical versus statistical prediction debates are discussed less today than they were in previous decades. In the *idiographic approach* to personality assessment, every person is considered to be a lawful, integrated system to be studied in his or her own right. In the *nomothetic approach*, which relies heavily on group norms or averages, general laws of behavior or personality that apply to all people are sought and applied. Rather than attempting to interpret the scores made by an individual on a set of tests, inventories, rating scales, and similar standardized instruments, psychologists of an idiographic persuasion study the consistencies and variations noted in observations, interviews, and personal records (diaries, biographies, etc.) of the individual.

The clinical versus statistical approach to personality assessment is discussed in Chapter 4, and response sets and dissimulation are discussed in Chapter 7. These controversies were still very much alive in the 1990s (e. g., Dawes, Faust, & Meehl, 1993; Kleinmuntz, 1990; Ones, Viswesvaran, & Reiss, 1996). Most practicing psychologists had accepted a compromise between the clinical and statistical approaches (Dawes, Faust, & Meehl, 1993; Kleinmuntz, 1990). And many, if not all, eagerly awaited the technological advances that would lead to more flexible and valid interactive multimedia assessments.

Traits and Situations

Trait/factor theorists of personality have traditionally assumed that behavior is influenced to a great extent by traits that are expressed in a consistent manner across different situations. Environment (the specific situation) is also considered important in determining behavior, but the emphasis has been on relatively stable personality traits and their measurement. Despite the preoccupation with traits, the fact that the situation is sometimes more important in determining specific behavior was clearly demonstrated over 70 years ago in Hartshorne and May's (1928) classic studies of children's character traits.

Four decades after the Hartshorne and May studies, Walter Mischel (1968) concluded that behavioral correlates of cognitive abilities are fairly consistent across situations but that personal-social behavior is highly dependent on the specific situation in which it occurs. Mischel maintained that inferences regarding personality dynamics or traits are less useful than a knowledge of situational variables in predicting behavior. He further argued that assessments of generalized traits of personality are not particularly useful because such traits typically show little cross-situational generality. Rather than analyzing personality in terms of a complex of traits or factors, Mischel (1986) proposed a social-learning approach. This approach stresses the fact that people learn to make different responses in different situations and that the accuracy with which an individual's behavior in a specific situation can be predicted must take into account the person's learning history in similar situations.

It is certainly true that social norms, roles, and other group-related conditions can exert powerful effects on people and override temperament or personal style as determiners of individual action and thoughts. As long as the social situation remains fairly constant, people may suppress their idiosyncrasies and adjust their behavior and thinking to the expectations and reward-punishment schedules provided by others in that situation. It has been amply demonstrated by research in social psychology and by candid television programs than when in Rome all kinds of people "do as the Romans do." Acceptance of this truism does not imply, however, that individual personality plays no role whatsoever in behavior.

Evidence pertaining to the trait-situation controversy is not all in favor of situationism. A number of investigators (e. g., Bem & Allen, 1974; Block, 1977; Underwood & Moore, 1981; Chaplin & Goldberg, 1984) found that the consistency of traits across situations is itself an individual difference variable. In the Bem and Allen investigation, people who believed themselves to be fairly consistent in friendliness and conscientiousness tended to be so; those who identified themselves as less consistent tended to be so.

Research has also demonstrated that some behaviors are more consistent than others. Certain behaviors are narrowly situation-specific, whereas other behaviors that do not require specific eliciting stimuli in a wide range of situations and hence are more reflective of broad personality variables (Funder & Colvin, 1991).

As with the clinical versus statistical prediction debate, most psychologists would probably agree that research findings have not supported a strict situationist viewpoint regarding behavior. Rather, behavior is seen as a joint product of personality characteristics and the particular situation in which the behavior occurs. In certain (strong) situations, the features of the situations themselves are more important in determining how people behave; in other (weak) situations, personality characteristics are more influential. More generally, it is the interaction between personality characteristics and the situation that determines behavior. Efforts to develop effective measures of personality are more productive if they begin by providing a conceptual model of how personality dispositions and situational characteristics interact and then proceed to develop measures of both sets of variables.

Public and Governmental Concerns

During their relatively short history, measures of personality have been repeatedly attacked by psychologists and nonpsychologists alike. Representative of the most extreme negative reactions to these instruments are the writings of William Whyte (1956) and Martin Gross (1962, 1965) on the applications of personality assessment in business and industry. In commenting on testimony before a special subcommittee of the U.S. House of Representatives, Gross (1965) severely criticized personality tests on the grounds of invalidity and immorality.

Whyte and Gross were, of course, not the first writers to criticize psychological testing and assessment. Indicative of the feelings of certain members of the public toward psychological testing and research was an order by the Houston School Board in June 1959 that led to the burning of thousands of attitude scales and other questionnaires. This bonfire was a result of the strenuous objections by a group of Houston parents to the fact that children in their school district had been required, as a part of an educational research project, to answer true-false items such as the following:
- I enjoy soaking in the bathtub.
- A girl who gets into trouble on a date has no one to blame but herself.
- If you don't drink in our gang, they make you feel like a sissy.
- Sometimes I tell dirty jokes when I would rather not.
- Dad always seems too busy to pal around with me. (Nettler, 1959, p. 682)

It is certainly understandable how a situation of this sort could arise, particularly when many members of our society do not share the scientific attitude and quest for understanding that supposedly characterizes behavioral scientists. Furthermore, it has been alleged that many personality test items, especially those concerned with sex, religion, and morals, are not only personally offensive but also potentially destructive to children's character. Strong emotional reactions over the meaning and validity of psychological testing and social science research in general also occurred in the debate over Project CAMELOT during the mid-1960s. This project, which was financed by the U.S. government, was designed to analyze the causes of counterrevolution and counterinsurgency in Latin America. Public awareness of the project resulted in a heated reaction by many private citizens and government officials in both the United States and Latin America. The Project CAMELOT debate, combined with civil suits and attacks on the use of selection tests, led to a congressional investigation of psychological testing in government, industry, and education. One practice that was examined at length in the congressional inquiry was the administration to job applicants of personality test items concerned with sex and religion. The following kinds of true-false items were singled out for special criticism: (1) My sex life is satisfactory; (2) I believe in God; (3) I don't get along very well with my parents. Although the results of hearings concerned with personality tests did not lead to an indictment of these tests, the concern manifested in these hearings prompted psychologists and other assessment specialists to be more attentive to the ethics, legality, and validity of their instruments and procedures.

Some years later, a similar situation regarding the administration of true-false personality test items occurred in the case of *Soroka v. Dayton-Hudson Corp.* (1991). The dispute centered on the administration of Psychscreen, a 700-item paper-and-pencil inventory that was developed from the MMPI and the CPI, to applicants for the position of security guard with Target Stores. Psychscreen had previously been used as a screening test for positions in law enforcement, air-traffic control, and nuclear power plants. Legal counsel for the plaintiff maintained that questions on Psychscreen like these were discriminatory with regard to religious and sexual preference:

— I believe the in second coming of Christ.
— I believe there is a devil and a hell in afterlife.
— I am very strongly attracted to members of my own sex.
— I have never indulged in any unusual sex practices.
    (Hager, 1991, p. A-20)

Attorneys for Dayton-Hudson Corporation argued that such questions were justified because the position of security guard with Target Stores was not one that emotionally unstable persons, whom Psychscreen was attempting to identify, could perform effectively. However, the appellate court ruled in favor of the plaintiff in concluding that questions on religion and sex violate a job seeker's right to privacy.

The American Psychological Association (APA) appealed to the California Supreme Court, which agreed to review the appellate court's decision, that such questions should not be considered singly but rather collectively in deciding whether the answers are indicative of emotional instability (Freiberg & DeAngelis, 1992). It can nevertheless be argued that questions having to do with sexual and religious preferences have no place on employment screening tests because the answers may well be misinterpreted by sexually intolerant, religiously bigoted, or psychometrically unsophisticated persons.

Another area of controversy regarding psychological assessment in industry and government is *integrity testing*. As a way of controlling for the problem of theft in business and industry, for many years polygraph (lie detector) tests were administered to employees and job applicants in critical or sensitive positions. The polygraph does not access lying as such, but rather indicates the increased arousal in bodily systems stemming from stress of any sort. By comparing the reactions of suspects to questions that are relevant with those that are irrelevant to a crime under investigation, an expert polygraph examiner may be able to judge whether or not the suspect is lying. However, it has been shown that in over one-third of the cases examiners err in the direction of concluding that innocent suspects are lying. This is because even innocent people can become emotionally aroused by questions pertaining to a crime. Various techniques, such as asking control questions that refer in a general way to prior misdeeds and applying a guilty knowledge test, may improve the accuracy of the polygraph. Although polygraph findings are typically not admissible as evidence in court, the technique continues to be used in law enforcement. However, as a consequence of the Employee Polygraph Protection Act of 1988, which banned the use of polygraph testing in preemployment interviews in both government and the private sector, employers were obliged to seek alternative methods. One approach was represented by paper-and-pencil tests of honesty or integrity, consisting of items designed to assess personality traits and thought patterns that are presumably associated with dishonesty. Some, but not all, of these integrity tests have been found, when used appropriately and in conjunction with additional selection procedures, to be valid (Ones, Viswesvaran, & Schmidt, 1995). Still, the practice of integrity testing remains controversial, particularly in regard to whether the administration of such tests compromises a person's right to privacy (Camara & Schneider, 1994, 1995; Lilienfeld, Alliger, & Mitchell, 1995).

Despite criticisms of personality testing in business and industry, it has continued to receive support in employee selection and other personnel procedures in the workplace. A number of psychologists are engaged in ongoing research programs concerned with determining the personality requirements of leadership positions and other jobs. Among the characteristics that are being studied are sociability, conscientiousness, and other traits delineated by the five-factor model (Hogan, Hogan, & Roberts, 1996; Landy, Shankster, & Kohler, 1994). In addition, inventories such as the MMPI continue to be used for detecting psychopathology and employee screening for highly sensitive positions.

Validity of Personality Assessment

In addition to ethical and legal concerns about personality assessment, the related questions of what is measured by such tests, whether those things are worth measuring, and how best to interpret and apply the results have received a great deal of professional attention during the past few decades. As we have seen, the psychometric characteristics of personality tests, and projective techniques in particular, often leave much to be desired. Criterion-keyed inventories tend to have higher validities than other assessment procedures, but the validity coefficients of these instruments often show significant declines when they are administered in new situations.

With regard to their validity in personnel selection and placement situations, personality inventories and projectives have sometimes contributed to such decisions. For example, the MMPI proved useful in the successful selection program of the Peace Corps during the 1960s (Hobbs, 1963; Wiggins, 1973). The utility of measures of cognitive abilities has also been enhanced on occasion by combining them with measures of temperament and motivation. More recently, Tett, Jackson, and Rothstein (1991) concluded that "Contrary to conclusions of certain past reviews, the present findings provide some grounds for optimism concerning the use of personality measures in employee selection."(p. 703) Furnham (1992) also concluded that sufficient evidence exists to justify the use of personality tests in the workplace.

Not only is there a need for more reliable and valid instruments in clinical and counseling contexts, but improvements in their theoretical bases and in the criteria against which they are validated are necessary. The disease model of mental disorders and the associated diagnostic classification system (DMS-III-R and DSM-IV) (American Psychiatric Association, 1987, 1994), which is basic to the development and scoring of many personality assessment procedures, is in many respects ambiguous and unreliable. Finally, there is the common problem of misinterpreting the results of personality assessments. Such misinterpretations can occur through failure to consider the base rate, or frequency of the event (criterion) being predicted. Misinterpretations of test scores can also be the results of what is referred to as "clinical insight" or "intuition," but is all too often a conglomeration of superficial stereotypes, truisms, and other overgeneralizations that may make sense to the personality analyst or psychodiagnostician but are actually misleading.

The solution to the validity problem in personality assessment lies in better research and development, but such efforts must be undertaken with a socially responsible attitude and a respect for the rights of the individual. Furthermore, test users should acquire a deeper understanding of statistical and other technical matters pertaining to test design, reliability, validity, and norms. Too many clinicians and counselors reject the technicalities of psychometrics as being the concern of academics and unrelated to the activities of practicing psychologists. Consequently, they may fail to consider such prediction-related factors as the base rates of particular conditions, the intercorrelations among various predictors, and the influence of regression toward the mean on scores obtained from repeated testings (L. R. Goldberg, 1991). Not surprisingly, research has shown that psychologists with lower levels of cognitive complexity are more likely than those with higher levels to form biased clinical judgments (Spengler & Strohmer, 1994; Walker & Spengler, 1995). Accurate clinical judgment requires a high level of cognitive ability, training and experience in problem-solving and judgment, and an awareness of one's own biases and the necessity of controlling them.

Even when a clinical or educational examiner has adequate knowledge and training and the test is satisfactory for its stated purposes, it is important to maintain a record of hits and misses and other indicators of successful and unsuccessful predictions made on the basis of test scores. Over the long run, such information can serve as a check on the validity of the test for its stated purposes.

Bias on Personality Tests

Related to both ethical issues and the question of test validity is the matter of whether personality tests are biased against a particular sex, social class, nationality, or racial group. Despite the pleas of Dana (1993, 1996, 1998) and others (e. g., Suzuki, Meller, & Ponterotto, 1996) for greater attention to culture, language, and belief systems of different cultures in constructing, administering, and interpreting tests, there has been relatively little systematic research on the matter of ethnic-group, social-class, or nationality-group bias in personality test performance. Statistical checks on gender and ethnic bias in test items have, however, become fairly routine in the construction of ability tests and interest inventories.

Research and action on the matter of gender bias in personality testing has flourished in recent years. Gender bias can affect the kinds of responses obtained on personality tests and the manner in which those responses are evaluated and interpreted. With respect to test content, the language of many personality and interest inventories has traditionally been somewhat sexist. For a long time gender bias on interest inventories was a topic of concern, with scores on these inventories reflecting sex stereotypes. But the fact that the mean scores of females were significantly higher than those of males on certain scales was not necessarily a reflection of gender bias but may simply have represented a socioeducational influence.

A traditional response to sex differences in test scores was the provision of separate norms for males and females. Efforts were made to construct tests in such a way that they are not biased toward either sex. By eliminating sexist language on inventories such as the Strong Interest Inventory (SII) and the MMPI-2, the test authors succeeded in devising instruments that are fairer to both males and females. Another procedure for reducing gender bias—devising items that were endorsed equally often by males and females—was employed in constructing instruments such as the Vocational Interest Inventory.

■ Prospects for Personality Assessment

For better or for worse, a 1918 to 2000 personality assessment time traveler would need to do less catching up than his counterparts in physics and biology. Much work remains to be accomplished before the diagnoses and prognoses of contemporary personality psychology are as impressive as those of the natural sciences. Nevertheless, the prize is still worth the effort, an effort that demands continuing foresight and patience on the part of researchers, theoreticians, and practitioners.

Despite the seeming disarray in the field of personality assessment, there is a great deal of activity on the current scene and a promise of clarification and restructuring of the field. Prompted by the methodological inadequacy of much research on personality, some of the current activity involves sophisticated methodologies such as structural equation modeling, path analysis, and taxometric methods. Other investigations are concerned with the administration of personality assessment instruments and the interpretations made from the results. Many of these investigations focus on the problem of reactivity, in which the very process of testing, including the biases and behavior of the examiner, influences the responses made by the examinee.

Writing in the mid-1980s, Ziskin (1986) concluded that clinical psychological assessment was in an unhealthy state due to the lack of an adequate system for classifying mental disorders, contamination of data by situational effects, evidence that clinical skills do not improve with practice, difficulties in differentiating normal from psychopathic behavior, and problems with computer interpretation of data. He advocated a broader approach to computer use in clinical diagnosis, including not only the MMPI and similar instruments, but also demographic data and information from structured interviews. He also predicted that in the future greater emphasis would be placed on personal assets (such as good looks) and psychosocial stresses and greater use of structured interviews. Ziskin also advised clinicians to become more aware of the fact that there are limits to what can be discovered about people by means of psychological assessment alone.

Over a decade later, much of what Ziskin wrote in the mid-1980s still seems like a reasonable forecast. Compared with the technical sophistication of ability testing, personality inventories and other affective instruments are fairly crude. Recent methodological progress in the construction of certain personality inventories suggests that general improvements in affective assessment are forthcoming. But even if, as recommended, shorter instruments with improved statistical characteristics and more representative standardization are developed, the validity of such instruments will probably not be much higher than those of existing inventories and scales (Megargee & Spielberger, 1992). Combining situational measures with scores on these personality assessment devices will perhaps improve predictive validity, but probably not markedly.

Regarding the longevity of current instruments, although it is unlikely that oldtimers such as the MMPI or the Rorschach will be replaced any time soon by more psychometrically sophisticated instruments, newer tests will force a continuing reevaluation of these and other time-honored clinical instruments.

Admittedly, personality assessment is not as popular in clinical and counseling psychology as it once was, but the character of the mental health professions and the types of people who enter these professions has changed substantially in recent years. One hears much about the "feminization of psychology" and "giving psychology away" by making it more "practical." Perhaps it has always been that way, but today's students seem less interested in the scientific and quantitative aspects of psychology and more interested in the humanistic and social service features of the discipline. As pointed out by Megargee and Spielberger (1992), education and training in psychological assessment appear to be declining. Although most training centers for clinical psychology interns continue to place a high priority on traditional psychological assessment, many centers have almost abandoned it. This is occurring despite the widely-advertised need for well-trained assessors and high-quality assessment instruments in various arenas.

Be that as it may, this author agrees with a prediction made over a decade ago by Weiner (1983, p. 456) that "Continued careful research on psychodiagnostic methods and the expert application of psychological test findings in clinical consultation should sustain a bright future for psychodiagnosis and its practitioners."

Some years later, Matarazzo (1992) continued to see a bright future for clinical psychodiagnosis with the construction of tests to identify and analyze more specific forms of psychopathology such as panic reactions and depressive disorders. Matarazzo also predicted that newer and better measures of personal competence in adapting to the environment, including scales of quality of life and adaptive behavior, will be devised.

Whatever the future may hold for personality and clinical assessment, there will be a continuing need to evaluate the effectiveness of psychometric instruments and procedures in these areas. Then, as now and in the past, the major questions pertaining to any personality or clinical assessment instrument or procedure will be concerned with its validity and the effectiveness of decisions made on the basis of the information supplied by the assessment. Measures of personality may also serve as vehicles to ideas and discoveries that will lead to new methods, measures, and ultimately contributions to the body of information and procedures known as psychological science.

Still, we must continue to ask whether our methods and devices fulfill their intended purposes—in research, psychodiagnosis, or in planning treatments or other interventions. Only by being constantly vigilant and questioning can we be assured that existing methods are serving their intended purposes. Of critical importance is the need to make certain that those who design, market and apply personality assessment instruments are adequately trained in what they do and that they practice it ethically and with a sensitivity to the welfare of the individual and society as whole.

■ Summary

This closing chapter deals with three topics: (1) physiological, perceptual, and cognitive measures of personality; (2) applications on personality assessment in health, forensic, marital and family counseling, sports, and consumer contexts; (3) issues in personality assessment.

A variety of bioelectric indicators or biological transducers, many of compact and even miniature size, are available for measuring general arousal and level of stress. Prominent among these instruments are measures of blood pressure, respiration rate, heart rate, and the galvanic skin response, which are combined in the polygraph. Other electrophysiological devices for determining when a person is under stress or physiologically activated are the voice stress analyzer, the plethysmograph, and the pupillometer.

Hans Eysenck and his coworkers have accumulated evidence for the differentiation of introversion and extraversion on the basis of specific perceptual and behavioral responses. Of related significance are Zuckerman's measurement and research program on the psychophysiological construct of sensation seeking.

Herman Witkin and his associates used scores on three perceptual tests to determine a person's standing on the field-independence/dependence perceptual dimension (or analytic vs. global cognitive style). These tests—the Body Adjustment Test, the Rod and Frame Test, and the Embedded Figures Test—assess a person's ability to distinguish an object from its context. People who score high on field independence are characterized as more secure, independent, controlled, psychologically mature, and self-accepting than those who score low. On the other hand, people who score high on field dependence are said to be more tense, insecure, psychologically immature, and passive, but less attuned to inner experiences and less insightful into oneself than those who score low on this variable. A number of other personality and sociocultural variables have also been found to be related to the field independence/dependence dimension.

Cognitive styles are strategies or approaches to perceiving, remembering, and thinking that a person comes to prefer in attempting to understand and cope with the world. Field independence/dependence is one of many different cognitive styles that have been studied. Another cognitive style that has received a great deal of research attention is the reflective versus impulsive style of responding, as measured by the Matching Familiar Figures Test.

Research and instrument development in health psychology, forensic psychology, marriage and family counseling, sport psychology, and consumer psychology are providing a better understanding, more accurate behavioral predictions, and more effective intervention programs. These fields are, however, only a few of the areas of application of personality assessment methods and practices in clinical and counseling, educational and school, business and industry, and government and military contexts.

Changing economic and social conditions, and the advances in technology that accompany them, will undoubtedly continue to create a need for new personality assessment methods and procedures.

Despite notable progress in the methodology and technology of psychological measurement, the assessment of personality continues to be a controversial practice characterized by numerous issues. Among the issues in personality assessment that are still being debated are clinical versus statistical prediction, idiographic versus nomothetic assessment, the ethics and morality of assessment, the importance of traits versus situations in predicting behavior, and the proper roles of computers and other technologies in assessment.

Due to some extent to the adoption of codes of ethics pertaining to psychological assessment and other activities of psychologists and other human service professionals, arguments concerning the ethics and morality of personality assessment are perhaps not as heated today as they once were. This is also true of the issue of whether personality traits or situational variables are more important in understanding and predicting behavior.

The validity of personality assessment instruments, and how it varies with culture, ethnicity, and gender, is and will continue to be a matter of concern. Efforts have been made to eliminate or at least to control for gender bias in interest inventories and other affective measures by rewriting items to make them relevant and fair to both males and females, and by providing both separate and combined sex norms. The construction of gender-free and race-free assessment instruments and procedures, however, does not reduce the need to measure and study bona fide gender differences in psychological characteristics and their origins and outcomes.

■ Questions and Activities

1. Numerous articles concerned with the validity and ethics of polygraph testing have appeared in popular magazines. Consult the *Reader's Guide*, the *New York Times Index*, and other reference sources on popular periodical literature under "polygraph" and "lie detector" for three or four recent articles on the topic. Summarize evidence for the utility of the procedure in criminal cases and the issues surrounding it.

2. Evaluate Witkin's research on field independence and dependence and Eysenck's research on introversion and extraversion. Consult several of the books and articles by Witkin and Eysenck in making your evaluations.

3. Use a stopwatch or wristwatch with a sweep second hand to determine how many seconds it takes each of several acquaintances or friends to find the hidden figures in the drawings in Figure 13-2. Follow the same procedure with Figure 13–3. Were there large individual differences in the response times of various people? What is the relationship to personality to differences in time required to locate embedded figures or to match familiar figures?

4. Provide some examples of contexts in which you would expect the situation to exert a more powerful effect on a person's behavior, and other contexts in which you would expect personality traits to have a greater effect.

5. Write one or two personality test items (true-false format) that are biased toward men, women, blacks, whites, Americans, Asians, and more highly educated people.
6. How can you account for the continuing, and even increasing, popularity of personality assessment when many of the most widely administered assessment instruments have relatively poor reliabilities and validities and are inadequately standardized?

■ Suggested Readings

Aiken, L.R. (1999). *Human differences* (Chs. 8 & 9). Mahwah, NJ: Erlbaum.

Anastasi, A. (1993). A century of psychological testing: Origins, problems, and progress. In T.K. Fagan & G.R. VandenBos (Eds.), *Exploring applied psychology: Origins and critical analyses* (pp. 13–36). Washington, DC: American Psychological Association.

Brebner, J., & Stough, C. (1995). Theoretical and empirical relationships between personality and intelligence. In D.H. Saklofske & M. Zeidner (Eds.), *International handbook of personality and intelligence* (pp. 321–347). New York: Plenum.

Butcher, J.N., & Rouse, S.V. (1996). Personality: Individual differences and clinical assessment. *Annual Review of Psychology, 47*, 87–111.

Epstein, S. (1997). This I have learned from over 40 years of personality research. *Journal of Personality, 65*(1), 3–32.

Hogan, R., Hogan, J., & Roberts, B.W. (1996). Personality measurement and employment decisions. *American Psychologist, 51*, 469–477.

Matarazzo, J.D. (1992). Psychological testing and assessment in the 21st century. *American Psychologist, 47*, 1007–1018.

Megargee, E.I., & Spielberger, C.D. (1992). Reflections on fifty years of personality assessment and future directions for the field. In *Personality assessment in America* (pp. 170–190). Hillsdale, NJ: Erlbaum.

Pervin, L.A. (1996). Personality: A view of the future based on a look at the past. *Journal of Research in Personality, 30*, 309–318.

Glossary

ABC approach. Behavioral assessment approach, involving the identification of the antecedent events (A) and consequences (C) of the behavior (B). The behavior is modified by controlling for A and changing C.

Accident proneness. Now largely discredited theory of a particular personality type associated with a greater tendency to have accidents.

Acquiescence response set. Tendency of a person to answer affirmatively ("yes" or "true") on personality test items and in other alternative response situations.

Actuarial approach. Combining quantified clinical information according to empirically established rules, and then making behavioral predictions or diagnoses on the basis of the results.

Affective assessment. Measurement of noncognitive (nonintellective) variables or characteristics. Affective variables include temperament, emotion, interests, attitudes, personal style, and other behaviors, traits, or processes that are typical of a person.

Anecdotal record. A written record of behavioral observations of a specified individual. Care must be taken to differentiate between observation and interpretation if the record is to be objective.

Anxiety. Vague feeling of uneasiness or apprehension, not necessarily directed toward a specific object or situation.

Assessment. Appraising the presence or magnitude of one or more personal characteristics. The assessment of human behavior and mental processes includes such procedures as observations, interviews, rating scales, checklists, inventories, projectives, and tests.

Astrology. Pseudoscience of interpreting an individual's personality and future circumstances from data on the individual's birth and the relative positions of the moon and planets at that time.

Attitude. Tendency to react positively or negatively to some object, person, or circumstance.

Attitude scale. A paper and pencil instrument, consisting of a series of statements concerning an institution, situation, person, event, etc. The examinee responds to each statement by endorsing it or indicating his or her degree of agreement or disagreement with it.

Attribution. Process of interpreting a person's behavior as caused by forces within (**internal attribution** or disposition) or outside (**external attribution** or situation) the person.

Aunt Fanny error. Accepting as accurate a trivial, highly generalized personality description that could pertain to almost anyone, even one's Aunt Fanny.

Authoritarian personality. Tendency to view the world in terms of a strict social hierarchy in which a person higher on the hierarchy demands cooperation and deference from those below him or her.

Barnum effect. Accepting as accurate a personality description phrased in generalities, truisms, and other statements that sound specific to a given person but are actually applicable to almost anyone. Same as **Aunt Fanny error.**

Base rate. Proportion of a specified population of people who possess a characteristic of interest. The base rate should be taken into account when evaluating the effectiveness of a psychometric instrument in identifying and diagnosing people who have that characteristic.

Behavior analysis. Procedures that focus on objectively describing a particular behavior and identifying the antecedents and consequences of that behavior. Behavior analysis may be conducted for research purposes or to obtain information in planning a behavior modification program.

Behavior modification. Psychotherapeutic procedures based on learning theory and research and designed to change inappropriate behavior to more personally and/or socially acceptable behavior. Examples of such procedures are systematic desensitization, counterconditioning, extinction, and implosion.

Biographical inventory. Questionnaire composed of items designed to collect information on a person's background, interests, and other personal data.

Bipolar disorder. Mental disorder in which a person's mood fluctuates between euphoric mania and depression.

Cardinal trait. According to G. W. Allport, a disposition or theme so dominant in a person's life that it is expressed in almost all of his or her behavior (e. g., power-striving, self-love).

Case study. Detailed study of an individual, designed to provide a comprehensive, in-depth understanding of personality. Information for a case study is obtained from biographical, interview, observational, and test data.

Central tendency error. General tendency to avoid extreme judgments in appraising or assessing a person, and to assign ratings in the middle categories of a continuum or scale.

Central trait. According to G. W. Allport, the tendency to behave in a particular way in various situations (sociability, affectionateness), but less general or pervasive than a **cardinal trait.**

Cerebrotonia. In William Sheldon's temperament typology, the tendency to be introversive and prefer mental to physical or social activities; most closely related to an ectomorphic body build.

Checklist. List of words, phrases, or statements descriptive of personal characteristics; respondents endorse (check) those items characteristic of themselves (self-ratings) or other people (other-ratings).

Classification. Assigning individuals to specified groups or categories on the basis of personal data obtained from various sources (observations, interviews, tests, inventories, etc.).

Client-centered therapy. A type of psychotherapy, pioneered by Carl Rogers, in which the client decides what to talk about and when, without direction, judgment, or interpretation on the part of the therapist. Unconditional positive regard, empathy, and congruence characterize the therapist's attitude in this type of therapy.

Clinical (impressionistic) approach. Approach to behavioral prediction and diagnosis in which psychologists assign their own judgmental weights to the predictor variables and then combine them in a subjective manner to make behavioral forecasts or diagnoses.

Cluster sampling. Sampling procedure in which the target population is divided into sections or clusters, and the number of units selected at random from a particular cluster is proportional to the total number of units in the cluster.

Coefficient alpha. An internal-consistency reliability coefficient, appropriate for tests composed of dichotomous or multipoint items; the expected correlation of one test with a parallel form containing the same number of items.

Coefficient of equivalence. A reliability coefficient (correlation) obtained by administering a test to the same group of people on two different occasions. See **Test-retest reliability.**

Coefficient of internal consistency. Reliability coefficient based on estimates of the internal consistency of a test (for example, split-half coefficient and alpha coefficient.

Coefficient of stability. A reliability coefficient (correlation) obtained by administering a test to the same group of people on two different occasions. See **Test-retest reliability.**

Coefficient of stability and equivalence. A reliability coefficient obtained by administering two forms of a test to a group of examines on two different occasions.

Cognitive assessment. Measurement of cognitive processes, such as perception, memory, thinking, judgment, and reasoning. See **Affective assessment.**

Cognitive style. Strategy or approach to perceiving, remembering, and thinking that a person seems to prefer in attempting to understand and cope with the world (for example, field independence-dependence, reflectivity-impulsivity, and internal-external locus of control).

Competency. Legal determination that a person's judgment is sound and that he or she is able to manage his or her own property, enter into contracts, and so forth.

Concordance reliability. Several raters or scorers make numerical judgments of a characteristic or behavior shown by a large sample of people. Then a coefficient of concordance, an index of agreement among the judgments of the scorers or raters, is computed.

Concurrent validity. The extent to which scores obtained by a group of people on a particular psychometric instrument are related to their simultaneously determined scores on another measure (criterion) of the same characteristic that the instrument is supposed to measure.

Confirmation bias. Tendency to seek and remember information that is consistent with one's beliefs or preconceptions.

Construct validity. The extent to which scores on a psychometric instrument designed to measure a certain characteristic are related to measures of behavior in situations in which the characteristic is supposed to be an important determinant of behavior.

Content analysis. Method of studying and analyzing written (or oral) communications in a systematic, objective, and quantitative manner to assess certain psychological variables.

Content validity. The extent to which a group of people who are experts in the material with which a test deals agree that the test or other psychometric instrument measures what it was designed to measure.

Contrast error. In interviewing or rating, the tendency to evaluate a person more positively if an immediately preceding individual was assigned a highly negative evaluation or to evaluate a person more negatively if an immediately preceding individual was given a highly positive evaluation.

Convergent validity. Situation in which an assessment instrument has high correlations with other measures (or methods of measuring) the same construct. See **Discriminant validity.**

Correlation. Degree of relationship or association between two variables, such as a test and a criterion measure.

Correlation coefficient. A numerical index of the degree of relationship between two variables. Correlation coefficients usually range from -1.00 (perfect negative relationship), through $.00$ (total absence of a relationship) to $+1.00$ (perfect positive relationship). Two common types of correlation coefficient are the product-moment coefficient and the point-biserial coefficient.

Criterion. A standard or variable with which scores on a psychometric instrument are compared or against which they are evaluated. The validity of a test or other psychometric procedure used in selecting or classifying people is determined by its ability to predict a specified criterion of behavior in the situation for which people are being selected or classified.

Criterion-related validity. The extent to which a test or other assessment instrument measures what it was designed to measure, as indicated by the correlation of test scores with some criterion measure of behavior.

Critical incident. A measure of performance, used primarily in industrial-organizational contexts, in which an individual's overall criterion score is determined by the extent to which behavior thought to be critical for effective performance in a given situation occurs.

Cross-validation. Readministering an assessment instrument that has been found to be a valid predictor of a criterion for one group of persons to a second group of persons to determine whether the instrument is also valid for that group. There is almost always some shrinkage of the validity coefficient on cross-validation, since chance factors spuriously inflate the validity coefficient obtained with the first group of people.

Diagnostic interview. An interview designed to obtain information on a person's thoughts, feelings, perceptions, and behavior; used in making a diagnostic decision about the person.

Discriminant validity. Situation in which a psychometric instrument has low correlations with other measures of (or methods of measuring) different psychological constructs.

Dispositional approach. Includes any one of the many different theories of personality based on the assumption of stable, enduring internal dispositions to feel, think, or act in certain ways. Different dispositions are considered to be characteristic of different individuals and to be expressed across a variety of situations.

Ectomorph. In William Sheldon's somatotype system, a person with a tall, thin body build; related to the cerebrotonic (thinking, introversive) temperament type.

Ego. In psychoanalytic theory, that part of the personality ("I" or "me") that obeys the reality principle and attempts to mediate the conflict between the id and superego.

Electroencephalograph (EEG). Electronic apparatus designed to detect and record brain waves from the intact scalp.

Electromyograph (EMG). Electronic apparatus designed to measure muscular activity or tension.

Endomorph. In William Sheldon's somatotype system, a person having a rotund body shape (fat); related to the viscerotonic (relaxed, sociable) temperament.

Equipercentile method. Traditional method of converting the score units on one test to the score units on a parallel test. The scores on each test are converted to percentile ranks, and a table of equivalent scores is produced by equating the score at the pth percentile on the first test to the score at the pth percentile on the second test.

Evaluation. To judge the merit or value of an examinee's behavior from a composite of test scores, observations, and reports.

Extrovert. Carl Jung's term for people who are oriented, in thought or social orientation, toward the external environment and other people rather than toward their own thoughts and feelings.

Face validity. The extent to which the appearance or content of the materials (items and the like) on a test or other psychometric instrument is such that the instrument appears to be a good measure of what it is supposed to measure.

Factor. A dimension, trait, or characteristic of personality revealed by factor analyzing the matrix of correlations computed from the scores of a large number of people in several different tests or items.

Factor analysis. A mathematical procedure for analyzing a matrix of correlations among measurements to determine what factors (constructs) are sufficient to explain the correlations.

Factor loadings. In factor analysis, the resulting correlations (weights) between tests (or other variables) and the extracted factors.

Factor rotation. A mathematical procedure applied to a factor matrix for the purpose of simplifying the matrix for interpretive purposes by increasing the number of high and low factor loadings in the matrix. Factor rotation may be either *orthogonal*, in which case the resulting factors are at right angles to each other, or *oblique*, in which the resulting factor axes form acute or obtuse angles with each other.

False negative. Selection error or diagnostic decision error in which an assessment procedure incorrectly predicts a maladaptive outcome (for example, low achievement, poor performance, or psychopathology).

False positive. Selection error or diagnostic decision error in which an assessment procedure incorrectly predicts an adaptive outcome (for example, high achievement, good performance, or absence of psychopathology).

Fantasy stage. The earliest stage in the development of interests, in which a child's interest orientations are not based on an accurate perception of reality.

Field dependence. A perceptual style in which the perceiver relies primarily on cues from the surrounding visual environment, rather than kinesthetic (gravitational) cues, to determine the upright position in H. A. Witkin's rod-and-frame test.

Field independence. A perceptual style in which the perceiver depends primarily on kinesthetic (gravitational) cues, rather than visual cues from the surrounding environment, to determine the upright position in H. A. Witkin's rod-and-frame test.

Forced-choice item. Item on a personality or interest inventory, arranged as a dyad (two options), a triad (three options), or a tetrad (four options) of terms or phrases. The respondent is required to select an option viewed as most descriptive of the personality, interests, or behavior of the person being evaluated and perhaps another option perceived to be least descriptive of the personality, interests, or behavior of the person being evaluated. Forced-choice items are found on certain personality inventories (for example, the Edwards Personal Preference Schedule, interest inventories (Kuder General Interest Survey), and rating forms to control for response sets.

Frequency distribution. A table of score intervals and the number of cases (scores) falling within each interval.

Fundamental attribution error. Tendency to attribute one's own behavior to situational influences but to attribute the behavior of other people to dispositional causes.

Gender identity. Inner sense of being male or female, resulting from child-rearing practices combined with genetic and hormonal factors.

Gender role. Patterns of appearance and behavior associated by a society or culture with being male or female and expected of the appropriate sex.

Generalizability theory. A theory of test scores and the associated statistical formulation that conceptualizes a test score as a sample from a universe of scores. Analysis of variance procedures are used to determine the generalizability from score to universe value, as a function of examinees, test items, and situational contexts. A generalizability coefficient may be computed as a measure of the degree of generalizability from sample to population.

Genital stage. The last of Freud's five stages of psychosexual development. Beginning with puberty, interest in the opposite sex becomes predominant during this stage, culminating in heterosexual union.

Graphic rating scale. A rating scale containing a series of items, each consisting of a line on which the rater places a check mark to indicate the degree of a characteristic that the ratee is perceived as possessing. Typically, at the left extremity of the line is a brief verbal description indicating the lowest degree of the characteristic, and at the right end is a description of the highest degree of the characteristic. Brief descriptions of intermediate degrees of the characteristic may also be located at equidistant points along the line.

Graphology. The analysis of handwriting to ascertain the character or personality of the writer.

Group test. A test administered simultaneously to a group of examinees by one examiner. See **individual test.**

Guess who technique. Procedure for analyzing group interaction and the social stimulus value of group members, in which children are asked to "guess who" in a classroom or other group situation possesses certain characteristics or does certain things.

Halo effect. Rating a person high on one characteristic merely because he or she rates high on other characteristics.

Hardiness. Personality trait characterized by commitment, challenge, and control, and associated with a lower rate of stress-related illness.

Health psychology. Branch of psychology concerned with research and applications directed toward the maintenance of health and the prevention of illness.

Hindsight bias. Tendency to believe, after an event has occurred, that one could have predicted it beforehand.

Ideal self. In Carl Rogers' phenomenological theory, the self that a person would like to be, as contrasted with the person's **real self.**

Identification. Taking on the personal characteristics of another person, as when a developing child identifies with a significant "other" person. Also, in psychoanalytic theory, an ego defense mechanism for coping with anxiety.

Idiographic approach. Approach to personality assessment and research in which the individual is viewed as a lawful, integrated system in his or her own right. See **Nomothetic approach.**

Illusory correlation. Focusing on the number of times that a symptom and a disorder have occurred together and overlooking the number of times they have not occurred together.

In-basket technique. A procedure for evaluating supervisors or executives in which the candidate is required to indicate what action should be taken on a series of memos and other materials of the kind typically found in a supervisor's or executive's in-basket.

Incident (event) sampling. In contrast to **time sampling,** an observational procedure in which certain types of incidents, such as those indicative of aggressive behavior, are selected for observation and recording.

Incompetency. Legal determination that a person is suffering from a disorder that causes a defect of judgment such that the person is unable to manage his or her own property, enter into contracts, and take care of his or her other affairs.

Individual test. A test administered to one examinee at a time.

Informed consent. A formal agreement made by an individual, or the individual's guardian or legal representative, with an agency or another person to permit use of the individual's name and/or personal information (test scores and the like) for a specified purpose.

Insanity. A legal term for a disorder of judgment or behavior in which a person is unable to tell the difference between right and wrong (McNaghten Rule) or cannot control his or her actions and manage his or her affairs.

Integrity (honesty) testing. Use of psychometric devices to screen employees for dishonesty and other undesirable characteristics; questions pertaining to attitudes toward theft and the admission of theft and other illegal activities are commonly found on such tests.

Intelligence. Many definitions of this term have been offered, such as "the ability to judge well, understand well, and reason well" (Binet) and "the capacity for abstract thinking" (Terman). In general, what is measured by intelligence tests is the ability to succeed in school-type tasks.

Interest inventory. A test or checklist, such as the Strong Interest Inventory or the Kuder General Interest Survey, designed to assess an individual's preferences for certain activities and topics.

Internal consistency. The extent to which all items on a test measure the same variable or construct. The reliability of a test computed by the Spearman-Brown, Kuder-Richardson, or Cronbach-alpha formulas is a measure of the test's internal consistency.

Interrater (interscorer) reliability. Two scorers assign a numerical rating or score to a sample of people. Then the correlation between the two sets of numbers is computed.

Interval scale. A measurement scale on which equality of numerical differences implies equality of differences in the attribute or characteristic being measured. The scale of temperature (Celsius, Fahrenheit) and, presumably, standard score scales z, T) are examples of interval scales.

Interview. A systematic procedure for obtaining information by asking questions and, in general, verbally interacting with a person (the interviewee).

Intraclass reliability. Several raters or scorers make a numerical judgment of a characteristic or behavior of a person. Then an **intraclass coefficient**, an index of agreement among the numbers assigned by the various judges, among the scores is computed.

Introvert. Carl Jung's term for orientation toward the self; primarily concerned with one's own thoughts and feelings rather than with the external environment or other people; preference for solitary activities.

Inventory. A set of questions or statements to which the individual responds (for example, by indicating agreement or disagreement), designed to provide a measure of personality, interest, attitude, or behavior.

Ipsative measurement. Test item format (e. g., forced-choice) in which the variables being measured are compared with each other, so that a person's score on one variable is affected by his or her scores on other variables measured by the instrument.

Item. One of the units, questions, or tasks of which a psychometric instrument is composed.

Item analysis. A general term for procedures designed to assess the utility or validity of a set of items on a test or other psychometric instrument.

Item characteristic curve. A graph, used in item analysis, in which the proportion of examinees passing a specified item is plotted against total test scores.

Item difficulty index. An index of the easiness or difficulty of an item for a group of examinees. A convenient measure of the difficulty of an item is the percentage (p) of examinees who select the designated answer.

Item discrimination index. A measure of how effectively an item discriminates between examinees who score high on a test as a whole (or on some other criterion variable) and those who score low.

Item-response curve. Graph showing the proportion of examinees who get a test item right, plotted against theoretical estimates of the examinees' standings on some latent trait continuum.

Item response theory (IRT). Theory of test items in which item scores are expressed in terms of estimated scores on a latent ability continuum.

Item sampling. Procedure for selecting subsets of items from a total item pool; different samples of items are administered to different groups of examinees.

Kuder-Richardson formulas. Formulas used to compute a measure of internal-consistency reliability from a single administration of a test having 0–1 scoring.

Leaderless group discussion (LGD). Six or so individuals (e. g., candidates for an executive position) are observed while discussing an assigned problem to determine their effectiveness in working with the group and reaching a solution.

Leniency error. Tendency to rate an individual higher on a positive characteristic and less severely on a negative characteristic than he or she actually should be rated.

Life-style. Composite of habits, attitudes, preferences, socioeconomic status, and other features constituting a person's manner of living.

Likert scale. Attitude scale in which respondents indicate their degree of agreement or disagreement with a particular proposition concerning some object, person, or situation.

Linear regression analysis. Procedure for determining the algebraic equation of the best-fitting line for predicting scores on a dependent variable from one or more independent variables.

Linking. Item-response based methodology for equating two tests by transforming the item parameters of one form of the test to those of a second form of the test so the corresponding parameters on the two tests will be on the same numerical scale.

Local norms. Percentile ranks, standard scores, or other norms corresponding to the raw test scores of a relatively small, local group of examinees.

Locus of control. J. B. Rotter's term for a cognitive-perceptual style characterized by the typical direction (internal or self versus external or other) from which individuals perceive themselves as being controlled.

Looking-glass theory. After C. H. Cooley, the idea that the self is formed as a result of the individual's perception of how others view her or his person and behavior.

M'Naughten rule. Standard of legal insanity stating that "the party accused was laboring under such a defect of reason, from disease of the mind, as not to know the nature and quality of the act he was doing . . ."

Machiavellianism. Personality trait in which the individual is concerned with manipulating other people or using them for his or her own purposes.

Man-to-man scale. Procedure in which ratings on a specific trait (e. g., leadership) are made by comparing each person to be rated with several other people whose standings on the trait have already been determined.

Measurement. Procedures for determining (or indexing) the amount or quantity of some construct or entity; assignment of numbers to objects or events.

Median. Score point in a distribution of scores below and above which 50% of the scores fall.

Medical model of mental disorders. The concept that mental disorders can be diagnosed on the basis of a pattern of symptoms (syndromes) and cured through physical or psychological therapies.

Mesomorph. William Sheldon's term for a person having an athletic physique; correlated with a somatotonic temperament (active, aggressive, energetic).

Mode. The most frequently occurring score in a group of scores.

Model Penal Code. Standard of legal insanity applied in most states that "A person is not responsible for criminal conduct, i. e., insane if, at the time of such conduct, as a result of mental disease or defect, he lacks substantial capacity either to appreciate the criminality (wrongfulness) of his conduct, or to conform his conduct to the requirement of the law."

Moderator variable. Demographic or personality variable (e. g., age, sex, cognitive style, compulsivity) affecting the correlation between two other variables (e.g, aptitude and achievement).

Multiple correlation coefficient (R). A measure of the overall degree of relationship, varying between −1.00 and + 1.00, of several variables with a single criterion variable. The multiple correlation of a group of scholastic aptitude tests with school grades is typically around .60 to .70, a moderate degree of correlation.

Multiple regression analysis. Statistical method for analyzing the contributions of two or more independent variables in predicting a dependent variable.

Multitrait-multimethod matrix. Matrix of correlation coefficients resulting from correlating measures of the same trait by the same method, different traits by the same method, the same trait by different methods, and different traits by different methods. The relative magnitudes of the four types of correlations are compared in evaluating the construct validity of a test.

National norms. Percentile ranks, standard scores, or other norms based on a national sample. See **Local norms, Norms.**

Need. A physiogenic or psychogenic drive or motive underlying behavior. Henry Murray's need/press theory of personality lists a number of physiogenic and psychogenic needs, several of which (e. g., need for achievement, need for affiliation, need for power) have been extensively investigated in research.

Need achievement. Motive to excel or attain success in some field or endeavor; measured and studied extensively by D. C. McClelland.

Neurosis (psychoneurosis). Nonpsychotic mental disorder characterized by anxiety, obsessions, compulsions, phobias, and/or bodily complaints or dysfunctions having no demonstrable physical basis.

Nominal scale. The lowest type of measurement, in which numbers are used merely as descriptors or names of things, rather than designating order or amount.

Nomination technique. Method of studying social structure and personality in which students, workers, or other groups of individuals are asked to indicate with which persons in the group they would like to do a certain thing or whom they feel possess(es) certain characteristics.

Nomothetic approach. A search for general laws of behavior and personality that apply to all individuals.

Nonverbal behavior. Any behavior in which the respondent does not make word sounds or signs. Nonverbal behavior serving a communicative function includes movements of large (macrokinesics) and small (microkinesics) body parts, interpersonal distance or territoriality (proximics), tone and rate of voice sounds (paralinguistics), and communications imparted by culturally prescribed matters relating to time, dress, memberships, and the like (culturics).

Normal distribution. A smooth, bell-shaped frequency distribution of scores, symmetrical about the mean and described by an exact mathematical function. The test scores of a large group of examinees are frequently distributed in an approximately normal manner.

Normalized standard scores. Scores obtained by transforming raw scores in such a way that the transformed scores are normally distributed with a mean of 0 and a standard deviation of 1 (or some linear function of these numbers).

Norm group. Sample of people on whom a test is standardized.

Norms. A list of scores and the corresponding percentile ranks, standard scores, or other transformed scores of a group of examinees on whom a test has been standardized.

Numerology. The study of numbers, such as the figures designating the year of one's birth, to determine their supposed influence on one's life and future.

Objective test. A test scored by comparing the examinee's responses to a list of correct answers (a key) prepared beforehand, in contrast to a subjectively scored test. Examples of objective test items and multiple-choice and true-false.

Oblique rotation. In a factor analysis, a rotation in which the factor axes are allowed to form acute or obtuse angles with each other. Consequently, the factors are correlated.

Observation method. Observing behavior in a controlled or uncontrolled situation and making a formal or informal record of the observations.

Ordinal scale. Type of measurement scale on which the numbers refer merely to the ranks of objects or events arranged in order of merit (e. g., numbers referring to order of finishing in a contest).

Orthogonal rotation. In factor analysis, a rotation that maintains the independence of factors, that is, the angles between factors are kept at 90 degrees and hence the factors are uncorrelated.

Palmistry (chiromancy). Telling fortunes and interpreting character from the lines and configurations in the palms of the hand.

Parallel forms. Two tests that are equivalent in the sense that they contain the same kinds of items of equal difficulty and are highly correlated. The scores made by examinees on one form of the test are very close to those made by them on the other form.

Parallel forms reliability. An index of reliability determined by correlating the scores of individuals on parallel forms of a test.

Participant observation. A research technique, used mainly by cultural anthropologists, in which an observer attempts to minimize the intrusiveness of his or her person and observational activities by becoming part of the group being observed, for example, by dressing and behaving like the other group members.

Percentile. The *p*th percentile is the test score at or below which *p* percent of the examinee's test scores fall.

Percentile band. A range of percentile ranks within which there is a specified probability that an examinee's true score on a test will fall.

Percentile norms. A list of raw scores and the corresponding percentages of the test standardization group whose scores fall below the given percentile.

Percentile rank. The percentage of scores falling below a given score in a frequency distribution or group of scores; the percentage corresponding to the given score.

Personal orientation. Generalized personality disposition, such as gender role or self-actualization, that directs behavior in a variety of situations.

Personality. The sum total of all the qualities, traits, and behaviors that characterize the thoughts, feelings, and behaviors of a person and by which, together with his or her physical attributes, the person is recognized as a unique individual.

Personality assessment. The description and analysis of personality by means of various techniques, including personality inventories, observations, interviews, checklists, rating scales, and projective techniques.

Personality disorder. Maladaptive behavioral syndrome originating in childhood but not characterized by psychoneurotic or psychotic symptomatology.

Personality inventory. A self-report inventory or questionnaire consisting of statements concerned with personal characteristics and behaviors. On a true-false inventory, the respondent indicates whether or not each test item or statement is self-descriptive; on a multiple-choice or forced-choice inventory, the respondent selects the statements that are self-descriptive.

Personality profile. Graph of scores on a battery or set of scales of a personality inventory or rating scale. The elevation and scatter of the profile assist in the assessment of personality and mental disorders.

Personality test. Any one of several methods of analyzing personality, such as checklists, personality inventories, and projective techniques.

Phenomenology. Study of objects and events as they appear to the experiencing observer; type of psychotherapy (Rogers, Maslow, etc.) which emphasizes the importance of self-perceptions and impressions of others in determining personality and behavior.

Phenotype. The way in which a genetically determined characteristic is actually manifested in a person's appearance or behavior.

Phrenology. Discredited theory and practice of Gall and Spurzheim relating affective and cognitive characteristics to the configuration (bumps) of the skull.

Physiognomy (anthroposcopy). A pseudoscience that maintains that the personal characteristics of an individual are revealed by the form or features of the body, especially the face.

Point-biserial coefficient. Correlation coefficient computed between a dichotomous variable and a continuous variable; derived from the product-moment correlation coefficient.

Polygraph. An apparatus that monitors respiration rate, blood pressure, pulse rate, and the galvanic skin response (GSR); formerly used to detect lying or verify truthfulness in responding to interrogation.

Predictive validity. Extent to which scores on a test are predictive of performance on some criterion measure assessed at a later time; usually expressed as a correlation between the test (predictor variable) and the criterion variable.

Press. As contrasted with **need**, external, environmental pressures influencing behavior. Henry Murray's need/press theory of personality differentiates between press from the objective environment (**alpha press**) and press from the perceived environment (**beta press**).

Privileged communication. Confidential communication between a person and his or her lawyer, doctor, pastor, or spouse. The information communicated is privileged against disclosure in court if the privilege is claimed by the person (client, patient, penitent, spouse).

Profile (psychograph). Graph depicting an individual's scores on several parts of the same test. By examining the profile of scores on a personality inventory such as the MMPI, a psychologist may obtain information useful in personality analysis and the diagnosis of psychopathology.

Projective technique. A relatively unstructured personality assessment technique in which the examinee responds to materials such as inkblots, ambiguous pictures, incomplete sentences, and other materials by telling what he or she perceives, making up stories, or constructing and arranging sentences and objects. Theoretically, because the material is fairly unstructured, whatever structure the examinee imposes on it represents a projection of his or her own personality characteristics (needs, conflicts, sources of anxiety, etc.).

Psychoanalysis. Developed by Sigmund Freud and his followers, psychoanalysis is a theory of personality concerned with the dynamic interaction between the conscious and unconscious, a psychotherapeutic method for dealing with personality problems, and a research method for studying personality.

Psychodiagnosis. Examination and evaluation of personality in terms of behavioral, cognitive, and affective characteristics and the interactions among them.

Psychodynamic theory. Theory emphasizing the interaction of conscious and unconscious mental process in determining thoughts, feelings, and behavior.

Psychographics. Study of the relationships of consumer behavior to personality characteristics and life-styles.

Psychohistory. Biography, such as E. H. Erikson's *Young Man Luther* or *Gandhi's Truth*, written from a psychoanalytic point of view.

Psychometrics. Theory and research pertaining to the measurement of psychological (cognitive and affective) characteristics.

Psychosexual stages. Sequence of stages in sexual development (oral, anal, phallic, latency, genital) characterized by a focus on different erogenous zones and associated conflicts.

Psychosis. Severe mental disorder characterized by faulty perception of reality, deficits of language and memory, disturbances in the emotional sphere, and other bizarre symptoms.

Psychosocial stages. Erik Erikson's modification of Freud's theory of psychosexual stages; emphasizes environmental and social problems, as contrasted with biological factors, in the progression of development from infancy through old age.

Pupillometrics. Procedure for measuring pupillary diameter as a measure of pleasure or interest in a specific stimulus.

Q technique (sort). Personality assessment procedure that centers on sorting decks of cards (Q sorts) containing statements that may or may not be descriptive of the rater.

Quartile. A score in a frequency distribution below which either 25% (first quartile), 50% (second quartile), 75% (third quartile), or 100% (fourth quartile) of the total number of scores fall.

Questionnaire. A list of questions concerning a particular topic, administered to a group of individuals to obtain information concerning their preferences, beliefs, interests, and behavior.

r. A symbol for the Pearson product-moment correlation coefficient.

Rapport. A warm, friendly relationship between examiner and examinee.

Rating scale. A list of words or statements concerning traits or characteristics, sometimes in the form of a continuous line divided into sections corresponding to degrees of the characteristic, on which the rater indicates judgments of either his or her own behavior and traits or the behavior and traits of another person (ratee).

Ratio scale. A scale of measurement, having a true zero, on which equal numerical ratios imply equal ratios of the attribute being measured. Psychological variables are typically not measured on ratio scales, but height, weight, energy, and many other physical variables are.

Real self. In C. R. Rogers' phenomenological theory, a person's perception of what he or she really is, as contrasted with what he or she would like to be (**ideal self**).

Realistic stage. Final stage in the development of vocational interests, usually occurring during late adolescence or early adulthood. At this stage the individual has a realistic notion about what particular occupations entail and the vocation he or she would like to pursue.

Reliability. The extent to which a psychological assessment device measures anything consistently. A reliable instrument is relatively free from errors of measurement, so the scores obtained on the instrument are close in numerical value to the true scores of examinees

Reliability coefficient. A numerical index, between .00 and 1.00, of the reliability of an assessment instrument. Methods for determining reliability include test-retest, parallel-forms, and internal consistency.

Repression-sensitization. Donald Byrne's conception of a personality continuum representing a person's typical response to threat; information-avoidance behaviors are at one end of the continuum and information-seeking behaviors are at the other end.

Response sets (styles). Tendencies for individuals to respond in relatively fixed or stereotypes ways in situations where there are two or more response choices, such as on personality inventories. Tendencies to guess, to answer true (acquiescence), and to give socially desirable answers are some of the response sets that have been investigated.

RIASEC model. John Holland's model of person-environment interest/personality types consisting of Realistic, Investigative, Artistic, Social, Enterprising, and Conventional themes.

Secondary trait. Less important personality traits, such as preferences or interests, that affect behavior less than central or cardinal traits.

Self. Perceived identity, individuality, or ego; that which consciously knows and experiences.

Self-actualization. In C. R. Rogers' phenomenological theory, attaining a state of congruence between one's real and ideal selves; developing one's abilities to the fullest; becoming the kind of person one would ideally like to be.

Self-concept. An individual's evaluation of her or his self as assessed by various psychometric instruments.

Self-efficacy. A person's judgment concerning his or her ability to accomplish a particular task in a certain situation successfully.

Self-fulfilling prophecy. Tendency for a person's expectations and attitudes concerning future events or outcomes to affect their occurrence; the tendency for children to behave in ways in which parents or teachers expect them to behave.

Self-monitoring. The extent to which people are sensitive to, or monitor, their own behavior according to environmental cues. High self-monitors are more sensitive to what is situationally appropriate and act accordingly. Low self-monitors are less sensitive to external cues and act more in response to their own internal attitudes and feelings.

Self-report inventory. A paper-and-pencil measure of personality traits or interests, comprised of a series of items that the examinee indicates as characteristic (true) or not characteristic (not true) of himself (herself).

Semantic differential. A rating scale, introduced by C. E. Osgood, for evaluating the connotative meanings that selected concepts have for a person. Each concept is rated on a seven-point, bipolar adjectival scale.

Sentence completion test. A projective test of personality consisting of a series of incomplete sentences that the examinee is instructed to complete.

Situation(al) test. A performance test in which the examinee is placed in a realistic but contrived situation and directed to accomplish a specified task. Situation tests are sometimes used to assess personality characteristics such as honesty and frustration tolerance.

Skewness. Degree of asymmetry in a frequency distribution. In a positively skewed distribution, there are more scores to the left of the mean (low scores); this is true when the test is too difficult for the examinees. In a negatively skewed distribution, there are more scores to the right of the mean (high scores); this is true when the test is too easy for the examinees.

Social desirability response set. Response set or style affecting scores on personality inventories. It refers to the tendency on the part of an examinee to respond to the assessment materials in a more socially desirable direction rather than responding in a manner that is truly characteristic or descriptive of his or her personality.

Social learning theory. Conceptualization that learning occurs by imitation or interactions with other people.

Sociogram. Diagram consisting of circles representing individuals in a group, with lines drawn indicating which people chose (accepted) each other and which people did not choose (rejected) each other. Terms used in referring to particular elements of a sociogram are star, clique, isolate, and mutual admiration society.

Sociometric technique. Method of determining and describing the pattern of acceptances and rejections in a group of people.

Somatotonia. Athletic, aggressive temperament type in W. H. Sheldon's three-component system of personality; most closely related to a mesomorphic (muscular) body build.

Somatotype. Classification of body build (physique) in W. H. Sheldon's three-component system (endomorphy, mesomorphy, ectomorphy).

Source traits. R. B. Cattell's term for organizing structures or dimensions of personality that underlie and determine surface traits.

Spearman-Brown prophecy formula. A general formula for estimating the reliability (r_{11}) of a test on which the number of items is increased by a factor of m. In the formula, $r_{mm} = mr_{11}/[1 + (m-1)r_{11}]$, r_{11} is the reliability of the original (unlengthened) test, and m is the factor by which it is lengthened.

Split-half coefficient. An estimate of reliability determined by applying the Spearman-Brown formula for m = 2 to the correlation between two halves of the same test, such as the odd-numbered items and the even-numbered items.

Standard deviation. The square root of the variance; used as a measure of the dispersion or spread of a group of scores.

Standard error of estimate. Degree of error made in estimating a person's score on a criterion variable from his (her) score on a predictor variable.

Standard error of measurement. An estimate of the standard deviation of the normal distribution of test scores that an examinee would theoretically obtain by taking a test an infinite number of times. If an examinee's obtained test score is X, then the chances are two out of three that he or she is one of a group of people whose true scores on the test fall within one standard error of measurement of X.

Standardization. Administering a carefully constructed test to a large, representative sample of people under standard conditions for the purpose of determining norms.

Standardization sample. Subset of a target population on which a test is standardized.

Standardized test. A test that has been carefully constructed by professionals and administered with standard directions and under standard conditions to a representative sample of people for the purpose of obtaining norms.

Standard scores. A group of scores, such as z scores, T scores, or stanine scores, having a desired mean and standard deviation. Standard scores are computed by transforming raw scores to z scores, multiplying the z scores by the desired standard deviation, and then adding the desired mean to the product.

Stanine. A normalized standard score scale consisting of the scores 1 through 9, stanine scores have a mean of 5 and a standard deviation of approximately 2.

State anxiety. A temporary state of anxiety, precipitated by a specific situation.

Statistic. A number used to describe some characteristic of a sample of test scores, such as the arithmetic mean or standard deviation.

Statistical (actuarial) approach. Combining quantified clinical information according to empirically established rules, and then making behavioral predictions or diagnoses on the basis of the results.

Stratified random sampling. A sampling procedure in which the population is divided into strata (e. g., men and women; blacks and whites, lower class, middle class, upper class), and samples are selected at random from the strata; sample sizes within strata are proportional to strata sizes.

Stress interview. Interviewing procedure in which the interviewer applies psychologically stressful techniques (critical and hostile questioning, frequent interruptions, prolonged silences, etc.) to break down the interviewee's defenses and/or determine how the interviewee reacts under pressure.

Structured interview. Interviewing procedure in which the interviewee is asked a planned series of questions.

Surface traits. Publicly manifested characteristics of personality; observable expressions of source traits.

T scores. Converted, normalized standard scores having a mean of 50 and a standard deviation of 10. Z scores are also standard scores with a mean of 50 and a standard deviation of 10, but in contrast to T scores they are not normalized.

Target behaviors. Specific, objectively defined behaviors observed and measured in behavioral assessments. Of particular interest are the effects on these behaviors of antecedent and consequent events in the environment.

Target population. The population of interest in standardizing a test or other assessment instrument; the norm group (sample) must be representative of the target population if valid interpretations of (norm-referenced) scores are to be made.

Test. Any device used to evaluate the behavior or performance of a person. Psychological tests are of many kinds—cognitive, affective, and psychomotor.

Test anxiety. A feeling of fear or uneasiness that one will not do well on a test.

Test bias. Condition in which a test unfairly discriminates between two or more groups.

Test-retest reliability. A method of assessing the reliability of a test by administering it to the same group of examinees on two different occasions and computing the correlation (**coefficient of stability**) between their scores on the two occasions.

Time sampling. Observational sampling procedure in which observations lasting only a few minutes are made over a period of a day or so.

Trait. A cognitive, affective, or psychomotor characteristic possessed in different amounts by different people.

Trait anxiety. Generalized level of anxiety expressed in a variety of situations.

Trait theory. Personality theory that conceptualizes human personality as consisting of a combination of traits.

Transitional stage. An intermediate stage in the development of interests; it falls between the fantasy stage of early childhood and the realistic stage of late adolescence and early adulthood.

Type. A larger dimension of personality that a **trait**; a combination of traits characterizing a particular kind of personality.

Type A personality. Personality pattern characterized by a combination of behaviors, including aggressiveness, competitiveness, hostility, quick actions, and constant striving; associated with a high incidence of coronary heart disease.

Type B personality. Personality pattern characterized by a relaxed, easygoing, patient, noncompetitive lifestyle; associated with a low incidence of coronary heart disease.

Unconditional positive regard. In client-centered therapy, an accepting, sincere attitude on the part of the therapist, regardless of the feelings or actions revealed by the client.

Unconscious. In psychoanalytic theory, that part of the personality that is below the level of conscious awareness and is brought into consciousness only in disguised form.

Unobtrusive observations. Observations made without the awareness of the person whose behavior is being observed.

Unstructured interview. Interviewing procedure in which the questions asked are not planned but vary with the progress or flow of the interview.

Validity. The extent to which an assessment instrument measures what it was designed to measure. Validity can be assessed in several ways: by analysis of the instrument's content (**content validity**), by relating scores on the test to a criterion (**predictive** and **concurrent validity**), and by a more thorough study of the extent to which the test is a measure of a certain psychological construct (**construct validity**).

Validity coefficient. The correlation between scores on a predictor variable and scores on a criterion variable.

Validity generalization. The application of validity evidence to situations other than those in which the evidence was obtained.

Variability. The degree of spread or deviation of a group of scores around their average value.

Variable. In contrast to a **constant**, any quantity that can assume more than one state or numerical value.

Variance. A measure of variability of test scores, computed as the sum of the squares of the deviations of raw scores from the arithmetic mean, divided by one less than the number of scores; the square of the standard deviation.

Viscerotonia. Jolly, sociable temperament type in W. H. Sheldon's three-component description of personality; most closely related to the endomorphic (rotund) body build.

Word association test. A list of words that is read aloud to an examinee who has been instructed to respond with the first word that comes to mind.

z **score.** Any one of a group of derived scores varying from $-\infty$ to $+\infty$, computed from the formula $z =$ (raw score $-$ mean)/standard deviation, for each raw score. In a normal distribution, over 99% of the cases lie between $z = -3.00$ and $z = +3.00$.

Commercial Suppliers of Psychological Assessment Materials

Ablin Press Distributors, 3332 Hadfield Greene, Sarasota, FL 34235.

Thomas M. Achenbach, University Associates in Psychiatry, Department of Psychiatry, University of Vermont, 1 South Prospect Street, Burlington, VT 05401-3456.

Addison-Wesley Testing Service, 2725 Sand Hill Road, Menlo Park, CA 94025.

American College Testing (ACT), 2201 North Dodge Street, P.O. Box 4060, Iowa City, IA 52243-4060. Tel. 800-498-6065 or 319-337-1000.

American Educational Research Association, 1230 Seventeenth Street, N.W., Washington, DC 20036-3078.

American Guidance Service (AGS), 4201 Woodland Road, P.O. Box 99, Circle Pines, MN 55014-1796. Tel. 800-328-2560. Fax: 612-786-9077. E-mail: agsmail@agsnet.com. Web site: www.agsnet.com.

American Orthopsychiatric Association, Inc., 49 Sheridan Avenue, Albany, NY 12210.

Assessment Systems Corporation, 2233 University Avenue, Suite 200, St. Paul, MN 55114-1629. Tel. 612-647-9220. Fax: 612-647-0412. Web site: www.assess.com.

Australian Council for Educational Research Ltd., 19 Prospect Hill Road, Private Bag 55, Camberwell, Victoria 3124, Australia. Tel. (03) 9277 5656. Fax: (03) 9227 5678. E-mail:sales@acer.edu.au. Web site: www.acer.edu.au.

Behavior Science Systems, Inc., P.O. Box 580274, Minneapolis, MN 55458.

Consulting Psychologists Press, Inc. (CPP), 3803 East Bayshore Road, P.O. Box 10096, Palo Alto, CA 94303. Tel. 800–624–1765.

CPPC, 4 Conant Square, Brandon, VT 05733. Tel. (800) 624-1765.

C.P.S., Inc., P.O. Box 83, Larchmont, NY 10538. Ph. 800/433–8324.

CTB/McGraw-Hill, 20 Ryan Ranch Road, Monterey, CA 93940–5703. Tel. 800-538-9547. Fax: 800-282-0266. TDD: 800-217-9190. Web site: www.ctb.com.

DLM Resources, One DLM Park, Allen, TX 75002. Tel. 800-527-4747.

Educational and Industrial Testing Service (EdITS), P. O. Box 7234, San Diego, CA 92167. Tel. 800-416-1666. Fax: 619-226-1666.

Educational Testing Service (ETS), Publication Order Services, P.O. Box 6736, Princeton, NJ 08541-6736. Web site: www.ets.org.

Harcourt Brace Educational Measurement, Educational Testing Division of TPC, 555 Academic Court, San Antonio, TX 78204-2498. Tel. 800-211-8378. Fax: 800-232-1223. TDD: 800-723-1318. Web site: www.hbem.com.

Harvard University Press, 79 Garden Street, Cambridge, MA 92138.

Hawthorne Educational Services Inc., 800 Gray Oak Drive, Columbia, MO 65201. Tel. 800-542-1673. Fax: 800-442-9509.

Hilson Research, Inc., P.O. Box 150239, 82–28 Abingdon Road, Kew Gardens, NY 11415-0239. Tel. 800-926-2258. Fax: 718-849-6238.

Hogan Assessment Systems, Inc., P.O. Box 521176, Tulsa, OK 74152-1176. Tel. 800-756-0632. Fax: 918-749-0635. Web site: www.hoganassessments.com.

Hogrefe & Huber Publishers, P.O. Box 2487, Kirkland, WA 98083. Tel. 800-228-3749 (orders), 425-820-1500. Fax: 425-823-8324. Web site: www.hhpub.com. E-mail: hh@hhpub.com.

IDS Publishing, P.O. Box 389, Worthington, OH 43085.

Industrial Psychology International, Ltd., 4106 Firestone Road, Champaign, IL 61821. Tel. 217-398-1437. Fax: 217-398-5798.

Institute for Personality and Ability Testing (IPAT), P.O. Box 1188, Champaign, IL 61824-1188. Tel. 800-225-IPAT. Web site: www.ipat.com.

Jastak Associates, Inc., P.O. Box 3410, Wilmington, DE 19804-0250. Tel. 800-221-WRAT.

London House, 9701 W. Higgins Road, Rosemont, IL 60018-4720. Tel. 800-227-7685. Fax: 847-292-3400.

Martin M. Bruce, 50 Larchwood Road, Box 248, Larchmont, NY 10538. Tel. 914-834-1555.

Metritech, Inc., 4106 Fieldstone Road, P.O. Box 6489, Champaign, IL 61826-6479. Tel. 217-398-4868.

Multi-Health Systems, Inc., 908 Niagara Falls Boulevard, North Tonawanda,

NY 14120-2060; Tel. 800-456-3003. Fax: 416-2324. E-mail: janice_b@mhs. com.

NCS Assessments, P.O. Box 1416, Minneapolis, MN 55440. Tel. 800-627-7271.

NCS Workforce Development Group, 9701 West Higgins Road, Rosemont, IL 60018-4720. Tel. 800-237-7685. Fax: 847-292-3400.

NFER-Nelson Publishing Company, Ltd., Darville House, 2 Oxford Road East, Windsor-Berkshire, SL4 1lDF, United Kingdom.

pro.ed, 8700 Shoal Creek Boulevard, Austin, TX 78757-6897. Tel. 512-451-3246 or 800-897-3202. Fax: 800-FXPROED. Web site: www.proedinc.com.

Psychological Assessment Resources, Inc. (PAR), P.O. Box 998, Odessa, FL 33556-0998. Tel. 800-331-TEST or 800-383-6595. Fax: 800-727-9329. Web site: www.parinc.com.

The Psychological Corporation, 555 Academic Court, San Antonio, TX 78204-2498. Tel. 800/211-8378. Fax: 800-232-1223. Tdd: 800-723-1318.

Psychological Publications, Inc., P.O. Box 3577, Thousand Oaks, CA 91359-0577. Tel. 800-345-TEST.

Psychological Test Specialists, Box 9229, Missoula, MT 59807.

Psychologists and Educators, Inc., P.O. Box 513, Chesterfield, MO 63006.

Psychometric Affiliates, Box 807, Murfreesboro, TN 37133-0807. Tel. 615-898-2565.

Publishers Test Service, CTB/McGraw-Hill, 20 Ryan Ranch Road, Monterey, CA 93940. Tel. 800-538-9547.

Riverside Publishing Company (The), 425 Spring Lake Drive, Itasca, IL 60143-2079. Tel. 800-323-9540. Fax: 630-467-7192. Web site: www.riverpub.com.

Scholastic Testing Service, Inc. (STS), 480 Meyer Road, P.O. Box 1056, Bensenville, IL 60106-1617. Tel. 800-766-7150 or 800-642-6STS. Fax: 630-766-8054. E-mail: STSLH25@aol.com.

Sigma Assessment Systems, Inc., P.O. Box 610984, Port Huron, MI 48061-0984. Tel. 800-265-1285. Fax: 800-361-9411. LE-mail: sigma@mgl.ca. Web site: www.mgl.ca-sigma.

Slosson Educational Publications, Inc., P.O. Box 280, East Aurora, NY 14052-0280. Tel. 818-756-7766. Fax: 800-655-3840.

SOI Systems, P.O. Box D, 45755 Goodpasture Road, Vida, OR 97488. Tel. 503-896-3936.

SRA/London House, 9701 Higgins Road, Rosemont, IL 60018. Tel. 800-221-8378.

Stoelting Co., 620 Wheat Lane, Wood Dale, IL 60191. Tel. 630-860-9700. Fax: 630-860-9775. E-mail: psychtests@stoeltingco.com.

Swets Test Services, Heereweg 347, NL-2161 CA Lisse, The Netherlands. Tel: +31-(0)2521-35128. Fax: +31-(0)2521-15888.

Thompson Patrick Association, 5838 Monte Verde, Sana Rosa, CA 95409.

Timao Foundation for Research and Development, 2828 B Alta View Drive, San Diego, CA 92139.

Western Psychological Services (WPS), 12031 Wilshire Boulevard, Los Angeles, CA 90025-1251. Tel. 800-648-8857. Fax: 310-478-7838.

Wide Range, Inc., P.O. Box 3410, Wilmington, DE 19804-0250. Tel. 800-2211-WRAT or 302-652-4990. Fax: 302-652-1644.

Wonderlic Personnel Test, Inc., 1509 N. Milwaukee Avenue, Libertyville, IL 60048-1387. Tel. 800-963-7542. Web site: www.wonderlic.com.

References

Aaker, J. (1997). Dimensions of brand personality. *Journal of Marketing Research, 34*(3), 347–356.

Abrahams, N. M., Neumann, I., & Gilthens, W. H. (1971). Faking vocational interests: Simulated vs. real life motivation. *Personnel Psychology, 24*(1), 5–12.

Achenbach, T. M. (1981). A junior MMPI? *Journal of Personality Assessment, 45*, 332.

Achenbach, T. M., & Edelbrock, C. (1983). *Manual of the Child Behavior Checklist and Revised Child Behavior Profile.* Burlington, VT: University of Vermont, Department of Psychiatry.

Achenbach, T. M., & Edelbrock, C. (1986). *Manual for the Teacher's Report Form and Teacher Version of the Child Behavior Profile.* Burlington, VT: University of Vermont, Department of Psychiatry.

Achenbach, T. M., & Edelbrock, C. (1987). *Manual for the Youth Self-Report and Profile.* Burlington, VT: University of Vermont, Department of Psychiatry.

Acklin, M. W. (1996). Personality assessment and managed care. *Journal of Personality Assessment, 66*, 194–201.

Adair, F. L. (1984). Coopersmith Self-Esteem Inventories. In D. J. Keyser & R. C. Sweetland (Eds.), *Test critiques* (Vol. I, pp. 226–232). Kansas City, MO: Test Corporation of America.

Adorno, T. W., Frenkel-Brunswik, E., Levinson, D., & Sanford, N. (1950). *The authoritarian personality.* New York: Harper.

Aiken, L. R. (1985). Three coefficients for analyzing the reliability and validity of ratings. *Educational and Psychological Measurement, 45*, 131–142.

Aiken, L. R. (1993). *Personality: Theories, research, and applications.* Englewood Cliffs, NJ: Prentice-Hall.

Aiken, L. R. (1996). *Rating scales and checklists: Evaluating behavior, personality, and attitudes.* New York: Wiley.

Aiken, L.R. (1997a). *Questionnaires and inventories: Surveying opinions and assessing personality.* New York: Wiley.

Aiken, L.R. (1997b). Review of MIPS: Millon Index of Personality Styles. *Journal of Psychoeducational Assessment, 15,* 380–382.

Aiken, L.R. (1997c). *Assessment of adult personality.* New York: Springer.

Aiken, L.R. (1998). *Tests and examinations: Measuring abilities and performance.* New York: Wiley.

Aiken, L.R., & Romen, L. (1984). Attitudes and experiences concerning psychological and educational testing. *Paper presented at the Annual Meeting of the Rocky Mountain Psychological Association, 1984* (ERIC Reports ED 247 322).

Aiken, L.R., & Zweigenhaft, R. (1978). Signature size, sex and status: A cross-cultural replication. *Journal of Social Psychology, 106,* 273–274.

Albert, S., Fox, H.M., & Kahn, M.W. (1980). Faking psychosis on the Rorschach: Can expert judges detect malingering? *Journal of Personality Assessment, 44,* 115–119.

Allard, G., Butler, J., Faust, D., & Shea, M.T. (1995). Errors in hand scoring objective personality tests: The case of the Personality Diagnostic Questionnaire. *Professional Psychology: Research and Practice, 26,* 304–308.

Allen, M.J. (1985). Review of Millon Behavioral Health Inventory. *Ninth Mental Measurements Yearbook,* 981–983.

Allport, G.W. (1937). *Personality: A psychological interpretation.* New York: Holt, Rinehart & Winston.

Allport, G.W. (Ed.). (1965). *Letters from Jenny.* New York: Harcourt, Brace & World.

Allport, G.W., & Allport, F.H. (1928). *The A-S Reaction Study.* Boston: Houghton Mifflin.

Allport, G.W., & Odbert, H.S. (1936). Trait names, a psycholexical study. *Psychological Monographs, 47* (Whole No. 211).

Alterman, A.I., Zaballro, A.R., Lin, M.M., Siddiqui, N., et al. (1995). Personality Assessment Inventory (PAI) scores of lower-socioeconomic African American and Latino methadone maintenance patients. *Assessment, 2*(1), 91–100.

Alvarado, N. (1994). Empirical validity of the Thematic Apperception Test. *Journal of Personality Assessment, 63,* 59–79.

American Educational Research Association, American Psychological Association, & National Council on Measurement in Education (1985). *Standards for educational and psychological testing.* Washington, DC: American Psychological Association.

American Law Institute (1956). *Model penal code.* Tentative Draft Number 4. Author.

American Psychiatric Association. (1980). *Diagnostic and statistical manual of mental disorders* (3rd ed.). Washington, DC: Author.

American Psychiatric Association. (1987). *Diagnostic and statistical manual of mental disorders* (3rd rev. ed.). Washington, DC: Author.

American Psychiatric Association. (1994). *Diagnostic and statistical manual of mental disorders* (4th ed.). Washington, DC: Author.

American Psychological Association, Committee on Professional Standards, & Committee on Psychological Tests and Assessment. (1986). *Guidelines for computer-based tests and interpretations.* Washington, DC: Author.

American Psychological Association. (1987). *General guidelines for providers of psychological services.* Washington, DC: Author.

American Psychological Association. (1992). Ethical principles of psychologists and code of conduct. *American Psychologist, 47,* 1597–1611.

Ames, L. B., Learned, J., Metraux, R. W., & Walker, R. N. (1974). *Child Rorschach responses.* New York: Paul B. Hoeber.

Anastasi, A., & Urbina, S. (1997). *Psychological testing* (7th ed.). Upper Saddle River, NJ: Prentice-Hall.

Anderson, H., & Anderson, G. (1955). *An introduction to projective techniques.* New York: Prentice-Hall.

Appelbaum, S. A. (1960). The word association test expanded. *Bulletin of the Menninger Clinic, 24,* 258–264.

Arbisi, P. A. (1995). Review of the schedule for affective disorders and schizophrenia (3rd ed.). *Twelfth Mental Measurements Yearbook,* 917–918.

Arbisi, P. A. (1998). Review of the Senior Apperception Test (1985 Revision). *Thirteenth Mental Measurements Yearbook,* 897–900.

Archer, R. P., et al. (1991). Psychological test usage with adolescent clients: 1990 survey findings. *Professional Psychology: Research and Practice, 22,* 247–252.

Arkes, H. R. (1994). Clinical judgment. In R.. J. Corsini (Ed.), *Encyclopedia of psychology* (2nd ed., Vol. 1, pp. 237–238). New York: Wiley.

Armstrong, R. B. (1994). Early recollections. In R. J. Corsini (Ed.), *Encyclopedia of psychology* (2nd ed., Vol. 1, pp. 450–451). New York: Wiley.

Aronow, E. (1995). Review of Children's Apperceptive Story-Telling Test. *Twelfth Mental Measurements Yearbook,* 180–181.

Aronow, E., Reznikoff, M., & Moreland, K. (1994). *The Rorschach technique: Perceptual basics, content interpretation, and applications.* Boston: Allyn & Bacon.

Aronow, E., Reznikoff, M., & Moreland, K. (1995). The Rorschach: Projective technique or psychometric test? *Journal of Personality Assessment, 64,* 213–228.

Arvey, R. D. (1979). Unfair discrimination in the employment interview: Legal and psychological aspects. *Psychological Bulletin, 86,* 736–765.

Ash, P. (1995). Review of the Eating Disorder Inventory-2. *Twelfth Mental Measurements Yearbook,* 334–335.

Atkinson, J. W. (Ed.). (1958). *Motives in fantasy, action, and society.* New York: Van Nostrand.

Atkinson, L. (1986). The comparative validities of the Rorschach and MMPI: A meta-analysis. *Canadian Psychology, 27,* 238–247.

Bailey, B. E., & Green, J. (1977). Black Thematic Apperception Test stimulus material. *Journal of Personality Assessment, 41,* 25–30.

Bandura, A. (1977). *Social learning theory.* Englewood Cliffs, NJ: Prentice-Hall.

Bandura, A. (1986). *Social foundations of thought and action: A social cognitive theory.* Englewood Cliffs, NY: Prentice Hall.

Barends, A., Westen, D., Leigh, J., Silbert, D., & Byers, S. (1990). Assessing affect-tone of relationship paradigms from TAT and interview data. *Psychological Assessment, 2,* 329–332.

Barley, W. D., Dorr, D., & Reid, V. (1985). The Rorschach Comprehensive System egocentricity index in psychiatric inpatients. *Journal of Personality Assessment, 49,* 137–140.

Bauerfeind, R. H. (1986). COPSystem Interest Inventory. In D. J. Keyser & R. C. Sweetland (Eds.), *Test critiques* (Vol. V, pp. 76–82). Kansas City, MO: Test Corporation of America.

Beck, A. T., & Steer, R. A. (1993). *Beck Depression Inventory: Manual*. San Antonio, TX: Psychological Corporation.

Beck, S. J. (1944). *Rorschach's test I: Basic processes*. New York: Grune & Stratton.

Bell, H. M. (1939). *The adjustment inventory*. Palo Alto, CA: Consulting Psychologists Press.

Bellack, A. S., & Hersen, M. (Eds.). (1998). *Behavioral assessment: A practical handbook* (4th ed.). Boston: Allyn & Bacon.

Bellak, L. (1942). A note about Adam's apple. *Psychoanalytic Review, 29*(3).

Bellak, L. (1993). *The T.A.T., C.A.T., and S.A.T. in clinical use*. Des Moines, IA: Longwood Division, Allyn & Bacon.

Bellak, L., & Bellak, S. (1949). *Children's Apperception Test*. Larchmont, NY: C.P.S., Inc.

Bellak, L., & Bellak, S. (1973). *Manual: Senior Apperception Test*. Larchmont, NY: C.P.S., Inc.

Bem, D. J., & Allen, A. (1974). On predicting some of the people some of the time: The search for cross-situational consistencies in behavior. *Psychological Review, 81*, 506–520.

Bem, S. L. (1974). The measurement of psychological androgyny. *Journal of Consulting and Clinical Psychology, 42*, 165–172.

Bender, L. (1938). A visual-motor gestalt test and its clinical use. *American Orthopsychiatric Association Research Monographs* (No. 3).

Bender, L. (1970). The visual-motor gestalt test in the diagnosis of learning disabilities. *Journal of Special Education, 4*, 29–39.

Benjamin, J., Li, L., Patterson, C., Greenberg, B. D., Murphy, D. L., & Hamer, D. H. (1996). Population and familial association between the D4 dopamine receptor gene and measures of Novelty Seeking. *Nature Genetics, 12*, 81–84.

Ben-Porath, Y. S. (1997). Use of personality assessment instruments in empirically guided treatment planning. *Psychological Assessment, 9*, 361–367.

Benton, A. L., Windle, C. D., & Erdice, F. (1957). *A review of sentence completion techniques* (Project NR, pp. 151–175). Washington, DC: Office of Naval Research.

Bergner, M., & Gilson, B. S. (1981). The Sickness Impact Profile. In L. Eisenberg & A. Kleinman (Eds.), *The relevance of social science to medicine* (pp. 135–15). Dordrecht, The Netherlands: Reidel.

Bernard, H. W., & Huckins, W. C. (1978). *Dynamics of personality adjustment* (3rd ed.). Boston: Holbrook.

Berne, E. (1966). *Principles of group treatment*. New York: Oxford University Press.

Bernreuter, R. G. (1931). *The personality inventory*. Stanford, CA: Stanford University Press.

Bernstein, L. (1956). The examiner as an inhibiting factor in clinical testing. *Journal of Consulting Psychology, 20*, 287–290.

Betz, N. E. (1992). Counseling uses of career self-efficacy theory. *Career Development Quarterly, 41*, 22–26.

Betz, N. E. (1994). Self-concept theory in career development and counseling. *Career Development Quarterly, 43*, 32–42.

Binet, A., & Simon, T. (1905). Methodes pour le diagnostic du niveau intelectual des anormaux. *Lanne Psychologique, 11*, 191–244.

Blanchard, W. H. (1968). The consensus Rorschach: Background and development. *Journal of Projective Techniques and Personality Assessment, 32*, 327–330.

Blatt, S. J., & Berman, W. H. (1984). A methodology for use of the Rorschach in clinical research. *Journal of Personality Assessment, 48*, 226–239.

Block, J. (1961). *The Q-sort method in personality assessment and psychiatric research.* Springfield, IL: C. C. Thomas.

Block, J. (1965). *The challenge of response sets.* New York: Appleton-Century-Crofts.

Block, J. (1977). Recognizing the coherence of personality. In D. Magnusson & N. S. Endler (Eds.), *Interactional psychology: Current issues and future prospects.* New York: LEA/Wiley.

Block, J. (1978). *The Q sort method in personality assessment and psychiatric research.* Palo Alto, CA: Consulting Psychologists Press.

Block, J. (1995). A contrarian view of the five-factor approach to personality description. *Psychological Bulletin, 117*, 187–215.

Blum, K., Cull, J. G., Braverman, E. R., & Comings, D. E. (1996). Reward deficiency syndrome. *American Scientist, 84*, 132–145.

Bogardus, E. S. (1925). Measuring social distances. *Journal of Applied Sociology, 9*, 299–308.

Bolton, B. (1985). Work Values Inventory. In D. J. Keyser & R. C. Sweetland (Eds.), *Test critiques* (Vol. II, pp. 835–843). Kansas City, MO: Test Corporation of America.

Bolton, B. (1992). Review of the California Psychological Inventory (rev. ed.). *Eleventh Mental Measurements Yearbook*, 138–139.

Bordin, E. S. (1943). A theory of interests as dynamic phenomena. *Educational and Psychological Measurement, 3*, 49–66.

Bostic, J. Q., & Tallent-Runnels, M. K. (1991). Cognitive styles: A factor analysis of six dimensions with implications for consolidation. *Perceptual and Motor Skills, 72*, 1299–1306.

Bowmas, D. A., & Bernardin, H. J. (1991). Suppressing illusory halo with forced-choice items. *Journal of Applied Psychology, 76*, 592–594.

Boyle, G. J. (1995). Review of the Personality Assessment Inventory. *Twelfth Mental Measurements Yearbook*, 764–766.

Bradley, R. H., & Caldwell, B. M. (1977). Home observation for measurement of the environment: A validation study of screening efficiency. *American Journal of Mental Deficiency, 81*, 417–420.

Brevik, G. (1996). Personality, sensation seeking and risk taking among Everest climbers. *International Journal of Sport Psychology, 27*(3), 208–320.

Bricklin, B. (1984). *Bricklin Perceptual Scales.* Furlong, PA: Village.

Brittain, H. L. (1907). A study of imagination. *Pediatric Seminars, 14*, 137–207.

Brookhart, S. M. (1995). Review of the Rokeach Value Survey. *Twelfth Mental Measurements Yearbook*, 878–879.

Brown, D. T. (1985). Review of Millon Adolescent Personality Inventory. *Ninth Mental Measurements Yearbook*, 978–979.

Bruhn, A. R. (1992). The Early Memories Procedure: A projective test of autobiographical memory, Part I. *Journal of Personality Assessment, 58*, 1–15.

Bruhn, A. R. (1995). Early memories in personality assessment. In J. N. Butcher (Ed.), *Clinical personality assessment: Practical approaches* (pp. 278–301). New York: Oxford University Press.

Bruner, J. S. (1957). Neural mechanisms in perception. *Psychological Review, 64,* 340–358.

Buck, J. N. (1948). The H-T-P technique: A quantitative and qualitative scoring manual. *Clinical Psychology Monographs, 5,* 1–20.

Buck, J. N. (1981). *The House-Tree-Person technique: A revised manual.* Los Angeles: Western Psychological Services.

Buck, J. N. (1992). *House-Tree-Person projective drawing technique (H-T-P): Manual and interpretative guide* (Revised by W. L. Warren). Los Angeles, CA: Western Psychological Services.

Bugliosi, V. (1991). *And the sea will tell.* New York: Ivy Books.

Bukatman, B. A., Foy, J. L., & De Grazia, E. (1971). What is competency to stand trial? *American Journal of Psychiatry, 127,* 1225–1229.

Burdock, E. L., Hardesty, A. S., Hakerem, G., Zubin, J., & Beck, Y. M. (1968). *Ward Behavior Inventory.* New York: Springer.

Burisch, M. (1984). Approaches to personality inventory construction. *American Psychologist, 39,* 214–227.

Burnett, P. C. (1998). Review of the Revised Hamilton Rating Scale for Depression. *Thirteenth Mental Measurements Yearbook,* 838–839.

Burns, R. C. (1982). *Self-growth in families: Kinetic Family Drawings (K-F-D) research and applications.* New York: Brunner/Mazel.

Burns, R. C., & Kaufman, S. H. (1970). *Kinetic Family Drawings (K-F-D): An introduction to understanding children through kinetic drawings.* New York: Brunner/Mazel.

Burns, R. C., & Kaufman, S. H. (1972). *Actions, styles, and symbols in Kinetic Family Drawings (K-F-D): An interpretative manual.* New York: Brunner/Mazel.

Butcher, J. N., Dahlstrom, W. G., Graham, J. R., Tellegen, A., & Kaemmer, B. (1989). *Minnesota Multiphasic Personality Inventory-2 (MMPI-2): Manual for administration and scoring.* Minneapolis: University of Minnesota Press.

Butcher, J. N., & Rouse, S. V. (1996). Personality: Individual differences in clinical assessment. In J. T. Spence, J. M. Darley, & D. J. Foss (Eds.), *Annual Review of Psychology, 47,* 87–111.

Butcher, J. N., Williams, C. L., Graham, J. R., Archer, R. P., Tellegen, A., Ben-Porath, Y. S., & Kaemmer, B. (1992). *Minnesota Multiphasic Personality Inventory-Adolescent (MMPI-A): Manual for administration, scoring, and interpretation.* Minneapolis: University of Minnesota Press.

Butt, D. S. (1987). *Psychology of sport* (2nd ed.). New York: Van Nostrand Reinhold.

Byrne, D. (1961). The Repression-Sensitization Scale: Rationale, reliability, and validity. *Journal of Personality, 29,* 334–349.

Camara, W. J., & Schneider, D. L. (1994). Integrity tests: Facts and unresolved issues. *American Psychologist, 49,* 112–119.

Camara, W. J., & Schneider, D. L. (1995). Questions of construct breadth and openness of research in integrity testing. *American Psychologist, 50,* 459–460.

Campbell, D. T., & Fiske, D. W. (1959). Convergent and discriminant validation by the multitrait-multimethod matrix. *Psychological Bulletin, 56,* 81–105.

Canton, E., & Mayor, L. (1994). The sensation of risk and motivational tendencies in sports: An empirical study. *Personality and Individual Differences, 16,* 777–786.

Carlson, J. F. (1998). Review of the Beck Depression Inventory. *Thirteenth Mental Measurements Yearbook,* 117–120.

Carson, K. P., & Gilliard, D. J. (1993). Construct validity of the Miner Sentence Completion Scale. *Journal of Occupational and Organizational Psychology, 66,* 171–175.

Carter, H. D. (1940). The development of vocational attitudes. *Journal of Consulting Psychology, 4,* 185–191.

Cattell, J. M. (1887). Experiments on the association of ideas. *Mind, 12,* 68–74.

Cattell, R. B. (1965). *The scientific analysis of personality.* New York: Penguin.

Cattell, R. B., Cattell, A. K., & Cattell, H. E. (1993). *Sixteen Personality Factor Questionnaire* (5th ed.). Champaign, IL: Institute for Personality and Ability Testing.

Chaplin, W. F., & Goldberg, L. R. (1984). A failure to replicate the Ben and Allen study of individual differences in cross-situational consistency. *Journal of Personality and Social Psychology, 47,* 1074–1090.

Chapman, L. J., & Chapman, J. P. (1967). Genesis of popular but erroneous psychodiagnostic observations. *Journal of Abnormal Psychology, 72,* 193–204.

Chapman, L. J., & Chapman, J. P. (1969). Illusory correlation as an obstacle to the use of valid psychodiagnostic signs. *Journal of Abnormal Psychology, 74,* 271–280.

Childs, A., & Klimoski, R. J. (1986). Successfully predicting career success: An application of the biographical inventory. *Journal of Applied Psychology, 71,* 3–8.

Choca, J. P. (1998). Review of the Millon Index of Personality Styles. *Thirteenth Mental Measurements Yearbook,* 668–670.

Christenson, S. L. (1992). Review of the Child Behavior Checklist. *Eleventh Mental Measurements Yearbook,* 164–166.

Ciechalski, J. C. (1998). Review of the Self-Directed Search, Form E (1990 Revision). *Thirteenth Mental Measurements Yearbook,* 893–896.

Ciminero, A. R., Calhoun, K. S., & Adams, H. E. (Eds.). (1986). *Handbook of behavioral assessment* (2nd ed.). New York: Wiley.

Ciminero, A. R., Nelson, R. O., & Lipinski, D. P. (1977). Self-monitoring procedures. In A. R. Ciminero, K. S. Calhoun, & H. E. Adams (Eds.), *Handbook of behavioral assessment.* New York: Wiley.

Clark, A. J. (1994). Early recollections: A personality assessment tool for elementary school counselors. *Elementary School Guidance & Counseling, 29,* 92–101.

Clark, R. (1944). A method of administering and evaluating the Thematic Apperception Test in group situations. *Genetic Psychology Monographs, 30,* 1–55.

Coan, R. W. (1972). Measurable components of openness to experience. *Journal of Consulting Psychology, 39,* 346.

Cohen, R. J., Swerdlik, M. E., & Phillips, S. M. (1996). *Psychological testing and assessment: An introduction to tests and measurement* (3rd ed.). Mountain View, CA: Mayfield.

Coleman, M. J., et al. (1993). The Thought Disorder Index: A reliability study. *Psychological Assessment, 5,* 336–342.

Conners, C. K. (1973). Rating scales for use in drug studies with children. *Psychopharmacology Bulletin* [Special issue, Pharmacotherapy of children], 24–84.

Conners, C. K., & Barkley, R. A. (1985). Rating scales and checklists for child psychopharmacology. *Psychopharmacology Bulletin* [Special issue, Rating scales and assessment instruments for use in pediatric psychopharmacology research], *21*, 809–815.

Conoley, J. C., & Impara, J. C. (Eds.). (1995). *The twelfth mental measurements yearbook.* Lincoln, NE: Buros Institute of Mental Measurements, University of Nebraska.

Cooper, A. (1981). A basic TAT set for adolescent males. *Journal of Clinical Psychology*, *37*, 411–414.

Coopersmith, S. (1981). *The antecedents of self-esteem.* Palo Alto, CA: Consulting Psychologists Press.

Copple, G. E. (1956). Effective intelligence as measured by an unstructured sentence-completion technique. *Journal of Consulting Psychology*, *20*, 357–360.

Corsini, R. J., & Marsella, A. J. (Eds.). (1983). *Personality theory, research and assessment.* Itasca, IL: F. E. Peacock.

Cosden, M. (1984). Piers-Harris Children's Self-Concept Scale. In D. J. Keyser & R. C. Sweetland (Eds.), *Test critiques* (Vol. I, pp. 511–521). Kansas City, MO: Test Corporation of America.

Costa, P. T., Jr., & McCrae, R. R. (1986). Personality stability and its implications for clinical psychology. *Clinical Psychology Review*, *6*, 407–423.

Costa, P. T., Jr., & McCrae, R. R. (1992). Normal personality assessment in clinical practice. The NEO Personality Inventory. *Psychological Assessment*, *4*, 5–13.

Costantino, G. (1978, Nov.). *Preliminary report on TEMAS: A new thematic apperception test to assess ego functions in ethnic minority children.* Paper presented at the Second American Conference on Fantasy and the Imaging Process, Chicago.

Costantino, G., Malgady, R., & Rogler, L. H. (1988). *Tell-Me-A-Story—TEMAS—Manual.* Los Angeles: Western Psychological Services.

Costantino, G., Malgady, R., & Vazquez, C. (1981). A comparison of Murray-TAT and a new thematic apperception test for urban Hispanic children. *Hispanic Journal of Behavioral Sciences*, *3*, 291–300.

Cowan, G. (1971). Achievement motivation in lower class Negro females as a function of the race and sex of the figures. *Representative Research in Social Psychology*, *21*, 42–46.

Cowan, G., & Goldberg, F. J. (1967). Need achievement as a function of the race and sex of figures of selected TAT cards. *Journal of Personality and Social Psychology 5*, 245–249.

Craig, R. J., & Horowitz, M. (1990). Current utilization of psychological tests at diagnostic practicum sites. *The Clinical Psychologist*, *43*, 29–36.

Cramer, P., & Blatt, S. J. (1990). Use of the TAT to measure change in the defense mechanisms following intensive psychotherapy. *Journal of Personality Assessment*, *54*, 236–251.

Crandall, E. (1975). A scale for social interest. *Journal of Individual Psychology*, *31*, 187–195.

Crites, J. O. (1969). *The maturity of vocational attitudes in adolescence.* Iowa City: University.

Cronbach, L. J. (1951). Coefficient alpha and the internal structure of tests. *Psychometrika*, *16*, 297–334.

Cronbach, L. J., Gleser, G. C., Nanda, H., & Rajaratnam, N. (1972). *The dependability of behavioral measurements: Theory of generalizability for scores and profiles.* New York: Wiley.

Crowne, D. P., & Marlowe, D. (1964). *The approval motive: Studies in evaluative dependence.* New York: Wiley.

Cundick, B. P. (1985). Review of The Holtzman Inkblot Technique. In J. V. Mitchell (Ed.), *The ninth mental measurements yearbook* (pp. 661–662). Lincoln, NE: Buros Institute of Mental Measurements, University of Nebraska.

Cutter, F., & Farberow, N. L. (1970). The consensus Rorschach. In B. Klopfer, M. M. Mayer, F. B. Brawer, & W. G. Klopfer (Eds.), *Developments in the Rorschach technique* (Vol. 3, pp. 209–261). San Diego, CA: Harcourt Brace Jovanovich.

D'Amato, R. C. (1995). Review of the Adult Personality Inventory. *Twelfth Mental Measurements Yearbook,* 52–54.

Dana, R. H. (1955). Clinical diagnosis and objective TAT scoring. *Journal of Abnormal and Social Psychology, 50,* 19–25.

Dana, R. H. (1959). A proposal for the objective scoring of the T.A.T. *Perceptual & Motor Skills, 9,* 27–43.

Dana, R. H. (1993). *Multicultural assessment perspectives for professional psychology.* Boston: Allyn & Bacon.

Dana, R. H. (1996). Culturally competent assessment practice in the United States. *Journal of Personality Assessment, 66,* 472–487.

Dana, R. H. (1998). Multicultural assessment of personality and psychopathology in the United States: Still art, not yet science, and controversial. *European Journal of Psychological Assessment, 14*(1), 62–70.

Darley, J. B., & Hagenah, T. (1955). *Vocational interest measurement.* Minneapolis: University of Minnesota Press.

Datel, W. E. & Gengerelli, J. A. (1955). Reliability of Rorschach interpretations. *Journal of Projective Techniques, 19,* 322–338.

Davidshofer, C. (1985). Review of Jackson Vocational Interest Survey. *Ninth Mental Measurements Yearbook,* 739–740.

Dawes, R. M., Faust, D., & Meehl, P. E. (1993). Statistical prediction versus clinical prediction: Improving what works. In G. Keren & C. Lewis (Eds.), *A handbook for data analysis in the behavioral sciences: Methodological issues* (pp. 351–367). Hillsdale, NJ: Erlbaum.

Day, S. X., & Rounds, J. (1998). Universality of vocational interest structure among racial and ethnic minorities. *American Psychologist, 53,* 728–736.

DeCato, C. M. (1994). Toward a training model for Rorschach scoring revisited: A follow-up study on a training system for interscorer agreement. *Perceptual and Motor Skills, 78,* 3–10.

De Pascalis, V., & Montirosso, R. (1988). Extraversion, neurotcism and individual differences in event-related potentials. *Personality and Individual Differences, 9,* 353–360.

Derogatis, L. R. (1994). *SCL-90-R: Symptom Checklist-90-R: Administration, scoring, and procedures manual* (3rd ed.). Minneapolis, MN: National Computer Systems.

Derogatis, L. R., & Lazarus, L. (1994). SCL-90-R, Brief Symptom Inventory, and matching clinical rating scales. In M. E. Maruish (Ed.), *The use of psychological testing for treatment planning and outcome assessment* (pp. 217–248). Hillsdale, NJ: Erlbaum.

DeStefano, L. (1998). Review of Personality Inventory for Youth. *Thirteenth Mental Measurements Yearbook, 755–757.*

Diamond, E. E. (1979). Sex equality and measurement practices. *New Directions for Testing and Measurement, 3, 31–78.*

Disbrow, M. A., Doerr, H. O., & Caulfield, C. (1977, March). *Measures to predict child abuse* (Final report of Grant MC-R530351, Maternal and Child Health). Washington, DC: National Institute of Mental Health.

Dittman, A. T. (1962). The relationship between body movements and moods in interviews. *Journal of Consulting Psychology, 26, 480.*

Domino, G., & Affonso, D. D. (1990). A personality measure of Erikson's life stages: The Inventory of Psychosocial Balance. *Journal of Personality Assessment, 54*(2 & 4), 576–588.

Dowd, E. T. (1992). Review of the Beck Hopelessness Scale. *Eleventh Mental Measurements Yearbook, 81–82.*

Dowd, E. T. (1998a). Review of the Beck Anxiety Inventory. *Thirteenth Mental Measurements Yearbook, 97–98.*

Dowd, E. T. (1998b). Review of the House-Tree-Person and Draw-A-Person as Measures of Abuse in Children: A Quantitative Scoring System. *Thirteenth Mental Measurements Yearbook, 486–487.*

Dowd, R., & Innes, K. M. (1981). Sport and personality: Effects of type of sport and level of competition. *Perceptual and Motor Skills, 53, 79–89.*

Drake, L. E. (1946). A social I.E. scale for the MMPI. *Journal of Applied Psychology, 30, 51–54.*

Drakeley, R. J., Herriot, P., & Jones, A. (1988). Biographical data, training success, and turnover. *Journal of Occupational Psychology, 61, 145–152.*

Dreger, R. M. (1982). The classification of children and their emotional problems: An overview-II. *Clinical Psychology Review, 2, 349–385.*

Dubious memories. (1994, May 23). *Time,* p. 51.

Duckworth, J. C., & Anderson, W. (1986). *Interpretation manual for counselors and clinicians* (3rd ed.). Munsey, IN: Excelerated Development.

Dunn, S., Bliss, J., & Siipola, E. (1958). Effects of impulsivity, introversion, and individual values upon association under free conditions. *Journal of Personality, 26, 61–76.*

Ebstein, R. P., Novick, O., Umansky, R., Priel, B., Osher, Y., Blaine, D., Bennett, E. R., Nemanov, L., Katz, M., & Belmaker, R. H. (1996). Dopamine D4 receptor (D4DR) exon III polymorphism associated with the personality trait of Novelty Seeking. *Nature Genetics, 12, 78–80.*

Edelbrock, C. (1988). Informant reports. In E. S. Shapiro & T. R. Kratchowill (Eds.), *Behavioral assessment in schools: Conceptual foundations and practical applications* (pp. 351–383). New York: Guilford Press.

Edelbrock, C., & Achenbach, T. M. (1984). The teacher version of the Child Behavior Profile: 2. Boys aged 6–11. *Journal of Consulting and Clinical Psychology, 52, 207–212.*

Edmonds, J. M. (1929). *The characters of Theophrastus.* Cambridge, MA: Harvard University Press.

Edwards, A. L. (1954). *Manual—Edwards Personal Preference Schedule.* New York: The Psychological Corporation.

Edwards, A. L. (1957). *The social desirability variable in personality assessment and research*. New York: Dryden.

Edwards, A. L. (1959). *Edwards Personal Preference Schedule: Manual*. New York: Psychological Corporation.

Edwards, A. L. (1970). *The measurement of personality traits by scales and inventories*. New York: Holt, Rinehart & Winston.

Egloff, B., & Gruhn, A. J. (1996). Personality and endurance sports. *Personality & Individual Differences, 21*, 223–229.

Ekman, P. (1965a). Communication through nonverbal behavior: A source of information about an interpersonal relationship. In S. S. Tomkins & C. E. Izard (Eds.), *Affect, cognition, and personality*. New York: Springer.

Ekman, P. (1965b). Differential communication of affect by head and body cues. *Journal of Personality and Social Psychology, 2*, 725–735.

Ekman, P., & Friesen, W. V. (1984). *Unmasking the face* (Reprint ed.). Palo Alto, CA: Consulting Psychologists Press.

Elliott, S. N., & Busse, R. T. (1992). Review of the Child Behavior Checklist. *Eleventh Mental Measurements Yearbook*, 166–169.

Engelhard, G., Jr. (1992). Review of the California Psychological Inventory (rev. ed.). *Eleventh mental measurements yearbook*, 139–141.

Entwisle, D. R. (1972). To dispel fantasies about fantasy-based measures of achievement motivation. *Psychological Bulletin, 77*, 377–391.

Epstein, S., Pacini, R., Denes-Raj, V., & Heier, H. (1996). Individual differences in intuitive-experiential and analytical-rational thinking styles. *Journal of Personality & Social Psychology, 71*, 390–405.

Erdman, P. E., Klein, M. J., & Greist, H. (1985). Direct patient computer interviewing. *Journal of Consulting and Clinical Psychology, 53*, 760–773.

Erikson, E. H. (1958). *Young man Luther: A study in psychoanalysis and history*. New York: Norton.

Erikson, E. H. (1963). *Childhood and society* (2nd ed.). New York: Norton.

Erikson, E. H. (1969). *Gandhi's truth: On the origins of militant nonviolence*. New York: Norton.

Eron, L. (1950). A normative study of the TAT. *Psychological Monographs, 64* (Whole No. 315).

Eron, L., & Ritter, A. M. (1951). A comparison of two methods of administration of the Thematic Apperception Test. *Journal of Consulting Psychology, 15*, 55–61.

Eron, L., Terry, D., & Callahan, R. (1950). The use of rating scales for emotional tone of TAT stories. *Journal of Consulting Psychology, 14*, 473–478.

Evans, B. J., Coman, G. J., & Stanley, R. O. (1988). Scores on the profile of nonverbal sensitivity: A sample of Australian medical students. *Psychological Reports, 62*, 903–906.

Exner, J. E. (1978). *The Rorschach: A comprehensive system. Vol. 2. Current research and advanced interpretation*. New York: Wiley.

Exner, J. E. (1986). *The Rorschach: A comprehensive system: Vol. 1. Basic foundations* (2nd ed.). New York: Wiley.

Exner, J. E. (1993). *The Rorschach: A comprehensive system. Vol. 2. Current research and advanced interpretation* (2nd ed.). New York: Wiley.

Exner, J. E., Armbruster, G. L., & Viglione, D. (1978). The temporal stability of some Rorschach features. *Journal of Personality Assessment, 42,* 474–482.

Exner, J. E., & Exner, D. E. (1972). How clinicians use the Rorschach. *Journal of Personality Assessment, 36,* 403–408.

Exner, J. E., Thomas, E. E., & Mason, B. (1985). Children's Rorschachs: Description and prediction. *Journal of Personality Assessment, 49,* 13–20.

Exner, J. E., & Weiner, I. B. (1982). *The Rorschach: A comprehensive system (Vol. 3). Assessment of children and adolescents.* New York: Wiley.

Exner, J. E., & Weiner, I. B. (1994). *The Rorschach: A comprehensive system. Vol. 3. Assessment of children and adolescents* (2nd ed.). New York: Wiley.

Exner, J. E., & Wylie, J. R. (1975). *Attempts at simulation of schizophrenia-like protocols by psychology graduate students* (Workshops Study No. 211, unpublished). Bayville, NY: Rorschach Workshops.

Eysenck, H. J. (1960). A rational system of diagnosis and therapy in mental illness. In H. G. Eysenck (Ed.), *Progress in clinical psychology* (Vol. 4, pp. 46–64). New York: Grune & Stratton.

Eysenck, H. J. (1962). Conditioning and personality. *British Journal of Psychology, 53,* 299–305.

Eysenck, H. J. (1965). The effects of psychotherapy. *International Journal of Psychiatry, 1,* 97–178.

Eysenck, H. J. (1967). *The biological basis of personality.* Springfield, IL: C. C. Thomas.

Eysenck, H. J. (Ed.). (1981). *A model for personality.* New York: Springer.

Eysenck, H. J. (1982). *Personality, genetics, and behavior.* New York: Praeger.

Eysenck, H. J. (1990). Biological dimensions of personality. In L. A. Pervin (Ed.), *Handbook of personality theory and research* (pp. 244–276). New York: Guilford Press.

Eysenck, H. J., & Eysenck, S. B. G. (1975). *Manual of the Eysenck Personality Questionnaire.* San Diego: Educational and Industrial Testing Service.

Eysenck, H. J., & Rachman, S. (1965). *The causes of neurosis.* San Diego: Robert R. Knapp.

Fabiano, E. (1989). *Index to tests used in educational disserta-tions.* Phoenix, AZ: Oryx Press.

Fadiman, C. (Ed.). (1945). *The short stories of Henry James.* New York: Random House.

Fals-Stewart, W., & Lucente, S. (1997). Identifying positive dissimulation by substance-abusing individuals on the Personality Assessment Inventory: A cross-validation study. *Journal of Personality Assessment, 68,* 455–469.

Farrell, A. D. (1993). Computers and behavioral assessment: Current applications, future possibilities, and obstacles to routine use. *Behavioral Assessment, 13,* 159–170.

Feldt, L. S., & Brennan, R. L. (1989). Reliability. In R. L. Linn (Ed.), *Educational measurement* (2nd ed., pp. 105–146). New York: American Council on Education.

Fernandez, E. (1998). Review of the Beck Hopelessness Scale. *Thirteenth Mental Measurements Yearbook,* 123–125.

Feshbach, S. (1961). The influence of drive arousal and conflict. In J. Kagan & G. Lesser (Eds.), *Contemporary issues in thematic apperception methods.* Springfield, IL: C. C. Thomas.

Fischer, J., & Corcoran, K. (1994). *Measures for clinical practice: A sourcebook* (2nd ed., Vols. 1–2). New York: Free Press.

Fitts, W. H. (1965). *Manual for the Tennessee Self-Concept Scale*. Nashville: Counselor Recordings and Tests.

Flanagan, J. C. (1954). The critical incident technique. *Psychological Bulletin, 51,* 327–358.

Foote, J., & Kahn, M. W. (1979). Discriminative effectiveness of the Senior Apperception Test with impaired and nonimpaired elderly persons. *Journal of Personality Assessment, 43,* 360–364.

Forer, B. R. (1948). A diagnostic interest blank. *Rorschach Research Exchange and Journal of Projective Techniques, 12,* 1–11.

Forer, B. R. (1949). The fallacy of personal validation: A classroom demonstration of gullibility. *Journal of Abnormal and Social Psychology, 44,* 118–123.

Forer, B. R. (1950). A structured sentence completion test. *Journal of Projective Techniques, 14,* 15–29.

Fowler, A. (1991). An even-handed approach to graphology. *Personnel Management, 23*(3), 40–43.

Fowler, O. L. (1890). *Practical phrenology* (rev. ed.). New York: Fowler & Wells.

Frank, L. K. (1948). *Projective methods*. Springfield, IL: C. C. Thomas.

Frauenhoffer, D., Ross, M. J., Gfeller, J., Searight, H. R., & Piotrowski, C. (1998). Psychological test usage among licensed mental health practitioners: A multidisciplinary survey. *Journal of Psychological Practice, 4*(1), 28–33.

Freedenfeld, R. N., Ornduff, S. R., & Kelsey, R. M. (1995). Object relations and physical abuse: A TAT analysis. *Journal of Personality Assessment, 64,* 552–568.

Freiberg, P., & DeAngelis, T. (1992, March). High court to review ruling on hiring tests. *APA Monitor,* 1–8.

Freud, S. (1905, reprinted 1959). Fragment of an analysis of a case of hysteria. In *Collected papers* (Vol. 3). New York: Basic Books.

Friedberg, L. (1975). Early recollections of homosexuals as indicators of their life styles. *Journal of Individual Psychology, 30,* 196–204.

Friedmann, E., & Lockwood, R. (1991). Validation and use of the Animal Thematic Apperception Test (ATAT). *Anthrozooes, 4,* 174–183.

Friedrich, W. N. (1984). Roberts Apperception Test for Children. In D. J. Keyser & R. C. Sweetland (Eds.), *Test critiques* (Vol. I, pp. 543–548). Kansas City, MO: Test Corporation of America.

Frueh, B. C., & Kinder, B. N. (1994). The susceptibility of the Rorschach Inkblot Test to malingering of combat-related PTSD. *Journal of Personality Assessment, 62,* 280–298.

Funder, D. C., & Colvin, C. R. (1991). Some behaviors are more predictable than others. *The Score* (Newsletter of Division of the American Psychological Association), *13*(4), 3–4.

Furnham, A. (1990). Personality and demographic determinants of leisure and sports preference and performance. *International Journal of Sport Psychology, 21,* 218–236.

Furnham, A. (1992). *Psychology at work*. London: Routledge.

Furst, D. M., & Hardman, J. S. (1988). The iceberg profile and young competitive swimmers. *Perceptual & Motor Skills, 67*(2), 478.

Gardner, W., Lidz, C. W., Mulvey, E. P., & Shaw, E. C. (1996). Clinical versus actuarial predictions of violence in patients with mental illnesses. *Journal of Consulting and Clinical Psychology, 64,* 602–609.

Garner, D. M. (1984). *Eating Disorder Inventory-II manual*. Odessa, FL: Psychological Assessment Resources.

Garwood, J. (1977). A guide to research on the Rorschach Prognostic Rating Scale. *Journal of Personality Assessment, 41*, 117–118.

Gendlin, E. T., & Tomlinson, T. M. (1967). The process conception and its measurement. In C. R. Rogers, E. T. Gendlin, D. J. Kiesler, & C. B. Truax (Eds.), *The therapeutic relationship and its impact: A study of psychotherapy with schizophrenics*. Madison: University of Wisconsin Press.

Giannetti, R. A. (1987). The GOLPH psychosocial history: Response-contingent data acquisition and reporting. In J. N. Butcher (Ed.), *Computerized psychological assessment* (pp. 124–144). New York: Basic Books.

Ginzberg, E., Ginsburg, S. W., Axelrad, S., & Herma, J. L. (1951). *Occupational choice: An approach to a general theory*. New York: Columbia University Press.

Glueck, B. C., & Reznikoff, M. (1965). Comparison of computer-derived personality profile and projective psychological test findings. *American Journal of Psychiatry, 121*, 1156–1161.

Goldberg, L. R. (1972). Parameters of personality inventory construction and utilization: A comparison of prediction strategies and tactics. *Multivariate Behavioral Research Monograph*, No. 72–2.

Goldberg, L. R. (1980, April). *Some ruminations about the structure of individual differences: Developing a common lexicon for the major characteristics of human personality*. Paper presented at the annual meeting of the Western Psychological Association, Honolulu, HI.

Goldberg, L. R. (1991). Human mind versus regression equation: Five contrasts. In D. Cicchetti & W. M. Grove (Eds.), *Thinking clearly about psychology: Essays in honor of Paul E. Meehl* (Vol. 1, pp. 173–184). Minneapolis: University of Minnesota Press.

Goldberg, L. R. (1994). Basic research on personality structure: Implications of the emerging consensus for applications to selection and classification. In M. G. Rumsey, C. B. Walker, & J. H. Harris (Eds.), *Personnel selection and classification* (pp. 247–259). Hillsdale, NJ: Erlbaum.

Goldberg, P. (1965). A review of sentence completion methods in personality assessment. *Journal of Projective Techniques and Personality Assessment, 29*, 12–45.

Goldfried, M. R., Stricker, G., & Weiner, I. B. (1971). *Rorschach handbook of clinical and research applications*. Englewood Cliffs, NJ: Prentice-Hall.

Goldfried, M. R., & Zax, M. (1965). The stimulus value of the T.A.T. *Journal of Projective Techniques, 29*(1), 46–57.

Golding, S. L., & Rorer, L. G. (1972). Illusory correlation and subjective judgment. *Journal of Abnormal Psychology, 80*, 249–260.

Goldman, B. A., Mitchell, D. F., & Egelson, P. E. (Eds.). (1997). *Directory of unpublished experimental mental measures* (Vol. 7). Washington, DC: American Psychological Association.

Goodenough, F. L. (1926). *Measurement of intelligence by drawings*. Yonkers, NY: World Book.

Gordon, R., & Peck, L. A. (1989). *The Custody Quotient*. Dallas, TX: Willington Institute.

Gottfredson, G. D., Holland, J. L., & Gottfredson, L. S. (1975). The relation of vocational aspirations and assessments to employment reality. *Journal of Vocational Behavior, 7,* 135–148.

Gough, H. G. (1957). *California Psychological Inventory: Manual* (rev. ed.). Palo Alto, CA: Consulting Psychologists Press.

Gough, H. G. (1975). *California Psychological Inventory manual.* Palo Alto, CA: Consulting Psychologists Press.

Gough, H. G. (1987). *California Psychological Inventory: Adminis trator's guide.* Palo Alto, CA: Consulting Psychologists Press.

Gough, H. G., & Bradley, P. (1996). *CPI manual* (3rd ed.). Palo Alto, CA: Consulting Psychologists Press.

Gough, H. G., & Heilbrun, A. B., Jr. (1983). *The Adjective Check List manual.* Palo Alto, CA: Consulting Psychologists Press.

Gregory, R. J. (1996). *Psychological testing: History, principles, and applications* (2nd ed.). Boston: Allyn & Bacon.

Gross, M. L. (1962). *The brain watchers.* New York: Random House.

Gross, M. L. (1965). Testimony before house special committee on invasion of privacy of the committee on government operations. *American Psychologist, 20,* 958–960.

Grotevant, H. D., Scarr, S., & Weinberg, R. A. (1977). Patterns of interest similarity in adoptive and biological families. *Journal of Personality and Social Psychology, 35,* 667–676.

Groth-Marnat, G. (1990). *Handbook of psychological assessment* (2nd ed.). New York: Wiley.

Groth-Marnat, G. (1997). *Handbook of psychological assessment* (3rd ed.). New York: Wiley.

Guilford, J. P. (1940). *An inventory of factors STDCR.* Beverly Hills, CA: Sheridan Supply.

Guilford, J. P., & Martin, H. G. (1943a). *Personnel Inventory: Manual of directions and norms.* Beverly Hills, CA: Sheridan Supply Company.

Guilford, J. P., & Martin, H. G. (1943b). *The Guilford-Martin Inventory of Factors GAMIN: Manual of directions and norms.* Beverly Hills, CA: Sheridan Supply.

Guilford, J. P., & Zimmerman, W. S. (1949). *The Guilford-Zimmerman Temperament Survey: Manual of instructions and interpretations.* Beverly Hills, CA: Sheridan Supply Company.

Hackett, G., & Lonberg, S. D. (1994). Career assessment and counseling for women. In W. B. Walsh & S. H. Osipow (Eds.), *Career counseling for women* (pp. 43–85). Hillsdale, NJ: Erlbaum.

Hager, P. (1991, Oct. 29). Court bans psychological tests in hiring. *Los Angeles Times,* p. A-20.

Haladyna, T. M. (1992). Review of the Millon Clinical Multiaxial Inventory-II. *Eleventh Mental Measurements Yearbook,* 532–533.

Hall, E. T. (1969). *The hidden dimension.* Garden City, NY: Doubleday.

Hall, H. V. (1987). *Violence prediction: Guidelines for the forensic practitioner.* Springfield, IL: C. C. Thomas.

Haller, N., & Exner, J. E. (1985). The reliability of Rorschach variables for inpatients presenting symptoms of depression and/or helplessness. *Journal of Personality Assessment, 49,* 516–521.

Hamilton, R. G., & Robertson, M. H. (1966). Examiner influence on the Holtzman Inkblot Technique. *Journal of Projective Techniques and Personality Assessment, 30,* 553–558.

Hammer, E. G., & Kleiman, L. S. (1988). Getting to know you. *Personnel Administrator, 33*(5), 86–92.

Hammill, D. D., Brown, L., & Bryant, B. R. (1992). *A consumer's guide to tests in print* (2nd ed.). Austin, TX: pro.ed.

Handler, L., & Habenicht, D. (1994). The Kinetic Family Drawing technique: A review of the literature. *Journal of Personality Assessment, 62,* 440–464.

Hanes, K. R. (1998a). Review of the Beck Scale for Suicide Ideation. *Thirteenth Mental Measurements Yearbook,* 125–126.

Hanes, K. R. (1998b). Review of the Early Memories Procedure. *Thirteenth Mental Measurements Yearbook,* 392–393.

Hanfman, E., & Getzels, J. W. (1953). Studies of the sentence completion test. *Journal of Projective Techniques, 17,* 280–294.

Hargrave, G. E., & Hiatt, D. (1980). Use of the California Psychological Inventory in law enforcement officer selection. *Journal of Personality Assessment, 53,* 267–277.

Harmon, L. W., Hansen, J.-I. C., Borgen, F. H., & Hammer, A. L. (1994). *Strong Interest Inventory: Applications and technical guide.* Palo Alto, CA: Consulting Psychologists Press.

Harris, M. M., & Schaubroeck, J. (1988). A meta-analysis of self-supervisor, self-peer, and peer-supervisor ratings. *Personnel Psychology, 41,* 43–62.

Harrison, R., & Rotter, J. B. (1945). A note on the reliability of the Thematic Apperception Test. *Journal of Abnormal and Social Psychology, 40,* 97–99.

Hartman, A. H. (1970). A basic T.A.T. set. *Journal of Projective Techniques and Personality Assessment, 34,* 391–396.

Hartmann, D. P., & Wood, D. D. (1990). Observational methods. In A. S. Bellack, M. Hersen, & A. E. Kazdin (Eds.), *International handbook of behavior modification and therapy* (2nd ed., pp. 107–138). New York: Plenum Press.

Hartshorne, H., & May, M. A. (1928). *Studies in the nature of character. Vol. 1: Studies in deceit.* New York: Macmillan.

Hathaway, S. R., & McKinley, J. C. (1943). *The Minnesota Multiphasic Personality Inventory.* New York: Psychological Corporation.

Hathaway, S. R., & McKinley, J. C. (1989). *MMPI-2.* Minneapolis: University of Minnesota Press.

Hatt, C. V. (1985). Review of Children's Apperception Test. In J. V. Mitchell, Jr. (Ed.), *The ninth mental measurements yearbook* (Vol. I, pp. 315–316). Lincoln, NE: Buros Institute of Mental Measurements, University of Nebraska.

Haynes, S. N. (1990). Behavioral assessment of adults. In G. Goldstein & M. Hersen (Eds.), *Handbook of psychological assessment* (2nd ed., pp. 423–463). New York: Pergamon.

Haynes, S. N. (1991). Behavioral assessment. In M. Hersen, A. E. Kazdin, & A. S. Bellack (Eds.), *The clinical psychology handbook* (2nd ed., pp. 430–464). New York: Pergamon Press.

Hays, J. R. (1997). Note on concurrent validity of the Personality Assessment Inventory in law enforcement. *Psychological Reports, 81,* 244–246.

Heilbrun, A. B., Jr. (1964). Social-learning theory, social desirability, and the MMPI. *Psychological Bulletin, 61,* 377–387.

Heilbrun, A. B., Jr. (1969). Parental identification and the patterning of vocational interests in college males and females. *Journal of Counseling Psychology, 16,* 342–347.

Herrington-Wang, L. E., & Taylor, E. R. (1997). A pilot study of the Personality Assessment Inventory (PAI) in corrections: Assessment of malingering, suicide risk, and aggression in male inmates. *Behavioral Sciences & the Law, 15,* 469–482.

Hess, A. K. (1998). Review of the Millon Multiaxial Inventory-III. *Thirteenth Mental Measurements Yearbook,* 665–667.

Hett, W. S. (Ed.). (1936). Physiognomics. In *Aristotle: Minor works* (pp. 81–137). Cambridge, MA: Harvard University Press.

Heymans, G., & Wiersma, E. (1906). Beitrage zur Speziellen Psychologie auf Grund einer Massenunterschung. *Zeitschrift für Psychologie, 43,* 81–127 and 258–301.

Hibbard, S., Farmer, L., Wells, C. Difillipo, E., Barry, W., Korman, R., & Sloan, P. (1994). Validation of Cramer's defense mechanism manual for the TAT. *Journal of Personality Assessment, 63,* 197–210.

Hibbard, S., & Porcerelli, J. (1998). Further validation of the Cramer Defense Mechanism Manual. *Journal of Personality Assessment, 70,* 460–483.

Hill, E. F. (1972). *The Holtzman Inkblot Technique: A handbook for clinical application.* San Francisco: Jossey-Bass.

Hilsenroth, M. J., & Handler, L. (1995). A survey of graduate students' experiences, interests, and attitudes about learning the Rorschach. *Journal of Personality Assessment, 64,* 243–257.

Hobbs, N. (1963). A psychologist in the Peace Corps. *American Psychologist, 18,* 47–55.

Hoch, A., & Amsden, G. S. (1913). A guide to the descriptive study of personality. *Review of Neurology and Psychiatry, 11,* 577–587.

Hodges, K., & Zeman, J. (1993). Interviewing. In T. H. Ollendick & M. Hersen (Eds.), *Handbook of child and adolescent assessment* (pp. 65–81). Boston: Allyn & Bacon.

Hodgins, H. S., & Koestner, R. (1993). The oroigins of nonverbal sensitivity. *Personality & Social Psychology Bulletin, 19,* 466–473.

Hogan, R. T. (1983). A socioanalytic theory of personality. In M. M. Page (Ed.), *1982 Nebraska symposium on motivation.* Lincoln: University of Nebraska Press.

Hogan, R. T., & Hogan, J. (1992). *Hogan Personality Inventory manual* (rev. ed.). Tulsa, OK: Hogan Assessment Systems.

Hogan, R., Hogan, J., & Roberts, B. W. (1996). Personality measurement and employment decisions. *American Psychologist, 51,* 469–477.

Holden, R. R., Fekken, G. C., Reddon, J. R., Helmes, E., & Jackson, D. N. (1988). Clinical reliabilities and validities of the Basic Personality Inventory. *Journal of Consulting and Clinical Psychology 56,* 766–768.

Holland, J. L. (1985). *Making vocational choices: A theory of careers: A theory of vocational personalities and work environments* (2nd ed.). Englewood Cliffs, NJ: Prentice-Hall.

Holland, J. L. (1996). Exploring careers with a typology: What we have learned and some new directions. *American Psychologist, 51,* 397–406.

Hollingworth, H. L. (1920). *The psychology of functional neuroses.* New York: D. Appleton.

Holsopple, J., & Miale, F. R. (1954). *Sentence completion: A projective method for the study of personality.* Springfield, IL: C. C. Thomas.

Holt, A. (1974). *Handwriting in psychological interpretations.* Springfield, IL: C. C. Thomas.

Holt, R. R. (1970). Yet another look at clinical and statistical prediction: Or, is clinical psychology worthwhile? *American Psychologist, 25,* 337–349.

Holtzman, W. H. (1981). Holtzman Inkblot Technique (HIT). In A. I. Rabin (Ed.), *Assessment with projective techniques* (pp. 47–83). New York: Springer.

Holtzman, W. H. (1988). Beyond the Rorschach. *Journal of Personality Assessment, 52,* 578–609.

Honigfeld, G., & Klett, C. (1965). The Nurses' Observation Scale for Inpatient Evaluation (NOSIE): A new scale for measuring improvement in schizophrenia. *Journal of Clinical Psychology, 21,* 65–71.

Horn, J. L., Wanberg, K. W., & Foster, F. M. (1990). *Guide to the Alcohol Use Inventory (AUI).* Minneapolis, MN: National Computer Systems.

Horowitz, R., & Murphy, L. B. (1938). Projective methods in the psychological study of children. *Journal of Experimental Education, 7,* 133–140.

Humm, D. G., & Wadsworth, G. W. (1935). The Humm-Wadsworth Temperament Scale. *American Journal of Psychiatry, 92,* 163–200.

Hunt, J. M. (1982). Personality. *Collier's Encyclopedia* (Vol. 18, pp. 594–594c). New York: Macmillan.

Hutt, M. L. (1969). *The Hutt adaptation of the Bender-Gestalt test* (2nd ed.). New York: Grune & Stratton.

Hutt, M. L. (1977). *The Hutt adaptation of the Bender-Gestalt test* (3rd ed.). New York: Grune & Stratton.

I was an imaginary playmate. (1965). *American Psychologist, 20,* 990.

Imada, A. S. (1982). Social interaction, observation, and stereotypes as determinants of differentiation in peer ratings. *Organizational Behavior and Human Performance, 29,* 397–415.

Impara, J. C., & Plake, B. S. (Eds.). (1998). *The thirteenth mental measurements yearbook.* Lincoln, NE: Buros Institute of Mental Measurements, University of Nebraska.

Interview questions that are (legally) acceptable. (1980, January 20). *News-Chronicle* (Thousand Oaks, CA), p. 8.

Isaacs, M., & Chen, K. (1990). Presence/absence of an observer in a word association test. *Journal of Personality Assessment, 55,* 41–51.

Jablonski v. United State of America, 712 F.2d 391 (1983).

Jackson, C. W., & Wohl, J. (1966). A survey of Rorschach teaching in the university. *Journal of Projective Techniques and Personality Assessment, 30,* 115–134.

Jackson, D. N. (1977). *Jackson Vocational Interest Survey manual.* Port Huron, MI: Research Psychologists Press.

Jackson, D. N. (1989a). *Basic Personality Inventory: BPI manual.* Port Huron, MI: Sigma Assessment Systems.

Jackson, D. N. (1989b). *Personality Research Form manual* (3rd ed.). Port Huron, MI: Sigma Assessment Systems.

Jackson, D. N. (1994). *Jackson Personality Inventory-Revised: Manual.* Port Huron, MI: Sigma Assessment Systems.

Jackson, D. N., Helmes, E., Hoffmann, H., Holden, R. R., Jaffe, P. G. Reddon, J. R., & Smiley, W. C. (1989). *Basic Personality Inventory manual*. Port Huron, MI: Sigma Assessment Systems.

Jackson, D. N., & Messick, S. (1958). Content and style in personality assessment. *Psychological Bulletin, 55*, 243–252.

Jackson, D. N., & Messick, S. (1962). Response styles and the assessment of psychopathology. In S. Messick & J. Ross (Eds.), *Measurement in pesonality and cognition* (pp. 129–155). New York: Wiley.

Jacobs, A., & Barron, R. (1968). Falsification of the Guilford-Zimmerman Temperament Survey: II. Making a poor impression. *Psychological Reports, 24*, 1271–1277.

Johnson, N. L., & Gold, S. N. (1995). The Defense Mechanism Profile: A sentence completion test. In H. R. Conte & R. Plutchik (Eds.), *Ego defenses: Theory and measurement* (pp. 247–262). New York: Wiley.

Jones, A. E. (1997). Reflection-impulsivity and wholist-analytic: Two fledglings? . . . or is R-I a cuckoo? *Educational Psychology, 17*(1–2), 65–77.

Jung, C. G. (1910). The association method. *American Journal of Psychology, 21*, 219–269.

Juni, S. (1998). Review of the Derogatis Psychiatric Rating Scale. *Thirteenth Mental Measurements Yearbook*, 344–346.

Kagan, J. (1966). Reflection-impulsivity: The generality and dynamics of conceptual tempo. *Journal of Abnormal Psychology, 71*, 17–24.

Kagan, J. (1994). *Galen's prophecy*. New York: Basic Books.

Kagan, J., Reznick, J. S., & Snidman, N. (1988). Biological bases of childhood shyness. *Science, 240*, 167–171.

Kaplan, B. J. (1998). Review of the Revised Hamilton Rating Scale for Depression. *Thirteenth Mental Measurements Yearbook*, 839–840.

Karon, B. P. (1981). The Thematic Apperception Test (TAT). In A. I. Rabin (Ed.), *Assessment with projective techniques* (pp. 85–120). New York: Springer.

Karp, S. A., Holmstrom, R. W., & Silber, D. E. (1990). *Apperceptive Personality Test Manual (Version 2.0)*. Orland Park, IL: International Diagnostic Systems, Inc.

Katkovsky, W. (1992). Review of the Draw-a-Story: Screening for Depression and Emotional Needs. In J. J. Kramer & J. C. Conoley (Eds.), *The eleventh mental measurements yearbook* (pp. 291–292). Lincoln, NE: Buros Institute of Mental Measurements, University of Nebraska.

Kaufman, A. S., Ford-Richards, J. M., & McLean, J. E. (1998). Black-white differences on the Strong Interest Inventory General Occupational Themes and Basic Interest Scales at ages 16 to 65. *Journal of Clinical Psychology, 54*, 19–33.

Kavan, M. G. (1995). Review of the Personality Assessment Inventory. *Twelfth Mental Measurements Yearbook*, 766–768.

Kavan, M. G. (1998). Review of The Senior Apperception Test (1985 Revision). *Thirteenth Mental Measurements Yearbook*, 900–901.

Keenan, P. A., & Lachar, D. (1988). Screening preschoolers with special problems: Use of the Personality Inventory for Children (PIC). *Journal of School Psychology, 26*, 1–11.

Kehoe, J. F. (1992). Review of the Career Assessment Inventory, (2nd ed., Vocational Version). *Eleventh Mental Measurements Yearbook*, 149–151.

Kelleher, K. (1996, August 19). In the world of psychology, the eyebrows surely have it. *Los Angeles Times*, p. E3.

Keller, H. R. (1986). Behavioral observation approaches to personality assessment. In H. M. Knoff (Ed.), *The assessment of child and adolescent personality* (pp. 353–397). New York: Guilford.

Kelly, E. L. (1994). Graphology. In R. J. Corsini (Ed.), *Encyclopedia of psychology* (2nd ed., Vol. 2, p. 83). New York: Wiley.

Kelly, E. L., & Fiske, D. W. (1951). *The prediction of performance in clinical psychology*. Ann Arbor, MI: University of Michigan Press.

Kelly, G. A. (1955). *The psychology of personal constructs: A theory of personality* (2 Vols.). New York: Norton.

Kendall, P. C., & Norton-Ford, J. D. (1982). *Clinical psychology: Scientific and professional dimensions*. New York: Wiley.

Kerr, J. H., & Cox, T. (1991). Arousal and individual differences in sport. *Personality and Individual Differences, 12*, 1075–1085.

Kerr, J. H., & Van Den Wollenberg, A. E. (1997). High and low intensity exercise and psychological mood states. *Psychology & Health, 12*(5), 603–618.

Keyser, D. J., & Sweetland, R. C. (Eds.). (1984–1994). *Test critiques* (Vols. I-X). Austin, TX: pro.ed.

Killian, G. A. (1987). House-Tree-Person technique. In D. J. Keyser & R. C. Sweetland (Eds.), *Test critiques compendium*. Kansas City, MO: Test Corporation of America.

King, A. D. (1978). Minnesota Multiphasic Personality Inventory. In O. K. Buros (Ed.), *The eighth mental measurements yearbook*. Highland Park, NJ: Gryphon.

King, L. A., & King, D. W. (1993). *Sex-Role Egalitarianism Scale manual*. Port Huron, MP: Sigma Assessment Systems.

Kinslinger, H. J. (1966). Application of projective techniques in personnel psychology since 1940. *Psychological Bulletin, 66*, 134–149.

Kirkcaldy, B. D., & Furnham, A. (1991). Extraversion, neuroticism, psychoticism and recreational choice. *Personality and Individual Differences, 12*, 737–745.

Kite, M. E., & Deaux, K. (1986). Attitudes toward homosexuality: Assessment and behavioral consequences. *Basic and Applied Social Psychology, 7*, 137–162.

Kitzinger, C., & Powell, D. (1995). Engendering infidelity: Essentialist and social constructionist readings of a story completion task. *Feminism & Psychology, 5*, 345–373.

Klein, M. H., Mathieu, P. L., Gendlin, E. T., & Kiesler, D. J. (1969). *The Experiencing Scale: A research and training manual* (Vol. 1). Madison: Wisconsin Psychiatric Institute.

Kleinmuntz, B. (1982). *Personality and psychological assessment*. New York: St. Martin's Press.

Kleinmuntz, B. (1990). Why we still use our heads instead of formulas: Toward an integrative approach. *Psychological Bulletin, 107*, 296–310.

Klopfer B., & Kelley, D. M. (1942). *The Rorschach technique*. Yonkers-on-Hudson, NY: World Book.

Klopfer, W. G. (1984). Application of the consensus Rorschach to couples. *Journal of Personality Assessment, 48*, 422–440.

Klopfer, W. G., & Taulbee, E. S. (1976). Thematic Apperception Test. *Annual Review of Psychology, 27*, 543–567.

Knoff, H. M. (1998a). Review of the Children's Apperception Test (1991 Revision). *Thirteenth Mental Measurements Yearbook*, 231–233.

Knoff, H. M. (1998b). Review of the House-Tree-Person and Draw-A-Person as measures of abuse in children: A quantitative scoring system. *Thirteenth Mental Measurements Yearbook*, 487–490.

Kohlberg, L. (1969). Stage and sequence: The cognitive-developmental approach to socialization. In D. Goslin (Ed.), *Handbook of socialization: Theory and research*. Chicago: Rand McNally.

Kohlberg, L. (1974). The development of moral stages: Uses and abuses. *Proceedings of the 1973 Invitational Conference on Testing Problems* (pp. 1–8). Princeton, NJ: Educational Testing Service.

Kohlberg, L., & Elfenbein, D. (1975). The development of moral judgments concerning capital punishment. *American Journal of Orthopsychiatry, 45*, 614–639.

Koppitz, E. M. (1975). *The Bender-Gestalt test for young children: Research and application, 1963–1973*. New York: Grune & Stratton.

Korchin, S. J., & Schuldberg, D. (1981). The future of clinical assessment. *American Psychologist, 36*, 1147–1158.

Kraeplin, E. (1892). *Über die Beeinflussung einfacher psychischer Vorgänge*. Jena, Germany: Fischer.

Kraiger, K. Hakel, M. D., & Cornelius, E. T. (1984). Exploring fantasies of TAT reliability. *Journal of Personality Assessment, 48*, 365–370.

Kratchowill, T. R., Doll, E. J., & Dickson, W. P. (1991). Use of computer technology in behavioral assessments. In T. B. Gutkin & S. L. Wis (Eds.), *The computer and the decision-making process* (pp. 125–154). Hillsdale, NJ: Erlbaum.

Kretschmer, E. (1925). *Physique and character*. New York: Harcourt, Brace & World.

Krug, S. E. (1993). *Psychware sourcebook* (4th ed.). Champaign, IL: MetriTech.

Lachar, D. (1992). Review of the Draw-a-Story: Screening for Depression and Emotional Needs. In J. J. Kramer & J. C. Conoley (Eds.), *The eleventh mental measurements yearbook* (pp. 292–293). Lincoln, NE: Buros Institute of Mental Measurements, University of Nebraska.

Lachar, D., & Gruber, C. P. (1995a). *Personality Inventory for Youth (PIY) manual: Administration and scoring guide*. Los Angeles: Western Psychological Services.

Lachar, D., & Gruber, C. P. (1995b). *Personality Inventory for Youth (PIY) manual: Technical guide*. Los Angeles: Western Psychological Services.

Landauer, T. K., & Dumais, S. T. (1997). A solution to Plato's problem: The latent semantic analysis theory of acquisition, induction, and representation of knowledge. *Psychological Review, 104*, 211–240.

Landy, F. J., Shankster, L. J., & Kohler, S. S. (1994). Personnel selection and placement. *Annual Review of Psychology, 45*, 261–296.

Lang, W. S. (1992). Review of the TEMAS (Tell-Me-A-Story). In J. J. Kramer & J. C. Conoley (Eds.), *The eleventh mental measurements yearbook* (pp. 925–926). Lincoln, NE: Buros Institute of Mental Measurements, University of Nebraska.

Langevin, R. (1983). *Sexual strands: Understanding and treating sexual anomalies in men*. Hillsdale, NJ: Erlbaum.

Lanyon, R. I. (1986). Psychological assessment procedures in court-related settings. *Professional Psychology: Research and Practice, 17*, 260–268.

Lanyon, R. I., & Goodstein, L. D. (1997). *Personality assessment* (3rd ed.). New York: Wiley.

Last, J., & Bruhn, A. R. (1991). *The Comprehensive Early Memories Scoring System—Revised.* Available from A. R. Bruhn.

Lastovicka, J. L., Murray, J. P., Joachimsthaler, E. A., Bhalla, G., & Scheurich, J. (1987). A lifestyle typology to model young male drinking and driving. *Journal of Consumer Research, 14,* 257–263.

Leigh, J., Westen, D., Barends, A., Mendel, M. J., & Byers, S. (1992). The assessment of complexity of representations of people using TAT and interview data. *Journal of Personality, 60,* 809–837.

Lerner, P. M. (1991). *Psychoanalytic theory and the Rorschach.* New York: Analytic Press.

LeUnes, A., Evans, M., Karnei, B., & Lowry, N. (1980). Psychological tests used in research with adolescents, 1969–1973. *Adolescence, 15,* 417–421.

LeUnes, A. D., & Nation, J. R. (1989). *Sport psychology: An introduction.* Chicago: Nelson-Hall.

Levenson, R. W. (1992). Autonomic nervous system differences among emotions. *Psychological Science, 3,* 23–27.

Lewinsohn, P. M. (1965). Psychological correlates of overall quality of figure drawings. *Journal of Consulting Psychology, 29,* 504–512.

Libby, W. (1908). The imagination of adolescents. *American Journal of Psychology, 19,* 249–252.

Lichtenstein, S., Fischoff, B., & Phillips, L. D. (1982). Calibration of probabilities: The state of the art to 1980. In D. Kahneman, P. Slovic, & A. Tversky (Eds.), *Judgment under uncertainty: Heuristics and biases.* New York: Cambridge University Press.

Lilienfeld, S. D., Alliger, G., & Mitchell, K. (1995). Why integrity testing remains controversial. *American Psychologist, 50,* 457–458.

Lindzey, G. (1950). An experimental examination of the scapegoat theory of prejudice. *Journal of Abnormal and Social Psychology, 45,* 296–309.

Lindzey, G. (1959). On the classification of projective techniques. *Psychological Bulletin, 56,* 158–168.

Lippa, R. (1998). Gender-related individual differences and the structure of vocational interests. *Journal of Personality & Social Psychology, 74,* 996–1009.

Lipsitt, P. D., Lelos, D., & McGarry, A. L. (1971). Competency for trial: A screening instrument. *American Journal of Psychiatry, 128,* 105–109.

Lisansky, E. S. (1956). The inter-examiner reliability of the Rorschach test. *Journal of Projective Techniques, 20,* 310–317.

Loepfe, A. (1925). Über Rorschachsche Formdeutversuche mit 10–13 jährigen Knaben. *Zeitschrift für Angewandte Psychologie, 26,* 202–253.

Loevinger, J., Wessler, R., & Redmore, C. (1970). *Measuring ego development: Vol. 1. Construction and use of a sentence completion test. Vol. 2. Scoring manual for women and girls.* San Francisco: Jossey-Bass.

Lubin, B., Larsen, R. M., & Matarazzo, J. D. (1984). Patterns of psychological test usage in the United States: 1935–1982. *American Psychologist, 39,* 451–454.

Lubin, B., Larsen, R. M., Matarazzo, J. D., & Seever, M. F. (1986). Selected characteristics of psychologists and psychological assessment in five settings: 1959–1982. *Professional Psychology: Research and Practice, 17,* 155–157.

Maccoby, E. E., & Maccoby, N. (1954). The interview: A tool of social science. In G. Lindzey (Ed.), *Handbook of social psychology* (pp. 449–487). Cambridge, MA: Addison-Wesley.

Machover, K. (1949). *Personality projection in the drawing of the human figure.* Springfield, IL: C. C. Thomas.

Machover, K. (1951). *Personality projection in the drawing of the human figure.* Springfield, IL: C. C. Thomas.

MacKinnon, D. W. (1962). The nature and nurture of creativity talent. *American Psychologist, 17,* 484–495.

Maddox, T. (Ed.). (1997). *Tests* (4th ed.). Austin, TX: pro.ed.

Mahl, G. F. (1968). Gestures and body movements in interviews. In J. Shlien, H. Hunt, J. D. Matarazzo, & C. Savage (Eds.), *Research in psychotherapy* (Vol. 3). Washington, DC: American Psychological Association.

Malgady, R., Costantino, G., & Rogler, L. (1984). Development of a Thematic Apperception Test for urban Hispanic children. *Journal of Consulting and Clinical Psychology, 52,* 986–996.

Manaster, G. J., & Perryman, T. B. (1974). Early recollections and occupational choice. *Journal of Individual Psychology, 30,* 232–237.

Marchant, G. J. (1998). Review of Personality Inventory for Youth. *Thirteenth Mental Measurements Yearbook,* 757–758.

Maslow, A. H. (1954). *Motivation and personality.* New York: Harper & Row.

Mastro, J. V., Sherrill, C., Gench, B., & French, R. (1987). Psychological characteristics of elite visually impaired athletes: The iceberg profile. *Journal of Sport Behavior, 10*(1), 39–46.

Matarazzo, J. D. (1980). Behavioral health and behavioral medicine: Frontiers for a new health psychology. *American Psychologist, 35,* 807–817.

Matarazzo, J. D. (1992). Psychological testing and assessment in the 21st century. *American Psychologist, 47,* 1007–1018.

McArthur, D. S., & Roberts, G. E. (1982). *Roberts Apperception Test for Children manual.* Los Angeles: Western Psychological Services.

McCabe, S. P. (1985). Career Assessment Inventory. In D. J. Keyser & R. C. Sweetland (Eds.), *Test critiques* (Vol. II, pp. 128–137). Kansas City: MO: Test Corporation of America.

McClelland, D. C. (1961). *The achieving society.* Princeton, NJ: Van Nostrand Reinhold.

McClelland, D. C. (1971). *Assessing human motivation.* Morristown, NJ: General Learning Press.

McClelland, D. C. (1985). *Human motivation.* Glenview, IL: Scott, Foresman.

McClelland, D. C., & Atkinson, J. W. (1948). The projective expression of needs: I. The effect of different intensities of the hunger drive on perception. *Journal of Psychology, 25,* 205–222.

McCrae, R. R., & Costa, P. T. (1987). Validation of the five-factor model of personality across instruments and observers. *Journal of Personality and Social Psychology, 52,* 138–155.

McGarry, A. L., et al. (1973). *Competency to stand trial and mental illness.* Washington, DC: U. S. Government Printing Office.

McGinnies, E. (1949). Emotionality and perceptual defense. *Psychological Review, 56*, 244–251.

McNair, D. M., Lorr, M., & Droppleman, L. F. (1971/1981). *Profile of Mood States manual*. San Diego, CA: EdITS.

Meehl, P. E. (1951). *Research results for counselees*. St. Paul, MN: Minnesota State Department of Education.

Meehl, P. E. (1954). *Clinical versus statistical prediction*. Minneapolis: University of Minnesota Press.

Meehl, P. E. (1962). Schizotaxia, schizotypy, schizophrenia. *American Psychologist, 17*, 827–838.

Meehl, P. E. (1965). Seer over sign: The first good example. *Journal of Experimental Research in Personality, 11*, 27–32.

Meehl, P. E. (1973). *Psychodiagnosis: Selected papers*. Minneapolis: University of Minnesota Press.

Megargee, E. I., & Spielberger, C. D. (1992). Reflections on fifty years of personality assessment and future directions for the field. In *Personality assessment in America* (pp. 170–186). Hillsdale, NJ: Erlbaum.

Mehrabian, A., & Weiner, M. (1967). Decoding of inconsistent communication. *Journal of Personality and Social Psychology, 6*, 109–114.

Meir, E. I., & Barak, A. (1974). A simple instrument for measuring vocational interests based on Roe's classification of occupations. *Journal of Vocational Behavior, 4*, 33–42.

Menendez v. The Superior Court of Los Angeles County, California, 3 Cal. 4th 435, 834 P.2d 786, 11 Cal.Rptr 2d 92 (1992).

Merten, T. (1995). Factors influencing word-association responses: A reanalysis. *Creativity Research Journal, 8*, 249–263.

Miller, F. E., (1986). The development and evaluation of an online computer-assisted Rorschach Inkblot Test. *Journal of Personality Assessment, 50*, 222–228.

Millon, T. (1969). *Modern psychopathology*. Philadelphia: Saunders.

Millon, T. (1981). *Disorders of personality: DSM-III—Axis II*. New York: Wiley Interscience.

Millon, T. (1982). *Millon Adolescent Personality Inventory manual*. Minneapolis: Interpretive Scoring Systems.

Millon, T. (1994). *Millon Index of Personality Styles (MIPS) manual*. San Antonio, TX: Psychological Corporation.

Millon, T., Davis, R. D., Millon, C. M., Wenger, A., Van Zuilen, M. H., Fuchs, M., & Millon, R. B. (1996). *Disorders of personality: DSM-IV and beyond* (2nd ed.). New York: Wiley.

Millon, T., Green, C. J., & Meagher, R. B., Jr. (1982). *Millon Adolescent Personality Inventory manual*. Minneapolis, MN: National Computer Systems.

Millon, T., Millon, C., & Davis, R. (1993). *Millon Adolescent Clinical Inventory (MACI) manual*. Minneapolis, MN: National Computer Systems.

Millon, T., Millon, C., & Davis, R. (1994). *MCMI-III manual: Millon Clinical Multiaxial Inventory-III*. Minneapollis, MN: National Computer Systems.

Mischel, W. (1968). *Personality and assessment*. New York: Wiley.

Mischel, W. (1986). *Introduction to personality* (4th ed.). New York: Holt, Rinehart & Winston.

Mooradian, T. A. (1996). Shopping motives and the five factor model: An integration and preliminary study. *Psychological Reports, 78*(2), 579–592.

Moore, M. M. (1985). Nonverbal courtship patterns in women: Context and consequences. *Ethology and Sociobiology, 6*(4), 237–247.

Moore, M. M. (1995). Courtship signaling and adolescents: "Girls just wanna have fun"? *Journal of Sex Research, 32,* 319–328.

Moore, S. M., Gullone, E., & Kostanski, M. (1997). An examination of adolescent risk-taking using a story completion task. *Journal of Adolescence, 20,* 369–379.

Morey, L. C. (1991). *Personality Assessment Inventory: Professional manual.* Odessa, FL: Psychological Assessment Resources.

Morgan, W. P. (1980). Test of champions. *Psychology Today, 14,* 92–108.

Mosak, H. H. (1969). Early recollections: Evaluation of some recent research. *Journal of Individual Psychology, 25,* 56–63.

Munroe, R. L. (1955). *Schools of psychoanalytic thought.* New York: Holt, Rinehart & Winston.

Murphy, K. R., & Constans, J. I. (1987). Behavioral anchors as a source of bias in rating. *Journal of Applied Psychology, 72,* 573–577.

Murphy, L. L., Conoley, J. C., & Impara, J. C. (Eds.). (1994). *Tests in print IV.* Lincoln: Buros Institute of Mental Measurements, University of Nebraska.

Murray, H. A. (and collaborators##). (1938). *Explorations in personality.* New York: Oxford University Press.

Murray, H. A. (1943). *Thematic Apperception Test.* Cambridge, MA: Harvard University Press.

Murstein, B. I. (1959). A conceptual model of projective techniques applied to stimulus variations with thematic techniques. *Journal of Consulting Psychology, 27,* 394–399.

Murstein, B. I. (1965). *Theory and research in projective techniques (emphasizing the TAT).* New York: Wiley.

Museum, of Modern Art (1955). *The family of man.* New York: Maco Magazine.

Mussen, P. H., & Scodel, A. (1955). The effects of sexual stimulation under varying conditions on TAT sexual responsiveness. *Journal of Consulting and Clinical Psychology, 19,* 90.

Myers, I. B., & McCaulley, M. H. (1985). *Manual: A guide to the development and use of the Myers-Briggs Type Indicator.* Palo Alto, CA: Consulting Psychologists Press.

Nachmann, B. (1960). Childhood experiences and vocational choices in law, dentistry, and social work. *Journal of Counseling Psychology, 7,* 243–250.

Naglieri, J. A., McNeish, T., & Bardos, A. (1991). *Draw-A-Person: Screening Procedure for Emotional Disturbance.* Austin, TX: pro.ed.

Naglieri, J. A., & Pfeiffer, S. I. (1992). Performance of disruptive behavior disordered and normal samples on the Draw A Person: Screening Procedure for Emotional Disturbance. *Psychological Assessment, 4,* 156–159.

Neter, E., & Ben-Shakhar, G. (1989). Predictive validity of graphological inferences: A meta-analytic approach. *Personality and Individual Differences, 10,* 737–745.

Netter, B., & Viglione, D., Jr. (1994). An empirical study of malingering schizophrenia on the Rorschach. *Journal of Personality Assessment, 62,* 45–57.

Nettler, G. (1959). Test burning in Texas. *American Psychologist, 14,* 682–683.

Newcombe, P. A., & Boyle, G. J. (1995). High school students' sports personalities: Variations across participation level, gender, type of sport, and success. *International Journal of Sport Psychology, 26*(3), 277–294.

Norusis, M. J. (1992). *SPSS/PC + professional statistics, version 5.0*. Chicago, IL: SPSS Inc.

O'Brien, W. H., & Haynes, S. N. (1993). Behavioral assessment in the psychiatric setting. In A. S. Bellack & M. Hersen (Eds.), *Handbook of behavior therapy in the psychiatric setting* (pp. 39–71). New York: Plenum Press.

Ochse, R., & Plug, C. (1986). Cross-cultural investigation of the validity of Erikson's theory of personality development. *Journal of Personality and Social Psychyology, 50,* 1240–1252.

Ollendick, T. H. (1983). Reliability and validity of the Revised Fear Survey Schedule for Children (FSSC-R). *Behavior Research and Therapy, 21,* 685–692.

Ollendick, T. H., & Green, R. (1990). Behavioral assessment of children. In G. Goldstein & M. Hersen (Eds.), *Handbook of psychological assessment* (2nd ed., pp. 403–422). New York: Pergamon.

Ones, D. S., Viswesvaran, C., & Reiss, A. D. (1996). Role of social desirability in personality testing for personnel selection: The red herring. *Journal of Applied Psychology, 81,* 660–679.

Ones, D. S., Viswesvaran, C., & Schmidt, F. L. (1995). Integrity tests: Overlooked facts, resolved issues, and remaining questions. *American Psychologist, 50,* 456–457.

Ornberg, B., & Zalewski, C. (1994). Assessment of adolescents with the Rorschach: A critical review. *Assessment, 1,* 209–217.

Osgood, C. E., Suci, G. J., & Tannenbaum, P. H. (1957). *The measurement of meaning.* Urbana, IL: University of Illinois Press.

Osipow, S. H. (1983). *Theories of career development* (3rd ed.). Englewood Cliffs, NJ: Prentice-Hall.

Ostendorf, F., & Angleitner, A. (1994). The five-factor taxonomy: Robust dimensions of personality description. *Psychologica Belgica, 34,* 175–194.

Ostrom, T. M., Bond, C. F., Jr., Krosnick, J. A., & Sedikides, C. (1994). Attitude scales: How we measure the unmeasureable. In S. Shavitt & T. C. Brock (Eds.), *Persuasion: Psychological insights and perspectives* (pp. 15–42). Boston: Allyn & Bacon.

O'Sullivan, D. M., Zuckerman, M., & Kraft, M. (1998). Personality characteristics of male and female participants in team sports. *Personality & Individual Differences, 25*(1), 119–128.

Owen, S. V. (1992). Review of the Beck Hopelessness Scale. *Eleventh Mental Measurements Yearbook,* 82–83.

Owens, T. A., & Stufflebeam, D. L. (1969, February). *An experimental comparison of item sampling and examinee sampling for estimating norms.* Paper presented at the meeting of the National Council on Measurement in Education, Los Angeles.

Padilla, A. M. (1979). Critical factors in the testing of Hispanic Americans: A review and some suggestions for the future. In R. Tyler & S. White (Eds.), *Testing, teaching and learning: Report of a conference on testing.* Washington, DC: National Institute on Education.

Pagano, R. R. (1994). *Understanding statistics in the behavioral sciences* (4th ed.). Minneapolis: West.

Pam, A., & Rivera, J. (1995). Sexual pathology and dangerousness from a Thematic Apperception Test protocol. *Professional Psychology: Research & Practice, 26,* 72–77.

Payne, A. F. (1928). *Sentence completions.* New York: New York Guidance Clinic.

Payne, F. D. (1985). Review of Bem Sex-Role Inventory. *Ninth Mental Measurements Yearbook,* 137–138.

Peck v. Counseling Service of Addison County, Vermont, 146 Vt 61, 499 A.2d 422 (1985).

Peterson, C. A. (1985a). Review of Bloom Sentence Completion Survey. *Ninth Mental Measurements Yearbook,* 204–205.

Peterson, C. A. (1985b). Review of Projective Assessment of Aging Method. *Ninth Mental Measurements Yearbook,* 1235–1237.

Peterson, R. A., & Headen, S. W. (1984). Profile of Mood States. In D. J. Keyser & R. C. Sweetland (Eds.), *Test critiques* (Vol. I, pp. 522–529). Kansas City MO: Test Corporation of America.

Petzelt, J. T., & Craddick, R. (1978). Present meaning of assessment in psychology. *Professional Psychology: Research and Practice, 9,* 587–591.

Phares, E. J. (1994). Incomplete sentences. In R. J. Corsini (Ed.), *Encyclopedia of psychology* (2nd ed., Vol. 2, pp. 221–222). New York: Wiley.

Phelps, L. (1998). Review of the Early Memories Procedure. *Thirteenth Mental Measurements Yearbook,* 393–394.

Piers, E. V. (1969). *Manual for the Piers-Harris Children's Self-Concept Scale.* Nashville, TN: Counselor Recordings and Tests.

Piotrowski, C., Belter, R. W., & Keller, J. W. (1998). The impact of "managed care" on the practice of psychological testing: Preliminary findings. *Journal of Personality Assessment, 70*(3), 441–447.

Piotrowski, C., & Keller, J. W. (1984). Attitudes toward clinical assessment by members of the AABT. *Psychological Reports, 55,* 831–838.

Piotrowski, C., Sherry, D., & Keller, J. W. (1985). Psychodiagnostic test usage: A survey of the Society for Personality Assessment. *Journal of Personality Assessment, 49,* 115–119.

Piotrowski, C., & Zalewski, C. (1993). Training in psychodiagnostic testing in APA-approved PsyD and PhD clinical psychology programs. *Journal of Personality Assessment, 61,* 394–405.

Piotrowski, Z. (1957). *Percept analysis.* New York: Macmillan.

Piotrowski, Z. (1964). Digital-computer interpretation of inkblot test data. *Psychiatric Quarterly, 38,* 1–26.

Pittenger, D. J. (1998). Review of the Jackson Personality Inventory—Revised. *Thirteenth Mental Measurements Yearbook,* 556–557.

Polich, J., & Martin, S. (1992). P300, cognitive capability, and personality: A correlational study of university undergraduates. *Personality and Individual Differences, 13,* 533–543.

Polyson, J., Norris, D., & Ott, E. (1985). The recent decline in TAT research. *Professional Psychology: Research and Practice, 16,* 26–28.

Polyson, J., Peterson, R., & Marshall, C. (1986). MMPI and Rorschach: Three decades of research. *Professional Psychology: Research and Practice, 17,* 476–478.

Pope, M. (1995). Review of the Kuder General Interest Survey, Form E. *Twelfth Mental Measurements Yearbook,* 543–545.

Prediger, D. J., & Hanson, G. R. (1976). Holland's theory of careers applied to men and women: Analysis of implicit assumptions. *Journal of Vocational Behavior, 8*, 167–184.

Pressey, S. L., & Pressey, L. W. (1919). Cross-out test, with suggestions as to a group scale of the emotions. *Journal of Applied Psychology, 3*, 138–150.

Pritchard, W. S. (1989). P300 and EPQ/STPI personality traits. *Personality and Individual Differences, 10*, 15–24.

Procter, M. (1993). Measuring attitudes. In N. Gilbert (Ed.), *Researching social life* (pp. 116–134). London: Sage.

Quay, H. C., & Peterson, D. R. (1983). *Interim manual for the Behavior Problem Checklist*. Unpublished manuscript, University of Miami.

Rabin, A. I., & Zlotogorski, Z. (1981). Completion methods: Word association, sentence and story completion. In A. I. Rabin (Ed.), *Assessment with projective techniques: A concise introduction* (pp. 121–149). New York: Springer.

Radcliffe, J. A. (1966). A note on questionnaire faking with the 16PFQ and MPI. *Australian Journal of Psychology, 18*, 154–157.

Ransford, H. E., & Bartolomeo, P. J. (1996). Aerobic exercise, subjective health and psychological well-being within age and gender subgroups. *Social Science & Medicine, 43*(11), 1555–1559.

Rapaport, D., Gill, M. M., & Schafer, R. (1946). *Diagnostic psychological testing*. Chicago: Year Book.

Rapaport, D., Gill, M. M., & Schafer, R. (1968). *Diagnostic psychological testing* (rev. ed.). New York: International Universities Press.

Reilly, R. R., & Chao, G. T. (1982). Validity and fairness of some alternative employee selection procedures. *Personnel Psychology, 35*, 1–62.

Reinehr, R. C. (1998). Review of the Children's Apperception Test (1991 Revision). *Thirteenth Mental Measurements Yearbook*, 233–234.

Reise, S. P., & Oliver, C. J. (1994). Development of a California Q-set indicator of primary psychopathy. *Journal of Personality Assessment, 62*, 130–144.

Repp, A. C., & Felce, D. (1990). A microcomputer system used for evaluative and experimental behavioural research in mental handicap. *Mental Handicap Research, 3*, 21–32.

Retzlaff, P. (1995). Review of the Millon Adolescent Clinical Inventory. *Twelfth Mental Measurements Yearbook*, 621–622.

Retzlaff, P. (1998a). Review of the Derogatis Psychiatric Rating Scale. *Thirteenth Mental Measurements Yearbook*, 346–347.

Retzlaff, P. (1998b). Review of the Millon Multiaxial Inventory-III. *Thirteenth Mental Measurements Yearbook*, 667–668.

Reynolds, C. R. (1985). Review of Personality Inventory for Children. *Ninth Mental Measurements Yearbook*, 1154–1157.

Reynolds, C. R. (1992). Review of the Millon Clinical Multiaxial Inventory—II. *Eleventh Mental Measurements Yearbook*, 533–535.

Reznikoff, M., Aronow, E., & Rauchway, A. (1982). The reliability of inkblot content scales. In C. D. Spielberger & J. N. Butcher (Eds.), *Advances in personality assessment* (Vol. 1, pp. 83–113). New York: Erlbaum.

Riding, R. J., & Read, G. (1996). Cognitive style and pupil learning preferences. *Educational Psychology, 16*(1), 81–106.

Ritter, A., & Effron, L. D. (1952). The use of the Thematic Apperception Test to differentiate normal from abnormal groups. *Journal of Abnormal and Social Psychology, 47*, 147–158.

Ritzler, B. (1993). Thanks for the memories! *Journal of Personality Assessment, 60*, 208–210.

Ritzler, B. A., Sharkey, K. J., & Chudy, J. F. (1980). A comprehensive projective alternative to the TAT. *Journal of Personality Assessment, 44*, 358–362.

Roback, H. (1968). Human figure drawings: Their utility in the clinical psychologist's armamentarium for personality assessment. *Psychological Bulletin, 70*, 1–19.

Robinson, J. P., Athanasiou, R., & Head, K. B. (1974). *Measures of occupational attitudes and occupational characteristics.* Ann Arbor: Institute for Social Research, University of Michigan.

Robinson, J. P., Rush, J. G., & Head, K. B. (1973). *Measures of political attitudes.* Ann Arbor: Institute for Social Research, University of Michigan.

Robinson, J. P., Shaver, P. R., & Wrightsman, L. S. (1991). *Measures of personality and social psychological attitudes.* New York: Academic Press.

Rodgers, D. A. (1972). Minnesota Multiphasic Personality Inventory. In O. K. Buros (Ed.), *The seventh mental measurements yearbook* (Vol. 1, pp. 243–250). Highland Park, NJ: Gryphon.

Roe, A. (1956). *The psychology of occupations.* New York: Basic Books.

Roe, A., & Klos, D. (1969). Occupational classification. *Counseling Psychologist, 1*, 84–92.

Roe, A., & Siegelman, M. (1964). *The origin of interests.* Washington, DC: American Personnel and Guidance Association.

Rogers, C. R., & Dymond, R. F. (Eds.), (1954). *Psychotherapy and personality change.* Chicago: University of Chicago Press.

Rogers, L. S., Knauss, J., & Hammond, K. R. (1951). Predicting continuation in therapy by means of the Rorschach Test. *Journal of Consulting Psychology, 15*, 368–371.

Rogers, R. (1984). *Rogers Criminal Responsibility Scales.* Odessa, FL: Psychological Assessment Resources.

Rogers, R. (1986). *Conducting insanity evaluations.* Odessa, FL: Psychological Assessment Resources.

Rogers, R. (1995). *Diagnostic and structured interviewing: A handbook for psychologists.* Odessa, FL: Psychological Assessment Resources.

Rogers, R., Ustad, K. L., & Salekin, R. T. (1998). Convergent validity of the Personality Assessment Inventory: A study of emergency referrals in correctional setting. *Assessment, 5*(1), 3–12.

Rohde, A. R. (1947). *Sentence completions test manual.* Beverly Hills, CA: Western Psychological Services.

Rokeach, M. (1973). *The nature of human values.* New York: Free Press.

Rokeach, M. (1979). Understanding human values. Palo Alto, CA: Consulting Psychologists Press.

Rome, H. P., et al. (1962). Symposium on automation techniques in personality assessment. *Proceedings of the Staff Meetings of the Mayo Clinic, 137*, 61–82.

Ronan, G. F., Colavito, V. A., & Hammontree, S. R. (1993). Personal problem-solving system for scoring TAT responses: Preliminary validity and reliability data. *Journal of Personality Assessment, 61*, 28–40.

Ronan, G. F., Date, A. L., & Weisbrod, M. (1995). Personal problem-solving scoring of the TAT: Sensitivity to training. *Journal of Personality Assessment, 64*, 119–131.

Rorer, L. G. (1965). The great response-style myth. *Psychological Bulletin, 63*, 129–156.

Rorschach, H. (1921). *Psychodiagnostik*. Bern: Bircher.

Rosenbaum, B. (1973). Attitude toward invasion of privacy in the personnel selection process and job applicant demographic and personality correlates. *Journal of Applied Psychology, 58*, 333–338.

Rosenberg, S. D., Blatt, S. J., Oxman, T. E., McHugo, G. J., et al. (1994). Assessment of object relatedness through a lexical content analysis of the TAT. *Journal of Personality Assessment, 63*, 345–362.

Rosenfeld, P., Doherty, L. M., Vincino, S. M., Kantor, J., et al. (1989). Attitudes assessment in organizations: Testing three microcomputer-based survey systems. *Journal of General Psychology, 116*, 145–154.

Rosenhan, D. L. (1973). On being sane in insane places. *Science, 179*(4070), 365–369.

Rosenheim, E., & Mane, R. (1984). Inferences of personality characteristics from earliest memories. *Israel Journal of Psychiatry & Related Sciences, 21*(2), 93–101.

Rosenman, R. H. (1986). Current and past history of Type A behavior pattern. In T. H. Schmidt, T. M. Dembroski, & G. Blumchen (Eds.), *Biological and psychological factors in cardiovascular disease* (pp. 15–40). New York: Springer.

Rosenthal, R. (1966). *Experimenter effects in behavioral research*. New York: Appleton-Century-Crofts.

Rosenthal, R., et al. (1979). *Sensitivity to nonverbal communication: The PONS test*. Baltimore: Johns Hopkins University Press.

Rosenzweig, S. (1978). *Aggressive behavior and the Rosenzweig Picture-Frustration Study*. New York: Praeger.

Rosenzweig, S. (1981a). *Adolescent Form supplement to the basic manual of the Rosenzweig Picture-Frustration (P-F) Study*. St. Louis, MO: Rana House.

Rosenzweig, S. (1981b). *Children's Form supplement to the basic manual of the Rosenzweig Picture-Frustration (P-F) Study*. St. Louis, MO: Rana House.

Rosenzweig, S. (1988). Revised norms for the Children's Form of the Rosenzweig Picture-Frustration (P-F) Study, with updated reference list. *Journal of Clinical Child Psychology, 17*, 326–328.

Rossini, E. D., & Moretti, R. J. (1997). Thematic Apperception Test (TAT) interpretation: Practice recommendations from a survey of clinical psychology doctoral programs accredited by the American Psychological Association. *Professional Psychology: Research and Practice, 28*, 393–398.

Rothenberg, M. G. (1990). Graphology. *Encyclopedia Americana* (Vol. 13, pp. 190–191). Danbury, CT: Grolier.

Rothermel, R. D., & Lovell, M. R. (1985). In D. J. Keyser & R. C. Sweetland (Eds.), *Test critiques* (Vol. II, pp. 570–578). Kansas City, MO: Test Corporation of America.

Rothstein, H. R., Schmidt, F. L., Erwin, F. W., Owens, W. A., & Sparks, C. P. (1990). Biographical data in employment selection: Can validities be made generalizable? *Journal of Applied Psychology, 75*, 175–184.

Rotter, J. B. (1946). The Incomplete Sentences Test for studying personality. *American Psychologist, 1*, 286.

Rotter, J. B. (1954). *Social learning and clinical psychology*. Englewood Cliffs, NJ: Prentice Hall.

Rotter, J. B. (1966). Generalized expectancies for internal versus external control of reinforcement. *Psychological Monographs, 80* (1, Whole No. 609).

Rotter, J. B., Lah, M. I., & Rafferty, J. E. (1992). *Rotter Incomplete Sentences Blank manual*. San Antonio, TX: Psychological Corporation.

Rounds, J. B. (1985). Review of Vocational Preference Inventory (7th ed.). *Ninth Mental Measurements Yearbook,* 1683–1684.

Rowley, A. J., Landers, D. M., Kyllo, L. B., & Etnier, J. L. (1995). Does the iceberg profile discriminate between successful and less successful athletes? A meta-analysis. *Journal of Sport & Exercise Psychology, 17*(2), 185–199.

Russell, M., & Karol, D. (1994). *16 PF Fifth Edition administrator's manual*. Champaign, IL: Institute for Personality and Ability Testing.

Ryan, J. M., Tracey, T. J., & Rounds, J. (1996). Generalizability of Holland's structure of vocational interests across ethnicity, gender, and socioeconomic status. *Journal of Counseling Psychology, 43*, 330–337.

Sackheim, K. K. (1991). *Handwriting analysis and the employee selection process*. Westport, CT: Quorum.

Sacks, J. M., & Levy, S. (1950). The Sentence Completion Test. In L. E. Abt & L. Bellak (Eds.), *Projective psychology*. New York: Knopf.

Sanford, E. E. (1995). Review of the Rokeach Value Survey. *Twelfth Mental Measurements Yearbook*, 879–880.

Sanford, R. N. (1943). Physique, personality and scholarship. *Monographs of the Society for Research in Child Development, 8*, 705.

Sattler, J. M. (1985). Review of the Hutt Adaptation of the Bender-Gestalt Test. *Ninth Mental Measurements Yearbook,* 184–185.

Schafer, R. (1954). *Psychoanalytic interpretation in Rorschach testing*. New York: Grune & Stratton.

Schaie, J. P. (1978). Review of Gerontological Apperception Test. In O. K. Buros (Ed.), *The eighth mental measurements yearbook* (Vol. I, pp. 829–830). Highland Park, NJ: Gryphon.

Schaie, K. W. (1978). Review of Senior Apperception Technique. In O. K. Buros (Ed.), *The eighth mental measurements yearbook* (Vol. I, p. 1060). Highland Park, NJ: Gryphon.

Scherer, K. R. (1974). Acoustic concomitants of emotional dimensions: Judging affect from synthesized tone sequences. In S. Wertz (Ed.), *Nonverbal communication*. New York: Oxford University Press.

Schinka, J. A. (1995). Personality Assessment Inventory scale characteristics and factor structure in the assessment of alcohol dependency. *Journal of Personality Assessment, 64*, 101–111.

Schinka, J. A., LaLone, L., & Broeckel, J. (1997). Statistical methods in personality assessment research. *Journal of Personality Assessment, 68*, 487–496.

Schinke, S. (1995). Review of the Eating Disorder Inventory-2. *Twelfth Mental Measurements Yearbook,* 335.

Schneider, M. F. (1989). *Children's Apperceptive Story-telling Test*. Austin, TX: Pro-Ed.

Schneider, M. F., & Perney, J. (1990). Development of the Children's Apperceptive Story-telling Test. *Psychological Assessment: A Journal of Consulting and Clinical Psychology*, 2, 175–185.

Schoenfeldt, L. F., & Mendoza, J. L. (1994). Developing and using factorially derived biographical scales. In G. S. Stokes, M. D. Mumford, & W. A. Owens (Eds.), *Biodata handbook: Theory, research, and use of biographical information in selection and performance prediction* (pp. 147–169). Palo Alto, CA: Consulting Psychologists Press.

Schroth, M. L. (1995). A comparison of sensation seeking among different groups of athletes and nonathletes. *Personality and Individual Differences*, 18, 219–222.

Schuldberg, D., & Korchin, S. J. (1994). Clinical assessment. In R. J. Corsini (Ed.), *Encyclopedia of psychology* (2nd ed., Vol. 1, p. 235–236). New York: Wiley.

Schwab, D. P., & Packard, G. L. (1973). Response distortion on the Gordon Personal Inventory and the Gordon Personal Profile in the selection context: Some implications for predicting employee behavior. *Journal of Applied Psychology*, 58, 372–374.

Schwartz, L. A. (1932). Social-situation pictures in the psychiatric interview. *American Journal of Orthopsychiatry*, 2, 124–132.

Sharkey, K. J., & Ritzler, B. A. (1985). Comparing diagnostic validity of the TAT and a new picture projective test. *Journal of Personality Assessment*, 49, 406–412.

Sheldon, W. H., & Stevens, S. S. (1942). *The varieties of temperament*. New York: Harper & Row.

Sheldon, W. H., Stevens, S. S., & Tucker, W. B. (1940). *The varieties of human physique*. New York: Harper & Row.

Shields, R. B. (1978). The usefulness of the Rorschach Prognostic Rating Scale—A rebuttal. *Journal of Personality Assessment*, 42, 579–582.

Shneidman, E. S. (1952). Manual for the Make a Picture Story Method. *Projective Techniques Monographs*, 2.

Siegelman, M., & Peck, R. F. (1960). Personality patterns related to occupational roles. *Genetic Psychology Monographs*, 61, 291–349.

Silver, R. (1988). Screening children and adolescents for depression through Draw-a-Story. *The American Journal of Art Therapy*, 26, 119–124.

Sines, J. O. (1970). Actuarial versus clinical prediction in psychopathology. *British Journal of Psychiatry*, 116, 129–144.

Sines, J. O. (1985). Review of Roberts Apperception Test for Children. In J. V. Mitchell, Jr. (Ed.), *The ninth mental measurements yearbook* (Vol. II, pp. 1290–1291). Lincoln, NE: Buros Institute of Mental Measurements, University of Nebraska.

Siipola, E. M. (1994). House-Tree-Person Test. In R. J. Corsini (Ed.), *Encyclopedia of psychology* (2nd ed., Vol. 2, p. 164). New York: Wiley.

Siipola, E. M., Walker, W. N., & Kolb, D. (1955). Task attitudes in word association. *Journal of Personality*, 23, 441–459.

Small, J. R. (1984). Taylor-Johnson Temperament Analysis. In D. J. Keyser & R. C. Sweetland (Eds.), *Test critiques* (Vol. I, pp. 652–659). Kansas City, MO: Test Corporation of America.

Smith, S. R., & Meyer, R. G. (1987). *Law, behavior, and mental health*. New York: New York University Press.

Solomon, I. L., & Starr, B. D. (1968). *The School Apperception Method*. New York: Springer.

Soroka v. Dayton-Hudson Corp.9 41. L. A. Daily Journal D.A. R. 13204 (Cal. Ct. App. 1991).

Sorrentino, R. M., Holmes, J. G., Lhanna, S. E., & Sharp, A. (1995). Uncertainty orientation and trust in close relationships: Individual differences in cognitive styles. *Journal of Personality & Social Psychology, 68,* 314–327.

Spence, J. T., & Helmreich, R. (1978). *Masculinity and femininity: Their psychological dimensions, correlates, and antecedents.* Austin, TX: University of Texas Press.

Spengler, P. M., & Strohmer, D. C. (1994). Clinical judgmental biases: The moderating roles of counselor cognitive complexity and counselor client preferences. *Journal of Counseling Psychology, 41,* 8–17.

Spitzer, R. L. (1976). More on pseudoscience in science and the case for psychiatric diagnosis: A critique of D. L. Rosenhan's "On Being Sane in Insane Places" and "The Contextual Nature of Psychiatric Diagnosis." *Archives of General Psychiatry, 33,* 459–470.

Spitzer, R. L., Williams, J. B. W., Gibbon, M., & First, M. B. (1992). The Structured Clinical Interview for DSM-III-R (SCID). *Archives of General Psychiatry, 49,* 624–629.

Stahmann, R. F. (1978). Review of Taylor-Johnson Temperament Analysis. *Eighth Mental Measurements Yearbook,* 1111–1112.

Stamoulis, D. T., & Hauenstein, N. M. A. (1993). Rater training and rating accuracy: Training for dimensional accuracy versus training for ratee differentiation. *Journal of Applied Psychology, 78,* 994–1003.

Steimel, R. J., & Suziedelis, A. (1963). Perceived parental influence and inventoried interests. *Journal of Counseling Psychology, 10,* 289–295.

Stelmack, R. M. (1990). Biological bases of extraversion: Psychophysiological evidence. *Journal of Personality, 58,* 293–311.

Stelmack, R. M., & Houlihan, M. (1995). Event-related potentials, personality, and intelligence: Concepts, issues, and evidence. In D. H. Saklofske & M. Zeidner (Eds.), *International handbook of personality and intelligence* (pp. 349–365). New York: Plenum.

Stelmack, R. M., Houlihan, M., & McGarry-Roberts, P. S. (1993). Personality, reaction time, and event-related potentials. *Journal of Personality and Social Psychology, 65,* 399–409.

Stenberg, G., Rosen, I., & Risberg, J. (1988). Personality and augmenting/reducing in visual and auditory evoked potentials. *Personality and Individual Differences, 9,* 571–580.

Stenberg, G., Rosen, I., & Risberg, J. (1990). Attention and personality in augmenting/reducing of visual evoked potentials. *Personality and Individual Differences, 11,* 1243–1254.

Stephenson, W. (1953). *The study of behavior: Q-technique and its methodology.* Chicago: University of Chicago Press.

Sternberg, C. (1955). Personality trait patterns of college students majoring in different fields. *Psychological Monographs, 69* (No. 18, Whole No. 403).

Sternberg, R. J., & Grigorenko, E. L. (Eds.). (1997). *Intelligence, heredity, and environment.* New York: Cambridge University Press.

Stewart, J. R. (1998). Review of the Beck Scale for Suicide Ideation. *Thirteenth Mental Measurements Yearbook,* 126–127.

Stewart, L. H. (1959). Mother-son identification and vocational interest. *Genetic Psychology Monographs, 60,* 31–63.

Stokes, G. S., Mumford, M. D., & Owens, W. A. (1994). *Biodata handbook: Theory, re-*

search, and use of biographical information in selection and performance prediction. Palo Alto, CA: CPP Books.

Stoloff, M. L., & Couch, J. V. (Eds.). (1992). *Computer use in psychology: A directory of software* (3rd ed.). Washington, DC: American Psychological Association.

Stone, A. A. (1986). Vermont adopts Tarasoff: A real barn-burner. *American Journal of Psychiatry, 143,* 352–355.

Streiner, D. L., & Norman, G. R. (1995). *Health measurement scales: A practical guide to their development and use* (2nd ed.). Oxford, England: Oxford University Press.

Stricker, G., & Healey, B. J. (1990). Projective assessment of object relations: A review of the empirical literature. *Psychological Assessment: A Journal of Consulting and Clinical Psychology, 2,* 219–230.

Stricker, L. J. (1969). Test-wiseness on personality scales. *Journal of Applied Psychology Monograph, 53*(3, Part 2).

Stuart, R. R. (1995). Review of the Millon Adolescent Clinical Inventory. *Twelfth Mental Measurements Yearbook,* 622–623.

Sulsky, L. M., & Day, D. V. (1994). Effects of frame-of-reference training on rater accuracy under alternative time delays. *Journal of Applied Psychology, 79,* 515–543.

Sundberg, N. D. (1977). *Assessment of persons.* Englewood Cliffs, NJ: Prentice-Hall.

Super, D. E. (1957). *The psychology of careers.* New York: Harper & Row.

Super, D. E. (1970). *Work Values Inventory.* Chicago: Riverside.

Super, D. E. (1972). Vocational development theory: Persons, positions, processes. In J. M. Whiteley & A. Resnikoff (Eds.), *Perspectives on vocational development* (pp. 13–33). Washington, DC: American Personnel and Guidance Association.

Super, D. E. (1973). The Work Values Inventory. In D. G. Zytowski (Ed.), *Contemporary approaches to interest measurement.* Minneapolis, MN: University of Minnesota Press.

Super, D. E., & Bohn, M. J., Jr. (1970). *Occupational psychology.* Belmont, CA: Wadsworth.

Sutherland, J. D., & Gill, H. S. (1970). *Language and psychodynamic appraisal.* London: Research Publication Services.

Sutton, P. M., & Swensen, C. H. (1983). The reliability and concurrent validity of alternative methods for assessing ego development. *Journal of Personality Assessment, 47,* 468–475.

Suzuki, L. A., Meller, P. J., & Ponterotto, J. G. (Eds.). (1996). *Handbook of multicultural assessment: Clinical, psychological, and educational applications.* San Francisco: Jossey-Bass.

Svebak, S., & Kerr, J. (1989). The role of impulsivity in preference for sports. *Personality and Individual Differences, 10,* 51–58.

Swartz, J. D. (1992). The HIT and HIT 25: Comments and clarifications. *Journal of Personality Assessment, 58,* 432–433.

Swartz, J. D., Reinehr, R. C., & Holtzman, W. H. (1983). *Holtzman Inkblot Technique, 1956–1982: An annotated bibliography.* Austin, TX: Hogg Foundation for Mental Health.

Swensen, C. (1957). Empirical evaluations of human figure drawings. *Psychological Bulletin, 54,* 431–466.

Swensen, C. (1968). Empirical evaluations of human figure drawings: 1957–1966. *Psychological Bulletin, 70,* 20–44.

Swenson, W. M., & Pearson, J. S. (1964). Automation techniques in personality assessment: A frontier in behavioral science and medicine. *Methods of Information in Medicine, 3,* 34–36.

Symonds, P. M. (1949). *Adolescent fantasy: An investigation of the picture-story method of personality study.* New York: Columbia University Press.

Tamkin, A. S. (1980). Rorschach experience balance, introversion, and sex. *Psychological Reports, 46,* 843–848.

Tarasoff v. Regents of the University of California, 17 Cal.3d 425, 435, 551, P.2d 334, 343, 131 Cal.Rptr. 14, 23 (1976).

Taylor, J. A. (1953). A personality scale of manifest anxiety. *Journal of Abnormal and Social Psychology, 48,* 285–290.

Teeter, P. A. (1985). Review of Adjective Check List. *Ninth Mental Measurements Yearbook,* 50–52.

Templer, D. I. (1985). Multiple Affect Adjective Check List—Revised. In D. J. Keyser & R. C. Sweetland (Eds.), *Test critiques* (Vol. IV, pp. 449–452). Kansas City, MO: Test Corporation of America.

Tendler, A. D. (1930). A preliminary report on a test for emotional insight. *Journal of Applied Psychology, 14,* 123–126.

Tett, R., Jackson, D., & Rothstein, M. (1991). Personality measures as predictors of job performance: A meta-analytic review. *Personnel Psychology, 44,* 703–735.

Thomas, A. D., & Dudek, S. Z. (1985). Interpersonal affect in Thematic Apperception Test Responses: A scoring system. *Journal of Personality Assessment, 49,* 30–36.

Thomas, E. E., Alinsky, D., & Exner, J. E. (1982). *The stability of some Rorschach variables in 9-year-olds as compared with non-patient adults.* Unpublished manuscript, Rorschach Workshops Study No. 441.

Thomas, R. G. (1985). Review of Jackson Vocational Interest Survey. *Ninth Mental Measurements Yearbook,* 740–742.

Thompson, A. E. (1986). An object relational theory of affect maturity: Applications to the Thematic Apperception Test. In M. Kissen (Ed.), *Assessing object relations phenomena* (pp. 207–224). Madison, CT: International Universities Press.

Thompson, C. (1949). The Thompson modification of the Thematic Apperception Test. *Journal of Projective Techniques, 13,* 469–478.

Thompson, D. (1995). Review of the Kuder General Interest Survey, Form E. *Twelfth Mental Measurements Yearbook,* 545–546.

Thompson, J. M., & Sones, R. (1973). *The Education Apperception Test.* Los Angeles: Western Psychological Services.

Thorpe, L. P., Clarke, W. W., & Tiegs, E. W. (1953). *Manual, California Test of Personality.* Los Angeles: California Test Bureau.

Thurstone, L. L. (1949). *Thurstone Temperament Schedule.* Chicago: Science Research Associates.

Timmons, L. A., Lanyon, R. I., Almer, E. R., & Curran, P. J. (1993). Development and validation of sentence completion test indices of malingering during examination for disability. *American Journal of Forensic Psychology, 11*(3), 23–38.

Tinsley, H. E. A. (1985). Personality Research Form. In D. J. Keyser & R. C. Sweetland (Eds.), *Test critiques* (Vol. III, pp. 499–509). Kansas City, MO: Test Corporation of America.

Tobey, L.H., & Bruhn, A.R. (1992). Early memories and the criminally dangerous. *Journal of Personality Assessment, 59,* 137–152.

Tokar, D.M., & Swanson, J.L. (1995). Evaluation of the correspondence between Holland's vocational personality typology and the Five Factor model of personality. *Journal of Vocational Behavior, 46,* 89–108.

Tolor, A., & Schulberg, H. (1963). *Evaluation of the Bender-Gestalt test.* Springfield, IL: C.C. Thomas.

Tomkins, S.S. (1947). *The Thematic Apperception Test.* New York: Grune & Stratton.

Trautscholdt, M. (1883). Experimentelle Untersuchungen über die Association der Vorstellungen. *Philosophische Studien, 1,* 213–250.

Tripathi, R.R., & Pillai, A. (1981). Diagnostic discrimination on the TAT. *Indian Journal of Clinical Psychology, 8,* 141–145.

Tuber, S.B. (1983). Children's Rorschach scores as predictors of later adjustment. *Journal of Consulting and Clinical Psychology, 51,* 370–385.

Tuma, J.M. (1985). Review of Personality Inventory for Children. *Ninth Mental Measurements Yearbook,* 1157–1159.

Turner, D.R. (1966). Predictive efficiency as a function of amount of information and level of professional experience. *Journal of Projective Techniques and Personality Assessment, 30,* 4–11.

Tversky, A., & Kahneman, D. (1981). The framing of decisions and the psychology of choice. *Science, 211,* 453–458.

Underwood, B., & Moore, B.S. (1981). Sources of behavioral consistency. *Journal of Personality and Social Psychology, 40,* 780–785.

Ungerleiter, S., & Golding, J.M. (1980). Mood profiles of masters track and field athletes. *Perceptual and Motor Skills, 68,* 607–617.

Urbina, S. (1995). Review of the Basic Personality Inventory. *Twelfth Mental Measurements Yearbook,* 105–106.

Utz, P., & Korben, D. (1976). The construct validity of the occupational themes on the Strong-Campbell Inventory. *Journal of Vocational Behavior, 9,* 31–42.

Van Hutton, V. (1996). *House-Tree-Person and Draw-A-Person as measures of abuse in children: A quantitative scoring system.* Odessa, FL: Psychological Assessment Resources.

Van Lennep, D.J. (1951). The Four-Picture Test. In H.H. Anderson & G.L. Anderson (Eds.), *An introduction to projective techniques* (pp. 149–180). Englewood Cliffs, NJ: Prentice-Hall.

Veldman, D.J., Menaker, S.L., & Peck, R.F. (1969). Computer scoring of sentence completion data. *Behavioral Science, 14,* 501–507.

Von Staabs, G. (1991). The Sceno-test (J.A. Smith, Trans.). Toronto: Hogrefe & Huber. (Original work published 1964)

Von Zerssen, D., Barthelmes, H., Poessl, J., Black, C., Garczynski, E., Wessel, E., & Hecht, H. (1998a). The Biographical Personality Interview (BPI): A new approach to the assessment of premorbid personality in psychiatric research: Part I. Development of the instrument. *Journal of Psychiatric Research, 32*(1), 19–25.

Von Zerssen, D., Barthelmes, H., Poessl, J., Black, C., Garczynski, E., Wessel, E., & Hecht, H. (1998b). The Biographical Personality Interview (BPI): A new approach to the assessment of premorbid personality in psychiatric research: Part II. Psychometric properties. *Journal of Psychiatric Research, 32*(1), 25–35.

Wade, T. C., & Baker, T. B. (1977). Opinions and uses of psychological tests: A survey of clinical psychologists. *American Psychologist, 32*, 874–882.

Wagner, E. E. (1985). Review of the Rosenzweig Picture-Frustration Study. *Ninth Mental Measure ments Yearbook*, 1297–1298.

Walker, B. S., & Spengler, P. M. (1995). Clinical judgment of major depression in AIDS patients: The effects of clinician complexity and stereotyping. *Professional Psychology: Research and Practice, 26*, 269–273.

Waller, N. G. (1998a). Review of the Beck Anxiety Inventory. *Thirteenth Mental Measurements Yearbook*, 98–100.

Waller, N. G. (1998b). Review of the Beck Depression Inventory. *Thirteenth Mental Measurements Yearbook*, 120–121.

Watkins, C. E., Jr., Campbell, V. L., & McGregor, P. (1988). Counseling psychologists' uses of the opinions about psychological tests: A contemporary perspective. *Counseling Psychologist, 16*, 476–486.

Watkins, C. E., Campbell, V. L., & Nieberding, R. (1994). The practice of vocational assessment by counseling psychologists. *Counseling Psychologist, 22*, 115–128.

Watkins, C. E., Campbell, V. L., Nieberding, R., & Hallmark, R. (1995). Contemporary practice of psychological assessment by clinical psychologists. *Professional Psychology: Research and Practice, 26*, 54–60.

Webb, E. (1915). Character and intelligence. *British Journal of Psychology Monograph Supplement, III*.

Weiner, I. B. (1983). The future of psychodiagnosis revisited. *Journal of Personality Assessment, 47*, 451–461.

Weiner, I. B. (1991). Editor's note: Interscorer agreement in Rorschach research. *Journal of Personality Research, 56*, 1.

Wells, R. L. (1914). The systematic observation of the personality—In its relation to the hygiene of the mind. *Psychological Review, 21*, 295–333.

Wertheimer, M. (1923). Untersuchungen zur Lehre von der Gestalt: II. *Psychologische Forschung, 4*, 301–350.

Westen, D. (1991). Clinical assessment of object relations using the TAT. *Journal of Personality Assessment, 56*, 56–74.

Westen, D., Lohr, N., Silk, K. R., Gold, L., & Kerber, K. (1990). Object relations and social cognition in borderlines, major depressives, and normals: A thematic apperception analysis. *Psychological Assessment, 2*, 355–364.

Westen, D., Muderrisoglu, S., Fowler, C., Shedlr, J., et al. (1997). Affect regulation and affective experience: Individual differences, group differences, and measurement using a Q-sort procedure. *Journal of Consulting & Clinical Psychology, 65*, 429–439.

Wewers, M. E., & Lowe, N. K. (1990). A critical review of visual analogue scales in the measurement of clinical phenomena. *Research in Nursing & Health, 13*(4), 227–236.

Wexley, K. N., & Klimoski, R. (1984). Performance appraisal: An update. In K. M. Rowland & G. R. Ferris (Eds.), *Research in personnel and human resources management* (Vol. 2, pp. 35–79). Greenwich, CT: JAI Press.

Wheeler, K. G. (1985). Review of Temperament and Values Inventory. *Ninth Mental Measurements Yearbook*, 1535–1536.

White, L. J. (1996). Review of the Personality Assessment Inventory: A new psychological test for clinical and forensic assessment. *Australian Psychologist, 31*(1), 38–40.

White, R. W. (1943). The personality of Joseph Kidd. *Character and Personality, 11,* 183–208, 318–360.

White v. United States of America, 780 F.2d 97, 250 U. S. App. D. C. 435 (1986).

Whyte, W. H., Jr. (1956). *The organization man.* Garden City, NY: Doubleday.

Widiger, T. A. (1985). Review of Millon Adolescent Personality Inventory. In J. V. Mitchell, Jr. (Ed.), *The ninth mental measurements yearbook* (Vol. 1, pp. 979–981). Lincoln, NE: Buros Institute of Mental Measurements, University of Nebraska.

Wiersma, U., & Latham, G. P. (1986). The practicality of behavioral observation scales, behavior expectation scales, and trait scales. *Personnel Psychology, 39,* 619–628.

Wiese, M. J. (1995). Review of Children's Apperceptive Story-Telling Test. *Twelfth Mental Measurements Yearbook,* 181–183.

Wiggins, J. S. (1959). Interrelationships among MMPI measures of dissimulation under standard and social desirability instructions. *Journal of Consulting Psychology, 23,* 419–427.

Wiggins, J. S. (1966). Substantive dimensions of self-report in the MMPI item pool. *Psychological Monographs, 80* (Whole No. 630).

Wiggins, J. S. (1973). *Personality and prediction: Principles of personality assessment.* Reading, MA: Addison-Wesley.

Wildman, R., et al. (1980). *The Georgia Court Competency Test: An attempt to develop a rapid, quantitative measure of fitness for trial.* Unpublished manuscript, Forensic Services Division, Center State Hospital, Milledgeville, GA.

Willis, C. G. (1984). Myers-Briggs Type Indicator. In D. J. Keyser & R. C. Sweetland (Eds.), *Test critiques* (Vol. I, pp. 482–490). Kansas City, MO: Test Corporation of America.

Wilson, G. (1978). Introversion/extroversion. In H. London & J. E. Exner (Eds.), *Dimensions of personality* (pp. 217–261). New York: Wiley.

Wilson, M. A., & Languis, M. L. (1990). A topographic study of differences in the P300 between introverts and extraverts. *Brain Topography, 2,* 269–274.

Winer, B. J., Brown, D. R., & Michels, K. M. (1991). *Statistical principles in experimental design* (3rd ed.). New York: Wiley.

Wink, P. (1992). Three narcissism scales for the California-set. *Journal of Personality Assessment, 58,* 51–66.

Winter, D. G. (1998). "Toward a science of personality psychology": David McClelland's development of empirically derived TAT measures. *History of Psychology, 1,* 130–153.

Winter, D. G., & Stewart, A. J. (1977). Power motive reliability as a function of retest instructions. *Journal of Consulting and Clinical Psychology, 45,* 436–440.

Wirt, R. D., & Lachar, D. (1981). The Personality Inventory for Children: Development and clinical applications. In P. McReynolds (Ed.), *Advances in psychological assessment* (Vol. 5, pp. 353–392). San Francisco: Jossey-Bass.

Wirt, R. D., Lachar, D., Klinedinst, J. K., & Seat, P. D. (1984). *Multidimensional description of child personality: A manual for the Personality Inventory for Children, Revised 1984.* Los Angeles: Western Psychological Services.

Wirt, R. D., Lachar, D., Klinedinst, J. K., & Seat, P. D. (1991). *Multidimensional description of child personality: A manual for the Personality Inventory for Children 1990 Edition.* Los Angeles: Western Psychological Services.

Witkin, H. A. (1973). The role of cognitive style in academic performance and in teacher-student relations. *Educational Testing Service Research Bulletin* (No. RB-73–11). Princeton, NJ: Educational Testing Service.

Witkin, H. A., & Berry, J. W. (1975). Psychological differentiation in cross-cultural perspective. *Journal of Cross-Cultural Psychology, 6*, 4–87.

Witkin, H. A., & Goodenough, D. R. (1977). Field dependence and interpersonal behavior. *Psychological Bulletin, 84*, 661–689.

Witkin, H. A., & Goodenough, D. R. (1981). *Cognitive styles: Essence and Origins—Field dependence and independence.* New York: International Universities Press.

Witkin, H. A., Lewis, H. B., Hertzman, M., Machover, K., Meissner, P. B., & Wapner, S. (1954). *Personality through perception.* New York: Harper.

Wolk, R., & Wolk, R. (1971). *The Gerontological Apperception Test.* New York: Behavioral Publications.

Woodruff, R. A., Goodwin, D. W., & Guze, S. B. (1974). *Psychiatric diagnosis.* London: Oxford University Press.

Woodworth, R. S. (1919). Examination of emotional fitness for warfare. *Psychological Bulletin, 16*, 59–60.

Wooten, K. C., Barner, B. O., & Silver, N. C. (1994). The influence of cognitive style upon work environment preferencdes. *Perceptual and Motor Skills, 79*, 307–314.

Worchel, F. F., & Dupree, J. L. (1990). Projective story-telling techniques. In C. R. Reynolds & R. W. Kamphaus (Eds.), *Handbook of psychological and educational assessment of children: Personality, behavior, and context* (pp. 70–88). New York: Guilford Press.

Wrightsman, L. S. (1994). *Adult personality development. Vol. 1. Theories and concepts.* Thousand Oaks, CA: Sage.

Wyatt, F. (1947). The scoring and analysis of the Thematic Apperception Test. *Journal of Psychology, 24*, 319–330.

Wynne, L., & Singer, M. (1963). Thought disorder and family relations of schizophrenics. II. A classification of forms of thinking. *Archives of General Psychiatry, 9*, 199–206.

Yelland, T. (1995). Review of the Basic Personality Inventory. *Twelfth Mental Measurements Yearbook*, 106–107.

Yeung, R. R. (1996). The acute effects of exercise on mood state. *Journal of Psychosomatic Research, 40*(2), 123–141.

Zachar, P. (1998a). Review of the Jackson Personality Inventory—Revised. *Thirteenth Mental Measurements Yearbook*, 557–560.

Zachar, P. (1998b). Review of the Millon Index of Personality Styles. *Thirteenth Mental Measurements Yearbook*, 670–674.

Zarske, J. A. (1985). Review of Adjective Check List. *Ninth Mental Measurements Yearbook, 52*–53.

Zhang, T., Xu, S., Cai, Z., Chen, Z., et al. (1993). Research on the Thematic Apperception Test: Chinese revision and its norm. *Acta Psychologica Sinica, 25*, 314–323.

Ziskin, J. (1986). The future of clinical assessment. In B. S. Plake & J. C. Witt (Eds.), *The future of testing* (pp. 185–201). Hillsdale, NJ: Lawrence Erlbaum.

Zlotogorski, Z., & Wiggs, E. (1986). Story- and sentence-completion techniques. In A. I. Rabin (Ed.), *Projective techniques for adolescents and children* (pp. 195–211). New York: Springer.

Zubin, J., Eron, L. D., & Schumer, F. (1965). *An experimental approach to projective techniques.* New York: Wiley.

Zuckerman, M. (1983). *Biological basis of sensation seeking, impulsivity, and anxiety.* Hillsdale, NJ: Erlbaum.

Zuckerman, M. (1985). Review of Temperament and Values Inventory. *Ninth Mental Measurements Yearbook,* 1536–1537.

Zuckerman, M. (1989). Personality in the third dimension: A psychobiological approach. *Personality and Individual Differences, 10,* 391–418.

Zuckerman, M. (1994). *Behavioral expressions and biosocial bases of sensation seeking.* New York: Cambridge University Press.

Zuckerman, M. (1995). Good and bad humors: Biochemical bases of personality and its disorders. *Psychological Science, 6,* 325–332.

Zuckerman, M., & Lubin, B. (1985). *Manual for the Multiple Affect Adjective Check List—Revised.* San Diego, CA: EdITS.

Zytowski, D. G. (1976). Predictive validity of the Kuder Occupational Interest Survey: A 12- to 19-year follow-up. *Journal of Counseling Psychology, 23,* 221–233.

Author Index

Assessment Instrument Index

Subject Index